LILLIAN ROXON'S

ROCK

ENCYCLOPEDIA

LILLIAN ROXON'S

ROCK

ENCYCLOPEDIA

The Universal Library
A WORKMAN PUBLISHING COMPANY BOOK
GROSSET & DUNLAP
A NATIONAL GENERAL COMPANY

NEW YORK

A Grosset & Dunlap Original
Universal Library Edition, 1971

Printed in the United States of America

It furthers one to install helpers. —I Ching

Many thanks

to Elisabeth Lohman, Margot Cates, Jane Altman, George Glassman and Jon Sokolski—for working so hard;

to Denver John Collins, Paul Dickson, Judy Edelman, Lyndall Erb, Mike Jahn, Linda Leibman, Donald Lyons, Mary Martin, Donald Peterson, Valerie Reardon, Carolyn Reynolds, Hope Ruff, Richard Skidmore, Jon Taplin, Dave Wynne and Tinkerbelle—for solving problems;

to all the music publicists—for never losing their patience with us (well, almost never) when we called to double-check dates;

to the musicians and managers and producers—for giving us something to write about in the first place;

and finally, to Gloria Stavers, Danny Fields, Linda Eastman, Susan and Peter Edmiston, Richard and Judith Goldstein, Albert Grossman, Derek Taylor, Steve Paul, Maggie Makeig in Australia, Penny Valentine in London, Howard Smith and Jann Wenner—for being stars as well as star-makers.

Special thanks to Mickey Ruskin. And to Darcy Waters, Mike Vaughan, Donald Horne, Craig McGregor, Richard Neville, Louise Ferrier, Aviva Layton, Judy Smith, Ruth Biegler, Lindsay Clinch and my brothers Jack and Milo—for moral support.

for Leon and Margaret Fink

Introduction to the Paperback Edition

A lot has happened since the hardcover edition of this book appeared. Crosby, Stills, Nash and Young happened—and unhappened. Led Zeppelin became the most popular band in the world. The Beatles called it a day. The Jackson Five filled Madison Square Garden to screaming capacity and so did Grand Funk Railroad. The Who played at the Met. Creedence Clearwater Revival threw a $250,000 party to tell the world how good they were—as though anybody needed to be told. Iggy Stooge emerged as the sexiest thing since Mick Jagger. And on a good strong cosmic night anyway, the Grateful Dead showed the rest of the nation what San Francisco had known all along, that it was the best live band of all time. Getting these and other changes into this edition simply hasn't been possible, but I am determined to get in one major event of 1970-71—the emergence of the so-called underground rock press as a vibrant and unified force. I would like to take this opportunity to thank, among many others, colleagues like Bobby Abrams, Vince Aletti, Lorraine Alterman, Karin Berg, Jean-Charles Costa, Henry Edwards, Jim Fouratt, Danny Goldberg, Don Heckman, Lenny Kaye, Richard Meltzer, Anne-Marie Micklo, Ed McCormick, Sandy Pearlman, Richard and Lisa Robinson, Bud Scoppa, and Bob Somma, not just for their friendship and support, but also for bringing so much vitality to the scene and making the words as magic as the music.

AUTHOR'S NOTE

Trying to get the rock world to keep still long enough for me to take its picture was one of the most difficult tasks in putting this book together. Groups split even as I wrote of their inner harmony, and got themselves together just as I had acknowledged their tragic demise. Baritones turned sopranos overnight; bands expanded and contracted their personnel like concertinas; fine performers degenerated swiftly and inexplicably while supposed second-raters found their promise all too late to make our deadlines.

Too many people blinked when I clicked the shutter—but then, isn't this restlessness exactly what rock is all about? The madness and desperation and constant shifts of power. I wanted to record the facts without losing the feelings. In the end, though, the music itself has to tell the story. This book is the companion to that story.

L.R.

New York City
August 1969

ROCK ENCYCLOPEDIA

ACID ROCK/Originally, acid rock was music that tried to reproduce the distorted hearing of a person under the influence of lysergic acid diethylamide (LSD). The idea was to recreate for someone who was not drugged the illusion of an LSD experience through music (an illusion heightened by light shows designed to reproduce *visual* aspects of a trip).

LSD hit San Francisco in 1965 just a little before the big dance scene started to happen there, a scene touched off by the general exuberance of a community that had just discovered chemical ecstasy. All the music did was mirror that ecstasy. It was slower and more languid than hard rock, incorporating much of the Oriental music that was providing background sounds for the drug experiences of that period. Numbers tended to run on longer as though time as we normally know it had lost its meaning. Notes and phrasings lurched and warped in a way that had not, until then, been considered acceptable in rock. Lyrics conjured up images previously confined to the verses of poets like Samuel Taylor Coleridge and William Blake.

The acid rock and light shows of the San Francisco ballrooms did provide for many a joyous journey to the center of the mind without any of the inconvenient side effects, let alone the expense, of hallucinatory drugs. However, there is not much doubt that a sizable percentage of those 1966-67 audiences did not need musical help so much as sympathetic musical companionship for a voyage that had already been triggered with chemicals. Thus, the term acid rock could be taken to mean *enhancing* as well as *inducing* psychedelic transports.

Is acid rock written by someone under the influence of LSD or at least while his memories of its effects are still fresh? The original acid rock was. Later, when the sound hit the national airwaves in 1967, there was a wave of ingenious reproductions which could have been composed after a trip to the nearest record shop. And today there are few groups or even single performers untouched by the music that came out of San Francisco's discovery of hallucinogens.
(see HEAD MUSIC)

DAVID ACKLES/A strong singer, pianist and a good songwriter, whose *Road To Cairo* was picked up in 1968 by Julie

Driscoll for her second single. He lives in California, has made an album and writes songs which manage to be at once gentle and forceful.

Albums/DAVID ACKLES (October 1968): *The Road To Cairo; When Love Is Gone; Sonny Come Home; Blue Ribbons; What A Happy Day; Down River; Laissez-Faire; Lotus Man; His Name Is Andrew; Be My Friend.*

THE AMBOY DUKES/*Ted Nugent (lead guitar), Steve Farmer (rhythm guitar), Dave Palmer (drums), Greg Arama (bass), Andy Solomon (piano, organ), Rusty Day (lead vocals).*

Three years cooking, with something like thirty-five changes in personnel, the Amboy Dukes finally made it late in 1968 with a number one single, *Journey to the Center of the Mind.*

Albums/AMBOY DUKES: *Let's Go Get Stoned; I Feel Free; Baby Please Don't Go; Young Love; Psalms Of Aftermath; Colors; Down On Philips Escalator; Lovely Lady; Night Time; It's Not True; Gimme Love.* JOURNEY TO THE CENTER OF THE MIND: *Mississippi Murder; Surrender To Your King; Flight Of The Bird; Scottish Tea; Journey To The Center Of The Mind; Dr. Slingshot; Ivory Castles; Why Is A Carrot More Orange Than An Orange; Missionary Mary; Death Is Life; St. Philip's Friend; I'll Prove I'm Right.*

Singles/*Baby Please Don't Go/Psalm Of Aftermath; Journey To The Center Of The Mind/Mississippi Murder; Scottish Tea/You Talk Sunshine, I Breathe Fire.*

AMERICAN BREED/*Chuck Colbert, Gary Loizzo, Lee Graziano, Al Ciner.*

Long before they had a national hit in *Bend Me, Shape Me,* the American Breed were major figures on the 1965 teen rock dance scene in the Midwest. They are typical of many hard-rock groups that build huge regional reputations and then hit the national and international jackpots with one strong single and never have to look back after that because the years of experience are all there behind them, standing them in good stead. The American Breed was not one of the fashionable groups of the late sixties—not enough psychedelica and mysticism.

Albums/AMERICAN BREED (November 1967): *Step Out Of Your Mind; Knock On Wood; We Gotta Get Out Of This Place; Don't Forget About Me; Same Old Thing; Lipstick Traces; My Girl; Short Skirts; Up Tight; I Don't Think You Know Me; Hi-Heel Sneakers.* BEND ME, SHAPE ME (April 1968): *Bend Me, Shape Me; Green Light; Don't It Make You Cry; Mindrocker; Bird; Something You've Got; Don't Make Me Leave You; I've Been Tryin'; Before and After; Sometime In The Morning; No Easy Way Down.* PUMPKIN, POWDER, SCARLET & GREEN (July 1968): *Pumpkin; Cool It (We're Not Alone); Welcome, You're In Love; The Right To Cry; Ready, Willing And Able; Take Me If You Want Me; Powder; Scarlet; Anyway That You Want Me; Master Of My Fate; Music To Think By; Train On A One-Track Mind; I'm Gonna Make You Mine; Green.* LONELY SIDE OF THE CITY (September 1968): *Always You; Walls; Partners In Love; Out In The Cold Again; Love Is Just A State Of Mind; New Games To Play; I've Got To Get You Off My Mind; Another Bad Morning; What Can You Do When You're Lonely; River Of No Regrets.*

Singles/*Step Out Of Your Mind/Same Old Thing; Don't Forget About Me/Short Skirts; Bend Me, Shape Me/Mindrocker; Green Light/Don't It Make You Cry; Keep The Faith/Private Zoo* (November 1968).

ERIC ANDERSEN/Gangling and innocent and perhaps just a little too beautiful, Eric Andersen came out of the same tight little second-generation Greenwich Village early sixties folk set that gave the world everyone from Bob Dylan and Phil Ochs to Judy Collins and the Lovin' Spoonful. (It wasn't a big money scene then, and the thought that it ever might be would have provoked nothing but laughter in those days down in the Gaslight and over in Gerdes' kitchen.) Eric was one of the first of the folksingers to write his own songs rather than interpret the songs of others. And in the early sixties that took courage. When Judy Collins recorded his song *Thirsty Boots* it marked a beginning for the singer-writer. Since then everyone from the Robbs to the Blues Project has recorded his most famous song, *Violets Of Dawn,* but his own tender version was the one that established him as master of the lyrical and

romantic ballad. Unlike some of his contemporaries, Eric
never did go big and blaring and electric. And he never made
the big, blaring electric money that went with it. Beatle
manager Brian Epstein was all set to sign him just before
Epstein died in 1967.

Albums/TODAY IS THE HIGHWAY (March 1965): *To-
day Is The Highway; Dusty Box Car Wall; Time For My
Returning; Plains Of Nebrasky-O; Looking Glass; Never
Coming Home; Come To My Bedside; Baby Please Don't Go;
Bay Of Mexico; Everything Ain't Been Said; Song To J.C.B.;
Bumblebee.* 'BOUT CHANGES 'N THINGS (February
1966): *Violets Of Dawn; Girl I Love; That's Alright Mama;
Thirsty Boots; The Hustler; Cross Your Mind; I Shall Go
Unbounded; You Been Cheatin'; Champion At Keepin' Them
Rollin'; Blind Fiddler; Close The Door Lightly When You
Go; My Land Is A Good Land.* 'BOUT CHANGES 'N
THINGS—TAKE TWO (July 1967): *Close The Door Light-
ly; That's All Right, Mama; Blind Fiddler; Hustler; Thirsty
Boots; My Land Is A Good Land; Hey Babe, Have You Been
Cheatin'; Cross Your Mind; Violets Of Dawn; Champion At
Keeping Them Rolling; I Shall Go Unbounded; Girl I Love.*
MORE HITS FROM TIN CAN ALLEY (March 1968): *Tin
Can Alley* (2 Parts); *Rollin' Home; 16 Year Grudge; Miss
Lonely Are You Blue; Mary Sunshine; Honey; Just A
Little Something; On The Edge Of You; Broken Hearted
Mama; Hello Sun; Woman Is A Prism.* AVALANCHE (June
1968): *It's Comin' And It Won't Be Long; An Old Song;
Louise; Think About It; So Hard To Fall; Good To Be With
You; We Were Foolish Like The Flowers; Avalanche; For
What Was Gained.*

Singles/*Think About It/So Hard To Fall* (October 1968).

ANIMALS (also ERIC BURDON and the NEW ANIMALS)
/*Eric Burdon (vocals), Andy Somers (guitar), Barry Jenkins
(drums, tambourine), John Weider (guitar, violin, bass),
Zoot Money (organ).*
*Previous Members: George Bruno, Charles Chandler, John
Skele, Dave Roweberry, Hilton Valentine, Alan Price, Vic
Briggs, Danny McCulloch.*
It was the long hot summer of 1964 and Beatlemania was

rampant when the hard, raspy voice of Eric Burdon hit the
airwaves with *The House Of The Rising Sun*. That was when
America knew the English meant business. With Eric up there
on the charts, they knew that the British invasion was for
real, that England had more than just the Beatles, perhaps
dozens more where that little foursome had come from. Take
the Animals. They were from Newcastle, a town just as rough
as Liverpool. Alan Price, the organist (who now has his own
group), was first with a quartet called the Alan Price Combo,
which Eric Burdon joined in 1962. The locals thought they
looked like animals, so the Animals they became. Eric was
very much into blues, as were so many other English groups
emerging at that time (a reaction against the polite, clean
rock of then top groups like the Shadows, who wore suits on
stage and sang songs to match). The Animals' sound, with
Eric's incredibly black, bluesy voice and Alan Price's black,
bluesy organ, was a big success on their several American
tours and on the album charts, not just with the teenies, but
with much of the black community, which considered Eric
and his music so funky they devoted five whole pages to him
in the national magazine *Ebony*. Then, in 1966, Eric Burdon
did one of the major somersaults in rock—he ceremoniously
killed off the old Animals (to the horror of the fans) and
emerged with a new group, a new sound and a new billing. By
this time Alan Price had already left to start the Alan Price
Set. Eric considered going solo, but eventually ended up with
a new team as Eric Burdon and the Animals.

Buried with the old Animals was the whole rhythm and
blues sound that had made Burdon famous. (Barry Jenkins,
the new drummer, had played with Carl Perkins, Bo Diddley
and Jerry Lee Lewis, and that made for a very rocking Chuck
Berry mood for a while.) But what eventually dominated all
the outside influences that the new group brought with it was
not the new Animals, but the new Eric. The rebirth was
dramatic. Funky Eric was dead as a doornail. The new Eric
had flipped out over a girl named Sandoz (the name of a
company which makes LSD), San Francisco and the Monterey Pop Festival. And that was exactly what his three
singles in 1967 were about, in that order. To old Eric fans,
especially the ones in England, it was a bit of a letdown.
They missed the rave-ups. The new Eric was too gentle and

tranquil and soppy for them. Fortunately for him he eventually settled down somewhere halfway between the two extremes
and produced *LOVE IS* in December, 1968, one of the finest
albums of that year. It was his farewell to rock, he said,
announcing he was leaving music for films.

Albums/THE ANIMALS (October 1964): *House Of The
Rising Sun; Blue Feeling; Girl Can't Help It; Baby Let Me
Take You Home; Right Time; Talkin' 'Bout You; Around
And Around; I'm In Love Again; Gonna Send You Back To
Walker; Memphis Tennessee; I'm Mad Again; I've Been
Around.* ANIMALS ON TOUR (March 1965): *Boom
Boom; How You've Changed; I Believe To My Soul; Mess
Around; Bright Lights, Big City; Worried Life Blues; Let The
Good Times Roll; Ain't Got You; Hallelujah, I Love Her So;
I'm Crying; Dimples; She Said Yeah.* ANIMAL TRACKS
(September 1965): *We Gotta Get Out Of This Place; Take It
Easy Baby; Bring It On Home To Me; Roberta; Story Of Bo
Diddley; I Can't Believe It; For Miss Caulker; Club A-Go-
Go; Don't Let Me Be Misunderstood; Bury My Body.* BEST
OF THE ANIMALS (February 1966): *It's My Life; Gonna
Send You Back To Walker; Bring It On Home To Me; I'm
Mad; House Of The Rising Sun; We Gotta Get Out Of This
Place; Boom Boom; I'm In Love Again; I'm Crying; Don't
Let Me Be Misunderstood.* ANIMALIZATION (September
1966): *Don't Bring Me Down; One Monkey Don't Stop The
Show; You're On My Mind; She'll Return It; Cheating;
Inside-Looking Out; See See Rider; Gin House Blues; Maud-
ie; What Am I Living For; Sweet Little Sixteen; I Put A
Spell On You.* ANIMALISM (December 1966): *All Night
Long; Shake; Other Side Of This Life; Rock Me Baby;
Lucille; Smoke Stack Lightning; Hey Gyp; Hit The Road,
Jack; Outcast; Louisiana Blues; That's All I Am To You;
Going Down Slow.* ERIC IS HERE (March 1967): *Help Me
Girl; In The Night; Mama Told Me Not To Come; I Think
It's Gonna Rain Today; This Side Of Goodbye; That Ain't
Where It's At; Wait Till Next Year; Losin' Control; It's Not
Easy; Biggest Bundle Of Them All; It's Been A Long Time
Comin'; True Love (Comes Only Once In A Lifetime).*
BEST OF ERIC BURDON AND THE ANIMALS—
VOLUME 2 (June 1967): *When I Was Young; Girl Named*

Sandoz; Don't Bring Me Down; She'll Return It; See See Rider; Other Side Of This Life; Hey Gyp; Inside-Looking Out; Help Me Girl; Cheating; You're On My Mind; That Ain't Where It's At. WINDS OF CHANGE (October 1967): *San Franciscan Nights; Good Times; Winds Of Change; Poem By The Sea; Paint It Black; Black Plague; Yes I Am Experienced; Man-Woman; Hotel Hell; Anything; It's All Meat.* TWAIN SHALL MEET (May 1968): *Monterey; Just The Thought; Closer To The Truth; No Self Pity; Orange And Red Beams; Sky Pilot; We Love You Lil; All Is One.* EVERY ONE OF US (July 1968): *White Houses; Uppers and Downers; Serenade To A Sweet Lady; The Immigrant Lad; Year Of The Guru; St. James Infirmary; New York 1963—America 1968.* LOVE IS (December 1968): *River Deep, Mountain High; I'm An Angel; I'm Dying, Or Am I; Ring Of Fire; Coloured Rain; To Love Somebody; As The Years Go Passing; Gemini—The Madman.*

Singles/*House Of The Rising Sun/Gonna Send You Back To Walker* (Summer 1964); *Blue Feeling/Boom Boom; Don't Let Me Be Misunderstood/Club A-Go-Go; Bring It On Home To Me/For Miss Caulker; We Gotta Get Out Of This Place/I Can't Believe It; Help Me Girl/Inside Looking Out; I'm Going To Change The World/You're On My Mind; It's My Life/See See Rider; Girl Named Sandoz/That Ain't Where It's At* (April 1967); *Don't Bring Me Down/When I Was Young* (Spring 1967); *San Franciscan Nights/Good Times* (July 1967); *Monterey/Ain't It So; Anything/It's All Meat* (March 1968); *Sky Pilot* (2 Parts) (1968); *River Deep, Mountain High/White Houses* (November 1968).

PAUL ANKA/In 1958, when he was fifteen, Paul Anka had a number one hit with a song he wrote called *Diana*. That was the teen agony era of American pop music—if you were fifteen and suffering over an older woman of seventeen or something and could write a song about it, you were in. By early 1959 Anka, at sixteen, had three major hits. At seventeen he'd made a million. At eighteen he made his nightclub debut. By twenty-one he'd written over two hundred songs and made millions, which was not at all surprising when you consider he had a huge following in different parts of the world and still does, especially in Europe. In France alone, twelve singers did French versions of *Diana,* but Anka's was still the best seller. Today he's doing better than most of the boys he grew up with (Tommy Sands, Avalon, Fabian, etc.).

Albums/SONGS I WISH I'D WRITTEN: *Ramblin' Rose; I Can't Stop Loving You; End Of The World; He'll Have To Go; All I Have To Do Is Dream; Can't Get Used To Losing You; Oh, Lonesome Me; Save The Last Dance For Me; Blue On Blue; Moon River; It's Not For Me To Say; Memories Are Made Of This; You Always Hurt The One You Love; Cry; Who's Sorry Now.* PAUL ANKA (January 1961). PAUL ANKA, 21 GOLDEN HITS (May 1963): *Diana; Put Your Head On My Shoulder; Time To Cry; Lonely Boy; Puppy Love; I Love You In The Same Old Way; You Are My Destiny; I Love You, Baby; Crazy Love; Don't Ever Leave Me; Summer's Gone; Adam And Eve; Don't Gamble With Love; I'm Still Waiting Here For You; It Doesn't Matter Any More; Love Land; Tonight My Love, Tonight; My Home Town; Cinderella; Dance On Little Girl; Longest Day.* STRICTLY NASHVILLE (August 1966): *Bonaparte's Retreat; I Wish; Oh, Such A Stranger; There Won't Be No Runnin' Back (To You); I Went To Your Wedding; Story Of My Life; Memphis, Tennessee; It's Only Make Believe; Truly Yours; Legend In My Time (I'd Be A); I Didn't Mean To Hurt You; Once A Day.* PAUL ANKA, LIVE (October 1967): *It Only Takes A Moment; Ev'rybody Has The Right To Be Wrong; How Insensitive; Satin Doll; When I Take My Sugar To Tea; Goin' Out Of My Head; Everybody Loves Somebody; What The World Needs Now Is Love; Memphis, Tennessee; Medley.*

Singles/*As If There Were No Tomorrow/Every Day A Heart Is Broken; Dream Me Happy/Loneliest Boy In The World; I Went To Your Wedding/I Wish; I Can't Get Along Very Well Without Her/I Can't Help Loving You; I'd Rather Be A Stranger/Poor Old World; Truly Yours/Oh, Such A Stranger; Until It's Time For You To Go/Would You Still Be My Baby; That's How Love Goes/Woman Is A Sentimental Thing; Can't Get You Out Of My Mind/When We Get There; Goodnight My Love/This Crazy World* (October 1968).

Also Appears On/ THREE GREAT GUYS: *I Can't Say A Word; No, No; Laugh, Laugh, Laugh; I Remember;* Other Songs are by Sam Cooke and Neil Sedaka. THE BEST OF THE BEST (June 1967): *Diana.*

ANTHONY AND THE IMPERIALS (formerly LITTLE ANTHONY AND THE IMPERIALS)/*Anthony Gourdine (vocals), Ernest Wright (vocals), Clarence Collins (vocals), Sam Strain (vocals), Kenny Seymour (guitar).*
The idea of head music astonishes Anthony. "We've been turning people on with our music since 1958," he says. They're a rhythm and blues group that *Variety* praises for being "relatively clean-cut" and employing "no weirdo techniques" or "costume put-ons." As a reward they get to play places like the Flamboyan Hotel in Puerto Rico, where their performances are based on old hits like *Going Out of My Head, Tears on My Pillow* and *Hurt So Bad.* It's really not a bad way to make a living.
Albums/BEST OF LITTLE ANTHONY & THE IMPERIALS: *Goin' Out Of My Head; Hurt So Bad; Hurt; Take Me Back; Shimmy Shimmy Ko-Ko Bop; Tears On My Pillow; I Miss You So; I'm On The Outside; Reputation; Our Song; Never Again; Get Out Of My Life.* BEST OF LITTLE ANTHONY & THE IMPERIALS, Vol. 2. (February 1968): *I'm Hypnotized; Beautiful People; Georgy Girl; Thousand Miles Away; You Only Live Twice; Goin' Out Of My Head; Two People In The World; Prayer & A Jukebox; When You Wish Upon A Star; You Better Take It Easy Baby; If I Remember To Forget.* GOIN' OUT OF MY HEAD: *Goin' Out Of My Head; What A Difference A Day Makes; Reputation; Hurt; It's Just A Matter Of Time; Never Again; Hurt So Bad; Who's Sorry Now; Where Are You; Take Me Back; I Miss You So; Get Out Of My Life.* GREATEST HITS OF LITTLE ANTHONY & THE IMPERIALS: *Tears On My Pillow; Two People In The World; Shimmy Shimmy Ko-Ko Bop; The Diary; Prayer & A Jukebox; I'm All Right; So Much; So Near & Yet So Far; When You Wish Upon A Star; I'm Still In Love With You; Over The Rainbow; River Path.* I'M ON THE OUTSIDE: *I'm On The Outside; People; Our Song; Where Did Our Love Go; Make It Easy On Yourself; Girl From Ipanema; Walk On By; Letter A Day; Please Go;*

Exodus; Funny; Tears On My Pillow. MOVIE GRABBERS (September 1967): *You Only Live Twice; Georgy Girl; Love Theme From 'The Sandpiper'; This Is My Song; I Will Wait For You; Somewhere My Love; Man And A Woman; Who Can Say; Watch What Happens; Born Free; Gentle Rain; Restless One.* PAYIN' OUR DUES (April 1966): *Better Use Your Head; Call Me The Joker; Good For A Lifetime; Cry My Eyes Out; You Better Take It Easy Baby; Hungry Heart; It's Not The Same; Wonder Of It All; Gonna Fix You Good; Lost Without You; You're Not That Girl Anymore; Your Own Little World.* REFLECTIONS (May 1967): *Don't Tie Me Down; My Love Is A Rainbow; If I Remember To Forget; Keep It Up; Hold On To Someone; Yesterday Has Gone; Trick Or Treat; Lost In Love; In The Mirrors Of Your Mind; I Love You; Better Off Without You; Thousand Miles Away.*

Singles/*Beautiful People/If I Remember To Forget; Better Use Your Head/Wonder Of It All; Don't Tie Me Down/ Where There's A Will There's A Way; Down On Love/It's Not The Same; Gonna Fix You Good/You Better Take It Easy Baby; Hold On To Someone/Lost In Love; Hungry Heart/I'm Hypnotized; My Love Is A Rainbow/You Only Live Twice; The Diary/So Much; I'm Alright/Shimmy, Shimmy Ko-Ko Bop; I'm Still In Love With You/When You Wish Upon A Star; Prayer And A Jukebox/Tears On My Pillow; Two People In The World/Wishful Thinking; My Love Is A Rainbow/Yesterday Has Gone; Flesh Failures/Gentle Rain* (1968).

Also Appear On/15 HITS: *Shimmy, Shimmy Ko-Ko Bop.* OLDIES BUT GOODIES, VOL. 3: *Two People In The World.* 12 PLUS 3 EQUALS 15 HITS: *When You Wish Upon A Star; Shimmy, Shimmy Ko-Ko Bop.* ALAN FREED'S MEMORY LANE. MURRAY THE K'S GASSERS FOR SUBMARINE RACE WATCHERS.

THE APOLLO is a theatre in New York's Harlem which features exclusively black talent—usually at very moderate prices. From time immemorial, white artists (Elvis Presley among them) have slipped into the audience to pick up more than a few useful pointers from their black brothers. Most of

the extravagant hip and leg action of the early white rockers
seems to have been taken, squirm by squirm, thrust by thrust,
from the Apollo stars. Wednesday night is a particular delight
because it's amateur night, and there's usually more talent
there even on an off-night than you'd hope to see in a dozen
clubs all together anywhere else. High-school girls from South
Carolina who sing better than the Supremes, making al-
lowances for a little lack of confidence; stock clerks from
New Jersey who could show Sam and Dave a thing or two;
and, for the sadistically inclined, just enough duds to give that
demanding and ruthless audience a chance to hiss and boo
anything less than the best. They say if you can survive an
Apollo audience on amateur night, you can survive anything.
Ella Fitzgerald, Billie Holliday, Leslie Uggams and Joe Tex
are a few who got their start there.

ARS NOVA/*Wyatt Day (rhythm guitar), John Pierson (lead
singer, bass trombone), Sam Brown (lead guitar), Jimmy
Owens (trumpet, cornet), Art Koenig (bass), Joe Hunt
(drums).*
*Previous Members: Maury Baker, Bill Folwell, Giovanni
Papalia, Jonathan Raskin.*
If small boys who could scarcely play an instrument could get
a hit, what could a group of classical musicians with years of
intensive musical training in every aspect of composition do?
Ars Nova emerged to show us. People who heard their
rehearsals in a New York loft in the fall of 1967 came away
with stories of barbaric splendor and medieval elegance plus a
rock beat. Their first single was *Pavane For My Lady* and
very courtly. Their instrument range covered such time and
space spans it could have been borrowed from a museum.
Nevertheless, all did not go well, and *Life* magazine, which
started off in its rock issue (of June 28, 1968) covering the
rise of Ars Nova finished up covering its rise, fall and
Phoenix-like reemergence. In July of 1968 it got itself together with new personnel to come up with what might very
well be the first really impressive baroque rock sound in
music.
Albums/ARS NOVA (April 1968): *Pavane For My Lady;
General Clover Ends A War; And How Am I To Know;
Album In Your Mind; Zarathustra; Fields Of People; Auto-*

matic Love; I Wrapped Her In Ribbons; Song Of The City; March Of The Mad Duke's Circus. SUNSHINE AND SHADOWS (June 1969).

Singles/*Pavane For My Lady/Zarathustra* (April 1968); *Fields Of People/March Of The Mad Duke's Circus* (September 1968).

THE ASSOCIATION/*Russ Giguere (vocals, guitar), Ted Bluechel Jr. (drums), Brian Cole (bass vocals, bass guitar, clarinet), Terry Kirkman (vocals, 23 instruments including tambourine, recorder, drums, fluegel horn), Larry Ramos (replaced Gary Alexander) (lead guitar, tenor vocals, ukulele, banjo, bass drums, harmonica), Jim Yester (rhythm guitar, tenor vocals, organ, piano, harmonica).*

Their first hit was *Along Comes Mary* and, even though it was a beautiful song and deserved to sell a million (which it did), one of the reasons it sold so well was that it came along in 1966 in the middle of a big messy controversy about ambiguous lyrics. Some of the songs on the air, it seemed, were not as innocuous as they sounded if you were familiar with drug slang. The Byrds' *Eight Miles High* was one that was immediately suspect and actually banned in some places. The title of Dylan's *Rainy Day Women No. 12 & 35* was said to be another term for marijuana cigarettes. Even *Puff The Magic Dragon* was taken apart, to Peter, Paul and Mary's amazement, to show its drug meanings. In the middle of this came the Association's Mary who cured traumas and psychodramas. Aha, said the knowledgeable, the only Mary that does that is Marijuana. And sales immediately tripled.

There were no possible second meanings in their subsequent million sellers *Cherish, Windy* and *Never My Love,* but somehow that happy misunderstanding got them off to an auspicious start. Clearly, the Association, though clean, wholesome and unrebellious, had their heads in the right place. They are one of those very professional, very well-rehearsed groups, and in the Midwest particularly people travel for miles to trip out on those vocal harmonies. Often they sound like a robust heavenly choir. They would probably blow more minds if they looked freakier, but what they lose on the roundabouts they get back on the roller coasters, selling more records to "straight" people than most groups on the rock scene today.

Albums/AND THEN . . . ALONG COMES THE ASSOCIA-TION (April 1966): *Along Comes Mary; Enter The Young; Your Own Love; Don't Blame It On Me; Blistered; I'll Be Your Man; Cherish; Standing Still; Message Of Our Love; Round Again; Remember; Changes.* RENAISSANCE (April 1967): *Pandora's Golden Heebie Jeebies; Memories Of You; Songs In The Wind; You Hear Me Call Your Name; I'm The One; You May Think; All Is Mine; Looking Glass; Come To Me; No Fair At All; Another Time, Another Place; Angeline.* INSIGHT OUT (August 1967): *Windy; Wasn't It A Bit Like Now; On A Quiet Night; We Love Us; When Love Comes To Me; Reputation; Never My Love; Happiness; Sometime; Wantin' Ain't Gettin'; Requiem For The Masses.* BIRTHDAY (April 1968): *Everything That Touches You; Come On In; Rose Petals, Incense And Kitten; Like Always; Toymaker; Barefoot Gentleman; Time For Livin'; Hear In Here; Time It Is Today; Bus Song; Birthday Morning.* ASSOCIATION'S GREATEST HITS (November 1968): *Cherish; Windy; Never My Love; Along Comes Mary; Enter The Young; Everything That Touches You; No Fair At All; Six Man Band; Time For Livin'; We Love; The Time It Is Today; Like Always; Requiem For The Masses.*

Singles/*Along Comes Mary/Cherish* (August 1966); *Windy /Sometime* (May 1967); *Never My Love/Requiem For The Masses* (August 1967); *Everything That Touches You/We Love Us* (January 1968); *Time For Livin'/Birthday Morning* (April 1968); *Like Always/Six Man Band* (August 1968); *Time It Is Today/Enter The Young* (November 1968).

CHET ATKINS/The magic of today's rock guitarist comes partly out of blues, partly out of the country and western tradition via Elvis. Chet Atkins, legendary country guitarist, Grand Ole Opry star, Nashville personality and vice-president of RCA Victor, inspired Elvis, Carl Perkins, Johnny Cash and all those country singers turned rockers of the middle fifties who helped put the guitar back up front where it counts. You hear a lot of Chet Atkins in the Beatle songs when they are in a country mood (especially in *RUBBER SOUL*). Although

Atkins is a senior executive, a prolific producer of albums, a star and undoubtedly a millionaire, he is still to be found, not occasionally, but often, doing session work in Nashville, not just for big names but for little names und newcomers. It's an old Nashville habit and hard to break. It's one reason people fly down there to get the Nashville sound—they could very well end up with Atkins playing lead guitar.

Albums/CHET ATKINS AT HOME (July 1958); SESSION WITH CHET ATKINS; STRINGIN' ALONG; IN THREE DIMENSIONS; FINGER STYLE GUITAR; CHET ATKINS IN HOLLYWOOD (July 1959); HUM AND STRUM ALONG (August 1959); MISTER GUITAR (January 1960); CHET ATKINS IN TEENSVILLE (February 1960); OTHER CHET ATKINS (September 1960); CHET ATKINS WORKSHOP (February 1961); CHET ATKINS AND HIS GUITAR (May 1961); MOST POPULAR GUITAR (July 1961); DOWN HOME (March 1962); CARIBBEAN GUITAR (September 1962); BACK HOME HYMNS (November 1962); OUR MAN IN NASHVILLE (February 1963); GUITAR GENIUS (May 1963); TRAVELIN' (June 1963); TEEN SCENE (September 1963); GUITAR COUNTRY (February 1964); BEST OF CHET ATKINS (June 1964); PROGRESSIVE PICKIN' (July 1964); REMINISCING (December 1964); MY FAVORITE GUITARS (April 1965); GUITAR COUNTRY (November 1965); CHET ATKINS PICKS ON THE BEATLES (May 1966); BEST OF CHET ATKINS (July 1966); MUSIC FROM NASHVILLE (August 1966); FROM NASHVILLE WITH LOVE (November 1966); GUITAR WORLD (April 1967); CHET ATKINS PICKS THE BEST (June 1967); CLASS GUITAR (November 1967); CHET (December 1967); SOLO FLIGHTS (March 1968); HOMETOWN GUITAR (August 1968).

AUTOSALVAGE/*Thomas Danaher (lead singer, rhythm guitar), Darius LaNoue Davenport (vocal, oboe, piano, drums, trombone, guitar, bass guitar, krummhorn, recorder), Rick Turner (lead guitar, banjo, dulcimer), Skip Boone (bass guitar, piano).*

The group was started in the middle of 1966 by Thomas Danaher, who was a folk and bluegrass freak, and Darius

LaNoue Davenport, who came from a musical family. Lead guitarist Turner, son of a poet and a painter, had worked with Ian and Sylvia and then with a long line of rock groups. Bass Skip Boone is the brother of Steve Boone, Lovin' Spoonful bass. Originally discovered by the Mothers, the group broke up when they saw it wasn't enough to be good; you also had to sell a lot of records to make the sort of money that made the whole hassle worthwhile. Their album, released in 1968, is full of quiet flashes, and there are people about still weeping at the demise of a group called Autosalvage—even if there is a fine album left to remember it by.

Album/AUTOSALVAGE (January 1968): *Auto Salvage; Bugular Song; Hundred Days; Rampant Generalities; Ancestral Wants; Land Of Their Dreams; Parahighway; Medley.* **Single**/*Parahighway/Rampant Dreams* (January 1968).

FRANKIE AVALON was one of the boy wonders of pre-Beatle rock and roll. In 1955, when he was only thirteen, he was a precocious child trumpet player who wowed them at the Horn and Hardart's Children's Hour. But by 1959, aged seventeen, his song *Venus* was on the number one spot for five weeks and his career as a singer and teen idol seemed set forever, putting him up with names like Tommy Sands, Ricky Nelson, Paul Anka and Dion. *The Beatles buried him.* There were people who never got over it and still regard the Beatles as little more than beasts for what they "did" to the boys with the pompadours and the silk suits of the 1956-64 era. For others, Avalon is a symbol of the sort of adult-controlled teen love scene the Beatles *saved* us from. However, lately there has been a sentimental swing back to that era. And like quite a few former idols, Frankie does very nicely on the cabaret circuit, being an "adult" entertainer and bringing back nostalgic memories of a million senior proms in the early sixties.

Album/15 GREATEST HITS (August 1964): *Venus; Why; Bobby Sox To Stockings; De De Dinah; Gingerbread; With All My Heart; Too Young To Love; Don't Let Love Pass Me By; Don't Make Fun Of Me; Where Are You; Who Else But You; Perfect Love; You Are Mine; I'll Wait For You; Don't Throw Away All Those Teardrops.*

Singles/*But I Do/Dancing On The Stars; Don't You Do It/ It's Over* (December 1968).

ALBERT AYLER TRIO/*Albert Ayler (saxophone), Gary Peacock (electric bass), Sonny Murray (drums).*
Although officially termed a jazz group, it was the Albert Ayler Trio's rollicking rhythm and blues sound that made it a favorite with the rock musicians of 1968—just one example of how much more into jazz rock groups are than the average person suspects.

Albums/MY NAME IS ALBERT AYLER: *Bye Bye Blackbird; Billie's Bounce; C.T.; Summertime; Green Dolphin Street.* ALBERT AYLER IN GREENWICH VILLAGE (October 1967): *For John Coltrane; Change Has Come; Truth Is Marching In; Our Prayer.* LOVE CRY (April 1968): *Love Cry; Ghosts; Omega; Dancing Flowers; Bells; Love Flower; Zion Hill; Universal Indians.* NEW GRASS (February 1969).

JOAN BAEZ/There must have been better and sweeter voices than early Joan Baez (Isla Cameron in England was one), but no one can remember them. She arrived in 1960 in a folk scene where to be flat, nasal and otherwise out of tune was a mark of authenticity; and though she sang too well to sound authentic, there were people ready to forgive her that. Jack Elliott, for one, Rambling Jack Elliott, came away from one of her early appearances at Gerdes' Folk City with his head reeling. He later went around for weeks telling people she'd made the best first album he'd ever heard. As well as this, and it didn't seem possible, she had a whole look that matched that voice. Raven hair, olive skin, a white smile—a romantic figure born to be a heroine, voice or no voice. She had never studied singing, this girl who started off in the small clubs of Cambridge, Mass., but at the age of twenty she was already getting top marks from the critics for the classical musts: pitch and diction. When she started coming across as a bargain-basement Pete Seeger, urging singalongs, she captivated a whole new generation of Seeger fans and, much more important, won over all the people who had never even considered liking folk music before. She *must* have won them over, because by November 1962 she had three albums on the charts (more than Sinatra) and a *Time* cover.

She was not the first of the folk singers, of course, merely the first to make it nationally and internationally on a mass-market basis. It may have taken Peter, Paul and Mary to put folk *singles* on the charts, but "Joanie" (people really did call her that) was the first to put folk *albums* in among the best sellers. She gave a young boy named Bob Dylan his start by dragging him on stage with her when he was still unknown. He would sing his strange songs and, because he laughed at her for singing her straight ones, the Childe Ballads and all that predictable folkie paraphernalia, she would sing his songs, and they knocked people out. There was one tentative move, in 1966, in the wake of Dylan, to go electric. A Baez rock album, produced by her brother-in-law Richard Fariña, was reportedly recorded but never released.

Although a million girls with raven hair, white smiles and olive skins took up guitars almost immediately after Baez emerged singing *Donna Donna* and *Plaisir D'Amour* to all who would listen, her impact has always been more social than musical. Like many other folk singers, though she was among the first to do so, she moved out of her classical and lyrical stage into protest; but unlike others, she never did move out of protest, extending it instead to the nonsinging part of her life: a school for nonviolence, which by 1967 was taking up most of her time and energy, with concert appearances and records playing a much smaller role. In the South and in Washington, she marched and sang for civil rights. In Berkeley she marched and sang for student rights. She unfurled herself like a banner at the head of almost every big demonstration of the troubled sixties. She had taken the folk singer off the stage and into the theatre of the streets. Then, finally, when everyone else was marching, when everyone like her was holding back taxes so they would not contribute to the war in Vietnam, she retired to her school for nonviolence, emerging only now and then to sing *Saigon Bride* or the Beatles' *Eleanor Rigby*. In 1968 there was an autobiography and an album of poems. She is obviously never destined to change the face of music again as she did when she first appeared with the perfect voice at the perfect moment. But she has made it clear she intends to change the face of society or die in the attempt.

Albums/JOAN BAEZ (October 1960): *Silver Dagger; East Virginia; Fare Thee Well; House Of The Rising Sun; All My Trials; Wildwood Flower; Donna Donna; Rake And Rambling Boy; Mary Hamilton; Henry Martin; Preso; John Riley; Little Moses.* JOAN BAEZ VOLUME 2 (September 1961): *Wagoner's Lad; Trees They Do Grow High; Lily Of The West; Silkie; Engine 143; Once I Knew A Pretty Girl; Lonesome Road; Banks Of The Ohio; Pal Of Mine; Barbara Allen; Cherry Tree Carol; Old Blue; Railroad Boy; Plaisir D'Amour.* JOAN BAEZ IN CONCERT (September 1962): *Babe, I'm Gonna Leave You; Geordie; Cooper Kettle; Kumbaya; Black Is The Color; Danger Waters; Gospel Ship; House Carpenter; Lady Mary; Pretty Boy Floyd; Ate Amanha; What Have They Done To The Rain; Matty Groves.* JOAN BAEZ IN CONCERT, PART 2 (November 1963): *Once I Had A Sweetheart; Jackaroo; Queen Of Hearts; Don't Think Twice, It's All Right; We Shall Overcome; Portland Town; Manha De Carnival; Te Adoro; Long Black Veil; 'Nu Bello Cardillo; Hush Little Baby; Rambler Gambler; Fennario; Three Fishers; Battle Hymn.* JOAN BAEZ/5 (October 1964): *I Still Miss Someone; When You Hear Them Cuckoos Hollerin'; Birmingham Sunday; So We'll Go No More A-Roving; O' Cangaceiro; Unquiet Grave; There But For Fortune; It Ain't Me Babe; Stewball; Death Of Queen Jane; Bachianas Brasileiras No. 5; Go 'Way From My Window.* FAREWELL ANGELINA (October 1965): *Farewell Angelina; Daddy, You Been On My Mind; It's All Over Now, Baby Blue; Wild Mountain Thyme; Ranger's Command; River In The Pines; Colours; Satisfied Mind; Pauvre Ruteboeuf; Where Have All The Flowers Gone* (In German); *Hard Rain's A-Gonna Fall.* NOEL (October 1966): *Good King Wenceslas; Bring A Torch, Jeanette, Isabella; Angels We Have Heard On High; Deck The Halls; Adeste Fidelis; O Come, O Come, Emmanuel; Coventry Carol; Little Drummer Boy; I Wonder As I Wander; Down In Yon Forest; Carol Of The Birds; Ave Maria; Mary's Wandering; Away In A Manger; Oh Holy Night; What Child Is This; Silent Night.* JOAN (August 1967): *Be Not Too Hard; Eleanor Rigby;*

Turquoise; La Colombe; Dangling Conversation; Lady Came From Baltimore; North; Children Of Darkness; Greenwood Side; If I Were A Carpenter; Annabelle Lee; Saigon Bride. BAPTISM—A JOURNEY THROUGH OUR TIME (June 1968): *Old Welsh Song; I Saw The Vision Of Armies; Minister Of War; Song In The Blood; Casida Of The Lament; Of The Dark Past; London; In Guernica; Who Murdered The Minutes; Oh, Little Child; No Man Is An Island; Portrait Of The Artist As A Young Man; All The Pretty Little Horses; Childhood III; The Magic Wood; Poems From The Japanese; Colours; All In Green Went My Love Riding; Gacela Of The Dark Death; The Parable Of The Old Man And The Young; Evil; Epitaph For A Poet; Old Welsh Song.* ANY DAY NOW (January 1969): *Love Minus Zero/No Limit; North Country Blues; You Ain't Goin' Nowhere; Drifter's Escape; I Pity The Poor Immigrant; Tears Of Rage; Sad-Eyed Lady Of The Lowlands; Love Is Just A Four-Letter Word; I Dreamed I Saw St. Augustine; The Walls Of Redwing; Dear Landlord; One Too Many Mornings; I Shall Be Released; Boots Of Spanish Leather; Restless Farewell.*

Singles/*Cantique De Noel/Little Drummer Boy* (June 1966); *Daddy, You Been On My Mind/There But For Fortune* (May 1967).

BAGATELLE/*Lee Mason (drums, lead singer), Fred Griffith (vocals), Steve Schrell (saxophone, clarinet, flute), Willie Alexander (piano, vocals), David "Redtop" Thomas (vocals), David "Turk" Bynoe (bass guitar, bass fiddle, harmonica, wooden flute, drums), Mark "Swifty" Gould (trumpet, flugelhorn, French horn, piano, organ), Rodney Young (drums, kazoo, clavets, cowbell, vocals), Marshall O'Connell (guitar).*
A black and white nine-man group specializing in soulful material, sometimes a bit tongue in cheek. In their first album, recorded live in 1968, there is a medley of songs from the pop charts of the fifties, full of doo-wah doo-wahs, and a nice piece of musical satire. This may be an indication that musical satire has arrived on the rock scene.

Album/11 PM SATURDAY (September 1968): *Soul Man; Got To Get You Into My Life; Shake; Mashed Potatoes;*

Such A Fuss About Sunday; Hey You; I'm Losin' You; Back On The Farm; Every Night; Everybody Knows; I've Been Trying; I Can't Stand It; I Feel Good (Medley).

Single/*Such A Fuss About Sunday/What Can I Do* (September 1968).

LONG JOHN BALDRY/A former English disc jockey, he is one of a long line of Englishmen who love to sing traditional American blues. He already has an album out in America, *LONG JOHN'S BLUES*, and his *Let The Heartaches Begin* was a number one record in England.

Album/LONG JOHN'S BLUES: *Got My Mojo Working; Gee Baby Ain't I Good To You; Roll 'Em Pete; You're Breaking My Heart; I'm Your Hoochie Coochie Man; Five Long Years; Everyday; Dimples; My Babe; Times Are Getting Tougher Than Tough; Goin' Down Slow; Rock The Joint.*

Singles/*Hey Lord You Made The Night Too Long/Let The Heartaches Begin; Hold Back The Daybreak/Since I Lost You Baby; Bring My Baby Back To Me/Cuckoo; Let Him Go (& Let Me Love You)/Only A Fool Breaks His Own Heart; Wise To The Ways Of The World/When The Sun Come Shining Thru* (September 1968).

FLORENCE BALLARD/She was with the Supremes and left to become a solo artist, probably, one suspects, because she is married (which the other Supremes weren't) and wanted to spend more time with her husband. But her voice is so good that she was at one stage considered to sing lead before it was finally decided Diana Ross would be the one. She has a few singles out, but there has been no full-scale push to promote her.
(see SUPREMES)

Singles/*Goin' Out Of My Head/It Doesn't Matter How I Say It; Forever Faithful/Love Ain't Love* (October 1968).

HANK BALLARD (and THE MIDNIGHTERS)/Hank Ballard ought to be as rich as Croesus. For one thing, back in 1960 or so he wrote a song called *The Twist* and we all know what *that* started. Every discotheque in the world should be giving him royalties for having single-handedly started the biggest dance revival in history. But that's not the way it has been, and even Chubby Checker who, in 1962, rose high on Hank's song (much to Hank's despair, since he'd been doing the song for some time), ended up working on the nostalgia circuit. Hank is still around though, playing his old hits, not just *The Twist* but a host of rhythm and blues hits, especially the beautiful Annie songs of 1954 that turned thousands of kids on to the r & b songs that were eventually to open up the door for rock and roll. The Annie records (*Work With Me Annie, Annie Had A Baby* and others), like most rhythm and blues hits but unlike the songs on the "white" hit parades, told it exactly like it was and white kids couldn't believe their ears. But although they sold millions they were swiftly yanked off the airwaves. *Work With Me Annie* was rewritten for youthful ears as *Dance With Me Henry* which, let's face it, wasn't the same thing at all. This was to set an interesting pattern that continued for some years of white bowdlerization of raunchy black r & b lyrics. The cleaned-up versions, sung by white singers and backed by large companies that could promote them, would end up high on the white charts, with few of the buyers realizing there was an original version that was bigger and better but had less money behind it to push it. Eventually all that changed and more and more of the originals got on the charts, but it was not early enough for Hank Ballard (who deserved to) to fully reap the benefits.

Albums/HANK BALLARD AND THE MIDNIGHTERS: *Work With Me Annie; Moonrise; Sexy Ways; Get It; Switchie Witchie Twitchie; It's Love Baby; Annie Had A Baby; She's The One; Annie's Aunt Fannie; Crazy Loving; Henry's Got Flat Feet; Tore Up Over You.* HANK BALLARD'S BIGGEST HITS: *Let's Go, Let's Go, Let's Go; Teardrops On Your Letter; Finger Poppin' Time; Let's Go Again; I'm Learning; Twist; It's Love Baby; Kansas City; Sugarfree; Work With Me Annie; Annie Had A Baby; Hoochi Coochi Coo.* THOSE LAZY, LAZY DAYS: *Let's Get The Show On The Road; Knock On Wood I Feel So Good; Somebody's Got To Help Me; That's Your Mistake; Handwriting On The Wall; You Don't Have To Cry; Watch What I Tell You; One Monkey Don't Stop No Show; I Done It; Seven Nights To*

Rock; Everybody Do Wrong; Winner Never Quits. GLAD
SONGS, SAD SONGS.

Singles/*If You'd Forgive Me/Let's Go, Let's Go, Let's Go;
I'm Just A Fool/Do It Zulu Style; My Sun Is Going Down/
Sloop And Slide; He Came Along/I Was Born To Move;
Dance Till It Hurtcha/Here Comes The Hurt; Unwind Your-
self/You're In Real Good Hands; Funky Soul Train/Which
Way Should I Turn; Come On Wit' It/I'm Back To Stay;
Finger Poppin' Time/I Love You, I Love You So-O-O; Annie
Had A Baby/She's The One; Work With Me, Annie/Until I
Die; Don't Say Your Last Goodbye/She's The One; Come On
Wit' It/I'm Back To Stay* (August 1968).

Also Appears On/18 KING SIZE RHYTHM AND BLUES
HITS (August 1967): *Work With Me Annie; Finger Poppin'
Time.*

THE BAND/*Rick Danko (bass, vocals), Levon Helm (drums,
vocals), Garth Hudson (organ, vocals), Richard Manuel
(piano, vocals), Robbie Robertson (lead guitar, vocals).*
When, in the middle of 1968, they released an album called
MUSIC FROM BIG PINK hardly anyone knew who they
were, which was remarkable because almost everyone agreed
it had to be the best and most honest record to come out in
months. The Hawks is who they were, and they had even
made some records as Levon and the Hawks. All but one
were from Canada and all, even that one, out of a long,
dusty, country tradition. They had been playing together since
1959, and one summer night in 1965 they were playing in
New Jersey when Bob Dylan phoned them. He had heard of
them but they claim they had barely heard of him. "Wanna
play Hollywood Bowl?" he said. Who else, they asked guard-
edly, would be on the bill? "Just us," said Dylan. And "just
us" it was in America, Asia, Australia, and Europe when the
new electrified Dylan made his bow. The shock of seeing a
folk singer of Dylan's integrity with a rock band is already
history. The Hawks heard more hissing in those few months
than they will ever hear in a lifetime. But the public recovered.
    When Dylan was hurt in a 1966 motorcycle accident, his
band holed up in Woodstock too, and was not heard from till

that LP came out at a time when rock was so complicated it only served to point up the album's simplicity. Reviewers saw the shadow of Dylan hovering over the album. He coauthored two songs on it and authored one, but from the start they were separate entities and remained so.

The album is very religious in mood. Several songs have Biblical references: Nazareth, the Devil, Moses and Luke in *The Weight,* the Golden Calf and the wreath of thistles and thorns in *To Kingdom Come.* Both *Caledonia Mission* and *I Shall Be Released* have religious overtones. All this is uncommon in rock (though not so uncommon in Dylan). The record is distinguished by its good taste. The use of the wah-wah pedal is so soft and soulful that Jimi Hendrix would barely recognize it. And the singing is freer, looser and more emotional than any other white record of that time. The instrumentation in the Big Pink album is directly influenced by the band that Dylan put together in his *BLONDE ON BLONDE* album, a band that greatly influenced the English group Procol Harum, which also uses the piano and organ combination. Lead guitarist Robbie Robertson is already being considered one of rock's more perfect guitarists and a songwriter of note. (His songs are on Cass Elliott's first solo album.) The group has been called everything from The Crackers, The Hawks, Dylan's Band and Big Pink to The Band. Its sound has been described as country rock, gospel blues, backwoods rock. But no name or label can describe it. It's simply music from Big Pink.

Album/MUSIC FROM BIG PINK (June 1968): *Tears Of Rage; To Kingdom Come; In A Station; Caledonia Mission; The Weight; We Can Talk; Long Black Veil; Chest Fever; Lonesome Swine; This Wheel's On Fire; I Shall Be Released.*

Single/*The Weight/I Shall Be Released.*

BAR-KAYS/They were a young, six-man group backing Otis Redding, and they had a hit out on their own: *Soulfinger.* Four of them died with Otis on December 10, 1967, when his private plane crashed. By October 1968 there was talk that the two surviving members were getting together a new group, which they did.

Album/SOUL FINGER: *Soul Finger; Knucklehead; With A Child's Heart; Bar-Kays Boogaloo; Hell's Angels; You Can't Sit Down; House Shoes; Don't Do That; Pearl High; I Want Someone; Hole In The Wall.*

Singles/*Soul Finger/Knucklehead; Don't Do That/Give Everybody Some; Hard Day's Night/I Want Someone.*

BAROQUE ROCK/On Procol Harum's *A Whiter Shade Of Pale* (1967), it's a Bach cantata. With Chrysalis (1968), it's a harpsichord on double speed. Two groups, the New York String Ensemble and the New York Rock and Roll Ensemble, are working at combining rock and baroque. And, of course, Ars Nova's whole (1967-68) sound is based on adding a rock beat to baroque music. In London Sebastian Jorgenson rewrote many baroque guitar pieces for electric guitar. The whole baroque rock movement is, at the moment, small, dedicated and not too commercially successful.

BEACH BOYS/*Al Jardine, Bruce Johnston, Mike Love, Brian Wilson, Carl Wilson, Dennis Wilson.*
Southern California has the sweetest and highest life style developed by the race. Its surface manifestations—riding in open cars, surfing, being in the sun, making love and watching tv—can be deceptive and puzzling, like Stonehenge and the Aztec temples. Pacific American civilization is a startling synthesis of opposites—sad rootlessness and loving homeyness, crazy speed and narcotic calm, ugly plastic and the orange sun—the wise mindlessness of extreme America. The great musical poets of this land are the Beach Boys (perhaps along with the astral Byrds). They arose, high-school boys from Hawthorne, with Mike and Brian's idea for a song about surfing. That song, *Surfin'*, a local hit, was the theme of their first album, *SURFIN' SAFARI,* which was released in November 1962. A celebration of airiness and speed, speed on the water or on the road (as in *409*), perfectly realized in the energetic melodies, cheerful repetitions and magical harmonies masterminded by Brian Wilson, this music, beautiful in itself, beautifully captured the bright simplicity of the early sixties' California life. (Live, the group, attired in matching striped shirts, became a great youth attraction in the same

bright simple way.) Their next twelve albums, vast hits with titles like *SURFER GIRL, LITTLE DEUCE COUPE* and *SUMMER DAYS,* worked this mindless joyfulness into exquisite songs, and the love songs, like *Wendy, In My Room, Barbara Ann* and, of course, *California Girls,* introduced a new softness and expressiveness.

The group produced a musical history of their place and time—summertime blues and chug-a-lug in 1962, noble surfers in 1963 (but also the getting away from the salty surf to the drama of black denim trousers and motorcycle boots. *Little Deuce Coupe* was immortalized as the contemporary gasoline-fed love goddess) and in 1964, when the Beatles were about to hit America, oblivious California was singing about *Fun, Fun, Fun* and *This Car Of Mine.* At the same time, the classic rock songs of Chuck Berry had a place in the Beach Boys' repertoire (as they did in the repertoires of most other rock groups of the pre-Beatle period), and so even when Bob Dylan made his first surprising appearances on the charts, the Beach Boys were able to absorb that, too—and his *The Times They Are A-Changin'* turns up on their party record, a gracious acknowledgment that there was, from time to time, something happening in the "outside" world.

That was the way it was for the Beach Boys—glorious harmonious oblivion—until their thirteenth album, *PET SOUNDS,* released in May 1966. *PET SOUNDS* represents a curious moment in the astounding development of Beach Boy composer-producer Brian Wilson—and an equally curious moment in the history of southern California. The hot rods and the gremmies gave way to a more interior theme. No more celebrations of mechanical exaltations. What was happening to southern California and to Wilson in 1966 was a more private matter, a thoughtful look inside the mind. For many in that sunny climate the new direction came through drugs and psychedelia via San Francisco. For others it came from religion or from a general contact high which became the occupational hazard of young Californians in the late sixties. Whatever it was for the Beach Boys, with the new private themes came a larger symphonic sound which suggested something of the expansions of Brain Wilson's musical and nonmusical mind. Significantly, the new complex orchestrations in *PET SOUNDS* were as disciplined, as clean and as well organized as the earlier, simpler Beach Boy sounds. Nothing was lost in the change. (Other groups were changing too. The Beatles' *RUBBER SOUL* album had appeared, and the creative interrelationship of the great groups had begun.) *Wouldn't It Be Nice* and *God Only Knows* typify the mood of this album, which began to achieve for the Beach Boys a following among serious pop musicians previously put off by a theme and style that seemed too superficial and too commercial.

Suddenly more deeply involved in production and composition, Brian Wilson stopped performing with the group (to be replaced by Bruce Johnston). He withdrew to his mansion and entered into a curious, perhaps ill-advised and certainly ill-fated symbiosis with composer Van Dyke Parks. Their planned album, *SMILES*, never appeared, and the Beach Boys' next album, *SMILEY SMILE,* contained only one memorable Wilson-Parks collaboration, *Heroes And Villains,* and the Brian Wilson-Mike Love song, *Good Vibrations,* which is still their masterpiece. *FRIENDS*, a more recent album and a rather minor one except for a few charming songs, like the title one, is most notable for the song *Transcendental Meditation,* a reflection of their unsurprising involvement with the Maharishi Mahesh Yogi, who joined them on a tour he never completed. In general, the second phase of the Beach Boys' music, from *PET SOUNDS* onwards, did the same as the first phase—it mirrored the rising and falling fortunes of the southern California culture. Just as the cars and the surf and the simplicity of the early sixties was recorded in the Beach Boys' earlier works, so the arrival of hallucinogenic drugs and religious interiorization of the late sixties are reflected in their songs of that period. Miraculously, while some things changed (including 'the Beach Boys' uniform and appearance, from surfie to psychedelic to English mod), other things remained the same. The sun will always shine in California, drugs or not, the surf will always break, so the Beach Boys, though larger in their scope, have managed to retain their freshness.

Albums/SURFIN' SAFARI (November 1962): *Surfin' Safari; County Fair; Ten Little Indians; Chug-A-Lug; Little Girl (You're My Miss America); 409; Surfin'; Heads You Win— Tails I Lose; Summertime Blues; Cuckoo Clock; Moon Dawg;*

The Shift. SURFIN' U.S.A. (March 1963): *Surfin' U.S.A.; Farmer's Daughter; Misirlou; Stoked; Lonely Sea; Shut Down; Noble Surfer; Honky Tonky; Lana; Surf Jam; Let's Go Trippin'; Finders Keepers.* SHUT DOWN (March 1963): *Shut Down; Chicken; Wide Track; Brontosaurus Stomp; Four On The Floor; Black Denim Trousers And Motorcycle Boots; 409; Street Machine; The Ballad Of Thunder Road; Hot Rod Race; Car Trouble; Cheater Slicks.* SURFER GIRL (September 1963): *Surfer Girl; Catch A Wave; The Surfer Moon; South Bay Surfer; The Rocking Surfer; Little Deuce Coupe; In My Room; Hawaii; Surfer's Rule; Our Car Club; Your Summer Dream; Boogie Woogie.* LITTLE DEUCE COUPE (October 1963): *Little Deuce Coupe; Ballad Of Ole' Betsy; Be True To Your School; Car Crazy Cutie; Cherry, Cherry Coupe; 409; Shut Down; Spirit Of America; Our Car Club; No-Go Showboat; A Young Man Is Gone; Custom Machine.* SHUT DOWN VOLUME 2 (March 1964): *Fun, Fun, Fun; Don't Worry Baby; In The Parkin' Lot; "Cassius" Love Versus "Sonny" Wilson; The Warmth Of The Sun; This Car Of Mine; Why Do Fools Fall In Love; Pom, Pom Play Girl; Keep An Eye On Summer; Shut Down, Part II; Louie, Louie; Denny's Drums.* ALL SUMMER LONG (August 1964): *Get Around; All Summer Long; Hushabye; Little Honda; We'll Run Away; Carl's Big Chance; Wendy; Do You Remember; Girls On The Beach; Drive-in; Our Favorite Recording Sessions; Don't Back Down.* BEACH BOYS CHRISTMAS ALBUM (October 1964): *Little Saint Nick; The Man With All The Toys; Santa's Beard; Merry Christmas, Baby; Christmas Day; Frosty The Snowman; We Three Kings Of Orient Are; Blue Christmas; Santa Claus Is Coming To Town; White Christmas; I'll Be Home For Christmas; Auld Lang Syne.* BEACH BOYS CONCERT (October 1964): *Fun, Fun, Fun; The Little Old Lady From Pasadena; Little Deuce Coupe; Long, Tall Texan; In My Room; The Monster Mash; Let's Go Trippin'; Papa-Oom-Mow-Mow; The Wanderer; Hawaii; Graduation Day; I Get Around; Johnny B. Goode.* BEACH BOYS TODAY (March 1965): *Do You Wanna Dance; Good To My Baby; Don't Hurt My Little Sister; When I Grow Up; Help Me, Rhonda; Dance, Dance, Dance; Please Let Me Wonder; I'm So Young; Kiss Me, Baby; She Knows Me Too Well; In The Back Of My Mind; Bull Session with* the *"Big Daddy."* SUMMER DAYS (June 1965): *The Girl From New York City; Amusement Parks U.S.A.; Then I Kissed Her; Salt Lake City; Girl Don't Tell Me; Help Me, Rhonda; California Girls; Let Him Run Wild; You're So Good To Me; Summer Means New Love; I'm Bugged At My Ol' Man; And Your Dream Comes True.* BEACH BOYS' PARTY (November 1965): *Hully Gully; I Should Have Known Better; Tell Me Why; Papa-Oom-Mow-Mow; Mountain Of Love; You've Got To Hide Your Love Away; Devoted To You; Alley Oop; There's No Other (Like My Baby); Medley; I Get Around; Little Deuce Coupe; The Times They Are A-Changin'; Barbara Ann.* PET SOUNDS (May 1966): *Wouldn't It Be Nice; You Still Believe In Me; That's Not Me; Don't Talk (Put Your Head On My Shoulder); I'm Waiting For The Day; Let's Go Away For Awhile; Sloop John B.; God Only Knows; I Know There's An Answer; Here Today; I Just Wasn't Made For These Times; Pet Sounds; Caroline, No.* BEST OF THE BEACH BOYS (June 1966): *Surfin' U.S.A.; Catch A Wave; Surfer Girl; Little Deuce Coupe; In My Room; Little Honda; Fun, Fun, Fun; The Warmth Of The Sun; Louie, Louie; Kiss Me, Baby; You're So Good To Me; Wendy.* BEST OF THE BEACH BOYS—VOLUME 2 (July 1967): *Barbara Ann; When I Grow Up; Long, Tall Texan; Please Let Me Wonder; 409; Let Him Run Wild; Don't Worry Baby; Surfin' Safari; Little Saint Nick; California Girls; Help Me, Rhonda; I Get Around.* SMILEY SMILE (September 1967): *Heroes And Villains; Vegetables; Fall Breaks And Back To Winter; Little Pad; She's Goin' Bald; Good Vibrations; With Me Tonight; Wind Chimes; Gettin' Hungry; Wonderful; Whistle In.* BEACH BOYS DELUXE SET (October 1967): *Wouldn't It Be Nice; You Still Believe In Me; That's Not Me; Don't Talk; I'm Waiting For The Day; Let's Go Away For Awhile; God Only Knows; Sloop John B.; I Know There's An Answer; Here Today; I Just Wasn't Made For These Times; Pet Sounds; Caroline, No; Girl From New York City; Amusement Parks U.S.A.; Then I Kissed Her; Salt Lake City; Girl Don't Tell Me; Help Me, Rhonda; Let Him Run Wild; California Girls; You're So Good To Me; Summer Means New Love; I'm Bugged At My Ol' Man; And Your Dream Comes True; Do You Wanna Dance; Good To My Baby;*

Don't Hurt My Little Sister; When I Grow Up; Dance, Dance, Dance; Please Let Me Wonder; Kiss Me, Baby; I'm So Young; She Knows Me Too Well; In The Back Of My Mind; Bull Session With The "Big Daddy." WILD HONEY (December 1967): *Wild Honey; Aren't You Glad; I Was Made To Love Her; Country Air; Thing Or Two; Here Comes The Night; Darlin'; I'd Love Just Once To See You; Let The Wind Blow; How She Boogalooed It; Mama Says.* FRIENDS (June 1968): *Meant For You; Friends; Wake The World; Be Here In The Mornin'; When A Man Needs A Woman; Passing By; Anna Lee, The Healer; Little Bird; Be Still; Busy Doin' Nothin'; Diamond Head; Transcendental Meditation.* THE BEACH BOYS 20/20 (March 1969): *Do It Again; I Can Hear Music; Bluebirds Over The Mountain; Be With Me; All I Want To Do; The Nearest Faraway Place; Cotton Fields; I Went To Sleep; Time To Get Alone; Never Learn Not To Love; Our Prayer; Cabinessence.*

Singles/*Surfin' Safari*/*409* (June 1962); *Surfin' U.S.A.*/*Shut Down* (March 1963); *Surfer Girl*/*Little Deuce Coupe* (July 1963); *Be True To Your School*/*In My Room* (October 1963); *Little Saint Nick*/*The Lord's Prayer* (December 1963); *Fun, Fun, Fun*/*Why Do Fools Fall In Love* (February 1964); *I Get Around*/*Don't Worry Baby* (May 1964); *Ten Little Indians*/*She Knows Me Too Well* (September 1964); *Four By The Beach Boys* (September 1964); *Dance, Dance, Dance*/*The Warmth Of The Sun* (November 1964); *Help Me, Rhonda*/*Do You Wanna Dance* (March 1965); *California Girls*/*Let Him Run Wild* (July 1965); *Barbara Ann*/*Girl Don't Tell Me* (January 1966); *Sloop John B.*/*You're So Good To Me* (March 1966); *God Only Knows*/*Wouldn't It Be Nice* (August 1966); *Good Vibrations*/*Let's Go Away For Awhile* (October 1966); *Heroes And Villains*/*You're Welcome* (July 1967); *Wild Honey*/*Wind Chimes* (October 1967); *Darlin'*/*Here Today* (December 1967); *Friends*/*Little Bird* (April 1968); *Bluebirds Over The Mountain*/*Never Learn Not To Love* (1968); *Do It Again*/*Wake The World* (1968).

BEACON STREET UNION/*Paul Tartachny (lead guitar, rhythm guitar, vocals), Wayne Ulaky (bass guitar, vocals),*

John Wright (lead singer, percussion), Richard Weisburg (drums), Robert Rhodes (keyboard, brass).
This is one of several groups that made their national debut as part of a 1968 Boston sound promotion. The problem was there *was* no Boston sound and the groups suffered in the ensuing confusion: no one would take them seriously. Beacon Street Union's members are all dropouts from Boston University who came to New York in the middle of the summer of 1967. They write their own songs *(Speed Kills,* which is anti-drug, and *Incident,* about a knifing) and their diversified sounds take in everything from hard rock to blues, with a little folk thrown in.

Albums/EYES OF THE BEACON STREET UNION (March 1968): *My Love Is; Beautiful Delilah; Sportin' Life; Four Hundred And Five; Mystic Mourning; Sadie Said No; Speed Kills; Blue Avenue; South End Incident; Green Destroys The Gold; The Prophet.* CLOWN DIED IN MARVIN GARDENS (August 1968): *The Clown Died In Marvin Gardens; The Clown's Overture; Angus Of Aberdeen; Blue Suede Shoes; A Not Very August Afternoon; Now I Taste The Tears; King Of The Jungle; May I Light Your Cigarette; Baby Please Don't Go.*

Singles/*South End Incident/Speed Kills* (March 1968); *Four Hundred And Five/Blue Suede Shoes* (August 1968); *May I Light Your Cigarette/Mayola* (November 1968).

THE BEATLES/*Paul McCartney (piano, fuzz bass, guitar, vocals), John Lennon (harmonica, guitar, piano, vocals), George Harrison (sitar, lead guitar), Ringo Starr (Richard Starkey) (drums, organ).*
Previous members: Peter Best (drums), Stu Sutcliffe.
The day Paul McCartney was born, the number one song on the hit parade was *Sleepy Lagoon* played by Harry James. If it wasn't Harry James in those days, it was Glenn Miller, and if not Glenn Miller, Benny Goodman or Guy Lombardo or Woody Herman. Paul, John, George and Ringo were born in the forties, the era of the Big Bands. The world was at war and the songs were escapist—moonlight cocktails, sleepy lagoons and white Christmases. Bing Crosby didn't want to be fenced in, the Andrews Sisters drank rum and Coca Cola, and

Perry Como was a prisoner of love when the Beatles were in
their young boyhood. Later it was Peggy Lee, Nat King Cole,
Dinah Shore and Frankie Laine who dominated the airwaves
and the best-seller charts. Popular music was sung by adults
for adults in the forties. Was there anyone else who mattered
in the forties but adults? No one else was buying records,
anyway, and that's what mattered.

It wasn't until the Beatles got into their teens, in the fifties
that something happened that was destined to change the face
of popular music and to lay the groundwork for the revolution the Beatles themselves were to bring about in the sixties.
That something was Bill Haley's *Rock Around The Clock,* a
song that, while it was sung by an adult, was distinctly
addressed to the younger generation. It had nothing to do
with cocktails and moonlight and a lot to do with being young
and rebellious. The Beatles were exactly the right age to be
hit hard by that song when it came out in 1955. That was the
year John, fifteen and still in school, started his own group,
the Quarrymen. When the historic meeting between Quarry-
man Lennon and new friend Paul McCartney took place on
June 15, 1956, Elvis Presley's first hit, *Heartbreak Hotel,* had
been number one on the U.S. hit parade for eight consecutive
weeks. One of the big attractions Paul, just fourteen, had for
the worldly sixteen-year-old John, was that he looked a bit
like Elvis. England was absolutely Elvis-happy at the time
and, of course, rock-happy. Plastic Elvises sprang up everywhere with Tommy Steele and Cliff Richard getting the same
hysterical screaming adulation in England that Elvis had in
the States. Paul joined the Quarrymen. He and John started
writing songs together and, in 1957, when Elvis was singing
All Shook Up and *Teddy Bear* and *Jailhouse Rock* and the
Everly Brothers were singing *Wake Up Little Susie,* John
and Paul wrote *Love Me Do,* which five years later in 1962
would be their first English (though not American) release.

In 1958 George Harrison, who wore tight pants and had a
group called The Rebels, disbanded it to join the Quarrymen.
In August of that year, when the group performed at the
Casbah Club in Liverpool, the big hit was *Volare* and the
latest plastic Elvis was Ricky Nelson. The Kingston Trio were
about to put folk on the charts with *Tom Dooley,* beginning a
folk revolution that would make Bob Dylan possible three

years later in 1961. And a young man named Phil Spector in a group called the Teddy Bears had a number one record, *To Know Him Is To Love Him.* A lot of big things were starting to happen in 1958, but who could possibly know then that the Beatles were among them?

In 1959 the Quarrymen changed their name several times, ending up with the Silver Beatles. Out in the world Frankie Avalon was singing *Venus* and Elvis was still king with *Are You Lonesome Tonight?* 1960 was the year of Mark Dinning's *Teen Angel* and Ray Charles' *Georgia On My Mind.* The Silver Beatles went to Hamburg to back up a singer named Tony Sheridan. You can still buy the recordings they made there, just as a backup group. They did a sort of rock version of *My Bonnie* with Sheridan around that time. They were pretty terrible. Or, to be more generous, utterly undistinguished. People are fond of saying now that there were a hundred groups in Liverpool playing better music than the Beatles in those days. Let's hope so. It was only in Hamburg that they started to get themselves together as a group. George, Paul, John, Peter Best on drums, Stu Sutcliffe on guitar. Their image was very rough-trade rocker, all leather and menace, as opposed to the more established rocker look of another English group in Hamburg at the time, Rory Storme and the Hurrycanes, who wore drape-shape suits with curved lapels and string ties. Their drummer, Ringo Starr, would eventually join the Beatles, but not before he learned to brush his hair forward instead of up and back in a greasy pompadour.

There were several Hamburg visits with increasingly triumphant returns to Liverpool. Then, just when kids were buying Ricky Nelson's *Travellin' Man,* in fact, the very week Dion's *Runaround Sue* was number one, someone asked Brian Epstein, a record salesman, for a record called *My Bonnie* by the Beatles. That was October 28, 1961, a big date, and if the rest isn't history, it ought to be. Epstein, made curious by this and other inquiries, tracked the group down to a place called the Cavern, where they were very popular. He became their manager and by the end of 1961 they were Liverpool's number one group—and the number one song was the Marvelettes' *Please Mr. Postman.* (Now you know why the Beatles recorded it). In 1962 everything happened. Epstein, after an eternity of pushing and wheedling and a million rejections, got the group a record contract. Ringo shaved his beard, took the grease out of his hair, put away the drape-shape suit and joined the group, replacing Peter Best. John Lennon got married. The Twist was the only thing happening on a very stale scene, but a young kid named Bob Dylan had just made a folk record and a new American group called the Beach Boys had a single out called *Surfin' Safari.* The week the Beatles' first single, *Love Me Do,* was released in England, the number one record in America was the Four Seasons' *Sherry,* which shows exactly where America was at that time. *Love Me Do* made the top twenty in England (but was not a number one record). It was released in the U.S., where everyone was listening to the *Monster Mash* and *Big Girls Don't Cry.* In the four weeks it took their next single, *Please Please Me,* to rocket its way to number one in England, America listened to *Go Away Little Girl* and *Hey Paula.* America would not hear of the Beatles for another two years.

Now it was the beginning of 1963 and the year Beatlemania happened in England. The *Please Please Me* album was number one on the charts for six months. In 1963 the group also released *From Me To You,* but it was *She Loves You* that clinched it for them and *I Want To Hold Your Hand* that set the final seal on Beatlemania. In America it was still Bobby Vinton singing *Blue Velvet,* but not for long. In a matter of weeks, at the beginning of 1964, the Beatles had displaced Vinton on the American hit parade with *I Want To Hold Your Hand,* number one for seven weeks (including the weeks the Beatles came to America, February 7 to February 21). *I Want To Hold Your Hand* was immediately followed by *She Loves You, Can't Buy Me Love* and *Love Me Do,* which meant that the Beatles were heading the U.S. charts from the beginning of February till the end of July, probably the biggest feat of its kind in history. When they finally were replaced, it was not by American groups but by other English groups, the Animals and Manfred Mann. The English invasion had started in earnest. The only American sound that was able to grow in influence during that British-dominated time was the Motown sound of the Supremes, which greatly influenced the Beatles and other English groups. Bob Dylan, at that time, was prophetically warning that *The Times They Are A-Changin'*, and in 1965 his prophecy came true. For the Beatles it was the end of being just another successful rock group and the beginning of serious musical maturity with *RUBBER SOUL* (in which the Beatles, for the first time, produced head music), an album very much influenced by Dylan, especially in Lennon and McCartney's lyrics. For Dylan it was another change: influenced by the Beatles—in *HIGHWAY 61 REVISITED* and *BRINGING IT ALL BACK HOME*—he went electric. As Dylan's folk went rock and the Beatles' rock went folk, 1965 was also the year of folk-rock and the Byrds (it was Byrd David Crosby who turned George Harrison on to the sitar).

The times continued to change. 1966 was the Beatles at their most Dylany with songs like the mocking *Nowhere Man,* a far cry from their early lyrics of teen love (Lennon directly, and frequently, credits Dylan for the change). And if the Beatles had changed, it was nothing to what was happening to the Beach Boys—and there were others. All of a sudden, in 1966: Simon and Garfunkel, the Mamas and the Papas, the Lovin' Spoonful, Donovan, the Stones—all coming out with something more than music had been till then. And to top it all, Dylan's *BLONDE ON BLONDE*. (Dylan, as usual, always a jump ahead.) By 1967 the Beatles were into the electronic intricacies of *SERGEANT PEPPER* (anything to top the Beach Boys' *PET SOUNDS, Good Vibrations* and a work in progress, *SMILE,* reportedly the greatest thing that had happened in rock to date). The Bee Gees and the Monkees dutifully stepped into the shoes the Beatles had by now outworn. Eventually *SMILE* didn't happen, Dylan was silenced by a motorcycle accident and the Beatles just about had the year to themselves, except for the emerging San Francisco scene. By 1968 Dylan was back, topping the elaborate *SERGEANT PEPPER* with an artfully simple *JOHN WESLEY HARDING;* the Beach Boys, cowed by the disaster of *SMILE,* were no longer, for the moment, a force to be reckoned with; but Cream and the Jimi Hendrix Experience and the San Francisco groups captured the popular imagination. Privately, it was a torturous time for the Beatles. Nevertheless (the Dylan influence again), they closed the year not with a new *PEPPER* but with a double album of great simplicity, a nostalgic look at rock styles.

The simplicity was misleading since, away from the studio, Beatle lives were increasingly complex. John divorced and married Japanese filmmaker Yoko Ono (with a lie-in here and a peace crusade there), Paul married American photographer Linda Eastman, George and his wife were busted, and Ringo landed in the movies. Their enthusiasm for Indian religion turned to an enthusiam for big business, with the group starting their own record company, Apple. On the Apple label, Paul presented Mary Hopkin; George presented Jackie Lomax; John presented Yoko Ono, the pair of them sweetly naked on the record's cover; Ringo stayed in the movies.

Albums/BEATLES—THIS IS WHERE IT STARTED with Tony Sheridan and the Titans: *My Bonnie; Cry For A Shadow; Saints; Why* (with Sheridan); *Johnson Rag; Darktown Strutters' Ball; Rye Beat; Summertime Beat* (the Titans); *Swanee River; You Are My Sunshine* (Sheridan & Beat Brothers). THIS IS THE SAVAGE YOUNG BEATLES with Peter Best and Tony Sheridan (Hamburg, 1961): *Cry For A Shadow; Let's Dance; If You Love Me; Baby What I Say; Why; Sweet Georgia Brown; Baby Jane; Ya-Ya.* MEET THE BEATLES (January 1964): *I Want To Hold Your Hand; I Saw Her Standing There; This Boy; It Won't Be Long; All I've Got To Do; All My Loving; Don't Bother Me; Little Child; Till There Was You; Hold Me Tight; I Wanna Be Your Man; Not A Second Time.* BEATLES' SECOND ALBUM (April 1964): *Roll Over Beethoven; Thank You Girl; Devil In Her Heart; You Really Got A Hold On Me; Money; You Can't Do That; Long Tall Sally; I Call Your Name; Please Mr. Postman; I'll Get You; She Loves You.* A HARD DAY'S NIGHT (June 1964): *A Hard Day's Night; I Should Have Known Better; If I Fell; I'm Happy Just To Dance With You; And I Love Her; Tell Me Why; Can't Buy Me Love; Any Time At All; I'll Cry Instead; Ringo's Theme (This Boy).* SOMETHING NEW (July 1964): *I'll Cry Instead; Things We Said Today; Any Time At All; When I Get Home; Slow Down; Matchbox; Tell Me Why; And I Love Her; I'm Happy Just To Dance With You; If I Fell; Komm, Gib Mir Deine Hand.* AIN'T SHE SWEET

(July 1964): *Ain't She Sweet; Sweet Georgia Brown; Nobody's Child; Take Out Some Insurance On Me Baby* (Beatles); *I Wanna Be Your Man; I Want To Hold Your Hand; She Loves You; How Do You Do It; Please Please Me; I'll Keep You Satisfied; I'm Telling You Now; From Me To You* (Swallows). BEATLES' STORY (January 1965): *On Stage With The Beatles; How Beatlemania Began; Beatlemania In Action; Man Behind The Beatles—Brian Epstein; John Lennon; Who's A Millionaire; The Beatles Look At Life; "Victims" Of Beatlemania; Beatle Medley; Ringo Starr; Liverpool And All The World!; Beatles Will Be Beatles; Man Behind The Music—George Martin; George Harrison; A Hard Day's Night; Paul McCartney; Sneaky Haircuts.* BEATLES '65 (January 1965): *No Reply; I'm A Loser; Baby's In Black; Rock And Roll Music; I'll Follow The Sun; She's A Woman; Mr. Moonlight; Honey Don't; I'll Be Back; I Feel Fine; Everybody's Trying To Be My Baby.* EARLY BEATLES (March 1965): *Love Me Do; Twist And Shout; Anna; Chains; Ask Me Why; Boys; Please Please Me; P.S. I Love You; Baby It's You; Taste Of Honey; Do You Want To Know A Secret.* BEATLES VI (June 1965): *Kansas City; Eight Days A Week; You Like Me Too Much; Bad Boy; I Don't Want To Spoil The Party; Words Of Love; Yes It Is; Dizzy Miss Lizzy; Tell Me What You See; Every Little Thing; What You're Doing.* HELP! (August 1965): *Help; Night Before; From Me To You Fantasy; You've Got To Hide Your Love Away; I Need You; In The Tyrol; Another Girl; Another Hard Day's Night; Ticket To Ride; Bitter End; You're Gonna Lose That Girl; The Chase.* RUBBER SOUL (December 1965): *I've Just Seen A Face; Norwegian Wood; You Won't See Me; Think For Yourself; The Word; Michelle; It's Only Love; Girl; I'm Looking Through You; In My Life; Wait; Run For Your Life.* YESTERDAY AND TODAY (June 1966): *Yesterday; Drive My Car; I'm Only Sleeping; Nowhere Man; Dr. Robert; Act Naturally; And Your Bird Can Sing; If I Needed Someone; We Can Work It Out; What Goes On; Day Tripper.* REVOLVER (August 1966): *Yellow Submarine; Eleanor Rigby; Taxman; Love To You; Here, There and Everywhere; She Said She Said; Good Day Sunshine; For No One; I Want To Tell You; Got To Get You Into My Life; Tomorrow Never Knows.* SERGEANT

PEPPER'S LONELY HEARTS CLUB BAND (June 1967):
*Sergeant Pepper's Lonely Hearts Club Band; A Little Help
From My Friends; Lucy In The Sky With Diamonds; Getting
Better; Fixing A Hole; She's Leaving Home; Being For The
Benefit Of Mr. Kite; Within You Without You; When I'm
Sixty-Four; Lovely Rita; Good Morning Good Morning; Ser-
geant Pepper's Lonely Hearts Club Band—Reprise; A Day In
The Life.* MAGICAL MYSTERY TOUR (November 1967):
*Magical Mystery Tour; The Fool On The Hill; Flying; Blue
Jay Way; Your Mother Should Know; I Am The Walrus;
Hello Goodbye; Strawberry Fields Forever; Penny Lane;
Baby You're A Rich Man; All You Need Is Love.* THE
BEATLES (November 1968): *Back In The U.S.S.R.; Dear
Prudence; Glass Onion; Ob-La-Di, Ob-La-Da; Wild Honey
Pie; The Continuing Story Of Bungalow Bill; While My
Guitar Gently Weeps; Happiness Is A Warm Gun; Martha
My Dear; I'm So Tired; Blackbird; Piggies; Rocky Raccoon;
Don't Pass Me By; Why Don't We Do It In The Road; I Will;
Julia; Birthday; Yer Blues; Mother Nature's Son; Everybody's
Got Something To Hide Except Me And My Monkey; Sexy
Sadie; Helter Skelter; Long, Long, Long; Revolution 1; Hon-
ey Pie; Savoy Truffle; Cry Baby Cry; Revolution 9; Good
Night.* YELLOW SUBMARINE (February 1969): *Yellow
Submarine; Only A Northern Song; All Together Now; Hey
Bulldog; It's All Too Much; All You Need Is Love; Pepper-
land Sea To Time & Sea Of Holes; March Of The Meanies;
Sea Of Monsters; Pepperland Laid Waste; Yellow Submarine
In Pepperland.*

Singles/*I Want To Hold Your Hand/I Saw Her Standing
There* (January 1964); *Can't Buy Me Love/You Can't Do
That* (March 1964); *A Hard Day's Night/I Should Have
Known Better* (July 1964); *I'll Cry Instead/I'm Happy Just
To Dance With You* (July 1964); *And I Love Her/If I Fell*
(July 1964); *Slow Down/Matchbox* (August 1964); *Ain't
She Sweet/Nobody's Child* (September 1964); *Sweet Georgia
Brown/Take Out Some Insurance On Me Baby* (September
1964); *I Feel Fine/She's A Woman* (November 1964); *Four
By The Beatles* (February 1965); *Eight Days A Week/I
Don't Want To Spoil The Party* (February 1965); *Ticket To
Ride/Yes It Is* (May 1965); *Help!/I'm Down* (July 1965);

Act Naturally/Yesterday (September 1965); *We Can Work It Out/Day Tripper* (December 1965); *Nowhere Man/What Goes On* (February 1966); *Paperback Writer/Rain* (May 1966); *Yellow Submarine/Eleanor Rigby* (August 1966); *Baby, You're A Rich Man/All You Need Is Love* (October 1966); *Strawberry Fields Forever/Penny Lane* (February 1967); *Hello Goodbye/I Am The Walrus* (November 1967); *Lady Madonna/The Inner Light* (March 1968); *Hey Jude/Revolution* (July 1968); *Get Back/Don't Let Me Down* (May 1969); *Ballad of John and Yoko/Old Brown Shoe* (June 1969).

BEAU BRUMMELS/*Sal Valentino (vocals), Ron Meagher (bass), Ron Elliott (guitar).*
They started off in 1964 doing the same thing a lot of other groups did then—copying the Beatles. But what happened was the beginning of a new *American* sound, not English. Their first big company album (they had done two for the small San Francisco company Autumn) was a collection of other people's hits. But the album that astonished everyone and blew a million minds was *TRIANGLE*, which featured guitarist Elliott as songwriter (or, as Paul Williams said in *Crawdaddy*, because the distinction was important—as composer). It was Williams, too, among others, who found Valentino's voice the best in rock.
Albums/BEAU BRUMMELS '66 (July 1966): *You've Got To Hide Your Love Away; Mr. Tambourine Man; Louie, Louie; Homeward Bound; These Boots Are Made For Walking; Yesterday; Bang Bang; Hang On Sloopy; Play With Fire; Woman; Mrs. Brown You've Got A Lovely Daughter; Monday, Monday.* BEST OF BEAU BRUMMELS (1967): *Laugh Laugh; Just A Little; You Tell Me Why; Sad Little Girl; Don't Talk To Strangers; Others.* TRIANGLE (July 1967): *Are You Happy; Only Dreaming Now; Painter Of Women; Keeper Of Time; It Won't Get Better; Nine Pound Hammer; Magic Hollow; And I've Seen Her; Triangle; Wolf Of Velvet Fortune; Old Kentucky Home.* BRADLEY'S BARN (October 1968): *Turn Around; Added Attraction; Cherokee Girl; Deep Water; Long Walking Down To Misery; Little Bird; I'm A Sleeper; Bless You California; Loneliest Man In Town; Love Can Fall A Long Way Down; Jessica.*

Singles/*Cry Just A Little* (May 1966); *Lower Level/Magic Hollow* (August 1967); *Are You Happy/Lift Me* (May 1968); *Long Walking Down To Misery/I'm A Sleeper* (October 1968).

JEFF BECK GROUP/*Rod Stewart (lead singer), Mike Waller (drums), Ron Wood (bass guitar, harmonica), Nicky Hopkins (piano), Jeff Beck (guitar).*
The Jeff Beck group is the strongest new-blues group to follow Cream over from England. Beck was the guitarist who replaced Eric Clapton on the original Yardbirds and he toured the States for several years in that capacity. When he broke from the Yardbirds in 1967, the English pop writers acted as if he had lost his sanity, and some disastrous early appearances seemed to bear them out. By summer 1968 Beck was back in the U.S. with his group and it was another story. Not only is he one of the best blues guitarists in the world today ("wild and visionary" said New York *Times'* Robert Shelton), but the group's lead singer, Rod Stewart, strongly influenced by the British blues scene, was a revelation. No one had heard Beck with a good singer before (Keith Relf, sex symbol of the Yardbirds, wasn't it). They worked together as excitingly as Romeo and Juliet.

The group's sound is very strong and frantic. In live performance, Beck doesn't exactly play faster than other rock musicians, just further. Sometimes the music seems to be coming from somewhere so unexpected that when it finally comes through the amp, it surprises Beck as much as anybody else. You might call the Jeff Beck Group one of the earliest of the second-generation rock groups. With groups splitting seemingly every minute by the score, more and more superstars of the Jeff Beck variety are out and about looking for action. Some of these will undoubtedly join with others of similar status to form impressive supergroups. Others, like Beck, will use their professional know-how to find exactly the kind of musicians they need from outside the immediate spotlight. Beck's drummer, for instance, was a very busy session musician before this. People saw the many group splits in 1967-68 as a sign that the rock scene was "dying." If Jeff Beck and his group are any indication, they may well be the sign of the upheaval necessary for a more logical rearrangement of talent.

Album/TRUTH (August 1968): *Shapes Of Things; Let Me Love You; Morning Dew; You Shook Me; Ol' Man River; Greensleeves; Rock My Plimsoul; Beck's Bolero; Blues Deluxe; I Ain't Superstitious.*
Single/*Ol' Man River/Blues Deluxe* (October 1968).

BEE GEES/*Barry Gibb (vocals), Maurice Gibb (bass), Robin Gibb (vocals, piano), Vince Melouney (guitar), Colin Petersen (drums).*
The Bee Gees first appeared in 1967 with a gimmick so brazen it just about took the public's breath away. They came on like the Beatles. Imagine that, people had been coming on like the Beatles since the Fabulous Four first made it outside Liverpool, and here was this new group, years later, doing it again, and what's more, doing it with a fanfare of trumpets. Why did they get away with it? Because they did it well. They did it so well in their startling first single, *New York Mining Disaster,* that it was like having a wonderful new Beatle single out on the market. For those who were bewailing the loss of the comparatively uncomplicated pre-*SERGEANT PEPPER* Beatles, the Bee Gees were a godsend and their first album a delight. The thing is that they sounded more like the Beatles than the Beatles ever did and that they wrote songs considerably better than the Beatles had done that early in their career. (An unfair comparison, though, that last, since once the Beatles had done it, it became easier for everyone else.)

The Bee Gees' defense was this: The three Gibb Brothers, nucleus of the group, were born in Manchester, not far from the Beatles' Liverpool, and subject to much the same musical influences. They were performing in public before the age of ten (they even preceded the Everly Brothers), and therefore claim that their so-called Beatle sound was the Bee Gee sound before the Beatles were ever heard of. In 1958 the family migrated to Australia, and the boys, still very young, made quite a name for themselves as performers there. They grew up in the middle of a very busy and very competitive rock scene in Australia. But they were *not,* as has been claimed (not by them), Australia's number one supergroup. In fact, it was a great source of distress, and later of great bitterness, to them that although they were good and they knew it, they were never fully appreciated by rock critics or played enough by disc jockeys. (Ironically, the Easybeats, the real number one group in Australia then, later moved to England where they watched the "lesser" group produce hit after hit and rake in a fortune, while they themselves battled for airplay.) After a while, the frustration of not being able to break into the Australian scene (they were constantly told they were too much like the Beatles) led them to decide to try London. On arrival there they were immediately signed up by another Australian, Robert Stigwood, who in partnership with the late Brian Epstein groomed them for stardom. No expense was spared in arrangements, production, studio time or publicity.

It was clear that Robin Gibb's heartrending vocal quaver, which became the one thing most closely identified with the Bee Gees' sound, was entirely his own. So were the lush orchestral backgrounds—and therein, lay a huge problem. Without a sixty-piece orchestra, the Bee Gees live did not sound like the Bee Gees on record. So although there were some appearances outside England (and one rather unfortunate concert at Saville) the Bee Gees did not face an English audience properly till one year after their first single was released. But when they did it, they did it in style. The Royal Albert Hall and a sixty-piece orchestra (some of those first violins are still recovering from the teenyboppers who rushed the stage). There was more—a forty-voice choir, for only one number (*Birdie Told Me*), and even more, a whole Royal Air Force Apprentice Band. It was the most spectacular concert in rock history. A few months later they did the whole thing again without the choir but with a sixty-piece band at Forest Hills Stadium in New York. It was impressive but it was no way to make a profit.

Illness stopped the rest of the tour and after that it was one problem after another for the group. First, lead singer Barry Gibb announced he was leaving to be A Star. Then guitarist Vince Melouney left to start his own group. Finally, just as Barry had been persuaded to stay and temporarily postpone his personal ambitions, younger brother Robin did leave to pursue a solo career. The future of the group as a performing unit may still be in doubt, but there is nothing dubious about their future as songwriters. Except for the Beatles, no other group has had as many of its songs recorded as successfully by top name stars as the Bee Gees.

Albums/BEE GEES' FIRST (October 1967): *Holiday; Turn Of The Century; Red Chair, Fade Away; One Minute Woman; In My Own Time; Every Christian Lion Hearted Man Will Show You; Craise Finton Kirk Royal Academy Of Arts; New York Mining Disaster 1941; To Love Somebody; Cucumber Castle; I Close My Eyes; I Can't See Nobody; Please Read Me; Close Another Door.* HORIZONTAL (January 1968): *World; And The Sun Will Shine; Lemons Never Forget; Really And Sincerely; Birdie Told Me; With The Sun In My Eyes; Harry Braff; Massachusetts; Day Time Girl; Earnest Of Being George; Change Is Made; Horizontal.* IDEA (August 1968): *Let There Be Love; Kitty Can; Indian Gin And Whiskey Dry; In The Summer Of His Years; I Have Decided To Join The Air Force; Down To Earth; I've Gotta Get A Message to You; Idea; When The Swallows Fly; I Started A Joke; Kilburn Towers; Swan Song.* RARE, PRECIOUS & BEAUTIFUL (November 1968): *What Are You; Spicks & Specks; Playdown; Big Chance; Glass House; How Many Birds; Second Hand People; I Don't Know Why I Bother With Myself; Monday's Rain; Tint Of Blue; Jingle Jangle; Born A Man.*

Singles/*I Can't See Nobody/New York Mining Disaster 1941* (May 1967); *Close Another Door/To Love Somebody* (June 1967); *Every Christian Lion Hearted Man Will Show You/Holiday* (September 1967); *Massachusetts/Sir Geoffrey Saved The World* (November 1967); *Sinking Ships/Words* (December 1967); *Singer Sang His Song/Jumbo* (March 1968); *I've Gotta Get A Message To You/Kitty Can* (August 1968); *I Started A Joke/Kilburn Towers* (December 1968).

CHUCK BERRY/Chuck Berry may be the single most important name in the history of rock. There is not a rock musician working today who has not consciously or unconsciously borrowed from his sound, the sound that was to become the definitive sound of fifties rock. The Beach Boys made their national reputation with a Chuck Berry song, *Surfin' U.S.A.* And both the Beatles and Stones started off in

the sixties by "reviving" Chuck Berry's fifties' material, songs
that were enormously popular at the height of the rock and
roll era, only to be forgotten as the hard-rock sound became
more and more watered down. Like Elvis, Jerry Lee Lewis
and other giants of rock, Berry was a raver. When the raving
quieted down, it was supposedly a sign that rock was growing
up. What, in fact, rock was doing was becoming very dull.
And the reason the Beatles (and the Stones) had so much
impact in 1963 and 1964 was that they brought the raving
back. Both groups had grown up to the sound of Chuck Berry
and Bill Haley and the old-guard rockers, only to see the
sound disappear prematurely. Both worked tirelessly to bring
it back; and every now and then when it seems in danger of
losing its basic punch, back they go, the Stones and the
Beatles, for new inspiration to the sounds of Chuck Berry and
hard rock.

Like Presley, Berry was half into rhythm and blues and half
into country and western and, again like Presley, what he
came up with, having combined the two, was what we now
know as rock and roll. His lyrics were for teenagers, but
always wry, not vapid. His music was intended to accompany
the rolling of an automobile on a highway, but not until
nearly fifteen years later did the songs come through as the
major rock classics they always were. Despite all this and the
awesome reputation Berry has with the rock cognoscenti, he
never had anything like the professional success his imitators
had. Part of the reason was some trouble he had with the law
at the height of his career. The rest, many believe, had to do
with his color. He emerged at a time when the black entertainer was still confined to the rhythm and blues charts and
white talent dominated. Later, when acceptance came to
black artists, it was apparently too late. Critic John Gabree is
one of many who feel that Berry, had he been white, would
have had as big a career as Presley. Meanwhile, it is interesting to note that the absence of black faces at concerts given
by Beatles and other white rock groups is due, in no small
part, to the resentment black Americans feel at having their
own music played back at them by white musicians from the
other side of the Atlantic.

Albums/AFTER SCHOOL SESSIONS (October 1958):

School Day; Wee Wee Hours; Brown Eyed Handsome Man;
Too Much Monkey Business; Deep Feeling; Rolli Polli; Berry
Pickin'; Together; No Money Down; Havana Moon; Down
Bound Train; Drifting Heart. ONE DOZEN BERRYS (October 1958): Sweet Little Sixteen; Reelin' And Rockin'; Rock
And Roll Music; Blue Ceiling; Rock At The Philharmonic;
Jaunda Espanol; Oh Baby Doll; Guitar Boogie; In-Go; Low
Ceiling; How You've Changed; I Don't Take But A Few.
CHUCK BERRY IS ON TOP: Almost Grown; Carol; Maybelline; Johnny B. Goode; Little Queenie; Anthony Boy;
Sweet Little Rock And Roller; Jo Jo Gunne; Around And
Around; Roll Over Beethoven; Hey Pedro; Blues For Hawaiians. ROCKIN' AT THE HOPS: Bye Bye Johnny; Worried
Life Blues; Down The Road A Piece; Confessin' The Blues;
Too Pooped To Pop; Mad Lad; I Got To Find My Baby;
Betty Jean; Childhood Sweetheart; Broken Arrow; Driftin'
The Blues; Let It Rock. NEW JUKE BOX HITS: I'm
Talking About You; Diploma For Two; Rip It Up; Thirteen
Question Method; Way It Was Before; Away With You;
Don't You Lie To Me; Little Star; Route 66; Sweet Sixteen;
Stop And Listen; Run Around. TWIST: Maybelline; Roll
Over Beethoven; Oh, Baby Doll; 'Round And 'Round; Come
On; Let It Rock; Reelin' And Rockin'; School Days; Almost
Grown; Sweet Little Sixteen; Thirty Days; Johnny B. Goode;
Rock And Roll Music; Back In The U.S.A. CHUCK BERRY
ON STAGE: Memphis; Sweet Little Sixteen; Rocking On The
Railroad; Maybelline; Surfing Steel; Go Go Go; Brown Eyed
Handsome Man; Still Got The Blues; Jaguar And The Thunderbird; I Just Want To Make Love To You; All Aboard;
Man And The Donkey; Trick Or Treat. CHUCK BERRY'S
GREATEST HITS (April 1964): Roll Over Beethoven;
School Days; Rock And Roll Music; Too Much Monkey
Business; Oh, Baby Doll; Johnny B. Goode; Nadine; Thirty
Days; Memphis; Maybelline; Sweet Little Sixteen; Brown
Eyed Handsome Man. CHUCK BERRY IN LONDON (May
1965): My Little Love-Lights; She Once Was Mine; After It's
Over; I Got A Booking; You Came A Long Way From St.
Louis; Night Beat; St. Louis Blues; His Daughter Caroline;
Dear Dad; Jamaica Farewell; Butterscotch; Song Of My
Love; Why Should We End This Way; I Want To Be Your
Driver. FRESH BERRY'S: It Wasn't Me; Run Joe; Every

Day We Rock And Roll; One For My Baby; Welcome Back Pretty Baby; It's My Own Business; Right Off Rampart Street; Vaya Con Dios; Merrily We Rock And Roll; My Mustang Ford; Ain't That Just Like A Woman; Wee Hour Blues. ST. LOUIS TO LIVERPOOL: *Little Marie; You Never Can Tell; Go Bobby Soxer; No Particular Place To Go; Merry Christmas Baby; Our Little Rendezvous; You Two; Night Beat; Promised Land; Things I Used To Do; Liverpool Beat; How Great Thou Art.* CHUCK BERRY'S GOLDEN DECADE (February 1967): *Maybelline; Deep Feeling; Johnny B. Goode; Wee Wee Hours; Nadine; Thirty Days; Brown Eyed Handsome Man; Roll Over Beethoven; No Particular Place To Go; Havana Moon; Almost Grown; Memphis; School Days; Too Much Monkey Business; Oh, Baby Doll; Too Pooped To Pop; Reelin' And Rockin'; You Can't Catch Me; Bye Bye Johnny; 'Round And 'Round; Sweet Little Sixteen; Rock And Roll Music; Anthony Boy; Back In The U.S.A.* CHUCK BERRY'S GOLDEN HITS (February 1967): *Sweet Little Sixteen; Memphis; Back In The U.S.A.; School Days; Maybelline; Johnny B. Goode; Rock And Roll Music; Thirty Days; Carol; Club Nitty Gritty; Roll Over Beethoven.* CHUCK BERRY IN MEMPHIS (August 1967): *Back To Memphis; I Do Really Love You; My Heart Will Always Belong To You; Ramblin' Rose; Sweet Little Rock And Roller; Oh, Baby Doll; Check Me Out; It Hurts Me Too; Bring Another Drink; So Long; Goodnight, Well It's Time To Go.* CHUCK BERRY LIVE AT THE FILLMORE AUDITORIUM (September 1967): *Driftin' Blues; Hoochie Coochie Man; Johnny B. Goode; See See Rider; Feelin' It; Flying Home; It Hurts Me Too; Fillmore Blues; Wee Baby Blues; Medley.* FROM ST. LOUIE TO FRISCO (November 1968): *Louie To Frisco; Ma Dear; The Love I Lost; I Love Her, I Love Her; Little Fox; Rock Cradle Rock; Soul Rockin'; I Can't Believe; Misery; My Tambourine; Oh Captain; Mum's The Word.*

Singles/*Brown Eyed Handsome Man/Too Much Monkey Business; Rock And Roll Music/Blue Feeling; Beautiful Delilah/Vacation Time; Sweet Little Rock And Roller/Jo Jo Gunne; Merry Christmas Baby/Run Rudolph Run; Anthony Boy/That's My Desire; Broken Arrow/My Childhood*

Sweetheart; Bye Bye Johnny/Worried Life Blues; I Got To Find My Baby/Mad Lad; Jaguar And The Thunderbird/Our Little Rendezvous; I'm Talking About You/Little Star; Come On/Go Go Go; Diploma For Two/I'm Talking About You; You Never Can Tell/Brenda Lee; Little Marie/Go Bobby Soxer; It Wasn't Me/Welcome Back Pretty Baby; Lonely School Days/Ramona, Say Yes; Sweet Little Sixteen/Maybelline; School Days/Memphis; Roll Over Beethoven/Back In The U.S.A.; Rock And Roll Music/Johnny B. Goode; It Hurts Me Too/Feelin' It.

BIG BOPPER/His real name was J. P. Richardson and he was a major figure in the post-Elvis rock era. He wrote and recorded *Chantilly Lace,* a Buddy Holly-type straight rock song, which was rated the third most played record in America in 1958 and had been released in 37 other countries. On the night of February 2, 1959, on leave from his job as a disc jockey, singer, and program director at station KTRM in Beaumont, Texas, Bopper appeared before 1,100 fans at the Surf Ballroom in Mason City, Iowa. Early next morning, with Buddy Holly and Ritchie Valens, he chartered a Beechcraft Bonanza to take them to Fargo, North Dakota. The plane came down five miles northwest of the airport and no one heard the crash. Bopper was twenty-four.

Album/CHANTILLY LACE (1958): *Chantilly Lace; Pink Petticoats; Walking Through My Dreams; The Clock; Someone Watching Over You; Old Maid; Big Bopper's Wedding; Little Red Riding Hood; Preacher And The Bear; It's The Truth, Ruth; White Lightning; Strange Kisses.*

Single/*Big Bopper's Wedding/Chantilly Lace* (1958).

BIG BROTHER AND THE HOLDING COMPANY/*Janis Joplin (lead vocals), Peter Albin (bass, vocals), Sam Andrew (lead and rhythm guitar, vocals), James Gurley (lead and rhythm guitar, vocals), David Getz (drums, vocals).*
Cameras play over those rugged features of hers as if she were an incredible beauty and, in her very own way, she is. Men's eyes go glassy as they think about her. Writers rape her with words as if there weren't any other way to deal with her. No one had gotten as excited about anyone in years as people

did about Janis Joplin. She was a whole new experience for everyone. People had to readjust their thinking because of her. Her voice, for instance. Chicks are not supposed to sing that way, all hoarse and insistent and footstamping. They're not supposed to sound as if they're shrieking for delivery from some terrible, urgent, but not entirely unpleasant, physical pain. For one thing, it is the age of cool (give or take Aretha and Levi Stubbs, and they're black and Janis is white). Janis has redefined the whole concept of the female vocalist. She's so beautiful it takes your breath away, and nothing makes you change that opinion—certainly not the knowledge that at any other time you'd have had to say the girl was homely. She lopes about, dressed like a dockside tart, funny little feathered hats, ankle bracelets, sleazy satins. Her hooker clothes, she calls them with a hooker laugh. And she drinks. Drinks—think of that—in a drug generation. She drinks Southern Comfort; a 24-year-old chick singer with the habits of another decade.

Big Brother and the Holding Company existed before Janis. They were a San Francisco group that used to jam around Chet Helms, head administrator of the Family Dog, a group designed to organize the musical community there. Janis was a Texan and so was Chet and it was he who thought Big Brother, one of the better bands of the many that had sprung up there, might use a girl singer. She'd sung country music and blues with a bluegrass band but she'd never had to sing as loud as she had to with Big Brother and that battery of amplifiers; and with all that rhythm going she found herself moving and dancing like another rhythm instrument. It was June 1966. She was a mean blues singer and she looked it, with her trailing draperies and tangled hair. San Francisco fell in love with her as if she were the first woman on earth. One year later, at the Monterey Pop Festival of 1967, everyone else did too. The press, the big music names from New York, everyone. The word was out: Janis Joplin is it. Albert Grossman, dean of the rock managers, with Dylan, Peter, Paul and Mary, and other major talent in his stable, snapped her and the band up on the spot. New York saw her finally at the Anderson Theatre and couldn't believe the voice actually carried all the way across Second Avenue to Ratner's Restaurant. Also unbelievable, the way she controlled the entire audience with her body, her hair, her stamping feet, her jewels, and breasts that were like something out of an erotic novel.

What a Jimi Hendrix or a Mick Jagger did to fainting girls, Janis did to fainting men—made her whole performance a frantic, sweating, passionate, demanding sexual act. Women watched for pointers through narrowed eyes. It was all very overwhelming for everyone: for Janis who couldn't believe she was a star until she saw it in *Time* magazine; for the media that hadn't heard anything like this since Tallulah Bankhead was a girl; for Big Brother, a good band that was nevertheless having difficulty keeping up. But all this abundance had to be captured on acetate, and their first album, which included *Down On Me*, got nowhere near it. A second album, done under the best circumstances possible, also got nowhere near it. When the news broke that Janis and the band would go their separate ways by the end of 1968, there was a general burst of anxiety that no matter what Big Brother's limitations Janis would lose whatever it was she had. Every time she sang, it seemed as if this was the time that rough, overworked whiskey voice would finally give. "I'd rather not sing than sing quiet," she said and she's right, the frenzy that's in her feet and hips is also in her throat. No wonder, after all that, there are times when she looks old and used. But there are also times when she looks young and vulnerable and the transition takes place sometimes in the matter of a minute. They're both there, those two extremes, and everything in between.

Janis' new band (still nameless) is into a big band-soul sound complete with horn section. Sam Andrews, former guitarist with Big Brother, has stayed with her. The band is not yet as tight as it could be and Janis' sound suffers for it. She seems to be leaving raunch and moving toward slick sounds. Whether she will maintain her vast popularity now remains to be seen.

Albums/*BIG BROTHER AND THE HOLDING COMPANY* (1968): *Bye, Bye, Baby; Easy Rider; Intruder; Light Is Faster Than Sound; Call On Me; Women Is Losers; Down On Me; Blind Man; All Is Loneliness; Caterpillar.* CHEAP THRILLS (1968): *Combination Of The Two; I Need A Man*

To Love; Summertime; Piece Of My Heart; Turtle Blues; Oh, Sweet Mary; Ball And Chain.

Singles/ *All Is Loneliness/ Blind Man* (1968); *Bye, Bye, Baby /Intruder* (1968).

THE BIG THREE/ *Cass Elliott, Tim Rose, and Denny Doherty.*
A folk group which evolved into the Mugwumps, which in turn fathered both the Mamas & the Papas and the Lovin' Spoonful.
(See MUGWUMPS, MAMAS & THE PAPAS, LOVIN' SPOONFUL)
Singles/ *Banjo Song/ Winkin' Blinkin'; Grandfather's Clock/ Nora's Dove.*

CILLA BLACK/ Born Priscilla White, she was discovered by Brian Epstein and the Beatles while she was working as a hatcheck girl at the Cavern. She went under the Epstein management, and while she never exactly set the world on fire, she has never starved for want of work.
Album/ IS IT LOVE: *Is It Love; I'm Not Alone Anymore; You've Lost That Lovin' Feelin'; Goin' Out Of My Head; Whatcha Gonna Do 'Bout It; You'd Be So Nice To Come Home To; Love Letters; Old Man River; Love Is Like A Heat Wave; This Empty Place; Anyone Who Had A Heart.*
Singles/ *You're My World/ You've Lost That Lovin' Feelin'; Step Inside Love/ I Couldn't Take My Eyes Off You; Only Forever Will Do/ What The World Needs Now Is Love* (November 1968).

BLIND FAITH/ *Eric Clapton (quitar, vocals), Ginger Baker (drums), Steve Winwood (organ, piano, guitar, vocals), Ric Grech (electric bass, electric violin).*
If Clapton, Baker and Bruce were the Cream, then Clapton, Baker, Winwood and Grech might very reasonably be expected to call themselves the Cream of the Cream, the supergroups' supergroup. Instead, with some humility and, as it happens, a lot of accuracy, they called themselves Blind Faith. What else can you have in a group too good to be true?

When Cream split at the end of 1968, guitarist Clapton and demon drummer Baker started jamming with Winwood, an escapee from Traffic, much the same as three divorced husbands might get together for the occasional amiable game of cards to while away the unfamiliar leisure of bachelorhood. But although Winwood is a multi-talent who plays organ, piano, guitar, and does most of the singing as well, the triangle remained as awkward a form as it had with Cream: just too much work and too many silences to work at filling. To solve that Ric Grech, electric bassist and electric violinist from an experimental group called Family, was added.

The group made its English debut on June 7, 1969 at a free concert in London, its American debut on July 11. Although their 24-concert eight-week maiden tour of the U.S. was expected to bring in a million dollars, no one has yet decided if the group should be called Blind Faith, Great Expectations, High Hopes or merely Mild Anti-Climax.

BLOOD, SWEAT AND TEARS/*David Clayton-Thomas (vocals), Bobby Colomby (drums), Jim Fielder (bass), Dick Halligan (keyboard), Jerry Hyman (trombone, recorder), Steve Katz (guitar, harmonica, vocals), Fred Lipsius (alto sax, piano), Chuck Winfield (trumpet, flügelhorn), Louis Soloff (trumpet, flügel horn).*

Credit whoever thought of the name with the sure gift of prophecy. Blood, sweat and tears was exactly what it took to get rock and jazz to marry in this nine- (formerly eight-) man combination. The band grew out of an idea that Al Kooper (formerly of the Blues Project) had nursed for a long time: to augment the more or less traditional rock quartet with a strong new four-man horn section. Of course others had thought of it too, getting away from the predictable guitar-bass-maybe-organ combination of rock. But enticing horn players away from jazz, the *right* horn players, and helping them fit into the new format, and then getting the rock players to adjust—none of that was easy. It was no small triumph when Kooper, having tried and discarded a variety of horn players, finally found what he wanted and unveiled, on what will be remembered as one of the weightiest rock and roll evenings of all time, his baby Big Band for all to see and hear.

And only that same band (which included Kooper's former Blues Project colleague, Steve Katz) knows why, with four fine horns blaring, and four of the best young rock musicians today, everything collapsed a few weeks later. To those who wanted to see rock and jazz meet constructively, and those who wanted to see music move in some new challenging direction, and the rest, who just wanted to hear some good sounds, it was tragic. By the time the new band's first album *THE CHILD IS FATHER TO THE MAN* was out, Kooper had left to become a producer and the band looked like it was finished. At least, no one could seriously imagine it without Kooper, who was one of the giants of the 1967 music scene.

But a miracle happened. Fred Lipsius, the saxophone player, breathed gently on the dying band and saw it revive There was a little rearranging among the horn personnel; David Clayton-Thomas, one of Canada's most respected blues singers, came to replace Kooper; everyone got their individual and collective heads together, and son of baby Big Band was flourishing.

The new Blood, Sweat and Tears was a pleasant surprise for everyone—from the scores of other bands who had seriously considered moving into a jazz direction to the New York fans who had missed having a band of their own since the demise of the Blues Project. There were, of course, those who thought that if 1968 rock was going to marry jazz, it should be jazz of that vintage and not the "outdated" big band style of Count Basie, which B, S and T (they already sound like a sandwich) had espoused. But that was a quibble. The thing was that Al Kooper's dream had come true.

Imagine a jazz-rock band that plays Tim Buckley, a band where a brass section dominates the lead guitar, and the singer is strong enough to dominate it all. That was Blood, Sweat and Tears at its best. But it wasn't at its best as often as it should have been. People would come from those BST concerts in 1968 gasping at all that fine musicianship packed into one group. Others, while acknowledging the sum total of talent there (far, far higher than in most groups around then), were somehow disappointed. Something wasn't jelling. There were factions *for* Kooper and against him and it became popular to argue whether Clayton-Thomas had saved the group or destroyed it. Criticism of the second album the one made without Kooper, blasted the wishy-washy material as Bar Mitzvah Soul. It still made number one on the charts, airplay was tremendous, BST concerts packed.

Nineteen sixty-nine saw many rock groups looking for a brass section in an effort to get what was soon called "The Blood, Sweat and Tears sound." The group was a huge technical and financial success. Clayton-Thomas was a star. Everyone in the group was a star. So what if the theatrics were programmed and the sound predictable? You can't have everything.

Albums/CHILD IS FATHER TO THE MAN (February 1968): *I Love You More Than You'll Ever Know; My Days Are Numbered; Morning Glory; Without Her; Just One Smile; I Can't Quit Her; House In The Country; Somethin' Goin' On; Meagan's Gypsy Eyes; Modern Adventures Of Plato; Diogenes And Freud; So Much Love.* BLOOD, SWEAT & TEARS: *Variations On A Theme By Eric Satie (1st & 2nd movements); Smiling Phases; Sometimes In Winter; More And More; And When I Die; God Bless The Child; Spinning Wheel; You've Made Me So Very Happy; Blues—Part II; Variations On A Theme By Eric Satie (1st Movement).*

Singles/I *Can't Quit Her/House In The Country* (May 1968); *You've Made Me So Very Happy/Blues—Part II; Spinning Wheel/More And More.*

MIKE BLOOMFIELD was originally a guitarist with the Paul Butterfield Blues Band and later with the Electric Flag, which he started. He became a star performer in his own right with *SUPER SESSION,* an album of jams (with Al Kooper and Steve Stills) which made the top fifty. His break from the Flag and the success of *SUPER SESSION* may very well herald a whole new golden era in music where performers are no longer tied down to the touring band format. An earlier Bloomfield jam record was Moby Grape's *GRAPE JAM,* and a later one was *TWO JEWS' BLUES* with Barry Goldberg. Bloomfield is regarded as being up there with the great blues guitarists—Eric Clapton, Jimi Hendrix and Johnny Winter (whom Bloomfield himself supposedly regards as one of the greatest blues guitarists). He can also be heard as a session musician on several Dylan records and was an integral part of Dylan's "new" electric sound in 1965. And he appears on a Mitch Ryder album, on John Hammond albums and on Sleepy John Estes albums. His latest record is *THE LIVE ADVENTURES OF MIKE BLOOMFIELD AND AL KOOPER,* recorded live at the Fillmore Auditorium. (See PAUL BUTTERFIELD BLUES BAND, ELECTRIC FLAG)

DAVID BLUE/Much influenced by Dylan, who was his friend in early Greenwich Village days, David Blue (born David Cohen) was in the first wave of singer-writers (along with Eric Andersen, Tom Rush and Phil Ochs) who moved away from folk into self-penned topical songs, sometimes protest, but mostly, in Blue's case, dealing with Dylanesque and surreal images. His *Grand Hotel* is a distant cousin of Presley's *Heartbreak Hotel*—but a much nicer place to visit, if not exactly to live in.

Albums/DAVID BLUE (August 1966): *Gasman Won't Buy Your Love; About My Love; So Easy She Goes By; If Your Monkey Can't Get It; Midnight Through Morning; It Ain't The Rain That Sweeps The Highway Clean; Arcade Love Machine; Grand Hotel; Justine; I'd Like To Know; The Street; It Tastes Like Candy.* 23 DAYS (March 1968): *These 23 Days In September; Ambitious Anna; You Need A Change; The Grand Hotel; The Sailor's Lament; You Will Come Back Again; Scales For A Window Thief; Slow An' Easy; The Fifth One.*

BLUE CHEER/*Paul Whaley (drums), Dick Peterson (bass), Randy Holden (replaced Leigh Stephens) (guitar).*
Nobody could accuse Blue Cheer of sneaking into the rock scene quietly in mid-1968. There are only three of them, and they're very young and very small, but there are people who still ache from the sheer loudness of those three small boys and their six gigantic Marshall amplifiers (probably the loudest sound in rock history). "They play so hard and so heavy they make cottage cheese out of the air," said Gut, the former Hell's Angel who co-manages them. In San Francisco, where they apparently like to be shaken up physically by noise, Blue Cheer is very big. They were less successful on the

East Coast, where they were put down for coming on as carbon copies of two other trios—Cream and the Jimi Hendrix Experience—without having either band's musical strength. Physical strength is something else. They have twenty-four speakers on those six amps, a guitarist who gets through four guitars a month without even trying (more when he's in the mood) and a drummer who wears thick gloves to protect his hands and files down his drumsticks for a blunter sound. Their version of the old Eddie Cochran song *Summertime Blues* was a summertime hit. There are people who see in their music, not the joyous versions of San Francisco acid rock, but the horrors of a bad STP trip, and *that*, they say, is what the sound is all about.

Albums/VINCEBUS ERUPTUM (July 1968): *Summertime Blues; Rock Me Baby; Dr. Please; Out Of Focus; Parchment Farm; Second Time Around.* OUTSIDEINSIDE (October 1968): *Feathers From Your Tree; Sun Cycle; Just A Little Bit; Gypsy Ball; Come And Get It; (I Can't Get No) Satisfaction; The Hunter; Magnolia Caboose; Babylon.* NEW! IMPROVED! BLUE CHEER (March 1969): *When It All Gets Old; West Coast Child Of Sunshine; I Want My Baby Back; Aces 'N' Eights; As Long As I Live; It Takes A Lot To Laugh, It Takes A Train To Cry; Peace Of Mind; Fruit And Iceburgs; Honey Butter Lover.*

Singles/*Summertime Blues* (2 parts) (June 1968); *Sun Cycle/ Feathers From Your Tree* (November 1968).

BLUEGRASS/Banjo, fiddles, bass, steel guitar, mandolin played at breakneck speed with high nasal voices in close harmony. Folk music of the Southeast dating from the twenties became a massive fad in the northern folk revival of the middle and late fifties. Every now and then in rock, particularly in the Lovin' Spoonful, what seems merely an accidental bit of goodtime or some trendy Nashville stage business, turns out to be an echo of the good old days of country strings that so many of the folk-oriented rock people grew up with.
(See NEW LOST CITY RAMBLERS and CHARLES RIVER VALLEY BOYS)

BLUES MAGOOS/*Ralph Scala (vocals, organ), Ron Gilbert*

(bass), Geoff Daking (drums), Mike Esposito (lead guitar), Emil "Peppy" Thielhelm (vocals, guitar).

The Blues Magoos have to be given due credit for trying. They got the best coif-genius in New York to cut their hair (the scowling Christopher Pluck at Vidal Sassoon); they got the wildest clothes-genius in New York to dress them (Diana Dew, the electric-dress girl who designed gear for them that lit up on stage); they were the first New York group (they came from the Bronx) to play psychedelic rock. And they called their first album *PSYCHEDELIC LOLLIPOP* late in 1966, when the word was still something to be marvelled at. On the title alone, the album must have sold tens of thousands in acid-happy San Francisco. On the back of it were instructions to play as loudly as possible. All that added up to a lot of effort. And it changed absolutely nothing.

Albums/PSYCHEDELIC LOLLIPOP (December 1966): *Nothin' Yet; Worried Life Blues; Tobacco Road; Love Seems Doomed; Queen Of My Nights; I'll Go Crazy; Gotta Get Away; One By One; Sometimes I Think About; She's Coming Home.* ELECTRIC COMIC BOOK (April 1967): *Pipe Dream; There's A Chance We Can Make It; Life Is Just A Cher O' Bowlies; Gloria; Intermission; Albert Common Is Dead; Baby, I Want You; Summer Is The Man; Let's Get Together; Take My Love; Rush Hour; That's All Folks.* BASIC BLUES MAGOOS (April 1968): *Sybil Green (Of In Between); I Can Hear The Grass Grow; All The Better To See You With; Yellow Rose; I Wanna Be There; I Can Move A Mountain; President's Council On Psychedelic Fitness; Scarecrow's Love Affair; There She Goes; Accidental Meditation; You're Getting Old; Subliminal Sonic Laxative; Chicken Wire Lady.*

Singles/*Nothin' Yet/Gotta Get Away* (December 1966); *Summer Is The Man/I Wanna Be There* (February 1967); *Life Is Just A Cher O' Bowlies/There She Goes* (April 1967); *Pipe Dream/There's A Chance We Can Make It* (April 1967); *One By One/Dante's Inferno* (June 1967); *Jingle Bells* (November 1967); *People Had No Faces/So I'm Wrong And You Are Right* (February 1968); *I Can Hear The Grass Grow* (August 1968).

BLUES PROJECT/*Andy Kulberg (flute, bass, piano), Roy Blumenfeld (drums), John Gregory (guitar, vocals), Donald Gretmar (bass saxophone); Richard Greene (violin).*
Previous Members: Tommy Flanders, Danny Kalb, Steve Katz, Al Kooper.

It was New York's first band—first band of its own, that is. The Cafe Au Go Go down on Bleecker Street in the Village was its home base when it wasn't working elsewhere, and there was always a special affection for it. Besides, it was incredibly good and none of its albums had ever done it justice (though every rock fan in New York has all three and loves them). The Blues Project never had a top ten single, though most likely that was because, like so many really good bands, it was before its time. By late 1967, when Cream and the Jimi Hendrix Experience and Canned Heat were all over the charts and the Blues Project certainly would have made it, it no longer existed. Even its name, not in any way unusual by then, was anomalous when it started in 1965. Actually *THE BLUES PROJECT* was the name of an album they had played on, a collection of blues tracks made by Dave Van Ronk, John Koerner, Geoff Muldaur, Eric Von Schmidt and Danny Kalb. But it seemed a better name than the one they had, the Danny Kalb Quartette.

Kalb, before then, had been either the best guitarist in folk or one of the best, depending on whom you were talking to. He's still to be heard in that capacity on a lot of folk records made at that time (Judy Collins' among them). But a funny thing happened to him—along with a lot of people in folk then—he fell in love with the idea of electric music. The new group probably did as much as anyone to make the average folk fan realize that electric music could be honest and valid and didn't have to be a sellout to Tin Pan Alley and commercialism. In any case, the Blues Project turned a lot of people on to a lot of things—on to blues, for one thing; on to Al Kooper and his incredible electric organ (which gave the group the characteristic "incandescence" *Times* critic Robert Shelton flipped out over); on to folk rock; on to the whole notion of a group that could play at a jazz festival, a folk festival and a pop festival, all in one year, and to wild applause. Nevertheless, other more commercially successful things started happening, things like the Spoonful. But the

Blues Project remained who they were, trying for a hit only because, well, why not?

By 1967 it was clear that something wasn't happening to New York's very own band, some quality was missing. Tommy Flanders, who had sung on their first album, was already off somewhere as a solo artist, and there were reports that both Kalb and Kooper wanted to do more singing than they were. Kooper announced he was through, off to England, to do something there on his own. Kalb became ill and abruptly left the group, disappeared, in fact—and Kooper returned. That, for some reason, did not work out either, and again Kooper was set to go. Farewell concerts were given, and to kill time before leaving he jammed with friends at the Au Go Go: Bobby Colomby, Steve Katz (of the Project) and Jim Fielder (formerly of the Mothers and the Buffalo Springfield). It worked so well, he decided to stay and form a new group, this time with horns. So was born Blood, Sweat and Tears. What was left of the Blues Project—without Kalb, Katz and Kooper—thought of keeping the name and the band going, but eventually re-formed with others into a new group called Sea Train. Danny Kalb stayed out of things so persistently that people started taking ads in the *Village Voice* asking, in large capital letters, "ANYONE KNOWING THE WHEREABOUTS OF DANNY KALB. . ." Rumors of his death were scotched by his sudden appearance. He is now producing for a record company and has gotten together a new group. Strangely enough, the death of the Blues Project hit New Yorkers badly. They still feel wounded and betrayed by it all. Those nights at the Au Go Go were a big part of the musical coming-of-age of a lot of people in the audience, as well as of the performers.
(see BLOOD, SWEAT AND TEARS, SEA TRAIN)

Albums/ BLUES PROJECT "LIVE" AT THE CAFE AU GO GO (May 1966): *Goin' Down Louisiana; You Go And I'll Go With You; Catch The Wind; I Want To Be Your Driver; Alberta; Way My Baby Walks; Violets Of Dawn; Back Door Man; Jelly Jelly Blues; Spoonful; Who Do You Love.* PROJECTIONS (January 1967): *I Can't Keep From Cryin'; Sometimes; You Can't Catch Me; Steve's Song; Fly Away; Wake Me, Shake Me; Cheryl's Going Home; Two*

Trains Running; Flute Thing; Caress Me Baby. BLUES PRO-
JECT "LIVE" AT TOWN HALL (September 1967): *Flute
Thing (Electric); I Can't Keep From Crying; Mean Old
Southern; No Time Like The Right Time; Love Will Endure;
Wake Me, Shake Me; Where There's Smoke, There's Fire.*
PLANNED OBSOLESCENCE (December 1968): *If You
Had To Make A Fool Of Somebody Calypso; The Endless
Sleep; Niartaes Hornpipe; Turtledove; Mojo Hanna; Frank
And Curt Incensed; She Raised Her Hand; Dakota Recollec-
tion.*

Singles/*No Time Like The Right Time*/*Steve's Song* (February 1967); *Gentle Dreams*/*Lost In The Shuffle* (August
1967).

BONZO DOG DOO-DAH BAND/*Vivian Stanshall (vocals),
"Legs" Larry Smith (drums), Neil Innes (piano), Rodney
Slater (saxophone), Roger Ruskin Spear (explosions), David
Claque.*
An English comedy group which for a long time was unknown in America in spite of one very funny album and an
appearance on the Beatles' *Magical Mystery Tour* in 1967.
Easily the freakiest group in England, though never as vicious
as our own dear Fugs and Mothers, the Bonzos had a singer
who wore silver lame and wiggled too lasciviously to be taken
entirely seriously, a drummer who wore Shirpley Temple
outfits and large wobbly plastic breasts and blew little kisses
(*before* Tiny Tim), and a robot who literally had his mind
blown on stage. There were parodies of fifties rock, of English
music hall and burlesque; there was out and out camp,
gadgetry, pop art construction, most unorthodox sound ac-
companiment (including an explosion) and much other
horseplay. The English adored them, but it took them a long
time to get a hit. They did it with *Urban Spaceman* and it was
only a matter of weeks to their first American tour, which
was extremely successful. They are the perfect example of at
least one direction rock may move into—more visual, more
comic, more theatrical.

Album/GORILLA (February 1968): *Cool Britannia; Eques-
trian Statue; I Left My Heart In San Francisco; Jollity Farm;
I'm Bored; Look Out, There's A Monster Coming; Jazz,*

Delicious Hot, Disgusting Cold; Deathcab For Cutie; Narcissus; Intro And The Outro; Mickey's Son And Daughter; Music For The Head Ballet; Piggy Bank Love; Sound Of Music.

BOOKER T & THE M.G.'s/*Steve Cropper (lead guitar), Al Jackson (drums), Donald "Duck" Dunn (bass), Booker T. Jones (organ).*

Besides recording on their own, Booker T & The M.G.'s back up most of the Stax-Volt artists—Sam & Dave, Wilson Pickett and Otis Redding—as well as writing many of their hits (*Midnight Hour, Knock On Wood,* etc.). They are the proverbial musicians' musicians, known for their elegant style of clean, tasteful soul. If you want to know exactly what the word "tight" means when referring to musicians, listen to them at work. Perfect rapport and no mistakes. There isn't a guitarist worth his strings who doesn't swoon over a Steve Cropper solo. Primarily studio musicians, they do leave their Memphis home base to play gigs. At first they traveled with the late Otis Redding, playing in his show and then backing him up. Now they play on their own, carrying their brand of Memphis funk all over the world, then rushing back to Tennessee to spend a month in session. The secret formula? Playing it the way they feel it, they say, no clever electronic trickery because their whole aim is to play in a way that touches the listener so deeply he *has* to buy the record. Very little overdubbing goes on at Stax, home of the so-called Memphis sound that dominated the 1968 charts, in strong contrast to the Detroit sound at Motown, which is very much controlled by the studio engineers.

Albums/GREEN ONIONS (November 1962): *Green Onions; Rinky-Dink; I Got A Woman; Mo' Onions; Twist & Shout; Behave Yourself; Stranger On The Shore; Lonely Avenue; One Who Really Loves You; I Can't Sit Down; Woman, A Lover, A Friend; Comin' Home Baby.* AND NOW: *My Sweet Potato; Working In The Coal Mine; In The Midnight Hour; Jericho; No Matter What Shape; One Mint Julep; Summertime; Don't Mess Up A Good Thing; Think; Taboo; Soul Jam; Sentimental Journey.* IN THE XMAS SPIRIT: *Jingle Bells; Santa Claus Is Coming To Town;*

Winter Wonderland; White Christmas; Christmas Song; Silver Bells; Merry Christmas Baby; Blue Christmas; Sweet Little Jesus Boy; Silent Night; We Three Kings; We Wish You A Merry Christmas. HIP HUG-HER: *Hip Hug-Her; Soul Sanction; Get Ready; Slim Jenkins Joint; Pigmy; Groovin'; Booker's Notion; Sunny; Double Or Nothing; Carnaby Street; Others.* BACK TO BACK: *Green Onions; Red Beans & Rice; Tic-Tac-Toe; Hip Hug-Her; Gimme Some Lovin'; Booker Loo; Outrage.* DOIN' OUR THING: *Expressway To Your Heart; Doin' Our Thing; You Don't Love Me; Never My Love; Exodus Song; Beat Goes On; Ode To Billie Joe; Blue On Green; You Keep Me Hanging On; Let's Go Get Stoned.* BEST OF BOOKER T. AND THE MG'S (November 1968): *Hip Hug-Her; Slim Jenkin's Place; Green Onions; Soul Dressing; Jelly Bread; Groovin'; Mo' Onions; Summertime; Boot-Leg; Can't Be Still; Tic-Tac-Toe; Red Beans And Rice.*

Singles/*Green Onions/Behave Yourself; Aw' Mercy/Jelly Bread; Big Train/Home Grown; Mo' Onions/Tic-Tac-Toe; MG Party/Soul Dressing; Can't Be Still/Terrible Things; Bootleg/Outrage; Be My Lady/Red Beans & Rice; Booker-Loo/My Sweet Potato; Jingle Bells/Winter Wonderland; Hip Hug-Her/Summertime; Groovin'/Slim Jenkin's Joint; Silver Bells/Winter Snow; Heads Or Tails/Soul Limbo; Hang 'Em High/Over Easy (1968).*

Also Appear On/HISTORY OF RHYTHM & BLUES, VOL. 5: *Green Onions.* MEMPHIS GOLD: *Bootleg.* MEMPHIS GOLD, VOL. 2: *Hip Hug-Her.* SUPER HITS, VOL. 1: *Hip Hug-Her.* TREASURE CHEST OF GOLDIES (April 1964): *Green Onions.*

PAT BOONE/Whether anyone wants to admit it or not, Pat Boone did much to popularize early rock and roll songs with a large segment of the public that might otherwise never have heard them or bought them. Songs which were totally unacceptable to cautious parents when sung by big, black, raunchy, rhythm and blues type singers somehow seemed safe emerging from the clean-cut, white, thoroughly wholesome and very happily married (with several kids) Pat Boone. Like many other white singers of the fifties and early sixties, he listened to the then all-black rhythm and blues hits which were played only on black stations, took what he liked and cut his own version. This practice, which was widely accepted and still is and is perfectly legal, was regarded with great bitterness by the original singers, who would see some other version of their song hit the number one spot and make a fortune and a reputation for someone else while the original version never got a hearing. Few white rock and roll stations gave black artists airplay then, though over the years this was to change considerably. Boone was often insipid, commercial and namby-pamby, but he *was* the answer to those who found it impossible to identify with a motorcycle hood like Elvis.

Albums/HYMNS WE LOVE (October 1957); STAR DUST (June 1958). PAT'S GREAT HITS (April 1959). SIDE BY SIDE (May 1959). HE LEADETH ME (September 1959). PAT'S GREAT HITS, VOL. 2 (December 1959). TENDERLY (April 1959). GREAT! GREAT! GREAT! (February 1961). MY GOD AND I (May 1961). MOODY RIVER (June 1961). GOLDEN HITS (September 1962). DAYS OF WINE AND ROSES (February 1963). STAR SPANGLED BANNER (June 1963). SING ALONG WITHOUT (November 1963). TOUCH OF YOUR LIPS (January 1964). PAT BOONE (April 1964). LORD'S PRAYER (June 1964). TWELVE GREAT HITS (June 1964). BOSS BEAT (September 1964). NEAR YOU (November 1964). GOLDEN ERA OF COUNTRY HITS (March 1965). 1965 (August 1965). MEMORIES (August 1966). WISH YOU WERE HERE (October 1966). TRUE LOVE: TENTH ANNIVERSARY WITH DOT. HOW GREAT THOU ART (April 1967). I WAS KAISER BILL'S BATMAN (May 1967). PAT BOONE'S GOLDEN HITS (August 1967).

Singles/*Moody River/Speedy Gonzales; Ain't That A Shame /Friendly Persuasion; April Love/Don't Forbid Me; I Almost Lost My Mind/I'll Be Home; Exodus Song/New Lovers; Hurry Sundown/What If They Gave A War And No One Came; Have You Heard/Me; Mirror Of Your Hand/Swanee Is A River; By The Time I Get To Phoenix/Ride, Ride, Ride; Green Kentucky Hills Of Home/You Mean All The*

World To Me; It's A Happening World/Emily; 500 Miles/I Had A Dream.

BOSTON SOUND/Poor Boston. Some very nice things have happened and are happening there, but the mere mention of a Boston sound gets people nervous. It happened like this. After the San Francisco sound clicked commercially in 1967 and 1968, a record company executive thought the musical happenings of Boston could be built up into a big Boston sound promotion. (*Newsweek* was taken in to the extent of a long, favorable article.) The trouble was that what was happening in Boston could not, even under the most optimistic circumstances, be described in terms of the explosion that had previously shaken San Francisco and the world. The Boston promotion bombed painfully, leaving some fine up-and-coming groups out in the cold, victims of what the critics immediately termed a hype. The groups involved are now battling their way with that strike against them. The point was there was no Boston sound then and there isn't now. The *real* Boston sound, in a considerably different sense, was the sound of Club 47, where Joan Baez, Tom Rush and the Cambridge folkies first became known early in the sixties. "Pure New England folk" is what the fans called it.

Meanwhile, current Boston rock groups include Orpheus, Ill Wind, Bagatelle, the Ultimate Spinach, Eden's Children, Phluph, Earth Opera—some more successful than others, but all fighting off that uncomfortable Boston tag.

THE ALAN BOWN/*Alan Bown (trumpet), Geoff Bannister (organist), John Anthony (tenor sax), Stan Haldane (bass guitar), Jess Roden (vocals), Vic Sweeny (drummer), Tony Catchpole (lead guitar).*
An English group, the Alan Bown, released their first album in the U.S. in 1968 without much fanfare. They have an extraordinarily calm sound, ironic little ditties about toys, magic handkerchiefs, dolls and violin shops. But they also do a wildly nightmarish version of Dylan's *All Along The Watchtower*. Like so many good English groups that aren't dabbling in whatever the current big fad is and don't have a hit on the charts, they are completely underrated in the United States.

Album/THE ALAN BOWN (August 1968): *Toyland; Magic Handkerchief; Little Lesley; All Along The Watchtower; Sally Green; Penny For Your Thoughts; Storybook; Technicolor Dream; Love Is A Beautiful Thing; Violin Shop; You're Not In My Class; My Girl; The Month Of May*
Single/*Magic Handkerchief/We Can Help You* (September 1968).

THE BOXTOPS/*Alex Chilton (lead singer), Billy Cunningham (bass guitar), Gary Talley (lead guitar), Danny Smythe (drums), John Evans (organ, guitar).*
No American group since the Righteous Brothers had looked whiter and sung blacker than the Boxtops on that sensational first single in 1967, *The Letter.* Alex Chilton's voice had more Memphis grit than was considered entirely proper for a white gentleman. But he learned to sing in Memphis (Elvis-country), where lots of people sing that way, and got his musicians from a town where musicians are pretty heavy whatever their color. You don't have to be black to sing that way, you just have to think that way.
Albums/BOX TOPS (October 1967): *The Letter; Neon Rainbow; She Knows How; Trains & Boats & Planes; Break My Mind; I'm Your Puppet; Whiter Shade Of Pale; People Make The World; Everything I Am; Happy Time; Gonna Find Somebody; I Pray For Rain.* CRY LIKE A BABY (March 1968): *Cry Like A Baby; Lost; Deep In Kentucky; Weeping Analeah; Trouble With Sam; Fields Of Clover; Good Morning Dear; You Keep Me Hanging On; I'm The One For You; Every Time.* NON-STOP (October 1968): *I'm Movin' On; She Shot A Hole In My Soul; People Gonna Talk; I Met Her In Church; Yesterday's Where My Mind;* Other titles.
Singles/*The Letter/Happy Times* (June 1967); *Neon Rainbow/Everything I Am* (October 1967); *Cry Like A Baby/Door You Closed To Me* (February 1968); *Choo Choo Train/Fields Of Clover* (May 1968); *I Met Her In Church/People Gonna Talk* (August 1968); *See Only Sunshine/Sweet Cream Ladies, Forward March* (December 1968).

BIG BILL BROONZY (William Lee Conley Broonzy)/One of the great country-blues singers and guitarists of the thirties, forties and fifties, Big Bill had a lot to do with helping to shape the Chicago blues sound. His music is extremely popular in folk as well as blues circles in England, Europe and America. He died in 1958.

Albums/BIG BILL BROONZY SINGS FOLK SONGS (May 1962): *Backwater Blues; This Train; I Don't Want No Woman To Try To Be My Boss; Martha; Tell Me Who; Bill Bailey; Alberta; Goin' Down This Road; Tell Me What Kind Of Man Jesus Is; John Henry; Glory Of Love.* BIG BILL BROONZY: *Plowhand Blues; C. C. Rider; Bill Bailey; Willie Mae Blues; This Train; Mule Riding, Talking Blues; Key To The Highway; Black, Brown And White; Joe Turner No. 1.* BIG BILL BROONZY SINGS COUNTRY BLUES: *In The Evenin'; When Things Go Wrong; Diggin' My Potatoes; Poor Bill Blues; Troublin' Mind; I Wonder When I'll Get To Be Called A Man; Louise, Louise; Frankie And Johnny; Southbound Train; Joe Turner No. 2; Hey Hey Baby; Good Evening Blues.* BIG BILL BROONZY SONGS AND STORY. BIG BILL BROONZY (November 1967): *Ridin' On Down; Feelin' Lowdown; St. Louis Blues; Baby Please Don't Go; I Got Up One Mornin' Blues; In The Evenin', Sixteen Tons; All I Got Belongs To You; Treat Everybody Right; See See Rider.* BIG BILL BROONZY WITH WASHBOARD SAM: *Little City Woman; Lonesome; Jacqueline; Romance Without Finance; By Myself; Shirttail; Diggin' My Potatoes; Bright Eyes; Minding My Own Business; Never, Never; Horseshoe Over My Door; I'm A Lonely Man.*

THE BROTHERHOOD/*Drake Levin (guitar), Phil Volk (bass), Michael "Smitty" Smith (drums), Ron Collins (organ, piano).*
The group is historically interesting because it was a sort of spinoff in the spring of 1967 from one of rock's most successful groups, Paul Revere and the Raiders. The original three members were Raiders who later added a fourth, on organ and piano. They left the Raiders mainly because they found the formula of comedy rock limiting and wanted to move into a sweeter, gentler thing. All three were very popular as Raiders. Can they still wow 'em out of Raider uniforms and into beads?

Single/ *Jump Out Of The Window/Box Guitar.*

CRAZY WORLD OF ARTHUR BROWN/ *Vincent Crane (organ), Drachian Theaker (drums), Sean Nicholas (bass), Arthur Brown (vocals).*
In mid-1968, when the pop scene had just about gimmicked itself out of existence, Arthur Brown arrived with the stunt to end all stunts—he appeared on stage wearing phosphorescent robes, black and white face paint and had flames shooting out of the top of his head. There was a lot of costume changing on stage, a series of metallic masks and an utterly astonishing voice that somehow went with the whole spectacle—a voice that shifted from gentle softness to raving maniac screeching, all in a matter of seconds. Probably the only voice like it in pop music. No one else (except Tiny Tim) has the range and power and ability to change so quickly. Finally, a strange spastic dancing like some sort of space-age ritual. This—with the masks, costumes and helmets, and what he swears is completely "safe" fire, along with swooping organ sounds and fierce drumming—is one of the most impressive examples of theatre rock combined with art rock and what might eventually be called ballet rock. "God of hell fire" they called him in London until the flames burned out.

Album/ CRAZY WORLD OF ARTHER BROWN (September 1968): *Nightmare; Fire Poem; Fire; Come & Buy; I've Got Money; Time; Confusion; I Put A Spell On You; Spontaneous Apple Creation; Rest Cure; Child Of My Kingdom.*

Singles/ *Fire/Rest Cure* (September 1968); *Nightmare/I Put A Spell On You* (December 1968).

JAMES BROWN/ The first time James Brown played white New York (he had played in Harlem's Apollo theatre before that) it was in 1966 at the old Madison Square Garden. It was at a time when American music was busy finding itself again after the English invasion of 1964-65, and whites were starting to take a closer look at all the Isley-Brothers-black-soul the Beatles and others were bringing back over. There on stage was soul brother number one, Mister Dynamite. A big, black, beautiful, shouting, raving, screaming presence in the good old-fashioned tradition of showmanship—buckets of perspiration, grimaces of unendurable pain, blaring brass, writhing girl dancers and a smooth, sleek male chorus. Although that sort of thing had been around the southern soul circuit for years, for the whites, those who had never ventured as far uptown as the Apollo, it was a penetrating experience. The concentration of it all. Cuff links hurled into the audience. The long, gasping collapse at the end. The colleagues running forward protectively with a brightly colored cape. Then, with a superhuman effort (a black Houdini), the struggle to throw off the cape and the protective arms. And again on stage for another sweating, agonized encore. Then, inevitably, another collapse and another race with the cloak, and the knees giving way and—oh, what's this?—muscles straining dreadfully, the whole body trembling in deathlike throes and, this time, more dead than alive, a return to the stage to thunderous applause.

He does it performance after performance, time after time, each cloak a different color to underline that—look folks—it's only a *performance,* but no one believes, no one wants to believe. Everything in the James Brown show is staged and contrived—the oohing and aahing, the little shuffles of everyone on stage, every rivulet of perspiration. It's the biggest show on earth, played for every possible angle, and James Brown does it 364 days a year, or something like that, in every town that will take him. They flock to see him (mostly black but sometimes white), and that keeps him in white shirts and shiny shoes and cuff links and cadillacs and great personal splendor. The man's rich, and he works for every penny. There must be better performers (there are) who sing better, look better, but James Brown gives the best show, the best value for money, and he's king. Others aspire, all the time, to his title, but somehow his act never palls. Once, during a riot season, he was put on television and everyone forgot the riot and stayed home to watch the king.

Albums/GRITS AND SOUL (May 1965): *Grits; Tempted; There; After You're Through; Devil's Den; Who's Afraid Of Virginia Woolf; Infatuation; Wee Wee; Mister Hip; Headache.* JAMES BROWN PLAYS JAMES BROWN TODAY AND YESTERDAY (January 1966): *Papa's Got A Brand New Bag; Oh, Baby Don't You Weep; Every Beat Of*

My Heart; Out Of Sight; Sidewinder; Maybe The Last Time; Hold It Song For My Father. HANDFUL OF SOUL (January 1967): *Our Day Will Come; Get Loose; Oh Henry; Let's Go Get Stoned; Hot Mix; Hold On, I'm Comin'; King; When A Man Loves A Woman; Message To Michael; 634-5789.* JAMES BROWN SHOW (January 1967): *Satisfaction; Don't Mess With Bill; Dog; Nowhere To Run; In The Midnight Hour; Stop And Think It Over; This Is My Story; 634-5789; Strung Out; Something's Got A Hold On Me.* JAMES BROWN PLAYS THE REAL THING (July 1967): *Jimmy Mack; What Do You Like; Peewee's Groove In 'D'; Bernadette; Mercy, Mercy, Mercy; I Never Loved A Man; 'D' Thing; Funky Broadway.* JAMES BROWN PLAYS NEW BREED (May 1968): *New Breed; Slow Walk; Fat Bag; Vonshelia; Jabo; Lost In The Mood Of Changes; All About My Girl; Hooks; Something Else.* AMAZING JAMES BROWN: *I Love You, Yes I Do; Lost Someone; You Don't Have To Go; Dancin' Little Thing; The Bells; Tell Me What You're Gonna Do; So Long; Just You And Me; And I Do Just What I Want; Come Over Here; I Don't Mind; Love Don't Love Nobody.* GOOD, GOOD, TWISTIN' WITH JAMES BROWN: *I Don't Mind; Shout And Shimmy; Tell Me What You're Gonna Do; Good, Good Lovin'; Have Mercy Baby; Begging, Begging; Love\Don't Love Nobody; Dancin' Little Thing; Come Over Here; You Don't Have To Go; Just Won't Do Right; It Was You.* JAMES BROWN AND THE FAMOUS FLAMES TOUR THE U.S.A.: *Mashed Potatoes U.S.A.; Three Hearts In A Tangle; Choo-Choo Locomotion; Doin' The Limbo; I Don't Care; Joggin' Along; I've Got Money; Sticky; Like A Baby; Every Beat Of My Heart; In The Wee Wee Hours; Cross Firing.* JAMES BROWN SHOW: *I'll Go Crazy; Lost Someone; You've Got The Power; Please, Please, Please; I Found Someone; Why Do You Do Me; I Want You So Bad; Night Train; Try Me; Think I Don't Mind; I Love You, Yes I Do; Bewildered; Why Does Everything Happen To Me; Please Don't Go.* PURE DYNAMITE: *Oh Baby Don't You Weep; These Foolish Things; Signed, Sealed And Delivered; Like A Baby; I'll Never Let You Go; Good, Good Lovin'; Please, Please, Please; Shout And Shimmy.* UNBEATABLE JAMES BROWN: *There Must Be A Reason; I Want You So Bad; Why Do You Do Me; Got To*

Cry; Strange Things Happen; Fine Old Foxy Self; Messing With The Blues; Try Me; It Was You; I've Got To Change; Can't Be The Same; It Hurts To Tell You; I Won't Plead No More; You're Mine, You're Mine; Gonna Try; Don't Let It Happen To Me. I GOT YOU: I've Got Money; Lost Someone; Three Hearts In A Tangle; Suds; Love Don't Love Nobody; Night Train; I Can't Help It; Good, Good Lovin'; You've Got The Power; Dancin' In The Street; Think; I Got You. MIGHTY INSTRUMENTALS: Hold It; Every Beat Of My Heart; Sticky; Night Train; Feel It; Cross Firing; Suds; James Brown's Houseparty; Doin' The Limbo; Papa's Got A Brand New Bag; Scratch; Choo-Choo. SOUL BROTHER NO. 1: The Scratch; Bewildered; The Bells; In The Wee Wee Hours Of The Night; I Don't Mind; Come Over Here; Just You And Me; I Love You, Yes I Do; Ain't That A Groove; It's A Man's, Man's, Man's World; Is It Yes Or Is It No. CHRISTMAS SONGS: Merry Christmas Baby; Christmas Song; Please Come Home For Christmas; Let's Make This Christmas Mean Something This Year; Christmas In Heaven; Merry Christmas, I Love You; Sweet Little Baby Boy; This Is My Lonely Christmas; Signs Of Christmas. RAW SOUL: Bring It Up; Don't Be A Drop Out; Till Then; Tell Me That You Love Me; Yours And Mine; Let Yourself Go; Money Won't Change You; Only You; Nearness Of You; Nobody Knows; Stone Fox. JAMES BROWN 'LIVE' AT THE GARDEN: Let Yourself Go; Out Of Sight; Bring It Up; Try Me; Hip Bag '67; Prisoner Of Love; It May Be The Last Time; I Got You; Ain't That A Groove; Please, Please, Please. COLD SWEAT: Cold Sweat (2 Parts); Stagger Lee; Fever; Kansas City; I Want To Be Around; Nature Boy; Come Rain Or Come Shine; I Loves You Porgy; Mona Lisa; Back Stabbin'; Good Rockin' Tonight. I CAN'T STAND MYSELF: There Was A Time; I Can't Stand Myself (2 Parts); Time After Time; Get It Together (2 Parts); Baby, Baby, Baby, Baby; Soul Of J.B.; Why Did You Take Your Love Away From Me; Need Your Love So Bad; You've Got To Change Your Mind; Funky Soul No. 1. I GOT THE FEELIN': I Got The Feelin'; You've Got the Power; If I Ruled The World; It Won't Be Me; Maybe I'll Understand; Maybe Good, Maybe Bad; Just Plain Funk; Shhhhhhh (For A Little While); Here I Go; Stone Fox. NOTHING BUT SOUL

(August 1968): *Soul With Different Notes; Go On Now;
Little Fellow; Gittin' A Little Hipper; Fat Soul; Buddy-E.*
PLEASE, PLEASE, PLEASE: *Please, Please, Please; Chon-
nie-On-Chon; Hold My Baby's Hand; I Feel That Old Feeling
Coming On; Just Won't Do Right; Baby Cries Over The
Ocean; I Don't Know; Tell Me What I Did Wrong; Try Me;
That Dood It; No, No, No, No; Begging, Begging; I Walked
Alone; That's When I Lost My Heart; Let's Make It; Love Or
A Game.* JAMES BROWN SINGS OUT OF SIGHT (Sep-
tember 1968): *Out Of Sight; Come Rain Or Come Shine; I
Loves You Porgy; Good Rockin' Tonight; Till Then; Nature
Boy; I Wanna Be Around; I Got You; Maybe The Last Time;
Only You; Else; Somethin'.*

Singles/*Good, Good Lovin'/Don't Let It Happen To Me; I
Know It's True/I'll Go Crazy; Please, Please, Please/Why Do
You Do Me; I Loves You Porgy/Yours And Mine; Hold
It/Scratch; Bewildered/If You Want Me; I Don't Mind/Love
Don't Love Nobody; Sticky/Suds; Baby, You're Right/I'll
Never, Never Let You Go; I Love You, Yes I Do/Just You
And Me, Darling; Cross Firing/Lost Someone; Night Train/
Why Does Everything Happen To Me; Every Beat Of My
Heart/Like A Baby; In The Wee Wee Hours/Please, Please,
Please; Think/Try Me; Papa's Got A Brand New Bag (2
Parts); I Can't Help It/I Got You; I'll Go Crazy/Lost
Someone; Ain't That A Groove (2 Parts); I've Got To
Change/Prisoner Of Love; Come Over Here/Tell Me What
You're Gonna Do; Is It Yes, Or Is It No/It's A Man's, Man's,
Man's World; This Old Heart/How Long Darling; Money
Won't Change You (2 Parts); Don't Be A Drop Out (2
Parts); Christmas Song (2 Parts); Bring It Up/Nobody
Knows; Let's Make This Christmas Mean Something This
Year (2 Parts); Sweet Little Baby Boy (2 Parts); Kansas
City/Stone Fox; Good Rockin' Tonight/Let Yourself Go;
Cold Sweat (2 Parts); America Is My Home (2 Parts); Get It
Together (2 Parts); Soul Of J.B./Funky Soul, Part 1; I Guess
I'll Have To Cry, Cry, Cry/Just Plain Funk; I Can't Stand
Myself/There Was A Time; You've Got The Power/You've
Got To Change Your Mind; I Got The Feelin'/If I Ruled The
World; Maybe Good, Maybe Bad (2 Parts); Here I
Go/Shhhhhh (For A Little While); Licking Stick, Licking*

Stick (2 Parts); Say It Loud—I'm Black And I'm Proud (2 Parts) (October 1968); *Goodbye My Love (2 Parts)* (November 1968).

Also Appears On/NIGHT TRAIN: *Hold It; Scratch; Night Train; Suds; Night Flying; Cross Firing.* 18 KING SIZE RHYTHM AND BLUES HITS (August 1967): *Please, Please, Please.*

JACKSON BROWNE/Some things take a long time to happen, said Danny Fields on WFMU when queried on the progress of young Californian singer-writer Jackson Browne. Browne's poem-songs appear on Steve Noonan's album and also on Nico's first solo album. (He was in New York playing guitar for Nico at the Dom in 1967.) And it's clear from them that when he does happen, when he's good and ready, the wait will have been worth it.

BUBBLEGUM MUSIC/Why did records like *Chewy Chewy* (October 1968) and *Yummy, Yummy, Yummy* (July 1968) dominate the charts during a period which is often described as the most sophisticated in rock? Because, statistically, there are more ten- and eleven-year-olds than ever and, not only that, more ten- and eleven-year-olds are buying more records than ever before, and more nine-year-olds and eight-year-olds too. Music that sells to subteens and sub-subteens is a comparatively recent phenomenon (give or take the red-nosed reindeer and the doggie in the window). Those who find the phenomenon deeply depressing have shrugged this music off as bubblegum music.

THE BUCKINGHAMS/*Denny Tufano (lead vocals), Carl Giammarese (lead guitar), Jon-Jon Poulos (drums), Nick Fortune (bass), Marty Grebb (replaced Dennis Miccoli) (organ).*
The Buckinghams are one of those sleek, expensively barbered, well-tailored, highly commercial rock groups—beloved by record companies, adored by fans and scorned by avant-garde rock critics and rock intellectuals. They came out of Chicago at the height of the rock boom and moved right into a hit formula, doing everything an efficient computer might recommend and never making a mistake. All this was only as

far as singles were concerned. The albums were something else; here, an ex-Mother, James William Guercio, took over completely. Produced. Arranged. Conducted. Directed. And, a lot of the time, composed. The sense of it was clear: be commercial with the singles, experiment with the albums. It was a brave try (and the albums have a high moment or two), but hard to reconcile with the Buckingham's commercial image.

Albums/KIND OF A DRAG: *Kind Of A Drag; I Call Your Name; I'll Go Crazy; Don't Want To Cry; Virginia Woolf; Beginners Love; Sweets For My Sweet; I've Been Wrong; Makin' Up And Breakin' Up; You Make Me Feel So Good, Summertime; Love Ain't Enough.* TIME AND CHARGES (July 1967): *Don't You Care; And Our Love; Pitied Be The Dragon Hunter; Why Don't You Love Me; You Are Gone; I'll Be Back; Remember; Mercy, Mercy, Mercy; Married Life; Foreign Policy.* PORTRAITS (March 1968): *Susan; Hey Baby; C'mon Home; I Love All Of The Girls; We Just Know; Inside Looking Out; Mail; Big Business Advisor; Have You Noticed You're Alive; Just Because I've Fallen Down; Any Place In Here.* IN ONE EAR AND GONE TOMORROW (September 1968): *Back In Love Again; Simplicity; Can I Get A Witness; Our Wrong To Be Right; Can't Find The Words; Song Of The Breeze; What Is Love; I Know I Think; Till The Sun Doesn't Shine; Are You There; Time Of My Life.*

Singles/*Don't Want To Cry/I'll Go Crazy; Kind Of A Drag/ You Make Me Feel So Good; Lawdy Miss Clawdy/I Call Your Name; Mercy, Mercy, Mercy/Don't You Care; Hey Baby/Susan; Back In Love Again/You Misunderstand; Where Did You Come From/Song Of The Breeze* (November 1968).

TIM BUCKLEY/Nothing in rock, folk rock, or anything else prepares you for a Tim Buckley album, and it's funny to hear his work described as blues, modified rock and roll, and raga rock when, in fact, there is no name yet for the places he and his voice go. He is a singer and a writer and often a lyricist. The voice is not a voice so much as a musical instrument of incredible range and sweetness. Robert Shelton of the New

York *Times* called him "not quite a counter-tenor but a tenor to counter with." His albums are some of the most beautiful in the new music, beautifully produced and arranged, always managing to be wildly passionate and pure at the same time. Women tend to play them thirty times over in one sitting. "His whole trip is a walk on the high wire, juggling insights," said another writer who understood you couldn't use ordinary words to talk about him.

On the first album he is untouched by the cold hard world around him and you don't want it any other way. On the second album, the protective wrapping is off. Life has begun to get to him. Because he's young and in the process of growing up, the beautiful pure choirboy of that first album dies a little every day. His best song yet, *Goodbye and Hello*, is only half innocence; the other half is experience. And his third album is the product of that experience. It is as if, not liking too much of the world outside, he chose to retreat to the warm and secure California where he has his home.

Tim Buckley may look like Huckleberry Finn lost in a blackberry patch, but in fact he's as tortuous and complicated as those ten thousand matted curls that cluster protectively around his head.

Albums/GOODBYE AND HELLO (September 1967): *No Man Can Find The War; Carnival Song; I Never Asked To Be Your Mountain; Pleasant Street; Hallucinations; Once I Was; Knight-Errant; Phantasmagoria In Two; Goodbye And Hello; Morning Glory.* TIM BUCKLEY (October 1968): *I Can't See You; Wings; Song Of The Magician; Strange Sweet Affair Under Blue; Valentine Melody; Aren't You The Girl; Song Slowly Song; It Happens Every Time; Song For Jainie; Grief In My Soul; She Is; Understand Your Man.* HAPPY/SAD (March 1969): *Strange Feelin'; Buzzin' Fly; Love From Room 109 At The Islander (On The Pacific Coast Highway); Dream Letter; Gypsy Woman; Sing A Song For You.*

Singles/*Morning Glory/Once I Was* (December 1967); *Aren't You The Girl/Strange Street Affair* (February 1967); *Wings/Grief In My Soul* (September 1966).

BUFFALO SPRINGFIELD/*Richie Furay (rhythm guitar and vocals), Neil Young (lead guitar and vocals), Jim Messina (bass*

*guitar), Dewey Martin (drums and vocals), Stephen Stills (guitar
and vocals). Previous Members: Doug Hastings, Bruce Palmer.*
The story of Buffalo Springfield is a sad one because this
could have been *the* group. One of its greatest assets was the
long and heavy experience of each of its members in a variety
of musical fields. It started in the spring of 1966 when two
singing guitarists, Steve Stills and Richie Furay, ran into two
Canadian musicians in a Los Angeles traffic jam. The Canadi-
ans were bass player Bruce Palmer and another guitarist, Neil
Young. Drummer Dewey Martin was added, and there it
was—Buffalo Springfield, a group that from the start had
impressive potential. During their first national tours (with
the Byrds and the Beach Boys), it was obvious that this was a
band with a very unique blend of styles—a folk song here, a
ballad there, hard rock, country. Their third single, written
by Steve Stills, *For What It's Worth,* gave the group the
national exposure it needed. But the first LP was less than
spectacular, less than it should have been. Although the
material had been performed live with great success, it came
through thin and weak. It was the old story of an essentially
"live" group having to learn what to do in the studio. One
song on that first LP was a milestone: *Go and Say Goodbye,*
written by Stills in 1965, was the first country-folk song and a
prophetic look ahead to the later emergence of country rock.
  Buffalo Springfield's second album, *BUFFALO SPRING-
FIELD AGAIN,* showed a marked change. This time there
was no attempt to record the song as performed. Instead, the
group concentrated on a good *recorded* sound. Arrangements
were expanded, and the old thin, flat, weak sound of the first
album was gone. (Only one song was recorded live—a jazzy
number called *Everydays.*) It was a giant step, this second
album, and the Buffalo Springfield were on their way. The
album was a best seller and the group one of the hottest in the
country. Then, suddenly, they disbanded. The material for a
third album had already been done and was released as
BUFFALO SPRINGFIELDS: THE LAST TIME AROUND.
It turned out to be the best album. Steve Stills and Neil
Young are now in the Anglo-American group Crosby, Stills,
Nash and Young. Richie Furay and Jim Messina, along with
two others, formed a country rock group, Poco.
(see CROSBY, STILLS, NASH AND YOUNG, POCO)

Albums/BUFFALO SPRINGFIELD (February 1967): *For What It's Worth; Burned; Nowadays Clancy Can't Even Sing; Flying On The Ground Is Wrong; Hot Dusty Roads; Go And Say Goodbye; Sit Down, I Think I Love You; Everybody's Wrong; Do I Have To Come Right Out And Say It; Leave; Out Of My Mind; Pay The Price.* BUFFALO SPRING-FIELD AGAIN (December 1967): *Mr. Soul; Rock 'n' Roll Woman; Child's Claim To Fame; Everydays; Expecting To Fly; Hung Upside Down; Sad Memory; Good Time Boy; Borken Arrows; Bluebird.* BUFFALO SPRINGFIELD LAST TIME AROUND (August 1968): *Un-Mundo; On The Way Home; It's So Hard To Wait; Pretty Girl Why; Four Days Gone; Carefree Country Day; Special Care; Hour Of Not Quite Rain; Questions; I Am A Child; Merry-Go-Round; Kind Woman.*

Singles/*Go And Say Goodbye/Nowadays Clancy Can't Even Sing* (August 1966); *Burned/Everybody's Wrong* (October 1966); *Do I Have To Come Right Out And Say It/For What It's Worth* (December 1966); *Bluebird/Mr. Soul* (June 1967); *Child's Claim To Fame/Rock 'n' Roll Woman* (September 1967); *Expecting To Fly/Everydays* (December 1967); *Four Days Gone/Un-Mundo* (March 1968); *On The Way Home/Four Days Gone* (September 1968).

SANDY BULL/The multi-instrumental virtuoso who, as early as 1963, was into Eastern music and instruments, moving easily from these to classical lute or Bach on electric guitar. Since Bull plays all the instruments on several of his songs, he regularly used overdubbing at a time when studio techniques were largely undeveloped. He is as good a musical technician as an improvisational performer. His two records made in 1963 and 1965 anticipate just about every style assimilated by the rock groups of 1968, with the exception of electronics. Although musicians and a hard core of dedicated fans have always known about Sandy Bull and his talents and innovations, he is only now becoming known to the general rock public.

Albums/SANDY BULL (FANTASIAS FOR GUITAR AND BANJO) (May 1963): *Blend; Carmina Burana Fantasy; Non Nobis Domine; Little Maggie; Gospel Tune.* INVENTIONS (FOR GUITAR, BANJO, OUD, FENDER BASS GUITAR,

ELECTRIC GUITAR) (July 1965): *Blend II; Gavotte No. 2 (Bach); Manha De Carnival; Triple Ballade; Memphis, Tennesee.* E PLURIBUS UNUM: *No Deposit-No Return; Electric Blend.*

ERIC BURDON (see ANIMALS)

GARY BURTON QUARTET/*Gary Burton (vibraharp), Jerry Hahn (replaced Larry Coryell) (guitar), Bob Moses (replaced Roy Haynes) (drums), Steve Swallow (bass).*
Gary Burton's long hair, hippie specs and rock look alone have won the rock people to his side, though his is at all times a jazz band. The rock people go to his concerts because they like his music and the way rock and pop have touched it without spoiling it. The more sophisticated are excited by his experiments. In one album Burton played all the instruments himself, taping them separately. In another he threw his jazz boys in with a bunch of fine Nashville country musicians and the result was *TENNESSEE FIREBIRD,* an interesting dialogue between country and jazz. Few jazz men have moved into the rock audience's sympathies, partly because they don't want to, partly because the rock people don't want them to. For those who would like to see rock and jazz flirting a little together, if not exactly marrying, Gary Burton seems to be the person to effect the match.
Albums/THE TIME MACHINE (September 1966): *Sunset Bell; Six-Nix, Quix, Flix; Interim I; Chega De Saudade; Childhood; Deluge; My Funny Valentine; Interim II; Norwegian Wood (The Bird Has Flown); Falling Grace.* TENNESSEE FIREBIRD (March 1967): *Gone; Tennessee Firebird; Just Like A Woman; Black Is The Color; Faded Love; I Can't Help It; I Want You; Alone And Forsaken; Walter L.; Born To Lose; Beauty Contest.* DUSTER (August 1967): *Ballet; Sweet Rain; Portsmouth Figurations; General Mojo's Well Laid Plan; One, Two, 1-2-3-4; Sing Me Softly Of The Blues; Liturgy; Response.* LOFTY FAKE ANAGRAM (February 1968): *June 15, 1967; Feelings And Things; I'm Your Pal; Fleurette Africaine; Lines; The Beach; Mother Of The Dead Man; Good Citizen Swallow; General Mojo Cuts Up.*
Singles/*Tennessee Firebird/Black Is The Color Of My True Love's Hair* (February 1967); *General Mojo's Well Laid*

Plan/Liturgy (October 1967); *Fleurette Africaine/General Mojo Cuts Up* (January 1968).

PAUL BUTTERFIELD BLUES BAND/*Paul Butterfield (harmonica, vocals), Buzzy Feiten (guitar), Steve Madaio (trumpet), Roderick Hicks (bass, vocals), Phil Wilson (drums), Gene Dinwiddie (tenor sax), Dave Sanborne (alto sax), Keith Johnson (trumpet, electric piano).*
Previous members: Mike Bloomfield (guitar), Sam Lay (drums), Jerome Arnold (bass), Billy Davenport (drums), Elvin Bishop (guitar), Mark Naftalin (keyboard), Bugsy Maugh (bass).
Paul Butterfield had the first of the white blues bands in 1965, when white blues was still regarded as an eccentricity and music people were into folk and, very tentatively indeed that year, folk rock and the beginnings of a switch to electricity. A white boy from Chicago, he brought electric black blues into homes that, until then, had heard nothing much louder than Joan Baez's top C and nothing more frenzied than Bob Dylan's harmonica. Butterfield, a harmonica player himself, took all the pieces he'd heard in the Chicago bars, pieces he'd played there because they used to let him *(Shake Your Money-Maker* and *I Got My Mojo Working)*, pieces that in the 1968 blues boom began to sound overworked and ridiculous, but were certainly fresh to white ears then—Butterfield took them and put them on record. And on that first album, *PAUL BUTTERFIELD BLUES BAND*, the earnest young white public first heard the sound of Mike Bloomfield's blues guitar. Some of the tunes on the second album, *EAST-WEST*, if you listened to them out of the corners of your ears, sounded like rock, some like jazz. The track *East-West* had more of the Eastern feeling the Yardbirds, the Byrds and Sandy Bull were offering up—in 1966, an innovation which anticipated the raga-rock of 1967.

In the third album Butterfield introduced horns, and was one of the first to do so. By 1968, when his fourth album came out and he had moved into progressive blues, the scene had changed completely. Bloomfield had left, become a personality in his own right, started his own band and talked up a storm about the blues. Cream, a blues-based rock band, had come over from England and completely won over the mass

American public which, until then, had not been receptive to blues. Its guitarist, Eric Clapton, graduate of early English blues bands like the Yardbirds and John Mayall's Bluesbreakers, had, along with Bloomfield and Jimi Hendrix, made the blues guitarist the single most magical figure on the rock scene (which was very nice for originals like Albert King and B.B. King who found themselves back in the spotlight they'd always deserved). Suddenly everyone saw that Paul Butterfield had been doing everything right all along, that it wasn't so eccentric really for a white boy to sing the blues. Surely they knew where he'd gotten it all from; they've learned now of the music of Little Walter, Muddy Waters and Howlin' Wolf, but it just made Butterfield more valuable for having brought their sound up front where everyone could hear it, not just the habitués of those smokey places in Chicago.

Albums/PAUL BUTTERFIELD BLUES BAND (October 1965): *Born In Chicago; Shake Your Money-Maker; Blues With a Feeling; Thank You Mr. Poobah; I Got My Mojo Working; Mellow Down Easy; Screamin'; Our Love Is Drifting; Mystery Train; Last Night; Look Over Yonder Wall.* EAST-WEST (August 1966): *Walkin' Blues; Get Out Of My Life; Woman; I Got A Mind To Give Up Living; All These Blues; Work Song; Mary, Mary; Two Trains Running; Never Say No; East-West.* RESURRECTION OF PIGBOY CRABSHAW (November 1967): *One More Heartache; Driftin' And Driftin'; Run Out Of Time; Pity The Fool; Born Under A Bad Sign; Double Trouble; Drivin' Wheel; Droppin' Out; Tollin' Bells.* IN MY OWN DREAM (July 1968): *Last Hope's Gone; Mine To Love; Just To Be With You; Get Yourself Together; Morning Blues; Drunk Again; In My Own Dream.*

Single/*I Got A Mind To Give Up Living/Come On In* (November 1966).

KENNETH BUTTREY/ Rock fans first heard him on Dylan's *BLONDE ON BLONDE* playing his drums with the lightest touch in the industry. He works out of Nashville, appears on many country albums, and although he is not a rock drummer, he has produced what must be some of the most tasteful drum work in modern pop. He's easy to recognize on Dylan's *JOHN WESLEY HARDING* and *NASHVILLE SKYLINE*—because he's so hard to copy.

BYRDS/*Roger McGuinn (guitar, lead vocals), Jay York (bass), Clarence White (guitar), Gene Parsons (drums).*
Previous Members: Gene Clark, David Crosby, Mike Clarke, Gram Parsons, Chris Hillman.
Until the Byrds, the very notion of a group of folk singers strengthening their sound with rock devices was unthinkable. Folk was highminded, pure and untouched by sordid commercial values. Rock was something you played for a quick buck. The most important thing the Byrds ever did was to recognize that rock could revitalize folk—with a finished product that was considerably more than the sum of its parts. Folk rock was officially born with the Byrds' early 1965 version of Dylan's *Mr. Tambourine Man,* the classic model for ten thousand imitations that year as folk rock swept the West and then the East.

The Byrds were the first of the *thinking* musicians. And they were articulate (at least Crosby and McGuinn were) at a time when the best that the Beatles could do was whip off a string of funny but not necessarily deep one-liners. The Byrds were the best innovators around. Folk and rock! It changed the face of American music and put them on the charts in a way no one in the business believed possible. At an early 1966 concert in New York, they were as mobbed and screamed over as the Beatles.

After the Byrds, it no longer became amazing to find someone like poet Allen Ginsberg backstage at a rock concert, or when they opened at the Village Gate a little later, Norman Mailer and Timothy Leary among the ringsiders. For the Byrds were not only musical but political and mystical. Later, acid rock would become commonplace. But the Byrds were the first acid rockers, the first head rockers, the first message rockers and, of course, the first outer space rockers. It's no wonder then that by the time everyone else caught up with it all, they lapsed happily back into the country sound that had been in their music all along, in with everything else they offered. Right from the start, the quality that had marked the Byrds as quite, quite different from the Beatles' imitators was a twangy uniquely American country harmony. No one since has ever been able to capture that sound any more than they could capture the distinctive jangle of McGuinn's electric twelve-string Rickenbacker.

Everyone knew they had to be the greatest group alive—everyone from the Beatles on down—but destiny was to plague them with a series of personnel changes that would weaken the group almost beyond repair. For a while they were a fixture at Ciros on Hollywood's Sunset Strip and the nucleus of all the good things that would be coming out of Los Angeles. They were five until Gene Clark, now of Dillard and Clark, left. Early in 1966 the remaining four came to New York with a sound that was newer than folk—raga rock (they cringed at the name) or rock with sitar, a David Crosby innovation that touched off a whole sitar craze. Their sitar song *Eight Miles High* was banned on some radio stations on the grounds that it glorified drugs. It was, however, like so many of their songs of that period, a song about jet airplanes, which they used to watch from airport observation towers. At the Village Gate they used a light show, the first in New York. The audience complained that it was distracting. By March 1967, the American music scene was jumping and in some ways the Byrds were being left behind. Their songs looked back in some anger, *"So You Want to be a Rock and Roll Star?"* asked one a little bitterly.

During the 1967–68 period when the first wave of success had receded, the group began having internal problems. Drummer Mike Clarke left, and so did David Crosby. Hillman and McGuinn kept going, though, and did an album *THE NOTORIOUS BYRD BROTHERS* with a little help from some friends. By the time they made *SWEETHEART OF THE RODEO* they had a strong new member, Gram Parsons, who brought out the country mood that had been there all along. However, neither it nor the next LP, *DR. BYRDS AND MR. HYDE,* had anything like their initial chart successes although they were albums everyone listened to and took note of. On *DR. BYRDS AND MR. HYDE* the only original Byrd left was McGuinn (Hillman and Parsons were in the Flying Burrito Brothers and Crosby had started his own group with the Hollies' Graham Nash and the Buffalo Springfield's Steve Stills.) Nevertheless, that strange mixture of country music and outer space that had always marked the Byrds remained. And the irony is that in sticking with what had always, more or less, been there, they still managed to produce an album that seemed fresh and timely.

Albums/MR. TAMBOURINE MAN (August 1965): *Mr. Tambourine Man; You Won't Have To Cry; I'll Feel A Whole Lot Better; Here Without You; Spanish Harlem Incident; Bells Of Rhymney; All I Really Want To Do; I Knew I'd Want You; It's No Use; Don't Doubt Yourself, Babe; Chimes Of Freedom; We'll Meet Again.* TURN TURN TURN (February 1966): *Turn, Turn, Turn; It Won't Be Wrong; Set You Free This Time; Lay Down Your Weary Tune; He Was A Friend Of Mine; World Turns All Around Her; Satisfied Mind; If You're Gone; Times They Are A-Changin'; Wait & See; Oh, Susannah.* FIFTH DIMENSION (September 1966): *5D (Fifth Dimension); Wild Mountain Thyme; Mr. Spaceman; I See You; What's Happening; I Come And Stand At Every Door; Eight Miles High; Hey Joe; Captain Soul; John Riley; 2–4–2 Fox Trot.* YOUNGER THAN YESTERDAY (April 1967): *So You Want To Be A Rock 'N' Roll Star; My Back Pages; Have You Seen Her Face; Why; C.T.A.–102; Renaissance Fair; Time Between; Mind Gardens; Girl With No Name; Thoughts & Worlds; Everybody's Been Burned.* BYRDS' GREATEST HITS (October 1967): *Mr. Tambourine Man; I'll Feel A Whole Lot Better; Bells Of Rhymney; Turn, Turn, Turn; All I Really Want To Do; Mr. Spaceman; So You Want To Be A Rock 'N' Roll Star; Eight Miles High; Chimes Of Freedom; My Back Pages; 5D (Fifth Dimension).* NOTORIOUS BYRD BROTHERS (March 1968): *Goin' Back; Artificial Energy; Natural Harmony; Draft Morning; Wasn't Born To Follow; Get To You; Change Is Now; Old John Robertson; Tribal Gathering; Dolphins' Smile; Space Odyssey.* SWEETHEART OF THE RODEO (November 1968): *You Ain't Going Nowhere; I Am A Pilgrim; Christian Life; You Don't Miss The Water; You're Still On My Mind; Pretty Boy Floyd; Hickory Wind; One Hundred Years From Now; Blue Canadian Rockies; Life In Prison; Nothing Was Delivered.* DR. BYRDS & MR. HYDE (February 1969): *This Wheel's On Fire; Old Blue; Your Gentle Way Of Loving Me; Child Of*

*The Universe; Nashville West; Drugstore Truckdrivin' Man;
King Apathy III; Candy; Bad Night At The Whiskey; My
Back Pages–B. J. Blues–Baby, What Do You Want Me To
Do.*

Singles/ *All I Really Want To Do/Mr. Tambourine Man;
Eight Miles High/Turn, Turn, Turn; My Back Pages/So You
Want To Be A Rock 'N' Roll Star; Goin' Back/Change Is
Now; Artificial Energy/You Ain't Going Nowhere; Pretty
Boy Floyd/I Am A Pilgrim.*

JOHN CAGE/ An American composer now in his fifties, who
has influenced many of the more advanced rock musicians.
The trouble is when you hear Cage you realize that rock isn't
all that bold and daring. One of his compositions is for twelve
radio sets and twenty-four players and a conductor. The score
gives the ratio of music to silence; the rest is up to chance.

CANADIAN SCENE/ A lot of good musicians, a lot of
talent, but very little money spent on promotion, and a strong
emphasis on good imitations of current U.S. hits. However,
some groups in Canada have actually developed their own
style in spite of the disadvantages. The Kensington Market is
one, though it is now working and recording in the States. The
Mandala is another, though it has had some shattering changes of personnel. Canada caught up on the Stones and Beatles
thing about the middle of 1965, and from then through 1966
each city had its Beatles, its Stones, its Manfred Manns. Very
big were the Haunted in Montreal, doing a strong Stones act
when everybody else was still imitating the Beatles. Also big
were Luke and the Apostles. Luke is now the lead singer with
Kensington Market, but he did beautiful Paul Jones imitations
then (Jones was Manfred Mann's lead singer before he went
solo). Another successful Canadian rock group was the Stac-
catos, who used to do a Gerry and the Pacemakers routine,
then switched to Four Seasons harmonies. And a group called
Influence might have done well in America if it had not split
early in 1968 because of internal problems. J.B. and the
Playboys, who later became the Carnival Connection, have
had some success in the States, as have a number of other
groups.

Zal Yanovsky of the Lovin' Spoonful was from Toronto,

but he did most of his musical developing in Greenwich Village. So did another Canadian, Denny Doherty of the Mamas and the Papas. Joni Mitchell is from Canada, as is Leonard Cohen, but they come from the folk scene that bred Gordon Lightfoot and Ian and Sylvia. Most of the Buffalo Springfield came from Canada, though the group got together in California (Canadian talent seems to develop best *outside* Canada). The Band, the Dylan group which did *MUSIC FROM BIG PINK*, is also mainly Canadian. And it was noted by observers of the scene that Canadian country rock was what was sounding freshest and newest in 1968.

THE CANDYMEN/*John Rainey Adkins (guitar), Rodney Justo (lead vocals), Dean Daughtry (organ, piano), Billy Gilmore (bass), Bob Nix (drums).*
The Candymen are a southern white group who specialize in extraordinary live reproduction of complex Beatle and Beach Boy material. Their ability to duplicate *in person* the recordings of such tributes to modern engineering as *Good Vibrations* by the Beach Boys and *Day In The Life* by the Beatles gave them quite a following when they first appeared in New York in the summer of 1967. (Before that they had spent several years touring around the world as Roy Orbison's backup group.) In spite of their good honest country-rock sound, well larded with Alabama soul, they have yet to come up with a substantial hit. Unfortunately, the group's *original* material was not quite up to those uncanny duplications of other people's electronic wizardries.

Albums/THE CANDYMEN (September 1967): *Roses Won't Grow In My Garden; Lonely Eyes; Strong Blues Man; Deep In The Night; See Saw; Georgia Pines; Hope; Movies In My Mind; Even The Grass Has Died; Happier Than Them; Stormy Monday Blues.* THE CANDYMEN BRING YOU CANDYPOWER (February 1968): *Ways; Great Society; Sentimental Lady; Crowded Room; Candy Man; Blues At Midnight; Memphis Blues Again; I've Lost My Mind; I'll Never Forget; Good Bye Mama; Bottled Up.*

Singles/*Georgia Pines/Movies In My Mind* (October 1967); *Deep In The Night/Stone Blues Man* (December 1967); *Ways/Sentimental Lady* (February 1968); *Candy Man/*

Crowded Room (May 1968); *Go And Tell The People/It's Gonna Get Good In A Minute* (October 1968).

CANNED HEAT/*Adolfo De La Parra (drums), Bob "The Bear" Hite (lead vocals), Larry Taylor (bass guitar), Henry Vestine (lead guitar), Alan Wilson (guitar).*
A Los Angeles based blues band that has a reputation for adapting old country blues and making them sound fresher and better than just about anyone else except "originals" like Muddy Waters and Howlin' Wolf. It also had the distinction of being the only young white blues band in the United States that did not have the word "blues" in its name. A useful omission since, until very recently, the word was the kiss of death to anyone hoping to sell a record on the straight rock market; blues was an archive word, something quaint, historic and not salable. That was the climate in late 1965 when the band started. It lasted a mere eight months. When it re-formed at the beginning of 1967, things had changed. Perhaps it was because by then Eric Clapton of Cream and Mike Bloomfield, then of the Butterfield Blues Band, were doing so much talking about blues. Whatever the reason, there was (and still is) a sudden interest in the roots of the new rock, and in the people like Butterfield and like the English blues-based groups who were digging them up. Canned Heat, superb archivists and collectors, were a walking, living and breathing college course in blues roots. Everyone enrolled. And as the roots revival gathers momentum, so does Canned Heat. Their first hit, *On the Road Again,* was one of the big singles of 1968.

Albums/CANNED HEAT (August 1967): *Rollin' And Tumblin'; Bullfrog Blues; Evil Is Going On; Goin' Down Slow; Catfish Blues; Dust My Broom; Help Me; Big Road Blues; The Story Of My Life; The Road Song; Rich Woman.* BOOGIE WITH CANNED HEAT (January 1968): *Evil Woman; My Crime; On The Road Again; World In A Jug; Turpentine Moan; Whiskey Headed Woman No. 2; Amphetamine Annie; An Owl Song; Marie Laveau; Fried Hockey Boogie.* LIVIN' THE BLUES (October 1968): *Pony Blues; My Mistake; Sandy's Blues; One Kind Favor; Going Up The Country; Walking By Myself; Boogie Music; Parthenogenesis; Refried Boogie (2 Parts).*

Singles/*Rollin' And Tumblin'/Bullfrog Blues* (June 1967); *Evil Woman/World In A Jug* (October 1967); *On The Road Again/Boogie Music* (April 1968); *One Kind Favor/Going Up The Country* (December 1968).

CAPTAIN BEEFHEART AND HIS MAGIC BAND/*Don Van Vliet, Alex Snoffer, Doug Moon, Gerald Handley, John French.*
A West Coast blues-based group with very savage vocals, good songs and all kinds of musical subtleties within a sound that doesn't seem especially new at first hearing (or even second—it's sometimes *that* subtle). When Frank Zappa was trying to get a band together in the days before the Mothers of Invention were invented, several of his early musicians left to form Captain Beefheart and his Magic Band, and the two groups do have some musical and lyrical approaches in common.

Albums/SAFE AS MILK (June 1968): *Sure 'Nuff 'N Yes I Do; Dropout Boogie; Zig Zag Wanderer; Yellow Brick Road; Autumn's Child; There's A Woman; Plastic Factory; Call On Me; Aba Zaba; Electricity; Grow So Ugly.* STRICTLY PERSONAL (December 1968).

JOHNNY CASH/One of the few country singers who has managed to transcend the narrowness of that classification, Johnny Cash came on the scene a little after Elvis first appeared on the country music circuit (and just before Elvis became a rock and roll star). By late 1955 he was recording for the same label Elvis started with, Sun records. Jerry Lee Lewis and Carl Perkins, also on that label, went on to Elvis-like rock 'n' roll fame (but when that ended, finished up back in the lucrative country field). Cash never climbed the big rock bandwagon in quite that way, but with songs like *I Walk The Line, Folsom Prison Blues* and *Ballad Of A Teenage Queen,* established himself as a big seller and has continued to make the charts with his own songs, regardless of whatever fad was current. Interestingly enough, by 1968 music started moving into exactly the area Cash had been in right from the start: the records that made the most impact— Bob Dylan's *JOHN WESLEY HARDING,* the Band's *MUSIC FROM BIG PINK,* the Byrds' *SWEETHEART OF THE*

RODEO—all had turned away from hard rock, psychedelics and electronic trickery to the purity and simplicity of the country rock Cash had been singing all along. He has never been anything but a big star and a big seller, and was always revered as much by folk and pop people as by country people, but the 1968 swing back to country might very well give him superstar instead of merely star stature. The fact that he has teamed up with Bob Dylan in an album hasn't hurt.

Albums/JOHNNY CASH WITH HIS RED & BLUE GUITAR: *Rock Island Line; I Heard That Lonesome Whistle; Country Boy; If The Good Lord's Willing; Cry Cry Cry; Remember Me; I Was There When It Happened; So Doggone Lonesome; I Walk The Line; Wreck Of Old '97; Folsom Prison Blues; Doin' My Time.* JOHNNY CASH SINGS THE SONGS THAT MADE HIM FAMOUS: *Ballad Of A Teenage Queen; There You Go; I Walk The Line; Don't Make Me Go; Train Of Love; Guess Things Happen That Way; Ways Of A Woman In Love; Next In Line; You're The Nearest Thing To Heaven; I Can't Help It; Home Of The Blues; Big River.* JOHNNY CASH SINGS HANK WILLIAMS: *I Can't Help It; You Win Again; I Could Never Be Ashamed Of You; Hey, Good Lookin'; I Walk The Line; I Love You Because;* Other Titles. GREATEST: *I Forgot To Remember To Forget; Katy Too; You Win Again; Hey, Good Lookin'; Goodbye Little Darlin'; You Tell Me; I Just Thought You'd Like To Know; Just About Time; I Could Never Be Ashamed Of You; Luther's Boogie; Get Rhythm.* JOHNNY CASH: *Sugartime; Down The Street To 301; Life Goes On; Port Of Lonely Hearts; Cry Cry Cry; My Treasurer; Oh Lonesome Me; Home Of The Blues; So Doggone Lonesome; You're The Nearest Thing To Heaven; Story Of A Broken Heart; Hey Porter.* ALL ABOARD THE BLUE TRAIN WITH JOHNNY CASH: *There You Go; So Doggone Lonesome; Wreck Of Old '97; Give My Love To Rose; Folsom Prison Blues; Blue Train; Hey Porter; Come In Stranger; Goodby Little Darling; Rock Island Line; Train Of Love; I Heard That Lonesome Whistle.* ORIGINAL SUN SOUND OF JOHNNY CASH: *Belshazah; Born To Lose; New Mexico; Big River; I Forgot To Remember To Forget; Two Timing Woman; Story Of A Broken Heart; Always Alone; Country Boy; Thanks A*

Lot; Goodnight Irene; Wide Open Road. HYMNS BY JOHN-
NY CASH (May 1959): *It Was Jesus; I Saw A Man; God
Will; Are All The Children In; Old Account; Swing Low,
Sweet Chariot; Lead Me Gently Home; Lead Me Father;
Snow In His Hair; These Things Shall Pass; I Call Him; He'll
Be A Friend.* SONGS OF OUR SOIL (July 1959): *Drink To
Me; Five Feet High And Rising; Man On The Hill; Hank And
Joe And Me; Clementine; Don't Step On Mother's Roses;
Great Speckled Bird; I Want To Go Home; Caretaker; Old
Apache Squaw; My Grandfather's Clock; It Could Happen
To You.* FABULOUS JOHNNY CASH (September 1959):
*Run Softly; Blue River; That's All Over; I Still Miss Someone;
Suppertime; That's Enough; Frankie's Man, Johnny; Trou-
badour; Don't Take Your Guns To Town; I'd Rather Die
Young; One More Ride; Pickin' Time; Shepherd Of My
Heart.* RIDE THIS TRAIN (September 1960): *Loading
Coal; Slow Rider; Lumberjack; Boss Jack; Dorraine Of Pon-
chartrain; Going To Memphis; When Papa Played The Do-
bro; Old Doc Brown.* THERE WAS A SONG! (December
1960): *Seasons Of My Heart; I Couldn't Keep From Crying;
I Feel Better All Over; My Shoes Keep Walking Back To
You; Time Changes Everything; I'd Just Be Fool Enough;
Why Do You Punish Me; Transfusion Blues; I Will Miss You
When You Go; I'm So Lonesome I Could Cry; Just One
More; Honky Tonk Girl.* HYMNS FROM THE HEART
(June 1962): *He'll Understand And Say Well Done; God
Must Have My Fortune Laid Away; I Got Shoes; When I've
Learned; Let The Lower Lights Be Burning; If We Never
Meet Again; When I Take My Vacation In Heaven; Taller
Than Trees; I Won't Have To Cross Jordan Alone; When He
Reached Down His Hand For Me; My God Is Real; These
Hands.* SOUND OF JOHNNY CASH (August 1962): *Lost
On The Desert; Accidentally On Purpose; In The Jailhouse
Now; Mr. Lonesome; You Won't Have Far To Go; In Them
Old Cottonfields Back Home; Delia's Gone; Sing It Pretty,
Sue; I Forgot More Than You'll Ever Know; You Remem-
bered Me; I'm Free From The Chain Gang Now; Let Me
Down Easy.* BLOOD, SWEAT AND TEARS (February
1963): *Legend Of John Henry's Hammer; Tell Him I'm
Gone; Another Man Done Gone; Busted; Nine Pound Ham-
mer; Casey Jones, Chain Gang; Waiting For A Train; Rough-*

neck. RING OF FIRE (August 1963): *Ring Of Fire; I'd Still Be There; What Do I Care; I Still Miss Someone; Forty Shades Of Green; Were You There; Rebel-Johnny Yuma; Bonanza; Big Battle; Remember The Alamo; Tennessee Flat-Top Box; Peace In The Valley.* CHRISTMAS SPIRIT (October 1963): *Christmas Spirit; I Heard The Bells On Christmas Day; Blue Christmas; Gifts They Gave; Here Was A Man; Christmas As I Knew It; Silent Night; Little Drummer Boy; Who Kept The Sheep; Ringing The Bells For Jim; We Are The Shepherds; Ballad Of The Harp Weaver.* I WALK THE LINE (July 1964): *I Walk The Line; Bad News; Folsom Prison Blues; Give My Love To Rose; Hey Porter; I Still Miss Someone; Understand Your Man; Wreck Of Old '97; Still In Town; Goodbye, Little Darlin' Goodbye; Big River; Troublesome Waters.* BITTER TEARS (December 1964): *As Long As The Grass Shall Grow; Ballad Of Ira Hayes; Apache Tears; Custer; White Girl; Vanishing Race; Talking Leaves; Drums.* ORANGE BLOSSOM SPECIAL (April 1965): *Orange Blossom Special; Long Black Veil; It Ain't Me Babe; Wall; Don't Think Twice, It's Alright; You Wild Colorado; When It's Springtime In Alaska; Mama, You've Been On My Mind; All Of God's Children Ain't Free; Danny Boy; Wildwood Flower; Amen.* TRUE WEST (September 1965): *Hiawatha's Vision; Road To Kaintuck; I Ride An Old Paint; Letter From Home; Shifting Whispering Sands; Ballad Of Boot Hill; Mr. Garfield; Hardin Wouldn't Run; Streets Of Laredo; Johnny Reb; Bury Me Not On The Lone Prairie; Mean As Hell; Sam Hall; 25 Minutes To Go; Sweet Betsy From Pike; Blizzard; Green Grow The Lilacs; Stampede; Reflections.* MEAN AS HELL (March 1966): *Shifting, Whispering Sands; I Ride An Old Paint; Road To Kaintuck; 25 Minutes To Go; Letter From Home; Mean As Hell; Blizzard; Mr. Garfield; Streets Of Laredo; Bury Me Not On The Lone Prairie; Sweet Betsy From Pike; Stampede.* EVERYBODY LOVES A NUT (June 1966): *Everybody Loves A Nut; One On The Right Is On The Left; Cup Of Coffee; Bug That Tried To Crawl Around The World; Singing Star's Queen; Austin Prison; Dirty Old Egg-Sucking Dog; Take Me Home; Please Don't Play Red River Valley; Boa Constrictor; Joe Bean.* THAT'S WHAT YOU GET FOR LOVIN' ME (November 1966): *Happiness Is You; Guess Things Happen*

That Way; Ancient History; You Comb Her Hair; She Came From The Mountains; For Lovin' Me; No One Will Ever Know; Is This My Destiny; Wound Time Can't Erase; Happy To Be With You; Wabash Cannon Ball. CARRYIN' ON (September 1967): *Long-Legged Guitar Pickin' Man; Shantytown; It Ain't Me, Babe; Fast Boat To Sydney; Pack Up Your Sorrows; I Got A Woman; Jackson; Oh, What A Good Thing We Had; You'll Be All Right; No, No, No; What'd I Say.* JOHNNY CASH'S GREATEST HITS (September 1967): *Jackson, I Walk The Line; Understand Your Man; Orange Blossom Special; One On The Right Is On The Left; Ring Of Fire; It Ain't Me, Babe; Ballad Of Ira Hayes; The Rebel; Five Feet High And Rising; Don't Take Your Guns To Town.* FROM SEA TO SHINING SEA (March 1968): *From Sea To Shining Sea; Whirl And The Suck; Call Daddy From The Mine; Walls Of A Prison; Frozen Four-Hundred-Pound Fair-To-Middlin'; Masterpiece; You And Tennessee; Another Song To Sing; Flint Arrowhead; Cisco Clifton's Fillin' Station; Shrimpin' Sailin'.* JOHNNY CASH AT FOLSOM PRISON (July 1968): *Give My Love To Rose; Jackson; Folsom Prison Blues; Dark As A Dungeon; I Still Miss Someone; Cocaine Blues; Long Black Veil; 25 Minutes To Go; Orange Blossom Special; Send A Picture Of Mother; I Got Stripes; The Wall; Dirty Old Egg-Sucking Dog; Flushed From The Bathroom Of Your Heart; Green, Green, Grass Of Home; Greystone Chapel.*

Singles/*So Doggone Lonesome/Folsom Prison Blues; Ballad Of A Teenage Queen/Big River; Belshazah/Wide Open Road; Blue Train/Born To Lose; Come In, Stranger/Guess Things Happen That Way; Don't Make Me Go/Next In Line; Down The Street To 301/Story Of A Broken Heart; Get Rhythm/I Walk The Line; Give My Love To Rose/Home Of The Blues; Goodbye Little Darlin'/You Tell Me; I Forgot To Remember To Forget/Katy Too; I Just Thought You'd Like To Know/It's Just About Time; I Love You Because/Straight A's In Love; Life Goes On/Oh Lonesome Me; Luther Played The Boogie/Thanks A Lot; Mean Eyed Cat/Port Of Lonely Hearts; My Treasure/Sugartime; There You Go/Train Of Love; Ways Of A Woman/You're The Nearest Thing To Heaven; Don't Take Your Guns To Town/Five Feet High &*

Rising (June 1962); *Bad News/Ballad Of Ira Hayes* (June 1964); *Sons Of Katie Elder/A Cert'in Kinda Hurtin'* (June 1965); *It Ain't Me Babe/Ring Of Fire* (September 1965); *Understand Your Man/It Ain't Me Babe* (March 1966); *Everybody Loves A Nut/Austin Prison* (May 1966); *I Walk The Line/Orange Blossom Special* (September 1966); *Boa Constrictor/One On The Right Is On The Left* (January 1967); *Long Legged Guitar Pickin' Man/You'll Be All Right* (May 1967); *Red Velvet/Wind Changes* (September 1967); *You Beat All I Ever Saw/Put The Sugar To Bed* (November 1967); *Jackson/Pack Up Your Sorrows* (December 1967); *Folk Singer/Folsom Prison Blues* (April 1968); *Ballad Of Ira Hayes/Rosanna's Going Wild* (June 1968).

CAT MOTHER AND THE ALL NIGHT NEWSBOYS/
Charley Chin (guitar, banjo, bass), Roy "Bones" Michaels (banjo, guitar, bass), Bob Smith (piano, drums), Michael Equine (drums, guitar, bass, piano, cello, arachnophone, clarumpetone), Larry Israel Packer (violin, guitar, mandolin, harmonica).
An American five-man group signed up in 1969 under the management of Jimi Hendrix with whom they subsequently went on tour. The New York-based group was originally folk and jug band in its sound (as were many of the groups hanging out in the Village in early '67) but gradually it moved into a rock format, which was where it was when "discovered" in Woodstock. The group has met with a universally enthusiastic reception.

CHAD & JEREMY/*Chad Stuart (vocals, guitar, banjo, harpsichord, organ, tack piano, ukelin, sitar), Jeremy Clyde (vocals, guitar).*
How could two polite well-bred long-haired lean-faced English gentlemen with nice California tans possibly go wrong with the fans in that early 1964 post-Beatle period when just to be English was practically all you needed for a number one record? Their second album was still English but mixed with Dylan and folk rock; and how could you go wrong with *that* in the fall of 1965 when *Mr. Tambourine Man* was the most important song around? By 1966 they were well established in what a year later they would contemptuously dismiss

as Muzak. Their sound in that Muzak period was Beatle-Everly Brothers harmony with Byrds-Beach Boys overtones, exactly what California teenyboppers wanted from their two tame Englishmen. Then, in 1967, came the realization that there had to be more to life than this, or at least this was the way they told it. The Beatles had just done *SERGEANT PEPPER,* so Chad and Jeremy put out *their* serious album: *OF CABBAGES AND KINGS* with most of the songs by Jeremy and arrangement and scoring by Chad and an entire side devoted to an elaborate *Progress Suite* in five movements. It wasn't exactly *SERGEANT PEPPER,* but it did establish once and for all that there was more to those two than Muzak. The duo no longer tour, each having found his own distinctive project (acting for Jeremy, composing musicals for Chad), but they still get together for occasional recording dates.

Albums/BEFORE AND AFTER (May 1964): *Before And After; Why Should I Care; For Lovin' Me; I'm In Love Again; Little Does She Know; Tell Me Baby; What Do You Want To Know.* I DON'T WANNA LOSE YOU BABY (September 1965): *I Don't Wanna Lose You Baby; Should I; Mr. Tambourine Man; Girl Who Sang The Blues; Funny How Love Can Be; The Woman In You; I Have Dreamed; Don't Think Twice, It's All Right; Baby Don't Go; There But For Fortune; These Things You Don't Forget.* BEST OF CHAD AND JEREMY (March 1966): *Summer Song; What Do You Want With Me; Too Soon; Only Those In Love; Like I Love You Today; If I Loved You; Willow Weep For Me; My How The Time Goes By; Yesterday's Gone; If You've Got A Heart; From A Window.* MORE CHAD AND JEREMY (June 1966): *September In The Rain; Girl From Ipanema; It Was A Very Good Year; Lemon Tree; No Tears For Johnny; Truth Often Hurts The Heart; Dirty Old Town; My Coloring Book; Four Strong Winds; Now And Forever; Donna, Donna.* DISTANT SHORES (August 1966): *Distant Shores; Ain't It Nice; Homeward Bound; Way You Look Tonight; Morning; You Are She; Everyone's Gone To The Moon; I Won't Cry; Early Mornin' Rain; Don't Make Me Do It.* OF CABBAGES AND KINGS (September 1967): *Rest In Peace; Gentle Cold Of Dawn; Busman's Holiday; Can I See*

*You; Family Way; I'll Get Around To It When And If I Can;
Progress Suite (Five Movements).* THE ARK (September
1968): *The Emancipation of Mister X; Sunstroke; The Ark;
The Raven; Imagination; Painted Dayglow Smile; Pipe
Dream; Transatlantic Trauma; Sidwalk Requiem, Los Ange-
les, June Fifth And Sixth; Pantheistic Study For Guitar And
Large Bird; Paxton Quigley's Had The Course; You Need
Feet.*

Singles/*Summer Song/Willow Weep For Me* (July 1966);
Yesterday's Gone/If I Loved You (July 1966); *You Are
She/I Won't Cry* (September 1966); *Family Way/Rest In
Peace* (October 1967); *Editorial/Painted Dayglow Smile*
(1968).

CHAMBERS BROTHERS/*George Chambers (bass), Willie
Chambers (guitar, vocals), Joe Chambers (guitar, vocals),
Brian Keenan (drums), Lester Chambers (tambourine, harmonica, cowbell, vocals).*
An explosive soul-rock group that has been playing the New
York discotheque circuit for a long time, adding a brother or
two along the way. It is currently made up of four black
musicians and one white drummer, and its sound is African
exuberance at every opportunity rather than merely good old
American Mississippi funk. Unlike most soul groups, the
Chambers Brothers play all their own instruments to back
themselves up in their soul-rock-gospel-Afro vocal free-for-
alls. Mississippi born, they went professional in 1961 and up
to 1965 were a gospel group. (They got their drummer when
they found they were too busy playing their instruments to
have time for hand claps.) Their big number, *Time Has Come
Today,* described by one critic as Afro-psychedelic-rock,
features screaming electric guitars and an African cowbell. It
runs from fifteen to thirty minutes in live performance, eleven
on the album. The version that got them on the national
charts is nowhere near the frantic original. And even their
interpretations of other people's material, including such overworked standards as *The Midnight Hour,* are wildly exciting.

Albums/CHAMBERS BROTHERS — NOW: *Hi Heel Sneakers; Baby Please Don't Go; What'd I Say; Long Tall Sally;
Bony Maronie; It's Groovin' Time; You Don't Have To Go;*

See See Rider; So Fine. PEOPLE GET READY: *People Get Ready; Call Me; Hooka Tooka; Yes, Yes, Yes; Tore Up; Reconsider Baby; You've Got Me Running; Money; You Can Run; Summertime; Your Old Lady; It's All Over Now.* TIME HAS COME (October 1967): *All Strung Out Over You; People Get Ready; I Can't Stand It; Romeo And Juliet; In The Midnight Hour; So Tired; Uptown; Please Don't Leave Me; What The World Needs Now Is Love; Time Has Come Today.* CHAMBERS BROTHERS SHOUT (September 1968): *Johnny B. Goode; Blues Get Off My Shoulder; I Got It; Shout; There She Goes; Seventeen; Pretty Girls; Rain The Day You Left; So Fine; Love Me Like The Rain.* NEW TIME—A NEW DAY (October 1968): *I Can't Turn You Loose; Guess Who; Do Your Thing; Where Have All The Flowers Gone; Love Is All I Have; You Got The Power—To Turn Me On; I Wish It Would Rain; Rock Me Mama; No, No, No, Don't Say Good-by; Satisfy You; A New Time—A New Day.*

Singles/*Call Me/Seventeen; Pretty Girls Everywhere/Love Me Like The Rain; All Strung Out Over You/Falling In Love* (December 1966); *I Can't Stand It/Summer Days And Summer Nights* (March 1967); *Please Don't Leave Me/I Can't Stand It* (April 1967); *Uptown/Love Me Like The Rain* (September 1967); *Time Has Come Today/People Get Ready* (1967); *New Time—A New Day* (October 1968).

Also Appear On/NEWPORT FOLK FESTIVAL '65 (1965): *Bottle Music; I Got It.* BARBARA DANE WITH THE CHAMBERS BROTHERS (May 1966): *It Isn't Nice; You Got To Reap; I Am A Weary And A Lonesome Traveler; We'll Never Turn Back.* WEST COAST LOVE-IN: *Don't Lose Your Cool; Girls, We Love You; There She Goes.*

THE CHARLATANS/In 1965 there were five of them and they were playing what was the San Francisco sound then (before the San Francisco sound went acid): a goodtimey, folksy, countryish sound. Three months in the Red Dog Saloon in Virginia City, Nevada, did it for them—and for Virginia City. They gave Virginia City and, though they did not know it then, the world, the first hippie rock dances ever. The saloon was very cowboy and very gold rush and so were they. When they got back to San Francisco, in the fall of 1965, the Family Dog was giving its historic first dances, the Fillmore was giving its historic Mime Benefits, the Warlocks were just emerging into what would later be the Grateful Dead, and the Jefferson Airplane was making its first appearances. The Charlatans were very big then, the first of the San Francisco groups to be big, and they were obviously bound for glory. They signed a contract, one of the very first San Francisco groups to do so, but for a variety of reasons it didn't work out. It was 1969 before an album came out. By then it was agreed that at least some of the magic was gone.

Album/THE CHARLATANS: *High Coin; Easy When I'm Dead; Ain't Got The Time; Folsom Prison Blues; The Blues Ain't Nothin'; Time To Get Straight; When I Go Sailin' By; Doubtful Waltz; Warbash Cannonball; Alabama Bound; When The Movies Are.*

RAY CHARLES (Ray Charles Robinson)/Ray Charles started his career singing like Nat King Cole. It was about as honest as if Janis Joplin were suddenly to sing like Joan Baez, and he soon made the change to his own hoarse, suffering voice, with all its gospel passion. Because he started in rhythm and blues and was in jazz before he moved into pop, his audience is enormous and his influence on a buying public considerably wider than any other black (or white) singer. In many ways and for many reasons, he has changed not only the face of pop music but also the habits of the people who buy its records. His historic country and western album *MODERN SOUNDS IN COUNTRY AND WESTERN MUSIC* sold a million copies to everyone from Nashville guitar pickers to boogaloo artists in the ghettos. His *own* sound first went on record in 1954 (he had recorded earlier on small labels in those other voices) with the great Jerry Wexler at Atlantic in charge. In those days Charles would have had more to teach Wexler than vice versa, and a lot of what Wexler learned then has been applied to the benefit of the artists he has recorded since. It is doubtful that producer Wexler could have brought out the "real" Aretha as effectively as he did without the man-hours he put in working with Charles. What Charles did, that was then very new (and in many circles unheard-of and shocking), was combine gospel music with the blues. Sacred and profane love, sung with all the intensity he could summon up on both levels. He called it soul.

Ray Charles later started moving into popular music, but there was no such thing as his taking on inferior material. He ennobled every song he sang. They're still talking about what he did to *You Are My Sunshine*. For rock fans, the best example is the Beatles' *Yesterday,* which he changed from a wistful and nostalgic ditty to a song of monumental despair and regret. He is the supreme interpreter (as well as a fine writer, fine pianist, fine saxophonist, fine musician). The greatest tribute to his musicianship is *I Believe To My Soul,* in which he dubs in four falsetto girls parts in close harmony. He is imitated by both black and white singers continually.

Albums/RAY CHARLES: *I Got A Woman; Come Back Baby; Don't You Know; Ain't That Love; Greenbacks; Drown In My Own Tears; Hallelujah I Love Her So; Sinner's Prayer; Funny (But I Still Love You); Losing Hand; Fool For You; Mary Ann; Mess Around; This Little Girl Of Mine.* YES INDEED (October 1958): *What Would I Do Without You; Yes Indeed; I Had A Dream; It's All Right; I Want To Know; Get On The Right Track Baby; Talkin' 'Bout You; Swanee River Rock; Lonely Avenue; I Want A Little Girl; Blackjack; Sun's Gonna Shine Again; Heartbreaker; Leave My Woman Alone.* RAY CHARLES AT NEWPORT (October 1958): *Right Time; In A Little Spanish Town; I Got A Woman; Blues Waltz; Hot Rod; Talkin' 'Bout You; Sherry; Fool For You.* WHAT'D I SAY (September 1959): *What'd I Say; Jumpin' In The Mornin'; You Be My Baby; Tell Me How Do You Feel; What Kind Of Man Are You; Rockhouse; Roll With My Baby; Tell All The World About You; My Bonnie; That's Enough.* GENIUS OF RAY CHARLES (October 1959)· *Let The Good Times Roll; Don't Let The Sun Catch You Cryin'; Alexander's Ragtime Band; Come Rain Or Come Shine; It Had To Be You; Two Years Of Torture; When Your Lover Has Gone; 'Deed I Do; Just For A Thrill; Tell Me You'll Wait For Me; Am I Blue; You Won't Let Go.* RAY CHARLES, IN PERSON (May 1960): *Right Time; What'd I Say; Yes Indeed;*

Tell The Truth; Spirit-Feel; Frenesi; Drown In My Own Tears. DO THE TWIST WITH RAY CHARLES: What'd I Say; I Got A Woman; Tell The Truth; Leave My Woman Alone; Tell Me How Do You Feel; Heartbreaker; Talkin' 'Bout You; You Be My Baby; I'm Movin' On. GREAT HITS OF RAY CHARLES: Tell Me How Do You Feel; I Had A Dream; Yes Indeed; Carrying That Load; Tell All The World About You; I Believe To My Soul; Tell The Truth; What'd I Say; I'm Movin' On; You Be My Baby; Right Time; My Bonnie; Early In The Mornin'. GREAT RAY CHARLES: Sweet Sixteen Bars; Doodlin'; There's No You; The Ray; My Melancholy Baby; Undecided; I Surrender Dear; Black Coffee; Ain't Misbehavin'. SOUL BROTHERS (With Milt Jackson): Blue Funk; Cosmic Ray; Soul Brothers; How Long Blues; Deed I Do. SOUL MEETING (With Milt Jackson): Hallelujah I Love Her So; Blue Genius; Soul Meeting; X-Ray Blues; Love On My Mind; Bags Of Blues. DEDI-CATED TO YOU (January 1961): Hard Hearted Hannah; Nancy; Margie; Ruby; Rosetta; Stella By Starlight; Cherry; Josephine; Candy; Marie; Diane; Sweet Georgia Brown. GENIUS PLUS SOUL EQUALS JAZZ (January 1961): From The Heart; I've Got News For You; Mister C; Moanin'; One Mint Julep; I'm Gonna Move To The Outskirts Of Town; Birth Of The Blues. GENIUS AFTER HOURS (June 1961): Genius After Hours; Ain't Misbehavin'; Ray; Dawn; Joy Ride; Hornful Soul; Man I Love; Charlesville; Music, Music, Music. RAY CHARLES SINGS THE BLUES (August 1961): Hard Times; Nobody Cares; Ray's Blues; Mr. Charles Blues; I Wonder Who; Feelin' Sad; Early In The Mornin'; I'm Movin' On; Right Time; I Believe To My Soul; Some Day Baby· Midnight Hour. RAY CHARLES AND BETTY CARTER (June 1961): Ev'ry Time We Say Good-bye; You And I; We'll Be Together Again; People Will Say We're In Love; Cocktails For Two; Side By Side; Baby, It's Cold Outside; Together; For All We Know; Takes Two To Tango; Alone Together; Just You, Just Me. MODERN SOUNDS IN COUNTRY AND WESTERN MUSIC (January 1962): Hey Good Looking; Just A Little Lovin'; Makes No Difference Now; Careless Love; Bye Bye Love; Move It On Over; Who Cares; Half As Much; I Can't Stop Loving You; You Don't Know Me; Born To Lose; I Love You So

Much It Hurts. GREATEST HITS (July 1962): *Them That
Got; Georgia On My Mind; Unchain My Heart; I'm Gonna
Move To The Outskirts Of Town; The Danger Zone; I've Got
News For You; Hit The Road Jack; Ruby; I Wonder; Sticks
And Stones; But On The Other Hand Baby; One Mint Julep.*
MODERN SOUNDS IN COUNTRY AND WESTERN MU-
SIC, VOL. II (October 1962): *You Are My Sunshine; No
Letter Today; Someday (You'll Want Me To Want You);
Don't Tell Me Your Troubles; Midnight; Oh, Lonesome Me;
Take These Chains From My Heart; Your Cheating Heart;
I'll Never Stand In Your Way; Making Believe; Teardrops In
My Heart; Hang Your Head In Shame.* RAY CHARLES
STORY, VOL. I (July 1962): *Sun's Gonna Shine Again;
Losing Hand; Mess Around; It Should've Been Me; Fool For
You; Don't You Know; Come Back Baby; I've Got A Wom-
an; This Little Girl Of Mine; Mary Ann; Hallelujah I Love
Her So; Lonely Avenue; Doodlin'; Sweet Sixteen Bars; Ain't
That Love.* RAY CHARLES STORY, VOL. II (July
1962): *Rockhouse; Swanee River Rock; Talkin' 'Bout You;
What Kind Of Man Are You; Yes Indeed; My Bonnie; Tell
All The World About You; Right Time; What'd I Say; Drown
In My Own Tears; Just For A Thrill; Come Rain Or Come
Shine; Let The Good Times Roll; I'm Movin' On.* INGREDI-
ENTS IN A RECIPE FOR SOUL (June 1963): *Busted;
Where Can I Go; Born To Be Blue; That Lucky Old Sun; Ol'
Man River; In The Evening (When The Sun Goes Down); A
Stranger In Town; Ol' Man Time; Over The Rainbow; You'll
Never Walk Alone.* RAY CHARLES STORY, VOL. III
(June 1963): *Sinner's Prayer; Funny (But I Love You);
Feelin' Sad; Hard Times (No One Knows Better Than I);
What Would I Do Without You; I Want To Know; Leave My
Woman Alone; It's All Right; Get On The Right Track Baby;
That's Enough; I Want A Little Girl; You Be My Baby; I
Had A Dream; Tell The Truth.* SWEET AND SOUR TEARS
(January 1963): *I Cried For You; I Cried A River; Willow
Weep For Me; Baby, Don't You Cry; Teardrops From My
Eyes; Don't Cry Baby; You Got Me Crying Again; No One
To Cry To; A Tear Fell; Cry; Guess I'll Have To Hang My
Tears Out To Dry; After My Laughter Came Tears.* RAY
CHARLES STORY, VOL. IV (June 1964): *Blackjack;
Alexander's Ragtime Band; Bit Of Soul; I Believe To My*

Soul; Greenbacks; In A Little Spanish Town; Undecided; When Your Lover Has Gone; It Had To Be You; Early In The Mornin'; Heartbreaker; Music, Music, Music; Tell Me How Do You Feel; You Won't Let Me Go. HAVE A SMILE WITH ME (July 1964): *Smack Dab In The Middle; Feudin' And Fightin'; Two Ton Tessie; I Never See Maggie Alone; Move It On Over; Ma (She's Making Eyes At Me); The Thing; The Man With The Weird Beard; The Naughty Lady Of Shady Lane; Who Cares (For Me).* RAY CHARLES 'LIVE' IN CONCERT (January 1965): *Swing A Little Taste; I Got A Woman; Margie; You Don't Know Me; Hide 'Nor Hair; Baby, Don't You Cry; Makin' Whoopee; Hallelujah I Love Her So; Don't Set Me Free; What'd I Say; Finale.* TOGETHER AGAIN (COUNTRY AND WESTERN MEETS RHYTHM AND BLUES) (August 1965): *Together Again; I Like To Hear It Sometime; I've Got A Tiger By The Tail; Please Forgive And Forget; I Don't Care; Next Door To The Blues; Blue Moon Of Kentucky; Light Out Of Darkness; Maybe It's Nothing At All; All Night Long; Don't Let Her Know; Watch It Baby.* CRYING TIME (January 1966): *Crying Time; No Use Crying; Let's Go Get Stoned; Going Down Slow; Peace Of Mind; Tears; Drifting Blues; We Don't See Eye To Eye; You're In For A Big Surprise; You're Just About To Lose Your Clown; Don't You Think I Ought To Know; You've Got A Problem.* RAY'S MOODS (July 1966): *Whatcha Doing In There; Please Say You're Fooling; By The Light Of The Silvery Moon; You Don't Understand; Maybe It's Because Of Love; Chitlins With Candied Yams; Granny Wasn't Grinning That Day; She's Lonesome Again; Sentimental Journey; A Born Loser; It's A Man's World; A Girl I Used To Know.* A MAN AND HIS SOUL (January 1967): *I Can't Stop Loving You; What'd I Say; Ol' Man River; One Mint Julep; Crying Time; Makin' Whoopee; Busted; Takes Two To Tango; Ruby; Let's Go Get Stoned; Cry; Unchain My Heart; Georgia On My Mind; Baby It's Cold Outside; Worried Mind; I Chose To Sing The Blues; I Don't Need No Doctor; Born To Lose; Hit The Road, Jack; You Are My Sunshine; From The Heart; Teardrops From My Eyes; No Use Crying; Chitlins With Candied Yams.* LISTEN (May 1967): *She's Funny That Way; How Deep Is The Ocean; You Made Me Love You; Yesterday; I'll Be*

Seeing You; Here We Go Again; All For You; Love Walked In; Gee Baby, Ain't I Good To You; People. A PORTRAIT OF RAY (March 1968): *Eleanor Rigby; Am I Blue; Never Say Naw; Sun Died; Yesterday; When I Stop Dreaming; I Won't Leave; Sweet Young Thing Like You; Bright Lights And You Girl; Understanding.*

Singles/*Midnight Hour/Roll With My Baby* (December 1952); *Funny But I Still Love You/Mess Around* (July 1953); *It Should've Been Me/Sinner's Prayer* (July 1954); *Don't You Know/Losing Hand* (September 1954); *A Fool For You/This Little Girl Of Mine* (August 1955); *Black-jack/Greenbacks* (November 1955); *Mary Ann/Drown In My Own Tears* (February 1956); *I Want To Know/Ain't That Love* (January 1957); *Get On The Right Track Baby/It's All Right* (April 1957); *Hallelujah I Love Her So/What Would I Do Without You* (May 1956); *Lonely Avenue/Leave My Woman Alone* (April 1957); *I Want A Little Girl/Swanee River Rock* (September 1957); *Rock-house* (2 Parts) (October 1958); *Tell Me The Truth/Sweet Sixteen Bars* (June 1959); *What'd I Say* (2 Parts) (June 1959); *Don't Let The Sun Catch You Crying/Let The Good Times Roll* (September 1959); *My Baby (I Love Her, Yes I Do)/Who You Gonna Love* (January 1960); *Heartbreaker/Just For A Thrill* (March 1960); *Sticks And Stones/Worried Life Blues* (May 1960); *I Had A Dream/Yes Indeed* (June 1960); *You Be My Baby/My Bonnie* (July 1960); *Georgia On My Mind/Carry Me Back To Old Virginny* (August 1960); *Them That Got/I Wonder* (October 1960); *Ruby/Hard Hearted Hannah* (November 1960); *Bit Of Soul/Early In The Mornin'* (February 1961); *Am I Blue/It Should've Been Me* (June 1961); *Hard Times/I Wonder Who* (August 1961); *Hit The Road Jack/The Danger Zone* (August 1961); *Unchain My Heart/But On The Other Hand Baby* (1961); *I Believe To My Soul/I'm Moving On; The Right Time/Tell All The World About You; Tell Me How Do You Feel/That's Enough; Doodlin'* (2 Parts) (1961); *Let's Go/One Mint Julep; I'm Gonna Move To The Outskirts Of Town/I've Got The News For You; Baby It's Cold Out-side/We'll Be Together Again* (January 1962); *At The Club/Hide 'Nor Hair* (March 1962); *I Can't Stop Loving You/*

Born To Lose (April 1962); *You Don't Know Me/Careless Love* (July 1962); *You Are My Sunshine/Your Cheating Heart* (1962); *Carrying That Load/Feelin' Sad* (November 1962); *Brightest Smile In Town/Don't Set Me Free* (February 1963); *Take These Chains From My Heart/No Letter Today* (March 1963); *No One/Without Love (There Is Nothing)* (May 1963); *Busted/Making Believe* (August 1963); *That Lucky Old Sun/Ol' Man Time* (November 1963); *Baby Don't You Cry/My Heart Cries For You* (1964); *My Baby Don't Dig Me/Something's Wrong* (May 1964); *A Tear Fell/No One To Cry To* (June 1964); *In A Little Spanish Town/Talkin' 'Bout You* (June 1964); *Smack Dab In The Middle/I Wake Up Crying* (September 1964); *Makin' Whoopee* (2 Parts) (November 1964); *Cry Teardrops From My Eyes* (January 1965); *I Got A Woman* (2 Parts) (March 1965); *Without A Song* (2 Parts) (April 1965); *I'm A Fool To Care/Love's Gonna Live Here* (June 1965); *The Cincinnati Kid/That's All I Am To You* (September 1965); *Crying Time/When My Dreamboat Comes Home* (October 1965); *Together Again/You're Just About To Lose Your Clown* (March 1966); *Let's Go Get Stoned/The Train* (May 1966); *I Chose To Sing The Blues/Hopelessly* (August 1966); *Please Say You're Fooling/I Don't Need No Doctor* (October 1966); *Something Inside Me/I Want To Talk About You* (February 1967); *Here We Go Again/Somebody Ought To Write A Book About It* (April 1967); *In The Heat Of The Night/Something's Got To Change* (August 1967); *Never Had Enough Of Nothing Yet/Yesterday* (October 1967); *Come Rain Or Come Shine/Tell Me You'll Wait For Me* (December 1967); *Go On Home/That's A Lie* (January 1968); *Eleanor Rigby/Understanding* (May 1968); *Sweet Young Thing Like You/Listen, They're Playing My Song* (1968).

Also Appears On/BLUES IN MODERN JAZZ: *Sweet Sixteen Bars*. CINCINNATI KID: *Cincinnati Kid*. DEFINITIVE JAZZ SCENE, VOL. II: *Without A Song*. GREATEST ROCK AND ROLL: *Mary Ann; Hallelujah I Love Her So*. HISTORY OF RHYTHM AND BLUES, VOL. II: *I've Got A Woman; Greenbacks*. HISTORY OF RHYTHM AND BLUES, VOL. IV: *What'd I Say*. HIS-

TORY OF RHYTHM AND BLUES, VOL. V: *Early In The Mornin'*. IN THE HEAT OF THE NIGHT: *In The Heat Of The Night*. THIS IS SOUL: *What'd I Say*.

CHARLES RIVER VALLEY BOYS/The Charles River Valley Boys were one of the best bands left over from the big bluegrass revival. Their album was *BEATLE COUNTRY,* Beatle songs done bluegrass style so nicely you wondered if they were ever meant to be played any other way. The album perfectly underscored just how country-influenced the Beatles were.

Album/BEATLE COUNTRY: *I've Just Seen A Face; Baby's In Black; And Your Bird Can Sing; I Feel Fine; Yellow Submarine; Ticket To Ride; I Saw Her Standing There; What Goes On; She's A Woman; Norwegian Wood; Help; Paperback Writer*.

CHUBBY CHECKER (Ernest Evans)/He was a Philadelphia boy and a good dancer and singer who, by 1960, had launched himself into a modest career. It was Mrs. Dick Clark who took one look at him and, thinking he looked like a young Fats Domino, named him Chubby Checker. When he first recorded a Hank Ballard number called *The Twist* in 1960, he had no idea that it would set off not just a national but an international craze, that it would put him in the Copacabana, make him a household word, and earn him close to a million dollars in one year. Kids were already doing the twist at high school dances—the white kids had learned it from the black kids—but adults in those days were about as enthusiastic about teenage dances as they were about acne. Chubby, nineteen years old, was about to change all that. At first the record took off just with the kids. They were twisting at a sleazy little bar just off New York's Times Square, a place called the Peppermint Lounge, when eventually they attracted some adult attention. After that—call it good press agentry, call it the Jet Set's perennial search for something new—the Lounge was *in*, and Chubby Checker was *in* as no single person had been since Elvis. (The only person who never did cash in was Hank Ballard, the man who wrote the song and was the first to perform it.)

Once the Jet Set took it up (and that included Elsa

Maxwell, the Duke and Duchess of Windsor and Greta Garbo
for a start), people at every other conceivable level started
twisting just to keep up. Not being able to twist became as
bad-mannered as leaving a party without thanking the hos-
tess. His record was number one, of course, and anyone who
got a twist number out fast enough made the charts till things
got glutted. Joey Dee's own *Peppermint Twist* did very well,
not to mention an ingenious *Oliver Twist* and Chubby's own
Let's Twist Again. What Chubby and the Twist did was to
move into a very stale season of a very stale year with
something so catchy it was irresistible. Once they got adults
dancing one teenage dance, they got them dancing all of them
(he had another number one hit with *Pony Time*). After that
it was a matter of finding somewhere to dance them, which
meant that the whole dead night scene revived (all you had to
do was put the word "twist" above the name of your club and
it was packed). Eventually this opened the way for the
private discotheque, and then the public. Dancing young
meant dressing young, which opened the way for Mary
Quant, youthquake fashion, the swinging England miniskirt
and, well, there's a lot Chubby Checker (and Hank Ballard if
you want to give credit where credit is due) should be
thanked for. But although Chubby is a huge success in Europe
(where they still dance the twist), a score of other fads left
him behind. Unless he's prepared to set himself on fire like
Arthur Brown or nibble at his guitar like Jimi Hendrix, he has
a lot to catch up on.
(See the TWIST)

Albums/TWIST (October 1962): *Twistin' U.S.A.; Coh- Poo-
Pah-Doo Shimmy; C. C. Rider Stroll; The Strand; The Chick-
en; Hucklebuck; The Twist; The Madison; Love Is Strange;
Calypso; Mexican Hat Twist; The Slop; The Pony.* DON'T
KNOCK THE TWIST (October 1962): *Twistin'; Bristol
Stomp; Paloma Twist; Bo Diddley; I Love To Twist; Don't
Knock The Twist; Do The New Continental; Salome Twist;
The Fly; Mashed Potatoes; Slow Twistin'; Mashed Potato
Time.* FOR TEEN TWISTERS ONLY (October 1962): *The
Fly; Peppermint Twist; Your Lips And Mine; Dear Lady
Twist; Twist Along; Shout; Lose Your Inhibitions Twist; Slow
Twistin'; Love Is Like A Twist; Runaround Sue; Twistin' The*

Blues; Twistin' Bones. IT'S PONY TIME (October 1962): *Pony Time; Watusi; Stroll; Hully Gully; Shimmy; Hi Ho Silver; Mashed Potatoes; We Like Birdland; Let's Dance, Let's Dance, Let's Dance; Charleston; Mess Around.* LET'S TWIST AGAIN (October 1962): *Let's Twist Again; I Could Have Danced All Night; Takes Two To Tango; Ballin' The Jack; Quarter To Three; Fishin'; Continental Walk; Peanut Butter; The Jet; I Almost Lost My Mind; Dance Along.* TWISTIN' ROUND THE WORLD (October 1962): *Twistin' Round The World; Alouette; O Sole Mio; Twist Marie; Paloma; Miserlou; Let's Twist Again; Twist Mit Mir; Twistin' Matilda; Tea For Two; Hava Nagila; Never On Sunday.* YOUR TWIST PARTY (October 1962): *Twist; Let's Twist Again; Hucklebuck; Rock Around The Clock; Twistin' U.S.A.; Whole Lotta Shakin' Going On; Ballin' The Jack; I Could Have Danced All Night; Blueberry Hill; Hound Dog; Mexican Hat Twist; Mr. Twister.* LIMBO PARTY (February 1963): *Man Smart, Woman Smarter; Mary Ann Limbo; Bossa Nova; Desafinado; La La Limbo; Baby, Come Back; Somebody Bad Stole The Wedding Bell; Limbo Rock; When The Saints Go Limbo In; Jamaica Farewell; Banana Boat Song; La Bamba.* CHUBBY CHECKER'S BIGGEST HITS (February 1963): *Popeye (The Hitchhiker); Slow Twistin'; Let's Twist Again; Limbo Rock; Hucklebuck; The Fly; Pony Time; Dance The Mess Around; The Twist; Dancin' Party; Good Good Lovin'.* LET'S LIMBO MORE (May 1963): *Let's Limbo Some More; Manana; Cindy Oh Cindy; Twenty Miles; How Low Can You Go; Girl With The Swingin' Derriere; Peanut Vendor; Rum And Coca Cola; Lotta Limbo; Run Chico, Run; Mama Look A Boo Boo; Mother.* BEACH PARTY (September 1963): *Birdland; Limbo Side By Side; Twist It Up; Mashed Potato Love; Surf Party; Killer; Oo-Kook-A-Boo; Surfin'; She Said; Nothin' But The Twist; She's A Hippy; Let's Surf Again.* TWIST IT UP: *Twist It Up; Kansas City; Rip It Up; Don't Let Go; Slow Twistin'; Twist; Don't You Just Know It; I'm Walkin'; Johnny B. Goode; Let's Twist Again; Maybelline; Hi-Ho Silver.* CHUBBY CHECKER: *Yes Indeed; Time After Time; It's Good Enough For Me; Absurd Bird; Everything's Gonna Be All Right;* Other Titles. CHUBBY CHECKER AND BOBBY RYDELL: *Jingle Bell Rock; Swingin' Together; Teach Me*

To Twist; Side By Side; Jingle Bells Imitations; What Are You Doing New Years Eve, My Baby Cares For Me; Voodoo; Walkin' My Baby Back Home; Medley; Other Songs By Bobby Rydell. CHUBBY CHECKER DISCOTHEQUE: 32 'Dance' Songs. CHUBBY CHECKER'S FOLK ALBUM (February 1964): *Loddy Lo; Hooka Tooka; Everybody Loves Saturday Night; Sippin' Cider Through A Straw; Go Tell My Baby; Hey, Bobba Needle; Doodang; Ole Anna; Ah Si Mon Moine; Tzena Tzena; 6-0-9; Doncha Get Tired.*

Singles/*Those Private Eyes/Dancing Dinosaur; The Twist/ Twistin' U.S.A.; Schooldays, Oh Schooldays/The Class; Hucklebuck/Whole Lotta Shakin'; Pony Time/Oh Susannah; The Mess Around/Good Good Lovin'; Let's Twist Again/Everything's Gonna Be All Right; The Fly/That's The Way It Goes; Slow Twistin'/Paloma Twist; Dancin' Part/Gotta Get Myself Together; Limbo Rock/Popeye (The Hitchhiker); Let's Limbo Some More/Twenty Miles; Birdland/Black Cloud; Twist It Up/Surf Party; Hooka Tooka/Loddy Lo; Hey, Bobba Needle/Spread Joy; Lazy Elsie Molly/Rosie; She Wants To Swing/You Better Believe It Baby; Lovely Lovely/Weekend's Here; Do The Freddie/Discotheque; Everything's Wrong/Cu Ma La Be-Stay; Hey You, Little Boo-Ga-Loo/Pussy Cat; You Got The Power/Looking At Tomorrow; Karate Monkey/Her Heart; Jingle Bell Rock/Jingle Bells Imitations; Swingin' Together/Teach Me How To Twist.*

CHER

Albums/ALL I REALLY WANT TO DO (November 1965): *All I Really Want To Do; I Go To Sleep; She Thinks I Still Care; Needles And Pins; Don't Think Twice; Dream Baby; Bells Of Rhymney; Girl Don't Come; See See Rider; Come And Stay With Me; Cry Myself To Sleep; Blowin' In The Wind.* SONNY SIDE OF CHER (June 1966): *Our Day Will Come; Bang Bang (My Baby Shot Me Down); Girl From Ipanema; Elusive Butterfly; It's Not Unusual; Like A Rolling Stone; Time; Where Do You Go; Come To My Window; Old Man River; Milord; Young Girl.* CHER (March 1967): *Alfie; Sunny, You Don't Have To Say You Love Me; Homeward Bound; Catch The Wind; Until It's Time For You To Go; I Want You; Cruel War; Twelfth Of Never, Will You Love Me Tomorrow; Pied Piper; Magic In The Air.* WITH

LOVE (January 1968): *You Better Sit Down, Kids; But I Can't Love You More; Hey Joe; Mama (When My Dollies Have Babies); Behind The Door; Sing For Your Supper; Look At Me; There But For Fortune; I Will Wait For You; Times They Are A-Changin'.* BACK STAGE (August 1968): *Go Now; Carnival; It All Adds Up Now; Take Me For A Little While; Reason To Believe; Masters Of War; Do You Believe In Magic; I Wasn't Ready; House Is Not A Home; Click Song; Impossible Dream; Song Called Children.* CHER'S GOLDEN GREATS (October 1968): *You Better Sit Down, Kids; Sunny; Come And Stay With Me; Alfie; Take Me For A Little While; All I Really Want To Do; Needles And Pins; Bang Bang; Dream Baby; Where Do You Go; Elusive Butterfly; Hey Joe.*

Singles/*All I Really Want To Do/Dream Baby; Bang Bang/ Alfie; Hey Joe/Our Day Will Come; You Better Sit Down, Kids/Elusive Butterfly; But I Can't Love You More/Click Song Number One; Song Called Children/Take Me For A Little While.*

Also Appears On/ORIGINAL GOLDEN GREATS (June 1967): *Bang Bang.* MORE ORIGINAL GOLDEN GREATS: *All I Really Want To Do.*
(see SONNY & CHER)

CHICAGO SOUND/When people talk about the Chicago sound they're not talking about the sound of Chicago-based rock bands like the Buckinghams, but rather about the sound of Chicago blues that traveled up from the Mississippi Delta as country blues and became "city" blues in Chicago, where you had to use electricity and amplification to make yourself heard. None of the basic simplicity and earthiness of the country blues was lost, and all the homesick southern Negroes who had migrated to Chicago looking for work in the postwar years drank in the blues like mother's milk. The big names were Muddy Waters, Willie Dixon, Little Walter, Howlin' Wolf, with later a new generation of younger men typified by Buddy Guy and Junior Wells. Eventually, and inevitably, the music attracted whites, especially young white musicians like Mike Bloomfield and Paul Butterfield. The Paul Butterfield Blues Band (with Mike Bloomfield in those days playing lead guitar) turned hundreds of young people of the rock gener-

ation on to blues and inspired other blues bands. Bloomfield's
Chicago blues guitar became very widely imitated and by
1968, a boom year for blues, the Chicago sound was all over
the rock scene. Before that, in 1964 and 1965, both the
Rolling Stones and the Yardbirds performed many Chicago
blues numbers, giving them back to American kids who didn't
have a clue they were hearing music that had always been
right on their own doorstep.

THE CHILDREN OF GOD/*Gerry Moore (lead vocals,
trumpet, saxophone, clarinet, rhythm guitar), Eddie Vernon
(lead vocals, harmonica, mouth harp, organ, tambourine),
Tom Everett (lead vocals, bass guitar, piano), Gil Silva (lead
vocals, lead guitar, banjo, accordion), Chris Sigwald (drums,
conga, tablas, percussion).*
The Children of God appeared on the scene late in 1968 with
a very healthy combination of soul, rhythm and blues, and
hard rock. Though they were making only live appearances
and their record album was still not finished, critics hailed
them as part of what became the new sound of 1969: rock 'n'
soul. The fact that they are a black *and* white group may or
may not have something to do with their musical effec-
tiveness; what *does* help is that the four lead singers were
formerly all single artists and that the group plays a combination of fourteen instruments.

CHRYSALIS/*Paul Album (bass), J. Spider Barbour (vocals,
rhythm cicada), Ralph Kotkov (keyboard, vocals), Nancy
Nain (vocals), John Sabin (guitar), Dahaud Shaar (percussion.)*
The lead singer's name is Spider and the group's name is
Chrysalis and their voices sometimes flit about like butterflies
and sometimes weave lacy spider webs—it all has a very
insect mood. Live, the group is much admired, with its songs
of melancholy whimsy, by such musical giants as Frank Zappa
and Al Kooper. On record, what with brass, strings and
woodwinds, they often come close to being overproduced, but
sometimes there's a harpsichord or double-speed piano doing
baroque things with some string instrument overdubbed in
exactly the right way to complement the song (one of those
genius touches that makes Jim Friedman *the* new producer to

watch). *Dr. Root's Garden* is maniac science fiction and shows how much the Mothers are starting to influence rock. *Cynthia Gerome*, a lonely Eleanor Rigby song, shows how much the Beatles are still influencing rock. The vocals are very unusual and the whole thing comes close, very close, to a theatrical performance. And now to spoil everything—they used to be around in Ithaca, New York, in 1966 (most of them anyway), and they were called something much less magical: the Rancid Years.

Album/DEFINITION (May 1968): *Baby Let Me Show You Where You Live; Fitzpatrick Swanson; Lake Hope; Piece Of Sun; Summer In Your Savage Eyes; Dr. Root's Garden; What Will Become Of The Morning; Lace Wing; Cynthia Gerome; April Grove; Father's Getting Old; 30 Poplar.*

THE CHURLS/*Brad Fowles (drums), Harry Southworth Ames III (lead guitar), Sam Hurrie (second guitar), John Barr (bass), Bob O'Neill (lead vocals).*
The Churls are a Canadian rock group who appeared on the U.S. scene in 1968.

CIRCUS MAXIMUS/*Jerry Jeff Walker (guitar, vocals), Bob Bruno (lead guitar, organ, piano, vocals, composer), David Scherstrom (drums), Gary White (bass, vocals), Peter Troutner (guitar, tambourine, vocals).*
Circus Maximus played psychedelic folk-rock-jazz-soul, and who didn't in 1967? It made an interesting appearance, though, at the end of that year, at Carnegie Hall with the New York Pro Musica (which specializes in medieval and Renaissance music) in a baroque-rock mix which neither the baroque nor rock worlds were ready for, though they both quite enjoyed it. It was also notable for having in its roster Jerry Jeff ("Mr. Bojangles") Walker. When Walker left to go solo (he had previously been a solo singer) and their second album produced little enthusiasm, the group disbanded.
(See JERRY JEFF WALKER)

Albums/CIRCUS MAXIMUS (October 1967): *Travelin' Around; Lost Sea Shanty; Oops I Can Dance; Rest Of My Life To Go; Bright Light Lovers; Chess Game; People's Games; Time Waits; Fading Lady; Short-Haired Fathers;*

Wind. NEVERLAND REVISITED (May 1968): *Hello Baby; Straight Guy Spy; Come Outside; Parallel; Trying To Live Right; Lonely Man; Mixtures; Dreamer Girl; Neverland Revisited; Hansel & Gretel.*

Singles/*Lonely Man*/*Negative Dreamer Girl* (April 1968).

CLANCY BROTHERS/*Tom Clancy, Paddy Clancy, Liam Clancy, Tommy Makem.*

The Clancy Brothers are an Irish-American group that started off in the middle-fifties folk scene and, as the folk boom grew and grew, made, along with Odetta, Judy Collins, Peter, Paul & Mary and others, the big time folk circuit—everything from New York's Carnegie Hall to London's Royal Festival Hall.

ERIC CLAPTON (see CREAM)

DAVE CLARK FIVE/*Dave Clark (drums), Lenny Davidson (guitar), Rick Huxley (guitar, banjo), Denis Payton (tenor sax, guitar, harmonica, clarinet), Mike Smith (lead vocals, piano, vibes).*

It's always important to know what groups paid their dues when they're toting up their gold cuff links later. The Dave Clark Five made a lot of money, and there are plenty of groups, some better, some worse, back in England, where they come from, who resent their success bitterly, who particularly resent their lack of musical creativity, and who like to point out that they never would have made it in England. Perhaps not. But the Dave Clark Five—who first met in a gym and originally played together to raise money for Dave's football club—managed to be in America in 1964, hot on the heels of the Beatles. They were armed with all you needed at that time: English haircuts and English accents. The whole key to the five is that Clark is not so much a musician as a business man and that the whole operation from the start, and still today, of course, has been run as a very efficient business. Everyone else has breakdowns and internal hassles and big creative triumphs. Dave Clark and his musical boys come on like young business executives and always have, and that's what they are.

The group plays uncomplicated rock that borrows freely from Motown and rhythm and blues. Mike Smith, the vocalist, who looks like one of those very handsome, very snooty, yet very deferential salesmen at Harrods in London, sings very black, which comes as a bit of a shock at first. He does *You Got What It Takes* the way Brook Benton might have, but it's all new to the fans. When the group finally did get a hit in England, it was all very nice, but they have no illusions about themselves. They don't pretend, as is now so fashionable, to be trailblazers; they just know they have something to sell that a sizable number of young Americans seem to want to buy. And when that ends, businessman Clark has all sorts of plans for film and television production.

Albums/GLAD ALL OVER (April 1964): *Glad All Over; All Of The Time; Chaquita; I Know You; Stay; Do You Love Me; No Time To Lose; Bits And Pieces; Doo Dah; Time; She's All Mine.* AMERICAN TOUR (October 1964): *Because; Who Does He Think He Is; Move On; Whenever You're Around; I Want You Still; Long Ago; Come On Over; Blue Monday; Any Time You Want Love; Sometimes; I Cried Over You; Ol' Sol.* DAVE CLARK FIVE RETURN (October 1964): *Can't You See That She's Mine; I Need You, I Love You; I Love You No More; Rumble; Funny; Zip-A-Dee-Doo-Dah; Can I Trust You; Forever And A Day; Theme Without A Name; On Broadway.* DAVE CLARK FIVE—COAST TO COAST (March 1965): *Any Way You Want It; Give Me Love; I Can't Stand It; I'm Left Without You; Everybody Knows (I Still Love You); Crying Over You; Say You Want Me; When; Don't You Know; It's Not True; To Me.* HAVING A WILD WEEKEND (June 1965): *Having A Wild Weekend; New Kind Of Love; Dum-Dee-Dee-Dum; I Said I Was Sorry; No Stopping; Don't Be Taken In; When I'm Alone; Catch Us If You Can; If You Come Back; On The Move; Sweet Memories; Don't You Realise.* I LIKE IT LIKE THAT (January 1966): *I Like It Like That; Pumping; I Need Love; I Am On My Own; Maybe It's You; That's How Long Our Love Will Last; Little Bit Of Love; I'll Be Yours My Love; Please Love Me; You Know You're Lying; Goodbye My Friends; She's A Loving Girl.* DAVE CLARK FIVE'S GREATEST HITS (April 1966): *Over And Over; Glad All Over; Catch Us If You Can; Bits And Pieces; I Like It Like That; Can't You See That She's Mine; Every-*

body Knows (I Still Love You); Because; Any Way You Want It; Do You Love Me. TRY TOO HARD *(August 1966): Try Too Hard; Today; I Never Will; Looking In; Ever Since You've Been Away; Somebody Find A New Love; I Really Love You; It Don't Feel Good; Scared Of Falling In Love; I Know.* SATISFIED WITH YOU *(October 1966): Satisfied With You; Do You Still Love Me; Go On; I Meant You; Look Before You Leap; Please Tell Me Why; You Never Listen; I Still Need You; Good Lovin'; It'll Only Hurt For A Little While.* MORE GREATEST HITS *(December 1966): Try Too Hard; Come Home; I'm Thinking; All Night Long; Look Before You Leap; Please Tell Me Why; Don't Let Me Down; Reelin' And Rockin'; At The Scene; Satisfied With You.* 5 BY 5 *(April 1967): Nineteen Days; Something I've Always Wanted; Little Bit Strong; Bernedette; Sitting Here Baby; You Don't Want My Loving; How Can I Tell You; Picture Of You; Small Talk; Pick Up Your Phone.* YOU GOT WHAT IT TAKES *(August 1967): You've Got What It Takes; I've Got To Have A Reason; You Don't Play Me Around; Thinkin' Of You Baby; Lovin' So Good; Doctor Rhythm; Play With Me; Let Me Be; Blueberry Hill; Tabatha Twitchit.* EVERYBODY KNOWS *(March 1968): Everybody Knows; Little Bit Now; At The Place; Inside And Out; Red And Blue; You Must Have Been A Beautiful Baby; Good Love Is Hard To Find; Lost In His Dreams; Hold On Tight; I'll Do The Best I Can; Concentration Baby.* WEEKEND IN LONDON *(May 1968): Come Home; We'll Be Running; I'm Thinking; Blue Suede Shoes; Hurting Inside; I'll Never Know; 'Til The Right One Comes Along; Your Turn To Cry; Little Bitty Pretty One; Remember, It's Me; Mighty Good Loving.*

Singles/*Because*/*Do You Love Me* (July 1964); *Glad All Over*/*Bits And Pieces* (September 1964); *Everybody Knows*/ *I Like It Like That* (September 1964); *Catch Us If You Can*/*On The Move* (August 1965); *Can't You See That She's Mine*/*Any Way You Want It* (October 1965); *Over And Over*/*I'll Be Yours* (October 1965); *At The Scene*/*I Miss You* (January 1966); *Try Too Hard*/*All Night Long* (March 1966); *Satisfied With You*/*Don't Let Me Down* (July 1966); *You've Got What It Takes*/*Doctor Rhythm* (March 1967); *You Must Have Been A Beautiful Baby*/*Man In The Pin*

Stripe Suit (May 1967); *A Little Bit Now/You Don't Play Around* (July 1967); *Red And Blue/Concentration* (October 1967); *Forget/Please Stay* (April 1968).

PETULA CLARK/The road to the top is a long and hard one for girl singers, and by the time they make it, unfortunately, they're not girls any more. Petula Clark, who wasn't a girl any more either by the time *Playboy* voted her top vocalist of 1967, was lucky because she looked like one. She's thirty-five and a mother, but she looks twenty-two when the lights are good. She was a showbiz celebrity in England in 1943 at the age of nine, made twenty-five films and recorded her first single when she was sixteen in 1950. She married a Frenchman, became a big singing star in France and the rest of Europe (the twist boom made her the leader of the rock and roll and disco set there), but with twenty million sales she didn't hit the U.S. until 1964 with *Downtown*. Hit after hit followed. In 1967 with *This Is My Song* she was signed to do a major film musical, *Finian's Rainbow* (her first film since childhood), with another former English pop star, Tommy Steele. And in 1968, with another big hit, *The Other Man's Grass,* she prepared to make a musical version of *Goodbye Mr. Chips* with Peter O'Toole. The Hollywood magnates say she's going to be another Julie Andrews. Which goes to show that there *is* a place for 35-year-old former teen idols when they outgrow their fans.

Albums/PETULA CLARK (March 1965): *Never On Sunday; You Can't Keep Me From Loving You; What Now My Love; Why Don't They Understand; Have I The Right; Nel Blu Dipinto Di Blu; Morgen; I Want To Hold Your Hand; Love Me With All Your Heart; Girl From Ipanema; I (Who Have Nothing); Hello, Dolly.* DOWNTOWN: *True Love Never Runs Smooth; Baby It's Me; Now That You've Gone; Tell Me; In Love; Let Me Tell You Baby; Crying Through A Sleepless Night; Music; Be Good To Me; This Is Goodbye; You Belong To Me; Downtown.* I COULDN'T LIVE WITHOUT YOUR LOVE: *Strangers In The Night; Monday, Monday; I Couldn't Live Without Your Love; Groovy Kind Of Love; Homeward Bound; Two Rivers Rain; Come Rain or Come Shine; Elusive Butterfly; There Goes My Love, There Goes My Life; Bang Bang; Wasn't It You.* I KNOW A

PLACE (July 1965): *I Know A Place; Dancing In The Street; In Crowd; Strangers & Lovers; Everything In The Garden; Heart; You're The One; Foggy Day; Gotta Tell The World; Every Little Bit Hurts; Call Me; Goin' Out Of My Head.* MY LOVE (May 1966): *My Love; Hold On To What You've Got; We Can Work It Out; Time For Love; Just Say Goodbye; Life & Soul Of The Party; Sign Of The Times; Thirty-first Of June; Where Did We Go Wrong; I Can't Remember Ever Loving You; Dance With Me; If I Were A Bell.* THIS IS PETULA CLARK (June 1966): *Day In Day Out; Darn That Dream; Too Darn Hot; That's How It Feels.* COLOR MY WORLD/WHO AM I (February 1967): *Color My World; Who Am I; England Swings; Cherish; Please Don't Go; What Would I Be; While The Children Play; Winchester Cathedral; Las Vegas; Reach Out, I'll Be There· Special People; Here, There & Everywhere.* THESE ARE MY SONGS (1967): *This Is My Song; Groovin'; Lover Man; San Francisco (Wear Some Flowers In Your Hair); Eternally; Resist; Don't Sleep In The Subway; Imagine; Love Is Here; How Insensitive; I Will Wait For You; On The Path Of Glory.* OTHER MAN'S GRASS IS ALWAYS GREENER (February 1968): *Smile; Cat In The Window; Black Coffee; Ile De France; Other Man's Grass Is Always Greener; For Love; Last Waltz; Answer Me My Love; Today, Tomorrow; I Could Have Danced All Night; At The Crossroads.* PETULA (August 1968): *Don't Give Up; Have Another Dream On Me; Your Love Is Everywhere; One In A Million; Beautiful In The Rain; This Girl's In Love With You; Kiss Me Goodbye; Sun Shines Out Of Your Shoes; We're Falling In Love Again; Days; Why Can't I Cry; Good Life.* FINIAN'S RAINBOW (1968). PETULA CLARK'S GREATEST HITS (November 1968): *Never On Sunday; You Can't Keep Me From Loving You; What Now My Love; Why Don't They Understand; Have I The Right; Nel Blu Dipinto Di Blu; Morgen; I Want To Hold Your Hand; Love Me With All Your Heart; Girl From Ipanema; I (Who Have Nothing); Hello, Dolly.*

Singles/*Cat In The Window/Fancy Dancin' Man; Color My World/Round Every Corner; Don't Give Up/Every Time I See A Rainbow; Don't Sleep In The Subway/Who Am I;*

Downtown/I Know A Place; I Couldn't Live Without Your Love/Sign Of The Times; Kiss Me Goodbye/Other Man's Grass Is Always Greener; My Love/This Is My Song; Look To The Sky/American Boys (November 1968).

CLEAR LIGHT/*Cliff De Young (vocals), Douglas Lubahn (bass), Michael Ney (drums), Bob Seal (guitar), Ralph Schuckett (keyboard), Dallas Taylor (drums).*
A young Los Angeles rock group that got together in 1966 and impressed Paul Rothchild, producer of the Doors, enough for him to sign them up and give them their name. There was Cliff De Young, a singer who came on like Jim Morrison (but was really very nice offstage), and not one but two drummers as well as the usual bass, guitar and organ players. The group's finest hour came when drunken customers in a Park Avenue club where they were playing heckled them so brutally that Ralph Schuckett, the usually gentle organist, hurled a few choice words back at them. They then walked off in a body, retired to the Albert Hotel to brood, and woke up next morning to find that they were underground heroes. Their album was extremely well received in England—they sounded very Californian and exotic there in all that London fog—but it was less successful in the U.S., and early in 1968 the group folded.
Album/CLEAR LIGHT (September 1967): *Black Roses; Sand; Child's Smile; Street Singer; Ballad Of Freddie And Larry; With All In Mind; Mr. Blue; Think Again; They Who Have Nothing; How Many Days Have Passed; Night Sounds Loud.*
Single/*Black Roses/She's Ready To Be Free.*

EDDIE COCHRAN/The Who loved Eddie Cochran and sang his *Summertime Blues* and so, in the summer of 1968, did Blue Cheer, who got a summer hit with it. Cochran was a classic rocker of the fifties, a James Dean figure, all leather and sexual arrogance, a sort of extension of what Elvis might have been if he hadn't gone soft and rich and Establishment. Eddie was killed in a car accident on April 17, 1960, while touring Britain with Gene Vincent. He was twenty-one.
Albums/SUMMERTIME BLUES (August 1958): *Summer-*

time Blues; Proud Of You; One Kiss; Tell Me Why; 6 Other Titles. EDDIE COCHRAN (February 1960): *C'mon Everybody; Three Steps To Heaven; Cut Across Shorty; Have I Told You Lately That I Love You; Hallelujah, I Love Her So; Sittin' In The Balcony; Summertime Blues; Lovin' Time; Somethin' Else; Tell Me Why; Teenage Heaven; Drive In Show.* NEVER TO BE FORGOTTEN (December 1963): *Weekend; Long Tall Sally; Lonely; Nervous Breakdown; Cherished Memories; Love Again; Twenty Flight Rock; Boll Weevil; Milk Cow Blues; Little Angel; Sweetie Pie; Blue Suede Shoes.*

Singles/*Jeannie, Jeannie, Jeannie/Pocketful Of Hearts* (January 1958); *Teresa/Pretty Girl* (May 1958); *Love Again/Summertime Blues* (June 1958); *Don't Ever Let Me Go/C'mon Everybody* (October 1958); *Teenage Heaven/I Remember* (January 1959); *Somethin' Else/Boll Weevil* (July 1959); *Hallelujah I Love Her So/Little Angel* (October 1959); *Cut Across Shorty/Three Steps To Heaven* (March 1960); *Lonely/Sweetie Pie* (August 1960); *Weekend/Lonely* (October 1961).

JOE COCKER/A white English singer with a strong soul voice like something out of Motown, whose version of the Beatles' *With A Little Help From My Friends,* complete with female gospel chorus, caused a sensation when it was released in the U.S. in 1968. Since then he and his Grease Band have toured the United States where they have been most enthusiastically received.

Singles/*Marjorine/New Age Of The Lily; With A Little Help From My Friends/Something's Coming On* (October 1968).

TOM COGBILL/He is the bass player and mainstay of the rhythm section of Atlantic's studio in Muscle Shoals, Alabama. He's the real star on many Aretha Franklin and Wilson Pickett records.

LEONARD COHEN/It has been fashionable to say, for some time now, that the young men writing and singing rock today are the same young men who in some past time might have been novelists and poets. Leonard Cohen, who is writing and singing for rock audiences today, *is* a novelist and poet. His reputation as a poet extends back more than ten years, especially in Canada where he comes from, but in America and England too. His reputation as a novelist extends back almost that far and both his novels, *The Favorite Game* and *Beautiful Losers,* have been more than well received, especially the last, which came out in 1966. So, it might be asked, what on earth would induce a man with that behind him to go into the business, at the age of thirty-three, not only of writing songs (both words and music) but also of performing them? Add to that question the additional caution that the man has no great voice to speak of. Cohen, who is dark and brooding and made to be a poet and a novelist, will tell you quickly that he started as a musician—a guitarist and singer of folk songs with his own square-dance group—and that that never died. Then came the heady example of Dylan, whose words splashed out of every jukebox. Poets have such small audiences, but songwriters. . . .

Judy Collins was the first to record a Cohen song, *Suzanne,* on her *IN MY LIFE* album in 1966. In the summer of 1967, when she did a concert in New York's Central Park, she brought him up on the stage with her. He was diffident, handsome, very vulnerable—and his voice was thin. But when his album came out in 1968 every one of those qualities worked for him. His face stared out compellingly in a picture he'd taken himself in a picture machine. His thin and diffident voice made for a realism that seemed to bring him right into the room with the listener. The songs are exactly in the mood of his novels and poems—and his life. The lyrics are always a poet's lyrics. You'd never say the tunes were *funky,* but there is a hypnotic repetitiousness that makes the album a calm antidote for loneliness. It's very easy to see how the whole album might not have worked. The fact that it does work might very well be merely a happy accident of fortune, but it still remains one of the most remarkable first albums ever. His second album is a gentle continuation of the first.

Albums/SONGS OF LEONARD COHEN (January 1968): *Suzanne; Master Song; Winter Lady; Stranger Song; Sisters Of Mercy; So Long, Marianne; Hey, That's No Way To Say Goodbye; Stories Of The Street; Teachers; One Of Us Cannot*

Be Wrong. SONGS FROM A ROOM (April 1969): *Bird On The Wire; Story Of Isaac; A Bunch Of Lonesome Heroes; The Partisan; Seems So Long Ago, Nancy; The Old Revolution; The Butchers; You Know Who I Am; Lady Midnight; Tonight Will Be Fine.*

Single/*Suzanne/Hey, That's No Way To Say Goodbye* (January 1968).

JUDY COLLINS started in the days when what a girl needed most was a trusty guitar, a soulful expression, a formidable repertoire of songs from other times and other places, and a fine clear voice to sing them in. There were a lot of them around in the folk boom of the late fifties and early sixties— soulful ladies singing *John Riley* and *I Know Where I'm Going*—but Judy was one of the few to survive that whole sweet, sad, gentle and unrealistic period. Who could mourn one long-lost love in 1963 when a whole world looked as if it were about to go up in flames? Once the gentle maid from Denver heard what Bob Dylan, Phil Ochs and Tom Paxton sang and wrote about the troubled, changing times, she knew that for her, anyway, there would be no more *John Rileys.* This was the beginning of her Stage Two, and if it seemed then, on *JUDY COLLINS NO. 3,* that she was just about the first to sing those songs of protest, it was because she was one of the first to sing them with conviction. When others saw that protest folk worked musically and aesthetically, as well as socially, they followed, and soon so many folk and pop-folk albums had their mandatory track of angry Dylan or ironic Ochs that it was easy to forget that Judy Collins had been one of those who made it possible.

With her point made, she was now able to move into Stage Three and return to lyricism and romance. On her last two albums she introduced the new lyricism of Leonard Cohen, Joni Mitchell, Donovan, Randy Newman and even of the wildly romantic songs she is now writing herself. Within this framework she has done a lot of moving: classical musicians on stage with her for some concerts; the songs from *Marat/ Sade;* a hard rocking single that was in the juke box at Berkeley's Blue Cue for a whole summer; her own three electric musicians traveling with her; a huge international hit with *Both Sides Now;* and even, in 1969, a budding career in the theatre as Peer Gynt's Solveig.

Albums/A MAID OF CONSTANT SORROW: *Maid Of Constant Sorrow; Prickilie Bush; Wild Mountain Thyme; Tim Evans; Sailor's Life; Bold Fenian Men; Wars Of Germany; O Daddy Be Gay; I Know Where I'm Going; John Riley; Pretty Saro; Rising Of The Moon.* GOLDEN APPLES OF THE SUN: *Golden Apples Of The Sun; Bonnie Ship The Diamond; Crow On The Cradle; Fannerio; Tell Me Who I'll Marry; Christ Child Lullaby; Great Selchie Of Shule Skerry; House Carpenter; Little Brown Dog; Minstrel Boy; Twelve Gates To The City; Lark In The Morning; Shule Aroon; Sing Hallelujah.* JUDY COLLINS NO. 3 (October 1963): *Anathea; Bullgine Run; Farewell; Dove; Hey Nellie; Town Crier; Masters Of War; Hills Of Shiloh; Bells Of Rhymney; Deportees; Settle Down; Come Away Melinda; Turn, Turn, Turn.* JUDY COLLINS CONCERT (August 1964): *Winter Sky; That Was The Last Thing On My Mind; Tear Down The Walls; Bonnie Boy Is Young; Me & My Uncle; Wild Rippling Water; Lonesome Death Of Hattie Carrol; Ramblin' Boy; Red-Winged Blackbird; Coal Tattoo; Cruel Mother; Bottle Of Wine; Medgar Evers Lullaby; Hey, Nellie, Nellie.* JUDY COLLINS 5TH ALBUM (August 1965): *Pack Up Your Sorrows; Coming Of The Roads; So Early, Early In The Spring; Daddy You've Been On My Mind; Thirsty Boots; Carry It On; Early Morning Rain; Tomorrow Is A Long Time; Lord Gregory; In The Heat Of The Summer; Mr. Tambourine Man; It Isn't Nice.* IN MY LIFE (November 1966): *Just Like Tom Thumb's Blues; Hard Lovin' Loser; Pirate Jenny; Suzanne; Colombe, La; Marat/Sade; I Think It's Going To Rain Today; Sunny Goodge Street; Liverpool Lullaby; Dress Rehearsal Rag; In My Life.* WILDFLOWERS (November 1967): *Albatross; Michael From Mountains; Hey, That's No Way To Say Goodbye; Chanson Des Vieux Amants; Since You Asked; Sisters Of Mercy; Priests; Ballata Of Francesco Landini; Both Sides Now; Sky Fell.* WHO KNOWS WHERE THE TIME GOES (November 1968): *Hello Hooray; Story Of Isaac; My Father; Someday Soon; Who Knows Where The Time Goes; Poor Immigrant; First Boy I Loved; Bird On The Wire; Pretty Polly.*

Singles/*I'll Keep It With Mine/Thirsty Boots* (November 1965); *Hard Lovin' Loser/I Think It's Going To Rain Today* (January 1967); *Both Sides Now/Who Knows Where The Time Goes* (October 1968).

COLWELL-WINFIELD BLUES BAND/*"Moose" Sorrento (vocals), Chuck Purro (drums), Jack Shroer (saxophone), Bill Colwell (guitar), Mike Winfield (bass), Collin Tilton (tenor saxophone, flute).*
There were blues bands around before the blues boom of 1968 but that was the year bands like the Colwell-Winfield Blues Band got signed up and recorded. The big companies suddenly saw commercial possibilities in a band that played "tough, educated, creative blues."

Album/COLD WIND BLUES (October 1968): *Free Will Fantasy; Got A Mind; Dead End Street; Cold Wind Blues; Whole Lot Of Lovin'; Going Down Slow; Govinda.*

ARTHUR CONLEY/A small soul shouter with a big voice, Conley was discovered (by Otis Redding) in 1965 when he was eighteen and singing with the Corvettes. Otis then produced his singles and co-wrote some of his songs. Following several releases, *Sweet Soul Music* was a national hit.

Albums/SHAKE, RATTLE & ROLL: *Shake, Rattle & Roll; I've Been Loving You Too Long; Love Got Me; Hand & Glove; Ha, Ha, Ha; Change Is Gonna Come; Don't Have To See Me; Baby What You Do To Me; I'll Take The Blame; Keep On Talking.* SOUL DIRECTIONS: *You Really Know How To Hurt A Guy; Funky Street; Burning Fire; Get Yourself Another Fool; Otis Sleep On; Hear Say; This Love Of Mine; Love Comes & Goes; Put Our Love Together; People Sure Act Funny.* SWEET SOUL MUSIC: *Sweet Soul Music; Take Me (Just As I Am); Who's Foolin' Who; There's No Place For Us; I Can't Stop (No, No, No); Wholesale Love; I'm A Lonely Stranger; I'm Gonna Forget About You; Let Nothing Separate Us; Where You Lead Me.*

Singles/*Burning Fire/People Sure Act Funny; Funky Street/ Put Our Love Together; I'm Gonna Forget About You/Take Me; Let's Go Steady/Sweet Soul Music; Love Comes & Goes/Whole Lotta Woman; Shake, Rattle & Roll/You Don't*

Have To See Me; Aunt Dora's Love Soul Shack/Is That You Love (October 1968).

Also Appears On/SMASH SOUNDS: *Sweet Soul Music.* THIS IS SOUL: *Sweet Soul Music.*

SAM COOKE/He had a tremendous influence on many Negro singers, and particularly on Otis Redding; it is one of those tragic coincidences that both men died in the midst of promising careers, within three years of each other almost to the day. (Otis died on December 10, 1967, in a plane crash. Sam, on December 16, 1964, when a motel operator shot him, she claimed, in self-defense because she thought he was going to attack her. The verdict was justifiable homicide.) Certain songs were particularly associated with him: *Another Saturday Night, Little Red Rooster* (which the Rolling Stones later recorded) and the unforgettable *Shake,* which Otis Redding always did as a tribute to Cooke, as did Mick Jagger. His very first release, in 1957, *You Send Me,* went to number one and sold two and a half million copies. The hits that followed were frankly pop—soul wasn't selling then as it does now. Just before he died, he had eight successive songs in the top ten.

Albums/HITS OF THE 50'S (August 1960): *Hey There; Mona Lisa; Too Young; Wayward Wind; Great Pretender; You, You, You; Cry; Unchained Melody; Secret Love; Song From Moulin Rouge; I'm Walking Behind You; Venus.* TWISTIN' THE NIGHT AWAY (April 1962): *Sugar Dumpling; Somebody's Gonna Miss Me; Whole Lotta Woman; Movin' And Groovin'; Camptown Twist; Somebody Have Mercy; Soothe Me; That's It—I Quit—I'm Movin' Out; Twistin' The Night Away; Twistin' In The Kitchen With Dinah; Twist; Twistin' In The Old Town Tonight.* THE BEST OF SAM COOKE (August 1962): *You Send Me; Only Sixteen; Everybody Loves To Cha Cha Cha; For Sentimental Reasons; Wonderful World; Summertime; Chain Gang; Twistin' The Night Away; Sad Mood; Having A Party; Bring It On Home To Me.* MR. SOUL (February 1963): *I Wish You Love; Willow Weep For Me; Chains Of Love; Smoke Rings; All The Way; Send Me Some Lovin'; Cry Me A River; Driftin' Blues;*

For Sentimental Reasons; Nothing Can Change This Love; Little Girl; These Foolish Things. NIGHT BEAT (September 1963): *Nobody Knows The Trouble I've Seen; Lost And Lookin'; Mean Old World; Please Don't Drive Me Away; I Lost Everything; Get Yourself Another Fool; Little Red Rooster; Laughin' And Clownin'; Trouble Blues; You Gotta Move; Fool's Paradise; Shake Rattle And Roll.* AIN'T THAT GOOD NEWS (March 1964): *Ain't That Good News; Meet Me At Mary's Place; Good Times; Rome Wasn't Built In A Day; Another Saturday Night; Tennessee Waltz; Change Is Gonna Come; Falling In Love; Home; Sittin' In The Sun; No Second Time; Riddle Song.* SAM COOKE AT THE COPA (October 1964): *Best Things In Life Are Free; Bill Bailey; Nobody Knows You When You're Down And Out; Frankie And Johnny; If I Had A Hammer; When I Fall In Love; Twistin' The Night Away; This Little Light Of Mine; Blowin' In The Wind; Tennessee Waltz; Medley.* SHAKE (February 1965): *Shake; Yeah Man; Win Your Love For Me; Love You Most Of All; Meet Me At Mary's Place; I've Got The Whole World Shakin'; Change Is Gonna Come; I'm In The Mood For Love; I'm Just A Country Boy; You're Nobody 'Til Somebody Loves You; Comes Love; Ease My Troublin' Mind.* THE BEST OF SAM COOKE—VOL. II (July 1965): *Frankie And Johnny; That's Where It's At; Shake; Baby, Baby, Baby; Another Saturday Night; Little Red Rooster; Ain't That Good News; Cousin Of Mine; Tennessee Waltz; Change Is Gonna Come; Basin Street Blues; Love Will Find A Way.* TRY A LITTLE LOVE (October 1965): *Try A Little Love; Don't Cry On My Shoulder; Bridge Of Tears; I Fall In Love Every Day; You're Always On My Mind; Love Song From 'Houseboat'; When A Boy Falls In Love; To Each His Own; Tammy; The Gypsy; The Little Things You Do; You Send Me.* THE UNFORGETTABLE SAM COOKE (March 1966): *I'm Gonna Forget About You; Sugar Dumpling; I Ain't Gonna Cheat On You No More; Soothe Me; With You; One More Time; Feel It; It's All Right; Wonderful World; Whole Lotta Woman; No One; That's All.* THE MAN WHO INVENTED SOUL (April 1968): *I Ain't Gonna Cheat On You No More; Falling In Love; Tain't Nobody's Business If I Do; Willow Weep For Me; Try A Little Love; Blowin' In The Wind; Ease My Troublin' Mind; Nobody Knows You When*

You're Down And Out; Danny Boy; Great Pretender; Send Me Some Lovin'.

Singles/*Teenage Sonata*/*If You Were The Only Girl* (February 1960); *You Understand Me*/*I Belong To Your Heart* (April 1960); *Chain Gang*/*I Fall In Love Every Day* (July 1960); *Sad Mood*/*Love Me* (November 1960); *That's It—I Quit—I'm Movin' On*/*What Did You Say* (February 1961); *Cupid*/*Farewell My Darling* (May 1961); *Feel It*/*It's All Right* (August 1961); *Twisting The Night Away*/*One More Time* (January 1962); *Having A Party*/*Bring It On Home To Me* (May 1962); *Somebody Have Mercy*/*Nobody Can Change This Love* (September 1962); *Send Me Some Lovin'*/*Baby, Baby, Baby* (December 1962); *Another Saturday Night*/*Love Will Find A Way* (April 1963); *Frankie And Johnny*/*Cool Train* (July 1963); *Little Red Rooster*/*You Gotta Move On* (October 1963); *Good News*/*Basin Street Blues* (January 1964); *Good Times*/*Tennessee Waltz* (May 1964); *Cousin Of Mine*/*That's Where It's At* (September 1964); *Shake*/*A Change Is Gonna Come* (December 1964); *It's Got The Whole World Shaking*/*Somebody Ease My Troublin' Mind* (March 1965); *When A Boy Falls In Love*/*The Piper* (May 1965); *Sugar Dumpling*/*Bridge Of Tears* (July 1965); *Feel It*/*That's All* (January 1966); *Let's Go Steady Again*/*Trouble Blues* (March 1966); *Meet Me At Mara's Place*/*If I Had A Hammer* (August 1966).

JAMES COTTON BLUES BAND/*James Cotton (harmonica, vocals), Luther Tucker (lead guitar), Bob Anderson (bass), Albert Gianquinto (piano), Francis Clay (drums).*
With everyone else and his mother (from the Rolling Stones on) making money and a reputation out of Chicago blues, some of the originals have finally ventured out of Chicago into the world, and about time. Cotton, a veteran of Muddy Waters' famous Chicago blues band, got his own band together in 1966 and was snapped up by all those places (like San Francisco's Fillmore Auditorium) that were bent on showing the paying customers what the real thing was like. Cotton, who grew up in Mississippi hearing Sonny Boy Williamson, the great blues harmonica player on the radio, ran away from home at the age of nine to find him. He told Williamson he

didn't have any family and was promptly adopted, taught the harp and sometimes allowed to play with the band. When Muddy Waters came to Memphis in 1954, Cotton was asked to sit in for one night and ended up sitting in for twelve years. As a performer, he's a bouncer around and a somersaulter, a shouter and a pleader. It's the Delta folk blues of Cotton's childhood and the urban blues of Muddy Waters' Chicago all in one. For those who've only heard the blues second-hand, it's a major revelation.

Albums/JAMES COTTON BLUES BAND (November 1967: *Good Time Charlie; Turn On Your Lovelight; Something On Your Mind; Don't Start Me Talkin'; Jelly, Jelly; Off The Wall; Feelin' Good; Sweet Sixteen; Knock On Wood; Oh Why; Blues In My Sleep.* PURE COTTON (June 1968): *Soul Survivor; I Remember; Worried Life Blues; Fallin' Rain; Heart Attack; Lovin' Cup; She's Murder; Something You Got; Who's Afraid Of Little Red Riding Hood; The Creeper; Down At Your Buryin'.*

Singles/*Complete This Order/Laying In The Woods; Off The Wall/Good Time Charlie* (April 1967); *Don't Start Me Talkin'/Feelin' Good* (August 1967).

COUNTRY JOE & THE FISH/*Joe McDonald (lead vocals, rhythm guitar, harmonica), Barry Melton (lead guitar, vocals), Bruce Barthol (bass, harmonica), Chicken Hirsch (drums), David Cohen (alternate lead guitar, organ).*
Country Joe lived with the Fish in Berkeley in 1963—before they were known as the Fish but after Joe had already made *his* name with his solo performances around the campus as a folk singer. Their first collective sounds came about in October 1965 when Joe's magazine *Rag Baby* put out a talking issue which presented *The I-Feel-Like-I'm-Fixin'-To-Die Rag* and *Superbird*, performed jugband style. A few months later, like so many folk people all over America, they went electric. After another *Rag Baby* talking issue, they made their debut at the Fillmore and eventually signed with a big recording company late in 1966. The blend of oriental, folk, rock and blues remains the basis for the Fish sound, but the balance of the four ingredients keeps shifting. As for the lyrics, they fall into two classes: social commentary and personal commentary, or, if you like, anti-Establishment

and love songs (one to Janis Joplin). In person they have a group sense of the absurd which can make a performance as personal and erratic as you would expect from a much-loved university "house" band. At times they use theatre—the Fish Cheer, the LSD commercial and other breaks in normal rock presentation such as the *Socking It To You Riff*.

Joe, right from his folksinging days, has had an acute sense of audience that operates through all this skylarking. From the start they were one of the free concert music-is-for-everyone bands, and at times it seemed as if no riot or rally at Berkeley in its big historic years, 1966 and 1967, was complete, or even possible, without the Fish. Because of this close identification with Berkeley, they seem just a little less charismatic away from it, especially in the East. One song that manages to bridge the gap between east and west is *Harlem Song*. Typical of the group's sense of humor, the song, done in a vaudevillian style, attempts to sell the ghetto as a summer resort.

Joe, once a folk purist, was turned on to protest rock by the late Richard Farina, who inspired him to try writing it. The result was *The Ballad of Lyndon Bird*. He may yet give protest and satire and witty social commentary a place in the rock scene, which it hasn't really had since the reaction against the protest folk of the early sixties.

Albums/ELECTRIC MUSIC FOR THE MIND AND BODY (May 1967): *Flying High; Not So Sweet Martha Lorraine; Death Sound; Porpoise Mouth; Section 43; Superbird; Sad And Lonely Times; Love; Bass Strings; Masked Marauder; Grace.* I-FEEL-LIKE-I'M-FIXIN'-TO-DIE (November 1967): *Janis; Fish Cheer And I-Feel-Like-I'm-Fixin'-To-Die Rag; Who Am I; Pat's Song; Rock Coast Blues; Magoo; Thought Dream; Thursday; Eastern Jam; Colors For Susan.* TOGETHER (August 1968): *Rock And Soul Music; Susan; Mojo Navigator; Bright Suburban Mr. & Mrs. Clean Machine; Good Guys/Bad Guys Cheer And The Streets Of Your Town; Fish Moan; Harlem Song; Away Bounce My Bubbles; Waltzing In The Moonlight; Cetacean; Untitled Protest.*

Singles/*Not So Sweet Martha Lorraine/The Masked Marauder* (June 1967); *Janis—2 Parts* (October 1967); *Thursday/Who Am I* (December 1967).

COWSILLS/ *John (vocals, drums), Bob (vocals, guitar), Barry (bass, vocals), Bill (vocals, guitar), Susan (vocals), Mom (vocals).*
When they first arrived there was a suspicion that the Cowsills weren't really a family (even the name sounded like something out of Disney) but a group of strangers, carefully matched personally and vocally, who had been brought together from all over the U.S. by clever promoters to do a stunning "family" act. Of course that's a joke because the family resemblance down to the last kiss-curl and tooth gap is there from Dad, who doesn't sing but takes care of things, and Mini-Mom Barbara, who does sing, right down to the boys and little Susan. Actually, the Cowsills are in an old tradition of family rock. Their sound is clean rock with plenty of early Beach Boy harmonizing. Those looking for revelation in the new music should forget about the Cowsills, at the same time remembering that the American Dairy Association loves them, families love them, and their manager loves them all the way to the bank and back.

Albums/ THE COWSILLS (September 1967): *Rain, The Park And Other Things; I'm The One You Need (Come Round Here); Pennies; La Rue Du Sole; Thinkin' About The Other Side; Is Anyone There (Stop, Look); Dreams Of Linda; River Blue; Gettin' Into That Sunny, Sunny Feelin' Again; That's My Time Of The Day; How Can I Make You See; Troubled Roses.* WE CAN FLY (March 1968): *We Can Fly; Gray, Sunny Day; Heaven Held; Time For Remembrance; Gotta Get Away From It All; What Is Happy; In Need Of A Friend; Yesterday's Girl; Beautiful Beige; Mister Flynn; One Man Show.* CAPTAIN SAD AND HIS SHIP OF FOOLS (August 1968): *Indian Lake; Captain Sad And His Ship Of Fools; Make The Music Flow; Ask The Children; Who Can Teach A Songbird To Sing; The Bridge; The Path Of Love; Newspaper Blanket; Meet Me At The Wishing Well; Fantasy World Of Harry Faversham; Can't Measure The Cost Of A Woman Lost; Painting The Day.* BEST OF THE COWSILLS (September 1968): *Rain, The Park And Other Things; Path Of Love; In Need Of A Friend; Mr. Flynn; Captain Sad And His Ship Of Fools; We Can Fly; Indian Lake; Gray, Sunny Day; Time For Remembrance; Gotta Get*

Away From It All; Poor Baby; Newspaper Blanket. COW-SILLS IN CONCERT.

Singles/ *Rain, The Park And Other Things/Mr. Blue* (August 1967); *Time For Remembrance/We Can Fly* (January 1968); *In Need Of A Friend/Mister Flynn* (February 1968); *Indian Lake/Newspaper Blanket* (April 1968); *Rain, The Park And Other Things/We Can Fly* (1968); *Captain Sad And His Ship Of Fools/The Path Of Love* (1968).

FLOYD CRAMER works out of Nashville, playing piano for literally hundreds of country records. When you think of country-style piano, it's Cramer's style you're thinking of.

CREAM/ *Eric Clapton (lead guitar), Ginger Baker (drums), Jack Bruce (bass, harmonica, vocals).*
Cream was the first of the superbluesgroups. Born of the musician's perennial dream of bringing together the cream of the current musical crop into one mind-boggling all-star group, Cream brought together Ginger Baker, master drummer, Eric Clapton, king of the English blues guitarists, and Jack Bruce, superbass. This was early 1967, when those who had outgrown early Beatles and early Beatles imitators were ready to get their teeth into some adult and substantial music, so their timing was perfect.

With Cream rock finally grew up, and Eric Clapton became the all-time rock hero, edging Lennon and Jagger from their pedestals. Although there's been plenty of blues playing around, it took Cream to fully tune a whole new generation in to that kind of music. Cream was almost entirely responsible for the blues revival of 1968 and for the great interest in the roots of the new blues-rock. Clapton and Mike Bloomfield (of the Paul Butterfield Blues Band and the Electric Flag) continually gave credit where it was due, talking of roots and sources, bringing up the names of blues originals like B. B. King, Muddy Waters and Howlin' Wolf. It worked two ways for them, for once some of the more astute heard the originals they were less impressed by what Cream and the Bloomfield bands were doing. But that was irrelevant because Cream conquered like no other band did, so that by the end of 1968, when they called it quits, they were able to sell out

New York's enormous Madison Square Garden weeks before their "farewell" concert.

To hear them was to be left stoned and stunned. No one had quite seen anything like the way Cream worked—not as an uninspired background for a brilliant soloist, but three major musicians giving it everything from start to finish. In spite of Clapton, there were no stars, just the music. There had been several seasons of delicate imagery, Donovan and the other poets; Cream gave it out hot and heavy and very physical, which is not to say there was no delicate imagery. Martin Sharp's lyrics for *Tales Of Brave Ulysses* are among the most beautiful in the new rock. Clapton's guitar (you knew he had listened and played with every blues record ever made, all the way back to the Mississippi Delta) was as lean and melancholy as his face. Jack Bruce—who could believe he had played on Manfred Mann's hit *Pretty Flamingo*—was the embodiment of music: instrumentalist, vocalist and composer. Ginger Baker was the devil with drumsticks. Each gave the others a run for their money, frantically competing for attention, though never at the cost of what they were playing. In any case, all of them were always winning, which was what made the music so heavy and rich.

Cream's music was essentially interpretative blues and rock, with all kinds of personal versatility but very little cheap flash, and no help from musical friends, except on their last album, in which they did use sidemen. The group always came off better live than on album, and when *WHEELS OF FIRE* was made, as a two-record set, one record was live. There were criticisms of the albums (after all, the standards set by Cream were high) and there were personal problems (Clapton, particularly, seemed unable to cope with the lack of time and thinking space), but all the same, it came as a great shock, just when they could be said to be the number one group in America, to hear their announcement that they would disband. The only possible consolation at that time was the thought that out of the break could come, after some cunning contractual reshuffling in other circles, not one supergroup like Cream, but three, with Bruce, Baker and Clapton each heading one.

And where was Cream when all the other English groups were happening, from 1964 on? Bruce, who started off singing

Scots folk songs, was in the Graham Bond Organization, an organ group with jazz and blues influences with which jazz-oriented Ginger Baker also played. Bruce also played with the highly commercial Manfred Mann group for a while, and with the blues-oriented John Mayall Blues Breakers, the group Eric Clapton went to after starting with the Yardbirds. You can hear echoes of all these groups in a Cream performance, for they all had a lot to teach a young musician, but the format had always been too rigid. Cream represented unheard-of freedom for the three, at first anyway. Now that the band is finished, its legacy is everywhere. Until Cream, few groups thought of having solos; now even Ginger Baker's drum solo *Toad* is widely imitated. Other groups, seeing Cream's huge success with albums rather than "commercial" singles, finally dared to move out of pop back into music—and record companies approved. There is a lot to thank Cream for: the new enthusiasm for blues, the new enthusiasm for rock generally.

Albums/FRESH CREAM (January 1967): *I Feel Free; N.S.U.; Sleepy Time Time; I'm So Glad; Toad; Dreaming; Sweet Wine; Cat's Squirrel; Four Until Late; Rollin' And Tumblin'.* DISRAELI GEARS (December 1967): *Strange Brew; Sunshine Of Your Love; Blue Condition; World Of Pain; Dance The Night Away; Tales Of Brave Ulysses; Swlabr; We're Going Wrong; Outside Woman Blues; Take It Back; Mother's Lament.* WHEELS OF FIRE (June 1968): *White Room; Sitting On Top Of The World; Passing The Time; As You Said; Pressed Rat And Warthog; Politician; Those Were The Days; Born Under A Bad Sign; Deserted Cities Of The Heart; Crossroads; Spoonful; Traintime; Toad. Goodbye; I'm So Glad; Politician; Sitting On Top Of The World; What A Bringdown; Doing That Scrapyard Thing; Badge. GOODBYE: Sitting on top of the World; Badge; Doing that Scrapyard Thing; What a Bringdown; I'm so Glad; Politician.*

Singles/*I Feel Free/N.S.U.* (January 1967); *Strange Brew/ Tales Of Brave Ulysses* (May 1967); *Spoonful* (2 Parts) (September 1967); *Swlabr/Sunshine Of Your Love* (December 1967); *Pressed Rat And Warthog/Anyone For Tennis*

(March 1968); *White Room/Those Were The Days* (September 1968).

Also Appear On/SAVAGE SEVEN: *Anyone For Tennis; Desert Ride.*

CREEDENCE CLEARWATER REVIVAL/*Doug Clifford (drums), Stuart Cook (electric bass, piano), John Fogerty (guitar, harp, piano, organ), Tom Fogerty (guitar).*
Rock and roll wasn't dead in 1968. It was just playing possum. Creedence Clearwater Revival proved that by reviving a mid-fifties hit *Suzie Q* and making it a mid-sixties hit, though they were an unknown group. Since then the group has established itself comfortably as one of the big groups of 1969.

Albums/CREEDENCE CLEARWATER REVIVAL: *Ninety-nine And A Half; I Put A Spell On You; Working Man; Walk On The Water; Gloomy; Get Down Woman; Suzie Q; Porterville.* BAYOU COUNTRY: *Born On The Bayou; Bootleg; Graveyard Train; Penthouse Pauper; Proud Mary; Keep On Chooglin'.*

Singles/*Suzie Q/I Put A Spell On You; Proud Mary/Born On The Bayou; Lodi/Bad Moon Rising* (May 1969).

CRITTERS/*Chris Darway (autoharp), Kenny Gorka (bass), Jeff Pelosi (drums), Jim Ryan (guitar), Bob Spinella (organ).*
A young rock group notable for being the first to do a John Sebastian song not already released by his own group as a single. The song was *Younger Girl* (and for a while the country seemed populated with younger girls who said they had met Sebastian, each claiming to be the younger girl he couldn't get out of his mind). The Critters' second song, also done in a sort of modified Lovin' Spoonful style, was *Mr. Dieingly Sad.* Since then they have not appeared on the charts.

Albums/YOUNGER GIRL (September 1966): *Younger Girl; It Just Won't Be That Way; Gone For A While; Children & Flowers; Everything But Time; Come Back On A Rainy Day; Mr. Dieingly Sad; I Wear A Silly Grin; Best Love You Ever Had; Forever Or No More; He'll Make You Cry;*

Blow My Mind. TOUCH 'N GO WITH THE CRITTERS: *Touch 'N Go; Younger Generation; Reason To Believe; Cool Sunday Morning; Good Morning Sunshine; Because You Came To See Me Today; Moment Of Being With You; Let's Love; Awake In A Dream; Margie Girl; Sweet Breezes; Forget It.*

Singles/<i>Bad Misunderstanding/Forever Or No More; Children & Flowers/He'll Make You Cry; Dancing In The Street/Little Girl; Don't Let The Rain Fall Down On Me/ Walk Like A Man Again; Gone For A While/Younger Girl; Good Morning Sunshine/Moment Of Being With You; Mr. Dieingly Sad/It Just Won't Be That Way; Marryin' Kind Of Love/New York Bound; Touch 'N Go/Younger Generation.</i>

Also Appear On/THE GENE PITNEY SHOW (August 1966): *Georgiana; I'm Gonna Give.*

CHRIS CROSBY, son of Bob Crosby and nephew of Bing, is beautiful and sings. He has released one single.

Single/<i>Hippy Lullaby/I Will Wait For You</i> (November 1967).

KING CURTIS & THE KINGPINS is one of the best and most imitated soul bands around. In the 1950s, Curtis, born Curtis Ousley, played on most of the early rock and roll records, then eventually formed his own group. Now in his thirties, he plays tenor sax, guitar, sings, writes and has a long string of hits.

Albums/HAVE TENOR SAX, WILL BLOW (November 1959): *Midnight Ramble; Linda; Shake; Peter Gunn; Jaywalk; Li'l Brother Groove; Snake Eyes; Cuban Twilight; Birth Of The Blues; Chili.* SAX IN MOTION (1963): *Jersey Bounce; Honeysuckle Rose; Stompin' At The Savoy; Movin' On; 6 others.* SOUL SERENADE (April 1964): *Tequila; Night Train; Java; Harlem Nocturne; Honky Tonk; Soul Twist; Memphis; Swingin' Shepherd Blues; Watermelon Man; My Last Date; Soul Serenade; Wiggle Wobble.* KING CURTIS (PLAYS THE HITS MADE FAMOUS BY SAM COOKE) (April 1965): *Ain't That Good News; Bring It On Home To Me; Having A Party; Good Times; You Send Me; Shake; Tennessee Waltz; Chain Gang; Cupid; Change Is*

Gonna Come; Send Me Some Lovin'; Twistin' The Night Away. THAT LOVIN' FEELING (October 1966): *Love Theme From "The Sandpiper"; Cryin' Time; Michelle; I Left My Heart In San Francisco; Moonglow; Spanish Harlem; And I Love Her; You've Lost That Lovin' Feeling; What Now My Love; Make The World Go Away; Girl From Ipanema; On Broadway*. KING CURTIS 'LIVE' AT SMALL'S PARADISE (February 1967): *Tough Talk; Philly Dog; Preach; Blowin' In The Wind; Pots And Pans; Road Runner; Love Theme From "The Sandpiper"; Something On Your Mind; Soul Theme; Medley*. KING CURTIS (PLAYS THE GREAT MEMPHIS HITS) (March 1967): *Knock On Wood; Good To Me; Hold On; I'm Comin'; When Something Is Wrong With My Baby; Green Onions; You Don't Miss Your Water; Fa-Fa-Fa-Fa-Fa (Sad Song); In The Midnight Hour; The Dog; I've Been Loving You Too Long; Last Night; Jump Back*. KING SIZE SOUL (December 1967): *Ode To Billie Joe; Whiter Shade Of Pale; For What It's Worth; To Sir, With Love; Memphis Soul Stew; When A Man Loves A Woman; I Never Loved A Man (The Way I Love You); I Was Made To Love Her; See See Rider; Live For Life*. BEST OF KING CURTIS (January 1968): *Tanya; Tennessee Waltz; Bill Bailey; Soul Twist; Misty; Sister Sadie; Night Train; One Mint Julep; Soul Serenade; Ain't That Good News; Peter Gunn*. SWEET SOUL (April 1968): *Theme From Valley Of The Dolls; Soul Serenade; I Heard It Through The Grapevine; Sweet Inspiration; By The Time I Get To Phoenix; Spooky; Honey; Up Up And Away; The Look Of Love; Sittin' By The Dock Of The Bay*. BEST OF KING CURTIS (November 1968): *Harper Valley PTA; Ode To Billie Joe; Soul Serenade; I Heard It Through The Grapevine; Sittin' On The Dock Of The Bay; Memphis Soul Stew; Spanish Harlem; Jump Back; Something On Your Mind; You've Lost That Loving Feeling; Makin' Hay; I Was Made To Love Her*.

Singles/*Soul Twist/Soul Serenade* (February 1957); *Honey Dripper* (2 Parts) (May 1959); *Boss/Spanish Harlem* (November 1959; *On Broadway/Quicksand* (March 1966); *Pots And Pans* (2 Parts) (November 1966); *Something On Your Mind/Soul Theme* (December 1966); *Jump Back/ When Something Is Wrong With My Baby* (April 1967);

Don't Miss Your Water/ Green Onions (June 1967); *In The Pocket/ Ode To Billie Joe* (August 1967); *Blue Nocturne/ Memphis Soul Stew* (August 1967); *Cook-Out/ For What It's Worth* (November 1967); *I Never Loved A Man/ I Was Made To Love Her* (December 1967); *Dock Of The Bay (Sitting On The)/ This Is Soul* (February 1968); *Valley Of The Dolls (Theme From)/ Eighth Wonder* (March 1968); *Makin' Hay/ Harper Valley P.T.A.* (September 1968).

THE CYRKLE/ *Don Dannemann (lead guitar), Tom Dawes (bass and 12-string guitar, 5-string banjo, harmonica, sitar), Marty Fried (drums), Mike Losekamp (organ, piano).*
The Cyrkle was the first of what were intended to be many American groups which Beatle manager Brian Epstein planned to take over. The group had been together since 1962 as the Rhondells (Epstein renamed them) and they were crisp and professional, if not exactly devastatingly sexy. They were launched in 1966 with a press conference presided over by a beaming Epstein and his equally beaming U.S. counterpart, Nat Weiss, who talked of a big American expansion. The Cyrkle's music was crystal-clear college rock, and their *Red Rubber Ball* (co-written by Paul Simon) and *Turn Down Day* were hits. In natty striped blazers, along with the sequined Ronettes, they did the Beatles' last U.S. tour. But in 1967 Epstein died and nothing was quite the same after that. The Cyrkle disappeared from the charts and finally disbanded.

Albums/ RED RUBBER BALL (June 1966); *Red Rubber Ball; Cloudy; How Can I Leave Her; Bony Moronie; Why Can't You Give Me What I Want; Baby, You're Free; Big, Little Woman; Cry; Turn Down Day; There's A Fire In The Fireplace; Money To Burn.* NEON (January 1967): *Don't Cry, No Fears, No Tears Comin' Your Way; Visit; Weight Of Your Words; I Wish You Could Be Here; It Doesn't Matter Anymore; Two Rooms; Our Love Affair's In Question; I'm Happy Just To Be With You; Problem Child; Please Don't Ever Leave Me; I'm Not Sure What I Wanna Do.*

Singles/ *Red Rubber Ball/ How Can I Leave Her* (April 1966); *Turn Down Day/ Big, Little Woman* (July 1966); *Please Don't Ever Leave Me/ Money To Burn* (October 1966); *I Wish You Could Be Here/ The Visit (She Was*

Here) (December 1966); *The Words/Penny Arcade* (July 1967); *Reading Her Paper/Friends* (January 1968).

DAVID AND JONATHAN/An English duo who happened a little after Peter and Gordon (and Chad and Jeremy)—that is, in early 1965—but did not really become known until late in 1965, when they were the first to record a new Beatles song, *Michelle,* which automatically hurled them headlong into the charts and gave them a mild form of fame. They faded away and finished up as a successful songwriting team. *You've Got Your Troubles,* which they wrote for the Fortunes, was a number one hit.

Singles/*Softly Whispering I Love You/Something's Gotten Hold Of My Heart; Michelle.*

Also Appear On/MODESTY BLAISE: *Modesty;* SUPER OLDIES, VOL. 3 (June 1968): *Michelle.*

DAVE DAVIES/Younger brother of Ray Davies, superstar leader of the Kinks, Dave Davies has done several solo records which made some chart impact in England but so far not in the U.S.

Singles/*Death Of A Clown/Love Me Till The Sun Shines* (August 1967); *Susannah's Still Alive/Funny Face* (January 1968).

SPENCER DAVIS GROUP/*Spencer Davis (rhythm guitar, harmonica, vocals), Ray Fenwick (lead guitar, vocals), Dee Murray (bass guitar), Dave Hynes (drums).*
Previous Members: Muff Winwood, Peter York, Eddie Hardin (replaced Steve Winwood), Phil Sawyer.
Where did Spencer Davis find Steve Winwood? many have wondered. He found him and Peter York, his drummer, and Steve's brother Muff all playing in Muff's band, which in the summer of 1963 was not doing especially well as far as work was concerned. Teaming up with the very bright (a degree from Birmingham University in England) and well-organized (he does his own managing) Spencer Davis was good for the Winwood boys and vice versa. By May 1964 the group was playing professionally and Steve had just turned sixteen. Steve's bluesy voice and bluesier organ playing was the "sound"

which got them to the top of the English charts with *Keep On Running, Somebody Help Me, Gimme Some Loving* (in Steve's roughest, grittiest voice) and *I'm a Man*. That was all America needed. The boys from Birmingham were asked to name their own price for an American tour. And that was when Steve decided he couldn't take the life. Some of the trade press in England said he left for money, some for glory, but Steve said he needed to catch up on being a kid and having time to write his own songs and getting together his sort of music. For Davis it must have been a blow, though he certainly must have expected it. A resourceful man, he announced he would do vocals himself for a while. And he seemed relieved *not* to be the Steve Winwood quartet anymore. The first post-Winwood album was called *WITH THEIR NEW FACE ON,* and with their new face on the Spencer Davis Group has been less fortunate in the hits department. Now, however, it has been announced that the Spencer Davis sound will be bluesier, heavily guitar and harmonica oriented, as opposed to its early sound, which accentuated the organ.

Albums/GIMME SOME LOVIN' (March 1967): *Gimme Some Lovin'; Keep On Running; Nobody Knows You When You're Down And Out; Hammer Song; When I Come Home; It Hurts Me So; Here Right Now; Somebody Help Me; Midnight Special; Trampoline; Sittin' And Thinkin'; Goodbye Steevie.* I'M A MAN (June 1967): *I'm A Man; Every Little Bit Hurts; Searchin'; I Can't Stand It; Dimples; Look Away; My Babe; Georgia On My Mind; I Can't Get Enough Of It; On The Green Light; Stevie's Blues; Midnight Train.* SPENCER DAVIS' GREATEST HITS (February 1968): *Gimme Some Lovin'; I'm A Man; Keeping On Running; Somebody Help Me; On The Green Light; Time Seller; Don't Want You No More; Midnight Special; Blues In F; Searchin'.* WITH THEIR NEW FACE ON (June 1968): *Time Seller; With His New Face On; Don't Want You No More; Alec In Transitland; Mr. Second Class; Morning Sun; Feel Your Way; Sanity Inspector; Stop Me I'm Falling; One Time Some Time Or Never.*

Singles/*High Time Baby/Keep On Running* (January 1966); *Somebody Help Me/Stevie's Blues* (April 1966); *After*

Tea/Looking Back (1967); *Gimme Some Lovin'/Blues In F;
I'm A Man/Can't Get Enough Of It; Somebody Help Me/On
The Green Light; Time Seller/Don't Want You No More;
After Tea/Looking Back; Short Change/Picture Heaven*
(November 1968).

DEATH ROCK (or neck-rock-philia)/From the Shangri-La's
Leader Of The Pack, Mark Dinning's *Teen Angel* and Eddie
Cochran's *Teenage Heaven* to Bobby Gentry's *Ode To Billie
Joe* and Bobby Goldsboro's *Honey*, songs about death tend to
sell well on the charts. Significantly, blues are more concerned
with the living. Country music does fairly well with death but
much better with sin. (But it's best when both are combined,
as in *Ode To Billie Joe* and The Band's *Long Black Veil*.) The
giants and rock intellectuals have tended to leave death alone
(except for Mick Jagger's *Paint It Black*), considering the
subject sloppy and sentimental. Death rock was at its best
when dealing with teenage death in the pre-Beatle heyday of
hot-rod music (*Dead Men's Curve*) and teen anguish (*Laura*). Nevertheless, *Billie Joe* was a big 1967 hit and *Honey* a
big 1968 hit. On the charts, death still sells.

DAVE DEE, DOZY, BEAKY, MICK, & TICH/*David Harmon (Dave Dee), Trevor Davies (Dozy), John Dymond
(Beaky), Michael Wilson (Mick), Ian Amey (Tich).*
There has always been a place in rock for good, honest
commercialism. Dave Dee, Dozy, Beaky, Mick and Tich, who
are English, are it. They used to be known as Dave Dee and
the Bostons, but then decided to use their old school nicknames. *Bend It* was banned in America for being too sexy,
which it certainly was (and even more so in live performance). In *Legend of Xanadu,* which was not banned, you
can hear the cracking of whips (the Velvet Underground did
it first, though). Again, to get the full impact of that, you
have to see ex-policeman Dee do it live at London's Royal
Albert Hall in front of an audience of very hip fourteen-year-olds. The group specializes in good, clean, wildly entertaining,
very sexy off-color fun, beautifully staged. They should have
made it in America by now. Almost everyone else has, and
they're better than some.

Albums/DAVE DEE, DOZY, BEAKY, MICK & TICH GREATEST HITS (June 1967): *Bend It; Touch Me, Touch Me; Hold Tight; I'm On The Up; Hideaway; Save Me; You Make It Move; Here's A Heart; You Know What I Want; Hands Off.* TIME TO TAKE OFF: *I've Got A Feeling; In A Matter Of A Moment; Mrs. Thursday; Zabadak; Mama, Mama; If I Were A Carpenter; Legend Of Xanadu; Look At Me; Tide Is Turning; Break Out; Medley.*

Singles/ *Bend It; Breakout/ Mrs. Thursday; Legend Of Xanadu/ Please; Master Llewellyn/ Okay; Sun Goes Down/ Zabadak.*

Also Appear On/ENGLAND'S GREATEST HITS: *Bend It.*

JOEY DEE AND THE STARLITERS/Joey Dee reigned supreme at the Peppermint Lounge in 1961 when the twist was the dance to dance and the Peppermint Lounge was the place to dance it. Cecil Beaton, Greta Garbo, Elsa Maxwell, the Duke and Duchess of Windsor, were among the gilded hordes who came to hear him in those days. His records were sensational best sellers. But the twist became passe, and the big names got excited about something else the next season. And Joey Dee faded out of the big time, though he stayed around playing, living on the memories of past glories. In those later, less heady days, some of the Rascals, before they were Rascals, played in his band, and from time to time someone on the current rock scene names the Starliters as one of his musical credits. Otherwise, little is heard from the man whose irresistibly bouncy sound got the whole world dancing. (See the TWIST)

Singles/*Peppermint Twist* (2 Parts); *Shout* (2 Parts); *Hot Pastrami, Mashed Potatoes/ What Kind Of Love Is This; Feel Good About It* (2 Parts)*; Dancing On The Beach/ Good Little You; It's Got You/ She's So Exceptional; Put Your Heart In It/ You Can't Sit Down Medley.*

DEEP PURPLE/*Rod Evans (vocals), Jon Lord (organ, vocals), Nicky Simper (bass, vocals), Ritchie Blackmore (lead guitar), Ian Paice (drums).*
With the scene as overcrowded and top-heavy as it was in late 1968, could there possibly be room for yet another group? Deep Purple made it with a single called *Hush.*

Albums/SHADES OF DEEP PURPLE (October 1968):
*Hush; Help; Hey Joe; Mandrake Root; And The Address;
Love Help Me; One More Rainy Day; Prelude; Happiness;
I'm So Glad.* BOOK OF TALIESYN (December 1968):
*Listen, Learn, Read On; Hard Road; Kentucky Woman;
Exposition; We Can Work It Out; The Shield; Anthem; River
Deep, Mountain High.*
Singles/*Hush/One More Rainy Day* (September 1968); *Kentucky Woman/Hard Road* (November 1968).

DETROIT SOUND/A few years ago the Detroit sound was
the sound of revving motors, the city being the automobile
capital of the world. Today the sound of Detroit is the sound
of Motown, the first Negro owned and operated record
company in America, and one of the most successful enter-
prises in music today. The company was started by Berry
Gordy Jr., a part-time songwriter who worked on a Ford
assembly line at $85 a week. Gordy went into the music
business in 1957, and by 1960 he had his own label. His first
million seller was *Shop Around* by the Miracles, his second
million-dollar seller was *Please Mr. Postman* by the Marvelettes—and from then on Motown was bound for glory. Their
secret formula was no secret: always a very danceable lead,
James Jameson's incredible bass lines, and a sort of watering
down of soul for the white pop market (some rhythm and
blues people did not quite approve of it, but it sold). The
formula worked, so it was always strictly adhered to. One of
the big criticisms of the Motown-Detroit sound was that there
was no room for spontaneity. The Four Tops, however, one
of Motown's biggest sellers, managed to work passion and
frenzy within that controlled framework. But the Supremes,
who really established Motown as major hitmakers, were
perfect examples of how discipline could work *for* music as
well as *against* it.

Motown also had its own writers (Holland-Dozier-
Holland) and its own producers. It worked out its artists'
choreography, stage routines and arrangements, and also
taught them dancing, grooming, dressing and even manners.
Gordy's ambition was to see every one of his acts headlining
at the Copacabana, and he has just about realized that. One of
his biggest assets is Smokey Robinson, a best-selling artist with

his group the Miracles, a brilliant songwriter and an even
more brilliant producer. The Detroit sound stands for a
sophisticated black sound. One of its biggest drawbacks is that
of late it's become just a little too commercial and predictable. Later, however, Mitch Ryder, the MC 5, the Stooges
and other artists from that city emerged to show that there's
more to the Detroit sound than just Motown.

NEIL DIAMOND/His special fame lies not in recording but
in songwriting, and when he does have a hit it's more because
of how he wrote it than of how he sings it. For the Monkees,
he has written *I'm A Believer* and *A Little Bit Me, A Little
Bit You*, both of which were perfect for them. He has had big
hits himself with *Cherry, Cherry, Girl You'll Be A Woman
Soon* and *Thank The Lord For The Night Time*. Live, the
26-year-old boy from Brooklyn is a bit of an anachronism for
the late sixties—there's still a lot of the Elvis era in him,
brushed back hair, sinister black cowboy gear. You would
never know to look at him that the Beatles or the psychedelic
revolution had ever happened.

Albums/FEEL OF NEIL DIAMOND (September 1966):
*Cherry, Cherry; Solitary Man; Monday, Monday; Red Rub-
ber Ball; Hanky Panky; New Orleans; La Bamba; Do It; I
Got The Feelin' Oh No No; I'll Come Running; Love To
Love*. JUST FOR YOU (July 1967): *I'm A Believer; It's
Such A Pretty World Today; Walk Through This World With
Me; Detroit City; My Cup Runneth Over; Get Out Of My
Life; You Pushed Me Too Far; Cryin' Time; Lonesome Out
Tonight; You Should Live My Life; Don't Hurt Me Any-
more; Bridge I Have Never Crossed*. NEIL DIAMOND'S
GREATEST HITS (June 1968): *Cherry, Cherry, Oh No No;
New Orleans; Do It; Girl You'll Be A Woman Soon; You Got
To Me; Solitary Man; Kentucky Woman; Red Red Wine;
Thank The Lord For The Night Time; Hanky Panky; Boat
That I Row*. VELVET GLOVES AND SPIT (November
1968): *Sunday Sun; A Modern Day Version Of Love; Hon-
ey-Drippin' Times; The Pot Smokers Song; Brooklyn Roads;
Two-Bit Manchild; Holiday Inn Blues; Practically Newborn;
Knackelflerg; Merry-Go-Round*.

Singles/*Do It*/*Solitary Man* (April 1966); *Cherry, Cherry*/

I'll Come Running (July 1966); *Boat That I Row/I Got The Feelin' Oh No No* (October 1966); *Someday Baby/You Got Me* (January 1967); *Girl, You'll Be A Woman Soon/You'll Forget* (March 1967); *Thank The Lord For The Night Time/Long Way Home* (June 1967); *Kentucky Woman/The Time Is Now* (October 1967); *Hanky Panky/New Orleans* (December 1967); *Red Rubber Ball/Red Red Wine* (March 1968); *Brooklyn Roads/Holiday Inn Blues; Broad Old Woman/Two-Bit Manchild; Sunday Sun/Honey-Drippin' Times* (September 1968); *Shilo/La Bamba* (September 1968).

BO DIDDLEY (Ellas McDaniel)/In the mid-fifties, before Elvis (and everyone else), the man with the beat was Bo Diddley. It was Bo Diddley at the Paramount and Loews piling them in during school vacations. Bo Diddley breaking attendance records. Bo Diddley and his bass player Jerome. Every kid in the world with a feeling for rhythm and blues had all the Bo Diddley singles—Checker label produced by the great Willie Dixon. Bo was The Man *before* Murray the K and Dick Clark and the later rock and roll disc jockeys; he was the man when Alan Freed was big and he was the man who started it all. Meanwhile, he was breaking records at the Apollo and not getting any recognition from whites. An all-time great in the rhythm and blues field, he somehow broke the pop barrier at a time when no one else was crossing those lines. He was the only r & b man to do a surfing album during the surfing craze. When Elvis came along doing Bo's thing, the world blew apart. There were times when it seemed that he would never recover. But over in England, the Yardbirds, the Stones, the Beatles, knew who Bo Diddley was all along—you only have to hear their early albums to know that.

Albums/BO DIDDLEY: *I Can Tell; Mr. Khrushchev; Diddling; Give Me A Break; Who May Your Lover Be; Babes In The Woods; Bo's Bounce; You Can't Judge A Book By Looking At The Cover; Sad Sack; Bo's Twist; Mama Don't Allow No Twistin'; You All Green.* BO DIDDLEY'S A TWISTER: *Detour; She's Alright; Doin' The Jaguar; My Babe; Who Do You Love; Shank; Road Runner; Twister; Hey, Bo Diddley; Hush Your Mouth; Bo Diddley; I'm Look-*

ing For A Woman; Here 'Tis; I Know. HAVE GUITAR,
WILL TRAVEL: *She's Alright; Cops And Robbers; Run
Diddley Daddy; Mumblin' Guitar; I Need You Baby; I Love
You So; Say Man; Back Again; Nursery Rhyme; Spanish
Guitar; Dancing Girl; Come On Baby.* BO DIDDLEY IS A
GUNSLINGER: *Gunslinger; Ride On Josephine; Doing The
Craw-Daddy; Cadillac; Somewhere; Whoa Mule (Shine); Six-
teen Tons; Cheyenne; No More Lovin'; Diddling.* BO DID-
DLEY IS A LOVER: *Not Guilty; You're Looking Good;
Love Is A Secret; Hong Kong; Mississippi; Congo; Bo's
Lover; Aztec; Back Home; Bo Diddley Is Loose; Quick
Draw.* ROAD RUNNER: *Detour; She's Alright; Doin' The
Jaguar; Who Do You Love; Shank; Road Runner; My Babe;
Twister; Hey, Bo Diddley; Hush Your Mouth; Bo Diddley;
I'm Looking For A Woman; Here 'Tis; I Know.* BO DID-
DLEY AND COMPANY: *Ben (Extra Read All About);
Help Out; Bo's A Lumber Jack; Diana; Lazy Woman; Met
You On Saturday; Mama Mia; Gimme Gimme; Put The
Shoes On Willie; Pretty Girl; Same Old Thing; Little Girl.*
SURFIN' WITH BO DIDDLEY: *White Silver Sands; Huck-
lebuck; Ol' Man River; What Did I Say; Surfboard Cha Cha;
Surf, Sink Or Swim; Piggy Back Surfers; Surfers Love Call;
Twisting Waves; Wishy Washy; Oops He Slipped; Low Tide.*
BO DIDDLEY'S BEACH PARTY: *Memphis; Gunslinger;
Hey, Bo Diddley; Old Smokey; Bo Diddley's Dog; I'm All
Right; Mr. Custer; Bo's Waltz; What's Buggin' You; Road
Runner.* BO DIDDLEY'S 16 ALLTIME GREATEST HITS
(June 1964): *Bo Diddley; Bring It To Jerome; Hey, Bo
Diddley; Dearest Darling; I'm A Man; She's Alright; Diddley
Daddy; Pretty Thing; You Can't Judge A Book By The
Cover; Say Man; Road Runner; I'm Sorry; I'm Looking For
A Woman; Bo Diddley's A Gunslinger; Who Do You Love;
Hush Your Mouth.* TWO GREAT GUITARS (With Chuck
Berry) (September 1964): *Liverpool Drive (C. Berry);
When The Saints Go Marching In* (Bo Diddley); *Chuck's
Beat; Bo's Beat* (Berry & Diddley). HEY GOOD LOOKIN'
(July 1965): *Hey, Good Lookin'; Mush Mouth Millie; Bo
Diddley's Hootenanny; London Stomp; Let's Walk Awhile,
Rooster Stew; La, La, La; Yeah, Yeah, Yeah; Rain Man; I
Wonder Why; Brother Bear; Mummy Walk.* 500 PER CENT
MORE MAN: *500 Per Cent More Man; Let Me Pass; Stop*

Tonight Is Ours; Root Hoot; Hey Red Ridinghood; Let The Kids Dance; He's So Mad; Soul Food; Corn Bread; Somebody Beat Me. ORIGINATOR: *Yakky Doodle; What Do You Know About Love; Puttentang; Pills; Jo Ann; Two Flies; Lazy Woman; You Ain't Bad; Love You Baby; Africa Speaks; Limbo; Background To A Music.* GO BO DIDDLEY: *Crackin' Up; I'm Sorry; Bo's Guitar; Willie And Lillie; You Don't Love Me; Say Man; Great Grandfather; Oh Yea; Don't Let It Go; Little Girl; Dearest Darling; Clock Strikes Twelve.* BO DIDDLEY: *Bo Diddley; I'm A Man; Bring It To Jerome; Before You Accuse Me; Hey, Bo Diddley; Who Do You Love; Dearest Darling; Hush Your Mouth; Say Bossman; Diddley Daddy; Diddey Wah Diddey; Pretty Thing.* SUPER BLUES (August 1967): *Long Distance Call; Who Do You Love; I'm A Man; Bo Diddley; You Can't Judge A Book By The Cover; I Just Want To Make Love To You; My Babe; You Don't Love Me.* SUPER SUPER BLUES BAND (April 1968): *Long Distance Call; Sweet Little Angel; Ooh, Baby; Wrecking My Love Life; Goin' Down Slow; Spoonful; Diddley Daddy; Red Rooster.*

Singles/*Diddley Daddy/She's Fine, She's Mine; Who Do You Love/I'm Bad; Hey, Bo Diddley/Mona; Dearest Darling/Hush Your Mouth; Say Man, Back Again/She's Alright; Crawdad/Walkin' And Talkin'; Aztec/Not Guilty; Call Me/Pills; I Can Tell/You Can't Judge A Book By The Cover; Bo's Beat/Chuck's Beat; You Ain't Bad/Hey Good Lookin'; 500 Per Cent More Man/Let The Kids Dance; Do The Frog/We're Gonna Get Married; Back To School/Oooh Baby; Wrecking My Love Life/Boo-Ga-Loo Before You Go; Another Sugar Daddy/I'm High Again.*

Also Appears On/THE BLUES, VOL. II (August 1963): *I'm A Man.* HEAVY HEADS (1968): *I'm A Man.*

DILLARD AND CLARK are a duo who started in 1968 consisting of Gene Clark, one of the original Byrds, and Doug Dillard, one of the original Dillards. Both are very country in mood, and if a country-rock sound really takes over, they'll be there and picking when it happens.
(See DILLARDS, BYRDS)

Album/FANTASTIC EXPEDITION OF DILLARD AND

CLARK (October 1968): *Out On The Side; She Darked The Sun; Don't Come Rollin'; Train Leaves Here This Mornin'; With Care From Someone; The Radio Song; Git It On Brother; In The Plan; Something's Wrong.*

Single/*Out On The Side/Train Leaves Here This Mornin'* (October 1968).

THE DILLARDS/*Rodney Dillard (rhythm guitar, dobro, lead guitar, pedal steel), Herb Pedersen (Nashville rhythm guitar, banjo), Dean Webb (mandolin), Buddy Emmons (pedal steel), Mitch Jayne (acoustic bass), Joe Osborn (electric bass), Toxey French (drums), Jimmy Gordon (drums).*
Previous Member: Douglas Dillard (guitar, banjo).
The Dillards are a much underrated bluegrass group that has been around for a long time. Although three of them came from Missouri, their professional career started in Los Angeles in 1962, when folk reigned. The man who became their manager later became the manager of the Byrds, which explains why from time to time one Dillard or another has turned up in the Byrds' wide and varied lineup. In 1968 Douglas Dillard joined Byrd Gene Clark to form a new country rock twosome.
(See DILLARD AND CLARK)

Albums/BACK PORCH BLUEGRASS (April 1963): *Old Joseph; Somebody Touched Me; Polly Vaughn; Banjo In The Hollow; Dooley; Doug's Tune; Lonesome Indian; Ground Hog; Rainin' Here This Mornin'; Old Home Place; Hickory Hollow; Old Man At The Mill; Cold Trailin'; Reuben's Train; Duelin' Banjo.* DILLARDS—LIVE! ALMOST! (August 1964): *Black-Eyed Susie; There Is A Time; Never See My Home Again; Old Blue; Sinkin' Creek; Whole World Round; Liberty; Dixie Breakdown; Walkin' Down The Line; Jody's Tune; Pretty Polly; Taters In Sandy Land; Gimme Chaw T'baccer; Buckin' Mule.* PICKIN' AND FIDDLIN' (February 1965): *Hamilton County; Fisher's Hornpipe; Paddy On The Turnpike; Jazz Bow Rag; Apple Blossom; Tom And Jerry; Cotton Patch; Durang's Hornpipe; Wagoner; Sally Johnson; Drunken Billy Goat; Crazy Creek; Black Mountain Rag; Twinkle, Twinkle; Wild John; Soppin' The Gravy.*
WHEATSTRAW SUITE (December 1968): *I'll Fly Away;*

Nobody Knows; Hey Boys; The Biggest Whatever; Listen To The Sound; Little Pete; Reason To Believe; Single Saddle; I've Just Seen A Face; Lemon Chimes; Don't You Cry; Bending The Strings; She Sang Hymns Out Of Tune.

Singles/*Dooley/Dough's Love; Nobody Knows/Reason To Believe* (December 1968).

DINO, DESI AND BILLY/*Dino Martin Jr. (guitar), Desi Arnaz Jr. (drums), Billy Hinsche (guitar).*
They were three rich Hollywood kids—one was Dean Martin's son, another Desi Arnaz's. The story goes that they "just happened to be playing" at Dino's house when Dad's friend F. Sinatra dropped in and heard them. And, what luck, Mr. Sinatra happened to have his own recording company. Well, they got in early. Dino was a good-looking boy; they were all young enough and cute enough for the teenies; and it didn't hurt that their dads were famous. Most of their songs were can't-fail versions of current hits.

Albums/OUR TIME'S COMING (January 1966): *Get Off My Cloud; Act Naturally; Turn, Turn, Turn; You've Got To Hide Your Love Away; Yesterday; Fun, Fun, Fun; She's So Far Out She's In; Hang On Sloopy; Let Me Be; Sheila; Everything I Do Is For You; Desi's Drums.* MEMORIES ARE MADE OF THIS (August 1966): *Memories Are Made Of This; Good Lovin'; Daydream; Girl Don't Tell Me; Homeward Bound; Baby, Scratch My Back; When You Walk In The Room; Tie Me Down; Just The Way You Are; Spanish Harlem Incident; Nowhere Man.* SOUVENIR (October 1966): *I Hope She's There Tonight; Josephine; Got To Get You Into My Life; Pretty Flamingo; Black Is Black; Turn Down Day; Without Hurtin' Some; Look Out Girls; She's So Far Out She's In; Sunny Afternoon.* I'M A FOOL (November 1967): *I'm A Fool; Satisfaction (Can't Get No); Mr. Tambourine Man; Like A Rolling Stone; Not The Lovin' Kind; Rebel Kind; Chimes Of Freedom; It Ain't Me, Babe; Boo-Hoo-Hoo; So Many Ways; Seventh Son.*

Singles/*Look Out Girls/She's So Far Out She's In* (June 1966); *I Hope She's There Tonight/Josephine* (October 1966); *If You're Thinkin' What I'm Thinkin'/Pretty Flamingo* (December 1966); *Good Luck, Best Wishes To You/*

Two In The Afternoon (April 1967); *I'm A Fool/Not The Lovin' Kind* (August 1967); *Kitty Doyle/Without Hurtin' Someone* (August 1967); *Inside Outside/My What A Shame* (January 1968).

DION AND THE BELMONTS/*Dion DiMucci (lead singer, guitar), Angelo D'Aleo, Fred Milano (piano), Carlo Mastrangelo (drums).*

They were the troubadours of the fifties generation, Dion and the Belmonts. After the rock and roll revolution demonstrated that teenagers were people, a whole new era of music opened up when just to put the word "teen" in a title of a song was to be already halfway to the top of the charts. Predictably, Dion and the Belmonts made it with *A Teenager In Love,* which adults found high pitched and whiny, but teenagers identified with perfectly. Dion's high sad voice had the nicely unbroken quality of adolescence. He was one of the first of the teen idols (along with Paul Anka, Frankie Avalon, Fabian, Ricky Nelson and other Elvis followers). There were ups and downs, Dion at one stage going solo. Then a long retreat from show business. In 1968, when everybody had written him off as a bad joke from a time of teenage proms and orchid corsages and Presley pompadours, Dion turned up with an album in a gentle Tim Hardin mood, in what might have been called folk rock once, and a hit single, *Abraham, Martin and John.*

Albums/PRESENTING DION AND THE BELMONTS. DION AND THE BELMONTS (April 1960). WHEN YOU WISH UPON A STAR (October 1960). DION ALONE. RUNAROUND SUE. LOVERS WHO WANDER. DION'S GREATEST HITS: *Teenager In Love; Teen Angel; Where Or When; Don't Pity Me; That's My Desire; No One Knows; I Wonder Why; In The Still Of The Night; When You Wish Upon A Star; Little Miss Blue; Lonely Teenager.* LOVE CAME TO ME. TOGETHER WITH THE BELMONTS (October 1966). SONGS TO SANDY (October 1966). 15 MILLION SELLERS (October 1966). GREATEST HITS (October 1966). TOGETHER AGAIN (March 1967): *Movin' Man; Berimbau; Come To My Side; All I Wanna Do; But Not For Me; New York Town; Loserville; For Bobbie; Jump Back Baby; My Girl The Month Of May; Baby You've*

Been On My Mind. DION (November 1968): *Abraham, Martin & John; He Looks A Lot Like Me; Purple Haze; From Both Sides, Now;* Other Titles.

Singles/*(Dion and the Belmonts)/Teenager In Love; I Wonder Why; Where Or When; When You Wish Upon A Star; That's My Desire; Don't Pity Me; Berimbau/My Girl The Month Of May; Movin' Man/For Bobbie; (Dion)/Runaround Sue; Lovers Who Wander/Born To Cry; Ruby Baby/Donna The Prima Donna; Abraham, Martin & John.*

DISCOTHEQUE/By 1961 music had the most kinetic beat since tom-toms. In France, clubs found they didn't need live musicians to get people to dance—just a disquaire who "programmed" dance records and moods for the evening. Such a place had a name too, a discotheque. The first one in New York, a private club called Le Club, was a raging success. Dozens and then thousands followed in the wake of the biggest dance craze of the decade, the twist. By 1964–65 there were 5,000 in America alone. Although many of these stick to the original formula of recorded music, others, including famous ones like Arthur, Cheetah, the Electric Circus, Trude Heller's, the Scene, Ondine, Salvation, also use live bands. Many big rock groups got a more than flying start in a discotheque (the Rascals in The Barge in Southampton, the Doors at the Whisky A-Go-Go in Los Angeles). Discotheques in America and in London, places like the Scene in New York and London's Speakeasy, are also meeting places of off-duty performers. On a good night you can see just about anyone you've ever wanted to see. If you can find them in the dark, that is.
(See the TWIST)

WILLIE DIXON/Now a producer for Chess records, Willie Dixon played bass on many of Muddy Waters' records in the early 1950s, when the modern Chicago blues styles that influenced so much of rock were emerging. He also produced all of Bo Diddley's singles. But he is best known for his unaffected blues compositions like the song Muddy does so well, *Hootchie Cootchie Man,* and all those Little Walter, Howlin' Wolf, Sonny Boy Williamson songs that all the blues-rock people, especially the ones from England, took over—and brought back. Namely, *Little Red Rooster, The Seventh Son, I Just Want To Make Love To You, Bring It On Home* and *Wang Dang Doodle.*

Songs Recorded by Others/*Little Red Rooster* (The Rolling Stones, Sam Cooke); *Seventh Son* (Mose Allison, The Challengers, Dino, Desi & Billy, John Hammond, Peggy Lee, The Mindbenders, Johnny Rivers, Ted Taylor); *I Just Want To Make Love To You* (Chuck Berry, Bo Diddley, Muddy Waters, Little Walter, Etta James, Ramsey Lewis Trio, Lou Rawls, The Rolling Stones); *Bring It On Home* (The Animals, Dirty Blues Band, Wilson Pickett, Sonny Boy Williamson); *Wang Dang Doodle* (Howlin' Wolf, Ko Ko Taylor); *Hootchie Cootchie Man* (Chuck Berry, John Hammond, Timmy Smith, Steppenwolf, Muddy Waters).

DR. JOHN, THE NIGHT TRIPPER/The album is the grisliest, eeriest, most magical example of voodoo rock. In fact, it's the *only* example. But Dr. John is no hoochie coochie man; just a studio musician named Mack Rebenneck who originally came from New Orleans and now lives in California. One critic dubbed his style, along with Arthur Brown's of the flaming headgear, as "jungle rock." His album, *GRIS-GRIS*, sounds more out of Haiti or the bayou than out of California. The Incredible String Band was once described as offering evidence of magic. So does Dr. John.

Album/GRIS-GRIS (July 1968): *Gris-Gris Gumbo Ya Ya; Croker Courtbullion; I Walk On Gilded Splinters; Danse Fambeaux; Mama Roux; Jump Sturdy; Danse Kalida Ba Doom.*

Single/*Jump Sturdy*/*Mama Roux* (December 1968).

FATS DOMINO (Antoine Domino)/The undisputed emperor of the pre-Elvis rock and roll scene. But, as he kept insisting, he'd never played anything else that he could remember; he'd just always known it as rhythm and blues. He played a honkytonk piano, singing in a grating voice that almost every post-Elvis rock and roll pianist-singer tried to imitate. In one of those curious cycles that are now happening in the new rock, Fats was in the odd position of recording, on a 1968 album, the Beatles' *Lady Madonna*, a 1968 single born out of nostalgia for the Domino sound. (But something was lost in translation

Domino's imitation of the Beatles imitating Domino some-how doesn't work.) When people get nostalgic for the mid-fifties rock period, it's Domino they think of. He broke all records at the Brooklyn Paramount in those days. And in the summer of 1968, when everyone started getting very serious about the new rock and its historical roots, it was the Brooklyn Paramount all over again in Central Park, with Fats making a triumphant reappearance in New York after all those years.

Albums/ROCK & ROLLIN': *Tired Of Crying; Rose Mary; All By Myself; You Said You Love Me; Ain't It A Shame; Fat Man; Poor Me; Bo Weevil; Don't Blame It On Me; Goin' Home; Going To The River; Please Don't Leave Me.* ROCK & ROLLIN': *My Blue Heaven; Swanee River Hop; Second Line Jump; Goodbye; I Love Her; I'm In Love Again; When My Dreamboat Comes Home; My Heart Is In Your Hands; Careless Love; Are You Going My Way; If You Need Me; Fats' Frenzy.* THIS IS FATS DOMINO: *Blueberry Hill; Blue Monday; Poor, Poor Me; Honey Chile; What's The Reason I'm Not Pleasing You; So Long; La La; Troubles Of My Own; You Done Me Wrong; Reeling And Rocking; Fat Man's Hop; Trust In Me.* HERE STANDS FATS DOMINO: *Detroit City Blues; Hide Away Blues; She's My Baby; New Baby; Cheatin'; Little Bee; I'm Walkin'; Every Night About This Time; You Can Pack Your Suitcase; I'm In The Mood For Love; Hey Fat Man; I'll Be Gone.* THIS IS FATS (September 1958): *As Time Goes By; Hey, La Bas; Rooster Song; My Happiness; Valley Of Tears; It's You I Love; Love Me; Don't You Hear Me Calling You; Where Did You Stay; Baby Please; You Know I Miss You; Thinking Of You.* FAB-ULOUS MR. D (September 1958): *Big Beat; I'll Be Glad When You're Dead You Rascal You; Barrel House; What Will I Tell My Heart; Little Mary; Sick And Tired; I Want You To Know; '44'; Mardi Gras In New Orleans; I Can't Go On; Long Lonesome Journey; Young School Girl.* LET'S PLAY FATS DOMINO: *I'm Gonna Be A Wheel, Someday; When The Saints Go Marching In; Margie; Lil' Liza Jane; I Want To Walk You Home; You Left Me; Ain't It Good; Howdy Podner; Stack And Billy; Would You; Hands Across The Table.* FATS DOMINO SINGS MILLION RECORD HITS: *You Said You Love Me; I Still Love You; Be My*

Guest; Country Boy; If You Need Me; I Want To Walk You Home; It's You I Love; I've Been Around; Margie; I'm Gonna Be A Wheel Someday; I'm Ready; I Want You To Know. 12,000,000 RECORDS (August 1959). I MISS YOU SO: *I Miss You So; It Keeps Rainin'; Ain't That Just Like A Woman; Once In A While; I Hear You Knocking; Isle Of Capri; What A Price; When I Was Young; Fell In Love On Monday; My Bleeding Heart; Easter Parade; I'll Always Be In Love With You.* FATS DOMINO SWINGS: *Fat Man; Blue Monday; Blueberry Hill; I'm Walkin'; I'm In Love Again; Going To The River; My Blue Heaven; Bo Weevil; Please Don't Leave Me; Goin' Home; Ain't It A Shame; Whole Lotta Loving.* MILLION SELLERS BY FATS: *Walking To New Orleans; My Real Name; My Girl Josephine; Three Nights A Week; Ain't Gonna Do It; Shu Rah; Natural Born Lover; What A Price; Let The Four Winds Blow; My Heart Is Bleeding; Jambalaya; You Win Again.* LOTS OF DOMINOS: *Put Your Arms Around Me Honey; Three Nights A Week; Shu Rah; Rising Sun; My Girl Josephine; Sheik Of Araby; Walking To New Orleans; Don't Come Knockin'; Magic Isles; You Always Hurt The One You Love; It's The Talk Of The Town; Natural Born Lover.* WALKING TO NEW ORLEANS: *Goin' Back Home; Oh Wee; Sailor Boy; Walkin' To New Orleans; How Can I Be Happy; One Of These Days; So Glad; Lazy Woman; My Love For Her; What's Wrong; Little Mama; I Guess I'll Be On My Way.* LET'S DANCE WITH DOMINO: *Ain't It A Shame; I Don't Want To Walk Without You; I Lived My Life; Someday; Telling Lies; When I See You; Just A Little While (To Stay Here); Oh Ba-a-by; When You're Smiling; Don't You Know I Love You; Yes My Darling; True Confession.* HERE HE COMES AGAIN: *Goin' Home; Trouble In Mind; Every Night; I Can't Give You Anything But Love; When I See You; Oh Ba-a-by; Ain't Gonna Do It; Lil' Liza Jane; Your Cheatin' Heart; Along The Navajo Trail; South Of The Border; Telling Lies.* HERE COMES FATS DOMINO (July 1963): *When I'm Walking; I've Got A Right To Cry; There Goes My Heart Again; Just A Lonely Man; Red Sails In The Sunset; Bye Baby, Bye Bye; Forever, Forever; I'm Livin' Right; Can't Go On Without You; Land Of 1,000 Dances; Tell Me The Truth, Baby.* FATS ON FIRE: *I Don't Want To Set The World On Fire;*

You Know I Miss You; Fat's On Fire; Land Of Make Believe; Old Man Trouble; Love Me; Mary, Oh Mary; Gotta' Get A Job; Fat Man; Valley Of Tears; Fat's Shuffle; I'm A Fool To Care. '65 (November 1965): *Blueberry Hill; Please Don't Leave Me; I'm Gonna Be A Wheel Someday; Domino Twist; Let The Four Winds Blow; I'm In The Mood For Love; Whole Lot Of Loving; Oh, What A Price; Jambalaya; Ain't That A Shame; So Long.* GETAWAY WITH FATS DOMINO (February 1966): *When My Dreamboat Comes Home; Trouble In Mind; Wigs; Man That's All; Kansas City; Reelin' And Rockin'; Slow Boat To China; Girl I'm Gonna Marry; Monkey Business; Heartbreak Hill; Why Don't You Do Right; Ballin' The Jack.* FATS DOMINO (June 1966): *One Night; Goin' Home; I Just Cry; I've Been Calling;* Six Other Titles. STOMPIN' FATS DOMINO (July 1967): *Every Night; She's My Baby; Domino Stomp; Don't Blame It On Me;* Six Other Titles. TROUBLE IN MIND: *South Of The Border; I Know; Hold Hands; Coquette; Trouble In Mind;* Five Other Titles. FATS IS BACK (September 1968): *My Old Friend; I'm Ready; So Swell When You're Well; Wait Till It Happens To You; I Know; Lady Madonna; Honest Papas Love Their Mamas Better; Make Me Belong To You; One For The Highway; Lovely Rita; One More Song For You.*

Singles/*Fat Man/Goin' Home; Ain't That A Shame/Goin' To The River; Blue Monday/I'm In Love Again; Blueberry Hill/I'm Walking; I Hear You Knocking/I'm Gonna Be A Wheel Someday; Walking To New Orleans/Please Don't Leave Me; Bo Weevil/Whole Lotta Loving; Let The Four Winds Blow/Valley Of Tears; Country Boy/My Blue Heaven; Jambalaya/You Always Hurt The One You Love; Isle Of Capri/One Night; Three Nights A Week/Your Cheatin' Heart; I Want To Walk You Home/Rosemary; I Don't Want To Set The World On Fire/I'm Living Right; Lady Madonna/One For The Highway* (1968); *Lovely Rita/Wait Till It Happens To You* (1968).

DONOVAN (Donovan Leitch)/Imitation is not just the most sincere form of flattery, it's a very good way to get a moving start in just about any of the creative arts. So it was not really the worst thing in the world that Donovan in 1965 came on like twelve million other Dylan freaks (after all, Dylan in *his* time came on like twelve million other Guthrie freaks). It didn't matter in the long run, but in the short run it was very sad when Scotsman Donovan came to America for the first time in February 1966 to play to a two-thirds empty Carnegie Hall and to be put down for presuming to do a Dylan on Dylan's own home ground (he even *looked* like Dylan). It was a disaster, and a pity because even then he'd done *Catch The Wind,* which was not only a beautiful love song but also a beautiful love poem.

He went back to England and went through a lot of the changes that produced, among other things, *SUNSHINE SUPERMAN* and *MELLOW YELLOW,* which were nothing like Dylan. Coming out as they did, when everyone's head was buzzing with talk of grass, trips, highs and turn-ons, they seemed to be telling Young America that here was a new Donovan and now his head was where theirs was, with the flowers flying and the bells ringing and the incense burning and the colors swirling in the air around him. Which was not exactly where Dylan was then. So this time, when Donovan arrived for his second visit, there was no empty Carnegie Hall with its handful of earnest folk and protest fans. This time there was the Philharmonic Hall at Lincoln Center, packed with the entire flower and feather population of greater New York City (and Westchester, New Jersey, and some of Connecticut), all under twenty or at least looking it, all dripping more love and beauty and tranquility than had been seen in Fun City since the first Easter Be-In. Brooklyn girls in panniered antique skirts, Bronx boys in ruffles and velvets.

And Donovan did it. Not the Beatles, not Elvis, not Dylan. Donovan. Nor did he let them down, this Sunshine Superman. No Dylan caps this time. Instead, in a piece of showmanship worthy of the Maharishi, Donovan stepped out on stage into a sea of massed flowers, feathered boas and burning incense, looking, in his floor-length white robe, like an escapee from the Last Supper (and, for one chilly moment, not entirely unlike its Guest of Honor). Perhaps one group too many had come out in love beads and Carnaby frills. Perhaps it was just the luxury of not having the eardrums damaged for once. But whatever it was, and though it must have all been very contrived (he did the same things at every concert), it was a heady night. Donovan sang, the incense burned and no one could stop hallucinating. Later, away from his sweetness and intoxicating presence, a Donovan backlash started. Yes, the showmanship and the musicianship was superb, but wasn't his public renunciation of drugs smug and pompous, considering? If America didn't take to Stage One Donovan, the folk minstrel, it certainly took to Stage Two Donovan, the musical trips man. About Stage Three Donovan, a product of success, the Maharishi, and Mickie Most, no one is yet decided. One thing is sure: he has written some of the most beautiful songs in the new rock.

Albums/CATCH THE WIND (December 1965): *Josie; Catch The Wind; The Alamo; Cuttin' Out; Car Car; Keep On Truckin'; Goldwatch Blues; To Sing For You; You're Gonna Need Somebody On Your Bond; Tangerine Puppet; Donna Donna; Ramblin' Boy.* SUNSHINE SUPERMAN (August 1966): *Sunshine Superman; Legend Of A Girl Child Linda; Three King Fishers; Ferris Wheel; Fat Angel; Bert's Blues; Season Of The Witch; The Trip; Guinevere; Celeste.* FAIRY TALES (December 1966): *Universal Soldier; Colours; Sunny Goodge Street; Jersey Thursday; To Try For The Sun; Circus Of Sour; Summerday Reflection Song; Candy Man; Belated Forgiveness Plea; Ballad Of The Crystal Man; Little Tin Soldier; Battle Of Geraldine.* REAL DONOVAN (December 1966): *Turquoise; Oh Deed I Do; Catch The Wind; Remember The Alamo; Ballad of The Crystal Man; Colours; Hey Gyp; Belated Forgiveness Plea; Ramblin' Boy; War Drags On; Josie; To Try For The Sun.* LIKE IT IS (January 1967): *Colours; Josie; Catch The Wind; Sunny Goodge Street; Universal Soldier; Summer Day Reflection Song; Do You Hear Me Now; Why Do You Treat Me The Way You Do; To Try For The Sun; Hey Gyp; War Drags On.* MEL-LOW YELLOW (January 1967): *Mellow Yellow; Writer In The Sun; Sand And Foam; The Observation; Bleak City Woman; House Of Jansch; Young Girl Blues; Museum; Hampstead Incident; Sunny South Kensington.* GIFT FROM A FLOWER TO A GARDEN (November 1967) PART 1: WEAR YOUR LOVE LIKE HEAVEN: *Wear Your Love Like Heaven; Mad John's Escape; Skip-A-Long-Sam; Sun; There Was A Time; Oh Gosh; Little Boy In*

Corduroy; Under The Greenwood Tree; Land Of Doesn't Have To Be; Someone's Singing. PART 2: FOR LITTLE ONES: *Song Of The Naturalist's Wife; Enchanted Gypsy; Voyage Into The Golden Screen; Isle Of Islay; Mandolin Man And His Secret; Lay Of The Last Tinker; Tinker And The Crab; Widow With Shawl; Lullaby Of Spring; The Magpie; Starfish-On-The-Toast; Epistle To Derroll.* DONOVAN IN CONCERT (July 1968): *Isle Of Islay; Young Girl Blues; There Is A Mountain; Poor Cow; Celeste; Fat Angel; Guinevere; Widow With Shawl; Preachin' Love; Lullaby Of Spring; Writer In The Sun; Pebble And The Man; Rules And Regulations; Mellow Yellow.* HURDY GURDY MAN (October 1968): *Hurdy Gurdy Man; Peregrine; Entertaining Of A Shy Girl; As I Recall It; Get Thy Bearings; Hi It's Been A Long Time; West Indian Lady; Jennifer Juniper; River Song; Tangier; Sunny Day; Sun Is A Very Magic Fellow; Teas.*

Singles/*Sunshine Superman/The Trip* (July 1966); *Catch The Wind/Why Do You Treat Me The Way You Do* (October 1966); *Colours/Josie* (October 1966); *Little Tin Soldier/You're Gonna Need Somebody On Your Bond* (October 1966); *Summer Day Reflection/Sunny Goodge Street* (November 1966); *To Try For The Sun/Sunny Goodge Street* (November 1966); *Hey Gyp/War Drags On* (November 1966); *Do You Hear Me Now/Why Do You Treat Me The Way You Do* (November 1966); *Do You Hear Me Now/Universal Soldier* (January 1967); *Mellow Yellow/Sunny South Kensington* (January 1967); *Mellow Yellow/Sunshine Superman* (May 1967); *There Is A Mountain/Sand And Foam* (July 1967); *Jennifer Juniper/Poor Cow* (February 1968); *Wear Your Love Like Heaven/There Is A Mountain* (April 1968); *Teen Angel/Hurdy Gurdy Man* (May 1968); *Lalena/Aye My Love* (September 1968).

THE DOORS/*Jim Morrison (vocals), Ray Manzarek (organ), Robbie Krieger (guitar), John Densmore (drums).*
More gloppy, pretentious, pseudosurrealistic, hyperliterary, quasi-mystical prose has been written about the Doors than about any rock group ever. Whenever the Doors are mentioned in print, the similes fly like shrapnel in an air raid. They are unendurable pleasure indefinitely prolonged, they are the messengers of the devil, they are the patricide kids, the Los

Angeles branch of the Oedipus Association, the boys next door (if you live next door to a penitentiary, a lunatic asylum or a leather shop). So say the metaphor makers anyway. The Doors seeped in through the underground early in 1967, a time when no one could possibly have predicted that a group that sang about the evil and the reptilian and the bloody was about to become not just the number one group in America, but the number one *teenybopper* group in America, which just shows what secret dreams of mayhem and vengeance and violent sexuality all those dear little suburban nymphets were harboring in the infant hearts beating under all those preteen bras.

Initially there was an album, *THE DOORS*, a growing reputation on the West Coast, and a ferocious single, *Break On Through*, that defined their sound and image perfectly but got nowhere. The album, on the other hand, scored up the biggest underground following any local group had ever had— there was an organ *before* Procol Harum, images more grimly surreal than Dylan's; there was poetry, violence, mystery, suspense and terror. Wow, they were saying in those days when the Doors first came in from the West, this is *adult* rock, and the adults of the underground settled down smugly to keep this group to itself. At Ondine and then Steve Paul's The Scene, it became clear that theatre was a very important part of what the Doors were doing: Ray Manzarek played the organ as if he were on leave from a black mass engagement. In person, singer Jim Morrison was cold, insolent, evil, slightly mad and seemed to be in some sort of drugged or hypnotic trance. His shrieks as he killed that imaginary father in *The End* (which is an eleven-and-one-half minute piece) were straight out of Truman Capote's *In Cold Blood*. At that stage it was probably one of the most exciting rock performances ever.

Then several things happened. The second single, *Light My Fire*, got on the charts and, as fire after fire was lit all over America, rocketed to number one. From that day on Morrison was lost to the underground forever. It's one thing to lick your lips and strain and sneer at Steve Paul's The Scene to a roomful of cognoscenti. It's another thing to do your thing, every nuance of it, not even bothering to change the order of each gesture, in front of five thousand screaming little girls. Jim Morrison's grimaces, Robbie Krieger's peasant-boy bewilderment, Ray Manzarek's satanic sweetness, John Densmore's wild drumming—they were all public property. As triumph piled on triumph for the Doors—packed auditoriums, television appearances, riots, hit after hit, albums in the top hundred, fees soaring and soaring—the underground drew back first in dismay, then in disgust. Incredible, incredible, the Doors, of all people, had sold out. First they sold out to *Sixteen* magazine, where Morrison allowed himself to be molded into a teeny idol. Then they sold out in performance by stereotyping all those seemingly spontaneous movements that had originally whacked half the underground out of its collective skull. It got so you couldn't go to a Doors concert because you'd seen it all before. An earthshaking second album might have saved the scene and allowed the Doors to win friends in both camps. But the second album was a repeat, a lesser repeat, of the first. And the third album, *WAITING FOR THE SUN,* strengthened dreadful suspicion that the Doors were in it just for the money (as did a single, *Hello I Love You,* that seemed to be a straight cop from an early Kinks hit). Then a magical thing happened to the Doors, the big beautiful bust in New Haven, which to this day has not been matched for theatre and excitement. Morrison in tight leather pants or less embracing a beautiful young girl in the dressing room. Enter police. Morrison makes one violent movement and is Maced on the spot. He is allowed to go on stage and perform, but the "performance" is a monologue telling what has just happened. Police rush on, and there, in front of the paying customers, looking for all the world like a crucified angel or Saint Sebastian, Morrison is dragged off. It is no accident that the picture blown up to monster size now graces the walls of his recording company. Millions wouldn't have bought publicity like that. Later, Morrison made national headlines again when Miami, Florida police issued six warrants for his arrest on charges involving, "lewd and lascivious behavior in public by exposing his private parts and by simulating masturbation and oral copulation" and for alleged public profanity and drunkenness during a March 2, 1969 concert in Miami.

Things are looking up for The Doors. One more bust and they'll be back in favor with the underground.

Albums/THE DOORS (January 1967): *Break On Through (To The Other Side); Soul Kitchen; Crystal Ship; Twentieth Century Fox; Alabama Song (Whisky Bar); Light My Fire; Back Door Man; I Looked At You; End Of The Night; Take It As It Comes; The End.* STRANGE DAYS (October 1967): *People Are Strange; Strange Days; You've Lost Little Girl; Love Me Two Times; Unhappy Girl; Horse Latitudes; Moonlight Drive; My Eyes Have Seen You; I Can't See Your Face In My Mind; When The Music's Over.* WAITING FOR THE SUN (July 1968): *Hello, I Love You; Love Street; Summer's Almost Gone; Not To Touch The Earth; Five To One; Wintertime Love; Unknown Soldier; Spanish Caravan; My Wild Love; Yes, The River Knows; We Could Be So Good Together.*

Singles/*Break On Through/End Of The Night* (January 1967); *Light My Fire/Crystal Ship* (April 1967); *People Are Strange/Unhappy Girl* (September 1967); *Love Me Two Times/Moonlight Drive* (November 1967); *Unknown Soldier/We Could Be So Good Together* (March 1968); *Hello, I Love You, Won't You Tell Me Your Name/Love Street* (June 1968); *Touch Me/Wild Girl* (January 1969).

SIR DOUGLAS QUINTET (PLUS 2)/*Doug Sahm (guitar, fiddle), George Rains (drums), Whitney 'Hershey' Freeman (bass), Bill Atwood (horn), Terry Henry, Mel Martin, Frank Morin (horns), PLUS 2: Martin Ferrio (horn), Wayne Talbert (piano).*
Sir Douglas Quintet without the plus two came out of the Texas blues scene like Janis Joplin, did the San Francisco dance palaces in the early days (1965–66) and then took off back to Texas for that peace and calm and head restoration that bands occasionally find important. They then reappeared (plus two) with an album bearing the honest but surprising title, *HONKY BLUES.* Critical comment indicated it was rather more honky than blues. Now they're back minus the plus two.

Albums/BEST OF SIR DOUGLAS QUINTET (August 1966): *She's About A Mover; Beginning Of The End; The Tracker; You're Out Walking The Streets Tonight; It Was In The Pines; In The Jailhouse Now; Quarter To Three; It's A*

Man Down There; Rains Came; Please Just Say So; We'll Take Our Last Walk Tonight; Walking The Streets. SIR DOUGLAS QUINTET PLUS 2 EQUALS HONKY BLUES (October 1968): *Are Inlaws Really Outlaws; Song Of Everything; Can You Dig My Vibrations; Glad For Your Sake; Whole Lotta Peace Of Mind; You Never Get Too Big And You Sure Don't Get Too Heavy, That You Don't Have To Stop And Pay Some Dues Sometimes.*

Singles/*She's About A Mover/We'll Take Our Last Walk Tonite; In Time/Story Of John Hardy; Rains Came/Bacon Fat; Quarter To Three/She's Gotta Be Boss; Beginning Of The End/Love Don't Treat Me Fair; When I Sing The Blues/She Digs My Love; I'm Sorry/Hang Loose; Are Inlaws Really Outlaws/Sell A Song* (October 1968); *Mendocino/I Wanna Be Your Mama Again* (November 1968).

THE DRIFTERS (with Clyde McPhatter) were a rhythm and blues group of the early sixties, as strong then as the Motown groups are now. They had a steady string of hits such as *Up On The Roof, On Broadway* and *Under The Boardwalk*. They and other groups like them played an important role, directly or indirectly, in forming the musical tastes of many of the post-Beatle groups.

Albums/ROCKIN' AND DRIFTIN' (October 1958): *Moonlight Bay; Ruby Baby; Drip Drop; I Gotta Get Myself A Woman; Fools Fall In Love; I Know; Hypnotized; Yodee Yakee; Soldier Of Fortune; Drifting Away From You; To Be Mine; Your Promise; It Was A Tear; Adorable; Steamboat.* DRIFTERS' GREATEST HITS (September 1960): *There Goes My Baby; Sadie My Lady; Dance With Me; Baltimore; Honky Tonky; Lonely Winds; This Magic Moment; Hey Senorita; Oh My Love; Suddenly There's A Valley; True Love, True Love; Souvenirs.* SAVE THE LAST DANCE FOR ME (February 1962): *Save The Last Dance For Me; I Count The Tears; Somebody New Dancin' With You; No Sweet Lovin'; Jackpot; Sweets For My Sweet; Mexican Divorce; When My Little Girl Is Smiling; Some Kind Of Wonderful; Please Stay; Nobody But Me; Room Full Of Tears.* UP ON THE ROOF (February 1963): *Up On The Roof; There Goes My Baby; Sweets For My Sweet; This*

Magic Moment; Mexican Divorce; Stranger On The Shore; What To Do; Save The Last Dance For Me; Loneliness Or Happiness; Another Night With The Boys; True Love, True Love (If You Cry); When My Little Girl Is Smiling; Room Full Of Tears; Ruby Baby. UNDER THE BOARDWALK (August 1964): *Under The Boardwalk; One Way Love; Didn't It; On Broadway; I Feel Good All Over; Up On The Roof; Vaya Con Dios; In The Land Of Make Believe; If You Don't Come Back; Let The Music Play; I'll Take You Home; Rat Race.* GOOD LIFE WITH THE DRIFTERS (July 1965): *Quando, Quando, Quando; I Wish You Love; As Long As She Needs Me; On The Street Where You Live, Tonight; More; What Kind Of Fool Am I; Good Life; Desafinado; Who Can I Turn To; Saturday Night At The Movies; Temptation.* I'LL TAKE YOU WHERE THE MUSIC'S PLAYING (July 1966): *I'll Take You Where The Music's Playing; I've Got Sand In My Shoes; At The Club· I Don't Want To Go On Without You; Answer The Phone; He's Just A Playboy; Follow Me; Spanish Lace; Chains Of Love; Far From The Maddening Crowd; Outside World; Come On Over To My Place.* DRIFTERS' GOLDEN HITS (December 1967): *I Count The Tears; Save The Last Dance For Me; On Broadway; Saturday Night At The Movies; Dance With Me; Under The Boardwalk; Up On The Roof; I've Got Sand In My Shoes; Some Kind Of Wonderful; This Magic Moment; True Love, True Love (If You Cry); There Goes My Baby.*

Singles/*Fools Fall In Love/It Was A Tear* (December 1956); *Drip Drop/Moonlight Bay* (April 1957); *Adorable/Steamboat* (August 1958); *Dance With Me/True Love, True Love* (September 1959); *Hey Senorita/Lonely Winds* (April 1960); *Oh My Love/There Goes My Baby* (June 1960); *I Count The Tears/Suddenly There's A Valley* (July 1960); *Honey Bee/Some Kind Of Wonderful* (March 1961); *Jackpot/Sometimes I Wonder* (October 1961); *Mexican Divorce/When My Little Girl Is Smiling* (October 1961); *No Sweet Lovin'/Please Stay* (November 1961); *Nobody But Me/Save The Last Dance For Me* (November 1961); *Room Full Of Tears/Somebody Been Dancin' With You* (December 1961); *Another Night With The Boys/Up On The Roof*

(September 1962); *Loneliness Or Happiness/Sweets For My Sweet* (November 1962); *Stranger On The Shore/What To Do* (December 1962); *Ruby Baby/Your Promise To Be Mine* (December 1962); *Didn't It/One Way Love* (March 1964); *I Don't Want To Go Without You/Under The Boardwalk* (April 1964); *I Feel Good All Over/I'll Take You Home* (April 1964); *If You Don't Come Back/Rat Race* (April 1964); *In The Land Of Make Believe/Vaya Con Dios* (May 1964); *Let The Music Play/On Broadway* (May 1964); *Christmas Song/I Remember Christmas* (November 1964; *Answer The Phone/At The Club* (January 1965); *He's Just A Playboy/I've Got Sand In My Shoes* (January 1965); *Chains Of Love/Come On Over To My Place* (March 1965); *Far From The Maddening Crowd/I'll Take You Where The Music's Playing* (April 1965); *Follow Me/Outside World* (April 1965); *Memories Are Made Of This/My Island In The Sun* (February 1966); *Nylon Stockings/We Gotta Sing* (April 1966); *Spanish Lace/Saturday Night At The Movies* (May 1966); *You Can't Love Them All/Up In The Streets* (May 1966); *Aretha/Baby What I Mean* (November 1966); *Ain't It The Truth/Up Jumped The Devil* (July 1967); *I Need You Now/Still Burning In My Heart* (December 1967).

JULIE DRISCOLL AND BRIAN AUGER & THE TRINITY/*Julie Driscoll (vocals), Brian Auger (organ), Clive Thacker (drums), Dave Ambrose (bass).*

There is a picture of Julie Driscoll about somewhere, taken ages ago, and she has long straight hair and looks like every other average-looking chick with long straight hair. The cleverest thing Julie Driscoll ever did was to get her Mum to perm her hair. Although it was one of those dreadful home permanents—Julie's hair frizzed out as though each individual hair had been struck by lightning, a huge freaky halo of electricity around her head—it was the most miraculous transformation since Bob Dylan and Jimi Hendrix let their hair grow. It was Instant Image. Nevertheless it was in Europe not in London that she got her break, along with Brian Auger and the Trinity. The song was *Save Me* and she's sick of hearing it. Later someone played her a demo of Dylan's *This Wheel's On Fire* with Dylan singing and she thought: "What a grotty record, what a drag." But it grew on her and she recorded it. The record was a huge success in England in the spring of 1968 and in New York in the summer. Meanwhile, with her hair and pale lips and star designs on her eyelids, her Chelsea Antique Market clothes (that all looked as if they had been owned by tatty old ladies) she turned on *Vogue* like nothing had ever turned them on before. (She got one whole page for her frizzed-out hair and another for her star eye-makeup.) She sings as if she were a cocktail singer who had asked her priest if she had a soul. When he affirmed that indeed she did, Julie decided she was a singer of depth and great emotion. She's one of the best examples of convent soul around. As for Brian Auger and the Trinity, they are always complaining about being upstaged by "Jools." Perhaps they should get their Mums to perm their hair too.

Albums/JOOLS (September 1968): *In And Out; Isola Natale; Black Cat; Lament For Miss Baker; Goodbye Jungle Telegraph; Tramp; Why (Am I Treated So Bad); A Kind Of Love-In; Break It Up; Season Of The Witch.* STREET NOISE: *Tropic Of Capricorn; Czechoslovakia; Take Me To The Water; A Word About Color; Light My Fire; Indian Rope Man; When I Was A Young Girl; The Flush Failures (Let The Sun Shine In); Ellis Island; In Search Of The Sun; Finally Found You Out; Looking In The Eye Of The World; Vauxhall To Lambeth Bridge; All Blues; I Got Life; Save The Country.*

Singles/*This Wheel's On Fire/Kind Of Love* (August 1968); *Road To Cairo/Shadows Of You* (November 1968).

DULCIMER/An instrument with *metal* strings which are struck with two small hammers by the player. The dulcimer was popularized outside of Appalachia by Jean Ritchie during the great folk revival of the early sixties. (What is often called a dulcimer in America is really more a zither, a flat-stringed folk instrument that is plucked and not struck.)

BOB DYLAN (Robert Zimmerman)/The moment of truth. Bob Dylan is a book, at the least. At the most he is a continuing autobiography of this country—its music, its confusions, the failure of its dream. Charting his course is the simplest and perhaps the most complete statement one can make at this time.

Fall 1960. Dylan arrives in New York from Hibbing, Minnesota, to visit the ailing Woody Guthrie, his idol. He hangs out in Greenwich Village—Gerde's Folk City, the Gaslight, Izzy Young's Folklore Center—and sings like Guthrie, but he soon discovers that that's not what is making money in the winter of 1960.

1961. Dylan survives the winter. He is writing a lot of songs. Robert Shelton hears him at Folk City and on September 29 writes in the New York *Times* that this boy who looks like "a cross between a choirboy and a beatnik" is "bursting with talent." John Hammond, Sr., producer, signs the young (twenty year old) unknown up on the spot. He cuts his first album, *BOB DYLAN,* and gives his first concert in Carnegie Recital Hall—to fifty-three people.

1962. The first album is released. Dylan writes more songs —among them, *Blowin' in the Wind,* which becomes the unofficial anthem of the Civil Rights Movement. (Eventually something like sixty people make records of that song—not just Peter, Paul and Mary who make it a number one record, but unlikely people like Sam Cooke, Marlene Dietrich, Duke Ellington, Percy Faith and the New Christy Minstrels.)

1963. Dylan's first solo concert at Town Hall, April 12, makes him a star. *FREEWHEELIN' BOB DYLAN* is released. He's invited on the Ed Sullivan Show, May 12, but CBS bans his *Talking John Birch Society Blues* and he refuses. He meets Joan Baez at the Monterey Folk Festival. That summer Baez and Dylan are the stars of the Newport Folk Festival. Peter, Paul and Mary have a hit with *Blowin' in the Wind.*

1964. The Times They Are A-Changin' is the song of 1964. Dylan is in *Life* and *Newsweek.* Dylan, whose songs have made a whole generation political (*A Hard Rain's A-Gonna Fall, Masters of War, Talking World War III Blues*), is slowly starting to move out of politics. *ANOTHER SIDE OF BOB DYLAN,* out that summer, seems like a betrayal to the protest movement. The Beatles and the Rolling Stones come to America.

1965. Dylan uses electric instruments on *BRINGING IT ALL BACK HOME,* released in March. He and Baez do a successful tour of London. In America, the Byrds do *Mr. Tambourine Man* with electric guitars and amplifiers and folk-rock is born. On July 25, Dylan appears on stage in Newport with an electric guitar on hand. He is booed and hissed. He loses many of the folk people, but already there is a rock generation growing up who understands him. *HIGH-WAY 61 REVISITED* reaches them, reaches more people than any other Dylan record yet. Forest Hills Stadium, August 28: thousands find the new Dylan unbearable; millions have a new hero. Elsewhere, especially in California, folk-rock takes over and wins over some of Dylan's harshest critics (some are never won over).

1966. The furor has settled down. Rock is respectable. *BLONDE ON BLONDE* is released and is superb. Everyone is playing Dylan and singing him (*Don't Think Twice, It's Alright* from the second album is eventually recorded by more than thirty people including, of all people, Lawrence Welk). The twenty-five year old troubador is now writing a novel, called *Tarantula.*

1967. The motorcycle accident. How bad was it really? More rumors. Was he crippled? disfigured? a mindless vegetable? or hurt just enough to have an excuse to take some time off? He hides out in Woodstock with wife, one, two or three children, depending what story you're hearing. The novel is dropped. *BOB DYLAN'S GREATEST HITS* comes out, but no new album. Nor will there be one for eighteen months.

1968. JOHN WESLEY HARDING gives some clues as to what happened in Woodstock, reflecting its (and perhaps Dylan's) rustic calm. He appears at a Memorial to Woody Guthrie in Carnegie Hall. He sings (with The Band) rockabilly. The acid generation is somewhat disappointed by *JOHN WESLEY HARDING,* but there are plenty more who welcome the new tranquillity. After JWH, both the Beatles and the Rolling Stones put out albums that are significantly simple. Later in the year Dylan turns up at a Johnny Cash concert.

1969. NASHVILLE SKYLINE is released early in the year, and all the people who had acquired a taste for that harsh Dylan voice now have to get used to the new voice. The album is very country and a continuation of the direction he took in JWH, only warmer and more personal. Almost sexy.

Even so, the change costs him a few friends. He appears on
the Johnny Cash tv show, singing with him *Girl From the
North Country*. He makes a surprise appearance in St. Louis
at a concert for The Band (is introduced as Elmer Johnson)
and sings four songs. As usual, he speaks best to his audience
through his work. They love him.

1970 . . .

Albums/BOB DYLAN (March 1962): *You're No Good;
Talkin' New York; See That My Grave Is Kept Clean; In My
Time of Dyin'; Man Of Constant Sorrow; Fixin' To Die; Song
To Woody; Pretty Peggy-O; Highway 51; House Of The Risin'
Sun; Gospel Plow; Baby, Let Me Follow You Down; Freight
Train Blues.* FREEWHEELIN' BOB DYLAN (May
1963): *Blowin' In The Wind; Down The Highway; Bob
Dylan's Blues; Hard Rain's A-Gonna Fall; I Shall Be Free;
Don't Think Twice, It's All Right; Oxford Town; Corrine,
Corrina; Honey, Just Allow Me One More Chance; Girl From
The North Country; Masters Of War; Talking World War III
Blues; Bob Dylan's Dream.* TIMES THEY ARE A-
CHANGIN' (January 1964): *Times They Are A-Changin';
Ballad Of Hollis Brown; With God On Our Side; One Too
Many Mornings; North Country Blues; When The Ship
Comes In; Only A Pawn In Their Game; Boots Of Spanish
Leather; Lonesome Death Of Hattie Carroll; Restless Fare-
well.* ANOTHER SIDE OF BOB DYLAN (August
1964): *All I Really Want To Do; Black Crow Blues; Spanish
Harlem Incident; Chimes Of Freedom; I Shall Be Free; To
Ramona; My Back Pages; Motorpsycho Nitemare; I Don't
Believe You; Ballad In Plain D; It Ain't Me Babe.* BRING-
ING IT ALL BACK HOME (March 1965): *Subterranean
Homesick Blues; She Belongs To Me; Maggie's Farm; Outlaw
Blues; On The Road Again; Bob Dylan's 115th Dream; Gates
Of Eden; Mr. Tambourine Man; It's Alright, Ma (I'm Only
Bleeding); It's All Over Now, Baby Blue; Medley.* HIGH-
WAY 61 REVISITED (August 1965): *Like A Rolling
Stone; Tombstone Blues; It Takes A Lot To Laugh; It Takes
A Train To Cry; From A Buick 6; Ballad Of A Thin Man;
Queen Jane Approximately; Desolation Row; Highway 61
Revisited; Just Like Tom Thumb's Blues.* BLONDE ON
BLONDE (May 1966). *Rainy Day Women No. 12 & 35;
Pledging My Time; Visions Of Johanna; One Of Us Must
Know (Sooner Or Later); I Want You; Memphis Blues*

Again; Just Like A Woman; Most Likely You Go Your Way And I'll Go Mine; Temporary Like Achilles; Absolutely Sweet Marie; 4th Time Around; Obviously 5 Believers; Sad-Eyed Lady Of The Lowlands. BOB DYLAN'S GREATEST HITS (March 1967): *Rainy Day Women No. 12 & 35; Blowin' In The Wind; Subterranean Homesick Blues; Like A Rolling Stone; Positively 4th Street; Times They Are A-Changin'; It Ain't Me Babe; Mr. Tambourine Man; I Want You; Just Like. A Woman.* JOHN WESLEY HARDING (January 1968): *John Wesley Harding; As I Went Out One Morning; I Dreamed I Saw St. Augustine; All Along the Watchtower; Ballad Of Frankie Lee and Judas Priest; Drifter's Escape; Dear Landlord; I Am A Lonesome Hobo; I Pity The Poor Immigrant; Wicked Messenger; Down Along The Cove; I'll Be Your Baby Tonight.* NASHVILLE SKYLINE (April 1969): *Girl From The North Country* (with Johnny Cash); *Nashville Skyline Rag; To Be Alone With You; I Threw It All Away; Peggy Day; Lay Lady Lay; One More Night; Tell Me That It Isn't True; Country Pie; Tonight I'll Be Staying Here With You.*

Singles/*Mixed Up Confusion/Corinna, Corinna* (December 1962); *On the Road Again/Bob Dylan's 115th Dream; Gates of Eden/She Belongs to Me* (March 1965); *Like a Rolling Stone; Gates of Eden* (July 1965); *From a Buick Six/Positively Fourth Street* (September 1965); *Can You Please Crawl Out Your Window/Highway 61 Revisited* (December 1965); *One of Us Must Know/Queen Jane Approximately* (February 1966); *Rainy Day Women/Pledging My Time* (March 1966); *I Want You/ Just Like Tom Thumbs Blues* (June 1966); *Just Like a Woman/Obviously Five Believers* (August 1966); *Rainy Day Women/Like a Rolling Stone* (September 1966); *Just Like a Woman/I Want You* (January 1967).

EARTH OPERA/*Peter Rowan (acoustic & electric guitars, tenor saxophone, vocals), David Grisman (mandolin, mandocello, piano, alto saxophone, vocals), Paul Dillon (drums, acoustic guitar, percussion, vocals), John Nagy (electric bass, cello, mandocello).*
Former Member: Bill Stevenson (vibes, piano, organ).
Because it came out of Boston early in 1968 at a time when a record company was pushing the Boston or Boss-town Sound,

it somehow got confused with it, and when the Boston sound turned out to be less than all had hoped, Earth Opera suffered slightly from the backlash. The group, in fact, is not at all connected with what later became known as the Boston hype. It is a very polished group that uses a mandolin and a grand piano and produces that blend of classical and contemporary music that is still without a classification. The leader, Peter Rowan, writes most of the group's material—a little country, a little jug band, a little classical, some jazz, rock and folk.

Albums/ EARTH OPERA (March 1968): *Red Sox Are Winning; As It Is Before; To Care At All; Dreamless; Home Of The Brave; Child Bride; Close Your Eyes And Shut The Door; Time And Again; When You Were Full Of Wonder; Death By Fire.* THE GREAT AMERICAN EAGLE TRAGEDY (March 1969): *Home To You; Mad Lydia's Waltz; Alfie Finney; Sanctuary From The Law; All Winter Long; The American Eagle Tragedy; Roast Beef Love; It's Love.*

THE EASYBEATS/ *Little Stevie Wright (lead vocals), Dick Diamonde (bass), Tony Cahill (replaced Snowy Fleet) (drums), George Young (rhythm guitar, vocals), Harry Vanda (lead guitar, vocals).*
They seemed to come out of nowhere with *Friday On My Mind,* one of the best songs and biggest sellers of 1966, but they had paid their dues by starving for years before. They started off like a million other groups, playing for fun, then for parties and dances, until they were discovered by a shrewd manager who made them Australia's number one rock group. It was the Beatle thing all over again—weeping fans, torn shirts, mob scenes. Finally, when it seemed they could go no further in Australia, they went to England and again, did the same starvation route they thought they'd left behind forever as they battled for an English hit. *Friday On My Mind,* their first try, was it, and they toured America in the summer of 1967 on the strength of it. But after that, nothing took off in England and when it didn't take off there, no one in the States wanted to know about it. It's a pity, because *Falling Off The Edge Of The World,* written by the *Friday* team, Harry Vanda and George Young, in 1967, was one of the great rock songs; so was *Come In Or You'll Get Pneumonia,* which was never released in the U.S., and *Hello How Are You,* which was a hit only in England. The Lemon Pipers, Buckinghams, Music Explosion and Los Bravos have recorded some of the

constant stream of new Easybeats material and the proceeds keep them going.

Their technique is the quiet start, slowly and systematically working its way to a frenzy (often with a Kink-like crescendo chorus). Musicians like them a lot and a 1969 change of label with a new single, *St. Louis,* could finally swing a change of fortune for them.

Albums/ FRIDAY ON MY MIND (May 1967): *Friday On My Mind, River Deep, Mountain High; Do You Have A Soul; Saturday Night; You Me, We Love; Pretty Girl; Happy Is The Man; Make You Feel Alright (Women); Who'll Be The One; Made My Bed, Gonna Lie In It; Remember Sam; See Line Woman.* FALLING OFF THE EDGE OF THE WORLD (December 1968): *Gonna Have A Good Time; What In The World; Falling Off The Edge Of The World; Music Goes Round My Head; Can't Take My Eyes Off Of You; Come In, You'll Get Pneumonia; See Saw; Land Of Make Believe; Fancy Seeing You Here; Hello, How Are You; Hit The Road Jack; I Can't Stand It.*

Singles/ *Friday On My Mind/Made My Bed, Gonna Lie In It* (June 1966); *Heaven And Hell/Pretty Girl* (July 1967); *Falling Off The Edge Of The World/Remember Sam* (November 1967); *Come In, You'll Get Pneumonia/Hello, How Are You* (July 1968).

ECLECTION/*Michael Rosen (guitar, vocals, trumpet), Trevor Lucas (vocals, bass), Kerrilee Male (vocals), Gerry Conway (drums), George Hultgreen (12-string guitar, vocals).*

Never was a group more appropriately named. It is made up of one Canadian, two Australians, a Norwegian and an Englishman. They have a little of Jefferson Airplane in them, a little of the Seekers, a little of the BeeGees, a little of everyone. Their sound is based on very complex four-part harmonies. Kerrilee Male, an Australian, looks and sings like Grace Slick of the Airplane when she isn't looking and singing like Judy Durham of the Seekers. Her voice cuts into the brain like an electric carving knife. Ossie Byrne, responsible for producing most of the BeeGees big hits, has made the album a textbook on the art of record production. But the group, formed in 1968 in London, has yet to visit the U.S. and make the personal impact necessary for serious chart success.

Album/ECLECTION (July 1968): *In Her Mind; Neverthe-less; Violet Dew; Will Tomorrow Be The Same?; Still I Can See; In The Early Days; Another Time Another Place; Morning Of Yesterday; Betty Brown; St. George And The Dragon (Up The Night); Confusion.*

DUANE EDDY/ His twanging guitar was the sound of early rock for many people. Scores of young musicians say they first started playing guitar when Duane Eddy turned them on in the mid-fifties. Eddy was a Lee Hazlewood discovery, so it's no surprise that years later when Hazlewood was looking for a sound to put Nancy Sinatra on the map, he used Eddy's distinctive growling bass guitar sound on *Boots,* exactly what it needed to become a hit.

Albums/ESPECIALLY FOR YOU (May 1961). HAVE TWANGY GUITAR, WILL TRAVEL (May 1961). MILLION DOLLARS WORTH OF TWANG (May 1961). TWANGS THE THANG (May 1961). TWANGY GUITAR (October 1962). DUANE EDDY PLAYS SONGS OF OUR HERITAGE (May 1964). LONELY GUITAR (March 1964). GIRLS, GIRLS, GIRLS (August 1964). DUANE EDDY WITH THE REBELS—IN PERSON (August 1964). MILLION DOLLARS WORTH OF TWANG, VOL. 2 (August 1964). SURFIN' (August 1964). TWISTIN' WITH DUANE EDDY (August 1964). TWANGIN' THE GOLDEN HITS (March 1965). TWANGSVILLE (September 1965); BEST OF DUANE EDDY (February 1966); BIGGEST TWANG OF ALL (September 1966). ROARING TWANGIES (March 1967).

Singles/*Avenger/Londonderry Air; Along Came Linda/My Blue Heaven; Along The Navajo Trail/Peter Gunn; The Battle/Trombone; Because They're Young/Rebel Walk; Bobbie/Theme From Ring Of Fire; Bonnie Came Back/Lost Island; Cannonball/Mason Dixon Line; Daydream/This Guitar Was Made For Twangin'; Detour/Pepe; Drivin' Home/Tammy; First Love, First Tears/Some Kinda Earthquake; Forty Miles Of Bad Road/Quiet Three; Gidget Goes Hawaiian/Theme From Dixie; Just Because/Runaway Pony; Kommotion/Theme For Moon Children; The Lonely One/Lost Friend; Monsoon/Roarin'; Movin' And Groovin'/Up And*

Down; Niki Hoeky/Velvet Night; Ram Rod/The Walker; Rebel Rouser/Stalkin'; The Secret Seven/Shazam; There Is A Mountain/This Town; Three-Thirty Blues/Yep.

EDEN'S CHILDREN/*Richard Schamach (guitar), Jimmy Sturman (drums), Larry Kiely (bass).*
Eden's Children is a Boston-based trio which inevitably, and unfortunately for them, invites a comparison with 1968's most famous rock trios, the Jimi Hendrix Experience and Cream.

Albums/EDEN'S CHILDREN (January 1968): *Knocked Out; Goodbye Girl; If She's Right; I Wonder Why; Stone Fox; My Bad Habit; Just Let Go; Out Where The Light Fish Live; Don't Tell Me.* SURE LOOKS REAL (1968): *Sure Looks Real; Toasted Fruit Call; Call It Design; Come When I Call; Awakening; Clock's Imagination; Things Gone Wrong; Invitation; Echoes.*

Single/*Goodbye Girl/Just Let Go.*

EIRE APPARENT/*Michael Cox (guitar), Chris Stewart (bass), Dave Lutton (drums), Ernie Graham (bass guitar).*
Eire Apparent is a rock group that came out of Ireland and in 1968 toured the U.S. with Jimi Hendrix and other acts also under the management of ex-Animals Mike Jeffries and Chas Chandler.

Album/SUNRISE (January 1969): *Yes, I Need Someone; Got To Get Away; The Clown; Mr. Guy Fawkes; Someone Is Sure To Want You; Morning Glory; Magic Carpet; Captive In The Sun; Let Me Stay; 1026.*

Single/*Yes, I Need Someone/Let Me Stay* (August 1968).

ELECTRIC FLAG/*Hoshal Wright (replaced Mike Bloomfield) (guitar), Harvey Brooks (bass), Buddy Miles (drums, vocals), Herbie Rich (replaced Barry Goldberg) (organ), John Simon (piano), Terry Clements (tenor), Marcus Doubleday (trumpet), Nick Gravenites (rhythm guitar, vocals), Virgil Gonsalves (baritone sax, soprano sax, flute), Stemsy Hunter (alto sax, vocals).*
The musicians that made up the Electric Flag had been around for a long time, but they hadn't been around *together*

for a long time, so what you got was a strange mixture of innocence and experience. The band, which made its debut at the 1967 Monterey Pop Festival, was the brainchild of Mike Bloomfield and was, in theory, a dream band. Bloomfield, former lead guitarist of the Paul Butterfield Blues Band and king of the white American guitarists, is the man who brought the magic back into lead guitars in the U.S. rock scene. He put Buddy Miles on drums, and Miles is one of the most energetic drummers in the world. And there was an organ player (at one stage Butterfield's Barry Goldberg) and horns— a saxophone and trumpet. The sound came out of the Chicago blues that Bloomfield had been playing with Butterfield, but it had been married to hard rock. *Rolling Stone* magazine, among others, hailed it as the newest of new sounds, new soul. For one thing, the use of brass was very innovative then. For another, what Buddy Miles was doing to those drums was unlike anything ever heard before.

What you had were two monster musicians and personalities like Bloomfield and Miles having to fight it out for supremacy. So when the band abruptly fell apart within about a year of being together, it looked as if that combination might have been the reason for it. Not that there was actual antagonism between them—Bloomfield was bursting with pride about his drummer. "Buddy is super power, everyone else is just human," he told critic Jann Wenner. But what goes into bands is very complicated—everything from major ego hassles to overwork, fatigue and flipouts. The miracle, as someone once said, is that they stay together at all. If lesser bands survived, it was perhaps because they had less invested. In any case, the Electric Flag should have been a superband and could have been, but first Bloomfield left and then Buddy Miles formed his own band, the Buddy Miles Express.

Bloomfield, who'd started off in folk and as a session musician, went off in search of something else. And he found it with Al Kooper—in the now famous *SUPER SESSION,* where he and Kooper and ex-Buffalo Steve Stills jam. The incredible success of the record in the fall of 1968 suggested that there was a need not so much for touring groups of musicians but for a pool of musicians who were willing from time to time to record and maybe perform together, but only on a temporary basis.

Albums/A LONG TIME COMIN' (March 1968): *Killing Floor; Groovin' Is Easy; Over-Lovin' You; She Could Have Just; Wine; Texas; You Don't Realize; Sittin' In Circles; Another Country; Easy Rider.* THE TRIP (soundtrack): *Peter's Trip; Green & Gold;* Background music from the film. THE ELECTRIC FLAG (December 1968): *Soul Searchin'; Sunny; With Time There Is Change; Nothing To Do; See To Your Neighbor; Qualified; Hey, Little Girl; Mystery; My Woman That Hangs Around The House.*
Singles/*Groovin' Is Easy/Over-Lovin' You* (September 1967); *Peter's Trip/Green & Gold.*

Also Appear On/YOU ARE WHAT YOU EAT: *Freakout* (with John Simon).

ELECTRIC PRUNES/*Ron Morgan (guitar), Mark Kincaid (guitar, vocals), Richard Whetstone (drums, guitar, lead vocals), Brett Wade (bass guitar, flute, vocals).*
Previous Members: John Herren (keyboard), Jim Lowe (auto harp, vocals), Weasel (rhythm guitar), Quent (drums), Ken Williams (lead guitar), Mark Tulin (bass).
I Had Too Much To Dream Last Night, the first successful single of this South California quintet, was a minor classic. Their *MASS IN F MINOR* album (complete with rosary on cover), sung in Latin, was described by one critic as sounding like "tone-deaf monks singing Gregorian chants." The piece is one of the earliest examples of God Rock.

Albums/ELECTRIC PRUNES (February 1967): *I Had Too Much To Dream (Last Night); Are You Lovin' Me More (But Enjoying It Less); Bangles; Onie; Train For Tomorrow; Sold To The Highest Bidder; Get Me To The World On Time; About A Quarter To Nine; King Is In The Counting House; Luvin'; Try Me On For Size; Tunerville Trolley.* UNDERGROUND (July 1967): *Great Banana Hoax; Children Of Rain; Wind-Up Toys; Antique Doll; It's Not Fair; Big City; I Happen To Love You; Dr. Do-Good; I; Hideaway; Captain Glory; Long Day's Flight.* MASS IN F MINOR (November 1967): *Kyrie Eleison; Gloria; Credo; Sanctus; Agnus Dei; Benedictus.*
Singles/*Dr. Do-Good/Hideaway* (May 1967); *Great Banana Hoax/Wind-Up Toys* (July 1967); *Get Me To The World On*

Time/I Had Too Much To Dream (Last Night) (August 1967); *Everybody Knows You're Not In Love/You Never Had It Better* (January 1968).

ELECTRONIC ROCK/The Beatles' *SERGEANT PEPPER* album, in the summer of 1967, marked the formal beginning of electronic rock. In *A Day In The Life,* a chord is sustained for forty seconds electronically to suggest a trancelike state. Before that is the famous crescendo that could not possibly be reproduced live. Only with electronics can you get those eerie nonhuman sounds, echoes, distortions, sound effects, and only in a studio can you produce them. People had experimented with electronics in rock before *SERGEANT PEPPER,* but until then the mechanical tinkerings tended to take away from rather than contribute to the emotion of the music. The triumph of *SERGEANT PEPPER* (was it a Beatle triumph or an engineering triumph or both?) was that the machines *elevated* the content. Electronic experiments before then had been mainly confined to avant-garde classical musicians. The Los Angeles group called the United States of America was made up of such musicians who decided to move into rock, designing their own electronic equipment so they could create studio effects on stage in live performance. They used oscillators and synthesizers, which were still comparatively new, though groups like the Stones and Moody Blues were starting to use them. The Pink Floyd uses abstract electronic music (musique concrète). The Silver Apples are two men and an electronic music machine. The Byrds used an oscillator and a theramin and other electronic soundmakers to get the mood of a spaceflight in *CIA-102.* Interest is growing, and the day will eventually come when bands will bristle with electronic equipment and use tapes, gadgets and trickery to get a variety of noises not yet heard on the rock stage.

ELEPHANT'S MEMORY/*Stan Bronstein (electric soprano sax, flute, clarinet, rothophone), Richard Frank (drums), Michal Shapiro (vocals), Richard Sussman (piano, organ), John Ward (bass guitar), Myron Yules (electric bass trombone).*
Elephant's Memory is a New York based group aiming for a big band jazz-rock sound by adding such instruments as the

electric bass trombone and electric soprano sax. They made rock history early in 1969 by appearing with inflatable stage sets (designed by Keith Nelson Payne), a huge inflatable plastic jungle.

Album/ELEPHANTS MEMORY (February 1969): *Yogourt Song; Hot Dog Man; Don't Put Me On Trial No More; Jungle Gym At The Zoo; Bard Of Love; Brief Encounter; Crossroads Of The Stepping Stones; Takin' A Walk; Super Heep; Rip; Old Man Willow.*

Single/*Keep Free* (2 parts) (November 1968).

ELIZABETH/*Steve Weingarten (lead guitar, organ), Jim Dahme (lead vocals, flute, guitar), Bob Patterson (rhythm guitar, vocals), Steve Bruno (bass, organ, piano), Hank Ransome (drums, bass, guitar).*

The group, which is from Philadelphia and got together in the summer of 1967, chose the name because "it evokes a memory in almost everyone." That's what they want to do in their music, too, which draws from classical, folk and jazz roots.

Album/ELIZABETH (September 1968): *Not That Kind Of Guy; Mary Anne; Dissimilitude; Similitude; You Should Be More Careful; The World's For Free; Fields Of Home; Alarm Rings Five; Lady "L"; When All Else Fails.*

Single/*Mary Anne/World's For Free* (September 1968).

CASS ELLIOTT/When the Mamas and the Papas split in 1968, Cass Elliott went solo, did an album, played Las Vegas (for one disastrous night) and did a tv show—all of which showed the lady had great talent. Getting that talent across, as a solo artist, remained her problem.
(See MAMAS & THE PAPAS)

Album/CASS ELLIOTT (November 1968): *Dream A Little Dream Of Me; California Earthquake; The Room Nobody Lives In; Talkin' To Your Toothbrush; Blues For Breakfast; You Know Who I Am; Rubber Band; Long Time Loving You; Jane, The Insane Dog Lady; What Was I Thinking Of; Burn Your Hatred; Sweet Believer.*

RAMBLIN' JACK ELLIOTT/How you feel about Jack Elliott depends on whether you heard him before or after you heard Bob Dylan. Elliott sounds just like early Dylan till you stop to think that he was doing it first and that it's early Dylan that sounds like Elliott. Elliott's career antedates Dylan's by a good twenty years, and if Dylan started off sounding like him it's because both of them took their style from the same man, Woody Guthrie. When Woody was still alive, it was sometimes exasperating to hear someone sounding as much like him as Rambling Jack did. But in England, where they had never met Woody, Jack was especially welcome, and when Woody was ill and no longer able to perform, and later, after his death, you wanted to thank Jack for what he had done. Besides, somewhere along the line Jack did become his own man. He was a Brooklyn boy (born Elliott Charles Adnopoz) in love with the West. He ran away from home and joined a rodeo where he met up with Woody and traveled with him. He became, as well as his own man, an extension of Woody. Same cracked old voice, same sweet, small impish face. (Early Dylan, too, bore an uncanny resemblance to Woody.)

Jack was before the folk boom, when it was a good strong respected scene and you could make a living out of it, just, but there was nothing like the worldwide idolatry, the massive teen audiences and the huge money that came later. Nothing. So Jack rambled and that was all right too, singing Woody's songs and songs of the West in a way that made you feel restless and nostalgic. Then came Dylan, doing the Guthrie-Elliott thing, and being laughed at and called a poor man's Elliott (Jack, in turn, had been called a poor man's Guthrie). But now the time was right, everything was right. Anyway, when it all happened, Jack, of course, was left behind. Left to continue doing his songs the same way he had always done them, still the most lovable and nostalgic figure at the Newport folk festivals. And that's the way it is now; he's still the folk-singer's folk singer, whose style was tried by many struggling young men before they evolved into other things. As for what Ramblin' Jack Elliott evolved into, the *YOUNG BRIGHAM* album has it all.

Albums/JACK ELLIOTT SINGS WOODY GUTHRIE SONGS (July 1961). RAMBLIN' JACK ELLIOTT (December 1961). RAMBLIN' COWBOY (August 1962): *Rocky Mountain Belle; Fifteen Cents And A Dollar; Chisolm Trail;*

Sadie Brown; 8 Other Titles. RAMBLIN' JACK ELLIOTT
SINGS GUTHRIE AND RODGERS (August 1962): *Do-
Re-Mi; Dead Or Alive; Grand Coulee Dam; Jimmy The Kid;
Dust Storm Disaster;* 7 Other Titles. HOOTENANNY (January 1964). JACK ELLIOTT (June 1964): *1913 Massacre;
House Of The Rising Sun; In The Shade Of The Old Apple
Tree; Will The Circle Be Unbroken; Black Snake Moan;
Portland Town; More Pretty Girls; Roving Gambler; Diamond Joe; Guabi Guabi; Sowing On The Mountain; Roll On
Buddy.* TALKING WOODY GUTHRIE (March 1966):
*Talking Columbia Blues; Pretty Boy Floyd; Ludlow Massacre; Talking Miner Blues; Hard Travelling; So Long It's
Been Good To Know You; Talking Dustbowl Blues; Talking
Sailor Blues.* JACK ELLIOTT (April 1967). JACK ELLIOTT (September 1967): *More Pretty Girls Than One; Roll
On Buddy; John Henry; Salty Dog Blues; Talking Blues; I'm
Gonna Walk The Street In Glory; San Francisco Bay Blues;
Cigarettes And Whiskey; Danville Girl; Worried Man Blues;
Roll In My Sweet Baby's Arms; I'm Going Down The Road.*
YOUNG BRIGHAM (February 1968): *If I Were A Carpenter; Talking Fisherman; Tennessee Stud; Night Herding Song;
Rock Island Line; Danville Girl; 912 Greens; Don't Think
Twice, It's Alright; Connection; Goodnight Little Arlo.*

THE EQUALS/*Pat Lloyd, Eddie Grant, Dervin Gordon,
Lincoln Gordon, John Hall.*
Baby Come Back by the Equals was a number one record in
England in July 1968. Funny, it was issued in 1967 there as a
B side, and no one noticed it.

Albums/SENSATIONAL EQUALS: *I Get So Excited; Is It
Right; Reincarnation; Cinderella; Look What You've Done
To My Daughter; The Guy Who Made Her A Star; Soul
Groovin'; Laurel And Hardy; I Don't Want You To Know;
The Skies Above; Butterfly Red White And Blue; Good Times
Are Gone Forever.* BABY COME BACK (September 1968):
*Baby, Come Back; Reincarnation; Police On My Back;
Teardrops; Guy Who Made Her A Star; Laurel And Hardy;
Soul Groovin'; Good Times Are Gone Forever; Leaving You
Is Hard To Do; Skies Above; Hold Me Closer.*
Singles/*Hold Me Closer/Baby, Come Back* (1967); *Softly,
Softly/Lonely Rita* (December 1968).

EVEN DOZEN JUG BAND is most famous for "hatching" such talents as the Jim Kweskin Jug Band's Maria D'Amato, Blood, Sweat & Tears' Steve Katz, producer Pete Siegel, arranger Josh Rifkin and the Lovin' Spoonful's John Sebastian. For some reason, at the time, all that talent wasn't enough to make the band the sensational success one would imagine it could have been.

Album/EVEN DOZEN JUG BAND (January 1964): *Take Your Fingers Off It; Come On In; Even Dozens; I Don't Love Nobody; Mandolin King Rag; Overseas Stomp; Evolution Mama; Rag Mama; France Blues; On The Road Again; Lonely One In This Town; Original Colossal Drag Rag; All Worn Out; Sadie Green.*

THE EVERLY BROTHERS (Don and Phil Everly)/They are one of the few original rock and roll acts to live through the English invasion and the psychedelic era without disappearing entirely from the pop scene. Unlike Conway Twitty, who retired to make a fortune in country and western, or Dion, who simply retired (though he did make a comeback in 1968), Don and Phil Everly have scarcely missed a beat since the golden days of rock. When there was talk of a rock revival, there they were waiting, as if nothing had happened. A sudden interest in the history of rock and its roots has put them on top again; if not exactly in the top 50, then close enough. Everyone knows by now that much of Beatle harmony came from the Everly Brothers (in the first Beatle album it's all you hear), and that their sound is everywhere in the new rock. You hear them in the new Byrds, in the Mamas and Papas, often in the Beach Boys, continually in England's big hit act of 1967, the Walker Brothers. Their harmony is straight out of country and western, which the Kentucky-born brothers grew up with, and yet another piece of evidence for the theory that most of the original rock from Elvis on came as much out of country as out of rhythm and blues.

The Everlys, like Elvis, Carl Perkins, Jerry Lee Lewis and others, easily straddle the two worlds of country and rock and, like all the others except Elvis, found it easy to return to country when the excitement abated in rock. By 1968 the Everlys, no longer wearing pompadours but suitably shaggy in what used to be known as Beatle cuts, were back with their harmonies. It wasn't quite the same as the old times—how could it be?—but it was nice to hear one early rock sound that had proved its timelessness.

Albums/DATE WITH THE EVERLY BROTHERS (January 1961): *Made To Love; That's Just Too Much; Stick With Me Baby; Baby What You Want Me To Do; Sigh, Cry, Almost Die; Always It's You; So How Come; Love Hurts; Lucille; Donna, Donna; Change Of Heart; Cathy's Clown.* BOTH SIDES OF AN EVENING (November 1961): *My Mammy; Muskrat; My Gal Sal; Bully Of The Town; Chlo-E; Grandfather's Clock; Now Is The Hour; Mention My Name In Sheboygan; Hi-Lili, Hi-Lo; Wayward Wind; Don't Blame Me; Little Old Lady; When I Grow Too Old To Dream; Love Is Where You Find It.* INSTANT PARTY (March 1962): *Step It Up And Go; Theme From 'Carnival'; Bye Bye Black-bird; Jezebel; True Love; When It's Night-Time In Italy, It's Wednesday Over Here; Oh Mein Papa; Trouble In Mind; Long Lost John; Autumn Leaves; Party's Over; Ground Hawg.* VERY BEST OF THE EVERLY BROTHERS (April 1962): *Bye Bye Love; Till I Kissed You; Wake Up Little Susie; Crying In The Rain; Walk Right Back; Cathy's Clown, Bird Dog; All I Have To Do Is Dream; Devoted To You; Lucille; So Sad (To Watch Good Love Go Bad); Ebony Eyes.* GOLDEN HITS OF THE EVERLY BROTHERS (June 1962): *That's Old Fashioned; How Can I Meet Her; Crying In The Rain; I'm Not Angry; Muskrat; Don't Blame Me; Ebony Eyes; Cathy's Clown; Walk Right Back; Lucille; So Sad; Temptation.* EVERLY BROTHERS SING GREAT COUNTRY HITS (October 1963): *Oh, Lonesome Me; Born To Lose; Just One Time; Send Me The Pillow You Dream On; I'm So Lonesome I Could Cry; Release Me; Sweet Dreams; Please Help Me; I'm Falling; I Walk The Line; Lonely Street; Silver Threads And Golden Needles; This Is The Last Song I'm Ever Going To Sing.* GONE, GONE, GONE (January 1965): *Donna, Donna; Lonely Island; Facts Of Life; Ain't That Lovin' You Baby; Love Is All I Need; Torture; Drop Out; Radio And TV; Ferris Wheel; Honolulu; It's Been A Long Dry Spell; Gone, Gone, Gone.* TWO YANKS IN ENGLAND (March 1965): *Somebody Help*

Me; So Lonely; Kiss Your Man Goodbye; Signs That Will Never Change; Like Every Time Before; Pretty Flamingo; I've Been Wrong Before; Have You Ever Loved Somebody; The Collector; Don't Run And Hide; Fifi The Flea; Hard Hard Year. ROCK 'N SOUL (March 1965): *That'll Be The Day; So Fine; Maybelline; I'm Gonna Move To The Outskirts Of Town; Susie Q; Dancing In The Street; Kansas City; I Got A Woman; Love Hurts; Slippin' And Slidin'; Hound Dog; Lonely Weekends.* BEAT 'N SOUL (August 1965): *Love Is Strange; Money; What Am I Living For; Hi-Heel Sneakers; See See Rider; My Babe; Lonely Avenue; Man With Money; Girl Can't Help It; People Get Ready; Walking The Dog; I Almost Lost My Mind.* IN OUR IMAGE (March 1966): *Leave My Girl Alone; Chained To A Memory (Why Am I); I'll Never Get Over You; Doll House Is Empty; Glitter And Gold; Power Of Love (You Got); Price Of Love; It's All Over; I Used To Love You; Lovely Kravezit; June Is As Cold As December; It Only Costs A Dime.* HIT SOUNDS OF THE EVERLY BROTHERS (February 1967): *Blueberry Hill; Devil's Child; I'm Movin' On; Trains And Boats And Planes; Sea Of Heartbreak; Oh Boy; Legend In My Time (I'd Be A); Let's Go Get Stoned; Sticks And Stones; House Of The Rising Sun; She Never Smiles Anymore; Good Golly, Miss Molly.* EVERLY BROTHERS SING (July 1967): *Bowling Green; Voice Within; I Don't Want To Love You; It's All Over; Deliver Me; I'm Finding It Rough; Talking To The Flowers; Mary Jane; Do You; Somebody Help Me; Mercy, Mercy, Mercy; Whiter Shade Of Pale.* ROOTS (November 1968): *Mama Tried; Less Of Me; T For Texas; You Done Me Wrong; I Wonder If I Care As Much; Ventura Boulevard; Shady Grove; Illinois; Living Too Close To The Ground; Sing Me Back Home; Turn Around.*

Singles/*All I have To Do Is Dream/Bye Bye Love* (1958); *Bird Dog/Wake Up Little Susie* (1958); *Devoted To You/ Claudette* (1958); *Till I Kissed You* (1959); *Cathy's Clown/ So Sad* (May 1960); *Walk Right Back* (1961); *This Little Girl Of Mine; Problems; Take A Message To Mary; Poor Jenny; Let It Be Me; That's Old Fashion; Ebony Eyes; Gone, Gone, Gone; Price Of Love; Crying In The Rain/Lucille; Mary Jane /Talking To The Flowers* (July 1967); *Love Of The Common*

People/Voice Within (August 1967); *Lord Of The Manor/ Milk Train* (August 1968).

EVERY MOTHER'S SON/*Lary Larden (lead vocals, rhythm guitar), Dennis Larden (lead guitar, vocals), Bruce Milner (piano, organ, vocals), Christopher Augustine (drums), Don Kerr (replaced Schuyler Larsen) (bass).*
In early 1967, when every other group was working very hard for a tousled, matted look, the beautifully groomed Every Mother's Son appeared on the scene, shouting "Look, Mom, clean hair," or so it seemed. The New York group made its name singing clean summer rock (with almost imperceptible echoes of the Beach Boys). But they made things hard for themselves when they posed with their mothers (some of them in mink stoles, yet) on an album cover. Later, when a press agent declared they were really psychedelic at heart, it was just too late. 1967 was absolutely no year to come on wholesome.

Albums/EVERY MOTHER'S SON (June 1967): *Come On Down To My Boat; I Won't; Brandy; Didn't She Lie; What Became Of Mary; Ain't It A Drag; Allison Dozer; I Believe In You; Ain't No Use; Sittin' Here (Peter's Tune); Come On Queenie.* EVERY MOTHER'S SON'S BACK (January 1968): *Pony With The Golden Mane; Put Your Mind At Ease; Rainflowers; Another Day, Another Song; Dolls In The Clock; I May Be Right; I'd Rather Be Right Than Wrong; Only Child; Sally (Life Story Number 3); Proper Four Leaf Clover; Lary's Birthday Party.*

Singles/*Come On Down To My Boat/I Believe In You* (April 1967); *Proper Four Leaf Clover/Put Your Mind At Ease* (August 1967); *Dolls In The Clock/Pony With The Golden Mane* (October 1967).

FABIAN (Fabian Forte)/Elvis Presleys are born, not made. Today we know that's true, but in 1959, when Elvis still seemed like just another fabulous freak, anybody with an eye to a bank balance was trying to reproduce the phenomenal formula. Get a good-looking boy, teach him to sing like Elvis, to move like Elvis, and wowee, a fortune. Fabian, who came from Philadelphia, was a good-looking boy, and he did resemble Elvis slightly. He wasn't a very good singer but a properly edited tape could remedy that, not to mention some good publicity. It very nearly worked, but in the end Fabian never did become a big rock star.

JOHN FAHEY/A guitar soloist from Maryland, Fahey has absorbed as much of the southern blues as possible, but with this as a basis, has developed his own style. He also uses his knowledge of classical and Spanish guitar forms. Well known on the West Coast, he was one of the people responsible for the 1968 blues revival and the popularization of old blues artists. His influence can be found in nearly everything from Arlo Guthrie to the Stones' *No Expectations*.

Albums/JOHN FAHEY (October 1966). JOHN FAHEY (November 1966). TRANSFIGURATION OF BLIND JOE DEATH (April 1967). DAYS HAVE GONE BY (October 1967). JOHN FAHEY (August 1968): *Requiem For Molly; Fight On Christians, Fight On; Requiem For John Hurt; Requiem For Russell Blaine Cooper; When The Catfish Is In Bloom.*

MARIANNE FAITHFULL/A gentle English folk singer in that whole tradition of gentle English folksinging. Her first single release in the United States, in 1964, was the Rolling Stones' *As Tears Go By*. Three years later, she and Rolling Stone Mick Jagger became one of the very few great couples in rock. English newspapers identified her as the nude girl wrapped in a rug found with Jagger and others during a police raid in 1967. It only served to enhance her image as Jagger's Juliet. Her latest venture has been to star on stage in Chekov's *Three Sisters* with great critical success. She also made a film with Alain Delon, *Girl on a Motorcycle*.

Albums/MARIANNE FAITHFULL (April 1965): *Come And Stay With Me; They Will Never Leave You; What Have They Done To The Rain: In My Time Of Sorrow; What Have I Done Wrong; I'm A Loser; As Tears Go By; If I Never Get To Love You; Time Takes Time; He'll Come Back To Me; Paris Bells; Plaisir D'Amour.* GO AWAY FROM MY WORLD (November 1965): *Go Away From My World; Yesterday; Come My Way; Last Thing On My Mind; How*

Should True Love; Wild Mountain; Summer Nights; Mary Ann; Scarborough Fair; Lullabye; North Country Maid; Sally Free And Easy. FAITHFULL FOREVER (July 1966): *Counting; I Will Wait For You; Tomorrow's Calling; First Time; With You In Mind; In The Night Time; Monday, Monday; Some Other Spring; That's Right Baby; Lucky Girl; I'm The Sky; I Have A Love.*

Singles/*As Tears Go By/Greensleeves* (August 1964); *What Have I Done Wrong/Come And Stay With Me* (January 1965); *This Little Bird/Morning Sun* (April 1965); *Summer Nights/The Sha La La Song* (August 1965); *Go Away From My World/Oh Look Around You* (November 1965); *Counting/Tomorrow's Calling* (July 1966); *Is This What I Get For Loving You?/Tomorrow's Calling* (January 1967).

GEORGIE FAME (Clive Powell)/Although known best in America for *The Ballad Of Bonnie And Clyde,* Georgie Fame was doing the rock and jazz combination (accompanying himself with a Hammond organ) in 1963 and 1964, before it was the trendy and obvious thing to do. In 1966 he was voted top British blues artist, top male jazz singer. All this time he was in the English charts, much admired by English musicians from the Beatles on (he went the same skiffle and struggle route as the Beatles, and at about the same time too, 1956–58). In May, 1967, he co-starred at the Royal Albert Hall with Count Basie. He has never made a major impact on American charts, which always amazes the English and also his many American jazz fans.

Albums/YEH YEH!: *Let The Sunshine In; Yeh Yeh; Get On The Right Track, Baby; Monkey Time; I'm In The Mood For Love; Preach And Teach; Gimme That Wine; Pride And Joy; I Love The Life I Live; Point Of No Return; Pink Champagne; Monkeying Around.* GET AWAY (October 1966): *Get Away; Sweet Thing; Ride Your Pony; See Saw; Funny How Time Slips Away; Sitting In The Park; Music Talk; Last Night; It's Got The Whole World Shakin'; World Is Round; El Bandido; In Crowd.* BALLAD OF BONNIE AND CLYDE (June 1968): *Ballad Of Bonnie And Clyde; Ask Me Nice; St. James Infirmary; When I'm Sixty-four; Blue Prelude; Exactly Like You; Someone To Watch Over Me; Bullets La Verne.*

Singles/*Yeh Yeh/In The Meantime; Hideaway/Kentucky Child; Bonnie And Clyde/Beware Of The Dog* (1968).

THE FAMILY/*Jim King (harmonica), Rob Townsend (drums), Ric Grech (electric violin, cello, bass), John Witney (lead guitar, sitar), Roger Charpman (lead vocals, tenor sax, harmonica, penny whistle).*
Apart from the conventional rock instruments, the Family, an English group that released its first album in the U.S. at the end of 1968, plays Eastern and Old English instruments, and all rather well. When Dave Mason left Traffic, they backed his first solo single without using⁀ one electrified instrument. Early in 1968, bass player Ric Grech left to join the new Clapton-Baker-Winwood group, Blind Faith.
Album/MUSIC IN A DOLLS HOUSE (November 1968): *Chase; Mellowing Grey; Never Like This; Be My Friend; Winter; Old Songs New Songs; Variation On A Theme Of The Breeze; Hey Mr. Policeman; See Through Windows; Peace Of Mind; Variation On A Theme Of Me My Friend; Voyage; Breeze; 3 By Time.*

FAMILY DOG was a group of people in San Francisco who ran the original dances at the Avalon, spawned rock groups and generally acted as a rock family under the benevolent leadership of Chet Helms. Other groups have followed, the most successful of which is New York's Group Image, which sponsored dances and a rock group and the Trans Love Energies commune out of which came Detroit's MC5.

RICHARD AND MIMI FARIÑA/She was Joan Baez's little sister and as beautiful as a summer day. He was a writer, dashing and handsome, half Cuban, half Irish, an irresistible combination. He came out of the early Greenwich Village folk scene, the immediately pre-Dylan heyday of Folk City, a place where, in 1959, the Clancy Brothers and their admiring entourage reigned supreme. It was the tail end of the urban folk revival that had started in 1956. He had been married briefly to folk singer Carolyn Hester. When he and Mimi got together they sang at major folk festivals and sometimes on stage with Joan. It was awesome then that anyone who wrote as well as he did sang well too, and that anyone who sang so well wrote such beautiful songs (this was long before performers' songwriting talents were taken, as they are today, as a matter of course). He was one of the earliest protest writers to be lyrical as well. *Pack Up Your Sorrows*, already a classic, was his masterpiece and was recorded by Johnny Cash and June Carter, Peter, Paul and Mary, Judy Collins and Joan Baez. And besides all this, and a million schemes, and reports of a rock album he was producing for his singing sister-in-law, there was a novel, *Been Down So Long It Looks Like Up To Me*, due to be launched early in 1966.

It was the night of the publication party and the night before Mimi's twenty-first birthday party and there had already been two beautiful albums and his star had never been higher. Sometime during the party he got on a motorcycle and there was an accident and Richard Fariña was dead. The book, a big, mad, exuberant, freaky story, became his epitaph. To this day, more than three years later, people still find it hard to talk about his death and his friends lament that he's not around to see the music scene in its full flower. A memorial album, *MEMORIES*, was released in December 1968. And as for the rock album that he was reportedly helping Joan get together, nothing more was ever heard about it. Mimi, recently remarried, made no attempt to become a solo singer, though she did join the Arlo Guthrie-Judy Collins 1967 tour of Japan as a dancer, and she sometimes sings along with Joan.

Albums/CELEBRATIONS FOR A GREY DAY (April 1965): *Dandelion River Run; Pack Up Your Sorrows; Tommy Makem Fantasy; Michael, Andrew And James; Dog Blue, V.; One-Way Ticket; Hamish; Another Country; Tuileries; Falcon; Reno Nevada; Celebration For A Grey Day.* REFLECTIONS IN A CRYSTAL WIND (January 1966): *Reflections In A Crystal Wind; Bold Marauder; Dopico; A Swallow Song; Chrysanthemum; Sell-Out Agitation Waltz; Hard-Loving Loser; Mainline Prosperity Blues; Allen's Interlude; House Un-American Blues Activity Dream; Raven Girl; Miles; Children Of Darkness.* MEMORIES (December 1968).

Single/*Reno Nevada/One Way Ticket.*

JOSE FELICIANO/A guitarist and singer who was "discovered" while playing the Greenwich Village folk clubs. Not a rock musician, he attracted attention with rock audiences when his slowed down version of the Doors' *Light My Fire* hit the charts more than a year after the Doors had their number one hit with it. In his repertoire are rock classics like *California Dreaming* and *Hey Jude*. His versions have a peculiar melancholy appeal and are not, as some might think, sacrilegious.

JULIE FELIX, an American folk singer who was never a big seller in the United States, is one of England's biggest folk names with a tv show of her own and all sorts of kudos. She arrived in England just when England was thinking it would be nice to have a Joan Baez all of its own. It got one.

Albums/JULIE FELIX: *Masters Of War; Old Maids Song; Hey Nelly Nelly; Cu Cu Tu Cu Cu Paloma; Tarrytown; Go Tell Aunt Rhody; Pastures Of Plenty; Tell Old Bill; Ship In The Sky; Buttermilk Hill; Sally Don't You Grieve; Don't Think Twice; Riddle Song; Plane Crash At Los Gatos.* JULIE FELIX—SECOND ALBUM: *Someday Soon; Needle Of Death; The Young Ones Move; Guantanamera; Road Makers; I've Got Nothing But Time; Days Of Decision; You Won, I Lost; A Rumbling In The Land; When The Ship Comes In; Port Mahon; Space Girl; Judge Jeffries; Last Thing On My Mind.*

FEVER TREE/*Dennis Keller (vocals) John Tuttle (percussion), Michael (guitar), E. E. Wolfe III (bass), Rob Landes (piano, organ, harp, flute, bass recorder, clavinette, harpsichord, cello).*
They got together early in 1967, and by 1968 their album—with a Bach Toccata and Fugue on it and an old Wilson Pickett song and a version of the Beatles' *Day Tripper* (with all sorts of other Beatles songs collaged into it) and original material (by their producer-manager) with echoes of everyone from Dylan, Hendrix and Ravel's *Bolero*—zipped up into the charts proving, once and for all, that 1968 was a good year for nice cheerful eclecticism, as long as it was done with style.

Albums/FEVER TREE (August 1968): *Imitation Situation No. 1; Where Do You Go; San Francisco Girls (Return Of The Native); Ninety-Nine & One Half; Man Who Paints The Pictures; Filigree & Shadow; Sun Also Rises; Day Tripper; We Can Work It Out; Nowadays Clancy Can't Even Sing; Unlock My Door; Come With Me.* WHAT TIME DID YOU SAY IT IS IN SALT LAKE CITY (December 1968).

Singles/*Hey Mister/I Can Beat Your Drum; Girl, Oh Girl/ Steve Lenore; Come With Me/San Francisco Girls (Return Of The Native); What Time Did You Say It Is In Salt Lake City/Where Do You Go* (November 1968).

FEEDBACK/An accidental high-pitched sound, feedback comes out of the speaker when a microphone or guitar pickup is put too close to it. In other words, the sound goes into the microphone, out of the speaker and into the microphone again. Musicians, like public speakers, used to consider it a nuisance; now they have come to make this shrill, piercing noise work *for* them instead of against them. The Who's Peter Townshend saw how it could work to sustain a sound in an eerie manner. The Yardbirds insist the deliberate use of feedback is one of the distinguishing marks of *their* sound, and it may very well be so. It does no good to check it out on records since both groups were recording in England before they recorded in America, and besides, they were playing long before they recorded, so who knows who copied whom, if anyone copied anyone (which is doubtful). What has happened since, of course, everyone knows. Once Clapton, Jeff Beck, Peter Townshend, Jimi Hendrix and other guitarists took up feedback as the new sound, there was no stopping the imitators. Its eerie sound was perfect for the chilling messages of the Velvet Underground. Later it became the backbone of acid-rock groups from the Jefferson Airplane on. By 1968 it was horribly overdone, but still a mandatory part of the rock scene. Does feedback feed back? Yes, ad infinitum.

THE FIFTH DIMENSION/*Ron Townson (vocals), Lamonte Lemore (vocals), Marylin McCoo (vocals), Florence LaRue (vocals), Billy Davis (guitar, vocals).*
If white singers like Mick Jagger and Steve Winwood choose to sing black, then black singers like the Fifth Dimension

certainly have all the right in the world to sing white. They used to be known as the Hi-Fi's and sang nothing but blues. By the time they became the Fifth Dimension, late in 1966, they had the white Californian male-female vocal harmonies of a revved-up Mamas and Papas, and significantly, their first hit, *Go Where You Wanna Go,* was a Papa John Phillips composition. *Up, Up and Away,* which made top-of-the-chart stars of them and a young songwriter named Jim Webb, may have been the whitest sound ever produced by a black group. It enchanted a national airline that bought the rights to it and hired a group to sing it, much to the dismay of the Fifth Dimension, who thought *they* should have sung the airline's commercial version if it was going to sound *that* much like them (which it did). On their later hits (especially Laura Nyro's *Stoned Soul Picnic),* a blacker sound emerged. Which is the *real* Fifth Dimension? It doesn't really matter; both are doing very nicely in the big white clubs where the audiences love the voices almost as much as they love the shiny American-English mod gear that is a Fifth Dimension trademark.

Albums/UP UP AND AWAY (April 1967): *Up Up And Away; Another Day, Another Heartache; Which Way To Nowhere; California My Way; Misty Roses; Go Where You Wanna Go; Never Gonna Be The Same; Pattern People; Rosecrans Boulevard; Learn How To Fly; Poor Side Of Town.* THE MAGIC GARDEN (November 1967): *Prologue; The Magic Garden; Summer's Daughter; Dreams; Carpet Man; Ticket To Ride; Requiem; 820 Latham; The Girls' Song; The Worst That Could Happen; Orange Air; Paper Cup; Epilogue.* STONED SOUL PICNIC (July 1968): *The Sailboat Song; Sweet Blindness; It'll Never Be The Same Again; It's A Great Life; Stoned Soul Picnic; California Soul; Lovin' Stew; Broken Wing Bird; Good News; Bobbie's Blues; The Eleventh Song.*

Singles/*I'll Be Lovin' You Forever/Train, Keep On Movin'* (October 1966); *Go Where You Wanna Go/Too Poor To Die* (December 1966); *Another Day, Another Heartache/ Rosecrans Boulevard* (March 1967); *Up Up And Away/ Which Way To Nowhere* (May 1967); *Paper Cup/Poor Side Of Town* (October 1967); *Stoned Soul Picnic/The Sailboat*

Song (May 1968); *Bobby's Blues/Sweet Blindness* (September 1968); *California Soul/It'll Never Be The Same* (December 1968).

FIFTH ESTATE/*Rik Engler (vocals, kazoo, electric clarinet, violin, bass guitar), Duck Ferrar (vocals, guitar, string bass, fuzz bass), Wads Wadhams (electric harpsichord, electric piano, fuzz organ), Furvus Evans (drums, maracas, combines), D. William Shute (electric mandolin, fuzz guitar).*
The Fifth Estate is a rock group that revived *Ding Dong The Witch Is Dead* and got it to the top of the charts in 1967, which just goes to show there is a place for everything, even in an ultrasophisticated rock scene.

Album/DING DONG THE WITCH IS DEAD: *Ding Dong The Witch Is Dead; Kisses For Breakfast; I'm A Believer; Goofin' Song; Midnight Hour; Tomorrow Is My Turn; It's Waiting There For You; That's Love; Lost Generation; Rub-A-Dub; Birds And Bees; Number One Hippy On The Village Scene.*

Singles/*Ding Dong The Witch Is Dead/Rub-A-Dub; Goofin' Song; Tomorrow Is My Turn/Coney Island Sally; It's Waiting There For You.*

FLATT AND SCRUGGS (Lester Flatt and Earl Scruggs)/ Earl Scruggs' brilliant banjo work set the style for the much imitated bluegrass sound in the fifties. Lester Flatt sings. Although both men made first the country scene, then the folk circuits, their real fame came in 1968 after they did the soundtrack for the film *Bonnie and Clyde*. Their albums, mainly country and western, include a recent one devoted entirely to topical songs. Flatt and Scruggs were performing together for over twenty years, which must have been long enough since they decided to split up early in 1969.

Albums/COUNTRY MUSIC (April 1958). FOGGY MOUNTAIN JAMBOREE; SONGS OF GLORY (April 1960); FLATT AND SCRUGGS WITH THE FOGGY MOUNTAIN BOYS (August 1960); FOGGY MOUNTAIN BANJO (March 1961); SONGS OF THE FAMOUS CARTER FAMILY (October 1961); HARD TRAVELIN' (March 1963); FLATT AND SCRUGGS AT CARNEGIE

HALL (October 1963); FLATT AND SCRUGGS WITH
THE FOGGY MOUNTAIN BOYS (August 1964); THE
FABULOUS SOUND OF FLATT AND SCRUGGS (De-
cember 1964); PICKIN', STRUMMIN' AND SINGIN' (July
1965); KINGS OF BLUEGRASS (November 1965); TOWN
AND COUNTRY (February 1966); WHEN THE SAINTS
GO MARCHING IN (August 1966); FLATT AND
SCRUGGS' GREATEST HITS (November 1966); SACRED
SONGS (February 1967); FLATT AND SCRUGGS WITH
JIM AND JESSE; STRICTLY INSTRUMENTAL (June
1967); HEAR THE WHISTLES (August 1967); CHANGIN'
TIMES (March 1968); NASHVILLE AIRPLANE (Novem-
ber 1968): *Like A Rolling Stone; Folsom Prison Blues; Gentle
On My Mind; If I Were A Carpenter; Frieda Florentine; I'll
Be Your Baby Tonight; Rainy Day Women #12 & 35; Catch
The Wind; Long Road To Houston; The Times They Are
A-Changin'; Universal Soldier.* FOGGY MOUNTAIN
BREAKDOWN (December 1968): *Bouquet In Heaven; No
Mother Or Dad; Cora Is Gone; Pike Co. Breakdown;* Six
Other titles.

Singles/*Foggy Mountain Breakdown/My Cabin In Caroline;
Ballad Of Jed Clampett/Go Home; California Up Tight
Band/Last Train To Clarksville; Mama, You've Been On My
Mind/Last Thing On My Mind; Down In The Flood/Foggy
Mountain Breakdown.*

FLEETWOOD MAC/*Peter Green (lead guitar, vocals, mouth
organ), John McVie (bass guitar), Mick Fleetwood (drums),
Jeremy Spencer (lead guitar, vocals), Danny Kirwan (lead
guitar).*
Three of them came out of the purest, most uncompromising
of the English blues bands, John Mayall's Bluesbreakers. In
fact, Peter Green, who is one of England's best blues guitarists, was Eric Clapton's replacement when Clapton left Mayall. But pure blues is not what this group is doing. Since they
first got together in England in the summer of 1967, they
have done a lot of very unbluesy and commercial things like
funny takeoffs of Elvis and other rock heroes, a whole B. B.
King guitar thing by Peter Green, an Elmore James routine
by Jeremy Spencer ("Why not," he says, "he's the greatest,
isn't he?"), some earthy blues, some melodic blues and plenty

of early rock and roll. Their first American album featured mainly songs written by Green and Spencer, songs that could easily have been written by the old blues men they are only too happy to admit they copy note for note (one is an old Howlin' Wolf song and the other, James' classic *Shake Your Moneymaker*). They're probably the only blues group around with *three* lead guitarists, which only serves to give their music a greater scope.

In England they are part of a whole group of bands who function as a respectful repository for the American blues style, which is important there where they don't always have a chance to hear the originals. Ironically, as the interest in blues touched off by Cream grew in 1968, English blues bands like Fleetwood Mac did as well as the U.S. originals who had inspired them.

Albums/FLEETWOOD MAC (August 1968): *My Heart Beat Like A Hammer; Merry Go Round; Long Grey Mare; Hellhound On My Trail; Shake Your Moneymaker; Looking For Somebody; No Place To Go; My Baby's Good To Me; If I Loved Another Woman; Cold Black Night; The World Keeps On Turning; Got To Move.* ENGLISH ROSE (January 1969): *Stop Messin' 'Round; Jigsaw Puzzle Blues; Doctor Brown; Something Inside Of Me; Evenin' Boogie; Love That Burns; Black Magic Woman; I've Lost My Baby; One Sunny Day; Without You; Coming Home; Albatross.*

Singles/*Black Magic Woman/Long Grey Mare; Stop Messing 'Round/I Need Your Love So Bad* (September 1968).

EDDIE FLOYD/Another of the soulful soul singers out of the Stax studios in Memphis, Eddie Floyd is also a particularly talented songwriter for others and did *634–5789* for Wilson Pickett and a lot of material for Otis Redding and Carla Thomas. He was with the Falcons from 1955 to 1962, a group that started as gospel but switched to more commercial rhythm and blues. His biggest hit was *Knock On Wood*.

Albums/KNOCK ON WOOD: *Knock On Wood; Warm And Tender Love; I Stand Accused; Something You Got; If You Gotta Make A Fool Of Somebody; But It's Alright; I Don't Want To Cry; Raise Your Hand; Got To Make A Comeback;*

634–5789; I've Just Been Feeling Bad; Hi-Heel Sneakers.
I'VE NEVER FOUND A GIRL (November 1968).

Singles/*Good Love, Bad Love/Things Get Better; Knock On
Wood/Got To Make A Comeback; Raise Your Hand/I've
Just Been Feeling Bad; This House/Don't Rock The Boat;
Under My Nose/On A Saturday Night; I've Never Found A
Girl/I'm Just The King Of Fools; Bring It On Home To
Me/Sweet Things You Do* (October 1968).

FLYING BURRITO BROTHERS/*Gram Parsons (rhythm
guitar, vocals), Chris Hillman (rhythm guitar, mandolin),
Sneeky Pete (steel guitar), Chris Ethridge (bass, piano).*
Two of them, Parsons and Hillman, are ex-Byrds. Here
Hillman, who never stopped being a country boy, comes into
his own. Parsons, who gave the Byrds' *SWEETHEART OF
THE RODEO* much of its Western sound, does the same
again but better with the Flying Burrito Brothers, a splendidly
bespangled team dressed in early Hank Snow. In early 1969,
when the country rock sound dominated, the Flying Burrito
Brothers did it all bigger and better and more relaxed. Interestingly enough, although the group was extremely well
received and the country mood albums of the new Byrds and
Bob Dylan were also successful, few country artists (the
genuine Nashville kind) made the charts in this period.
(See BYRDS)

Album/THE GILDED PALACE OF SIN (March 1969):
*Christine's Tune; Sin City; Do Right Woman; Dark End Of
The Street; My Uncle; Wheels; Juanita; Hot Burrito #1;
Hot Burrito #2; Do You Know How It Feels; Hippie Boy.*

FOLK ROCK/Marrying rock to folk, blues, gospel, raga,
Bach or anything else you can think of is so much the thing to
do that it is difficult to recall those weeks in August and
September of 1965 when the idea of giving a folk song a rock
beat seemed blasphemous. Folk was integrity, purity, the
people. Rock was Tin Pan Alley, corruption, payola, the
Establishment. Who could have foretold then that the two
would meet? When Dylan sang with electricity for the first
time at the Newport Folk Festival and Forest Hills, it seemed
like a major sellout. There are still people who feel that way.

Actually, like everyone else, he was moving with the changin'
times. Before the Byrds came up with the first of the folk-
rock hits, *Mr. Tambourine Man,* rocking Dylan was as unlikely, as unsavory and easily as sacrilegious as producing a Hard
Rain's Gonna Fall Cha-Cha, a Masters of War Twist or a Girl
from the North Country Bossa Nova. But the Byrds were
different. The Byrds were mystic and holy. The Byrds could
do no wrong. And the rock they played wasn't Tin Pan Alley
but music from another planet. They could have rocked the
Bible and gotten away with it (and they did). *Newsweek*
called them Dylanized Beatles when the whole point was they
were Beatlized Dylans. In any case, the Byrds were first with
the new sound in March of 1965 when Dylan had already
recorded an electrical *Subterranean Homesick Blues* in
BRINGING IT ALL BACK HOME. After that, the folk
rockers came in droves. Sonny and Cher with nice imitation
Dylan like *I Got You Babe,* Donovan, more Byrds, Barry
McGuire's *Eve of Destruction* (rock protest), the Turtles' *It
Ain't Me Babe.*

1965 was the year of the folk rocker, the year when
1963–64 protest went pop and made the top of the charts. The
two biggest things in music in those years—the Beatles and
Dylan—had come together in an absolutely foolproof formula. By the end of 1965, everyone who had been into folk was
ready to go electric. By 1966, two new groups, the Lovin'
Spoonful and the Mamas and the Papas, had absorbed the
new form so completely, had built their sound so much on its
premise, that folk rock was taken for granted. Even to use the
word was passé. The new sound had arrived. It was ready to
move on to other things.

FOUNDATIONS/*Clem Curtis (vocals), Tim Harris (drums),
Peter Macbeth (bass guitar), Eric Allan Dale (trombone),
Allan Warner (lead guitar), Tony Gomez (organ), Pat Burke
(tenor sax), Mike Elliott (tenor sax)*
The English adore soul but have usually had to import it from
America. Now they have started growing their own. The
Foundations are three white Londoners, two Jamaicans, one
Trinidadian, one Dominican and one Ceylonese, whose first
release early in 1968, *Baby, Now That I've Found You,* was a
number one record in England and very soulful indeed. They

were one of the first English bands to add horns to the usual rock instruments.

Album/BABY, NOW THAT I'VE FOUND YOU (1968): *Baby, Now That I've Found You; I Can Take Or Leave Your Loving; Just A Little While Longer; Come On Back To Me; Love Is A Five Letter Word; Call Me; Show Me; Jerking The Dog; I'm A Whole New Thing; I've Seen The Writing On The Wall; Mr. Personality Man.*

Singles/*Baby, Now That I've Found You/Come Back To Me* (1968); *Back On My Feet Again/I Can Take Or Leave Your Loving; Any Old Time (You Are Lonely And Sad)/We Are Happy People.*

THE FOUR SEASONS/*Frankie Valli (vocals), Bob Gaudio (vocals), Tommy De Vito (vocals), Joe Long (vocals).*
From 1962 on, the Four Seasons sold far too well to the older generation to enchant the rock generation as much as did those groups it was able to discover and keep for itself. Nevertheless, they did sneak up on that segment of the listening and record-buying public from time to time. *Sherry* sold 180,000 copies in one day and *Big Girls Don't Cry* was a big hit from the teen-love period of rock, before the post-Beatle era of the erudite lyric. But with a sale of eighty million in the last six years, why should they care about erudite teens? They have recently released a "modern album" complete with protest, symbolic lyricism, and complex arrangement and orchestration. It was not well received.

Albums/BORN TO WANDER (January 1964): *Born To Wander; Don't Cry Elena; Ballad For Our Time; Where Have All The Flowers Gone; Cry Myself To Sleep; Silence Is Golden; New Town; Golden Ribbon; Little Pony Get Along; No Surfin' Today; Searching Wind; Millie.* DAWN (March 1964): *Big Man's World; You Send Me; Life Is But A Dream; Mountain High; Church Bells May Ring; Dawn (Go Away); Only Yesterday; Don't Let Go; Sixteen Candles; Breaking Up Is Hard To Do; Earth Angel; Do You Want To Dance.* RAG DOLL (July 1964): *Save It For Me; Touch Of You; Danger; Rag Doll; No One Cares; Marcie; Angel Cried; Funny Face; Huggin' My Pillow; On Broadway Tonight; Setting Sun; Ronnie.* FOUR SEASONS ENTERTAIN YOU

(March 1965): *Show Girl; Where Is Love; One Clown Cried; My Prayer; Little Darlin'; Bye Bye Baby; Betrayed; Somewhere; Living Just For You; Little Angel; Big Man In Town; Sunday Kind Of Love.* FOUR SEASONS SING BIG HITS (November 1965): *What The World Needs Now Is Love; Anyone Who Had A Heart; Always Something There To Remind Me; Make It Easy On Yourself; Walk On By; What's New Pussycat; Queen Jane Approximately; Mr. Tambourine Man; All I Really Want To Do; Blowin' In The Wind; Like A Rolling Stone; Don't Think Twice.* FOUR SEASONS GOLD VAULT OF HITS (November 1965): *Let's Hang On; Rag Doll; Ronnie; Big Man In Town; Silence Is Golden; Bye, Bye Baby; Dawn; Save It For Me; Girl Come Running; Betrayed; Toy Soldier; Cry Myself To Sleep.* WORKING MY WAY BACK TO YOU (December 1965): *Working My Way Back To You; Pity; I Woke Up; Living Just For You; Beggars Parade; One Clown Cried; Can't Get Enough Of My Baby; Sundown; Too Many Memories; Show Girl; Comin' Up In The World; Everybody Knows My Name.* LOOKING BACK (November 1966): *Silhouettes; Sincerely; Yes Sir, That's My Baby; Why Do Fools Fall In Love; Long Lonely Nights; Lucky Lady Bug; Since I Don't Have You; Teardrops; Tonight, Tonight; Honey Love; Happy, Happy Birthday Baby; Goodnight My Love (Pleasant Dreams).* FOUR SEASONS XMAS ALBUM (November 1966). FOUR SEASONS SECOND VAULT OF HITS (January 1967): *Sherry; Walk Like A Man; Candy Girl; Stay; Alone; Marlena; I've Got You Under My Skin; Big Girls Don't Cry; Working My Way Back To You; Opus 17 (Don't Worry 'Bout Me); Connie-O; Peanuts.* FOUR SEASONS NEW GOLD HITS (June 1967): *C'mon Marianne; Let's Ride Again; Beggin'; Around And Around; Goodbye Girl; I'm Gonna Change; Tell It To The Rain; Dody; Puppet Song; Lonesome Road.* GENUINE IMITATION LIFE (December 1968): *American Crucifixion Resurrection; Mrs. Stately's Garden; Look Up Look Over; Somebody's On Her Mind; Saturday's Father; Wall Street Village; Day Genuine Imitation Life; Idaho; Wonder What You'll Be; Soul Of A Woman.*

Singles/*Rag Doll/Ronnie; Marlena/Stay; Let's Hang On/ Working My Way Back To You; Goodbye Girl/Saturday's*

Father; Girl Come Running/Walk Like A Man; Dawn/Save It For Me; C'mon Marianne/Tell It To The Rain; Candy Girl/Peanuts; Bye, Bye Baby/I've Got You Under My Skin; Big Man In Town/Sherry; Big Girls Don't Cry/Opus 17; Beggin'/Watch The Flowers Grow; Around And Around/Connie-O; Alone/Will You Love Me Tomorrow.

THE FOUR TOPS/*Levi Stubbs Jr. (lead vocals), Renaldo "Obie" Benson (vocals), Abdul "Duke" Fakir (vocals), Lawrence Payton (vocals).*

In the fierce battle for supremacy between the Memphis sound of Stax and the Detroit sound of Motown, the Four Tops are Motown's biggest asset. When the pro-Memphis faction accuses Motown of producing "black muzak," computerized, slick, preplanned, predictable, commercialized emotion (as opposed to Memphis where it's all just allowed to happen), all the Detroit people have to do in return is point to the Four Tops. Certainly everything *around* the Four Tops is preplanned and blueprinted, but all this does is give the group a stable framework to work *against*. The resulting stress, as critic Jon Landau has pointed out, is what gives the Four Tops' work its excitement. They are like swimmers battling their way upstream against the current—and winning. In the beginning they must have been like a thousand other singing groups. They got together at high school in 1954 and battled for professional work until 1964, when the Motown "machine" gave them the backing and polish and purpose they needed. Their first release that year, *Baby I Need Your Loving,* was an immediate hit, all passions unleashed, a frantic cry for love (as are all their songs), and all the more so for being played against the restrained background of impeccable Motown arrangements.

And the Four Tops play it sophisticated, never stooping to cheap trickery, flashy costuming or any other distracting trappings. They come on stage beautifully rehearsed and disciplined and looking for all the world like a team of British bankers in their white shirts and well-cut suits. Then, when they *do* start flipping out (these seemingly sleek and polished entertainers), it comes with double the shock. You expect mad ravings from Little Richard and James Brown, but Levi Stubbs Jr.? Hardly. The Four Tops, more than anyone in rock, soul or whatever you want to call it today, have managed to find the perfect ratio of abandon and restraint. It transforms just about any song they care to pick up—*Standing In The Shadows Of Love, Shake Me, Wake Me, Bernadette, It's The Same Old Song* and, of course, their classic *Reach Out*, which, no matter where they sing it, has every hand in the audience reaching out for them in one great involuntary reflex. Just as Motown helped to establish the Four Tops, the Four Tops helped to establish Motown. They had an especially strong influence in London, and it was their enormous success with the English (everyone from the Beatles on) that, once and for all, turned younger American fans on to them. For every black musician who thinks the Tops and Motown have sold out to commercial values, there is a white fan for whom the Tops have opened up the door into the whole new rich world of black music. Their backings and arrangements alone are a musical education for anyone who as listened to little more than top-forty rock.

Albums/ FOUR TOPS (January 1965): *Baby I Need Your Loving; Without The One You Love; Where Did You Go; Ask The Lonely; Sad Souvenirs; Your Love Is Amazing; Don't Turn Away; Tea House In Chinatown; Left With A Broken Heart; Love Has Gone; Call On Me.* FOUR TOPS SECOND ALBUM (November 1965): *Something About You; I Can't Help Myself; It's The Same Old Song; Love Feels Like A Fire; Is There Anything I Can Do; Helpless; Just As Long As You Need Me; I Like Everything About You; Since You've Been Gone; Stay In My Lonely Arms; I'm Grateful.* ON TOP (July 1966): *Shake Me, Wake Me; Michelle; I Got A Feeling; Brenda; Loving You Is Sweeter Than Ever; Until You Love Someone; There's No Love Left; Matchmaker; In The Still Of The Night; Bluesette; Quiet Nights Of Quiet Stars; Then.* FOUR TOPS LIVE! (November 1966): *Reach Out, I'll Be There; You Can't Hurry Love; It's The Same Old Song; It's Not Unusual; Baby I Need Your Loving; I'll Turn To Stone; I Left My Heart In San Francisco; I Can't Help Myself; Ask The Lonely; Climb Ev'ry Mountain; If I Had A Hammer; I Like Everything About You.* FOUR TOPS ON BROADWAY (March 1967): *On The Street Where You Live; What Did I Have That I Don't*

Have; Make Someone Happy; Hello Broadway; Maria; Climb Ev'ry Mountain; Mame; I Want To Be With You; Sound Of Music; For Once In My Life; My Way; Nice 'N' Easy. REACH OUT (July 1967): *Reach Out I'll Be There; Standing In The Shadows Of Love; Bernadette; Seven Rooms Of Gloom; If I Were A Carpenter; Walk Away Renee; Last Train To Clarksville; I'll Turn To Stone; I'm A Believer; Cherish; What Else Is There To Do; Wonderful Baby.* FOUR TOPS GREATEST HITS (July 1967): *Shake Me, Wake Me; I Can't Help Myself; Ask The Lonely; Loving You Is Sweeter Than Ever; Baby I Need Your Loving; Seven Rooms Of Gloom; Bernadette; Something About You; It's The Same Old Song; Without The One You Love; Standing In The Shadows Of Love; Reach Out I'll Be There.* YESTERDAY'S DREAMS (August 1968): *Yesterday's Dreams; Can't Seem To Get You Out Of My Mind; I'm In A Different World; We've Got A Strong Love On Our Side; By The Time I Get To Phoenix; Remember When; Sonny; Never My Love; Daydream Believer; Once Upon A Time; The Sweetheart Tree; A Place In The Sun.*

Singles/*Baby I Need Your Loving/Call On Me* (July 1964); *Without The One You Love/Love Has Gone* (November 1964); *Ask The Lonely/Where Did You Go* (January 1965); *I Can't Help Myself/Sad Souvenirs* (April 1965); *It's The Same Old Song/Your Love Is Amazing* (July 1965); *Something About You/Darling, I Hum Our Song* (October 1965); *Shake Me, Wake Me/Just As Long As You Need Me* (February 1966); *Loving You Is Sweeter Than Ever/I Like Everything About You* (May 1966); *Reach Out I'll Be There/Until You Love Someone* (August 1966); *Standing In The Shadows Of Love/Since You've Been Gone* (November 1966); *Bernadette/I Got A Feeling* (February 1967); *Seven Rooms Of Gloom/I'll Turn To Stone* (May 1967); *You Keep Running Away/If You Don't Want My Love* (August 1967); *Walk Away Renee/Your Love Is Wonderful* (January 1968); *If I Were A Carpenter/Wonderful Baby* (April 1968); *Yesterday's Dreams/For Once In My Life* (June 1968); *Remember When/I'm In A Different World* (October 1968).

Also Appear On/BOSS GOLDIES (November 1966): *Ain't That Love.* 16 ORIGINAL BIG HITS, VOL 4: *Baby I Need*

Your Loving. VOL 6: *It's The Same Old Song.* VOL 7: *Shake Me, Wake Me.* VOL 8: *Loving You Is Sweeter Than Ever.*

ARETHA FRANKLIN/That she's America's best-selling female singer is not as important as why. In an age of cool, Aretha has made it cool to be hot. Musically, she's the epitome of unleashed female passion. She's what female singers have been trying for from time immemorial, but if you don't have it you can't sing it. And even if you do have it you can't always sing it. Aretha must have had it for the six years she was with Columbia, but she didn't sing it. She came on like a road-company Nancy Wilson, said Pete Hamill—all polish, no feeling. She moved to Atlantic, where her producer. Jerry Wexler, had cut his teeth on Ray Charles for six years and all that Charles passion—physical, moral and spiritual —is in there in Aretha, Lady Soul. In 1968 Aretha was only twenty-six when it was all unleashed. She does gospel shouts that are holy, then her voice husks up and she bashes you with it *Respect, You Make Me Feel Like a Natural Woman, Satisfaction*—they are all a great big raucous shout for women's rights, looking for love, getting it and suffering when you lose it, but always how good it is when you've got it. The suffering is important. At twenty-seven she's paid her dues.

Albums/ARETHA (March 1961): *Won't Be Long; Over The Rainbow; Love Is Long; Who Needs You; Right Now; Are You Sure; Maybe I'm A Fool; It Ain't Necessarily So; By Myself; Today I Sing The Blues.* ELECTRIFYING ARETHA FRANKLIN: *You Made Me Love You; I Told You So; Rockabye Your Baby With A Dixie Melody; Nobody Like You; Exactly Like You; It's So Heartbreakin'; Rough Lover; Blue Holiday; Just For You; That Lucky Old Sun; I Surrender Dear; Ac-Cent-Tchu-Ate The Positive.* TENDER, MOVING, SWINGING—ARETHA FRANKLIN (August 1962): *Don't Cry, Baby; Try A Little Tenderness; I Apologize; Without The One You Love; Look For The Silver Lining; I'm Sitting On Top Of The World; Just For A Thrill; God Bless The Child; I'm Wandering; How Deep Is The Ocean; I Don't Know You Anymore; Lover Come Back To Me.* LAUGHING ON THE *OUTSIDE* (August 1963): *Skylark; For All We Know; Make*

*Someone Happy; I Wonder (Where Are You Tonight);
Solitude; Laughing On The Outside; Say It Isn't So; Until The
Real Thing Comes Along; If Ever I Would Leave You; Where
Are You; Mr. Ugly; I Wanna Be Around.* UNFORGET-
TABLE (March 1964): *Unforgettable; Cold, Cold Heart;
What A Difference A Day Made; Drinking Again; Evil Gal
Blues; Nobody Knows The Way I Feel This Morning; Don't
Say You're Sorry Again; This Bitter Earth; If I Should Lose
You; Soulville.* SONGS OF FAITH (September 1964): *There
Is A Fountain Filled With Blood; You Grow Closer; Precious
Lord; Day Is Past And Gone; Never Grow Old; He Will
Wash You White As Snow; While The Blood Runs Warm;
Yield Not To Temptation.* RUNNIN' OUT OF FOOLS
(November 1964): *Mockingbird; How Glad I Am; Walk On
By; My Guy; Every Little Bit Hurts; Shoop Shoop Song;
You'll Lose A Good Thing; I Can't Wait Until I See My
Baby's Face; It's Just A Matter Of Time; Runnin' Out Of
Fools; Two Sides Of Love; One Room Paradise.* YEAH (May
1965): *This Could Be The Start Of Something; If I Had A
Hammer; Once In A Lifetime; More; Misty; There Is No
Greater Love; Love For Sale; Muddy Water; Today I Love
Everybody; Without The One You Love; Trouble In Mind;
Impossible.* SOUL SISTER (May 1966): *Until You Were
Gone; You Made Me Love You; Follow Your Heart; Ol'
Man River; Sweet Bitter Love; Mother's Love; Swanee; I'm
Losing You (No, No); Take A Look; Can't You Just See Me;
Cry Like A Baby.* TAKE IT LIKE YOU GIVE IT (March
1967): *Why Was I Born; I May Never Get To Heaven;
Tighten Up Your Tie, Button Up Your Jacket; Lee Cross;
Her Little Heart Went To Loveland; Take It Like You Give
It; Only The One You Love; Deeper; Remember Me; Land
Of Dreams; Little Bit Of Soul.* ARETHA FRANKLIN'S
GREATEST HITS (April 1967): *Running Out Of Fools;
Rock-A-Bye Your Baby With A Dixie Melody; Today I Sing
The Blues; Cry Like A Baby; Without The One You Love;
One Step Ahead; Evil Gal Blues; Try A Little Tenderness;
Sweet Bitter Love; God Bless The Child; If Ever I Would
Leave You.* I NEVER LOVED A MAN: *I Never Loved A
Man; Do Right Woman; Do Right Man; Respect; Drown In
My Own Tears; Soul Serenade; Don't Let Me Lose This
Dream; Baby, Baby, Baby; Dr. Feelgood; Good Times; Save*

Me; Change Is Gonna Come. ARETHA FRANKLIN'S
GREAT HITS, VOL. 2 (February 1968): *Lee Cross; Say It
Isn't So; Skylark; Take It Like You Give It; Take A Look;
Mockingbird; Soulville; Every Little Bit Hurts; Don't Cry,
Baby; Just For A Thrill.* ARETHA ARRIVES: *Baby I Love
You; Satisfaction; You Are My Sunshine; 96 Tears; Prove It;
Night Life; I Wonder; That's Life; Ain't Nobody; Going
Down Slow.* LADY SOUL (1968): *Chain Of Fools; Natural
Woman; Come Back Baby; Money Won't Change You; People Get Ready; Niki Hoeky; Since You've Been Gone; Good
To Me As I Am To You; Groovin'; Ain't No Way.* ARETHA
NOW (1968): *Think; You Send Me; I Say A Little Prayer;
See Saw; Night Time Is The Right Time; You're A Sweet
Sweet Man; I Take What I Want; Hello Sunshine; A Change;
I Can't See Myself Leaving You.* ARETHA IN PARIS
(1968): *Satisfaction; Don't Let Me Lose This Dream; Soul
Serenade; Night Life; Baby, I Love You; Groovin'; Natural
Woman; Come Back Baby; Dr. Feelgood; Since You've Been
Gone; I Never Loved A Man; Chain Of Fools; Respect.*

Singles/*Precious Lord* (2 Parts) (September 1964); Runnin'
Out Of Fools/Cry Like A Baby (1965); *Mother's Love/
Mockingbird* (April 1966); *Follow Your Heart/Take A Look*
(May 1966); *Do Right Woman, Do Right/I Never Loved A
Man The Way I Love You* (February 1967); *Lee Cross/Until
You Were Gone* (March 1967); *Dr. Feelgood/Respect* (April
1967); *Soulville/If Ever I Would Leave You* (April 1967);
Baby, I Love You/Going Down Slow (July 1967); *Baby,
Baby, Baby/Natural Woman* (September 1967); *Chain Of
Fools/Prove It* (November 1967); *Ain't No Way/Since You've
Been Gone* (February 1968); *House That Jack Built/I Say A
Little Prayer* (July 1968); *Think/You Send Me* (August 1968);
My Song/See Saw (November 1968).

ERMA FRANKLIN/Like her singing sister Aretha, 29-year-
old Erma socks and punches her way through songs like a
prizefighter. *Piece Of My Heart* was a memorable single
(1967) *before* Janis Joplin got to it in 1968. Some say Erma
did it better.

Singles/*Big Boss Man/Don't Catch The Dog's Bone* (1967);
Piece Of My Heart/Baby What You Want Me To Do

(1967); *I'm Just Not Ready For Love/Open Up Your Soul* (June 1968).

JOHN FRED AND THE PLAYBOY BAND/*John Fred (vocals, harmonica), Andrew Bernard (baritone sax), Ronnie Goodson (trumpet), Charlie Spin (trumpet), Jimmy O'Rourke (guitar), Harold Cowart (bass), Tommy De Generes (organ), Joe Micely (drums).*

John Fred had a big teenybopper hit with *Judy In Disguise* in March, 1968, a huge hard-rocking song that had clever words and echoes of *Lucy In The Sky*. Even the music snobs liked it a bit. But they didn't like him because they thought he was a one-hit artist, a one-teenybopper-hit artist. John Fred and his Playboys, from Baton Rouge, Louisiana, fall into the southern white rhythm and blues category (like the Box Tops, Bobbie Gentry and the Candymen). Their album *AGNES ENGLISH* was beautiful but in spite of the big hit didn't sell especially well. The high pop people are very snobbish about what they feel is low pop. But, as critic Robert Christgau pointed out, the Beatles started off by turning on twelve-year-olds.

Albums/JOHN FRED AND HIS PLAYBOYS (February 1968): *Boogie Children; When I Meet My Girl; How Can I Prove It; Can't I Get (A Word In); Out Of Sight; My Babe; Don't Fight It; Wrong To Me; Making Love To You; Play With Fire; Night Owl; Harlem Shuffle.* AGNES ENGLISH (February 1968): *Judy In Disguise; Off The Wall; Up & Down; Out Of Left Field; She Shot A Hole In My Soul; Most Unlikely To Succeed; Agnes English; When The Lights Go Out; No Good To Cry; Sometimes You Just Can't Win; Sad Story; Achenall Riot.* 34:40 (February 1968): *We Gotta Get Out Of This Place; Sun City; Leave Her Never; I've Been Loving You Too Long; Doing The Best I Can; Got To Get You Out Of My Life; Outta My Head; Knock On Wood; You're On My Mind; Down To The Boogaloo; Loves Come In Time; Something's Going On.* PERMANENTLY STATED (October 1968): *Little Dum Dum; We Played Games; Hey Hey Bunny; Surprise, Surprise; Lonely Are The Lonely; What Is Happiness; Mary Jane; Who Could Love You; Tissue Paper; Before The Change; Permanently Stated.*

Singles/*Up & Down/Wind Up Doll* (August 1967); *Agnes*

English/Sad Story (January 1968); *Judy In Disguise/When
The Lights Go Out* (March 1968); *Hey Hey Bunny/No
Letter Today* (May 1968); *We Played Games/Lonely Are
The Lonely* (June 1968); *Little Dum Dum/Tissue Paper*
(October 1968); *Sometimes You Just Can't Win/What Is
Happiness* (November 1968).

FREDDIE AND THE DREAMERS/Because they were doing it all in England just about the time the Beatles emerged
in 1962 and 1963, it has been popular in some circles to say
that Freddie and the Dreamers could have been the Beatles
with a little more luck and a little more pushing and a little
more help from their friends. That is, they could have been up
there at the top, the group from which all others were
destined to draw nourishment. But all that these people were
saying was that at the time the Beatles were coming to the
fore, literally hundreds of other English groups played better
music, Freddie and the Dreamers among them. In the end,
though, the Beatles did it and the Dreamers didn't. The
Dreamers had two big hits, *The Freddie,* which introduced a
new dance, and *I'm Telling You Now.* They remained
bouncy, mildly popular, very danceable but never at any time
managed to rise to the rarefied levels that made the Beatles
stars.

Albums/FRANTIC FREDDIE (January 1966): *Windmill
In Old Amsterdam; Short, Shorts; Zip-A-Dee-Do-Dah; Drink
This Up, It'll Make You Sleep; Crying; Camptown Races;
How's About Trying Your Luck With Me; Cut Across Shorty;
Jailer Bring Me Water; I'm A Hog For You; What'd I Say;
See You Later, Alligator.*

Also Appear On/I'M TELLING YOU NOW: *I'm Telling
You Now; What Have I Done To You.* THREE AT THE
TOP: *I'm Telling You Now; You Were Made For Me; What
Have I Done To You; Send A Letter To Me.* SUPER
OLDIES, VOL. 2 (September 1966): *I'm Telling You Now.*
INSTANT REPLAY (February 1969): *I'm Telling You
Now; You Were Made For Me.*

Singles/*The Freddie; I'm Telling You Now.*

THE FUGS/*Ed Sanders (vocals), Ken Weaver (vocals,*

drums, routines), Tuli Kupferberg (vocals, function), Ken Pine (vocals, guitar), Bill Wolf (bass), Bob Mason (drums).
Chorus: Leslie Dorsey, Bob Dorough, Barbara Calabria, Marlys Trunkhill, Bob Hanson, James Jarvis, Kenneth Bates, Earl Baker, Jennifer Brown, Doug Franklin (conductor).
Previous Members: John Anderson, Vinny Leary, Peter Stampfel, Steve Weber, Lee Crabtree, Pete Kearney, Betsy Klein, Allen Ginsberg, Dan Kootch, Maretta Greer, Gregory Corso.
Who could start to describe the Fugs? In the beginning people couldn't even believe their name was for real—and if it was, their performance couldn't possibly live up to what that name implied. Didn't it just? They first started out in a very small theatre on St. Mark's Place, a team of assorted East Village poets and other types who had decided to sing some of the poetry they were writing (why not? everyone else did), and to follow to logical and honest conclusions what other popular songs were perenially hinting at and skirting around. At that stage, it was unthinkable for poets to form a rock group, and especially freaky-looking poets. (No one was to know then that within a few years a group that didn't look freaky wouldn't stand a chance.) When they moved to the Village's main drag on MacDougal Street, they marked up something like nine hundred performances in a row. In any case, they were the first of the underground rock groups, the first of the rock-satire groups (and no one has equaled them, not even the Mothers, with whom they're sometimes confused and who, in fact, do something quite different).

Someone said the Fugs were the Lenny Bruces of music. Certainly, right from the start they went out of their way to be "offensive," particularly on such musically taboo subjects as explicit physical sex and drugs. (Songs like *I Couldn't Get High* and *Coca Cola Douche* were the rule, not the exception). Like Bruce, they are comics and satirists, except that they happen to have come up with some beautiful lyrics (on both beautiful and unbeautiful subjects) and all kinds of melodic tunes, though they never pretend to be great musicians. They are outrageous at every turn—outrageous in their obscene gestures on stage, outrageous in their use of taboo four-letter words (to be heard even on their first album, in which they are blipped out only now and then), outrageous in their hippiness, their honesty, and outrageous in their pacifism (with songs like *Kill For Peace*). Later, when it became fashionable to be outrageous (and they preceded that), they found themselves on the cover of Establishment publications like *Life* and the *Saturday Evening Post*. All this time they never stopped working on their various projects as individuals, as East Village leaders, poets and political figures. But they were continually touring and adding to their repertoire. Much much later, in 1968, Beatle George Harrison talked of breaking the four-letter barrier in pop songs, and other groups started tentatively using pale versions of their crunching satire. But no one was able to reproduce the lushness of Fugs lyrics, and particularly the lushness of Fug pornography. It was like Henry Miller's novels set to music. And it was theatre too. About ten years from now, and not before, it will suddenly be clear how much ahead of their time the Fugs were.

Albums/THE FUGS FIRST ALBUM: *Slum Goddess; Sunflower Weary Of Time; Supergirl; Swineburne Stomp; I Couldn't Get High; How Sweet I Roamed From Field To Field; Seize The Day; My Baby Done Left Me; Boobs A Lot; Nothing.* THE FUGS: *Frenzy; I Want To Know; Skin Flowers; Group Grope; Coming Down; Dirty Old Man; Kill For Peace; Morning, Morning; Doin' All Right; Virgin Forest.* THE VIRGIN FUGS: *We're The Fugs; New Amphet Amine Shriek; Saran Wrap; The Ten Commandments; Hallucination Horrors; I Command The House Of The Devil; C.I.A. Man; Coca Cola Douche; My Bed Is Getting Crowded; Caca Rocka; I Saw The Best Minds Of My Generation Rot.* TENDERNESS JUNCTION: *Turn On/Tune In/Drop Out; Knock Knock; The Garden Is Open; Wet Dream; Hare Krishna; Exorcising The Evil Spirits From The Pentagon, October 21, 1967; War Song; Dover Beach; Fingers Of The Sun; Aphrodite Mass.* IT CRAWLED INTO MY HAND, HONEST (October 1968): *Crystal Liaison; Ramses II Is Dead, My Love; Burial Waltz; Wide Wide River; Life Is Strange; Johnny Pissoff Meets The Red Angel; Marijuana; Leprechaun; When The Mode Of The Music Changes; Whimpers From The Jello; The Divine Toe* (Part I); *We're Both Dead Now, Alice; Life Is Funny; Grope Need* (Part I); *Tuli,*

Visited By The Ghost Of Plotinus; More Grope Need (Grope Need-Part II); Robinson Crusoe; Claude Pellieu And J. J. Lebel Discuss The Early Verlaine Bread Crust Fragments; The National Haiku Contest; The Divine Toe (Part II); *Irene.*

Single/*Frenzy/I Want To Know.*

FUTURE ROCK/Some people believe that by 2001 rock will be entirely machine-made. Machines will be programmed so that combinations of different sounds will be left to chance. At-home listeners will have controls that will make it possible for them to "produce" a record—speed it up, slow it down, make it louder and softer, and separate the tracks, adding, subtracting, overdubbing—to create their own version of a hit. There will be no live performances, no stages. Music will be heard with a small circle of friends, not with a group of strangers. The sound will possibly be closest to that of the United States of America, an electronic-rock group. So many groups of the sixties have gone after a future-rock sound, however (the Byrds in their explorations of jets and space; the Jefferson Airplane in its explorations of the mind), that 2001 may very well bring a reaction against these "prophetic" sounds and move into something quite different, perhaps more along the line of Oriental music. Already the sitar, which was regarded as "boring" by musically uneducated westerners, has been taken up—and discarded. Thousands of fads are sure to come and go before 2001. There will probably be no more records, just tapes sold in combinations that can be mixed and mingled. And there will be Sunday producers (like Sunday painters) playing with sound on their home sets. Then it will be possible to have the Byrds and Beatles singing together with the New York Philharmonic. Or Aretha Franklin and Donovan and the New Lost City Ramblers. The sort of thing that has been happening informally in jam sessions, and more formally on the *SUPER SESSION* albums, the mixing of performers who don't usually play together, will be taken for granted on tape.

FUZZ BOX/Originally invented to give the guitar a saxophone sound, it is a small box operated by foot, which, when connected to the instrument, gives it fuzz tone, a fuzzy, distorted sound that "fills" gaps and creates a new dimension in playing—and listening. The Yardbirds, being the first really experimental group, were the first to use it (then it became popular with many lead guitarists—Eric Clapton, Jeff Beck, Jimi Hendrix), but it gained real fame when the Rolling Stones used it in *Satisfaction*. Since then it's been used, but more frequently abused, by most groups.

MARVIN GAYE/He started his singing career in a church choir (it seems to be a good place to start), became one of the Moonglows and eventually joined Motown as a solo artist in 1961. He racked up an impressive number of hits, got to play the Copa in the best Motown tradition and was recently named top rhythm and blues vocalist by *Cashbox* magazine.

Albums/SOULFUL SOUNDS OF MARVIN GAYE (June 1961). THAT STUBBORN KINDA' FELLOW (January 1963): *That Stubborn Kinda' Fellow; Hitch Hike; It Hurt Me Too; Soldier's Plea; I'm Yours, You're Mine; Hello There Angel; Get My Hands On Some Lovin'; Taking My Time; Pride And Joy; Wherever I Lay My Hat.* LIVE ON STAGE (September 1963): *Stubborn Kinda' Fellow; Hitch Hike; One Of These Days; Days Of Wine And Roses; You Are My Sunshine.* WHEN I'M ALONE I CRY (April 1964): *You've Changed; I Was Telling Her About You; I Wonder; I'll Be Around; Because Of You; I Don't Know Why; I've Grown Accustomed To Her Face; When Your Lover Has Gone; When I'm Alone I Cry; If My Heart Could Sing.* GREATEST HITS (April 1964): *Pride And Joy; Stubborn Kinda' Fellow; Can I Get A Witness; You're A Wonderful One; One Of These Days; I'm Crazy 'Bout My Baby; I'm Yours, You're Mine; Hitch Hike; It Hurt Me Too; Hello There Angel; Taking My Time; Sandman.* HELLO BROADWAY (November 1964): *Walk On The Wild Side; What Kind Of Fool Am I; Party's Over; Days Of Wine And Roses; People; My Way; On The Street Where You Live; Hello, Dolly; Hello Broadway; My Kind Of Town; This Is The Life.* HOW SWEET IT IS (January 1965): *How Sweet It Is (To Be Loved By You); Try It Baby; Baby Don't You Do It; You're A Wonderful*

*One; Now That You've Won Me; Me & My Lonely Room;
Need Somebody; Stepping Closer To Your Heart; No Good
Without You; One Of These Days; Need Your Lovin'; For-
ever.* A TRIBUTE TO THE GREAT NAT KING COLE
(November 1965): *Nature Boy; Ramblin' Rose; Too Young;
Pretend; Straighten Up & Fly Right; Mona Lisa; Unforgetta-
ble; To The Ends Of The Earth; Sweet Lorraine; It's Only A
Paper Moon; Send For Me; Calypso Blues.* MOODS OF
MARVIN GAYE (May 1966): *Take This Heart Of Mine;
Little Darling; I Worry 'Bout You; Ain't That Peculiar; I'll Be
Doggone; One More Heartache; Hey Diddle Diddle; Night
Life; You've Been A Long Time Coming; Your Unchanging
Love; You're The Only One For Me; One For My Baby.*
TAKE TWO (with Kim Weston) (August 1966): *It Takes
Two; I Love You, Yes I Do; Baby I Need Your Loving; It's
Got To Be A Miracle; Baby Say Yes; What Good Am I
Without You; Till There Was You; Love Fell On Me; Secret
Love; I Want You 'Round; Heaven Sent You I Know;
When.* UNITED (Recorded with Tammi Terrell) (August
1967): *Ain't No Mountain High Enough; You Got What It
Takes; If I Could Build My World Around You; Somethin'
Stupid; Your Precious Love; Hold Me Oh My Darling; Two
Can Have A Party; Little Ole Blue, Little Ole Girl; If This
World Were Mine; Sad Wedding; Give A Little Love; Oh How
I'd Miss You.* GREATEST HITS, VOL. 2 (August 1967): *Try
It Baby; Baby Don't You Do It; How Sweet It Is (To Be
Loved By You); I'll Be Doggone; Pretty Little Baby; Ain't
That Peculiar; One More Heartache; Take This Heart Of
Mine; Little Darling; Forever; Hey Diddle Diddle; Your
Unchanging Love.* YOU'RE ALL I NEED TO GET BY
(Recorded with Tammi Terrell) (August 1968): *You're All I
Need To Get By; Ain't Nothing Like The Real Thing; Keep
On Lovin' Me Honey; Baby Dontcha Worry; You Ain't Livin'
Till You're Lovin'; Give In, You Can't Win; When Love
Comes Knockin' At My Heart; Come On And See Me; I
Can't Help But Love You; I'll Never Stop Loving You;
Memory Chest.* IN THE GROOVE (August 1968): *You;
Tear It Down; I Heard It Through The Grapevine; At Last;
Some Kind Of Wonderful; Loving You Is Sweeter Than Ever;
It's Love I Need; Change What You Can; Every Now &
Then; You're What's Happening; There Goes My Baby.*

Singles/*Let Your Conscience Be Your Guide*/*Never Let You Go* (May 1961); *Sandman*/*I'm Yours, You're Mine* (January 1962); *Soldier's Plea*/*Taking My Time* (May 1962); *Stubborn Kind Of Fellow*/*It Hurt Me Too* (July 1962); *Hitch Hike*/*Hello There Angel* (December 1962); *Pride And Joy*/*One Of These Days* (April 1963); *Can I Get A Witness*/*Crazy About My Baby* (September 1963); *You're A Wonderful One*/*When I'm Alone I Cry* (February 1964); *Try It Baby*/*If My Heart Could Sing* (May 1964); *Baby Don't You Do It*/*Walk On The Wild Side* (September 1964); *What Good Am I Without You*/*I Want You 'Round* (September 1964); *How Sweet It Is*/*Forever* (November 1964); *I'll Be Doggone*/*You've Been A Long Time Coming* (February 1965); *Pretty Little Baby*/*Now That You Won Me* (June 1965); *Ain't That Peculiar*/*She's Got To Be Real* (September 1965); *One More Heartache*/*When I Had Your Love* (January 1966); *Take This Heart Of Mine*/*Need Your Lovin'* (May 1966); *Little Darling (I Need You)*/*Hey Diddle Diddle* (July 1966); *It Takes Two*/*It's Got To Be A Miracle* (December 1966); *Ain't No Mountain High Enough*/*Give A Little Love* (April 1967); *Your Unchanging Love*/*I'll Take Care Of You* (June 1967); *Your Precious Love*/*Hold Me Oh My Darling* (August 1967); *You*/*Change What You Can* (December 1967); *If I Could Build My Whole World Around You*/*If This World Were Mine* (November 1967); *Ain't Nothing Like The Real Thing*/*Little Ole Boy, Little Ole Girl* (March 1968); *You're All I Need To Get By*/*Two Can Have A Party* (July 1968); *Chained*/*At Last (I Found A Love)* (August 1968); *What's The Matter With You Baby*/*Once Upon A Time; At Last*/*Chained* (September 1968); *Keep On Lovin' Me Honey*/*You Ain't Livin' Till You're Lovin'* (October 1968); *I Heard It Through The Grapevine*/*You're What's Happening* (November 1968).

Also Appears On/16 ORIGINAL HITS: VOL 1, *Stubborn Kind Of Fellow; Pride & Joy*. VOL 2, *Hitch Hike*. VOL 3, *Can I Get A Witness; You're A Wonderful One*. VOL 4, *I'm Crazy 'Bout My Baby; Try It Baby*. VOL 5, *I'll Be Doggone*. VOL 6, *Ain't That Peculiar*. VOL 7, *I'll Be Doggone*. VOL 8, *Your Unchanging Love*.

BOBBIE GENTRY/She took us by surprise that summer of

1967 with a story of death on the Tallahatchie Bridge that took her right to the number one spot on the charts. She was a California girl who had spent her early years in Chickasaw County, Mississippi, where her *Ode To Billie Joe* was set. In fact, though she never did reveal what had been thrown over the bridge in the song (a baby, it was rumored by some; a ring, said others), there were many indications that the tragic story of Billie Joe was a true one, and one close to her. The song was well written and well sung (so soulfully that, at first, everyone was convinced Miss Gentry was black) and a sensation till it was killed by overplay on the air. But the real sensation was Miss Gentry, a true beauty—tall, leggy, long-haired, photogenic. She never did come up with anything that got even close to matching *Billie Joe,* but she did win a Grammy that year, and in June of 1968 she revealed she was booked up till the following February. There was a color tv series in England, films, Las Vegas. Bobbie Gentry didn't have another hit but she didn't *need* one. The success of her record proved that there is a huge audience for a good country song, and there always has been.

Albums/ODE TO BILLIE JOE (September 1967): *Mississippi Delta; I Saw An Angel Die; Chickasaw County Child; Sunday Best; Niki Hoeky; Ode To Billie Joe; Papa, Won't You Let Me Go To Town With You; Bugs; Hurry, Tuesday Child; Lazy Willie.* DELTA SWEETIE (February 1968): *Okolona River Bottom Band; Big Boss Man; Reunion; Parchman Farm; Mornin' Glory; Sermon; Tobacco Road;* **Penduli** *Pendulum; Jessye' Lisabeth; Refractions; Courtyard;* **Louisiana Man.**

Singles/*Requiem For Love/Stranger In The Mirror* (with Jody Reynolds) (1966); *Boney And Claude/Sugar* (with the Geezinslaw Brothers) (1966); *Mississippi Delta/Ode To Billie Joe* (July 1967); *Louisiana Man/Courtyard* (December 1967); *Okolona River Bottom Band/Penduli Pendulum* (December 1967); *Hushabye Mountain/Sweete Peony.*

BOB GIBSON/A prolific folk singer who dates back to the early folk revival of the middle fifties. He faded out later only to re-emerge in 1969 for some club dates. Although he is almost unknown by a whole new musical generation, you only have to listen to his albums to know how much he influenced just about everyone else who came into the folk scene and, then, out of that scene into rock. Probably only Pete Seeger had more influence than Gibson.

GOD ROCK/Those who wonder if rock may yet become the new religious medium (and probably message) should listen thoughtfully to the Electric Prunes' *MASS IN F MINOR,* the Association's *Requiem For The Masses* and the Gregorian Chant sounds to be found on BeeGees and Simon and Garfunkel tracks. Bob Dylan's songs are full of seemingly religious references, as are several of the songs on his band's album *MUSIC FROM BIG PINK.* There are several intelligent, well-read men, both in the U.S. and in England, who believe God is speaking to the world through Beatles songs, especially *Lady Madonna* and *Hey Jude* (no one has made that claim for the Rolling Stones). At the funeral of English playwright Joe Orton, the Beatles' *A Day In The Life* was played instead of the usual funeral music, and it seemed more appropriate than Bach for a young man who died in 1968.

BARRY GOLDBERG/Organist with the Electric Flag and before that with the Paul Butterfield Blues Band, Goldberg left to form his own group, the Barry Goldberg Blues Band, and recorded *BLOWING MY MIND.* Then, as more and more groups split up, more and more musicians slipped out of the comparative obscurity of groups into the limelight of solo careers—and so did Barry Goldberg. His next album, *BARRY GOLDBERG RÉUNION,* was made with musicians he'd worked with in the past, though not in any sense *his* band or *a* band. This bringing together of musicians for an album, rather than for an extended touring career, was one of the ideas that came out of the chaos of late 1968—a revolutionary idea doing away with old concepts of rigid group format and encouraging more flexible, less pemanent arrangements.

Albums/BLOWING MY MIND: *Gettin' It Down; Mean Old World; Twice A Man; Whole Lotta Shakin' Goin' On; Put Me Down; Big Boss Man; Blowing My Mind; That'll Be The Day; Can't Stand To See You Go; Think.* BARRY GOLD-BERG REUNION (October 1968): *Fool On The Hill; Sittin' In Circles; Hole In My Pocket; It Hurts Me Too; Capricorn*

Blues; Sugar Coated Lover; Strung And Young; I Think I'm Gonna Cry; Answers In Your Head. TWO JEWS' BLUES (March 1969): *You're Still My Baby; That's Alright, Mama; Maxwell Street Shuffle; Blues For Barry And; Jimi The Fox; A Lighter Blue; On The Road Again; Twice A Man; Spirit Of Trane.*

Single/*Sittin' In Circles/Hole In My Pocket* (October 1968).

GOLDIE AND THE GINGERBREADS were one of the few all-girl groups to get any attention. They came on very tough, and for a time, during the big dancing craze of the middle sixties, if you were a jet-setter and a with-it party giver like photographer Jerry Schatzberg, and the Rolling Stones came to your parties, the group you had providing the music was invariably Goldie and her Gingerbreads. She went to England for a while, and when she returned the dance boom had died down, the big party boom had died down and all-girl groups were having as rough a time of it as ever.

Singles/*That's Why I Love You/What Kind Of Man Are You* (May 1965); *Please, Please/Think About The Good Times* (July 1966); *Song Of The Moon/Walking In Different Circles* (March 1967).

ROOSEVELT GOOK/Whatever happened to "Rosie" Gook? is a question often asked in musical circles. He played piano on Tom Rush's *Take A Little Walk With Me* but has never been heard from since that day. His style reminds many people of Bob Dylan in earlier Minnesota piano-playing days, but there are those who detect Gookian overtones when former Blood, Sweat and Tears lead singer and now producer Al Kooper sits at the piano and plays. There are some mysteries that remain unsolved. The Musicians' Union does not have him listed.

GOODTIME MUSIC/It started to invade rock about the time that folk people moved in on electric music. The Lovin' Spoonful provided the most notable examples of goodtime music, their single, *Daydream* (1966), being the classic. After the Spoonful, most of the big bands had one goodtimey song in their live repertoire, if not always on record. The

Beatles' *Good Day Sunshine* (1966) is in a goodtimey mood, with its suggestion of country strings. The Sopwith Camel hinted at goodtime but moved into high camp like the New Vaudeville Band, which was all banjos and jokes. It's sometimes difficult to know where goodtime music ends and simply good times start. Whether the Kinks' *Sunny Afternoon* (1967) is goodtime music or not can be argued endlessly. Small Faces' *Lazy Sunday* (1968) is. The goodtime sound never became quite the big seller it looked like it would be early in 1966, but it has sneaked into a lot of American rock.

JIM GORDON is a drummer who went to Los Angeles three years ago, started playing on record sessions and hasn't had a vacation since. In an age when drummers tend to overplay, he is all restraint and taste. People cancel sessions for weeks to get Gordon. He has played on Mamas and Papas albums and is reported to have used fifteen tom-toms on the Fifth Dimension's *Stoned Soul Picnic*.

LESLEY GORE/In her day (1963) she was the reigning queen of teen-suffering then so musically fashionable (and commercially successful) on Tin Pan Alley. For a whole summer she bleated *It's My Pa-a-arty and I'll Cry If I Want To* and the song shot to the top of the charts as a million or so teen buyers empathized with the plight of being dumped on. The rule then for female singers was for the voice to be insistently high, penetrating and shrewish (a steal, consciously or otherwise, from country and western music in which the women sing darkly of sin and retribution in a voice that cuts right into the male conscience.) You could savor every bitchy second of Lesley's triumph with her sequel *Judy's Turn To Cry*. It took the Beatles to put a finish to shrill female nastiness. And from 1964 on, there was a long period of reaction against almost any female singer who was noisy about it. As America grew out of that sort of thing, so did Lesley Gore, who took herself off to college for a little educational, emotional and presumably musical gentling.
Albums/I'LL CRY IF I WANT TO (June 1963): *It's My Party; Cry Me A River; Cry; Just Let Me Cry; Cry & You Cry Alone; No More Tears; Judy's Turn To Cry; I Understand; I Would; Misty; What Kind Of Fool Am I; Party's*

Over. LESLEY GORE SINGS OF MIXED-UP HEARTS
(October 1963): *She's A Fool; Old Crowd; Fools Rush In;
My Foolish Heart; Young Lovers; You Don't Own Me;
Sunshine, Lollipops And Rainbows; Young And Foolish; Run,
Bobby, Run; I Struck A Match; If That's The Way You Want
It; Time To Go.* BOYS, BOYS, BOYS (April 1964): *That's
The Way Boys Are; Boys; It's Gotta Be You; Something
Wonderful; You Name It; Danny; I Don't Wanna Be A
Loser; That's The Way The Ball Bounces; Leave Me Alone;
I'll Make It Up To You; Don't Call Me; I'm Coolin', No
Foolin'.* GOLDEN HITS OF LESLEY GORE (June 1965):
*It's My Party; She's A Fool; Judy's Turn To Cry; Just Let Me
Cry; All Of My Life; You Don't Own Me; That's The Way
Boys Are; I Don't Wanna Be A Loser; Maybe I Know; Hey
Now; Look Of Love; Sunshine, Lollipops And Rainbows.*
LESLEY GORE SINGS ALL ABOUT LOVE (January
1966): *Young Love; I Won't Love You Anymore; With Any
Other Girl; Too Young; Start The Party Again; That's What
I'll Do; Only Last Night; To Know Him Is To Love Him; I
Can Tell; We Know We're In Love; Will You Love Me
Tomorrow; I Just Can't Get Enough Of You.* CALIFORNIA
NIGHTS (April 1967): *California Nights; Love Goes On
Forever; Treat Me Like A Lady; Bad; I'm Going Out (The
Same Way I Came In); Maybe Now; Off And Running;
Lilacs And Violets; Bubble Broke; Cry Like A Baby.* GIRL
TALK (October 1967): *Hey Now; Look Of Love; Wonder
Boy; Live And Learn; Say Goodbye; 5 Other Titles.* GOLD-
EN HITS OF LESLEY GORE, VOL. 2 (October 1968):
*California Nights; Off And Running; Love Goes On Forever;
Summer And Sunday; I Won't Love You Anymore (Sorry);
My Town, My Guy And Me; He Loves Me (La La La);
Young Love; We Know We're In Love; Brink Of Disaster; I
Can't Make It Without You.*

Singles/*It's My Party*/*She's A Fool* (1963); *Judy's Turn To
Cry*/*You Don't Own Me* (1963); *Brink Of Disaster*/*On A
Day Like Today; It's A Happening World*/*Magic Colors*
(November 1967); *Brand New Me*/*He Gives Me Love (La
La La); Say What You See*/*Small Talk* (February 1968);
Look The Other Way/*I'll Be Standing By* (November 1968).

GRAPEFRUIT/*George Alexander (bass guitar), John Perry*

(lead guitar), Pete Swettenham (rhythm guitar), Geoff Swet-tenham (drums).
Grapefruit was the first rock group to come out of the Beatles' own company, Apple Corps. Launched at a star-studded party late in 1967, they turned out to be four personable, perky little English pixies. They made their debut in the spring of 1968 (at the bottom of a distinguished bill headed by the BeeGees) wearing grapefruit yellow suits and jaunty smiles. Their sound was fresh and young to match. At later concerts, like naughty schoolboys, they took to rolling autographed grapefruits down the aisles. After so much publicity and a couple of hits (written by bass player George Alexander), there was the inevitable slowdown. Were the Grapefruit just a Beatles hype? Not really, said the Grape-fruit, settling down to *real* work. It was just a matter of too much, too soon. No group with George Alexander could possibly ever bomb. And the Beatles know it.

Single/*Ain't It Good/C'mon Marianne* (October 1968).

THE GRATEFUL DEAD/*Jerry Garcia (lead guitar), Phil Lesh (bass), Ron "Pig Pen" McKernan (conga drums, harp), Bob Weir (rhythm guitar), Mikey Hart (replaced Bill Som-mers) (drums), Bill Kruetzmann (drums), Tom Constanten (organ).*
They were not so much a band as a social institution. It would be impossible to tell the story of the Grateful Dead without telling the story of what happened when love hit San Francis-co in 1966, just as it would be impossible to talk about that period of San Francisco without talking about the Dead. The two were inextricably intertwined. Most bands tend to live an existence somewhat removed from their fans. The Dead lived right in Haight-Ashbury where it all started. They were an integral part of the community.

They didn't, as might be expected, play what we now call acid or psychedelic rock but instead produced fine, strong, straightforward traditional blues. (Much of the San Francisco music of that period came out of blues, but because of the whole psychedelic coloring of that culture, moved out of blues into the wilder realms of acid rock.) Nevertheless, their *ANTHEM OF THE SUN* album is said to be a good com-panion for an acid trip. They were a performing rather than a recording band and are still uneasy in a studio setting. Their contribution to the free society of San Francisco was the free concert. They must have given more free concerts than any band in the history of music. For this, and all sorts of other nonmusical reasons, they were San Francisco heroes. And their unwillingness to play the rock game with a record company (which earned them the name inside the business of the Ungrateful Dead) endeared them even further to their anti-Establishment fans. San Francisco is prouder of them than of the scores of other local groups that are considered to have sold out in one way or another. As for their influence, it could be said that just about every band that has ever given a free concert, and certainly every *name* band that has, has been influenced directly by the Dead.

Albums/THE GRATEFUL DEAD (March 1967): *Golden Road (To Unlimited Devotion); Cold Rain And Snow; Good Morning, Little School Girl; Beat It On Down The Line; Sitting On Top Of The World; Cream Puff War; Morning Dew; New, New Minglewood Blues; Viola Lee Blues.* ANTHEM OF THE SUN (August 1968): *That's It For The Other One; Cryptical Envelopment; Quadlibet For Tenderfeet; The Faster We Go The Rounder We Get; New Potato Caboose; Born Cross-eyed; Alligator; Caution (Do Not Stop On Tracks).*

Single/*Born Cross-eyed/Dark Star* (April 1968).

GREAT SOCIETY/*Grace Slick (vocals), Darby Slick (lead guitar), Jerry Slick (drums), David Minor (rhythm guitar), Peter Vandegilder (bass).*
A band that was one of the originators of the zonked-out folk-rock sound that eventually became known as "acid rock" or the "San Francisco sound." Great Society's claim to fame today is that it featured Grace Slick, now of the Jefferson Airplane. But the group was a big part of the San Francisco band scene right from the start in 1965, playing everywhere the bands played and often appearing on the same bill as the Jefferson Airplane. The group had Grace's husband, Jerry, on drums and her brother-in-law, Darby Slick, on lead guitar. When David Minor (rhythm guitar) and Peter Vandegilder (bass) split, wanting to get into Indian music, so did the

group. Just then, the Airplane's vocalist left to look after her
new baby; Grace took over, and the rest is history. Great
Society made two albums for Columbia, which were released
only after the band broke up and Grace was nationally known
as the Airplane vocalist. Armed with hindsight, it is easy to
find all the signs of primordial San Francisco psychedelics in
their two albums, particularly in *White Rabbit* and *Somebody
To Love,* the two great Airplane underground classics that
were the first San Francisco songs to crash into the top-forty
charts.
(See JEFFERSON AIRPLANE)

Albums/CONSPICUOUS ONLY IN ITS ABSENCE: *Sally
Go 'Round The Roses; Didn't Think So; Grimly Forming;
Somebody To Love; Outlaw Blues; Father Bruce; Often As I
May; White Rabbit; Arbitration.* HOW IT WAS (September
1968): *That's How It Is; Darkly Smiling; Nature Boy; You
Can't Cry; Daydream Nightmare; Everybody Knows; Born
To Be Burned; Father.*

THE GROUP IMAGE/*Dr. Hok (lead guitar), Freddy
Knuckles (guitar), William Guy Merrill (rhythm guitar),
Black Doug (bass), Professor Leon Luther Rix (drums),
Sheila Darla (vocals).*
A New York community enterprise consisting of artists,
musicians, writers, technicians and organizers. In 1968 the
combined efforts of the Group Image resulted in a light show,
a rock group, a self-produced and arranged record album,
and a once-a-week Wednesday night ballroom scene that
lasted for over a year. The rock group produces music which
is straight rock and roll with a little blues for color. They
represented American culture at the 1968 Olympics in Mexico.

Album/A MOUTH IN THE CLOUDS (November 1968):
*Aunt Ida; A Way To Love You All The Time; Moonlit Dip;
Voices Calling Me; New Romancing; Hiya; Banana Split; My
Man; Grew Up All Wrong; The Treat.*

GROUPIES/The concept of the groupie is not new but the
term is. An extension of the wartime "camp followers,"

groupies are girls whose sexual favors extend exclusively to rock musicians. The term came into use late in 1965 or early 1966 with the emergence of local rock bands. Those fans who were turning out to meet and greet visiting English players now found that with the flood of local bands and their increased availability, being a fan could be a fuller occupation than merely shrieking outside the stage door. (It wasn't easy to get to the Rolling Stones or the Yardbirds and the competition was heavy, but the local groups were friendlier and there were more of them.) Thus, a girl could confine her activities to rock musicians and shut any other sort of person out of her romantic life. There are many kinds of groupies: sad groupies who never get further than screaming and wishful thinking; apprentice groupies who cut their teeth on the local high school band; compromise groupies who are prepared to settle for the road manager or even his friend; daring groupies who bravely scale walls or dangle from helicopters to get their prey; bold groupies who ride up and down hotel elevators until one of "them" gets in and then minces no words in propositioning him. There are expert groupies who can get to anyone, who have guards bribed, hotel managers snowed, desk clerks distracted and bell boys and house maids on their payroll. There are socialite groupies who give big dances and have the singer later. The most clever groupies get jobs in the industry and often persuade themselves they aren't groupies at all. Finally there are groupies who just don't kid themselves: they know what they are; they know what they want.

Groupies can be high class and rich, they can be gentle confidantes, they can be ribald courtesans or ugly desperate children that English stars contemptuously call "scrubbers" or "band molls." But they are what give rock its sex appeal and its magic. They are fans who have dared to break the barriers between the audience and the perfromer, fans with one thing to give, love, who want nothing in return but a name to drop.

GROUPIES (Male)/Not all groupies are female. Male stars have male groupies who envy them and want to identify with them, run errands for them, breathe in the golden air around them (and perhaps even pick up a female groupie on the side). There are also discreetly homosexual male groupies, many of them sublimating it all by finding themselves jobs in the business side of rock—management, etc. Male groupies for female performers are less common, female performers on the road being, on the whole, less available than male ones. Janis Joplin was one of the few female performers to bewail the shortage of male groupies. The truth is female performers are groupies of the very worst kind, eternally forming alliances with the most starstudded of their colleagues. They would never be seen with a male groupie.

BLINDBOY GRUNT/For a long time it was supposed that Blindboy Grunt was a legendary blind boy discovered by Bob Dylan. Or so, at least, he was described on the notes to Volume I of *BROADSIDE BALLADS* (1963). He sang several tracks on this LP in a voice so like Dylan's that suspicions were aroused from the start. But it was not until 1968 in a *Sing Out* interview that Dylan let outsiders in on the inside joke that the mysterious Mr. Grunt was none other than Dylan himself. That was the way the scene used to be back in 1963—all whimsy and pranks. The revelation of Grunt's true identity came as a deep disappointment to those who secretly hoped this unknown Dylanesque figure would come up with an LP called *BLINDE ON BLINDE*.

ARLO GUTHRIE/Arlo Guthrie, star, was born on New York's underground station WBAI in the spring of 1967 when that station first played a tape of *Alice's Restaurant*. WBAI received so many requests that it was eventually played every night. A few months later Arlo and *Alice* were the stars of the 1967 Newport Folk Festival. Arlo had been singing all his life, but he only turned in his amateur status in February 1966. Before *Alice,* he had done the small-club folk route and a concert tour of Japan with Judy Collins. His father was Woody Guthrie, the great folk-poet, writer and singer of the thirties and forties. He grew up in a house where Pete Seeger, Cisco Houston, Jack Elliott and, much later, Bob Dylan were frequent visitors, but he has developed his own style, dry and witty to match the material he writes. No one holds an audience better with between-song raps than Arlo, no one is more beloved by the young. With a flawless sense of the

comic and the absurd, he comes on like a new young gentle
Lenny Bruce.

Albums/ ALICE'S RESTAURANT (September 1967): *Alice's
Restaurant Massacree; Chilling Of The Evening; Ring-
Around-A-Rosy Rag; Now And Then; I'm Going Home;
Motorcycle Song; Highway In The Wind.* ARLO (October
1968): *The Motorcycle Song; Wouldn't You Believe It; Try
Me One More Time; John Looked Down; Meditation (Wave
Upon Wave); Standing At The Threshold; The Pause Of Mr.
Claus.*

Singles/ *Motorcycle Song/Now And Then* (September 1967):
Motorcycle Song (2 Parts) (November 1968).

NORAH GUTHRIE/ Arlo's sister (and Woody's daughter),
Norah has started a singing career of her own and so far has
released one single.

Single/ *Emily's Illness/Home Before Dark.*

WOODY GUTHRIE/ Once Arlo was known as Woody's son,
now inevitably Woody has to be described as Arlo's father.
Folk singer, folk poet, writer, rambler, chronicler of the
thirties and forties, he was a friend of Leadbelly, Pete
Seeger, Ramblin' Jack Elliott, Cisco Houston and later Bob
Dylan. Dylan came to New York from Minnesota in 1960
just to visit Woody, and if he sang a lot like Woody in those
days, well, that's all right, so did a lot of kids. Woody is
the man you sang like in the early sixties. Woody wrote
hundreds of songs—talking blues, protest songs, ballads—
which went on to form a large part of the repertoire of
every folk singer of the fifties. By then Woody lay in a
hospital with the illness that would finally kill him in 1968.
Woody was the father of the folk revival, the father of protest, the father, as it happens, of country-folk. After all
these years you can hear him most in Dylan's *JOHN
WESLEY HARDING.*

Albums/ BOUND FOR GLORY. CHAIN GANG SONGS.
COWBOY SONGS. FOLK SONGS BY WOODY GUTHRIE
AND CISCO HOUSTON. WOODY GUTHRIE SINGS
FOLK SONGS. LONESOME VALLEY. MORE SONGS

BY WOODY GUTHRIE AND CISCO HOUSTON. POOR
BOY. SOIL AND THE SEA. SONGS OF THE SPANISH
CIVIL WAR. SONGS TO GROW ON. BALLADS OF
SACCO AND VANZETTI (December 1960). WOODY
GUTHRIE SINGS WITH LEADBELLY (March 1962).
DUST BOWL BALLADS (May 1964). WOODY GUTHRIE
(October 1964). LIBRARY OF CONGRESS RECORDINGS
(October 1964. BED ON THE FLOOR (June 1965).
WOODY GUTHRIE (November 1965). BONNEVILLE
DAM (October 1966). LEGENDARY WOODY GUTHRIE
(December 1967).

BUDDY GUY/A B.B. King protégé, Buddy Guy is probably
the best blues guitarist in the world, and if not yet, then
destined to be any day. Known, until recently, as the brilliant
accompanist of Junior Wells, Buddy's work was to be heard
only on those records. Now, at last, he has his own album, *A
MAN AND HIS BLUES* (he also made a rock and roll
record never released because he had been typed as a blues
man). Although he is originally from Louisiana, his musical
coming-of-age was in Chicago and Chicago city blues is what
he plays. Only just turned thirty, he's proud of the fact that at
one stage Muddy Waters, Howlin' Wolf and Willie Dixon
wouldn't record without Buddy's backing them. For a long
time he worked only in Chicago (though he had made three
European tours), but as rock personalities like Eric Clapton
started to sing his praises he moved further afield, winning a
growing national recognition.

Albums/MAN AND THE BLUES (February 1968): *I Can't
Quit The Blues; Money; Thousand Miles From Nowhere;
Mary Had A Little Lamb; Just Playing My Axe; Sweet Little
Angel; Worry Is All That I Can Do; Jam On A Monday
Morning; Man And The Blues.* THIS IS BUDDY GUY
(December 1968): *I Got My Eyes On You; Things I Used
To Do; Fever Knock On Wood; I Had A Dream Last Night;
24 Hours Of The Day; You Were Wrong; I'm Not The Best.*

Singles/*First Time I Met The Blues/I Got My Eyes On You;
Broken Hearted Blues/Shop Around; Let Me Love You
Baby/Ten Years Ago; Skippin'/Stone Crazy; Treasure Un-
told/When My Left Eye Jumps; I Dig Your Wig/My Time*

After While; Crazy Love/Leave My Girl Alone; Sweet Little Angel/Mary Had A Little Lamb.
Also Appears On/THE BLUES, VOL. 1 (June 1963): *First Time I Met The Blues.* THE BLUES, VOL. 2 (June 1963): *Ten Years Ago.*

BILL HALEY AND THE COMETS/His band was originally a country band and later what must have been the first white instrumental rhythm and blues band. Bill Haley himself was probably the first white face on what was still, in 1954, a basically black rock and roll scene. He wrote and recorded *Rock Around The Clock* in 1954, but the record never took off and everyone wrote it off then as a very small-time hit. Then, a whole year later, it turned up again as the theme song of the film *Blackboard Jungle,* and that was another story. In the context of that film of teenage rebellion, the song took on a whole new meaning. It became the first song to have a special secret defiant meaning for teenagers only. It was the first inkling teenagers had that they might be a force to be reckoned with, in numbers alone. If there could be one song, there could be others; there could be a whole world of songs, and then, a whole world. Unwittingly, Bill Haley, basically a very square man, had opened up a Pandora's box of teenage emotions. He had done so unwittingly because he was not *for* what he started. And he was always apologizing for the monster he created. Musically he was proud though. Proud that as far back as 1951 he was combining Dixie, rhythm and blues, country and western, and pop in what was to become one of the basic rock and roll sounds. He always said that he had developed rock and roll, while Alan Freed, the disc jockey, had only *named* it and *exploited* it. Well, to say *Rock Around The Clock* was a sensation is a gross understatement. It was the *Marseillaise* of the teenage revolution. Later he followed up with his own version of Joe Turner's rhythm and blues hit *Shake Rattle and Roll.* And there were a lot of other hits. Haley was enormously successful, not just in America but all over the world. Wherever he went there were riots, and years after the rock and roll craze had abated in the United States, it still went on dizzily in other countries. When the boom died down, he never did stop working. During England's rock revival of 1968 Bill was back there, with scores of old rockers at the airport to greet him, all drape-shape suits and boot-lace ties, obviously dying to tear up more seats and wreck more cinemas. Oh, how they had been waiting for this day!

Historically, Haley had the first international rock hit. He gave teenagers the first heady taste of a music of their own. But while he was moving into that sound, so, in other places, were others. Fats Domino. Jerry Lee Lewis. Buddy Holly. Little Richard. Elvis. It wasn't that Haley happened and everyone else copied so much as that some of the country people were casting an interested eye at rhythm and blues and arriving at much the same thing independently. What Haley did with rock and roll, or whatever it was in those early days, was to make it a commercial proposition for the charts. When *Rock Around The Clock* worked for him, a score of others said, "Why, that's exactly the sort of music I'm playing," and moved in. Others still simply imitated. It was a fad. It was an explosion. It was a revolution. After that, a million things became possible. Black rock like Fats Domino. Black country rock like Chuck Berry. Elvis. Polite white rock like Pat Boone. And eventually a teenage scene so mewling and insipid that only the Beatles could save it.

Albums/BILL HALEY AND HIS COMETS: *Caldonia; ABC Rock; Fool Such As I; Dragon Rock; Walkin' Beat;* 7 Other Titles. BILL HALEY AND HIS COMETS: *Joey's Song; Ooh, Look-A There, Ain't She Pretty; Shaky; Caldonia.* ROCK AND ROLL STAGE SHOW: *Calling All Comets; Rockin' Through The Rye; Hook, Line And Sinker; Rudy's Rock; Rocking Little Tune; Hide And Seek; Choo Choo Ch' Boogie; Blue Comet Blues; Hey Then, There Now; Goofin' Around; Hot Dog Buddy Buddy; Tonight's The Night.* ROCK AROUND THE CLOCK (November 1962): *Razzle-Dazzle; Two Hound Dogs; Burn That Candle; Rock-A-Beatin' Boogie; Rock Around The Clock; Shake Rattle And Roll; Thirteen Women; A. B. C. Boogie; Dim Dim The Lights; Happy Baby; Birth Of The Boogie; Mambo Rock.* ROCKIN' THE JOINT: *New Rock The Joint; Move It On Over; It's A Sin; Rock Lommond; How Many; Beak Speaks; See You Later Alligator; Forty Cups Of Coffee; Saints Rock And Roll; Sway With Me; Burn That Candle; Rip It Up.* BILL HALEY'S

GREATEST HITS (June 1968): *Rock Around The Clock; Thirteen Women; See You Later, Alligator; Sway With Me; Choo Choo Ch' Boogie; Razzle-Dazzle; Burn The Candle; Shake, Rattle And Roll; Skinny Minnie; Saints Rock 'N Roll; Joey's Song.*

Singles/*Lean Jean/Skinny Minnie; Rock Around The Clock/ Thirteen Women; A.B.C. Boogie/Shake, Rattle And Roll; Birth Of The Boogie/Mambo Rock; Burn That Candle/Rock-A-Beatin' Boogie; See You Later, Alligator/Paper Boy; Joey's Song/Ooh, Look-A-There, Ain't She Pretty; Corrine, Corrina Green Door* (June 1969).

JOHN HAMMOND/A fine harp and guitar player, he was one of the first (in 1963) of what was to be a long line of whites to be bitten by the blues bug. John Hammond, white, sings the blues black. His backing group, the Screaming Nighthawks, once had Jimi Hendrix in there screaming (before he was a star). On his latest LP, *I CAN TELL* (on which Rolling Stone Bill Wyman can be heard on bass), he has Robbie Robertson (from the Big Pink band) on lead guitar, playing even blacker than Hammond sings.

Albums/JOHN HAMMOND (October 1963): *Two Trains Running; Give Me A 32-30; Louise; Maybelline; This Train; Going Back To Florida; East St. Louis Blues; Mean Old Frisco; I Got A Letter This Morning; Hoochie Coochie Man; Alabama Woman Blues; See That My Grave Is Kept Clean, Crossroads Blues.* BIG CITY BLUES (November 1964): *I'm Ready; My Starter Won't Start; I'm A Man; Barbecue Blues; Barrelhouse Woman Blues; Midnight Hour Blues; Backdoor Man; I Live The Life I Love; No Money Down; When You Got A Good Friend; My Babe; Baby, Won't You Tell Me.* SO MANY ROADS (March 1965): *Rambling Blues; O Yea; You Can't Judge A Book By The Cover; Gambling Blues; Baby, Please Don't Go; Big Boss Man; Down In The Bottom; Long Distance Call; Who Do You Love; I Want You To Love Me; Judgement Day; So Many Roads, So Many Trains.* COUNTRY BLUES (January 1966): *Traveling Riverside Blues; Hitchhiking Woman; Statesborough Blues; Milk Cow's Calf Blues; Crawling Kingsnake; Bull Frog Blues; Drop Down Mama; Little Rain Falling; Seventh Son; Who Do You Love;*

32-20 Blues; Goin' Down Slow. MIRRORS (January 1968):
*I Wish They Would; Statesborough Blues; They Call It
Stormy Monday; Keys To The Highway; I Just Got Here;
Traveling Riverside; Stones In My Passway; Walking Blues;
Get Right Church; Death Don't Have No Mercy; Motherless
Willie Johnson; When You Are Gone; Rock Me Mama.* I
CAN TELL (June 1968): *I Wish You Would; I'm In The
Mood; I Can Tell; Spoonful; Coming Home; My Baby Is
Sweeter; Brown-Eyed Handsome Man; Smokestack Light-
ning; Going To New York; Five Long Years; You're So Fine;
Forty Days And Forty Nights.*

HAPPENINGS/*Ralph De Vito (vocals), Bob Miranda (vocals), Tom Guiliano (vocals), Dave Libert (organ).*
Those who believe it's all in the name will be interested to
know that nothing happened to the Happenings until they
changed their name from the Four Graduates. They are
basically a vocal group, with a great many comedy touches,
and their bit is to sing old hits like *Mammy* and *I Got Rhythm*
in a tongue-in-cheek way which is both old-fashioned and
contemporary.
Albums/THE HAPPENINGS (September 1966): *See You
In September; Girl On A Swing; Love Me, Really Love Me;
Tonight I Fell In Love; Go Away Little Girl; Sealed With A
Kiss;* Other Titles. BACK TO BACK: *I Got Rhythm; Good
Night My Love; Impatient Girl; Lilies By Monet; He Thinks
He's A Hero; I Believe In Nothing;* Other side of this album is
by the Tokens. PSYCLE: *Why Do Fools Fall In Love; I Got
Rhythm; I Believe In Nothing; That Cold Feeling; Down,
Down, Down; Growing Old; My Mammy; When I Lock My
Door; I'm Always Chasing Rainbows; When The Summer Is
Through; Every Year About This Time; Bye, Bye Blackbird.*
HAPPENING'S GOLDEN HITS: *I Got Rhythm; Go Away
Little Girl; See You In September; My Mammy; Sealed With
A Kiss; Breaking Up Is Hard To Do; Tea For Two; Randy;
Girl On A Swing; Goodnight My Love; Why Do Fools Fall In
Love; Music, Music, Music.*
Singles/*Anyway/Breaking Up Is Hard To Do; Go Away
Little Girl/Tea Time; Goodnight My Love/Lilies By Monet;
He Thinks He's A Hero/See You In September; I Believe In
Nothing/My Mammy; I Got Rhythm/You're In A Bad Way;*

*Love Song For Mommy & Daddy/Randy; When I Lock My
Door/Music, Music, Music; When The Summer Is Through/
Why Do Fools Fall In Love; Crazy Rhythm/Love Song Of
Mom And Dad* (October 1968).

HARD ROCK/This is the uncomplicated early rock sound
of the era that began with Elvis Presley and Bill Haley in
1955 and 1956. Later embellishments like the intrusion of
folk into the sound, the meanderings and distortions of acid
rock (which had some roots in folk), the hundred and one
frills and twirls that musicians introduced, diluted the hard-
rock sound. Groups never stopped being in love with hard
rock, and in 1968 especially, as the psychedelic sound died
away, hard rock, though not exactly early rock and roll, came
back hot and heavy.

TIM HARDIN/He started as one of the very best of the
white blues singers. And when *the* scene in American music
was not rock but folk, and everyone else who mattered
(including Dylan) was playing acoustic guitar, he went electric and sang a sort of jazz-flavored blues. That alone was
enough to make him a legend long before his fabulous first
album, the one with *Don't Make Promises* on it, came out at
the end of 1966. And before the term folk rock was a tired
cliche, or even very much in use, Hardin managed to work
the lyricism of folk in with the gutsiness of rock. He also had
a legendary reputation as a writer, which the general public
latched on to only after Bobby Darin popularized *If I Were A
Carpenter*. (Hardin's bitterness over this was not so much at
having his song cheapened as at Darin's taking over of the
characteristic Hardin vocal style before there had been time
to establish it as his own.) Hardin's first album was two
years in the making. The third album was made from early
blues tapes that were never intended for release, but give an
idea of what he was doing before he moved into the gentle,
vulnerable mood of *Misty Roses, Lady From Baltimore* and
all those songs from his second album that were played night
after night on the jukeboxes of 1967 and '68. The point about
Hardin was that there was nothing thin about his soft-

pedalling. His never bitter, simply resigned view of the way relationships between two people had to end was considerably more substantial than that airy romanticism of Donovan, with whom he's often been compared—both create beauty rather than noise. Much later when Bob Dylan did *JOHN WESLEY HARDING* (from whom Hardin is descended) there was a lot of talk about the new calm, the new simplicity of rock. Hardin had never been doing anything else.

Albums/TIM HARDIN (September 1966): *Don't Make Promises; Green Rocky Road; How Long; Smugglin' Man; While You're On Your Way; It'll Never Happen Again; Reason To Believe; Never Too Far; Part Of The Wind; Ain't Gonna Do Without; Misty Roses; How Can I Hang On To A Dream.* TIM HARDIN - VOLUME II (July 1967): *If I Were A Carpenter; Red Balloon; Black Sheep Boy; Lady Came From Baltimore; You Upset The Grace Of Living When You Lie; See Where You Are And Get Out; Baby Close Its Eyes; Speak Like A Child; It's Hard To Believe In Love For Long; Tribute To Hank Williams.* THIS IS TIM HARDIN (September 1967): *I Can Slow Down; Blues On The Ceilin'; I'm Your Hoochie Coochie Man; Stagger Lee; I've Been Working On The Railroad; House Of The Rising Sun; Fast Freight; Cocaine Bill; You Got To Have More Than One Woman; Danville Dame.* TIM HARDIN 3 LIVE IN CONCERT (November 1968): *The Lady Came From Baltimore; Reason To Believe; You Upset The Grace Of Living When You Lie; Misty Roses; Black Sheep Boy; Lenny's Tune, Don't Make Promises; Danville Dame; If I Were A Carpenter; Red Balloon; Tribute To Hank Williams; Smugglin' Man.* TIM HARDIN 4 (April 1969): *Airmobile; Whiskey Whiskey; Seventh Son; How Long; Danville Dame, Ain't Gonna Do Without* (Part I); *Ain't Gonna Do Without* (Part II); *House Of The Rising Sun; Bo Diddley; I Can't Slow Down; Hello Baby.* TIM HARDIN SUITE FOR SUSAN MOORE AND DAMION-WE ARE-ONE, ONE, ALL IN ONE (April 1969): *First Love Song; Everything Good Become; More True; Question Of Birth; Once-Touched By Flame; Last Sweet Moments; Magician; Loneliness She Knows; The Country I'm Living In; One, One, Tne Perfect Sum; Susan.*

Singles/*Green Rocky Road*/*Never Too Far* (February 1967);
Black Sheep Boy/*Misty Roses* (March 1967); *Tribute To
Hank Williams*/*You Upset The Grace Of Living When You
Lie* (June 1967).

HARPER'S BIZARRE/*Ted Templeman (drums, trumpet),
Dickie Scoppettone (guitar), Eddie James (guitar), John
Petersen (drums), Dick Yount (guitar, bass drums).*
Harper's Bizarre, which started in California in 1963, will
always be remembered for doing the Song of the Year in
1967 (well, one of several Songs of the Year anyway)—
official title: *Fifty-ninth Street Bridge Song;* unofficial title:
Feelin' Groovy—a celebration of the particular ecstasies of
city life on a good day. Written by Simon and Garfunkel, it is
sung happily enough by the noted duo, but the Harper's
Bizarre version seems to have champagne bubbles in it,
exactly like the superhigh Paul Simon had in mind. The
Bizarre sound is California sunshine rock (the Turtles have it
too), a sort of extension of the folk song scene two of its
members originally came out of, and yet another example of
how folk people brought harmony and melody to rock.

Albums/FEELIN' GROOVY (June 1967): *59th St. Bridge
Song (Feelin' Groovy); Come To The Sunshine; Happy Talk;
Raspberry Rub; Come Love; I Can Hear The Darkness;
Simon Smith & The Amazing Dancing Bear; Happyland;
Peter & The Wolf; Debutante's Ball.* ANYTHING GOES
(December 1967): *Anything Goes; This Is Only The Begin-
ning; Two Little Babes In The Wood; Biggest Night Of Her
Life; Pocketful Of Miracles; Snow; Chattanooga Choo Choo;
Hey You In The Crowd; Louisiana Man; Milord; Virginia
City; You Need A Change; Jessie; High Coin.* SECRET LIFE
OF HARPER'S BIZARRE: *Look To The Rainbow; Battle Of
New Orleans; When I Was A Cowboy; Sentimental Journey;
Mananitas; Me, Japanese Boy; I'll Build A Stairway To
Paradise; Green Apple Tree; Sit Down You're Rocking The
Boat; I Love You Mama; Funny How Love Can Be; Mad;
Drifter; Medley.* HARPER'S BIZARRE 4 (April 1969):

Singles/*Anything Goes*/*Chattanooga Choo Choo; Battle Of
New Orleans*/*Green Apple Tree; Both Sides Now*/*Small
Talk; Come To The Sunshine*/*59th St. Bridge Song (Feelin'*

Groovy) (1967); *Cotton Candy Sandman/Virginia City; Look To The Rainbow/ I Love You Alice B. Toklas* (October (1968).

SLIM HARPO plays authentic country blues, the kind Canned Heat and other white blues bands work hard at reproducing. (The Rolling Stones' *King Bee* is one of his songs, as is *Moody Blues,* from which England's Moody Blues got their name.) Harpo is not as flashy as the black bluesmen who finally got through to white audiences in 1967; the audiences he usually plays to are in the South and they're black. However, he is slowly starting to become known to blues-loving audiences in the North, where he is now occasionally appearing.

Albums/SLIM HARPO SINGS RAININ' IN MY HEART: *Rainin' In My Heart; Blues Hangover; I Got Love If You Want It; Bobby Sox Baby; I'm A King Bee; Snoopin' Around; Buzz Me Baby; What A Dream; Don't Start Cryin' Now; My Home Is A Prison; Moody Baby; Dream Girl.* BABY, SCRATCH MY BACK. TIP ON IN WITH SLIM HARPO: *Tip On In; Te-Ni-Nee-Ni-Nu; Mailbox Blues; I've Been A Good Thing For You; Hey Little Lee; I'm Gonna Keep What I Got; I've Got To Be With You Tonight; I'm So Sorry; My Baby; She's Got It; I Just Can't Leave You.*

Singles/*I Got Love If You Want It/I'm A King Bee; Strange Love/Wondering And Worryin'; One More Day/You'll Be Sorry One Day; Buzz Me Babe/Late Last Night; Rainin' In My Heart/Don't Start Crying Now; I Love The Life I'm Living/Buzzin'; I Need Money/Little Queen Bee; Still Rainin' In My Heart/We're Two Of A Kind; Harpo's Blues/Please Don't Turn Me Down; Baby, Scratch My Back/I'm Gonna Miss You; Midnight Blues/Shake Your Hips; I'm Your Bread Maker, Baby/Loving You; Tip On In (2 Parts); I'm Gonna Keep What I've Got/I've Got To Be With You Tonight; Mailbox Blues/Te-Ni-Nee-Ni-Nu; Mohair Sam/I Just Can't Leave You* (October 1968); *Just For You/That's Why I Love You* (April 1969).

NOEL HARRISON/Son of actor Rex Harrison, Noel was singing in London clubs before he came to the United States.

Although he has been mainly an actor in America his first love is music, and he has recorded, in a light and pleasant voice, a lot of Dylan and Lennon and McCartney. He made rock news, however, in the summer of 1967 when he released as a single Leonard Cohen's *Suzanne*, which got the then fairly unknown song a lot of airplay. The following year he put another Cohen song, *So Long, Marianne,* on his album He makes no secret of his wistful longings to be back in the California music establishment, but acting on stage and television seems to be occupying most of his time.

Albums/NOEL HARRISON (March 1966): *It's All Over Now, Baby Blue; God Bless The Child; She's A Woman; Love Minus Zero; Nothing But A Fool; Mr. Tambourine Man; Young Girl; To Ramona; Much As I Love You; Like Strangers; All Blues; Tomorrow Is My Turn.* COLLAGE (October 1967): *Suzanne; Just Like A Woman; People In The Rain; Woman; Lucy In The Sky With Diamonds; Sign Of The Queen; Museum; Go Ask Your Man; Whiter Shade Of Pale; When I'm Sixty-Four; Mrs. Williams' Roses; Strawberry Fields Forever.* SANTA MONICA PIER (March 1968): *Santa Monica Pier; So Long, Marianne; In Your Childhood; Let's Not; I Shall Remember; Ring Around A Rosie Rag; Same Thing Has Happened To You; Leitch On The Beach; Dress Rehearsal Rag; Highway In The Wind; Show Me The Way To Go Home.*

Singles/*Marieke/Man Behind The Red Balloon* (June 1966); *Cheryl's Going Home/In A Dusty Old Room* (October 1966); *Fly Sing Song/Out For The Day* (February 1967); *Mrs. Williams' Roses/Sign Of The Queen* (May 1967); *Suzanne/Life Is A Dream* (August 1967); *In Your Childhood/Santa Monica Pier* (February 1968); *Leitch On The Beach/Windmills On Your Mind* (February 1968); *I'll Be Your Baby Tonight/Great Electric Experiment Is Over* (1968).

BOBBY HATFIELD

Singles/*Soul Cafe/Hang Ups* (April 1968); *I Wish I Didn't Love You So/My Prayer* (May 1969).
(see THE RIGHTEOUS BROTHERS)

RICHIE HAVENS/He is a folk singer who has done something that seems impossible: he has transcended color and the whole dreary controversy of black versus white sound. He was playing the coffee houses in the Village during the 1962 folk boom that he wasn't quite in on and suddenly came into his own in 1968, when his guru-like gentleness, his occasional flashes of real pain, his grainy Dylan interpretations, hit the bull's-eye exactly—especially for the young who were trying to get away from the noise. His music is all the more tranquilizing for the knowledge that behind him is a wild boyhood in the ganglands of Brooklyn's Bedford-Stuyvesant. He wears beads and plays the sitar (he was one of the first to use the electric sitar), and on an ex-gang kid that's touching. His sound is described as progressive blues folk. His voice is rough but his songs are simple and personal; and he makes sincerity work in 1968, which is no mean achievement.

Albums/MIXED BAG (September 1967): *High Flyin' Bird; I Can't Make It Anymore; Morning, Morning; Adam; Follow; Three Day Eternity; Sandy; Handsome Johnny; Like A Woman; San Francisco Bay Blues; Eleanor Rigby.* SOMETHIN' ELSE AGAIN (January 1968): *No Opportunity Necessary, No Experience Needed; Inside Of Him; The Klan; Don't Listen To Me; Sugarplums; From The Prison; New City; Run Shaker Life; Maggie's Farm; Somethin' Else Again.* RICHIE HAVENS RECORD: *I'm Gonna Make You Glad; It Hurts Me; Chain Gang; Drown In My Own Tears; I'm On My Way; Babe, I'm Leanin'; Nora's Dove; Daddy Roll 'Em; The Bag I'm In.* ELECTRIC RICHIE HAVENS (November 1968): *Oxford Town; 900 Miles From Home; I'm A Stranger Here; My Own Way; Boots Of Spanish Leather; C. C. Rider; 3:10 To Yuma; Shadow Town.* RICHARD P. HAVENS, 1983 (November 1968): *Stop pulling And Pushing Me; For Heaven's Sake; Strawberry Fields Forever; What More Can I Say John; I Pity The Poor Immigrant; Lady Madonna; Priests; Indian Rope Man; Cautiously; Just Above My Hobby Horse's Head; She's Leaving Home; Putting Out The Vibration, And Hoping It Comes Home; The Parable Of Ramon; A Little Help From My Friends; Wear Your Love Like Heaven; Run Shaker Life; Do You Feel Good.*

Single/*No Opportunity Necessary, No Experience Needed/ Three Day Eternity* (January 1968).

ROGER HAWKINS/The drummer at the Atlantic studios in Muscle Shoals, Alabama, and the other half of bass player Tom Cogbill's rhythm section. It's Hawkins who gives characteristic Alabama muscle and punch to the Aretha Franklin-Wilson Pickett recordings.

LEE HAZLEWOOD/He is the man who, in 1967, told a young and hitless Nancy Sinatra that she was singing too high and too pure. What she needed, he told her nicely, was to drop her voice down a bit and put a bit of funk into it. Splendid advice that launched Nancy into impressive stardom. Since then Hazlewood, who is nudging forty, has become a sort of teeny idol himself. He and Nancy sing duos like a country and western version of Jeannette MacDonald and Nelson Eddy. He also sings alone. He produces. He arranges. He writes songs. A childhood in Oklahoma and Texas has put a pinch of country in his sound, and an early, pre-Beatle association with guitarist Duane Eddy helped him come up with that relentless guitar sound that made his song *These Boots Are Made for Walking* a turning point in Nancy Sinatra's career.

Albums/WORLD OF LEE HAZLEWOOD (March 1966): *These Boots Are Made For Walkin'; For One Moment; When A Fool Loves A Fool; Not The Lovin' Kind; Your Sweet Love; Sand; My Baby Cried All Night Long; I Move Around; So Long, Babe; Bugles In The Afternoon; My Autumn's Done Come.* HAZLEWOODISM—ITS CAUSE AND CURE (December 1966): *Girls In Paris; Jose; Old Man And His Guitar; The Nights; I Am A Part; Home (I'm Home); After Six; Suzi Jane Is Back In Town; In Our Time; Dark In My Heart.* LOVE AND OTHER CRIMES (July 1968): *Love And Other Crimes; Morning Dew; She Comes Running; Rosacoke Street; She's Funny That Way; The House Song; Wait And See; Forget Marie; Pour Man; Love And Other Crimes.* HOUSTON (December 1968): *Houston; By The Way; Hutchinson Jail; Real Live Fool;* Plus six other titles. TROUBLE IS A LONESOME TOWN (April 1969).

Single/*Ode To Billie Joe/Charlie Bill Nelson* (August 1967).

HEAD ARRANGEMENTS/Not at all related to head music, head arrangements are those for which musicians don't use sheet music but because they have worked together so long and so harmoniously the music is just allowed to "happen" and comes off sounding better than anything preplanned. Most Nashville studio musicians work that way, as do those in the Stax studios in Memphis and the Muscle Shoals studios in Alabama where Aretha Franklin records.

HEAD MUSIC/In its most common use, head music can be defined as music that enhances the marijuana experience— gentle, soothing, calm, but at the same time with enough happening to engage heightened perceptions. (Marijuana is said to increase the awareness of instrumental passages often "lost" in the overall sound when heard under normal conditions.) Some music is more appropriate to certain chemical states than to others. There is music that doesn't even start to make sense, say drug aficionados, until the mind has been suitably altered or bent to receive it. Ravi Shankar's sitar music, not entirely to his pleasure, is highly regarded head music, as are Shankar-influenced tracks like the Beatles' *Norwegian Wood*, the Byrds' *Eight Miles High* and the Stones' *Paint It Black*, all of which have sitar sounds. There are people who claim you can't possibly know what's going on in Van Dyke Parks' album *SONG CYCLE* if you are listening to it straight. *Day In The Life*, from the Beatles' *SERGEANT PEPPER*, is the ultimate in head music with sound effects that are guaranteed to turn on a little old lady from Dubuque with not as much as an aspirin to help. But no "head" would dream of listening to it unaided. The Beach Boys' *Good Vibrations* with its screaming theramin and its unearthly harmonies is such a good piece of head music that it could be a million dollar seller if it were expanded into an album or, better, an hour-long tape.
(See ACID ROCK)

BOBBY HEBB/He had a big hit in August 1966 with the soulful and emotional *Sunny* but has not reappeared at the top of the charts since then.
Album/SUNNY (August 1966): *Sunny; Where Are You; Got You On My Mind; Yes Or No Or Maybe Not; Good Good Lovin'; Love, Love, Love; Satisfied Mind; You Don't*

Know What You Got Until You Lose It; I Am Your Man; Crazy Baby; Bread; For You.

Singles/*Betty Jo From Ohio/Sam Hall Jr.; I Love Mary (2 Parts); Satisfied Man/Love, Love; Love Me/Crazy Baby; My Pretty Sunshine/Ooh La La; Some Kind Of Magic/I Love Everything About You; Bound By Love/Everything's Coming Up Roses; Sunny/Satisfied Mind.*

THE JIMI HENDRIX EXPERIENCE/*Jimi Hendrix (guitar), Mitch Mitchell (drums), Noel Redding (bass).*

Jimi Hendrix was one of the experiences of 1968—or 1967, if you were on the ball and found him early. An unlikely hybrid, the Seattle-born Negro with years of orthodox rhythm and blues tours behind him was snatched from a New York discotheque, where he was playing brilliant backup guita' zipped over to England by trans-Atlantic jet and exposed to a London in the most extreme throes of freaked-out frilled-out flower power, lace power and velvet power. And then when the time was ripe and this escapee from the southern music trap was considered sufficiently Anglicized, he was zipped right back across the Atlantic with his ruffles, his velvet hat, his guitar and his two English sidemen. It was the summer of 1967 and the Monkees tour, and no mother who had taken her apple-cheeked little daughter to shriek over Peter, Mike, Mickey and Davy was ready for what Hendrix got into that hot night out at the Forest Hills stadium. Lyne Randell, who was little and blonde and wholesome, had just sung her numbers in her sequined jump suit. It was a bit daring, *Going Out Of My Head,* and Mom got very protective about that. But wait. That was nothing. On stage now with that insolent saunter came the Jimi Hendrix Experience. Three huge frizzy dandelion heads. Three decadent Regency rakes. Amplifiers turned up to infinity. And now the star, like Christ between his two thieves, black hair flying from his head in electric fright, doing things to his guitar so passionate, so concentrated and so intense that anyone with halfway decent manners had to look away. And that was the way the act began, not ended. By the time it was over he had lapped and nuzzled his guitar with his lips and tongue, caressed it with his inner thighs, jabbed at it with a series of powerful pelvic thrusts. Even the little girls who'd come to see the Monkees understood what this was about. What Mick Jagger and the early rockers had so saucily promised and hinted at, Jimi Hendrix delivered. And was there ever a row! The Mothers of American Girl Monkee Watchers or some such association had him taken off the tour at once. (Exactly what his gleeful manager had hoped would happen. The publicity was perfect.) After that they could hardly go wrong. Nothing changed except the guitar-nuzzling was even more intimate, the caresses more intense and the thrusts so furious that from time to time the guitar at the end of it all would burst into flames and no one would seem the least surprised. Jimi Hendrix was hotter and sexier and more explicit than Jim Morrison, the Rolling Stones, the Beatles, Mae West and a battalion of strippers. And though there had been some pretty acrobatic bumping and grinding along the rhythm and blues route and up at Harlem's Apollo, this was not one of your come-back-to-Africa performances in shiny suit and processed hair. This was the Wild Man of Borneo, all right, but crossed with all the languid, silken, jewelled elegance of a Carnaby Street fop. It was a very erotic combination, and no doubt a shrewdly calculated one. First layer: noble savage. Second layer: San Francisco acid freak. Third layer: swinging London dandy. How *could* he lose?

Chas Chandler found him in a New York club, playing backings as he had always done (but not without hopes and dreams and a million jam sessions all over America). Chandler, an ex-Animal, who knew audiences, knew that Hendrix had it and that England was ready for a black superhero. Hendrix was a fantastic success in England, which could have been predicted, but Chandler couldn't wait to play his hunches in America. He had done everything right first, like getting Mitch Mitchell, a pale frail drummer who played faster than the speed of light, and Noel Redding, a pale frail bass player. The whole notion of a rock trio then was very new (though Cream, which emerged about the same time, was to make it a very popular form). When the excitement died down it became apparent that there was music there. Hendrix was, for one thing, a very good writer. Much of the material was his own. He also did Dylan material and took it one step further (his interpretation of *All Along the Watchtower* was masterful). His guitar playing was admired by the one man whose opinion counted, Cream guitarist Eric Clapton, who warned that you have to be there when Hendrix is really trying, and that Hendrix only tries when he has to. If he can get away with theatre and pyrotechnics, he will do so. But if it's music people want, and he senses it, he gives the pelvic girdle a rest and no longer feels compelled to roar out his words like a randy lion. Instead he settles down to some very serious blues guitar work, the kind that makes other musicians' voices drop with respect when they mention his name.

Albums/ARE YOU EXPERIENCED (September 1967): *Purple Haze; Manic Depression; Hey Joe; I Don't Live Today; Love Or Confusion; May This Be Love; Wind Cries Mary; Third Stone From The Sun; Fire; Foxey Lady; Are You Experienced*. GET THAT FEELING (With Curtis Knight) (November 1967): *How Would You Feel; Simon Says; Get That Feeling; Hush Now; Welcome Home; Gotta Have A New Dress; No Business; Strange Things*. AXIS: BOLD AS LOVE (March 1968): *EXP; Up From The Skies; Little Miss Lover; Spanish Castle Magic; Wait Until Tomorrow; Ain't No Telling; Little Wing; If 6 was 9; You Got Me Floatin'; Castles Made Of Sand; One Rainy Wish; So Fine Bold As Love*. ELECTRIC LADY LAND (August 1968): *And The Gods Made Love; Have You Ever Been; Crosstown Traffic; Voodoo Chile; All Along The Watchtower; Still Raining, Still Dreaming; House Burning Down; Voodoo Child; Little Miss Strange; Long Hot Summer Night; Come On; Gypsy Eyes; Burning Of The Midnight Lamp; Rainy Day, Dream Away; 1983; Moon, Turn The Tides*.

Singles/*Hey Joe/51st Anniversary* (May 1967); *Wind Cries Mary/Purple Haze* (June 1967); *Foxey Lady/Hey Joe* (November 1967); *One Rainy Wish/Up From The Skies; All Along The Watchtower/Burning Of The Midnight Lamp* (September 1968); *Crosstown Traffic/Gypsy Eyes*.

JUDY HENSKE/A bluesy folk singer or, if you like, a folky blues singer, Judy made a splash in 1963, then vanished from the scene. She is married to Jerry Yester who replaced Zal Yanovsky in the Lovin' Spoonful till the group folded in 1968.

Albums/DEATH DEFYING JUDY HENSKE (February

1963): *Hey Babe; Betty And Dupree; Sing A Rainbow; Saved; I've Been Loving You Too Long; Ace In The Hole; Danny Boy; Nobody Knows.* JUDY HENSKE (May 1963): *Low Down Alligator; Empty Bed Blues; Wade In The Water; Ballad Of Little Romy; Hooka Tooka; I Know You Rider; Lily Langtree; Lilac Wine; Love Henry; Every Night When The Sun Goes In; Salvation Army Song.* HIGH FLYING BIRD (November 1963): *High Flying Bird; Buckeye Jim; Till The Real Thing Comes Along; Oh, You Engineer; Blues Chase Up A Rabbit; Baltimore Oriole; Duncan And Brandy; Crawdad Song; Columbus; God Bless The Child; Lonely Train; Good Old Wagon; You Are Not My First Love; Charlotte Town.*

Single/*Day To Day*/*Dolphins In The Sea* (February 1963).

THE HERD/*Andy Brown (guitar, organ, piano, harmonica, bass guitar), Andrew Steele (drums), Gary Taylor (bass guitar), Peter Frampton (lead vocals, guitar, bass, piano, organ, drums, harmonica).*
The Herd has been not so much a group as a face—Peter Frampton's seventeen-year-old face. It was the old story. The Beatles had grown too old and complicated for the young and uncomplicated to love. The Herd was one of several young groups that emerged to fill the gap. They started in England in 1967 with a hit, *From The Underworld.* The trouble was they had to be seen to be appreciated. Until Frampton and his face make a personal appearance in the U.S., the Herd, which happens to be musically good, will have to wait for its American hits.

Album/LOOKIN THRU YOU (September 1968): *I Don't Want Our Loving To Die; Come On—Believe Me; Our Fairy Tale; On My Way Home; Goodbye; Groovy; From The Underworld; Paradise Lost; Sweet William; I Can Fly; Understand Me.*

Singles/*Sweet William*/*From The Underworld*; *Come On—Believe Me*/*Paradise Lost*; *I Don't Want Our Love To Die*/*Our Fairy Tale.*

HERMAN'S HERMITS/*Peter Noone (piano, guitar, vocals), Keith Hopwood (guitar), Karl Green (guitar, harmoni-*

ca), Barry Whitwam (drums), Derek Leckenby (guitar). No one is going to say Herman's Hermits were the great innovators of pop music, but their sense of timing was inspired. No sooner had the Beatles happened in America, in 1964, leaving the young American public quiveringly open to anything young, English and perky, when Herman's Hermits arrived. In England, where they were known as the Heartbeats, they were just another bunch of boys from Manchester with Beatle-like aspirations. In America, they were undiluted, goopy, squishy, adorable bundles from Britain; dear little marshmallow-soft English boys that a girl of thirteen could listen to without effort, bear-hug to death in her Barbie-doll dreams, and scream over without upsetting her mother and, particularly, her father. It was quite a role for the winsome Peter Noone, who seemed to have been tailored for it. He was the Mr. Clean of rock and the only pop star that Ed Sullivan could cope with painlessly. His music was pleasant and trivial, with lyrics concentrating mostly on the joys of teenage love. In a way he could be said to be the Paul Anka of the Beatle era, and it was his success that made the idea of a group like the Monkees possible. Ironically, in spite of his string of hits in America, he was virtually unknown in his own country, or if not unknown, then looked down upon and considered a bit of a joke by "serious" musicians. But some of his records *(No Milk Today,* for instance) were so gentle and innocuous and nicely put together that they ended up making the British charts anyway. He has now gotten into acting, for which his bright blue eyes and little-boy look have made him a natural. And recently he bought half of a New York men's boutique called Zoo (which manufactures, among other things, a vinyl suit for men).

Albums/INTRODUCING HERMAN'S HERMITS (March 1965): *I'm Into Something Good; Mrs. Brown You've Got A Lovely Daughter; Kansas City Loving; I Wonder; Sea Cruise; Walkin' With My Angel; Show Me Girl; I Understand; Your Hand In Mine; Mother-In-Law; I Know Why; Thinking Of You.* HERMAN'S HERMITS ON TOUR (July 1965): *I'm Henry VIII, I Am; End Of The World; Can't You Hear My Heartbeat; I Gotta Dream On; Don't Try To Hurt Me; I'll Never Dance Again; Heartbeat; Travelin' Light; Tell Me*

Baby; Silhouettes. BEST OF HERMAN'S HERMITS—VOL. 1 (December 1965): *I'm Henry VIII, I Am; Mrs. Brown You've Got A Lovely Daughter; Mother-In-Law; I'm In To Something Good; Silhouettes; Just A Little Bit Better; Can't You Hear My Heartbeat; End Of The World; Sea Cruise; I Gotta Dream On; Wonderful World.* HOLD ON (March 1966): *Must To Avoid; Hold On; Got A Feelin'; Wild Love; George And The Dragon; Leaning On The Lamp Post; Where Were You When I Needed You; Things I Do For You Baby; Gotta Get Away; Make Me Happy.* BOTH SIDES OF HERMAN'S HERMITS (September 1966): *This Door Swings Both Ways; Bus Stop; For Love; L'Autre Jour; Dial My Number; Future Mrs. 'Awkins; Oh Mr. Porter; Man With The Cigar; Two Lovely Black Eyes; My Reservations Been Confirmed; My Old Dutch.* BEST OF HERMAN'S HERMITS—VOL. 2 (December 1966): *Dandy; Must To Avoid; Leaning On The Lamp Post; Listen People; Bus Stop; Story Of My Life; Hold On; For Your Love; Take Love, Give Love; This Door Swings Both Ways; Little Boy Sad.* THERE'S A KIND OF HUSH (April 1967): *There's A Kind Of Hush; East West; You Won't Be Leaving; Saturday's Child; If You're Thinkin' What I'm Thinkin'; No Milk Today; Little Miss Sorrow Child Of Tomorrow; Gas Light Street; Rattler; Dandy; Jezebel.* BLAZE (October 1967): *Museum; Don't Go Out Into The Rain; Busy Line; Moonshine Man; Green Street Green; I Call Out Her Name; One Little Packet Of Cigarettes; Last Bus Home; Ace, King, Queen, Jack; Upstairs, Downstairs.* BEST OF HERMAN'S HERMITS— VOLUME 3 (January 1968): *There's A Kind Of Hush; No Milk Today; Big Man; Moonshine Man; What Is Wrong What Is Right; East West; Wings Of Love; Museum; Mum And Dad; Last Bus Home; Don't Go Out Into The Rain (You're Gong To Melt).*

Singles/*Man with The Cigar/Must To Avoid* (November 1965); *Got A Feeling/Listen People* (February 1966); *Leaning On The Lamp Post/Hold On* (March 1966); *This Door Swings Both Ways/For Love* (June 1966); *Dandy/My Reservation's Been Confirmed* (September 1966); *East West/What Is Wrong What Is Right* (November 1966); *Don't Go Out Into The Rain (You're Going To Melt)/Moonshine Man*

(June 1967); *Last Bus Home/Museum* (August 1967); *I Can Take Or Leave Your Loving/Marcel's* (December 1967); *Just One Girl/Sleepy Joe* (May 1968); *No Milk Today/ There's A Kind Of Hush* (September 1968).

BILLIE HOLIDAY/Queen of the blues in the forties, Billie Holiday died tragically in 1959 at the age of forty-four. Everyone from Frank Sinatra to Janis Joplin has learned from her.

Albums/BODY AND SOUL. BILLIE HOLIDAY. LADY DAY. LADY LOVE. LADY SINGS. LADY SINGS THE BLUES. MUSIC FOR TORCHING. RECITAL BY BILLIE HOLIDAY. SOLITUDE. STAY WITH ME. BLUES ARE BREWIN' (April 1958). LADY IN SATIN (May 1958). LOVER MAN (October 1958). SONGS FOR DISTINGUE LOVERS (January 1959). ALL OR NOTHING AT ALL (September 1959). BILLIE HOLIDAY STORY (September 1959). UNFORGETTABLE LADY DAY (February 1960). ESSENTIAL BILLIE HOLIDAY (August 1961). GOLDEN YEARS, VOL. 1 (March 1962). ONCE UPON A TIME (December 1964). LADY (December 1965). GOLDEN YEARS, VOL. 2 (April 1966). SHADES OF BLUE (January 1967). BILLIE HOLIDAY'S GREATEST HITS (April 1967). LADY LOVE (April 1969).

Singles/*Lover Man/The Old Devil Called Love, Solitude/ There Is No Greater Love; Crazy He Calls Me/You're My Thrill; Please Don't Talk About Me When I'm Gone/ Travelin' Light.*

HOLLIES/*Bernard Calvert (replaced Eric Haydock) (bass guitar), Allan Clarke (lead singer), Bobby Elliott (drums), Tony Hicks (lead guitar, vocals), Graham Nash (rhythm guitar, vocals).*
The Hollies' big tragedy in America right from the start was a lack of image. They didn't come on as meanies, or cuties, or groovies, or heavies. They didn't go in for gimmickry and stunts. They just sang well, and as everyone knows that's not always enough for the sort of giant promotion campaign needed to establish an English group in the United States. In England (and Europe) it was another story: fifteen consecu-

tive hits in the top ten, some of which eventually seeped through to the U.S. charts. But they were never (until 1966 and *Bus Stop*) the big hit group in the States that they were in England. Rather, their clean, witty rock sound won them a kind of inside fame which quickly got them labelled "the group's group." Their first tour with Herman's Hermits got them a useful backwash of Herman fans who have stuck with them ever since. In contrast with the style of their earlier hits *(HOLLIES GREATEST HITS, 1967)*, the Hollies, who write a lot of their own material, now lean toward the softer, gentler sound of *Butterfly* with eight orchestrated tracks. In 1969 singer and guitarist Nash left to join Crosby and Stills in the group, Crosby, Stills & Nash.

Albums/HEAR, HERE (December 1965): *I'm Alive; Very Last Day; You Must Believe Me; Put Yourself In My Place; Down The Line; That's My Desire; Look Through Any Window; Lawdy Miss Clawdy; When I Go Home To You; Lonely; I've Been Wrong; Too Many People.* HERE I GO AGAIN (December 1965): *Memphis; Stay; Just One Look; Talkin' 'Bout You; You Better Move On; Keep Off That Friend Of Mine; Rockin' Robin; Do You Love Me; Lucille; What Kind Of Girl Are You; It's Only Make Believe.* BEAT GROUP (June 1966): *I Can't Let Go; That's How Strong My Love Is; Running Through The Night; Oriental Sadness (She'll Never Trust In Anybody No More); A Taste Of Honey; Mr. Moonlight; Don't You Ever Care; Hard Hard Year; Take Your Time; Fifi The Flea; I Take What I Want.* BUS STOP (October 1966): *Bus Stop; Candy Man; That's All; I Am A Rock; Sweet Little Sixteen; We're Through; Don't Run And Hide; Oriental Sadness; Mickey's Monkey; Little Lover; You Know He Did; Whatcha Gonna Do 'Bout It.* STOP, STOP, STOP (February 1967): *Stop Stop Stop; What's Wrong With The Way I Live; Pay You Back With Interest; Tell Me To My Face; Clown; Suspicion; Look In Your Eyes; It's You; High Classed; Peculiar Situation; What Went Wrong; Crusader; Don't Ever Think About Changing.* HOLLIES' GREATEST HITS (April 1967): *On A Carousel; Bus Stop; Pay You Back With Interest; Here I Go Again; Tell Me To My Face; I'm Alive; Look Through Any Window; Stop Stop Stop; Whatcha Gonna Do 'Bout It; Just One*

Look; Memphis; I Can't Let Go. EVOLUTION (June 1967):
*Carrie-Ann; Stop Right There; Rain On The Window; Then
The Heartaches Begin; Ye Olde Toffee Shoppe; You Need
Love; Heading For A Fall; Games We Play; Lullaby To Tim;
Have You Ever Loved Somebody.* DEAR ELOISE/KING
MIDAS IN REVERSE (December 1967): *Dear Eloise;
Wishyouawish; Charlie & Fred; Butterfly; Leave Me; Post-
card; King Midas In Reverse; Would You Believe; Away
Away Away; Maker; Step Inside.* THE HOLLIES: WORDS
AND MUSIC BY BOB DYLAN (August 1969).

Singles/*I'm Alive/Look Through Any Window* (1965); *Just
One Look/Bus Stop; I Can't Let Go/Stop, Stop, Stop; On A
Carousel/Pay You Back With Interest; I'll Be True To
You/If I Need Someone; Carrie-Anne/Signs That Will Never
Change* (May 1967); *King Midas In Reverse/Water On The
Brain* (September 1967); *When Your Lights Turned On/
Dear Eloise* (November 1967); *Jennifer Eccles/Try It* (Feb-
ruary 1968); *Do The Best You Can/Elevated Observation;
Listen To Me/Everything Is Sunshine; Sorry Suzanne* (March
1969).

BUDDY HOLLY/(Charles Hardin Holly)/He was one of
the giants of early rock, a figure so important in the histroy
of popular music that it is impossible to hear a song on the
charts today that does not owe something to the tall, slim,
bespectacled boy from Lubbock, Texas. He started off in
1956, as so many of those early rock figures did, as a country
singer, but from the summer of 1957 until his death in
February 1959 he recorded scores of rock songs—the great
classic *Peggy Sue, That'll Be The Day, Maybe Baby* (with
the Crickets), *Oh Boy, Early In The Morning.* Just how
prolific he was in a career that was only a matter of
months came to light recently in England during the great
rock revival of 1968 when four albums (47 tracks) of his
were released under the title *THE IMMORTAL BUD-
DY HOLLY.* More than any other singer of that era, he
brings back a time when music was fun, when rock was fun,
when no one was trying to push it as an art form and when
sheer animal exuberance was what counted As well as his

own material (co-written with manager Norman Petty), he did all the standards of the day: *Shake Rattle and Roll, Blue Suede Shoes, Rip It Up.* Like a lot of country boys of that time who automatically headed for country music, he was sidetracked by the success other country musicians were having in the new field of rock—Elvis Presley, Bill Haley, Johnny Cash, Jerry Lee Lewis, Carl Perkins. Once he got going, he became one of the big hitmakers of rock. You only have to listen to those hits to know where a lot of the early Beach Boys and Beatles come from, not to mention the hundreds of groups that literally wouldn't have been possible without him. At the time, of course, there was no such thing as the serious rock appreciation that sprang up in 1967 and 1968. People didn't know much about music, they just knew what they liked. Adults put him down with the rest of the Presley era as shock rock. Kids just remembered it was impossible not to dance, not to groove, while he sang. Most of the giants of ten years later, of the booming rock scene of the late sixties, were teenagers when Holly was king and their music reflects it. Looking back from the twin peaks of psychedelia and electronic gadgetry, he comes through fresher than ever. It would be nice to speculate where Buddy Holly would be today if he had lived. But he didn't. He died with two others who were just beginning to make their names in rock, Richie Valens and Big Bopper, in a plane crash in Mason City, Iowa, on February 3, 1959. There are people who still weep at the thought of the talent that went down that day.

Albums/BUDDY HOLLY (March 1958): *I'm Gonna Love You Too; Peggy Sue; Listen To Me; Everyday; Look At Me; Valley Of Tears; Ready Teddy; Mailman, Bring Me No More Blues; Words Of Love; You're So Square Baby; Rave On; Little Baby.* THAT'LL BE THE DAY (April 1958): *Rock Around The Ollie Vee; Ting-A-Ling; I'm Changing All Those Changes; Girl On My Mind; That'll Be The Day.* BUDDY HOLLY STORY (February 1957): *Raining In My Heart; Early In The Morning; It Doesn't Matter Anymore; Heartbeat; Peggy Sue; Maybe Baby; Everyday; Rave On; That'll Be The Day; Think It Over.* BUDDY HOLLY STORY. VOL. 2 (March 1960); *Oh Boy; It's So Easy; Peggy Sue Got Married,*

Crying, Waiting, Hoping; Learning The Game; That Makes It Tough; Well Alright; Now We're One; What To Do; Take Your Time; True Love Ways; Little Baby; Moondreams; That's What They Say. REMINISCING (February 1963): *Reminiscing; Slippin' And Slidin'; Bo Diddley; Wait Till The Sun Shines Nellie; It's Not My Fault; Baby, Won't You Please Come Home; Brown-Eyed Handsome Man; Because I Love You; I'm Gonna Set My Foot Down; Rock-A-Bye-Rock; Changing All Those Changes.* BUDDY HOLLY AND THE CRICKETS (April 1962): *Oh, Boy, Not Fade Away; You've Got Love; Maybe Baby; It's Too Late; Tell Me How; I'm Lookin' For Someone To Love; That'll Be The Day; Empty Cup; Send Me Some Lovin'; Last Night; Rock Me Baby.* BUDDY HOLLY SHOWCASE (May 1964): *Shake, Rattle And Roll; Rock Around With Ollie Vee; Honky Tonk; I Guess I Was Just A Fool; Ummm, Oh Yeah; You're The One; Blue Suede Shoes; Come Back Baby; Rip It Up; Love's Made A Fool Of You; Gone; Girl On My Mind* HOLLY IN THE HILLS (January 1965): *I Wanna Play House With You; Door To My Heart; Fool's Paradise; Gotta Get You Near Me Blues; I Gambled With My Heart; What To Do; Wishing; Down The Line; Soft Place In My Heart; Lonesome Tears; Flower Of My Heart; You And I Are Through.* BEST OF BUDDY HOLLY (April 1966): *Peggy Sue; Blue Suede Shoes; Learning The Game; Brown-Eyed Handsome Man; Everyday; Maybe Baby; Early In The Morning; Ready Teddy; It's Too Late; What To Do; Rave On; True Love Ways; It Doesn't Matter Anymore; Crying, Waiting, Hoping; Moondreams; Rock Around With Ollie Vee; Raining In My Heart; Bo Diddley; That'll Be The Day; I'm Gonna Love You Too; Peggy Sue Got Married; That Makes It Tough; Shake, Rattle And Roll; Wishing.* BUDDY HOLLY'S GREATEST HITS (March 1967): *Peggy Sue; True Love Ways; Bo Diddley; What To Do; Learning The Game; It Doesn't Matter Anymore; That'll Be The Day; Oh, Boy; Early In The Morning; Brown-Eyed Handsome Man; Everyday; Maybe Baby.* GREAT BUDDY HOLLY (October 1967): *Blue Days, Black Nights; Girl On My Mind; That'll Be The Day; Love Me;* Six Other titles. BROWN-EYED HANDSOME MAN: *Brown-Eyed Handsome Man; Wishing; True Love Ways; Bo Diddley.*

Singles/*Peggy Sue*/ *Everyday* (September 1957); *Bo Diddley*/ *True Love Ways* (April 1963); *Brown-Eyed Handsome Man*/*Wishing* (September 1963); *I'm Gonna Love You Too*/*Rock Around With Ollie Vee* (January 1964); *Love Is Strange*/*You're The One* (March 1969).

Also Appears On/MILLION-AIRS: *Peggy Sue.* ROCK AROUND THE BLOCK: *I'm Gonna Love You Too.*

HOLY MODAL ROUNDERS/*John Wesley Annis (bass), Steve Webber (guitar), Richard Tyler (piano), Sam Shepard (drums), Peter Stampfel (banjo).*
The Holy Modal Rounders are a late sixties phenomenon, an underground group whose songs most companies were afraid to put on record and most promoters were afraid to put on stage. Their songs are sometimes pretty, sometimes funny and invariably as spaced out as the Sahara desert. Their drummer, Sam Shepard, is also the well-known off-off-Broadway playwright who was chosen by Antonioni to write for his first American movie, *Zabriskie Point.*

Album/MORAY EELS EAT THE HOLY MODAL ROUNDERS: *Bird Song; One Will Do For Now; Take-Off Artist Song; Drano; Werewolf; Interlude; Dame Fortune; Mobile Line; Duji Song; STP Song; Interlude 2; Half A Mind; The Pledge.*

JOHN LEE HOOKER/The simple, citified country blues of John Lee Hooker have touched almost every rock musician around today (the Animals and Stones do his material). Hooker, who began playing and singing in the late forties, has, thanks to Newport Folk Festivals and the folk circuit, had more exposure to the new generation than most blues artists, many of whom have never been heard outside their own hometowns. He is particularly known for his guitar style that is said to go back to Civil War days.

Albums/HOUSE OF THE BLUES (January 1960): *Wailin' The Boogie; Love Blues; It's My Own Fault; Union Station Blues; Leave My Wife Alone; Ramblin' By Myself; Sugar Mama; Down At The Landing; Louise; Ground Hog Blues; High Priced Woman; Women And Money.* JOHN LEE HOOKER PLAYS AND SINGS THE BLUES (April 1961):

Journey; I Don't Want Your Money; Hey, Baby; Mad Man Blues; Bluebird; Worried Life Blues; Apologize; Lonely Boy Boogie; Please Don't Go; Dreamin' Blues; Hey Boogie; Just Me And My Telephone. DON'T TURN ME FROM YOUR DOOR (February 1963): *Stuttering Blues; Wobbling Baby; You Lost A Good Man; Love My Baby; Misbelieving Baby; Drifting Blues; Don't Turn Me From Your Door; My Baby Don't Love Me; I Ain't Got Nobody; Real Real Gone; Guitar Lovin' Man; Talk About Your Baby.* IT SERVES YOU RIGHT TO SUFFER (February 1966): *Shake It Baby; Country Boy; You're Wrong; Bottle Up And Go; Sugar Mama; Money; It Serves You Right To Suffer; Decoration Day.* AND SEVEN NIGHTS (July 1966): *Bad Luck And Trouble; Waterfront; No One Pleases Me But You; It's Raining Here; It's A Crazy Mixed Up World; Seven Days And Seven Nights; Mai Lee; I'm Losin' You; Little Girl Go Back To School; Little Dreamer; Don't Be Messin' With My Bread.* LIVE AT THE CAFE AU GO GO (December 1966): *I'm Bad Like Jesse James; She's Long, She's Tall; When My First Wife Left Me; I Don't Want No Trouble; Heartaches And Misery; One Bourbon, One Scotch, One Beer; I'll Never Get Out Of These Blues Alive; Seven Days.* URBAN BLUES (January 1968): *Cry Before I Go; Boom Boom Boom; Back Biters And Syndicaters; Mr. Lucky; My Own Blues; I Can't Stand To Leave You; Think Twice Before You Go; I'm Standing In Line; Hot Spring Water* (2 Parts); *Motor City Is Burning.* REAL FOLK BLUES (March 1968): *Let's Go Out Tonight; Peace Lovin' Man; I'll Never Trust Your Love Again; Stella Mae; I Put My Trust In You; In The Mood; You Know, I Know; One Bourbon, One Scotch, One Beer; Waterfront.*

Singles/*In The Mood/Let's Go Out Tonight; Motor City Is Burning/Want Ad Blues; Back Biters And Syndicaters/Think Twice Before You Go; Mr. Lucky/Cry Before I Go; I Don't Want To Go To Vietnam/Simply The Truth* (March 1969).

MARY HOPKIN was still a schoolgirl in the provinces in 1968 when Twiggy heard her sing and turned the Beatles on to her. The Beatles signed her to their company, Apple Corps, and made her single their first release. Within weeks, it was not only number one in England (and high in America), but it actually pushed the Beatles' own single, *Hey Jude,* from the number one spot. Mary is one of those sweet, delicate, innocent-looking girls who could have stepped out of a Botticelli painting. Her voice is superb musical comedy style (and so is her song *Those Were The Days*). She has everything going for her, except that one touch of soul, which, in 1968–69 music, was just about essential.

Album/POSTCARD (March 1969): *Lord Of The Reedy River; Happiness Runs; Love Is The Sweetest Thing; Y Blodyn Gwyn; The Honeymoon Song; The Puppy Song; Inchworm; Voyage Of The Moon; Lullaby Of The Leaves; Young Love; Those Were The Days; Prince En Avignon; The Game; Show Business.*

Singles/*Those Were The Days/Turn, Turn, Turn* (August 1968); *Goodbye/Sparrow* (April 1969).

LIGHTNIN' (SAM) HOPKINS/An itinerant Texas country blues singer of the fifties and disciple of Blind Lemon Jefferson, his literally hundreds of records have affected almost every rock-blues singer around today. Lightnin' Hopkins could tell the story of a man wronged by a woman with such dry wit and pathos it became an art form.

Albums/COUNTRY BLUES (January 1960). LIGHTNIN' HOPKINS (February 1960). AND THE BLUES: *Worried Life; Change Your Way; Drinkin' Woman; Unpredictable Woman; I Just Don't Care; Tell It Like It Is; Miss Loretta; I Can't Stay Here In Your Town; Sugar On My Mind; You're Gonna Miss Me; Someday Baby; Mama's Baby Child.* BLUES. KING OF THE BLUES. LIGHTNIN' SAM HOPKINS (July 1962). EARLY RECORDINGS (December 1963). FIRST MEETIN' (March 1964) (With Brownie McGhee, Sonny Terry, Big Joe Williams): *Ain't Nothin' Like Whiskey; Penitentiary Blues; If You Steal My Chickens You Can't Make 'Em Lay; First Meetin'; How Long Have It Been Since You've Been Home; Wimmin From Coast To Coast.* MY LIFE IN THE BLUES (June 1965). ROOTS OF LIGHTNIN' HOPKINS (June 1965): *Penitentiary Blues; Bad Luck And Trouble; Come And Go With Me; Trouble Stay 'Way From My Door Goin' Back To Florida; She's Mine; Fan It;* Four Other Ttiles. LIGHTNIN' STRIKES

(December 1965): *Mojo Hand; Little Wail; Cotton; Take Me Back; Nothin' But The Blues; Hurricane Betsy; Guitar Lightnin'; Woke Up This Morning; Shake Yourself.* SOUL BLUES (February 1966). SOMETHING BLUE (April 1967): *Shaggy Dad; I'll Be Gone; Shining Moon; Goin' Back Home; Shake It Baby; Good Times; Don't Wake Me; What'd I Say; Talk Of The Town.* BEST OF LIGHTNIN' HOPKINS (May 1967): *Short-Haired Woman; Bottle It Up And Go; Long Time; Foot Race Is On; Prison Blues Come On Me; Bunion Stew; Mama And Papa Hopkins; Get Off My Toe; Trouble In Mind; Till The Gin Runs Out; Gonna Pull A Party; When The Saints Go Marchin' In.* BLUE (October 1967). TALKIN' SOME SENSE (June 1968).

Singles/*I Like To Boogie/Let's Go Sit On The Lawn; Automobile Blues/Mo Jo; T Model Blues/You Cook Alright; Got To Move Your Baby/Sinner's Prayer; I'm Gonna Build Me A Heaven Of My Own* (2 Parts); *Mama Blues/Pneumonia Blues; Merry Christmas/Happy New Year.*

JOHNNY HORTON/A country singer who decided to break into the pop-rock charts and occasionally managed it. It can happen.

Albums/SPECTACULAR JOHNNY HORTON (June 1959): *Plaid And Calico; Coal, Smoke, Valve Oil And Steam; Devilish Love Light; Done Rovin'; Mean, Mean, Mean Son Of A Gun; Gobbler, The Houn' Dog; Shadows On The Old Bayou; In My Home In Shelby County; Go And Wash Your Dirty Feet; Smokey Joe's Barbeque; Long Rocky Road; Words.* JOHNNY HORTON MAKES HISTORY (July 1960): *O'Leary's Cow; Battle Of New Orleans; Johnny Reb; Sink The Bismarck; Johnny Freedom; Jim Bridger; Young Abe Lincoln; Show-Shoe; Comanche; John Paul Jones; Battle Of Bull Run; Sinking Of The Reuben James.* JOHNNY HORTON'S GREATEST HITS (December 1960): *North To Alaska; Whispering Pines; Johnny Reb; Mansion You Stole; I'm Ready, If You're Willing; When It's Springtime In Alaska; Battle Of New Orleans; All For The Love Of A Girl; Sink The Bismarck; Comanche; Jim Bridger; Johnny Freedom.* HONKY-TONK MAN (March 1963): *Honky-Tonk Man; I'm A One-Woman Man; I'm Coming Home; I Got A Hole In*

My Pirogue; She Knows Why; Goodbye, Lonesome, Hello, Baby Doll; They'll Never Take Her Love From Me; Ole Slew-Foot; Sleepy-Eyed John; Wild One; Everytime I'm Kissing You; Honky-Tonk Hardwood Floor. I CAN'T FORGET YOU (February 1965): *Hot In The Sugar Cane Field; Lonesome And Heartbroken; Seven Come Eleven; I Can't Forget You; Wise To The Ways Of A Woman; Out In New Mexico; Same Old Tale The Crow Told Me; Tetched In The Head; Just Walk A Little Closer; Don't Use My Heart For A Stepping Stone; I Love You, Baby; Lost Highway.* JOHNNY HORTON ON STAGE (September 1966). JOHNNY HORTON ON THE LOUISIANA HAYRIDE (September 1966); *First Train Heading South; Lost Highway; Rock Island Line; Battle Of New Orleans; All For The Love Of A Girl; Got The Bull By The Horns; Whispering Pines; Sal's Got A Sugar Lip; Sink The Bismarck; North To Alaska.* UNFORGETTABLE JOHNNY HORTON (December 1968).

Singles/*Sink The Bismarck/When It's Springtime In Alaska* (June 1962); *North To Alaska/The Battle Of New Orleans* (May 1967); *Battle Of New Orleans/All For The Love Of A Girl* (1968).

HOT-ROD MUSIC/California started with surf music in 1963, but in 1965, with the discovery that a teenager's first love is his car, came hot-rod music. The Beach Boys did a whole album of it. No hot rod was more famous than the one driven by Jan and Dean's *Little Old Lady From Pasadena,* a drag-racing spinster. *Dead Man's Curve* was about teenage lovers who crack up their new car. The hot-rod sound was quite similar to the surf sound, very California and summery and, naturally, easy to drive to. (One of the hot-rod classics of sorts was Chuck Berry's *Cruising Along In My Automobile.*)

ENGELBERT HUMPERDINCK/As "Gerry Dorsey" he was one of hundreds of singers who never made it. As Engelbert Humperdinck his was the original Cinderella story of 1967, for his first single, *Release Me,* sold millions, as did every other single that followed. Why the difference? He looked the same, a handsome man. The voice must have been the same before and after. And the name could only draw attention to what was there. The secret really was a formula that his manager, Gordon Mills, had already applied to former rock singer Tom Jones. As Jones' popularity as a rock star faded, Mills gently eased him into country-flavored ballads with sentimental and universal appeal. It made millions for both of them. And the formula worked again for Humperdinck. *Release Me (And Let Me Love Again)* was a country song from Nashville which, sung in the rich Humperdinck voice, was apparently irresistible to all but progressive rock fans. He has never *not* had a hit since.

Albums/RELEASE ME (May 1967): *Release Me; Quiet Nights; Yours Until Tomorrow; There's A Kind Of Hush; Take My Heart; How Near Is Love; Walk Through This World With Me; Talking Love; Il Mondo; Ten Guitars; This Is My Song; There Goes My Everything.* THE LAST WALTZ (November 1967): *Last Waltz; Place In The Sun; Misty Blue; If I Were You; Two Different Worlds; If It Comes To That; Am I That Easy To Forget; Everybody Knows; To The Ends Of The Earth; To Miss Elaine E. S. Jones; All This World And The Seven Seas; Long Gone.*

Singles/*Release Me (And Let Me Love Again)/Ten Guitars* (January 1967); *There Goes My Everything/You Love* (May 1967); *The Last Waltz/That Promise* (August 1967); *Am I That Easy To Forget/Pretty Ribbons* (November 1967); *A Man Without Love/Call On Me* (April 1968); *Three Little Words/Bicyclettes De Belsize* (October 1968).

MISSISSIPPI JOHN HURT/The Mississippi-born Delta-style singer enjoyed a great success during the resurgence of interest in music roots in the middle sixties. He died in 1966 at the age of 73.

Albums/TODAY (November 1966): *Pay Day; I'm Satisfied; Candy Man; Make Me A Pallet On The Floor; Talking Casey; Hot Time In The Old Town Tonight; If You Don't Want Me, Baby; Corrine, Corrina; Coffee Blues; Louis Collins; Spike Driver Blues; Beulah Land.* IMMORTAL MISSISSIPPI JOHN HURT (February 1968): *Since I've Laid My Burden Down; Moaning The Blues; Buck Dance; Lazy Blues; Rich Land Women Blues; Tender Virgins; Hop Joint; Monday Morning Blues; I've Got The Blues And I Can't Be Satisfied;*

Keep On Knockin'; Chicken; Stagolee; Nearer My God To Thee.

JANIS IAN/This prodigious child was singing and writing songs at fifteen. By the time she was sixteen she had an album out. Her single *Society's Child* (white-girl-meets-black-boy, girl-loses-boy, girl-blames-society) was not the sort of song the disc jockeys were accustomed to playing, and they obviously would never have done so but for the intervention of Leonard Bernstein, conductor of the New York Philharmonic, who in a tv special on rock made a point of featuring the diminutive Miss Ian (four foot seven) and her ballad of miscegenation. That was it. The record took off and so did Janis. Her songs are concerned with the hypocrisies of modern society. She has clearly been influenced by Bob Dylan, Joan Baez and Tim Buckley, but her style is her own and her following, especially among earnest middle-class sixteen-year-old girls who are also concerned with the hypocrisies of modern society, is enormous.

Albums/JANIS IAN (March 1967): *Society's Child; Go 'Way Little Girl; Hair Of Spun Gold; Then Tangles Of A Mind; I'll Give You A Stone If You'll Throw It; Pro-Girl; New Christ Cardiac Hero; Younger Generation Blues; Lover Be Kindly; Mrs. McKenzie; Janey's Blues.* FOR ALL THE SEASONS OF YOUR MIND (January 1968): *Insanity Comes Quietly To The Structured Mind; Song For All The Seasons Of Your Mind; And I Did Ma; Honey D'Ya Think; Bahimsa; Sunflakes Fall, Snowrays Call; Lonely One; Queen Merkin And Me; There Are Times; Shady Acres; Evening Star.* THE SECRET LIFE OF J. EDDY FINK (August 1968): *Everybody Knows; Mistaken Identity; Friends Again; 42nd St. Psycho Blues; She's Made Of Porcelain; Sweet Misery; When I Was A Child; What Do You Think Of The Dead; Look To The Rain; Son Of Love; Baby's Blue.*

Singles/*Younger Generation Blues/I'll Give You A Stone If You'll Throw It* (February 1967); *Insanity Comes Quietly To The Structured Mind/Sunflakes Fall, Snowrays Call* (November 1967); *Song For All The Seasons Of Your Mind/Lonely One* (January 1968); *Society's Child/Letter To Jon* (August 1968).

IAN AND SYLVIA/*Ian Tyson (guitar), Sylvia Fricker Tyson (autoharp).*
Canada breeds its folk musicians on a diet of Nashville and Grand Ole Opry, the sounds of which are to be heard on many a northern radio. Ian was a Canadian cowboy and Sylvia a backwoods girl. They brought all that musical background together and in 1962 produced a first album that had everything from a work song to a cappella to country to bluegrass to traditional. As they moved on, they showed an adventurous willingness to record original folk material at a time when it was just about heretical in folk circles to sing anything written after 1800. They were also among the first to value and make use of sidemen on records, which was absolutely not done in folk music either. Their voices were honest, raw, good and strong. Ian's song *Four Strong Winds* is still the unofficial national anthem of Canada. They were often the first, or among the first, to record what are now much recorded songs and destined to be classics of their kind—Gordon Lightfoot's *Early Morning Rain*, Phil Och's *Changes*, Joni Mitchell's *Circle Game*. They are one of the few folkrock groups born directly out of folk. In 1968 they cut their ninth album in Nashville, joining Bob Dylan, the Byrds and Buffy Sainte-Marie, but like them, not because it was a trend, but because they had never been too much out of country in their sound all along.

Albums/IAN AND SYLVIA (July 1962): *Rocks And Gravel; Old Blue; See See Rider; Canadien Errant; Handsome Molly; Mary Anne; Pride Of Petrovar; Makes A Long Time Man Feel Bad; Rambler Gambler; Down By The Willow Garden; Got No More Home Than A Dog; When First Unto This Country; Live A-Humble.* FOUR STRONG WINDS (February 1964): *Tomorrow Is A Long Time; Katy Dear; Four Strong Winds; Long, Lonesome Road; V'La Le Bon Vent; Royal Canal; Lady Of Carlisle; Greenwood Sidie; Every Time I Feel The Spirit; Jesus Met The Woman At The Well; Poor Lazarus* (Ian and Sylvia); *Ella Speed; Every Night When The Sun Goes Down* (Sylvia Fricker); *Spanish Is A Loving Tongue* (Ian Tyson). NORTHERN JOURNEY (July 1964): *You Were On My Mind; Moonshine Can; Four Rode By; Jealous Lover; Brave Wolfe; Nova Scotia Farewell;*

Some Day Soon; Little Beggarman; Texas Rangers; Ghost Lover; Captain Woodstock's Courtship; Green Valley; Swing Down, Chariot. EARLY MORNING RAIN (May 1965): *Come In Stranger; Early Morning Rain; Nancy Whiskey; Awake Ye Drowsy Sleepers; Darcy Farrow; Marlborough Street Blues; Song For Canada; For Lovin' Me; I'll Bid My Heart Be Still; Red Velvet; Traveling Drummer; Maud's Blues.* PLAY ONE MORE (February 1966): *Short Grass; French Girl; When I Was A Cowboy; Changes; Gifts Are For Giving; Molly And Tenbrooks; Hey What About Me; Lonely Girls; Satisfied Mind; Twenty-Four Hours From Tulsa; Friends Of Mine; Play One More.* SO MUCH FOR DREAM-ING (February 1967): *Circle Game; So Much For Dream-ing; Wild Geese; Child Apart; Summer Wages; Hold Tight; Cutty Wren; Si Les Bateaux; Catfish Blues; Come All Ye Fair And Tender Maidens; January Morning; Grey Morning.* LOVIN' SOUND (April 1967): *Windy Weather; Hang On To A Dream; I Don't Believe You; Where Did All The Love Go; Mr. Spoons; National Hotel; Sunday; Reason To Believe; Pilgrimage To Paradise; Big River Trilogy; Lovin' Sound.* BEST OF IAN AND SYLVIA (February 1968): *You Were On My Mind; So Much For Dreaming; Early Morning Rain; Four Rode By; Canadien Errant; Twenty-Four Hours From Tulsa; Changes; See See Rider; Darcy Farrow; Catfish Blues; V'La Le Bon Vent; Four Strong Winds.* NASHVILLE (June 1968): *The Mighty Quinn; Wheels On Fire; Farewell To The North; Taking Care Of Business; Southern Comfort; Ball Of The Ugly Man; 90° x 90°; She'll Be Gone; London Life; The Renegade; House Of Cards.* FULL CIRCLE (September 1968): *Here's To You; I Learned From Leah; Women's World; Mr. Spoons; Shinbone Alley; Please Think; Stories He'd Tell; Jinkson Johnson; Tears Of Rage; The Minstrel.*

Singles/*House Of Cards/Ninety Degrees Times Ninety De-grees* (December 1962); *Pilgrimage To Paradise/Lovin' Sound* (March 1967).

THE IMPRESSIONS/*Curtis Mayfield (lead vocals), Samuel Gooden (bass vocals), Fred Cash (tenor vocals).*
They formed in Chicago, where they used to be called the Roosters, and have been singing together since 1958. Singer Jerry Butler was with them then, before he went solo. They've

had a string of hits: *Gypsy Woman, It's All Right, People Get Ready*. The group does better with originals. Curtis writes most of their material (and other artists do his songs as well).

Albums/IMPRESSIONS (September 1963): *Gypsy Woman; Grow Closer Together; Little Young Lover; You've Come Home; Never Let Me Go; Can't You See; Minstrel And Queen; I'm The One Who Loves You; I Need Your Love; As Long As You Love Me; Sad, Sad Girl & Boy; Twist & Limbo.* KEEP ON PUSHING (September 1964): *Keep On Pushing; I've Been Trying; I Ain't Supposed To; Dedicate My Song To You; Long Long Winter; Somebody Help Me; Theme From Lilies Of The Field; I Thank Heaven; Don't Let It Hide; Talking About My Baby; I Love You (Yeah); I Made A Mistake.* PEOPLE GET READY (March 1965): *Woman's Got Soul; Emotions; Sometimes I Wonder; We're In Love; Just Another Dance; Can't Work No Longer; People Get Ready; Get Up & Move; I've Found That I've Lost; Hard To Believe; See The Real Me; You Must Believe Me.* IMPRESSION'S GREATEST HITS (April 1965): *Gypsy Woman; Talking About My Baby; I'm So Proud; Keep On Pushing; Never Let Me Go; I'm The One Who Loves You; It's All Right; Grow Closer Together; You Must Believe Me; Sad, Sad Girl & Boy; Minstrel & Queen; Amen.* RIDIN' HIGH (April 1966): *Ridin' High; I'm A-Tellin' You; No One Else; Gotta Get Away; I Need To Belong To Someone; Right On Time; I Need A Love; Too Slow; Man's Temptation; That's What Mama Say; Let It Be Me.* FABULOUS IMPRESSIONS (July 1967): *You Always Hurt Me; It's All Over; Little Girl; Hundred Pounds Of Clay; Love's A-Comin'; You Ought To Be In Heaven; I Can't Stay Away From You; Aware Of Love; Isle Of Sirens; I'm Still Waitin'; She Don't Love Me.* NEVER ENDING (March 1964): *Sister Love; Little Boy Blue; Satin Doll; I Gotta Keep On Movin'; Girl Don't You Know Me; You Always Hurt The One You Love; I'm So Proud; That's What Love Will Do; Lemon Tree; September Song; Ten To One; Woman Who Loves Me.* ONE BY ONE (October 1965): *Twilight Time; I Wanna Be Around; Nature Boy; Just One Kiss From You; I Want To Be With You; Answer Me, My Love; It's Not Unusual; Without A Song; Falling In Love With You; Mona Lisa; Lonely Man.*

WE'RE A WINNER (March 1968): *We're A Winner; Moonlight Shadows; Let Me Tell The World; I'm Getting Ready; Nothing Can Stop Me; No One To Love; Little Brown Boy; I Loved & I Lost; Romancing To The Folk; Up-Up & Away.* THIS IS MY COUNTRY (November 1968). YOUNG MODS' FORGOTTEN STORY (April 1969): *My Deceiving Heart; Seven Years; Choice Of Colors; Mighty Mighty; Young Mods' Forgotten Story; Girl I Find; Wherever You Leadeth Me; Loves Miracle; Jealous Man; Soulful Love.*

Singles/*Amen/Long Long Winter; As Long As You Love Me/Gypsy Woman; Can't Satisfy/This Must Be The End; Falling In Love With You/Since I Lost The One I Love; Get Up And Move/Woman's Got Soul; I Can't Stay Away From You/You Ought To Be In Heaven; I Love You/Keep On Pushing; I Loved & I Lost/Up Up & Away; I Need You/Never Could You Be; It's All Over/We're A Winner; It's All Right/You'll Want Me Back; It's Hard To Believe/You've Got Me Running; I've Been Trying/People Get Ready; Just One Kiss From You/Twilight Time; Little Girl/You Always Hurt Me; Love's A Comin'/Wade In The Water, Never Too Much Love/Talking About My Baby; No One Else/Too Slow; Sad, Sad Girl & Boy/Twist & Limbo; See The Real Me/You Must Believe In Me; We're Rollin' On* (Part I) *We're Rollin' On* (Part II); *Fool For You/I'm Loving Nothing; Don't Cry My Love/Sometimes I Wonder* (November 1968); *This Is My Country/My Woman's Love* (December 1968).

THE INCREDIBLE STRING BAND/*Mike Heron (vocals, guitar, sitar, recorder, Hammond organ, hammer dulcimer, harpsichord), Robin Williamson (vocals, guitar, mandolin, gimbri, whistle, drums, chahanai, percussion, pan pipe, piano, oud, jews' harp, water harp, harmonica). Previous Member: Clive Palmer.*

Two eccentric Scottish hippies make up a string (and not so string) band that is, indeed, incredible. Between them they play not just sitar, harmonica and hammond organ, but also jews' harp, dulcimer and other musical exotica. Their voices hum, buzz and slide around a world populated with witches, cherry rings and fire king's daughters. Over all this they sprinkle ancient mythology, church ritual and primitive philosophy. The result is a cauldron filled with a resonant mixture that is influenced by every sound from the buzzing of bees to an Indian dance festival. It's all a very odd combination but it works and sells (in England better than any other "folk material). And why not? It's a hundred acts for the price of one. There is something occult and mysterious and unexplained about the Incredible String Band, as if it were conjured out of nowhere with a magic spell, and perhaps it was.

Albums/THE INCREDIBLE STRING BAND (April 1967): *Maybe Someday; October Song; When The Music Starts To Play; Schaeffer's Jig; How Happy I Am; Womankind; The Tree; Whistle Tune; Dandelion Blues; Empty Pocket Blues; Smoke Shovelling Song; Can't Help Me Here; Good As Gone; Footsteps Of The Heron; Niggertown; Everything's Fine Right Now.* SPIRITS (THE LAYERS OF THE ONION) (October 1967): *Way Back In The 1960's; Painting Box; Eyes Of Fate; Blues For The Muse; Chinese White; No Sleep Blues; Mad Hatter's Song; Little Cloud; Hedgehog's Song; First Girl I Loved; You Know What You Could Be; My Name Is Death; Gently Tender.* HANGMAN'S BEAUTIFUL DAUGHTER (May 1968): *Koeedaddi There; Minotaur's Song; Witches Hat; Very Cellular Song; Mercy I Cry City; Waltz Of The New Moon; Water Song; Three Is A Green Crown; Swift As The Wind; Nightfall.* WEE TAM (March 1969): *Job's Tears; Puppies; Beyond The Sea; The Yellow Snake; Log Cabin Home In The Sky; You Get Brighter; The Half-Remarkable Question; Air; Ducks On A Pond.* THE BIG HUGE (March 1969): *Maya; Greatest Friend; The Son Of Noah's Brother; Lordly Nightshade; The Mountain Of God; Cousin Caterpillar; The Iron Stone; Douglas Traherne Harding; The Circle Is Unbroken.*

INFLUENCE/*Louis Campbell McKelvey (guitar), Andrew Keiler (lead vocals), Dave Wynne (drums), Jack Geisinger (bass), Walter Rossi (guitar), Bobo Island (organ, piano).*
A band that came out of Canada late in 1967 and put on something very new for America—a rock opera, a mini rock opera. Musically, it had more echoes of Weill's *Threepenny Opera* than of anything around in rock. The group was also notable for a song (all their material was original) that told

the story of a brief love affair between a girl and a donkey. Within a few months of getting itself together in New York, Influence became yet another casualty of the rock bands' internal strife syndrome.

Album/INFLUENCE (January 1968): *I Admire; I Don't Know Why; I Met Her At The County Fair; Pieces Of Me; Baby, That's My Bag; Sir Archibald; We Are Here; Natural Impulse; Dream Woman; Mad Birds Of Prey (A Mini Opera).*

IRISH ROVERS/*Will Millar (banjo), George Millar (guitar), Wilcil McDowell (accordian), Jimmy Ferguson (vocals).*
It wasn't exactly Irish rock, but *The Unicorn* went over fairly big early in 1968, suggesting that there is always room for a good Irish song.

Albums/FIRST OF THE IRISH ROVERS (February 1967): *Irish Rover; My Boy Willie; Rattling Bog; Coulter's Candy; My Old Man's A Dustman; Patsy Fagan; I Don't Mind If I Do; Many Young Men Of Twenty; Donald Where's Your Trousers; Mick Maguire; Nancy Whiskey.* THE UNICORN (January 1968): *The Unicorn; Bonnie Kellswater; Orange And The Green; Hiring Fair; Bridget Flynn; Come In; Goodbye Mrs. Durkin; Pat Of Mullingar; Wind That Shakes The Corn; First Love In Life; Black Velvet Band.*

Singles/*Orange And Green/Whiskey On A Sunday (Puppet Song)* (June 1967); *The Unicorn/Black Velvet Band* (January 1968); *Biplane, Ever More/Liverpool Lou* (September 1968).

IRON BUTTERFLY/*Erik Brann (lead guitar), Lee Dorman (bass), Ron Bushy (drums), Doug Ingle (organ, vocals).*
Iron Butterfly is the perfect name for a group playing heavy rock ("heavy-handed" say its critics). The group started in Los Angeles in 1967 but did not attract attention nationally until 1968, when its very raw and powerful sound hit the airwaves and the charts. It's worth noting here that the loud and heavy music of this period emerged as a West rather than East Coast phenomenon, almost as if it needed the noise to make its impact from so far away.

Albums/HEAVY (1968): *Possession; Unconscious Power; Get Out Of My Life, Woman; Gentle As It May Seem; You Can't Win; So-Lo; Look For The Sun; Iron Butterfly Theme; Fields Of The Sun; Stamped Ideas.* IN-A-GADDA-DA-VIDA (August 1968): *Most Anything You Want; Flowers And Beads; My Mirage; Termination; Are You Happy; In-A-Gadda-Da-Vida.* BALL (February 1969): *In The Time Of Our Lives; Soul Experience; Lonely Boy; Real Fright; In The Crowds; It Must Be Love; Her Favorite Style; Filled With Fear; Belda-Beast.*

Singles/*Unconscious Power/Possession; Iron Butterfly Theme/In-A-Gadda-Da-Vida; In The Crowds/Soul Experience* (February 1969); *In The Time Of Our Lives/It Must Be Love* (April 1969).

ISLEY BROTHERS/*Ronald, Rudolph and O'Kelly Isley.* Best known for two major hits, *Shout* and *Twist and Shout,* the Isley Brothers' sound has been imitated by everyone from early Beatles onwards. In March 1966 *This Old Heart Of Mine* (their first record for Motown) was a big hit. In November 1968 it flew into the top ten in England. Record companies never try to explain these phenomena. They have no idea themselves how it happens.

Albums/TWIST AND SHOUT: *Twist And Shout; I Say Love; You Better Come Home; Never Leave Me Baby;* Other Titles. TAKE SOME TIME OUT. FAMOUS ISLEY BROTHERS (January 1964): *Surf And Shout; Please, Please, Please; Do The Twist; She's The One; Tango; What'cha Gonna Do; Stagger Lee; You'll Never Leave Him; Let's Go, Let's Go, Let's Go; Shake It With Me Baby; She's Gone; Long Tall Sally.* THIS OLD HEART OF MINE (October 1966): *This Old Heart Of Mine; Stop, In The Name Of Love; Nowhere To Run; Take Some Time Out For Love; I Guess I'll Always Love You; Baby Don't You Do It; Who Could Ever Doubt My Love; Put Yourself In My Place; I Hear A Symphony; Just Ain't Enough Love; There's No Love Left; Seek And You Shall Find.* SOUL ON THE ROCKS (February 1968): *Got To Have You Back; That's The Way Love Is; Whispers (Gettin' Louder); Tell Me It's Just A Rumor Baby; One Too Many Heartaches; It's Out Of*

The Question; Why When Love Is Gone; Save Me From The Misery; Little Miss Sweetness; Good Things; Catching Up On Time; Behind A Painted Smile.

Singles/*Shout* (2 Parts); *Twist And Shout/Wa Watusi; Shine On Harvest Moon/Standing On The Dance Floor; Write To Me/Your Old Lady; Fool For You/Just One More Time; Last Girl/Looking For Love; Simon Says/Wild As A Tiger; This Old Heart Of Mine/There's No Love Left; Who Could Ever Doubt My Love/Take Some Time Out For Love; I Guess I'll Always Love You/I Hear A Symphony; Got To Have You Back/Just Ain't Enough Love; One Too Many Heartaches/That's The Way Love Is; Why When Love Is Gone/Take Me In Your Arms; All Because I Love You/Behind A Painted Smile* (November 1968).

MAHALIA JACKSON/She is the queen of the gospel singers. Much of the fervor of the blues and the soul singers today is inspired by Mahalia's work. For her part, she has listened to blues and learned from them, but her dedication has always been to sacred music. To those who find the two rather alike she concedes that they may come from the same source, but the *internal* emphasis is quite different.

Albums/MAHALIA JACKSON—THE WORLD'S GREATEST GOSPEL SINGER. BLESS THIS HOUSE. NEWPORT 1958 (December 1958). GREAT GETTIN' UP MORNING (September 1959). COME ON CHILDREN LET'S SING (May 1960). THE POWER AND THE GLORY (September 1960). I BELIEVE (February 1961). EVERYTIME I FEEL THE SPIRIT (September 1961). MAHALIA JACKSON—RECORDED IN EUROPE (March 1962). GREAT SONGS OF LOVE AND FAITH (September 1962). SILENT NIGHT—SONGS FOR CHRISTMAS (December 1962). MAKE A JOYFUL NOISE UNTO THE LORD (February 1963). MAHALIA JACKSON'S GREATEST HITS (October 1963). LET'S PRAY TOGETHER (April 1964). MAHALIA SINGS (March 1966). GARDEN OF PRAYER—THE OLD RUGGED CROSS (November 1966). MY FAITH (March 1967). IN CONCERT (September 1967). BEST LOVED HYMNS OF DR. MARTIN LUTHER KING (August 1968). MIGHTY FORTRESS

(September 1968). YOU'LL NEVER WALK ALONE (September 1968). CHRISTMAS WITH MAHALIA (September 1968).

Singles/*Sunrise, Sunset/Like The Breeze Blows; We Shall Overcome/Take My Hand Precious Lord; Lord's Prayer/Silent Night.*

ELMORE JAMES influenced many of today's blues guitarists, especially Eric Clapton, who learned from his records to play Mississippi Delta guitar in the bottleneck style also used by Mike Bloomfield. James died in 1964.

TOMMY JAMES (and the SHONDELLS)/Whenever anyone wants to put down rock, they pick on Tommy James as an example of the worst of it. Nevertheless, he's had eleven hits and several number one records. He made his first big hit, *Hanky Panky,* on his own and formed the Shondells only after that was a success. When *Money Money* made number one on the English charts in the summer of 1968, George Harrison sent him some Beatles songs. If you want to call it bubblegum music, Tommy won't stop you. As long as people keep buying, you can call it anything you want to. In 1969, he finally got away from the bubblegum with a nice piece of head music called *Crimson and Clover.*

Albums/HANKY PANKY: *Hanky Panky; I'll Go Crazy; I'm So Proud; Lover; Love Makes The World Go 'Round; Lots Of Pretty Girls; Good Lovin'; Say I Am; Cleo's Mood; Don't Throw Our Love Away; Shake A Tail Feather; Soul Searchin' Baby.* IT'S ONLY LOVE: *It's Only Love; Hold On A Little Bit Longer; I'm So Lonesome I Could Cry; It's Alright; Juanita (Nobody's Gonna Stop Our Love); Ya Ya; We'll Have A World; Don't Let My Love Pass You By; Fanny Mae; Some.* I THINK WE'RE ALONE NOW. SOMETHING SPECIAL: *Out Of The Blue; Say I Am; Gettin' Together; Run, Run, Baby Run; I Like The Way; Love's Closin' In On Me; I Think We're Alone Now; Real Girl; Mirage; Don't Let My Love Pass You By; It's Only Love; Hanky Panky.* GETTIN' TOGETHER: *Gettin' Together; Sometimes I'm Up (Sometimes I'm Down); I Want To Be Around You; Lost In Your Eyes; Some Happy Day;*

You Better Watch Out; Other Titles. SHONDELLS AT THE SATURDAY HOP.

Singles/*Baby I Can't Take It No More/I Like The Way; Don't Let My Love Pass You By/It's Only Love; Get Out Now/Wish It Were You; Gettin' Together/Real Girl; Gone, Gone, Gone/I Think We're Alone Now; Hanky Panky/Thunderbolt; Lots Of Pretty Girls/Say I Am; Love's Closin' In On Me/Out Of The Blue; Mirage/Run, Run, Run; Mony Mony /One Two Three & I Fell; Do Something To Me/Ginger Bread Man* (October 1968); *Crimson And Clover/Taken* (December 1968); *Breakaway/Sweet Cherry Wine* (March 1969).

Also Appears On/INCENSE & OLDIES: *I Think We're Alone Now; Mirage.*

JAMES JAMESON has been house bass player for Motown for the last four years and has played on all their great singles. His bass work on the Four Tops' *Reach Out I'll Be There* is classic.

JAN AND DEAN (Jan Berry and Dean Torrence)/To hear Jan and Dean in 1963 was to see the world as one great big California where life revolved around the beach, the sea and the California freeways. Jan and Dean were around before the Beach Boys but they didn't really make their name until they moved into the Beach Boys' special province—surf. Having introduced their public to the pleasures of Surf City ("Two girls to every boy"), they explored another California phenomenon: the love of a man for his car. And *Dead Man's Curve* showed just where it could finish. Like the Beach Boys and other lesser-known California groups, they became as obsessed with speed as they had been with water, the subject changing but the sound, high surfy harmonies, as familiar as ever. You only have to hear *Little Old Lady From Pasadena* to know that riding the highway is not that different from riding the waves. Later, when the boom died away, so did Jan and Dean, who went on to record such unsurfy sounds as *Norwegian Wood.*

Albums/JAN AND DEAN TAKE LINDA SURFIN' (May 1963): *Linda; Walk Like A Man; Surfin' U.S.A.; Mr. Bass*

Man; Let's Turkey Trot; Rhythm Of The Rain; Walk Right
In; Best Friend I Ever Had; Gypsy Cried; My Foolish Heart;
When I Learn How To Cry; Surfin' Safari. SURF CITY AND
OTHER SWINGIN' CITIES (June 1963): Surf City; Memphis,
Tennessee; Detroit City; Manhattan; Philadelphia, Pa.; Way
Down Yonder In New Orleans; Honolulu Lulu; Kansas City;
I Left My Heart In San Francisco; You Came A Long Way
From St. Louis; Tallahassee Lassie; Soul City. DRAG CITY
(November 1963): Drag City; I Gotta Drive; Drag Strip
Girl; Surfin' Hearse; Dead Man's Curve; Schlock Rod Part 1;
Schlock Rod Part 2; Popsicle Truck; Surf Route 101; Sting
Ray; Little Deuce Coupe; Hot Stocker. DEAD MAN'S
CURVE/THE NEW GIRL IN SCHOOL (May 1964): Dead
Man's Curve; Three Window Coupe; Bucket "T"; Rockin'
Little Roadster, "B" Gas Rickshaw; My Mighty G. T. O.; The
New Girl In School; Linda; Barons, West L. A.; School Day;
It's As Easy As 1, 2, 3; Hey Little Freshman. RIDE THE
WILD SURF (August 1964): Ride The Wild Surf; Tell 'Em
I'm Surfin'; Waimea Girl; She's My Summer Girl; The Rest-
less Surfer; Skateboarding Part 1; Sidewalk Surfin'; Surfin'
Wild; Down At Malibu Beach; A Surfer's Dream; Walk On
The Wet Side; The Submarine Races. THE LITTLE OLD
LADY FROM PASADENA (September 1964): The Little
Old Lady From Pasadena; Memphis; When It's Over; Horace
The Swingin' School-Bus Driver; Old Ladies Seldom Power
Shift; Sidewalk Surfin'; The Anaheim, Azusa And Cucamonga
Sewing Circle, Book Review And Timing Association; Sum-
mer Means Fun; It's As Easy As 1, 2, 3; Move Out Little
Mustang; Skateboarding Part 2; One-Piece Topless Bathing-
suit. COMMAND PERFORMANCE—"LIVE" IN PERSON
(January 1965): Surf City; Little Honda; Dead Man's Curve;
I Get Around; All I Have To Do Is Dream; Theme From The
Tami Show; Rock And Roll Music; The Little Old Lady From
Pasadena; Do Wah Diddy Diddy; I Should Have Known
Better; Sidewalk Surfin'; Louie Louie. JAN AND DEAN'S
GOLDEN HITS (August 1965): Baby Talk; Heart And
Soul; Jennie Lee; We Go Together; Tennessee; Palisades
Park; Who Put The Bomp; Sunday Kind Of Love; Queen Of
My Heart; In A Turkish Town; Poor Little Puppet; Barbara
Ann. JAN AND DEAN'S GOLDEN HITS—VOLUME 2
(September 1965): Linda; Surf City; Honolulu Lulu; Drag

City; Dead Man's Curve; The New Girl In School; The Little
Old Lady From Pasadena; The Anaheim, Azusa And Cu-
camonga Sewing Circle, Book Review And Timing Associa-
tion; Ride The Wild Surf; Sidewalk Surfin'; From All Over
The World; You Really Know How To Hurt A Guy. FOLK
'N ROLL (November 1965): I Found A Girl; Hang On
Sloopy; I Can't Wait To Love You; Eve Of Destruction; It's
A Shame To Say Goodbye; Where Were You When I Needed
You; A Beginning From An End; Yesterday; The Universal
Coward; It Ain't Me Babe; Folk City; Turn! Turn! Turn!
FILET OF SOUL (April 1966): Norwegian Wood; 1-2-3;
Lightnin' Strikes; You've Got To Hide Your Love Away;
Let's Hang On; Hang On Sloopy; Honolulu Lulu; Gonna
Hustle You; Dead Man's Curve; Michelle; I Found A Girl;
Everybody Loves A Clown. JAN AND DEAN MEET BAT-
MAN (March 1966): Batman; The Origin Of Captain Jan
And Dean The Boy Blunder; Robin The Boy Wonder; A
Vi-Ta-Min A Day; Mr. Freeze; The Doctor's Dilemma; A
Stench In Time; Batman Theme; A Hank Of Hair And A
Banana Peel; The Fireman's Flaming Flourish; The Joker Is
Wild; Tiger Tiger, Burning; Flight Of The Batmobile; A Hot
Time In The Old Town Tonight. POPSICLE (June 1966):
Popsicle; The Restless Surfer; She's My Summer Girl; Down
At Malibu Beach; Summer Means Fun; Tennessee; Norwe-
gian Wood; A Surfer's Dream; Surf Route 101; Surfin' Wild;
Waimea Bay; One-Piece Topless Bathing Suit. JAN AND
DEAN'S GOLDEN HITS—VOLUME 3 (August 1966):
Batman; Do Wah Diddy Diddy; Detroit City; Eve Of De-
struction; 1-2-3; Hang On Sloopy; Little Deuce Coupe; Louie
Louie; Memphis; Yesterday; Walk Right In; Everybody Loves
A Clown. SAVE FOR A RAINY DAY (March 1967):
Yellow Balloon; Here Comes The Rain; Like Summer Rain;
Lullaby In The Rain; Pocketful Of Rainbows; When Sunny
Gets Blue; Rain On The Roof; Raindrops; Cryin' In The
Rain; Taste Of Rain; Save For A Rainy Day Theme.

Singles/A Sunday Kind Of Love/Poor Little Puppet (No-
vember 1961); Tennessee/Your Heart Has Changed Its
Mind (April 1962); My Favorite Dream/Who Put The Bomp
(August 1962); Baby Talk/Jeanette Get Your Hair Done
(September 1962); Frosty/She's Still Talking Baby Talk

(November 1962); *When I Learn How To Cry/Linda* (January 1963); *She's My Summer Girl/Surf City* (May 1963); *Honolulu Lulu/Someday* (August 1963); *Drag City/Schlock Rod* (November 1963); *The New Girl In School/Dead Man's Curve* (February 1963); *The Little Old Lady From Pasadena/My Mighty G. T. O.* (June 1964); *Ride The Wild Surf/The Anaheim, Azusa And Cucamonga Sewing Circle, Book Review And Timing Association* (August 1964); *Sidewalk Surfin'/When It's Over* (October 1964); *Freeway Flyer/From All Over The World* (February 1965); *You Really Know How To Hurt A Guy/It's As Easy As 1, 2, 3* (April 1965); *It's A Shame To Say Goodbye/Folk City* (September 1965); *A Beginning From An End/Folk City* (December 1965); *Batman/Bucket "T"* (February 1966); *Norwegian Wood/Popsicle* (May 1966); *A Surfer's Dream/Fiddle Around* (July 1966); *The New Girl In School/School Day* (October 1966); *Love And Hate/Only A Boy* (February 1968); *I Know My Mind/Laurel And Hardy* (June 1968); *In The Still Of The Night/Girl, You're Blowing My Mind* (October 1968).

BERT JANSCH first appeared in the States in 1966 on an album built from the best of two British records. In Britain he has for a long time been considered one of the best guitarists in folk and he played lead guitar on several cuts in Donovan's first album. *Bert's Blues* in Donovan's *SUNSHINE SUPERMAN* and *The House of Jansch* on *MELLOW YELLOW* refer to the man who greatly influenced Donovan. His style comes from blues and classical guitar. His solos are light and graceful. He was given one big promotional push as the next Donovan, which never took off. His fame in America is mainly underground, though he nas made many albums in England, where he is very highly regarded. In 1968 he got together a group called Pentangle.
(See PENTANGLE)

Albums/LUCKY THIRTEEN (May 1966): *Angie; Been On The Road So Long; Running From Home; Tinker's Blues; I Have No Time; Lucky Thirteen; Needle Of Death; Ring A Ding Bird; Casbah; Courting Blues; Oh My Babe; Veronica; Rambling's Gonna Be The Death Of Me; The Wheel.* STEPPING STONES (March 1969).

JAY AND THE AMERICANS/*Jay Black (lead vocals), Kenny Vance (vocals), Sandy Deane (vocals), Marty Sanders (guitar).*
Previous member: Howie Kane.

These four Brooklyn boys get today's new music people jittery because without the Beatles that's the way popular music might still be. Jay and the Americans had a number one record in 1963, *She Cried*, and then *Only In America, Come A Little Closer, Cara Mia* and others. It was clean American rock, and good for television, European tours and plenty of record sales. Not everyone liked the changes the Beatles brought, and since Jay and the Americans continue to sell records and tickets in some parts of the country, one can only surmise that in some cases staying the same pays off as much as changing.

Albums/SHE CRIED (May 1963): *Drums; Kansas City; My Clair De Lune; Save The Last Dance For Me; Dawning; She Cried; Yes; Stand By Me; Moon River; Tonight; Other Girls; Spanish Harlem.* JAY AND THE AMERICANS AT THE CAFE WHA? (July 1963): *Gypsy In My Soul; I Hear Music; Song Is You; Certain Smile; This Land Is Your Land; Lot Of Living To Do; Percolator Song; Riddle; Girls, Girls, Girls; Gonna Build Me A Mountain; Lawrence; Golden Vanity; Kansas City; Baby, That Is Rock 'n Roll; For All We Know.* COME A LITTLE BIT CLOSER (November 1964): *Come A Little Bit Closer; She Doesn't Know It; Strangers Tomorrow; What's The Use; To Wait For Love; Only In America; Look In My Eyes Maria; Friday; This Is It; Come Dance With Me; Tomorrow; Goodbye Boys Goodbye.* BLOCKBUSTERS (May 1965): *When It's All Over; Something In My Eye; Cara Mia; Think Of The Good Times; Somebody's Gonna Cry; If You Were Mine, Girl; Run To My Lovin' Arms; Let's Lock The Door (And Throw Away The Key); Twenty-Four Hours From Tulsa; Please Let Me Dream; Silly Girl, Silly Boy; Hang Around.* JAY AND THE AMERICANS—GREATEST HITS (October 1965): *Some Enchanted Evening; Come A Little Bit Closer; Only In America; When It's All Over; Think Of The Good Times; Goodbye Boys Goodbye; Cara Mia; Something In My Eye; Girl; Let's Lock The Door (And Throw Away The Key); If*

You Were Mine, Girl; Run To My Lovin' Arms; Through This Doorway. SUNDAY AND ME (February 1966): *Sunday And Me; Granada; Crying; 'Til; I Miss You (When I Kiss You); I Don't Need A Friend; Why Can't You Bring Me Home; Maria; Baby Stop Your Cryin'; Chilly Winds; She's The Girl (That's Messin' Up My Mind).* LIVIN' ABOVE YOUR HEAD (August 1966): *Livin' Above Your Head; Grass Will Sing (For You); Too Many Times; Diana; Over The Mountain; I'll Remember; Sun Ain't Gonna Shine Anymore; Reason For Living; Monday, Monday; Baby Come Home; Stop The Clock; Look At Me—What Do You See.* JAY AND THE AMERICANS—GREATEST HITS, VOLUME 2 (November 1966): *Crying; Sunday And Me; Stop The Clock; Hang Around; Granada; 'Til; Twenty-Four Hours From Tulsa; Monday, Monday; Livin' Above Your Head; Maria; Why Can't You Bring Me Home; Silly Girl, Silly Boy.* TRY SOME OF THIS (March 1967): *You Ain't As Hip As All That Baby; Always Something There To Remind Me (There's); Where's The Girl; Show Must Go On; Truly Julie's Blues; Where Is The Village; Nature Boy; Here There And Everywhere; He's Raining In My Sunshine; What To Do With Laurie; It's A Big Wide Wonderful World.*

Singles/*She Cried/Tonight* (April 1963); *My Clair De Lune /Only In America* (September 1964); *I'll Remember You/Let's Lock The Door (And Throw Away The Key)* (September 1965); *Come A Little Bit Closer/Goodbye Boys Goodbye* (March 1966); *Don't Let The End Begin/Up And Over* (August 1966) (Jay alone); *Cara Mia/When It's All Over* (November 1966); *You Ain't Gonna Wake Up Cryin'/Gemini* (October 1968); *This Magic Moment* (December 1968).

JAY AND THE TECHNIQUES/*Jay Proctor (vocals), Karl Landis (vocals), Dante Dancho (lead guitar), Ronnie Goodly, John Walsh, George Lloyd, Chuck Crowl.*

Jay and the Techniques had been around Pennsylvania, where they came from, for some time but surfaced nationally in 1967 with a single, *Apples, Peaches, Pumpkin Pie,* and a good follow-up, *Keep the Ball Rolling.* Their black sound comes from the group's two lively black singers, Jay Proctor and Karl Landis. The five-man backing group is white.

Albums/APPLES, PEACHES, PUMPKIN PIE (July 1967):
*Apples, Peaches, Pumpkin Pie; Contact; Hey Diddle Diddle;
Been So Long (Since I Loved You); Power Of Love; Victo-
ry; Ain't No Soul (Left In These Old Shoes); Lovin' For
Money; Here We Go Again; Stronger Than Dirt; Keep The
Ball Rollin'.* LOVE, LOST AND FOUND (February 1968):
*Strawberry Shortcake; I Want You So Bad (I Can Taste It);
Don't Let It Go To Your Head; If I Should Lose You; When
Love Slips Away; I'm 'Gonna Make You Love Me; Still (In
Love With You); You Gave Me Somebody To Love; Girl I
Want To Marry You; Dig A Little Deeper; Locked In (Your
Love); Mexico.*

Singles/Here We Go Again/Keep The Ball Rolling (June
1967); *Strawberry Shortcake/Still (In Love With You)* (De-
cember 1967); *Singles Game/Baby, How Easy Your Heart
Forgets Me, Baby, Make Your Own Sweet Music/Help
Yourself To All My Lovin'; Apples, Peaches, Pumpkin Pie/
Stronger Than Dirt* (1967); *Baby How Easy Your Heart
Forgets Me/Singles Game* (August 1968); *No I Don't Know
Her/When You Dance* (April 1969); *Are You Ready For
This/Change Your Mind* (April 1969).

JAZZ/There have been many jazz musicians, from all styles
and periods of jazz, who have exerted a strong influence on
rock. Principally, however, the jazz musicians who have made
the greatest impression on the rock musicians—the jazzmen
whom many rock players acknowledge listening to and learning from—are those who belong to the current jazz avant-
garde. The standard-bearers of the movement are pianist-
composer Cecil Taylor; saxophonists Ornette Coleman, Albert Ayler, Archie Shepp, Pharoah Sanders and the late John
Coltrane; trumpeter Don Cherry; drummer Sunny Murray
and band leader-pianist Sun Ra.

With most rock groups the influence of jazz is largely subtle
and covert; more spiritual than specific. But many rock
musicians have had considerable experience in jazz, and
groups such as Jeremy & the Satyrs, Blood, Sweat & Tears and
Traffic are very jazz-oriented. Of course as rock has itself
ascended to the level of art, many jazz musicians have come
to look to it as a source of material and energy. Jazz groups

like those of Gary Burton, Charles Lloyd and Hugh Masekela have begun to use the rock sound in their music.

BLIND LEMON JEFFERSON/One of the great country-blues singers of the twenties and a big influence on men like Leadbelly and B. B. King.
Album/BLIND LEMON JEFFERSON: 1926–1929 (June 1968).

JEFFERSON AIRPLANE/*Jorma Kaukonen (lead guitar), Jack Casady (bass), Spencer Dryden (replaced Skip Spence) (drums), Paul Kantner (rhythm guitar), Marty Balin (vocals), Grace Slick (replaced Signe Andersen) (bass & rhythm guitar, vocals).*
Jefferson Airplane was the first of the big San Francisco bands to make it, the first to snap up a big contract, the first to get big national promotion, the first with a big national hit (*Somebody to Love* in 1967). The implications of that are enormous. Until then, in spite of the minor eccentricities of the Byrds and the Lovin' Spoonful, the national rock scene was reasonably sedate. A Beatles cut here, a touch of Carnaby Street there, but little that was really freaky. The arrival of the Jefferson Airplane changed all that forever. Even the New York hippies had to do some serious readjusting when the Airplane first arrived (their first piece of promotion was the first of the psychedelic hippie-nouveau San Francisco style posters most New Yorkers had never seen). This was early 1967, when San Francisco and Haight-Ashbury and Flower Power were in full bloom, and the Airplane breezed into New York to plant those first seeds of love power in the East. Initially, the nation as a whole was a little suspicious, a little afraid of being taken in by a San Francisco hype. But you only had to hear Grace Slick and Marty Balin sing and Casady on bass and those incredible songs that told you, between the lines, swirling tales of chemical journeys and wondrous discoveries—and you knew it was real. After all those years of Frankie Avalon and Pat Boone, it was startling to hear Gracie singing about acid and drugs and pills on your friendly neighborhood station.

The commercial (as well as the artistic) success of the Airplane was immediate and enormous. Record companies rushed to sign up every other San Francisco band (after having completely ignored them). None ever equaled the Airplane in draw power, though Big Brother and the Holding Company, thanks only to Janis Joplin, was to get a number one album. In any case, we now had on a national level what San Francisco had had all along since the golden days of the fall of 1965—the San Francisco sound. Apart from the goodtimey noises of the Spoonful and the Mamas and Papas, the San Francisco sound was the first original sound the United States had since the English invasion of 1964. (And the English loved it too.) It was a time of be-ins and bells and flowers and incense, and the oriental undertones of the San Francisco sound were the right background music for it all. There were bands that played good music and bands that were a total environment happening. The Jefferson Airplane hit you from all sides. They had Grace Slick, the first girl singer with a big band (she had, however, replaced another girl singer). Grace was an ex-model, a great beauty with a piercing voice. And though she tended to dominate, the band also had Marty Balin, one of the great singers of love songs in modern rock. They sang around each other and around the music like dancers.

The Airplane has a very wide musical range. In the beginning, when they were playing for dances at the Fillmore in San Francisco—where, if the participants weren't exactly zonked out of their minds, they at least wanted to feel that way—anything went. They could freak out all over the stage; they could get into jazz improvisations, into folk, into blues, into anything. There was no form in the usual rigid sense. There was no "audience" sitting rigidly with rigid expectations. Everything was flowing and free form, with just one important discipline, the usual one: give the customers what they came for. In this case, the customers came to be made one with the music. So there would be long instrumental passages, when everyone wanted to move and dance, and then the voices confirming for them what they knew already. *Triad* is about three people who all love one another, or at least, that's the only way out for them. *White Rabbit* reminds you that *Alice in Wonderland* was probably about drugs. In *Ulysses* you realize that James Joyce was ahead of his time and belongs to the age of McLuhan after all. And so on.

Away from the hot, heavy, sensual atmosphere of the San Francisco Fillmore (and do they ever miss it), the Jefferson Airplane has to come on like any other band. In a recording studio it was hard for them, since so much of their act was dependent upon their contact with their fans. And even in a concert hall without the feedback of that glazed, stoned Fillmore audience, without patterns and images swirling around them, it's very hard. Whenever possible they take Glenn McKay's Headlights with them, a light show that produces visually what the Airplane does with music. (Or is it the other way around?) But when they play, something does happen, even if it's not always their best. And Donovan sings *Fly Jefferson Airplane*, not just because the band has the right name but because it is one of those bands you fly with. That's the whole thing about acid rock. Having experienced, as most San Francisco bands did (as most young San Francisco people did), the sometimes frightening, sometimes ecstatic but always overwhelming effects of lysergic acid diethylamide, the Airplane could not conceive of music in any other way. The group grew with San Francisco, with Timothy Leary's drug revolution, with everything that followed.

In 1965 Grace was with another group, the Great Society, which often appeared on the same bill as the Airplane. When the Airplane's girl singer left and the Great Society split, Grace moved in with the Airplane, taking a lot of her songs with her. (Grace says it was the Airplane that inspired her and her husband and brother-in-law to start their own group.) Since then a lot has happened. The magic went out of San Francisco. The San Francisco sound was imitated, cheapened and weakened, so that by 1968 it was stale. And the Airplane became America's top group anyway. This should have meant the kiss of death for the group—the usual death from over- work, overpromotion and too much money—and it's true that the hard core is unhappy about the Airplane's playing class gigs like the Whitney Museum and the Waldorf on New Year's Eve. Nevertheless, that mixture of jazz, folk, blues and surrealistic electronic tinkering works, and even when they're not performing well they never sound uptight. Years, or maybe centuries from now, someone will discover that there really was a music of the spheres, and it will sound not unlike the music the Airplane plays in the moments of its highest flight.

Albums/JEFFERSON AIRPLANE TAKES OFF (August 1966): *Blues From An Airplane; Let Me In; It's No Secret; Bringing Me Down; Tobacco Road; Come Up The Years; Run Around; Let's Get Together; Don't Slip Away; Chauffeur Blues; And I Like It.* SURREALISTIC PILLOW (February 1967): *She Has Funny Cars; Somebody To Love; My Best Friend; Today; Comin' Back To Me; How Do You Feel; 3/5 Of A Mile In 10 Seconds; D.C.B.A.-25; Embryonic Journey; White Rabbit; Plastic Fantastic Lover.* AFTER BATHING AT BAXTER'S (January 1968): *Ballad Of You And Me And Pooneil; Two Heads; Last Wall Of The Castle; Rejoyce; Watch Her Ride; Spare Chaynge; Won't You Try/Saturday Afternoon; Wild Tyme; Martha; Small Package Of Value Will Come To You, Shortly; Young Girl Sunday Blues.* CROWN OF CREATION (September 1968): *Lather; In Time; Triad; Star Track; Share A Little Joke; Chusingura; If You Feel; Ice Cream Phoenix; Crown Of Creation; Greasy Heart; House At Pooneil Corners.* BLESS ITS POINTED LITTLE HEAD (March 1969): *Clergy; 3/5's Of A Mile In 10 Seconds; Somebody To Love; Fat Angel; Rock Me Baby; The Other Side Of This Life; It's No Secret; Plastic Fantastic Lover; Turn Out The Lights; Bear Melt.*

Singles/*It's No Secret/Runnin' Round This World* (February 1966); *Come Up The Years/Blues From An Airplane* (May 1966); *Bringing Me Down/Let Me In* (September 1966); *My Best Friend/How Do You Feel* (December 1966); *Somebody To Love/She Has Funny Cars* (February 1967); *White Rabbit/Plastic Fantastic Lover* (June 1967); *Ballad Of You And Me And Pooneil/Two Heads* (August 1967; *Watch Her Ride/Martha* (November 1967); *Greasy Heart/Share A Little Joke* (March 1968); *White Rabbit/ Somebody To Love* (September 1968); *Crown Of Creation/ Lather* (October 1968); *Other Side Of This Life/Plastic Fantastic Lover* (May 1969).

JEREMY & THE SATYRS/*Jeremy Steig, Donald MacDonald, Edgar Gomez, Adrian Gulilleroy, Warren B. Bernhardt.*

If the theory ever comes true that in the bands of the future, there will be a total merging of blues, rock, rhythm and blues, jazz and classical music, it will be historically interesting to know that Jeremy and the Satyrs did it before their time. What's more, that they were unable to conceive of any other kind of music but just this kind of merging. Anti-label and pro-music, Jeremy Steig feels a band should be able to do *anything* musically. That's just what they have been doing since late 1967, as often as not, in places where until then not much more than rock had been heard. If they didn't always educate their rock audiences completely, they at least let them know that other things existed. Jeremy and the Satyrs may very well be showing us where rock is heading—toward total music. Interestingly enough, it may also be where jazz is heading, too.

Album/JEREMY & THE SATYRS (February 1968): *In The World Of Glass Teardrops; Foreign Release; She Didn't Even Say Goodbye; Do It; Superbaby; First Time I Saw You, Baby; Lovely Child Of Tears; Movie Show; Mean Black Snake; Canzonetta; Satyrized.*

Single/*Lovely Child Of Tears/Movie Show.*

TOM JONES/He came out of the poverty-stricken Welsh mine territory that Richard Burton had already put on the map. He was tough and hard and very masculine and sang like that—hard rock all the way (that was where the money was then). Then, in one of those master strokes that a manager comes up with from time to time, he was switched to ballads with a strong country and western mood. The first, late in 1966, *Green, Green Grass of Home,* sold a million almost immediately, teary and sentimental as it was. The record was particularly successful in the United States, where no one had ever heard of Tom Jones (unless they'd heard him sing the title song on the sound track of *What's New Pussycat?*). When Elvis Presley went to see him in Las Vegas, he told Jones how much that song had moved him (Presley has never lost his country roots). In the good old tradition of not bucking good fortune when it's going your way, Jones did a second country ballad, *Detroit City,* with the same overwhelming success. He never announced them as country songs—

that would have put some people off—he just did them. Soon good old rocking Jonesy, who had, in fact, been getting a little long in the tooth for the youth-obsessed English rock scene, was moving out of that slightly scruffy world into a world of dinner suits, champagne, cigars and big houses. He was also getting fantastic attention from American managers—even, it was rumored, from Presley's own manager, the wily Colonel Parker, who may have had thoughts of creating another Elvis. Through the whole country-ballad thing, Jones is now bringing hard English rock, with some very heady hip action indeed, into the American nightclub scene. The Copacabana is still recovering.

Albums/IT'S NOT UNUSUAL (May 1965): *It's Not Unusual; Memphis Tennessee; I Need Your Loving; Whatcha Gonna Do; Skye Boat Song; Worried Man; Once Upon A Time; Spanish Harlem; If You Need Me; When The World Was Beautiful.* WHAT'S NEW PUSSYCAT? (August 1965): *What's New Pussycat; With These Hands; Some Other Guy; I've Got A Heart; Little By Little; One More Chance; Bama Lama Bama Loo; Untrue Unfaithful; To Wait For Love; And I Tell The Sea; The Rose; Endlessly.* A-TOM-IC JONES (December 1965): *Thunderball; Promise Her Anything; True Love Comes Only Once In A Lifetime; Key To My Heart; These Things You Don't Forget; Dr. Love; I'll Never Let You Go; A Little You; In A Woman's Eyes; More; Face Of A Loser; Where Do You Belong.* GREEN, GREEN GRASS OF HOME (January 1967): *Green, Green Grass Of Home; Taste Of Honey; Georgia On My Mind; That Old Black Magic; If Ever I Would Leave You; Any Day Now; Someday (You'll Want Me); You Came A Long Way From St. Louis; My Mother's Eyes; My Prayer; Kansas City; When I Fall In Love.* FUNNY, FAMILIAR FORGOTTEN FEELINGS (June 1967): *Funny, Familiar Forgotten Feelings; He'll Have To Go; Riders In The Sky; Sixteen Tons; Two Brothers; All I Get From You Are Heartaches; Detroit City; Ring Of Fire; Field Of Yellow Daisies; Cool Water; Say No To You (I Wish I Could); Mohair Sam.* TOM JONES "LIVE" (September 1967): *Good News; Hello Young Lovers; I Can't Stop Loving You; What's New Pussycat; Not Responsible; My Yiddishe Momma; That Lucky Old Sun; I*

Believe; Green, Green Grass Of Home; It's Not Unusual; Land Of 1,000 Dances. FEVER ZONE (May 1968): *Don't Fight It; You Keep Me Hanging On; Hold On, I'm Coming; I Was Made To Love; Keep On Running; Get Ready; Delilah; I Know; I Wake Up Crying; Funny How Time Slips Away; It's A Man's Man's World; Danny Boy.*

Singles/*It's Not Unusual/To Wait For Love (Is to Waste Your Life Away)* (February 1965); *What's New Pussycat?/Once Upon A Time* (May 1965); *With These Hands/Some Other Guy* (August 1965); *Thunderball/Key To My Heart* (November 1965); *Promise Her Anything/A Little You* (January 1966); *Not Responsible/Once There Was A Time* (May 1966); *What A Party/City Girl* (August 1966); *Green, Green Grass Of Home/If I Had You* (November 1966); *Detroit City/Ten Guitars* (February 1967); *Funny Familiar Forgotten Feelings/I'll Never Let You Go* (April 1967); *Sixteen Tons/Things I Wanna Do* (July 1967); *I'll Never Fall In Love Again/Once Upon A Time* (August 1967); *I'm Coming Home/The Lonely One* (November 1967); *Delilah/Smile Your Blues Away* (February 1968).

JANIS JOPLIN (see BIG BROTHER AND THE HOLD-ING COMPANY)

KALEIDOSCOPE/*David Lindley (lead guitar, violin, banjo, vocals), Soloman Feldthouse (guitar, oud, clarinet, caz, jumbus, vocals), Templeton Parcely (lead violin, organ, vocals), Stuart A. Brotman (bass, vocals), Paul Lagos (drums, vocals), Maxwell Buda (harmonica).*
Previous Members: Christopher Darrow, John Vadican.
Solomon plays caz, bouzoukee, oud, dobro, tair, rhythm guitar, bass, tablas and he sings lead. David can play anything with strings. Max sings some lead, plays violin, viola, bass organ, harpsichord, piano, harmonica. Chris plays bass, mandolin, violin, banjo, autoharp, harmonica and clarinet, and sings.
    They were around San Francisco for a while and had already made two albums when they suddenly found themselves the stars of the 1968 Newport folk festival. Their sound is half rock and roll, half traditional music. But they play and assimilate nearly everything: Eastern music, Western music,

folk (of all countries), hard rock, soft rock and classical rock. It's the very variety of musical influences that makes the group interesting and entertaining, for when they emerged in 1968, being eclectic worked.

Albums/SIDE TRIPS (April 1967): *Egyptian Gardens; If The Night; Hesitation Blues; Please; Keep Your Mind Open; Oh Death; Pulsating Dream; Come On In; Why Try; Minnie The Moocher.* BEACON FROM MARS (November 1967): *I Found Out; Greenwood Sidee; Life Will Pass You By; Taxim; Baldheaded End Of A Broom; Louisiana Man; You Don't Love Me; Beacon From Mars.* KALEIDOSCOPE (June 1968): *Lie To Me; Let The Good Love Flow; Tempe Arizona; Petite Fleur; Banjo; Cuckoo; Seven-Ate Sweet.*

Singles/*Elevator Man/Please* (December 1966); *Why Try/ Little Orphan Annie* (August 1967); *I Found Out/Rampé Rampé* (October 1967); *Nobody/*(Flip side not done by Kaleidoscope) (November 1967); *Hello Trouble/Just A Taste* (May 1968).

KANGAROO/*John Hall (bass), Teddy Speleos (lead guitar), Norman Dow Smart II (drums), Barbara Keith (vocals).*
Kangaroo is a young rock group which came out late in 1968 with a young "cute" sound. The best tracks on their first album are *Frog Giggin'* and *Daydream Stallion,* two of their singles.

Album/KANGAROO (November 1968): *Such A Long Long Time; You're Trying To Be A Woman; Daydream Stallion; Make Some Room In Your Life; Frog Giggin'; You Can't Do This To Me; If You Got Some Love In Mind; I Never Tell Me Twice; Tweed's Chicken Inn; Happy Man; The Only Thing I Had; Maybe Tomorrow.*

Singles/*I Never Tell Me Twice/Such A Long Long Time; Daydream Stallion/Only Thing I Had; Frog Giggin'/Maybe Tomorrow.*

KASENETZ-KATZ SINGING ORCHESTRAL CIRCUS/
Two producers had a bunch of bands they didn't think were getting enough exposure. Not wanting to put on just another dreary tour, they put them all together in one big monster forty-six-member orchestra. This group, named after their

producers, actually put on a circus rock extravaganza at Carnegie Hall. It didn't set the night on fire but it was ingenious and a thought for the future. The member bands are the 1910 Fruitgum Company, the Music Explosion, Ohio Express, Lieutenant Garcia's Magic Music Box, the JCW Rat Finks, the 1989 Musical Marching Zoo, the St. Louis Invisible Band and the Teri Nelson Group—some, because of single hits, a little more famous than others. While the orchestral circus is really just a promotion stunt, Kasenetz and Katz may have started something. For one thing, the group has a single on the charts in England.

Album/KASENETZ-KATZ SINGING ORCHESTRAL CIRCUS: *Place In The Sun; Mr. Jensen; Hey Joe; Little Bit Of Soul; Simon Says; We Can Work It Out; You've Lost That Lovin' Feeling; Mrs. Green; Latin Shake; Yesterday.*

Singles/*Down In Tennessee/Mrs. Green; Mr. Jensen/Quick Joey Small.*

KEITH (James Barry Keefer)/There were two really inspired things about this wistful Philadelphia boy: the use of one name, just like that, and his first song, *98.6*, which was sung at body temperature. His voice was sexy and shy and on stage so was he. The song was a huge success. The second song, *Easy as Pie,* was not.

Albums/KEITH (February 1967): *98.6; Ain't Gonna Lie; To Whom It Concerns; Pretty Little Shy One; You'll Come Running Back To Me; White Lightnin'; Tell It To Me; Sweet Dreams (Do Come True); Mind If I Hang Around; Our Love Started All Over Again; I Can't Go Wrong; Teeny Bopper Song.* OUT OF CRANK (September 1967): *Sugar Man; Candy Candy; Easy As Pie; Hope Girl; Making Every Minute Count; Sweet And Sour; There's Always Tomorrow; Daylight Savin' Time; Times Gone By; Happy Walking Around; Be My Girl.* THE ADVENTURES OF KEITH (May 1968): *Alone On The Shore; Trixon's Election; Waiting To Be; Melody; The Problem; Marstrand; Mr Hyde; China Clipper; Elea-Elea; Charley Cinders.*

Singles/*98.6/The Teeny Bopper Song; Easy As Pie/Sugar Man* (July 1967); *Candy Candy/I'm So Proud* (August 1967); *Pleasure Of Your Company/Hurry* (1968); *There's*

Always Tomorrow/I Can't Go Wrong (1968); *Marstrand/ The Problem* (April 1969).

KENSINGTON MARKET/*Alex Darou (bass), Luke Gibson (vocals), Gene Martynec (vocals, guitar, electric piano), Keith McKie (guitar, vocals), Jimmy Watson (drums, sitar).*
Kensington Market is a rock group that emerged in 1968 from Canada, where its lead singer headed a big group called Luke and the Apostles. The group sounds good and could become big, not the least of its advantages being that its producer, Felix Pappalardi, was the producer for 1968's top rock trio, Cream.

Albums/KENSINGTON MARKET — AVENUE ROAD (June 1968): *I Would Be The One; Speaking Of Dreams; Colour Her Sunshine; Phoebe; Aunt Violet's Knee; Coming Home Soon; Presenting Myself Lightly; Looking Glass; Beatrice; Girl Is Young.* AARDVARK (April 1969): *Help Me; If It Is Love; I Know You; The Thinker; Half Closed Eyes; Said I Could Be Happy; Ciao; Ow-Ing Man; Side I Am: Think About The Times; Have You Come To See; Cartoon; Dorian.*

ALBERT KING/He's the real thing. He's what every other blues guitarist in the world is imitating. But until 1967–68, when the blues guitarists started talking about where they'd gotten it from in the first place, the teenies, the average rock audience, had never heard of him. Now the whites have discovered him. Now they know where Jimi Hendrix and Eric Clapton and Mike Bloomfield and all the other monster guitarists learned to bend their notes. Now they know where all those screaming guitars came from. Now they see that the white boys play too loud, too fast, that Albert King can say it all in his quiet, unhurried way, that it doesn't do to play the blues with too much of that psychedelic nonsense messing up your head.

Albums/BORN UNDER A BAD SIGN: *Born Under A Bad Sign; Crosscut Saw; Oh, Pretty Woman; Kansas City; Down Don't Bother Me; Hunter; I Almost Lost My Mind; Personal Manager; Laundromat Blues; As The Years Go Passing By; Very Thought Of You.* YEARS GONE BY (May 1969).

Singles/*Funk-Shun*/*Pretty   Woman;   Crosscut   Saw*/*Down Don't Bother Me; Born Under A Bad Sign*/*Personal Manager; Cold Feet*/*You Sure Drive A Hard Bargain; You're Gonna Need Me*/*Lucy (I Love)*.

B. B. KING/He was playing the blues before Eric Clapton was born—but not too many people knew about it. Not too many people knew too much about B.B. King except that Clapton (and other blues guitarists like Mike Bloomfield) kept mentioning him in interviews, and that when he did his voice turned pale with respect. That was it until one night early in 1968 at the Cafe Au Go Go in New York. The Cream were at the top, then, and Eric Clapton, their guitarist, was going to be jamming there that night. Also due to play were Elvin Bishop (lead guitarist for Paul Butterfield) and B.B. King. B.B. King?

So now we are inside and the stage lights are on and there's Clapton, decked out from head to foot in psychedelia, complete with flaming painted guitar and Afro-fuzz hair. And Elvin Bishop, more Afro-fuzz, funky as all get-out, and chewing away on a toothpick. And beside him—now, just a moment, hold it, what?—sittin' back, relaxin' on a stool in a corner, is this middle-aged spade, shiny suit, slicked-down hair, smoking a Tiparillo while his candy apple Guild just rests on his lap. The show starts. Everybody gets together for basic blues number one—bass player, drummer, everyone's sort of struggling to hang on in there. Elvin steps forward, intent, toothpick clamped down hard between his teeth. Solo. A few complicated blues riffs, nothing too flashy, but you know it's good 'cause it just looks so hard. And now it's Eric's turn. Swaying, moccasined foot stomping the floor. Flash, flash. Such dexterity. The crowd is wild, and Eric's done it again. The solo ends. And now, oh yeah, the chubby spade in the corner. Well, for a start, old B. doesn't even stand up. He doesn't have to. He just sits back in his chair, still relaxin', smilin' a little and smokin' his Tiparillo, and suddenly he just lets go a little pure and ever-so-simple soul. Like he's been doin' this for a long time. No fancy playing now, just a couple of strokes, and—well, the whole room is wiped out. A great collective gasp. It goes on just long enough to prove his point.

The point: contemporary white guitarists learned the blues

from B.B. King. His slow, easy style of playing and singing has long made him a hit artist on the rhythm and blues charts. But it wasn't until recently, until people like Clapton talked about their sources, that he came to the attention of the vast white audience that knew the blues only as interpreted by other whites. Once they heard him play, and others like him, it was all different, because you couldn't see B. at work without thinking of how many other unknown masters were still lurking behind the scene, undiscovered by a whole generation. It was probably because of B.B. King that the 1968 audiences suddenly became interested in musical roots and the men who had influenced the music they were buying up in such huge quantities. And it's one of the great ironies in music today that American kids had to learn about one of their own big blues men from a bunch of English kids (the Rolling Stones, Cream) who, as always, had had much more respect for America's black heritage than most people in America. In any case, success or no success, B.B. King has been around for years and is likely to continue to be. That kind of musician doesn't ever stop playing.

Albums/MR. BLUES (June 1963): *Young Dreamers; By Myself; Chains Of Love; A Mother's Love; Blues At Midnight; Sneakin' Around; On My Word Of Honor; Tomorrow Night; My Baby's Comin' Home; Guess Who; You Ask Me; I'm Gonna Sit In 'Til You Give In.* B.B. KING "LIVE" AT THE REGAL (January 1965): *Every Day I Have The Blues; Sweet Little Angel; It's My Own Fault; How Blue Can You Get; Please Love Me; You Upset Me Baby; Worry, Worry; Woke Up This Mornin'; You Done Lost Your Good Thing Now; Help The Poor.* CONFESSIN' THE BLUES (October 1965): *See See Rider; Do You Call That A Buddy; Wee Baby Blues; I'd Rather Drink Muddy Water; In The Dark; Confessin' The Blues; Goin' To Chicago Blues; I'm Gonna Move To The Outskirts Of Town; World Of Trouble; How Long; How Long Blues; Cherry Red; Please Send Me Someone To Love.* BLUES IS KING (January 1967): *Waitin' On You; Gamblers' Blues; Tired Of Your Jive; Night Life; Buzz Me; Don't Answer The Door; Blind Love; I Know What You're Puttin' Down; Baby Get Lost; Gonna Keep On Loving You.* BLUES ON TOP OF BLUES (January 1968): *Heart-*

breaker; Losing Faith In You; Dance With Me; That's Wrong Little Mama; Having My Say; I'm Not Wanted Anymore; Worried Dream; Paying The Cost To Be The Boss; Until I Found You; I'm Gonna Do What They Do To Me; Raining In My Heart; Now That You've Lost Me. BEST OF B. B. KING: *Walking Dr. Bill; Hold That Train; You're Breaking My Heart; Did You Ever Love A Woman; Going Down Slow; Sneaking Around; Sweet Sixteen; Partin' Time; You Upset Me; My Own Fault, Baby; Bad Luck; Three O'clock Blues; Woke Up This Morning; Every Day I Have The Blues; Ten Long Years; Sweet Little Angel.* ROCK ME BABY: *You Know I Love You; Bad Case Of Love; You Upset Me Baby; Rock Me Baby; Woke Up This Morning; Three O'clock Blues; When My Heart Beats Like A Hammer; Sweet Sixteen; Ten Long Years; Sneakin' Around; Every Day I Have The Blues; Sweet Little Angel; Please Love Me.* LET ME LOVE YOU: *You're Gonna Miss Me; I'm Gonna Quit My Baby; Come By Here; Whole Lot Of Lovin'; I've Got A Right To Love My Baby; I Can't Explain; Walkin' Dr. Bill; Hold That Train; Let Me Love You; Driving Wheel; Did You Ever Love A Woman; Troubles Don't Last.* B. B. KING LIVE ON STAGE. SOUL OF B. B. KING: *Good Man Gone Bad; Beautician's Blues; You Won't Listen; Someday Baby; Please Remember Me; Long Nights; You Never Know; You Shouldn't Have Left; Partin' Time; Ruby Lee; What A Way To Go; Come Back Baby.* THE JUNGLE: *The Jungle; Eyesight To The Blind; Ain't Nobody's Business; Five Long Years; Blue Shadows; Worst Thing In My Life; Blues Stay Away; Beautician Blues; I Stay In The Mood; I Can Hear My Name; Got 'Em Bad; It's A Mean World.*

Singles/*I'm Gonna Sit In Till You Give In/You Ask Me* (March 1962); *Blues At Midnight/My Baby's Comin' Home* (June 1962); *Sneakin' Around/Chains Of Love* (March 1963); *Mother's Love/Tomorrow Night* (March 1963); *Guess Who/By Myself* (April 1963); *Young Dreamers/On My Word Of Honor* (June 1963); *How Do I Love You/Slowly Losing My Mind* (October 1963); *How Blue Can You Get/Please Accept My Love* (January 1964); *Help The Poor/I Wouldn't Have It Another Way* (April 1964); *The Hurt/Whole Lotta Lovin'* (July 1964); *Never Trust A*

Woman/Worryin' Blues (October 1964); *Please Send Me Someone To Love/Stop Leading Me On* (January 1965); *Every Day I Have The Blues/It's My Own Fault* (March 1965); *Night Owl/Tired Of Your Jive* (May 1965); *All Over Again/The Things You Put Me Through* (August 1965); *I'd Rather Drink Muddy Water/Goin' To Chicago Blues* (October 1965); *Tormented/You're Still A Square* (April 1966); *Don't Answer The Door* (Parts 1 and 2) (October 1966); *Night Life/Waitin' On You* (December 1966); *I Don't Want You Cuttin' Off Your Hair/Think It Over* (April 1967); *Worried Dream/That's Wrong Little Mama* (July 1967); *Heartbreaker/Raining In My Heart* (December 1967); *Sweet Sixteen* (Parts 1 and 2) (December 1967); *Paying The Cost To Be The Boss/Having My Say* (February 1968); *I'm Gonna Do What They Do To Me/Losing Faith In You* (June 1968); *Dance With Me/Please Send Me Someone To Love* (December 1968).

JONATHAN KING/He was a student in Cambridge, England (1963-66) when he took up singing, songwriting, and made himself a company. It was all right to do that sort of thing if you were a Liverpool plumber or a Manchester hairdresser, but it certainly wasn't the sort of thing Cambridge was accustomed to. Never mind, Jonathan King is the kind to revel in the shock waves. He isn't a terribly good singer but he's certainly a personality in the English rock scene, though not always a beloved one. For one thing, he has the most outspoken pop column in all of England—in all the world, if it comes to that. For another, he's violently antidrug and was so during that flower-power summer of 1967 when psychedelic smiles wreathed every face on the King's Road. He had his own tv show, produced records, had his songs done by others, wrote an antidrug novel, and generally proved that a Cambridge education need not be a drawback in the musical advancement of an English lad.

Album/JONATHAN KING OR THEN AGAIN (January 1968): *Everyone's Gone To The Moon; Time And Motion; Land Of The Golden Tree; Just Like A Woman; Passions Of Ancient Egypt; Seagulls; Round Round; Green Is The Grass; It's Good News Week; Where The Sun Has Never Shone; Keep Your Feet On The Ground; Brother John.*

Singles/*Everyone's Gone To The Moon*/*Summer's Coming* (June 1965); *Just Like A Woman*/*Land Of The Golden Tree* (July 1965); *Where The Sun Has Never Shone*/*Green Grass* (November 1965); *Icicles*/*A Hundred Years From Now* (September 1966); *Round Round*/*Time And Motion* (March 1967); *A Message To The Presidential Candidates* (2 Parts) (March 1968).

THE KINGSTON TRIO/*Bob Shane, John Steward (replaced Dave Guard), Nick Reynolds.*
Who would have guessed that when *Tom Dooley* zipped up the charts to the number one spot in 1959—and stayed there—that history was being made? The Kingston Trio were three fresh-faced college boys, wholesome when wholesomeness was in, and a welcome change. They could have sung all of Hamlet's soliloquies and got them to the number one spot. Instead they sang folk songs, making them once and for all widely acceptable and commercially successful with a huge audience. Others before them had made a few tentative stabs at the big money with folk material, but the few who did succeed made it with one or at the most two songs and then never again. These others were able to sell *a* folk song to the public, but not the notion of folk *songs* as a commercial commodity. The Kingston Trio sold folk—and look what they started. They inspired Albert Grossman (now a legendary manager and pop superhero, then still a comparatively small-scale promoter) to create Peter, Paul and Mary— a Kingston Trio with sex appeal. The Kingston Trio, then, set the stage for the big early sixties commercial success of Peter, Paul and Mary, Joan Baez and Bob Dylan, who in turn sparked off the notion of folk rock, which of course was one half of what the Beatles were about, and so forth. The Kingston Trio had a lot to answer for. Mainly they brought the folk revival out of concert halls into the jukeboxes, radios and home television screens. With so many other people doing their thing, the Trio eventually lost some of its banjo-picking freshness—but never all of it. And when Dave Guard announced he was leaving the group to go to Australia, there were loyal Americans accusing him of treason. The group hasn't played professionally since 1966, but the several groups that still play in their now quaintly old-fashioned

nine-year-old style still do well commercially outside the trendy new rock circles.

Albums/KINGSTON TRIO (May 1958). FROM .THE HUNGRY I (December 1958). STEREO CONCERT (February 1959). AT LARGE (May 1959). HERE WE GO AGAIN! (September 1959). SOLD OUT (March 1960). STRING ALONG (August 1960). MAKE WAY (January 1961). GOIN' PLACES (June 1961). CLOSE-UP (September 1961). COLLEGE CONCERT (January 1962). BEST OF THE KINGSTON TRIO (March 1962). SOMETHING SPECIAL (June 1962). NEW FRONTIER (November 1962). NUMBER 16 (May 1963). SUNNY SIDE (September 1963). SING A SONG (November 1963). TIME TO THINK (January 1964). BACK IN TOWN (May 1964). FOLK ERA (December 1964). NICK-BOB-JOHN (December 1964). BEST OF THE KINGSTON TRIO, VOL. 2 (February 1965). STAY AWHILE (May 1965). SOMETHIN' ELSE (November 1965). CHILDREN OF THE MORNING (May 1966). BEST OF THE KINGSTON TRIO, VOL. 3 (October 1966).

Singles/*Tom Dooley/M.T.A.; Worried Man/Scotch And Soda; Greenback Dollar/Reverend Mr. Black; My Ramblin' Boy/Hope You Understand; I'm Going Home/Little Play Soldiers; One Too Many Mornings/Scotch & Soda* (April 1969).

THE KINKS/*Peter Quaife (bass guitar, vocals), Mick Avory (drums), Ray Davies (harmonica, rhythm guitar, vocals), Dave Davies (vocals, lead guitar).*
The Kinks are probably the one group most admired by other musicians and certainly the one invariably held up as an example when someone is trying to prove that the Beatles aren't all that good and there are groups that were doing cleverer things earlier. *You Really Got Me,* the first of their singles to be released in the States, came out in August 1964—a time when music, even the Beatles' music, was fairly simple—yet it was an incredibly complex number with the voices doing all sorts of elaborate things, things most other groups wouldn't even try (although the Beach Boys did eventually, months later). The Kinks instinctively anticipated

all the complexities of post-*Good Vibrations* and post-*SERGEANT PEPPER* music, but intricate as their vocal harmonies were, the sound was never anything but delicate and subtle. *All Day and All of the Night* in 1965 was another single no one dared imitate, until 1968 when the Doors did *Hello I Love You,* a song so similar the Kinks thought of suing. Ray Davies, Kink leader and writer, had already established himself as a composer and lyricist equaled only by Bob Dylan and the Beatles. *A Well Respected Man* and *Dedicated Follower of Fashion* showed the particular gift for light, wry satire that put him up there with the masters. *Well Respected Man,* a put-down of the English middle class, was done at the end of 1965, scarcely a breath behind the Beatles' first *real* album, *RUBBER SOUL.* All this time one thing was apparent to Kinks fans (many in London, a loyal few in America, and every musician of note in either place), and that was that the Kinks were suffering commercially because of all sorts of basic problems—no image, not enough hard sell. In places like New York, they never got anything like the major airplay they should have gotten. In cities where they did, they were right on top of the charts, but no one seemed to learn that lesson. They never had the big ballyhooed tours lesser groups had. None of the usual big-group apparatus was used to help them along. Yet every single and every album was masterly. *Dandy,* sung sweetly by the Hermits, was another Davies put-down when sung by the Kinks. *Sunny Afternoon* was one of the beautiful songs of rock. So was *Dead End Street.* Soon it became obvious that so much of Ray Davies' energy was going into writing and recording that little was left over to promote the group as a live performing unit. People have written a lot about the Kinks, but there is little to say because there is no spectacle, no drama, no intrigue—just that music.

Albums/KINKS (YOU REALLY GOT ME) (November 1964): *Beautiful Delilah; So Mystifying; Long Tall Shorty; Just Can't Go To Sleep; You Really Got Me; Cadillac; Bald-Headed Woman; Too Much Monkey Business; I've Been Driving On Bald Mountain; Stop Your Sobbing; Got Love If You Want It.* KINKS-SIZE (May 1965): *Tired Of Waiting For You; Louie, Louie; Come On Now; I've Got That*

Feeling; Revenge; I'm A Lover Not A Fighter; I Gotta Move; Things Are Getting Better; I Gotta Go Now; All Day And All Of The Night. KINDA KINKS (October 1965): *Look For Me Baby; Dancing In The Street; So Long; Got My Feet On The Ground; Don't Ever Change; Nothin' In The World Can Stop Me Worryin' 'Bout That Girl; Wonder Where My Baby Is Tonight; Set Me Free; Ev'rybody's Gonna Be Happy; You Shouldn't Be Sad; Something Better Beginning.* KINKS KINKDOM (January 1966): *A Well Respected Man; Such A Shame; Wait 'Til The Summer Comes Along; Naggin' Woman; Never Met A Girl Like You Before; See My Friends; Who'll Be The Next In Line; Don't You Fret; I Need You; It's All Right; Louie, Louie.* KINKS' GREATEST HITS (November 1966): *Dedicated Follower Of Fashion; Tired Of Waiting For You; All Day And All Of The Night; You Really Got Me; Well Respected Man; Who'll Be The Next In Line; Everybody's Gonna Be Happy; Till The End Of The Day; Set Me Free; Something Better Beginning.* FACE TO FACE (January 1967): *Fancy; Party Line; Rosy Won't You Please Come Home; Dandy; Too Much On My Mind; Session Man; Rainy Day In June; House In The Country; Holiday In Waikiki; Most Exclusive Residence For Sale; Little Miss Queen Of Darkness; You're Lookin' Fine; Sunny Afternoon; I'll Remember.* "LIVE" KINKS (September 1967): *Well Respected Man; Till The End Of The Day; You're Lookin' Fine; Sunny Afternoon; Dandy; I'm On An Island; Come On Now; You Really Got Me; Medley; Milk Cow Blues; Batman Theme; Tired Of Waiting For You.* KINK KONTROVERSY (October 1967): *Milk Cow Blues; Ring The Bells; Gotta Get The First Plane Home; You Can't Win; I Am Free; World Keeps Going 'Round; It's Too Late; Till The End Of The Day; I'm On An Island; Where Have The Good Times Gone; What's In Store For Me; When I See That Girl Of Mine.* SOMETHING ELSE (February 1968): *David Watts; Death Of A Clown; Two Sisters; No Return; Harry Rag; Tin Soldier Man; Love Me Till The Sun Shines; Situation Vacant; End Of The Season; Lazy Old Sun; Afternoon Tea; Funny Face; Waterloo Sunset.* THE KINKS ARE THE VILLAGE GREEN PRESERVATION SOCIETY (March 1969): *The Village Green Preservation Society; Do You Remember Walter; Picture Book; Johnny Thunder; Last Of The Steam-*

Powered Trains; Big Sky; Sitting By The Riverside; Animal Farm; Village Green; Starstruck; Phenomenal Cat; All Of My Friends Were There; Wicked Annabella; Monica; People Take Pictures Of Each Other.

Singles/*You Really Got Me/It's Alright* (August 1964); *Two Sisters/Waterloo Sunset* (July 1967); *Well Respected Man/ Set Me Free* (August 1967); *Dedicated Follower Of Fashion/Who'll Be The Next In Line* (August 1967); *Sunny Afternoon/Dead End Street* (August 1967); *All Day And All Of The Night/Tired Of Waiting For You* (August 1967); *David Watts/Autumn Almanac* (November 1967); *Days/ She's Got Everything* (August 1968).

GLADYS KNIGHT AND THE PIPS/*Gladys Knight, Merald Knight, Edward Patten, William Guest.*
We could have had Gladys Knight without the Pips back in 1948 (she won first place in the Ted Mack Amateur Hour three times in a row, first time at the age of four, and was besieged with offers) but her mother wanted her to have an education. There's no keeping talent down, however, and when she was still a kid, she and her brother and two cousins used to harmonize gospel hymns so divinely she became the star of the local church scene. In 1958, when Gladys was fourteen, she was joined by the Pips and they did the school-dance route. From there it was a long road to Ed Sullivan and the Copa, but thanks to *I Heard It Through The Grapevine*, which sold two million copies, Gladys was recognized as the personification of soul. Her refined voice hardly needs a microphone, the choreography of the Pips is the tightest thing around, and when those perfectly timed and blended voices get going, it's just impossible to keep still. Even at the Copa it was all frenzy and emotion for the audience.

Albums/EVERYBODY NEEDS LOVE (August 1967): *I Heard It Through The Grapevine; Yes, I'm Ready; I'll Be Standing By; He's My Kind Of Fellow; Everybody Needs Love; My Bed Of Thorns; Since I've Lost You; Just Walk In My Shoes; Since You Don't Love Me No More; Do You Love Me Just A Little, Honey; Take Me In Your Arms And Love Me; Ain't No Sun Since You've Been Gone.* GLADYS

KNIGHT AND THE PIPS' TASTIEST HITS (January 1968): *Letter Full Of Tears; Either Way I Lose; If Ever I Should Fall In Love; Daybreak; Maybe, Maybe Baby; Every Beat Of My Heart; Giving Up; Stop And Get A Hold Of Myself; Lovers Always Forgive; Tell Her You're Mine; Operator.* FEELIN' BLUESY (April 1968): *It Should Have Been Me; End Of The Road; Don't You Miss Me Just A Little Bit Baby; Boy From Crosstown; That's The Way Love Is; Don't Turn Me Away; What Good Am I Without You; It's Time To Go Now; Ain't You Glad You Chose Love; I Know Better; Don't Let Her Take Your Love From Me; Your Old Standby.*

Singles/*Just Walk In My Shoes/Stepping Closer To Your Heart* (June 1966); *Take Me In Your Arms And Love Me/Do You Love Me Just A Little, Honey* (March 1967); *Everybody Needs Love/Stepping Closer To Your Heart* (June 1967); *I Heard It Through The Grapevine/It's Time To Go Now* (September 1967); *The End Of Our Road/Don't Let Her Take Your Love From Me* (January 1968); *It Should Have Been Me/You Don't Love Me No More* (May 1968); *I Wish It Would Rain/It's Summer* (August 1968).

AL KOOPER/Originally singer and organist with the Blues Project, and later with Blood, Sweat & Tears, Kooper became a star in his own right with *SUPER SESSION,* an album of jam sessions made with former Electric Flag guitarist Mike Bloomfield and former Buffalo Springfield guitarist Steve Stills (it made the top fifty). He also recorded a live album with Bloomfield called the *LIVE ADVENTURES OF MIKE BLOOMFIELD AND AL KOOPER.* He appears in other jams (*GRAPE JAM* with Moby Grape and a cut on *ELECTRIC LADYLAND* with Jimi Hendrix), and is currently working as a producer at Columbia. His first album is *I STAND ALONE.* Other credits: a boyhood stint in the Royal Teens of *Short Shorts* fame, a gold record, *This Diamond Ring,* sung by Gary Lewis, and the organ playing on Bob Dylan's *BLONDE ON BLONDE,* which forever linked the organ with the Dylan sound, influencing such important groups as Procol Harum, The Band and Traffic.
(See BLUES PROJECT and BLOOD, SWEAT & TEARS)

THE JIM KWESKIN JUG BAND/*Jim Kweskin (guitar, vocals), Geoff Muldaur (washboard, guitar, kazoo, vocals), Richard Greene (fiddle), Maria d'Amato (kazoo, tambourine, vocals), Bill Keith (banjo, pedal steel, guitar), Fritz Richmond (jug, washtub bass).*

The Jim Kweskin Jug Band was never put together. It *came* together in Cambridge, Massachusetts, in 1963. That was when the Cambridge folkies were still denying rock and roll, and the Club 47 (birthplace of Joan Baez's folksinging career) was half empty because kids wanted to dance, not listen. That was when the Kweskin band moved in, a happy tribe with fiddles, spoons, washboards, jugs, anything that would produce a sound. (In England there were bands something like this called skiffle bands, with which the Beatles and many of the modern English groups got their teenage starts.) They cavorted on stage, singing old-time ragtime and just goodtime. Often they sounded like old 78s, and that was good too. The band went on, intermarried, bore children, changed members and still they played and sang and made people laugh. Sometimes they would go on with four people, sometimes eleven. At one stage, in the wake of the New Vaudeville Band's *Winchester Cathedral*, it looked as if goodtime music might make it on the charts, and indeed, Dr. West's Medicine Show and Jug Band had a big hit with *The Eggplant That Ate Chicago*, but it was the only one. The Jim Kweskin Jug Band hung on and did all right, but by 1968 they announced enough was enough and said they were calling it quits. No one who has heard them believes they will stop.

Albums/JIM KWESKIN AND THE JUG BAND (October 1963): *Newport News; My Gal; Borneo; Hawaii; I'm Satisfied With My Gal; Beedle Um Bum; Wild About My Loving; Going To Germany; Boodle Am Shake; Washington At Valley Forge; Sweet Sue; Overseas Stomp; Coney Island Washboard; Mobile Line.* JUG BAND MUSIC (February 1965): *K. C. Moan; Good Time Charlie; Jug Band Waltz; Whoa Mule Get Up In The Alley; I'm A Woman; Memphis; Ukulele Lady; Rag Mama; Blues My Naughty Sweetie Gives To Me; Jug Band Music; Morning Blues; Sadie Green; Don't You Leave Me Here; Somebody Stole My Gal.* RELAX YOUR MIND (January 1966): *I Got Mine; Buffalo Skin-*

ners; Make Me A Pallet On Your Floor; Guabi Guabi; My Creole Belle; Relax Your Mind; Hannah; Bye And Bye; Cuckoo; I Ain't Never Been Satisfied; Eight More Miles To Louisville; Sister Kate's Night Out Medley. JIM KWESKIN AND THE JUG BAND (December 1966): *Blues In The Bottle; Chevrolet; Christopher Columbus; Never Swat A Fly; Richland Woman; Downtown Blues; Turn The Record Over; Fishing Blues; Storybook Ball; That's When I'll Come Back To You; Viola Lee; Papa's On The Housetop; Onyx Hop.* JUMP FOR JOY (May 1967): *Moving Day; Memphis Blues; Kicking The Gong Around; You're Not The Only Oyster In The Stew; He's In The Jailhouse Now; Melancholy Baby; There'll Be Some Changes Made; Jazzbo Brown; Staggerlee; I Can't Give You Anything But Love; Louisiana; Medley.* GARDEN OF JOY (September 1967): *If You're A Viper; Minglewood; Garden Of Joy; Circus Song; My Old Man; Sheik Of Araby; Kaloobafak; When I Was A Cowboy; Mood Indigo; I Ain't Gonna Marry; Ella Speed; Gee Baby, Ain't I Good To You.* BEST OF JIM KWESKIN AND THE JUG BAND (January 1968): *Good Time Charlie; Jug Band Music; I'm A Woman; Christopher Columbus; Sweet Sue; Boodle Am Shake; Fishing Blues; Blues My Naughty Sweetie Gives To Me; Never Swat A Fly; Coney Island Washboard; K. C. Moan; Crazy Words, Crazy Tune.* WHAT EVER HAPPENED TO THOSE GOOD OLD DAYS (September 1968): *Mississippi Mud; Buddy Bolden Blues; Bill Bailey, Won't You Please Come Home; Ain't She Sweet; La Boma; Good Morning, Little Schoolgirl; I Had A Dream Last Night; Five Foot Two, Eyes Of Blue; Ella Speed; Blues; Sheik Of Araby.*

Singles/*Minglewood*/*Sheik Of Araby; I'll Be Your Baby To-night*/*Circus Song.*

DENNY LAINE/He was the leader and sad-voiced singer of the Moody Blues until 1966 (before the group had its recent big revival), when he left to start an electric string band. The band, four very straight musicians from the Royal Academy of Music in London, played electrified violins and cellos. A solo single, *Say You Don't Mind,* had an underground success in London, but that's all. Laine is currently away from the rock scene and plans to stay away from it (and study flamenco guitar) until he finds people who want to play the same sort of music he wants. But he's a very major force in the English rock world behind the scenes.

LAMP OF CHILDHOOD/Whatever happened to James Hendricks, who was once in the Mugwumps? He burned brightly in the Lamp of Childhood with Fred Olson, Mick Tani and drummer Billy Mundi. Then the group split. Hendricks went solo and Mundi became drummer for the Mothers of Invention and later for Rhinoceros.

Singles/*Season Of The Witch*/*You Can't Blame Me* (1968): *Two O'Clock In The Morning*/*First Time Last Time* (1968); *Two O'Clock In The Morning*/*No More Running Around* (1968).

LEADBELLY (Huddie Ledbetter)/By the time he died in 1949, aged sixty-one, Leadbelly had influenced most of the folksingers of the 40s, especially Pete Seeger and Woody Guthrie, who in turn gave so much to the folk people of the 50s and early 60s. There are people around today who think they're singing like Bob Dylan when they're actually singing like Bob Dylan singing like Woody Guthrie singing like Leadbelly. One of the first folk songs ever to make the hit parade, and it was number one for thirteen weeks in 1950, was *Goodnight Irene*, written by Leadbelly and sung by the Weavers.

Albums/EASY RIDER: *There's A Man Goin' Round Taking Names; Easy Rider; Red Bird; Line 'Em; T. B. Blues; Jim Crow; Bourgeois Blues; Army Life; Hitler Song.* LEADBELLY (January 1966): *Bourgeois Blues; Looky, Looky Yonder; Poor Howard; Black Betty; Green Corn; Yellow Woman's Doorbells; Borrow Love And Go; De Kalb Woman; Gallis Pole; Noted Rider; Big Fat Woman; Bring Me Li'l Water Silvay; Line 'Em; Whoa Back Buck; John Hardy; Julie Ann Johnson.* LEADBELLY, HIS GUITAR, VOICE & PIANO (January 1963): *Irene; Grasshoppers In My Pillow; Western Plain; Eagle Rocks; Rock Island Line; Ella Speed; Backwater Blues; Take This Hammer; Tell Me, Baby; Eagle Rock Rag; Sweet Mary Blues; On A Christmas Day.* LEADBELLY (Library Of Congress Recording): Collection Of 50 Songs

Of: *Penitentiary; Spirituals; Blues; Ballads; Square Dances; Sooky Jumps And Reels; Topical-Protest; Texas, Louisiana And Barrel House.* LEADBELLY. . .FROM LAST SESSIONS (March 1967): *Easy Rider; Nobody Knows You When You're Down And Out; Hesitation Blues; Darktown Strutters Ball; Careless Love; Cry For Me (Mr. Tom Hughes' Town); How Come You Do Me Like You Do, Do, Do; Midnight Special; Sweet Jenny Lee; Yellow Gal; 4, 5 & 9.* LEADBELLY'S LAST SESSIONS: Set Composed of Four Records Containing 94 Songs. LEADBELLY'S LEGACY: *Fort Worth And Dallas Blues; Roberta;* Five Other Titles. MIDNIGHT SPECIAL (September 1964): *Easy Rider; Good Morning Blues; Pick A Bale Of Cotton; Sail On, Little Girl, Sail On; New York City; Rock Island Line; Roberta; Gray Goose; Midnight Special; Alberta; You Can't Lose-A Me Cholly; T.B. Blues; Red Cross Store Blues; Whoa Back Buck; Don't You Love Your Daddy No More; I'm On My Last Go-Round.* PLAY PARTY SONGS. 12 STRING GUITAR. LEADBELLY MEMORIAL.

LED ZEPPELIN/*Jimmy Page, John Paul Jones, Robert Plante, John Bonham.*
Led Zeppelin is the new name for what was left of the Yardbirds (namely Jimmy Page) after they folded in 1968. They play heavy blues with a great deal of improvisational techniques.
(See YARDBIRDS)

Albums/LED ZEPPELIN (February 1969): *Good Times Bad Times; Babe I'm Gonna Leave You; You Shook Me; Dazed & Confused; Your Time Is Gonna Come; Black Mountain Side; Communication Breakdown; I Can't Quit You Baby; How Many More Times.* LED ZEPPELIN II (August 1969).

Single/*Communication Breakdown/Good Times Bad Times* (March 1969).

BRENDA LEE/She was only a little girl but she made seventy-four singles. She had a nice big run in the late fifties when shrill female tones, often complaining, always piercing, were *in. I'm Sorry* was a number one record for three weeks in the summer of 1960, and it took Elvis and the twist to push it off the top. But she was back at the number one spot again two months later with *I Want To Be Wanted*. In 1961 she had at least four singles in the top ten—*You Can Depend On Me, Emotions, Fool Number One* and *Dum Dum*. She doesn't get number one records anymore, but she's still moving, entertaining brightly in clubs in America and Europe. Her latest album, *FOR THE FIRST TIME*, done with Pete Fountain, features such current hits as *Windy* and *59th St. Bridge Song (Feelin' Groovy)*.

Albums/BRENDA LEE (August 1960). THIS IS BRENDA (January 1961). EMOTIONS (May 1961). BRENDA LEE, ALL THE WAY (September 1961). SINCERELY, BRENDA LEE (April 1962). THAT'S ALL, BRENDA (December 1962). ALL ALONE AM I (April 1963). LET ME SING (JANUARY 1964). BY REQUEST (July 1964). TOP TEEN HITS (April 1965). VERSATILE (July 1965) TOO MANY RIVERS (November 1965). BYE BYE BLUES (May 1966). TEN GOLDEN YEARS (July 1966). MERRY CHRISTMAS FROM BRENDA LEE. THANKS A LOT. COMING ON STRONG (January 1967). HERE'S BRENDA LEE (June 1967). REFLECTIONS IN BLUE (December 1967). FOR THE FIRST TIME (June 1968). JOHNNY ONE TIME (May 1969).

Singles/*Ain't Gonna Cry No More/It Takes One To Know One; Am I/Save All Your Lovin' For Me; Alone With You/My Dreams; Anybody But Me/Fool No. 1; As Usual/ Lonely, Lonely, Lonely Me; Bigelow 6–200/Jambalaya; Bill Bailey/Hummin' The Blues Over You; Born To Be By Your Side/Take Me; Break It To Me Gently/So Deep; Christmas Will Be Just Another Lonely Day/This Time Of The Year; Christy Christmas/I'm Gonna Lasso Santa Claus; Coming On Strong/You Keep Coming Back To Me; Crying Game/ Thanks A Lot; Dum Dum/Eventually; Each Day Is A Rainbow/Kansas City; Emotions/I'm Learning About Love; Everybody Loves Me But You/Here Comes That Feeling; Fantasy/That's All Right; Grass Is Greener/Sweet Impossible You; Heart In Hand/It Started All Over Again; He's So Heavenly/Losing You; He's Sure To Remember Me/When You Loved Me; I Still Miss Someone/Truly, Truly, True; I Want To Be Wanted/Just A Little; I Wonder/My Whole*

World Is Falling Down; If You Don't/Rusty Bells; I'm Sorry/That's All You Gotta Do; Is It True/Just Behind The Rainbow; It's Never Too Late/You Can Depend On Me; Jingle Bell Rock/Winter Wonderland; Let's Jump The Broomstick/Some Of These Days; Lonely People Do Foolish Things/Ride, Ride, Ride; My Heart Keeps Hangin' On/ Where Love Is; No One/Too Many Riders; Papa Noel/Rockin' Around The Christmas Tree; Save Me For A Rainy Day/Where's The Melody; She'll Never Know/Your Used To Be; Sweet Nothins/Weep No More My Baby; Think/Waiting Game; Time & Time Again/Too Little Time; Bring Me Sunshine/You Don't Need Me Anymore (May 1969).

GARY LEEDS/When the Walker Brothers split in 1967, at the height of their fame and glory, drummer Gary Leeds gradually got together his own group, Rain. They have still to release any records in the United States.

LEFT BANKE/*Rick Brand (banjo, mandolin), Steve Martin (vocals), Tom Finn (bass), Mike Brown (organ, piano, harp, clavichord), George Cameron (vocals).*
For every hundred groups getting by on little more than noise and effrontery in the 1967 rock boom, there was one group whose members played organ, piano, harp, clavichord, mandolin and more, and played as if they had just walked out of music school, which the Left Banke had. Their songs (especially *Walk Away Renee* and *Pretty Ballerina*, with all those chamber strings and all that classical discipline), were almost too pretty for rock. This New York based group was among the first, as early as 1966, to try to combine rock and the classics. It made for some very beautiful music. The only thing that was missing was noise, effrontery and internal harmony. And they probably could have done better with a little more of all three.

Album/WALK AWAY RENEE/PRETTY BALLERINA (March 1967): *Pretty Ballerina; Walk Away Renee; Let Go Of You Girl; She May Call You Up Tonight; Barterers And Their Wives; I've Got Something On My Mind; Evening Gown; What Do You Know; Shadows Breaking Over My Head; I Haven't Got The Nerve; Lazy Day.*

Singles/*I've Got Something On My Mind/Desire; Dark Is The Bark/My Friend Today.*

THE LEMON PIPERS/*Bill Albaugh (drums), R. G. Nave (organ, green tambourine), Bill Bartlett (lead guitar), Steve Walmsley (bass), Ivan Browne (rhythm guitar, lead vocals).*
The Lemon Pipers are what could be called Happy Rock. They had a hit in 1968 with *Green Tambourine* and seem to be concentrating on bright, listenable singles.

Album/GREEN TAMBOURINE (1968):*Green Tambourine; Rice Is Nice; Turn Around And Take A Look; Through With You; Shoeshine Boy; Blueberry Blues; Ask Me If I Care; 50 Year Void; Shoemaker Of Leatherwear Square; Stragglin' Behind; Rainbow Tree.*

Singles/*Green Tambourine/No Help From Me; Blueberry Blue/Rice Is Nice; Here I Go/Jelly Jungle (Of Orange Marmalade).*

GARY LEWIS (and the PLAYBOYS)/He never claimed to be an innovator. But in 1966-67, at a time when a lot of fancy experimenting was falling flat on its face, comedian Jerry Lewis' son Gary and his band were providing easy and uncomplicated music for that whole segment of the rock audience that didn't want to be confused by feedback, psychedelic hi-jinks and lyrics with forty-five levels of significance. When the last big tally is done, it will be remembered that Gary Lewis' records sold well at a very very competitive time in rock. That's no mean accomplishment, even for a kid born with a silver spoon in his mouth.

Albums/THIS DIAMOND RING (February 1965): *This Diamond Ring; Dream Lover; All Day And All Of The Night; Forget Him; Needles And Pins; Love Potion Number Nine; Keep Searchin'; The Birds And The Bees; Sweet Little Rock And Roller; Go To Him; The Night Has A Thousand Eyes; The Best Man.* A SESSION WITH GARY LEWIS AND THE PLAYBOYS (August 1965): *Count Me In; Travelin' Man; Concrete And Clay; Walk Right Back; For Your Love; Save Your Heart For Me; Palisades Park; Without A Word Of Warning; Voo-doo Woman; Free Like Me; Little Miss Go-Go; Runaway.* EVERYBODY LOVES A

CLOWN (November 1965): *Everybody Loves A Clown; Mr. Blue; Chip Chip; I Gotta Find Cupid; Let Me Tell Your Fortune; I Kissed You; Tossin' And Turnin'; My Special Angel; We'll Work It Out; Sha La La; Time Stands Still; Dreamin'.* SHE'S JUST MY STYLE (February 1966): *She's Just My Style; Lies; All I Have To Do Is Dream; You've Got To Hide Your Love Away; I Won't Make That Mistake Again; A Hundred Pounds Of Clay; Run For Your Life; Take Good Care Of My Baby; Down In The Boondocks; You Didn't Have To Be So Nice; Someone I Used To Know; Heart Full Of Soul.* GARY LEWIS HITS AGAIN! (April 1966): *Look Through My Window; It's Too Late; Face In The Crowd; A Well Respected Man; Rubber Ball; Green Grass; Autumn; One Track Mind; You Baby; I Can Read Between The Lines; Daydream; Sure Gonna Miss Her.* GOLDEN GREATS (September 1966): *This Diamond Ring; Count Me In; She's Just My Style; Tina; Without A Word Of Warning; Sure Gonna Miss Her; Everybody Loves A Clown; I Won't Make That Mistake Again; Save Your Heart For Me; Little Miss Go-Go; Time Stands Still; Green Grass.* PAINT ME A PICTURE (January 1967): *My Heart's Symphony; Barefootin'; Down On The Sloop John B; Tina; String Along; Paint Me A Picture; Where Will The Words Come From; You're Sixteen; When Summer Is Gone; Linda Lu; Looking For The Stars; Wild Thing.* NEW DIRECTIONS (June 1967): *Girls In Love; Double Good Feeling; Keepin' Company; Here I Am; Hello Sunshine; Neighborhood Rock 'n Roll Band; New In Town; Slow Movin' Man; A Little Love From You; Let's Be More Than Friends; Me About You; Sunshine.* LISTEN! (September 1967): *Jill; Don't Make Promises; She'd Rather Be With Me; Look, Here Comes The Sun; Happiness; Bring The Whole Family; Reason To Believe; New Day; Small Talk; Angel On The Corner; Six O'Clock; Young And Carefree.* GARY LEWIS NOW (July 1968): *Young Girl; Sealed With A Kiss; Windy; What Am I Gonna Do; I Wonder What She's Doing Tonight; Pretty Thing; Judy In Disguise; How Can I Thank You; Elusive Butterfly; Sara Jane; Sunny.* MORE GOLDEN GREATS (October 1968): *Sealed With A Kiss; Where Will The Words Come From; Jill; Girls In Love; You Don't Have To Paint Me A Picture; My Heart's Symphony; Eyes; Ice Melts In The*

Sun; Down On The Sloop John B.; The Loser With A Broken Heart; You're Sixteen; Needles And Pins.

Singles/*This Diamond Ring/Tijuana Wedding* (January 1965); *Count Me In/Little Miss Go-Go* (March 1965); *Save Your Heart For Me/Without A Word Of Warning* (June 1965); *Everybody Loves A Clown/Time Stands Still* (August 1965); *She's Just My Style/I Won't Make That Mistake Again* (November 1965); *Sure Gonna Miss Her/I Don't Wanna Say Goodnight* (February 1966); *Green Grass/I Can Read Between The Lines* (April 1966); *My Heart's Symphony/Tina* (July 1966); *Where Will The Words Come From/May The Best Man Win* (November 1966); *The Loser/Ice Melts In The Sun* (February 1967); *Girls In Love/Let's Be More Than Friends* (April 1967); *Jill/New In Town* (July 1967); *Has She Got The Nicest Eyes/Happiness* (November 1967); *Sealed With A Kiss/Sara Jane* (May 1968); *See See Rider/Main Street* (November 1968); *Mister Melody/Rhythm Of The Rain* (March 1969).

JERRY LEE LEWIS/It was the golden age of rock, that period from 1956 to 1960, but scarcely anyone in it—except Elvis—was destined to come out of it unscathed by scandal, or in some cases, even alive. Jerry Lee Lewis, the boy from Louisiana who sang such all-time classic rock hits as *Great Balls of Fire* and *Whole Lotta Shakin' Going On* in 1957, was no exception. He was Elvis's contemporary, worked out of the same Memphis studio that gave Elvis his big start, and went in for the same hillbilly rave-up performances that characterized early rock, only his freaking was done at the keyboard and he belted the piano with all madness, energy, fists, feet and elbows. He was twenty-two, married to the daughter of his bass player—she was thirteen (and his cousin, some say). It was one of those young marriages not unusual in the South. And as Lewis said himself, "I know lots of people married to thirteen-year-olds." And she said, "I'd marry him a million times," and that was nice. But on his May 1957 English tour the hotel asked him to leave. The twenty-seven shows that were booked were canceled. Silence greeted his first appearance. "I sho' hope yawl ain't half as dead as you sound," said Jerry Lee. "Go home, crumb, baby snatcher" was the answer. "It's just jealousy," said young wife Myra. But there it was.

The ball was over. The fire had gone out. Jerry Lee faded away but, like some others of that time, was able to keep going on a local, if no longer national or international, level. In 1968 Jack Good produced a rhythm and blues version of *Othello* starring Lewis as Iago. It was very well received. In the same year he also began a highly successful comeback in the country and western field.

Albums/JERRY LEE LEWIS: *Don't Be Cruel; Goodnight Irene; Put Me Down; It All Depends On Who'll Buy The Wine; Ubangi Stomp; Crazy Arms; Jambalaya; Fools Like Me; When The Saints Go Marchin' In; High School Confidential; Matchbox; It'll Be Me.* JERRY LEE'S GREATEST: *Breakup; Home; Great Balls Of Fire; Hello, Hello Baby; Frankie And Johnny; Money; As Long As I Live; Country Music Is Here To Stay; Let's Talk About Us; What'd I Say; Cold Cold Heart; Hello Josephine.* GOLDEN HITS OF JERRY LEE LEWIS: *Whole Lotta Shakin' Goin' On; Great Balls Of Fire; Breathless; High School Confidential; Fools Like Me; I'll Make It All Up To You; Down The Line; End Of The Road; Breakup; Crazy Arms; Your Cheating Heart; You Win Again.* GREATEST LIVE SHOW ON EARTH (November 1964): *Jenny Jenny; Who Will The Next Fool Be; I Got A Woman; Memphis; Hound Dog; Hi-Heel Sneakers; No Particular Place To Go; Long Tall Sally; Together Again; Whole Lotta Shakin' Goin' On.* RETURN OF ROCK (April 1965). COUNTRY SONGS—JERRY LEE LEWIS (November 1965). BY REQUEST (November 1966): *Johnny B. Goode; Green Grass Of Home; Money; Roll Over Beethoven; You Win Again; Little Queenie; I'll Sail My Ship Alone; How's My Ex Treating You; What'd I Say; Crying Time.* RETURN OF ROCK (June 1967): *I Believe In You; Maybelline; Johnny B. Goode; Roll Over Beethoven;* Six Other Titles. SOUL, MY WAY (November 1967): *Turn On Your Love Light; It's A Hang Up Baby; Dream Baby (How Long Must I Dream); Just Dropped In; Wedding Bells; He Took It Like A Man; Hey Baby; Treat Her Right; Holdin' On; Shotgun Man; I Betcha Gonna Like It.* JERRY LEE LEWIS MEMPHIS BEAT (March 1968): *Mathilda; Sticks And Stones; Lincoln Limousine; Big Boss Man; Whenever You're Ready; Memphis Beat; The Urge; She Thinks I Still Care; Hallelujah I Love*

Her So; Too Young; Just Because; Drinkin' Wine (Spo-Dee-O-Dee). ANOTHER PLACE, ANOTHER TIME (May 1968): *What's Made Milwaukee Famous (Has Made A Loser Out Of Me); Play Me A Song I Can Cry To; On The Back Row; Walking The Floor Over You; All Night Long; I'm A Lonesome Fugitive; Another Place, Another Time; Break My Mind; Before The Next Teardrop Falls; All The Good Is Gone; We Live In Two Different Worlds.*

Singles/*Crazy Arms/End Of The Road; Whole Lotta Shakin' Goin' On/It'll Be Me; Great Balls Of Fire/You Win Again; Breathless/Down The Line; High School Confidential/Fools Like Me; Return Of Jerry Lee/Lewis Boogie; Breakup/I'll Make It Up; I'll Sail My Ship Alone/It Hurt Me; Big Blon' Baby/Lovin' Up A Storm; Ballad Of Billy Joe/Let's Talk About Us; Little Queenie/I Could Never Be Ashamed Of You; Baby, Baby, Bye, Bye/Old Black Joe; Hang Up My Rock And Roll Shoes/John Henry; Love Made A Fool Of Me/When I Get Paid; What'd I Say/Livin' Lovin' Wreck; Cold Cold Heart/It Won't Happen With Me; As Long As I Live/Save The Last Dance For Me; Money/Bonnie B; Ramblin' Rose/I've Been Twistin'; Sweet Little Sixteen/How's My Ex Treating You; Good Golly Miss Molly/I Can't Trust Me; Teenage Letter/Seasons Of My Heart; I Know What It Means/Carry Me Back To Old Virginia; Breathless/Whole Lotta Shakin' Goin' On; Great Balls Of Fire/High School Confidential; Holdin' On/It's A Hang Up, Baby; Turn On Your Love Light/Shotgun Man; Another Place, Another Time/Walkin' The Floor Over You; What's Made Milwaukee Famous/All The Good Is Gone; She Still Comes Around/Slipping Around; Don't Let Me Cross Over/We Live In Two Different Worlds* (May 1969).

LIGHT SHOWS/"At last, music for the deaf!" said someone ecstatically on seeing his first light show. Conceivably, the light show *could* translate sound into color, line, shape, pattern, image and movement. But so far it has not tried to replace sound but merely enhance it. As the music plays, so does the light and the color, usually on a large screen above and behind the players, often on the players themselves, and on the audience and walls and ceiling, breaking down yet another barrier between the spectacle and the spectators.

Light shows emerged as public entertainment in San Francisco late in 1965 along with the dance halls and acid rock, both of which involved rock audiences more than they had ever been involved before (a happy extension of the fainting-over-Elvis and jitterbugging-in-the-aisles phenomena of earlier ages). They employed all sorts of mechanics—films, slides, strobe lights, spotlights, oil paints swirling in saucers of water —in all sorts of combinations that commented on the content and even the lyrics of the music, and throbbed and pulsated with the beat like another instrument. The light shows were doing visually what acid rock was doing aurally—expanding the consciousness and reproducing mechanically and harmlessly what LSD, mescalin and other hallucinogens were doing chemically. For the nonusers they were, like acid rock, a *safe* turn-on and a short cut to rapture; for the users, a blissful backdrop to private transports. Because of the dance halls and the psychedelic orientation of San Francisco, the light shows soon became an indispensable part of every dance concert at the rock palaces of the Avalon and the Fillmore. On the East Coast, acceptance was slower. Lights by Cassen and Stern at the Village Gate performances of the Byrds in late 1966 were thought to be distracting from rather than enhancing the music. When a dance-hall scene started in the form of Andy Warhol's Exploding Plastic Inevitable, the light show (a perfect medium for Warhol's film tedium) got off the ground. The Electric Circus, which replaced the Inevitable, helped establish it further, and when Fillmore East, though not a dancing place but a rock concert hall, opened in 1968, light shows became a permanent fixture along with the music And light-show producers, such as Joshua, Pablo, Headlights, etc., became artists in their own right. There are light-show people who believe that eventually each rock album will come along with a spool of its own filmed light show especially "composed" to accompany the music. Others predict that eventually all visual art will move and will be accompanied by a tape of music especially planned to complement it. Either way, multimedia is moving in and the rock light show will be a big part of it.

GORDON LIGHTFOOT/Voted Canada's top folk singer in 1966 and Canada's top male vocalist in 1967, he started off as a country singer and moved into song writing. Peter, Paul and Mary first gained national recognition with a Lightfoot tune, *For Loving Me,* which became one of their biggest selling singles. Judy Collins' memorable song *Early Morning Rain* is Lightfoot's. And Marty Robbins and George Hamilton IV have topped country charts with his *Ribbon of Darkness* and *Steel Rail Blues.* He has a little of Johnny Cash and a little of Bob Dylan (with whom he shares a manager), and if he sings like anyone, he sings like a cowboy. He's yet another example of how country music is sneaking in on the pop-rock-folk scene.

Albums/LIGHTFOOT (June 1966): *Rich Man's Spiritual; Long River; The Way I Feel; For Lovin' Me; First Time Ever I Saw Your Face; Changes; Early Mornin' Rain; Steel Rail Blues; Sixteen Miles; I'm Not Sayin'; Pride Of Man; Ribbon Of Darkness; Oh, Linda; Peaceful Waters.* WAY I FEEL (May 1967): *Walls; If You Got It; Softly; Crossroads; Minor Ballad; Go-Go Round; Rosanna; Home From The Forest; I'll Be Alright; Song For A Winter's Night; Canadian Railroad Trilogy; Way I Feel.* LIGHTFOOT (January 1968): *Wherefore And Why; Last Time I Saw Her; May I; Black Day In July; Magnificent Outpouring; Does Your Mother Know; Mountain And Maryann; Pussywillows, Cat-Tails; I Want To Hear It From You; Something Very Special; Boss Man; Did She Mention My Name.*

Single/*Black Day in July/Pussywillows, Cat-Tails* (January 1968).

BOB LIND/The success of his delicate *Elusive Butterfly* in early 1967 opened up a place on the charts for a whole breathy, wistful, wispy, lyrical kind of song, the kind that until then had been thought to be too slow to be commercial. Others (Tim Buckley, Tim Hardin) benefited greatly from the breakthrough. Bob Lind, who should have, didn't.

Albums/DON'T BE CONCERNED: *Elusive Butterfly; Mr. Zero; You Should Have Seen It; Counting; Drifter's Sunrise; Unlock The Door; Truly Julie's Blues; Dale Anne; World Is Just A ('B' Movie); Cheryl's Goin' Home; It Wasn't Just The Morning; I Can't Walk Roads Of Anger.* ELUSIVE BOB LIND: *Fennario; Wandering; Times They Are A-Changin';*

Black Night; White Snow; Cool Summer; Hey Nellie Nellie; The Swan; What Color Are You; Gold Mine Blues; Hard Road. BOB LIND (PHOTOGRAPHS OF FEELING): *Go Ask Your Man; Oh Babe Take Me Home; I Just Let It Take Me; West Virginia Summer Child; Elinor; San Francisco Woman; But It Is; World Is Just A 'B' Movie Meets Reno, Funtown, U.S.A.; Nameless Request; We've Never Spoken; Remember The Rain.*

Singles/*Elusive Butterfly/Cheryl's Goin' Home* (1967); *Goodbye Neon Lies/We May Have Touched; Good Time Special/Just My Love.*

LINDA AND THE STONE PONEYS/*Linda Ronstadt (guitar), Bob Kimmel (rhythm guitar), Ken Edwards (lead guitar).*
The group is a trio that got together in Arizona and Los Angeles playing the kind of melodic folk pop that only started getting underway in 1967 when early Beatles hard rock (and its imitators) had given way to the folky sound of the Spoonful and the Mamas and Papas, and, as a matter of fact, the folky sound of middle and late Beatles. Their big hit, *Different Drum*, was written by Mike Nesmith of the Monkees.

Albums/STONE PONEYS (January 1967): *Sweet Summer Blue And Gold; If I Were You; Just A Little Bit Of Rain; Bicycle Song; All The Beautiful Things; Orion; Wild About My Lovin'; Back Home; Meredith (On My Mind); Train And The River; 2:10 Train.* EVERGREEN—VOLUME 2 (June 1967): *December Dream; Song About The Rain; I'd Like To Know; Autumn Afternoon; Different Drum; Evergreen (2 Parts); Driftin'; Back On The Street Again; Toys In Time; New Hard Times.* STONE PONEYS—VOLUME 3 AND FRIENDS (February 1968).

Singles/*Some Of Shelley's Blues/Hobo (Morning Glory)* (January 1965); *Sweet Summer Blue And Gold/All The Beautiful Things* (February 1967); *Different Drum/I've Got To Know* (July 1967); *Carnival Bear/Up To My Neck In High Muddy Water* (March 1968).

BUZZ LINHART/He came out of the legendary Greenwich Village coffee-house period of the early to middle sixties when

Tim Hardin, Fred Neil and John Sebastian (among many others) were finding themselves, influencing others, and being influenced (as often as not by each other). It was a period of hanging out, of song writing, of soaking in everything from folk to blues to rock. Like Fred Neil, who taught him a lot, Linhart has a strong, gritty, emotional voice. Like Hardin, his life has been racked with almost insurmountable personal problems, and his voice and lyrics reflect it. In 1968, after a long absence and with many of the personal problems apparently solved, he made some brief appearances in New York, where critical reaction was consistently favorable. He's also much sought after as sideman on vibes.

Album/BUZZY (February 1969): *Yellow Cab; Willie Jean; Step Into My Wildest Dreams; Wish I Could Find; Sing Joy; End Song.*

Single/*End Song*/*Yellow Cab* (April 1969).

LINN COUNTY/*Fred Walk (guitar, electric sitar), Larry Easter (soprano saxophone, assorted reeds, woodwinds), Dino Long (bass), Stephen Miller (organ, vocals), Snake McAndrew (drums).*

One of those groups still in the process of finding themselves, Linn County is not the best of the American blues bands, but one with some of the most talented musicians. There are hard-rock and jazz influences in their work.

Albums/LINN COUNTY (September 1968): *Think; Lower Lemons; Moon Food; Cave Song; Protect And Serve; Bad Things; Fast Days.* FEVER SHOT (May 1969): *Girl Can't Help It; Elevator Woman; Too Far Gone; Suspended; Fever Shot; Lonely Avenue; Ground Hog Blues.*

Singles/*Cave Song*/*Think* (October 1968); *Fever Shot*/*Girl Can't Help It* (April 1969).

MANCE LIPSCOMB/A famous country-blues singer from Texas now in his sixties, Lipscomb greatly influenced Bob Dylan, but not as many others as might be supposed, since his records are not widely circulated outside Texas, and his appearances are few.

LITERARY ROCK/Rock-producer Phil Spector wants to

produce films. Mick Jagger, Tiny Tim, Bob Dylan, John Lennon and Paul Jones have starred in them. The Fugs sing William Blake. The late Richard Fariña, a songwriter, singer and producer, wrote a novel. Leonard Cohen, a poet and novelist, writes songs and sings them. Joan Baez wrote an autobiography—and Bob Dylan was supposed to. Tim Buckley, a singer and songwriter, uses the poems of Larry Beckett as lyrics. The songs of Arlo Guthrie and Tom Paxton are outlines for twenty comic novels. It's still not agreed to what extent the most poetic of the new rock lyrics are poetry. The college professors are still fighting *that* out amongst themselves, but one way or another it is fairly well agreed that in the future it will be impossible to study accurately the literature of the sixties without close attention to the literature of rock.

LITTLE RICHARD/His pompadour was high and his hip action wicked when Elvis was still a pimply kid mowing lawns in Memphis. He was the model for 99 percent of the screaming, jet-propelled pelvic freakouts of the post-Elvis early rock era, down to the shiny suits, lurid showmanship and acrobatic piano-playing. Little Richard was wildly frantic and intense, all urgency and fervor, given to wild falsetto shrieks and a lot of showy costuming. He was the reason that much later everyone realized there wasn't one thing in those feverish rock years that wasn't copped straight from what was then known as "race" music (black rhythm and blues). Pat Boone rode to fame on his songs and the Beatles took a lot from his style. Mick Jagger and James Brown have never stopped doing the raving Little Richard thing. Richard Penniman had fought hard, though, but when he finally came into his own, he decided to leave rock for religion. Happily he did come back. Once you have seen Little Richard it is very difficult to take any other rocker seriously. He did it all first.

Albums/HERE'S LITTLE RICHARD (December 1958): *Long Tall Sally; Miss Ann; She's Got It; Can't Believe You Wanna Leave; Slippin' And Slidin'; Ready Teddy; Oh Why; Baby; Tutti-Frutti; Rip It Up; True, Fine Mama; Jenny, Jenny.* LITTLE RICHARD (December 1958): *Keep A-Knockin'; By The Light Of The Silvery Moon; Lucille; Hey-Hey-Hey-Hey; Ooh, My Soul; All Around The World; Good*

Golly Miss Molly; Baby Face; Boo-Hoo-Hoo-Hoo; Girl Can't Help It; Send Me Some Lovin'; Heeby-Jeebies. FABULOUS LITTLE RICHARD (April 1959): *Shake A Hand; Chicken Little Baby; All Night Long; Most I Can Offer; Lonesome And Blue; Wonderin'; She Knows How To Rock; Kansas City; Directly From My Heart; I'm Just A Lonely Guy; Maybe I'm Right; Whole Lotta Shakin'.* COMING HOME (November 1963): *Just A Closer Walk With Thee; Coming Home; Search Me Lord; I Want Jesus To Walk With Me; Milky White Way; Need Him; Everytime I Feel The Spirit; Does Jesus Care; God Is Real; I'm Trampin'; Jesus Walked This Lonesome Valley; Precious Lord.* LITTLE RICHARD'S BIGGEST HITS (December 1963): *Rip It Up; Lucille; Jenny Jenny; All Around The World; Good Golly Miss Molly; Long Tall Sally; Slippin' And Slidin'; Send Me Some Lovin'; Boo-Hoo-Hoo-Hoo; True Fine Mama; Keep A Knockin'; Tutti Frutti.* KING OF THE GOSPEL SINGERS (October 1964): *Joy, Joy, Joy; Do You Care; Captain Calls For You; Do Lord, Remember Me; Ride On, King Jesus; Peace In The Valley; He's Not Just A Soldier; My Desire; He's My Star; It Takes Everything To Serve The Lord.* EXPLOSIVE LITTLE RICHARD (January 1967): *I Don't Want To Discuss It; Land Of 1,000 Dances; Commandments Of Love; Money; Poor Dog; I Need Love; Never Gonna Let You Go; Don't Deceive Me (Please Don't Go); Function At The Junction; Well.* LITTLE RICHARD'S GREATEST HITS (June 1967): *Lucille; Girl Can't Help It; Tutti Frutti; Send Me Some Lovin'; Long Tall Sally; Get Down With It; True Fine Mama; Jenny, Jenny; Good Golly Miss Molly; Whole Lotta Shakin' Goin' On; Anyway You Want Me; You Gotta Feel It.*

Singles/*Tutti Frutti/I'm Just A Lonely Guy; Long Tall Sally/Slippin' And Slidin'; Ready Teddy/Rip It Up; Heeby Jeebies/She's Got It; All Around The World/Girl Can't Help It; Lucille/Save Me Some Lovin'; Jenny Jenny/Miss Ann; Can't Believe You Wanna Leave Me/Keep A-Knockin'; Good Golly Miss Molly/Hey, Hey, Hey, Hey; Ooh, My Soul/True Fine Mama; Baby Face/I'll Never Let You Go; Early One Morning/She Knows How To Rock; By The Light Of The Silvery Moon/Wonderin'; Lonesome And Blue/Kansas City; All*

Night Long/Shake A Hand; Maybe I'm Right/Whole Lotta Shakin'; Baby/I Got It; Annie Is Back/Bama Lama Bama Loo; Commandments Of Love/I Need Love; Hurry Sundown/I Don't Want To Discuss It; Don't Deceive Me/Never Gonna Let You Go; Little Bit Of Something/Money; Try Some Of Mine/She's Together; Can I Count On You/Soul Train.

LITTLE WALTER/The young man who played amplified harmonica on most of Muddy Waters' records for about ten years (1950–60), Little Walter was considered the single most original instrumentalist ever to come out of Chicago. Cream's version of a record he made of Muddy Waters' *Rollin' and Tumblin'* (with a singer other than Muddy) is very very close to the original (and people who are knocked out by it should know that). He originated that whole harmonica style that Paul Butterfield (and Junior Wells) made familiar to the current music generation, and is almost entirely responsible for the way almost every young harp player in blues or rock plays today. Ironically, he developed his unique harp style because he had originally wanted a saxophone and couldn't afford it, so he played his harp like a sax. The Chicago blues sound wouldn't have been possible without Little Walter. Yet, when he died in 1968 (at the age of 38) of a cerebral hemorrhage, after a beating it was rumored, the Chicago newspapers dismissed it in a few lines.

Album/BEST OF LITTLE WALTER (March 1968): *My Babe; Blues With A Feeling; Last Night; Mean Old World; Sad Hours; You're So Fine; Can't Hold Out Much Longer; Juke; Tell Me Mama; Off The Wall; You Better Watch Yourself; Blues Light.*

Singles/*Ah'w Baby/I Had My Fun; As Long As I Have You/I Don't Play; Back Track/Everything Gonna Be Alright; Blue And Lonesome/Mean Ole Frisco; Boom, Boom Out Goes The Lights/Temperature; Break It Up/Me And Piney Brown; Confessin' The Blues/The Toodle; Crazy For My Baby/Crazy Legs; Crazy Mixed Up World/My Baby Is Sweet; Dead Presidents/I'm A Business Man; I Got To Go/Roller Coaster; My Babe/Thunderbird; Southern Feeling/Up The Line.*

Also Appears On THE BLUES/Vols. 1–4, LOVE THOSE GOODIES & SUPER BLUES. ALAN FREED'S GOLDEN PICS.

THE CHARLES LLOYD QUARTET/Although they play jazz and not rock, the Charles Lloyd Quartet has won a rock following because of their long-hair-and-beads image, an image not usually associated with jazz. (Gary Burton's following, too, comes from fans attracted more by his costuming than his music.) The main point, though, is that once the jazz-rock barrier is broken, no matter by what means, some of the rock fans stay to listen.

Albums/DISCOVERY (October 1964). CHARLES LLOYD AT MONTEREY. DREAM WEAVER. CHARLES LLOYD IN EUROPE. JOURNEY WITHIN. OF COURSE, OF COURSE (January 1966). LOVE-IN. FOREST FLOWER. NIRVANA (May 1968).

LOADING ZONE/*Paul Fauerso (lead vocals, piano, organ), Linda Tillery (lead vocals, string bass, drums, bassoon, harmonica), Peter Shapiro (lead guitar), Steve Dowler (rhythm guitar), Bob Kridle (bass), George Newcom (drums), Todd Anderson (tenor, alto, soprano saxophone, piano, accordion, clarinet), Patrick O'Hara (trombone).*

This eight-man, or rather seven-man, one-woman group was supposed to be one of the best rhythm and blues groups to come out in years, and it's all white except for singer Linda Tillery, who comes on like a junior Aretha. It came out of San Francisco and played at all the band scenes there during the San Francisco boom before moving East and elsewhere for concerts.

Album/THE LOADING ZONE (April 1968): *No More Tears; Love Feels Like Fire; Don't Lose Control (Of Your Soul); I Can't Please You; Shop Around; The Bells; Kali Yuga-Loo; God Bless The Child; Danger Heartbreak Dead Ahead; Can I Dedicate.*

Singles/*Don't Lose Control/Danger Heartbreak Dead Ahead* (May 1968); *No More Tears/Can I Dedicate* (August 1968).

JACKIE LOMAX is an English singer who, in 1966, headed a rock group called the Lomax Alliance for which Beatle manager Brian Epstein had big plans. After Epstein died, the group seemed to fade out, but in 1968 the Beatles' Apple records brought Lomax out as a solo singer in one of its earliest releases. (Among the musicians backing him on that single was Eric Clapton of Cream).

Singles/*Genuine Imitation Life/One Minute Woman; Eagle Laughs At You/Sour Milk Sea* (October 1968); *New Day/ Thumbin' A Ride* (June 1969).

LOS ANGELES SOUND/It started as Sunshine Dylan—that is, New York protest folk married to California sunshine rock—the Byrds and the Turtles rocking Dylan and getting the sound and themselves into the charts and the national eye. That was 1965, *after* the Beatles but *before* San Francisco and acid rock. It was the first faint indication that America was not about to take the English invasion completely lying down. Sonny and Cher were the Los Angeles sound with *I Got You Babe* and other early folk rock. The Byrds were folk rock with the first hints of the coming acid-rock revolution in music. Love was British-influenced Los Angeles folk rock. (The Beach Boys, Jan and Dean, and all that surf and hot-rod music, dubbed in the early pre-Beatles sixties as the California sound, have to be in a class by themselves.) Later came the California sound of the Mamas and the Papas in *California Dreaming*, with echoes of the Beach Boys; and just in time came Beatles publicist Derek Taylor to tell the world about the Mamas and the Papas, the Byrds, Paul Revere and the Raiders and the genius of Brian Wilson, which transcended everything. Even when the whole paisley day-glo San Francisco explosion shook the world of rock, it never more than temporarily overshadowed Los Angeles with its suntanned Chad and Jeremy action, the Monkees hoopla and the San Francisco-influenced renaissance which took in the Doors, Clear Light, Tim Buckley and the Buffalo Springfield.

LOS BRAVOS/*Michael Kogel (vocals), Manuel Fernandez (organ), Juan-Pablo Sanllehi (drums), Antonio Martinez (rhythm & lead guitar), Miguel Luis Vicens Danus (bass).*
The first Spanish group to win worldwide fame, Los Bravos has been together since the summer of 1965. Their 1966 single *Black Is Black* was one of the great hits of that year.

Not too much happened till three singles later with *Bring A Little Lovin'* (a song written for them by Easybeats' George Young and Harry Vanda), which also hit the charts, though not as hard as their first single.

Albums/BLACK IS BLACK (September 1966): *Black Is Black; Trapped; Baby, Baby; I Want A Name; Make It Easy For Me; She Believes In Me; I Don't Care; Stop That Girl; I'm Cuttin' Out; Don't Be Left Out In The Cold; You Won't Get Far; Baby, Believe Me.* BRING A LITTLE LOVIN' (June 1968): *Bring A Little Lovin'; Make It Last; You Got Until The Morning; Then The Sun Goes Down; Show Me; Play With Fire And You'll Get Burned; Don't Get In My Way; Sympathy; She's My Girl; If I Were A River; Black Is Black.*

Singles/*Black Is Black/I Want A Name* (June 1966); *Going Nowhere/ Brand New Baby* (November 1966); *I'm All Ears /You'll Never Get The Chance Again* (May 1967); *Bring A Little Lovin'/Make It Last* (April 1968); *Two People In Me/Dirty Street* (April 1969).

LOTHAR AND THE HAND PEOPLE/*John Emelin (lothar-theremin), Tom Flye (drums), Kim King (lead guitar), Paul Conly (rhythm guitar), Rusty Ford (bass guitar).*
Lothar and the Hand People were already big in Denver, Colorado, when they won a respectable following in New York in the fall of 1966, thanks to Lothar, who is not a person but a theremin. A theremin is an electronic wand that makes weird shrieking sounds when hands are waved around it. (The electronic shrieks heard in so many horror movies are produced by a theremin. It also forms the basis for some of the more interesting sounds in the Beach Boys' *Good Vibrations*.) The Hand People themselves, tall, pale, thin, mysterious (when the whimsy isn't showing), have a touch of eeriness that goes beautifully with Lothar. You'd never guess they were mostly nice upper-class boys from Connecticut—unless you look closely.

Album/LOTHAR AND THE HAND PEOPLE (November 1968): *Machines; This Is It; This May Be Goodbye; That's Another Story; Kids Are Little People; Ha; Sex And Violence; Bye Bye Love; Milkweed Love; You Won't Be Lonely; It Comes On Anyhow; Woody Woodpecker; Paul, In Love.*

Single/*Have Mercy*/*Let The Boy Pretend* (July 1968).

LOVE/*Arthur Lee (guitar, lead vocals, piano, accordion, drums, harp, organ), John Echols (lead guitar), Bryan Maclean (guitar, vocals), Ken Forssi (electric bass), Michael Stuart (percussion).*
Previous Members: Alban "Snoopy" Pfisterer, Tjay Cantrelli.
One of the earliest of the Los Angeles rock groups, Love emerged late in 1965 before anyone could see that there would be a San Francisco music scene, let alone a successful one. Until then Los Angeles had produced only the Byrds and Sonny & Cher and the Raiders—and that explains why a "serious" group like Love was an underground success then. Their first album had a hard Beatles-Byrds sound (a marriage of English and Los Angeles rock). The second album used a lot of orchestration and came across as arty. The third had everything—hard rock, folk, and soft orchestration with singer Arthur Lee having written nine out of its eleven cuts. Love has never made it as a supergroup, and yet it was one of the first groups with a strong underground following (especially in England). Also, it was one of the first integrated groups. (Arthur Lee produced one of the most amusing paradoxes in rock—a Negro, he came on like Mick Jagger, a white singer who built his whole style around accurate imitations of Negroes.) And Love was one of the first groups to cover an entire side, 18.57 minutes, with one cut. And the first album had one of the first versions of Dino Valente's *Hey Joe*. The only thing Love never did was make the best-seller lists.

Albums/LOVE (March 1966): *My Little Red Book; Can't Explain; A Message To Pretty; My Flash To You; Softly To Me; No Matter What You Do; Emotions; You'll Be Following; Fazing; Hey Joe; Signed C. D.; And More; Colored Balls Falling; Mushroom Clouds.* DA CAPO (January 1967): *Stephanie Knows Who; Orange Skies; Que Vida; Seven And Seven Is; The Castle; She Comes In Colors; Revelation.* FOREVER CHANGES (November 1967): *Alone Again Or; A House Is Not A Motel; Andmoreagain; The Daily Planet; Old Man; The Red Telephone; Maybe The People Would Be The Times Or Between Clark And Hilldale; Live And Let Live; The Good Humor Man He Sees Everything Like This;*

Bummer In The Summer; You Set The Scene. LOVE FOUR
SAIL (July 1969): *August; Your Friend And Mine; Neil's
Song; I'm With You; Good Times; Singing Cowboy; Dream;
Robert Montgomery; Nothing; Talking In My Sleep; Always
See Your Face.*

Singles/*A Message To Pretty/My Little Red Book* (March
1966); *Number Fourteen/Seven And Seven Is* (July 1966);
She Comes In Colors/Orange Skies (November 1966); *Alone
Again Or/House Is Not A Motel* (February 1968).

LOVE AFFAIR/*Maurice Bacon (drums), Steve Ellis (vocals),
Rex Brayley (lead guitar), Mick Jackson (bass guitar), Morgan Fisher (replaced Lynton Guest) (organ).*
Love Affair is probably the youngest group around in England
(their drummer is only fifteen). The group came together
when the youthful drummer told his father he wanted a
group. They advertised, got four people, cut a record and
were surprised when it became a hit so soon. But it wasn't
quite that simple. They were the center of a very interesting
row early in 1968 when that first single, *Everlasting Love,*
hit the English charts. It seems that the only member of the
group who had appeared on the disc (a cover of Robert
Knight's U.S. record) was singer Ellis. Everyone else playing
was a session musician. This raised some vital points (points
that came up early in the Monkees' career): When is a group
not a group? Should session musicians, since even the Stones
and the Beatles use them, be credited or not? In the rough
and competitive world of rock, what trickery is ethical and
what trickery isn't? Over in England, they're still fighting it
out. Needless to say, the boys are doing all their own playing
on subsequent releases and meticulously acknowledging any
professional help they're getting. But they say indignantly, in
their defense, that the practice has gone on for years. And it
has.

Singles/*Everlasting Love/Gone Are The Songs Of Yesterday*
(February 1968); *Rainbow Valley/Someone Like Me* (May
1968); *Day Without Love/I'm Happy* (November 1968);
Let Me Know/One Road (June 1969).

H. P. LOVECRAFT/*George Edwards (vocals, guitar), Dave*

Michaels *(vocals, organ, harpsichord, piano)*, Tony Cavallari *(vocals, guitar)*, Mike Tegza *(vocals, drums)*, Jeffrey Boyan *(replaced Jerry McGeorge) (vocals, bass)*.

The band took its name from a novelist and poet of the twenties who specialized in the bizarre. (The group's manager has a dog named after a character in one of Lovecraft's works and that's how it started, or so they say.) The music is very sad and haunting; the harmonies, with two very strong lead singers, are as involved as those of the Mamas and the Papas and the Association. The band got together in Chicago in 1967. It has done everything from folky material like *Wayfaring Stranger* to Dino Valente's *Let's Get Together* and Randy Newman's *I've Been Wrong Before*.

Albums/H. P. LOVECRAFT (October 1967): *Wayfaring Stranger; Let's Get Together; I've Been Wrong Before; The Drifter; That's The Bag I'm In; The White Ship; Country Boy And Bleecker Street; The Time Machine; That's How Much I Love You; Gloria Patria*. H. P. LOVECRAFT II (October 1968): *Spin, Spin, Spin; It's About Time; Blue Jack Of Diamonds; Electrallentando; At The Mountains Of Madness; Mobius Trip; High Flying Bird; Nothing's Boy; Keeper Of The Keys*.

Single/*Blue Jack Of Diamonds/Keeper Of The Keys* (December 1968).

LOVIN' SPOONFUL/*Steve Boone (bass), John Sebastian (harmonica, autoharp, lead vocals), Jerry Yester (replaced Zal Yanovsky) (lead guitar), Joe Butler (drums)*.

For a lot of people in America, the Lovin' Spoonful was Liverpool—in Manhattan. Our own little moptops, born, bred and raised right here in the streets we walked each day, hanging around outside the coffee shops, playing in the basket houses, making a nuisance of themselves in Izzy Young's Folklore Centre. Scores of kids must have gone the Lovin' Spoonful route at the same time as the Spoonful, but John Sebastian, son of a great musician, had talent. And when all his folky friends started making it before he did, he was only playing harp on their albums. Before the Spoonful there was a strong, very creative folk scene which had already spawned Dylan, among others. There was a country scene down in

Nashville that wasn't really being felt in New York—except by Sebastian, who had been in a jug band, and by the Spoonful's producer, Erik Jacobsen, who had played banjo in a country string group. And there were a lot of leftovers from pre-Beatles hard rock, tough commercial little groups playing at dances. And in California there was a burgeoning folk-rock scene with the Byrds and Sonny and Cher. And then, of course, there were the English groups—no American group had anything like their stature in America or out of it.

There had been an attempt to change all this but they had failed. And the Spoonful, with all their talent, weren't that good, weren't clicking or jelling. The story goes—and it's such a legend now that everyone has forgotten what's true—that they were at the Night Owl and terrible, and that Joe Marra, the owner, told them to go away and practice. Zally and Joe had a room at the Albert Hotel then, mainly to store equipment. When they rehearsed there, there were complaints. So Miss Feldman, the assistant manager, suggested the basement. And that was it. The group made it. The basement became a shrine; and no musician feels he's a musician unless he's stayed at the Albert and rehearsed among the pools of water and the cockroaches. The Albert became *the* hotel and the Spoonful became *the* group that eventually turned the hurricane eye of rock away from Liverpool and London to New York and Los Angeles (and later San Francisco). The tide had turned. *Daydream*, written and sung by Sebastian, was the big hit of early '66 along with the Mamas and the Papas' *California Dreamin'*, a beautiful coincidence, since the two groups were friends. It was winter and both songs were about good times and good climes. Later, much later, people were to say that the Spoonful never developed, that the songs after a while were all the same, that there was never anything like the maturing of the Beatles or Stones, or even the Byrds or the Rascals. But at the time it seemed like one perfect hit followed another and that each had the happiness of jug-band music and country strings and some of the sweetness of folk, with all the punch of rock.

Off stage and on, the Spoonful were such *characters*. John had sidies and steel glasses when both were new. Zally wore a cowboy hat all the time and sometimes great bear-like furs. None of the four ever dressed mod-English as other groups did but from the start wore the striped shirts and vests that were the uniform of every Village kid. American kids couldn't believe their luck, that they had their own group. On tour, to Americans the Spoonful seemed so real and human. And when they visited England they wowed them. (They even made friends with the Beatles.) Joe got some of the most English gear in creation but he still looked, in his undertaker's coat, like a Greenwich Village kid playing Carnaby Street. Even if the songs weren't developing, and they were no longer America's only moptops, things looked like they might remain rosy forever. Then, and this was before rock busts were a frequent occurrence, there was a bust in San Francisco. It was revealed later that huge pressures were put on Zally, who could very easily have been deported. All anyone knew was that Zally and Steve had fingered their source, and that they were free but the source wasn't. In San Francisco in 1967 their name was mud, their albums were used as doormats, groupies were urged not to ball them. Later, Ralph Gleason said for heaven's sake, forgive and forget, remember what Lenny Bruce said about how easy it is to blurt out everything when the hot lead is on its way to your interior. But later was too late. Zally left to go solo and was replaced by Jerry Yester. Yester was a fine musician, but already it wasn't the same. Sebastian left to go into other ventures, a musical, a solo album. And Zally, who hadn't done too well solo, returned. But it was over. The group split. They had done what they had set out to do, and on the way changed the whole musical scene.

Albums/DO YOU BELIEVE IN MAGIC (December 1965): *Do You Believe In Magic; Blues In The Bottle; Sportin' Life; My Gal; You Baby; Fishin' Blues; Do You Ever Have To Make Up Your Mind; Wild About My Lovin'; Other Side Of This Side Of Life; Younger Girl; On The Road Again; Night Owl Blues.* DAY DREAM (May 1966): *Day Dream; There She Is; It's Not Time Now; Warm Baby; Day Blues; Let The Boy Rock And Roll; Jug Band Music; Didn't Want To Have To Do It; You Didn't Have To Be So Nice; Big Noise From Speonk; Butchie's Tune; Bald Headed Lena.* WHAT'S UP, TIGER LILY (July 1966): *Respoken; Grey Prison Blues; Introduction To Flick; Pow; Pow Revisited; Unconscious*

Minuet; Fishing Blues; Cool Millions; Phil's Love Theme; Speaking Of Spoken; Looking To Spy; Theme From "What's Up, Tiger Lily." HUMS OF THE LOVIN' SPOONFUL (January 1967): *Summer In The City; Rain On The Roof; Full Measure; Lovin' You; Bes' Friends; Voo-doo In My Basement; Darlin' Companion; Henry Thomas; Coconut Grove; Nashville Cats; Four Eyes.* YOU'RE A BIG BOY NOW (January 1967): *Darling Be Home Soon; You're A Big Boy Now; Lonely; Wash Her Away; Kite Chase; Try And Be Happy; Peep Show Percussion; Letter To Barbara; Girl, Beautiful Girl; Dixieland Big Boy; Miss Thing's Thang; March.* BEST OF THE LOVIN' SPOONFUL (March 1967): *You Didn't Have To Be So Nice; Did You Ever Have To Make Up Your Mind; Butchie's Tune; Jug Band Music; Night Owl Blues; Younger Girl; Day Dream; Do You Believe In Magic; Didn't Want To Have To Do It; Wild About My Lovin'; Blues In The Bottle; Summer In The City.* EVERYTHING IS PLAYING (November 1967): *Six O'clock; Money; She Is Still A Mystery; Younger Generation; Old Folks; Only Pretty, What A Pity; Try A Little Bit; Close Your Eyes; Priscilla Millionaira; Boredom; Forever.* BEST OF THE LOVIN' SPOONFUL—VOLUME 2 (March 1968): *Money; She Is Still A Mystery; Six O'clock; Darling Be Home Soon; Lovin' You; Boredom; Full Measure; Nashville Cats; Rain On The Roof; Old Folks; Darlin' Companion; Younger Generation.* REVELATION: REVOLUTION '69 (November 1968): *Amazing Air; Never Going Back; The Prophet; Only Yesterday; War Games; Till I Run With You; Jug Of Wine; Revelation: Revolution '69; Me About You; Words.*

Singles/*Do You Believe In Magic/On The Road Again* (July 1965); *You Didn't Have To Be So Nice/My Gal* (October 1965); *Day Dream/Night Owl Blues* (January 1966); *Did You Ever Have To Make Up Your Mind/Didn't Want To Have To Do It* (April 1966); *Summer In The City/Butchie's Tune* (June 1966); *You And Me And Rain On The Roof/Pow* (September 1966); *Nashville Cats/Full Measure* (November 1966); *Darlin' Be Home Soon/Darlin' Companion* (January 1967); *Six O'clock/You're A Big Boy Now* (April 1967); *Lonely (Amy's Theme)/You're A Big Boy Now* (May 1967); *She Is Still A Mystery/Only Pretty, What*

A Pity (September 1967); *Close Your Eyes/Money* (December 1967); *Forever/Never Going Back.*

LULU/She is the little-girl-with-the-big-voice, 1967 version. (There was a whole bunch of them in the late fifties and early sixties—Lesley Gore, Brenda Lee and the rest—all shrieking away about teenage love. Lulu's cooler than that.) Small, cute and comfortably padded with the merest quilting of baby fat, Lulu is capable of belting it out like Ethel Merman. Born Marie Laurie in Scotland, she was fairly big in London when she appeared in the film *To Sir, With Love* and sang its corny but somehow poignant theme. It made her a star in America.

Albums/FROM LULU WITH LOVE (October 1967): *Shout; Here Comes The Night; When He Touches Me; I'll Come Running; Call Me; Surprise, Surprise; Leave A Little Love; She Will Break Your Heart; Lies; Take Me As I Am; Tossin' And Turnin'; Tell It Like It Is.* LULU SINGS TO SIR WITH LOVE (December 1967): *To Sir With Love; Boat That I Row; Rattler; Morning Dew; Love Loves To Love Love; Best Of Both Worlds; Day Tripper; Let's Pretend; Take Me In Your Arms (And Love Me); To Love Somebody; You And I.*

Singles/*Have A Little Love/He Don't Want Your Love Anymore* (June 1965); *Try To Understand/Not In This Whole World* (September 1965); *To Sir With Love/The Boat That I Row* (June 1967); *Let's Pretend/Dreary Nights And Days* (July 1967); *Shout/When He Touches Me* (October 1967); *Best Of Both Worlds/Love Loves To Love Love* (November 1967); *Me, The Peaceful Heart/Look Out* (February 1968); *Boy/Sad Memories* (May 1968); *Morning Dew/You And I* (July 1968); *Without Him/This Time* (November 1968); *I'm A Tiger/Rattler* (December 1968).

FRANKIE LYMON (and the TEENAGERS)/Detroit-born Frankie Lymon was only thirteen when he and the Teenagers recorded *Why Do Fools Fall In Love?* in 1956—a song he wrote. It sold a million copies in America alone and was revived with great success by the Happenings in 1967—a year before Frankie died tragically of an overdose of drugs. He was the first of the teeny rockers and one of the most successful.

Album/THE TEENAGERS: *Why Do Fools Fall In Love; Please Be Mine; Who Can Explain; Share; Love Is A Clown; I Promise To Remember; I Want You To Be My Girl; I'm Not A Know It All; Baby, Baby; ABC's Of Love; Am I Fooling Myself Again; I'm Not A Juvenile Delinquent.*

Singles/*Why Do Fools Fall In Love/I'm Not A Juvenile Delinquent; Itty Bitty Pretty One/Paper Castles; Creation Of Love/Goody Goody; ABC's Of Love/I Promise To Remember; I Want You To Be My Girl/Out In The Cold Again; Teenage Love.*

MAD RIVER/*David Roberts (lead guitar), Rick Bochner (vocals, second lead guitar, 12-string guitar), Lawrence Hammond (lead vocals, bass), Thomas Manning (vocals, 12-string guitar, bass), Gregory LeRoy Dewey (vocals, drums, fence, worms, recorder).*
A white blues group with head-music overtones, Mad River formed at Antioch College a few years ago but released its first album in the fall of 1968 with long, long tracks and a good lead singer named Lawrence Hammond. Their first single was *High All The Time* and *Amphetamine Gazelle,* which gives you at least some idea of what they're about.

Album/MAD RIVER (October 1968): *Merciful Monks; High All The Time; Amphetamine Gazelle; Eastern Light; Wind Chimes; War Goes On; Hush Julianne.*

Single/*High All The Time/Amphetamine Gazelle* (September 1968).

TAJ MAHAL/The irony with the traditional country blues is that black singers, whose people originated them, have outgrown them emotionally and feel the need to move into something more sophisticated. So young white singers have taken them on, caring for them with the love of a true archivist. For Taj Mahal, who is black, to do these blues is an even further turn of the screw. One of the very few *sophisticated* young black singers, he brought back the sound of authentic country blues, flatly refusing to gloss over or stylize. The son of a noted jazz arranger and pianist, Taj Mahal was once told he would never be a musician. So he taught himself piano, guitar, harmonica, electric bass, banjo, tambourine, vibes, mandolin and dulcimer. It's what you might call healthy overcompensation for being put down. He's an admirer of Howlin' Wolf, Muddy Waters, Wilson Pickett and Otis Redding.

Albums/TAJ MAHAL (January 1968): *Leaving Trunk; Statesboro Blues; Checkin' Up On My Baby; Everybody's Got To Change Sometime; E Z Rider; Dust My Broom; Diving Duck Blues; Celebrated Walkin' Blues.* THE NATCH'L BLUES (January 1969): *Good Morning Miss Brown; Corinna; I Ain't Gonna Let Nobody Steal My Jellyroll; Going Up To The Country, Paint My Mailbox Blue; Done Changed My Way Of Living; She Caught The Katy And Left Me A Mule To Ride; The Cuckoo; You Don't Miss Your Water ('Til Your Well Runs Dry); A Lot Of Love.*

Singles/*Everybody's Got To Change Sometime/Statesboro Blues* (November 1967); *E Z Rider/Leaving Trunk* (November 1967); *Let The Good Times Roll/I Wish I Could Shimmy Like My Sister Kate* (November 1967).

MAMAS AND THE PAPAS/*Denny Doherty (vocals), Cass Elliot (vocals), John Phillips (vocals, guitar), Michelle Phillips (vocals).*
The Mamas and the Papas were the royal family of American rock—not because their music keeps growing and progressing to plateau after plateau of greatness (it doesn't), but because they were the first, with the Spoonful, of the *big* American groups, the first, that is, since the Beatles. Besides, they look regal. John Phillips, tall and stately, looks like Everyking, Cass Elliot, majestic earth mother, like Everyqueen, and Michelle and Denny the essence of princehood and princesshood. They came to us, that dreary winter of 1965–66, singing that all the leaves were brown and the sky was grey and that it was a good time to dream of California. Until then, everything new and interesting and commercially successful (all those things *can* go hand in hand) was English and had been since 1964 and the Beatles. Now, with the Mamas and the Papas, the spotlight that had been fixed so firmly on Liverpool and London suddenly swiveled over to America (and caught the Spoonful's *Daydream* as well). America had had Dylan, of course, but not a group scene

with any sort of style, and nothing like those first three singles the Mamas and the Papas brought out in less than a year.

The story of the group was new then, though by 1968 there must have been a thousand groups that told variants of it. They came out of the Village folk scene that had developed around Dylan and those who followed him. Cass had been with groups before (the Mugwumps and the Big Three), but these were not particularly successful. As the Mamas and the Papas tell it, the four met in the Virgin Islands, where there was not too much more to do than sing, but still the blend was not quite perfect till a piece of piping fell on Cass and changed her voice. Back in California the sound impressed people in the business who, having made one adjustment already to English moptops, found it difficult to readjust their vision to this motley quartet. The word "hippie" was not then in common use, but the concept existed. Groups in beards and boots and funny hats and strange drag were still new at the end of 1966 and not the cliché they became in 1968. The way this group looked, once the music business got over the shock of it all, was a novelty and very promotable. And the Mamas and the Papas were a sensation musically, visually and commercially. And what was really exciting was that they managed to establish the fact that there *was* an American scene. This was America's answer to the British invasion. Because of all this, it's quite incidental that the Mamas and the Papas never did live up to the glorious promise of their first year and that although every album they did sold, by the time they got to their fourth, in 1967, they just couldn't do it, couldn't put out another bland, predictable, salable, repetitive product. So in the middle of it all, in the middle of the taping, they just cut out, splitting to England and Europe to clear their heads, rethink their music and their lives, and give themselves a rest. It was a case of too much too soon—too much work, too much touring, too much freshness expected of them and too much to think about. No one really minded. Everyone understood. By 1968 Cass decided she wanted to sing solo. They had never intended to stay together any longer anyway, they all said. John Phillips, particularly, wanted to be not so much a performer as a writer, producer and discoverer of talent. Always there was much more to say about the Mamas and the Papas than the sweet-sad harmonies and the number one hits. They really *were* the first hippies to make it big and strike it rich, living in luxury in Bel Air and setting a bad example for the neighbors. Later, when other hippie groups made it, it no longer seemed unusual. But it was the Mamas and the Papas who established the precedent. (See MUGWUMPS, BIG THREE, CASS ELLIOT)

Albums/IF YOU CAN BELIEVE YOUR EYES AND EARS (January 1966): *Monday, Monday; Straight Shooter; Got A Feelin'; I Call Your Name; Do You Wanna Dance; Go Where You Wanna Go; California Dreamin'; Spanish Harlem; Somebody Groovy; Hey Girl; You Baby; In Crowd.* THE MAMAS AND THE PAPAS (September 1966): *No Salt On Her Tail; Trip, Stumble And Fall; Dancing Bear; Words Of Love; My Heart Stood Still; Dancing In The Street; I Saw Her Again; Strange Young Girls; I Can't Wait; Even If I Could; That Kind Of Girl; Once Was A Time I Thought.* THE MAMAS AND THE PAPAS DELIVER (January 1967): *Dedicated To The One I Love; My Girl; Creeque Alley; Sing For Your Supper; Twist And Shout; Free Advice; Look Through My Window; Boys And Girls Together; String Man; Frustration; Did You Ever Want To Cry; John's Music Box.* FAREWELL TO THE FIRST GOLDEN ERA (October 1967): *Dedicated To The One I Love; Go Where You Wanna Go; Words Of Love; Look Through My Window; Dancing In The Street; Monday, Monday; Creeque Alley; Got A Feelin'; Twelve-Thirty (Young Girls Are Coming To The Canyon); I Call Your Name; I Saw Her Again Last Night; California Dreamin'.* THE PAPAS AND THE MAMAS PRESENT THE MAMAS AND THE PAPAS (April 1968): *The Right Somebody To Love; Safe In My Garden; Meditation Mama (Transcendental Woman Travels); For The Love Of Ivy; Dream A Little Dream Of Me; Mansions; Gemini Child; Nothing's Too Good For My Little Girl; Too Late; Twelve-Thirty; Rooms; Midnight Voyage.* MAMAS AND PAPAS GOLDEN ERA (October 1968) *My Girl; Sing For Your Supper; No Salt On Her Tail; Twist And Shout; Glad To Be Unhappy; Nothing's Too Good For My Little Girl; For The Love Of Ivy; You Baby; String Man; Even If I Could; Spanish Harlem; Dream A Little Dream Of Me.*

Singles/*California Dreamin'/Somebody Groovy* (November 1965); *Monday, Monday/Got A Feelin'* (March 1966); *I Saw Her Again/Even If I Could* (June 1966); *Look Through My Window/Once Was A Time I Thought* (September 1966); *Words Of Love/Dancing In The Street* (November 1966); *Dedicated To The One I Love/Free Advice* (February 1967); *Creeque Alley/Did You Ever Want To Cry* (April 1967); *Twelve-Thirty/Straight Shooter* (August 1967); *Glad To Be Unhappy/Hey Girl* (October 1967); *Dancing Bear/John's Music Box* (November 1967); *Safe In My Garden/Too Late* (May 1968); *Dream A Little Dream Of Me/Midnight Voyage* (June 1968).

THE MAGNIFICENT MEN/There's lots of talk of blue-eyed soul, but most of it has never measured up to brown-eyed soul standards. The Magnificent Men apparently have measured up. They were one of the very few white acts asked to perform in Harlem's Apollo Theatre.

Albums/MAGNIFICENT MEN (January 1967): *Misty; Much, Much More Of Your Love; I Wish You Love; Peace Of Mind; Just Walk In My Shoes; Maybe, Maybe Baby; Cry With Me Baby; Stormy Weather; I Got News; Keep On Climbing; Do A Justice To Your Heart.* MAGNIFICENT MEN "LIVE" (June 1967): *Show Me; I'm Gonna Miss You; Just Be True; Doin' The Philly Dog; Stormy Weather; You Don't Know Like I Know; Misty; Whispers; Peace Of Mind; I've Been Trying; Function At The Junction; Sweet Soul Medley.* WORLD OF SOUL (August 1968).

Singles/*Babe, I'm Crazy About You/Forever Together; Sweet Soul Medley* (2 Parts); *Tired Of Pushing/By The Time I Get To Phoenix; I Found What I Wanted In You/Almost Persuaded; So Much Love Waiting/Save The Country* (October 1968).

MANDALA/*Roy Kenner (replaced George Olliver) (vocals), Dominic Troiano (lead vocals, guitar), Hugh Sullivan (replaced Joey Chirowski) (organ, vibraphone), Don Elliott (bass), Whitey Glan (drums, percussion).*
Screaming white hot Southern gospel-type soul—from Canada? That was the Mandala in 1967, all uplifted arms and

bleached white heads and a sweating singer who wanted you to confess your sins. The kids loved it. After George Olliver went solo, the Mandala's soul crusade wasn't quite what it had been.

Album/SOUL CRUSADE (June 1968): *World Of Love; One Short Year; Love-Itis; Come On Home; Every Single Day; Mellow Carmellow Palumbo; Can't Hold Out; Don't Make Me Cry; Stop Cryin' On My Shoulder.*

Single/*Love-Itis/Mellow Carmellow Palumbo.*

MANFRED MANN/*Manfred Mann (organ, piano), Mike Hugg (drums), Tom McGuiness (bass), Michael D'Abo (replaced Paul Jones) (lead vocals), Klaus Voorman (replaced Mike Vickers) (flute).*

In October 1964, not long after *I Want To Hold Your Hand* and *Can't Buy Me Love,* Manfred Mann became the third English group to have a number one record in America (the Animals came after the Beatles with *House of the Rising Sun).* The song was *Do Wah Diddy Diddy.* In England Manfred Mann has had something like fourteen consecutive hits since. He's been less lucky in America but very recently made it with Bob Dylan's *Mighty Quinn,* and it's reported that Dylan especially likes the way the group does his material.

Apart from having launched Paul Jones (star of the film *Privilege* and now a solo artist), it is a quiet, sober group ("I really am rather a boring person," says Mann). And Klaus Voorman, its flute player, was the artist responsible for the Beatles' *REVOLVER* cover. The group has a comfortable sideline doing radio jingles and recently did the sound track and songs for the film *Up the Junction,* which is considered the best pop film score ever.

Albums/MANFRED MANN ALBUM (November 1964): *Do Wah Diddy Diddy; Sock O' Woe; Don't Ask Me What I Say; What You Gonna Do; Got My Mojo Working; I'm Your Hoochie Coochie Man; Smokestack Lightning; It's Gonna Work Out Fine; Down The Road Apiece; Untie Me; Bring It To Jerome; Without You.* FIVE FACES OF MANFRED MANN (February 1965): *Sha La La; Come Tomorrow; She; Can't Believe It; John Hardy; Did You Have To Do That; Watermelon Man; I'm Your Kingpin; Hubble Bubble;*

You've Got To Take It; Dashing Away With The Smoothing Iron; Groovin'. MY LITTLE RED BOOK OF WINNERS (August 1965): *My Little Red Book; Oh No, Not My Baby; What Am I To Do; One In The Middle; You Gave Me Somebody To Love; You're For Me; Poison Ivy; Without You; Brother Jack; Love Like Yours; I Can't Believe What You Say; With God On Your Side.* MANN MADE (February 1966): *Since I Don't Have You; You're For Me; Way You Do The Things You Do; Look Away; Bare Hugg; Abominable Snowman; Watch Your Step; Stormy Monday Blues; I Really Do Believe; Hi Lili, Hi Lo; You Don't Know Me; L.S.D.; I'll Make It Up To You.* PRETTY FLAMINGO (October 1966): *Pretty Flamingo; Let's Go Get Stoned; Tired Of Trying, Bored With Living, Scared Of Dying; I Put A Spell On You; It's Getting Late; You're Standing By; Machines; Stay Around; Tennesse Waltz; Driva Man; Do You Have To Do That.* MANFRED MANN'S GREATEST HITS (November 1966): *Do Wah Diddy Diddy; Sha La La; Pretty Flamingo; Oh No, Not My Baby; You Don't Know; I Got You Babe; Let's Go Get Stoned; Got My Mojo Workin'; Come Tomorrow; My Little Red Book; Hi Lili, Hi Lo; Satisfaction (I Can't Get No).* UP THE JUNCTION (March 1967): *Up The Junction; Sing Songs Of Love; Walking Round; Love Theme From "Up The Junction;" Just For Me; Sheila's Dance; Belgravia; Wailing Horn; I Need Your Love.* MIGHTY QUINN (March 1968): *Mighty Quinn; Ha Ha Said The Clown; Every Day Another Hair Turns Grey; It's So Easy Falling; Big Betty; Cubist Town; Country Dancing; Semi-Detached Suburban Mr. James; Vicar's Daughter; Each And Every Day; No Better, No Worse.*

Singles/*Do Wah Diddy Diddy/What You Gonna Do* (October 1964); *Come Tomorrow/What Did I Do Wrong* (January 1965); *Hi Lili, Hi Lo/She Needs Company* (January 1966); *I Can't Believe What You Say/My Little Red Book* (May 1966); *John Hardy/Sha La La* (October 1966); *By Request—Edwin Garvey/Mighty Quinn* (January 1968); *My Name Is Jack/There Is A Man* (June 1968); *Fox On The Run/Too Many People* (December 1968).

MARTHA AND THE VANDELLAS/*Martha Reeves, Rosalind Ashford, Lois Reeves (replaced Betty Kelly).*

There must have been a time when every kid in Detroit dreamed of being snapped up by Berry Gordy's Motown machine and turned into a star. Martha Reeves joined Motown as a secretary, which is something like, in the old days, getting to work the switchboard at Twentieth Century-Fox in the hopes of being discovered. And just like in the movies, one day in 1962 there was an emergency session and Martha and two schoolmates with whom she'd sung in the school choir volunteered to fill in. (Their group at high school—Martha, Rosalind Ashford and Annette Sterling—was called the Del Phis). After that, it was no more shorthand. At first the original Vandellas did Motown backings, but they soon graduated to the big time. Then it was *Dancing In The Streets, Jimmy Mack, Lovebug Leave My Heart Alone* and *Honey Chile*. On their first tour in 1962 they performed every night for seventy nights. Betty Kelly took over from Annette; and when Betty recently decided to go solo (still with Motown) she was replaced by Martha's nineteen-year-old sister Lois. The Vandellas are an elegant lot, the pride of Motown, and they *have* played the Copacabana, a date without which no Motown star can regard his or her career properly crowned.

Albums/COME AND GET THESE MEMORIES (June 1963): *Come & Get These Memories; Can't Get Used To Losing You; Moments To Remember; This Is When I Need You Most; Love Like Yours; Tears On My Pillow; To Think You Would Hurt Me; Old Love; There He Is; I'll Have To Let Him Go; Give Him Up; Jealous Lover.* HEAT WAVE (September 1963): *My Boy Friend's Back; If I Had A Hammer; Wait Till My Bobby Gets Home; More; Then He Kissed Me; Hey There Lonely Boy; Danke Schoen; Mocking Bird; Hello Stranger; Just One Look.* DANCE PARTY (April 1965): *Dancing In The Street; Dancing Slow; Wild One; Nowhere To Run; Nobody'll Care; There He Is; Mobile Lil The Dancing Witch; Dance Party; Motoring; The Jerk; Mickey's Monkey, Hitch Hike.* GREATEST HITS (May 1966): *Love (Makes Me Do Foolish Things); My Baby Loves Me; Quicksand; Wild One; Come And Get These Memories; In My Lonely Room; Love Like Yours; Live Wire; You've Been In Love Too Long; Heatwave; Dancing In The Street; Nowhere To Run.* WATCH OUT (December

1966): *I'm Ready For Love; One Way Out; Jimmy Mack; Let This Day Be; Keep It Up; I'll Follow You; No More Tear Stained Makeup; Go Ahead & Laugh; What Am I Going To Do Without Your Love; Tell Me I'll Never Be Alone; He Don't Live Here Anymore.* MARTHA/VANDELLAS, "LIVE" (August 1967): *Love Bug Leave My Heart Alone; I'm Ready For Love; For Once In My Life; Love Is Like A Heat Wave; Nowhere To Run; I've Found A Love; My Baby Loves Me; Jimmy Mack; You've Been In Love Too Long; Love Makes Me Do Foolish Things; Do Right Woman; Medley.* RIDIN' HIGH (April 1968): *I Promise To Wait My Love; Honey Chile; To Sir, With Love; I Say A Little Prayer; Love Bug Leave My Heart Alone; Always Something There To Remind Me; Leave It In The Hands Of Love; Honey Love; Without You; Show Me The Way.*

Singles/*I'll Have To Let Him Go*/*My Baby Won't Come Back* (September 1962); *Come & Get These Memories*/*Jealous Lover* (February 1963); *Heat Wave*/*Love Like Yours* (July 1963); *Quicksand*/*Darling, I Hum Our Song* (November 1963); *Live Wire*/*Love (Makes Me Do Foolish Things)* (January 1964); *In My Lonely Room*/*A Tear For The Girl* (March 1964); *Dancing In The Street*/*There He Is (At My Door)* (July 1964); *Wild One*/*Dancing Slow* (November 1964); *You've Been In Love Too Long*/*Love (Makes Me Do Foolish Things)* (July 1965); *Motoring*/*Never Leave Your Baby's Side* (January 1966); *What Am I Going To Do Without Your Love*/*Go Ahead And Laugh* (May 1966); *I'm Ready For Love*/*He Doesn't Love Her Anymore* (October 1966); *Jimmy Mack*/*Third Finger, Left Hand* (February 1967); *Love Bug Leave My Heart Alone*/*One Way Out* (September 1967); *Honey Chile*/*Show Me The Way* (October 1967); *I Promise To Wait My Love*/*Forget Me Not* (April 1968); *I Can't Dance To That Music You're Playing*/*I Tried* (July 1968); *Sweet Darlin'*/*Without You* (October 1968); *I'm In Love (And I Know It)*/*Honey Love* (April 1969).

MARVELETTES/*Wanda Rogers (lead vocals), Katherin Schaffner (vocals), Ann Bogan (replaced Gladys Horton) (vocals).*
The Marvelettes are one of those Motown groups whose

harmony, grooming and movement are so impeccable and letter-perfect that it's frightening. But they sounded beautifully bitchy in *Don't Mess With Bill,* and, of course, their 1961 hit *Please Mr. Postman* went on the Beatles' second album. Like so many kids (especially Detroit kids), they started off harmonizing at parties for fun while they were still in high school, but when they sang at a talent show someone was impressed enough to turn them on to Berry Gordy at Motown, and vice versa. *Please Mr. Postman,* which went to number one, was their first try and they've consistently come out with big sellers ever since. The only thing they haven't done yet is play the Copacabana.

Albums/PLEASE MR. POSTMAN (November 1961): *Please Mr. Postman; Angel; I Want A Guy; Way Over There; Happy Days; You Don't Have To Want Me No More; All The Love I Got; I Apologize.* MARVELOUS MARVELETTES (February 1963): *Strange I Know; Locking Up My Heart; Too Strong To Be Strung Out; My Daddy Knows Best; I Forgot About You; Which Way Did He Go; Silly Boy; It's Gonna Take A Lot Of Doing; Smart Aleck; Why Must You Go.* LIVE ON STAGE (June 1963): *Beechwood 4-5789; Twistin' Postman; Strange I Know; Locking Up My Heart; So Long Baby; Someday, Someway; Tossing & Turning; Playboy.* MARVELETTES SING (November 1963): *Mashed Potato Time; Love Letters; Lover Please; Hey Baby; One Who Really Loves You; Slow Twist; Twistin' The Night Away; Good Luck Charm; Dream Baby; Twistin' Postman.* PLAYBOY (November 1963): *Beechwood 4-5789; Playboy; Someday, Someway; Goddess Of Love; Forever; Mix It Up; I'm Hooked; I Think I Can Change You; I've Got To Cry Over You.* MARVELETTES' GREATEST HITS (February 1966): *Don't Mess With Bill; You're My Remedy; Locking Up My Heart; As Long As I Know He's Mine; Too Many Fish In The Sea; Beachwood 4-5789; Danger Heartbreak Dead Ahead; Forever; Please, Mr. Postman; Playboy; Strange I Know; Twistin' Postman.* THE MARVELETTES (March 1967): *Hunter Gets Captured By The Game; I Know Better; Message To Michael; Barefootin'; When You're Young & In Love; I Can't Turn Around; He Was Really Sayin' Somethin'; Day You Take One; When I Need You;*

Keep Off No Trespassing; This Night Was Made For Love; I Need Someone. SOPHISTICATED SOUL (August 1968): *My Baby Must Be A Magician; Destination: Anywhere; I'm Gonna Hold On As Long As I Can; Here I Am Baby; You Are The One For Me Bobby; Reachin' For Something I Can't Have; Your Love Can Save Me; You're The One; Don't Make Hurting Me A Habit; What's Easy For Two Is Hard For One; The Stranger; Some Way Somehow.*

Singles/*Please Mr. Postman/Someday Someway* (August 1961); *Twistin' Postman/I Want A Guy* (December 1961); *Playboy/All The Love I've Got* (April 1962); *Beechwood 4-5789/So Long Baby* (July 1962); *Strange I Know/Too Strong To Be Strung Along* (October 1962); *Locking Up My Heart/Forever* (February 1963); *My Daddy Knows Best/Tie A String Around Your Finger* (July 1963); *As Long As I Know He's Mine/Little Girl Blue* (October 1963); *He's A Good Guy/Goddess Of Love* (January 1964); *You're My Remedy/A Little Bit Of Sympathy, A Little Bit Of Love* (June 1964); *Too Many Fish In The Sea/A Need For Love* (October 1964); *I'll Keep Holding On/No Time For Tears* (May 1965); *Danger Heartbreak Dead Ahead/Your Cheating Ways* (July 1965); *Don't Mess With Bill/Anything You Wanna Do* (November 1965); *You're The One/Paper Boy* (April 1966); *The Hunter Gets Captured By The Game/ I Think I Can Change You* (December 1966); *When You're Young & In Love/The Day You Take One You Have To Take The Other* (April 1967); *My Baby Must Be A Magician/I Need Someone* (November 1967); *Here I Am Baby/ Keep Off, No Trespassing* (May 1968); *Destination: Anywhere/What's Easy For Two Is Hard For One* (August 1968).

Also Appear On/16 ORIGINAL HITS: VOL 1, *Beechwood 4-5789; Please, Mr. Postman.* VOL 2, *Playboy; As Long As I Know He's Mine.* VOL 3, *Locking Up My Heart; Forever.* VOL 4, *Too Many Fish In The Sea.* VOL 5, *I'll Keep Holding On.* VOL 6, *Don't Mess With Bill.* VOL 7, *Hunter Gets Captured By The Game.* NOTHING BUT A MAN: *Come On Home.* MOTOR-TOWN REVUE. MOTOWN HITS.

JOHN MAYALL'S BLUES BREAKERS/*John Mayall (vocals, harmonica, piano, harpsichord, organ, harmonium, gui-*

tars), Chris Mercer (tenor and baritone saxes) (formerly Rip Kant on baritone sax), Dick Heckstall-Smith (tenor and soprano saxes), Jon Hiseman (replaced Keif Hartley) (drums, percussion), Henry Lowther (cornet, violin), Mick Taylor (guitar, Hawaiian guitar), Tony Reeves (replaced John McVie) (bass).

There is probably no more prestigious position in the world of rock than the one John Mayall has taken—the position of doing things for art instead of money. In an industry in which the fast buck is, to say the least, much respected and the position of a record on the chart is taken into consideration far too often by people who should know better, John Mayall is an almost holy figure. Devoted to music and seemingly indifferent to financial pressures, he has never had a hit. And only now at the age of thirty-five is he getting anything like the notice he deserves as proably the most potent force in British blues. He fell in love with blues in 1956, when everyone else was in love with "trad" jazz (Dixieland), and formed a blues group, the Powerhouse Four. In 1962 he formed the Blues Breakers in London and in 1963 went professional. The climate at that time was sympathetic to blues, but in direct contrast to the then burgeoning pop and rock scene progress was very gradual, which suited Mayall perfectly, for all he was concerned with anyway was the band's musical accomplishment. The lack of pressure is very important to musicians, Mayall believes, which may explain why Eric Clapton did some of his best work when he was with the Blues Breakers. On the other hand, the very fidelity to the blues form is restricting, and when Clapton left it was to break out into a wider field (though he has since said he plans to go back to straight blues). Significantly, Clapton's replacement, Peter Green, eventually left to start a band with a less rigid format. Meanwhile in 1967, in the wake of Cream's bluesy success, other blues bands, most of them lesser ones, made hits and money in the very blues boom Mayall touched off. Mayall, who has seen the hassles that go with success, is unruffled. "People who dig blues," he says, "stick with you for life." And with no frantic promotion and no compromises, Mayall and his albums have been received well in America, especially by those who saw the roots of Cream and others in them. His is a special talent. On *THE BLUES ALONE*, a

1968 LP, Mayall, accompanied only by a drummer, plays harmonica, six- and nine-string guitar, piano, bass, drums, organ and celeste, and sings. Were he to achieve the very success he has never struggled for, everyone would agree to the old chestnut that it couldn't have happened to a better person.

Albums/BLUES BREAKERS (January 1967): *All Your Love; Hideaway; Little Girl; What'd I Say; Another Man; Double-Crossing Time; Key To Love; Parchman Farm; Have You Heard; Ramblin' On My Mind; Steppin' Out; It Ain't Right.* A HARD ROAD (July 1967): *Hard Road; It's Over; You Don't Love Me; Stumble; Another Kind Of Love; Hit The Highway; Leaping Christine; Dust My Blues; There's Always Work; Same Way; Someday, After A While; Super-Natural; Top Of The Hill; Living Alone.* CRUSADE (January 1968): *Oh, Pretty Woman; Stand Back Baby; My Time After A While; Snowy Wood; Man Of Stone; Tears In My Eyes; Driving Sideways; Death Of J.B. Lenoir; I Can't Quit You Baby; Me And My Woman; Streamline; Checking On My Baby.* THE BLUES ALONE (May 1968): *Brand New Start; Please Don't Tell; Down The Line; Sonny Boy Blow; Marsha's Mood; No More Tears; Catch That Train; Cancelling Out; Harp Man; Brown Sugar; Broken Wings; Don't Kick Me.* BARE WIRES (September 1968): *Where Did I Belong; I Started Walking; Fire; Open Up A New Door; I Know Now; Look In The Mirror; I'm A Stranger; No Reply; Hartley Quits; Killing Time; She's Too Young; Sandy.*

Singles/*Parchman Farm/Key To Love* (October 1966); *All Your Love/Hideaway* (March 1967); *Suspicions/Oh, Pretty Woman* (November 1967); *Broken Wings/Sonny Boy Blow* (June 1968).

CHARLIE McCOY/They call him the dean of the Nashville studio musicians. When musicians go south to get the Nashville sound, it's McCoy and his team they're after. Probably one of the best guitarists in the country, he's also a horn and harmonica player of note. He has played with Bob Dylan on every record since *HIGHWAY 61 REVISITED.*

McCOYS/*Rick Zehringer (guitar, vocals), Randy Zehringer (drums), Randy Hobbs (bass), Bobbie Peterson (organ).*

Can a group make the switch from commercial pop-schlock to high-class art-rock? Apparently so. In 1965 the McCoys had a number one record, *Hang On Sloopy*, but that was all. The success was financial but not critical. And that's the way it continued. Then, suddenly, in 1968 this little group from Ohio and Indiana broke out into a brand new area of operation. They brought a freshness to what was that summer a very jaded pop scene. With a change of record label came a change of image and a change of direction. The jazz-influenced *Resurrection* showed exactly how the McCoys were expanding.

Albums/HANG ON SLOOPY (1965): *Hang On Sloopy; Fever; Papa's Got A Brand New Bag; Sorrow; If You Tell A Lie; I Don't Mind; Stubborn Kind Of Fellow; Hi Heel Sneakers; I Can't Help Falling In Love; I Can't Explain; All I Really Want To Do; Call It Stormy Monday.* YOU MAKE ME FEEL SO GOOD (1966): *Say Those Magic Words; Everyday I Have To Cry; The Dynamite; Mr. Summer; Stagger Lee; Sweets For My Sweet; Smokey Joe's Cafe; Little People; Runaway; C'mon Let's Go.* INFINITE MC COYS (June 1968): *Faces; Genesis Through A Window; Jesse Brady; Resurrection; Rosa Rodriguez; Hell; Song For Janie; He Likes It; Open Your Eyes; Eldorado; Melodrama; Union City Waltz.*

Singles/*Hang On Sloopy/I Can't Explain It* (August 1965); *Fever/Sorrow* (December 1965); *Up And Down/If You Tell A Lie* (February 1966); *C'mon Let's Go/Little People* (April 1966); *You Make Me Feel So Good/Runaway* (June 1966); *Don't Worry Mother/Ko-Ko* (October 1966); *I Gotta Go Back/Dynamite* (January 1967); *Beat The Clock/Like You Do To Me* (June 1967); *Say Those Magic Words/I Wonder If She Remembers Me* (January 1968); *Resurrection* (2 Parts) (October 1968); *Daybreak/Epilogue* (March 1969); *Love Don't Stop/Only Human* (May 1969).

Also Appears On/GANG AT BANG (1965): *Hang On Sloopy; Fever; Sorrow; I Can't Explain It.* GANG AT BANG (1966).

MC 5/*Rob Tyner (vocals, saxophone), Fred Smith (guitar), Michael Davis (bass), Dennis Thompson (drums), Wayne Kramer (lead guitar).*

The MC 5 is an exuberant white hard-rock band from Detroit that was "discovered" late in 1968. It has been described as a second Rolling Stones, a second Grateful Dead and a guerrilla rock band. The group came out of a multi-media community called Trans Love Energy.

Album/MC 5 (March 1969): *Ramblin' Rose; Kick Out The Jams; Come Together; Rocket Reducer No. 62 (Rama Lama Fa Fa Fa); Borderline; Motor City Is Burning; I Want You Right Now; Starship.*

BROWNIE McGHEE/A singer and guitarist now in his fifties, Brownie McGhee first learned to sing the blues in Tennessee, where he grew up. In partnership with harmonica player Sonny Terry since the thirties, he was a familiar figure on the folk scene in the fifties and sixties, greatly influencing all those rock personalities who started off, like Dylan and others, in a folk setting.
(See SONNY TERRY)

Album/BLUES BY BROWNIE MC GHEE: *Sporting Life; Good Morning Blues; Betty And Dupree; Careless Love Blues; Move To Kansas City; Worried Mind; Pawnshop Blues; Me And Sonny.*
(See SONNY TERRY for albums they recorded together)

BARRY McGUIRE/He is famous for more things than having sung the first rock protest song ever—*Eve of Destruction,* which he recorded in 1965. He is mentioned in the Mamas and Papas' autobiographical song *Creeque Alley* and was responsible, along with *16* editor Gloria Stavers, for getting them started in their career. He's still a lively part of the Los Angeles music scene though no longer a hitmaker or protest singer.

Albums/EVE OF DESTRUCTION (September 1965): *Eve Of Destruction; Sins Of The Family; It's All Over Now, Baby Blue; What Exactly's The Matter With Me; She Belongs To Me; You Never Had It So Good; Sloop John B.; Try To Remember; Mr. Man On The Street; You Were On My Mind; Ain't No Way I'm Gonna Change My Mind; Why Not Stop And Dig While You Can.* THIS PRECIOUS TIME (February 1966): *This Precious Time; California Dreamin';*

*Let Me Be; Do You Believe In Magic; Hang On Sloopy;
Yesterday; Just Like Tom Thumb's Blues; Upon A Painted
Ocean; Hide Your Love Away; I'd Have To Be Outa My
Mind; Child Of Our Times; Don't You Wonder Where It's
At.* WORLD'S LAST PRIVATE CITIZEN (April 1968):
*Top O' The Hill; Cloudy Summer Afternoon; Secret Saucer
Man; There's Nothin' Else On My Mind; Walkin' My Cat
Named Dog; Hang On Sloopy; Masters Of War; Inner-
Manipulations; Grasshopper Song; This Precious Time; Why
Not Stop And Dig It While You Can; Eve Of Destruction.*

Singles/*Eve Of Destruction/What Ever's The Matter With
Me; Child Of Our Times/Upon A Painted Ocean; Don't You
Wonder Where It's At/This Precious Time; Cloudy Summer
Afternoon/I'd Have To Be Outa My Mind; Masters Of
War/Why Not Stop And Dig It While You Can; Lollipop
Train/President's Analyst; Grasshopper Song/Top Of The
Hill.*

SCOTT McKENZIE/He emerged at just the right moment
(summer 1967) with his song warning people that if they
were going to come to San Francisco they would have to be
sure to wear a flower in their hair. A long-time friend of Papa
John Phillips, he had been one of the Journeymen with him
and had almost become a Papa. But he didn't, and his solo
records that followed *San Francisco* did not do very well. The
trouble was he was so closely associated through the song with
San Francisco and flower power that it hurt his other singles
on other subjects. Besides, a lot of people *did* go to San
Francisco wearing flowers in their hair and it didn't do them a
bit of good. They still haven't forgiven Scott McKenzie.

Album/VOICE OF SCOTT MC KENZIE (November 1967):
*Like An Old Time Movie; San Francisco (Wear Some Flow-
ers In Your Hair); Celeste; It's Not Time Now; What's The
Difference; Reason To Believe; No, No, No, No, No; Don't
Make Promises; Twelve-Thirty (Young Girls Are Coming To
The Canyon); Rooms.*

Singles/*San Francisco (Wear Some Flowers In Your Hair)/
What's The Difference* (May 1967); *I Want To Be
Alone/No, No, No, No, No* (With McKenzie Musicians)
(May 1967); *All I Want Is You/Look In Your Eyes* (July

1967); *Like An Old Time Movie/What's The Difference— Chapter II* (September 1967).

CLYDE McPHATTER/*Money Honey*, his 1953 hit with the Drifters, is still held up as an example of how lively the rock and roll milieu was long before Elvis Presley's name brought it worldwide publicity. McPhatter later went solo and toured with big rock names like Bill Haley and Fats Domino. He was an integral part of early rock and roll and did much to solidify the sound. In 1968 his albums were re-released in England as part of a rock "revival."

Albums/CLYDE MC PHATTER AND THE DRIFTERS: *Without Love; I Make Believe; Thirty Days; Treasure Of Love; Someday You'll Want Me To Want You; Seven Days; I'm Not Worthy Of You; Bells Of St. Mary's; White Christmas; Warm Your Heart; Money Honey; What'cha Gonna Do; Such A Night; Honey Love.* LOVE BALLADS (October 1958): *Heartaches; Come What May; Rock And Cry; That's Enough For Me; I Gotta Have You; Bip Bam; Just To Hold My Hand; Lucille; Long Lonely Nights; When You're Sincere; No Matter What; No Love Like Her Love; You'll Be There; Love Has Joined Us Together.* CLYDE (September 1959): *Lovey Dovey; My Island Of Dreams; Lover's Question; I Can't Stand Up Alone; Since You've Been Gone; Let Me Know; I'm Lonely Tonight; Way I Feel; Hot Ziggity; Try Try Baby; Everyone's Laughing; Gone.* BEST OF CLYDE MC PHATTER (June 1963): *Lover's Question; Treasure Of Love; Just To Hold My Hand; Without Love; Long Lonely Nights; Seven Days; Lovey Dovey; Money Honey; Honey Love; Such A Night; Someday You'll Want Me To Want You; Warm Your Heart; What'cha Gonna Do; White Christmas.* CLYDE MC PHATTER'S GREATEST HITS (June 1963): *Lover Please; Money Honey; Sixty Minute Man; Such A Night; Maybe; Stop; Ta Ta; I Do Believe; Without Love; Little Bitty Pretty One; Best Man Cried; Bells.* SONGS OF THE BIG CITY (April 1964): *Deep In The Heart Of Harlem; My Block; Up On The Roof; Spanish Harlem; Three Rooms With Running Water; Second Window, Second Floor; Chinatown; Coney Island; Shelter Of Your Arms; In My Tenement; Broadway.* LIVE AT THE APOLLO: *Baby Baby; Ta Ta; Lover's Question; Hold My Hand; Second*

Window, Second Floor; Such A Night; Lucille; What's Love To Me; Deep In The Heart Of Harlem; Mercy Mercy Baby; Without Love. MAY I SING FOR YOU: *Harbor Lights; You Belong To Me; That's My Desire; 7 Other Titles.*

Singles/ *Bells Of St. Mary's/ White Christmas; Bip Bam/ Someday; Come What May/ Let Me Know; Deep Sea Ball/ Let The Boogie Woogie Roll; Don't Dog Me/ Just Give Me A Ring; Everyone's Laughing/ Hot Ziggity; Heartaches/ Long Lonely Nights; Honey Love/ Warm Your Heart; I Can't Stand Up Alone/ Lover's Question; I Gotta Have You/ Love Has Joined Us Together; I Make Believe/ Without Love; I'm Lonely Tonight/ Thirty Days; I'm Not Going To Work Today/ Shot Of Rhythm And Blues; I'm Not Worthy Of You/ Seven Days; Lavender Lace/ Sweet And Innocent; Lover Please/ Lover's Question; Lovey Dovey/ My Island Of Dreams; Lucille/ Such A Night; Money Honey/ Way I Feel; No Love Like Her Love/ That's Enough For Me; Since You've Been Gone/ Try Try Baby; There You Go/ You Went Back On Your Word; Treasure Of Love/ When You're Sincere.*

BILL MEDLEY

Albums/ BILL MEDLEY, 100 PER CENT (June 1968): *Brown-Eyed Woman; Let The Good Times Roll; You Don't Have To Say You Love Me; Run To My Loving Arms; You're Nobody 'Til Somebody Loves You; Impossible Dream; I Can't Make It Alone; That's Life; One Day Girl; Show Me; Goin' Out Of My Head; Who Can I Turn To.*

Singles/ *I Can't Make It Alone/ One Day Girl* (March 1968); *Brown-Eyed Woman/ Let The Good Times Roll* (April 1968).
(see THE RIGHETOUS BROTHERS)

MELLOTRON/ An advanced synthesizer, a mellotron contains tapes of any number of recorded sounds so that when the player touches a certain button he can reproduce the chord he is playing in any given sound. English groups have started to use them a lot. The Stones and Beatles have them (they're very expensive). Jimmy Page, formerly of the Yardbirds, may use one in his new group Led Zeppelin. The Moody Blues have two cut down and put in one organ body, which enables them to produce violin sounds on stage when there are no violins.

MEMPHIS SOUND/The first "sound" to come out of Memphis was Elvis. Elvis and Carl Perkins and Jerry Lee Lewis and Roy Orbison, all of whom started their careers with a small recording company in Memphis called Sun Records. Before long, the company, and the town, became famous for that blend of country-and-western and rhythm-and-blues that music people named rock and roll. That was Memphis in the early fifties, and the success of those early names lured scores of others over to try their luck with the new sound. When rock and roll fizzled out in the late fifties, so did Memphis, as a recording center. But by the middle sixties Memphis was a name to be reckoned with again. What was coming out of Memphis now was not the old style rock and roll anymore, but the sound of blues, rhythm and blues, and soul, a sound familiar enough to black Americans but quite new and wonderfully exciting to the white buyers who were first discovering it. It took some of the English groups (they had always been big rhythm and blues freaks over there) to tell white Americans about their own sounds.

Now what was happening in Memphis was Carla Thomas, Sam and Dave, the late Otis Redding, Booker T and the MG's—some of the best music in the country. It wasn't the Memphis air, but Stax, a recording company with its own house group of seven handpicked studio musicians who played on all the records in almost telepathic accord not only with each other but with every artist they backed. The seven were Booker T and the MG's (on organ, guitar, bass and drums, plus three horn players collectively known as the Mar-keys). No one else gets to play on Stax records, and no one outside the company gets to use the studio, let alone its musicians (despite constant and heartfelt pleadings from everyone from the Rolling Stones down). It's a very personal freewheeling sound and they themselves say that the difference between Memphis sound and Motown's Detroit sound is that the Memphis people play what they feel and the Detroit people play what they're told to. Another big studio is a mere hour's drive from Memphis at Muscle Shoals, Alabama. This is where Aretha Franklin, Wilson Pickett and

Percy Sledge recorded their biggest hits in 1967. Muscle Shoals is said to be a little more country than the already countrified Stax studio, with an emphasis also on a gospel sound. The Boxtops live and record in Memphis, which explains why they sound so black and soulful. Albert King records in Memphis too. It's important to note that the original country and rock sound that put Memphis on the map still creeps into the recordings there, giving them that special little extra something that other studios have found completely impossible to duplicate.

LEE MICHAELS is a Californian who in 1968 cut a first album, *CARNIVAL OF LIFE,* and decided that guitars and the usual rock backing weren't him. Later in the year he put out an album that *was* him: Michaels on bass, Michaels on piano, Michaels on harpsichord, Michaels on organ (his main instrument) and Michaels doing the vocals. He also wrote, arranged, mixed, mastered and produced it. Heads are still reeling at the virtuosity of it all.

Albums/CARNIVAL OF LIFE (April 1968): *Hello; Another One; Streetcar; Love; Why; Carnival Of Life; Tomorrow; Sounding The Sleeping; My Friends.* RECITAL (October 1968): *If I Lose You; Time Is Over; No Part Of It; Fell In Love Today; Blind; Grocery Soldier; What Can He Do; Basic Knowledge; Gonna Leave; War; Spare Change.*

Singles/*Hello/Love; Sounding The Sleeping/Tomorrow; If I Lose You/My Friends; Goodbye, Goodbye/The War* (March 1969).

THE BUDDY MILES EXPRESS/*Jim McCarty (guitar), Herbie Rich (organ), Virgil Gonsalves (baritone sax), Terry Clements (tenor sax), Marcus Doubleday (trumpet), Billy Rick (bass), Bob McPherson (tenor sax), Ron Woods (drums), Buddy Miles (drums, vocals).*
Born in August 1968 out of the original Electric Flag, with four members of the Flag and five new members, the Buddy Miles Express made its inspired debut at Hollywood's Whisky A Go-Go in September. Since high-powered Miles, around whom the band was built, is one of the heavy drummers of the rock scene, this could yet become one of the new super-groups—combining jazz, rock and blues to the best effect.

Albums/EXPRESSWAY TO YOUR SKULL (November 1968): *Train; Let Your Lovelight Shine; Don't Mess With Cupid; Funky Mule; You're The One (That I Adore); Wrap It Up; Spot On The Wall.* ELECTRIC CHURCH (June 1969): *Miss Lady; 69 Freedom Special; Cigarettes & Coffee; Destructive Love; Texas; My Chant; Wrap It Up.*

Single/*Train* (2 Parts) (December 1968).

MRS. ELVA MILLER/She couldn't carry a tune. She was no beauty. But in 1966 this middle-aged lady was one of the great hit-making phenomena of rock. Mrs. Miller's gimmick: a non-voice. Listening to her struggling and screeching her way through the top forty was one of the funniest experiences in years. Like so many *in* things of that trendy year, it was high camp. And high camp made funnier by the fact that Mrs. Miller honestly believed people liked her voice. Or at least she was shrewd enough to let people think so. It seems that she had always fancied herself a singer and had often made, at her own expense, records of herself singing sacred and inspirational tunes. The pianist and organist who accompanied her for these private recordings thought it might be "interesting" to hear her on more contemporary material. He got her to do four sides and took them along to a friend who was a producer. The result, in April 1966, was *MRS. MILLER'S GREATEST HITS.* They had her making personal appearances in Hawaii, on the Ed Sullivan show, and at the Royal Tahitian Hotel in Ontario. She had a marvelous time but faded out after about a year. By 1968 someone came along who did Mrs. Miller's high-camp thing bigger and better: Tiny Tim. Even Mrs. Miller couldn't beat that one.

Albums/MRS. MILLER'S GREATEST HITS (April 1966): *Downtown; The Shadow Of Your Smile (Love Theme From "The Sandpiper"); Hard Day's Night; Dear Heart; Chim Chim Cher-ee; These Boots Are Made For Walkin'; The Lover's Concerto; Let's Hang On; Catch A Falling Star; Gonna Be Like That; My Love.* WILL SUCCESS SPOIL MRS. MILLER? (November 1966): *Strangers In The Night; Bill Bailey, Won't You Please Come Home; Somewhere, My Love; A Groovy Kind Of Love; Melody; The Girl From Ipanema; Yellow Submarine; Every Little Movement; Moon*

River; Second-Hand Rose; Sweet Pea; Monday, Monday.
COUNTRY SOUL OF MRS. MILLER (May 1967): *I've Got*
A Tiger By The Tail; There Goes My Everything; Memphis;
Little Bitty Tear; Oh, Lonesome Me; May The Bird Of
Paradise Fly Up Your Nose; Misty Blue; Shutters And
Boards; This Ole House; Act Naturally; Waitin' In Your
Welfare Line.

STEVE MILLER BAND (formerly STEVE MILLER
BLUES BAND)/*Steve Miller (lead guitar, lead vocals),*
William Bozz Scaggs (replaced Curly Cooke) (rhythm gui-
tar), Tim Davis (drums), Lonnie Turner (bass), Jim Peter-
man (organ).
Steve Miller was originally with organist Barry Goldberg in
the Barry Goldberg Blues Band in Chicago. When he left to
start the Steve Miller Blues Band, he developed a huge
following in Chicago but was virtually unknown elsewhere.
Nevertheless, when the San Francisco band boom happened
he was besieged with offers to record from a variety of labels.
After holding out for months, he eventually succumbed to
one of the biggest royalty advances in the history of rock—
$50,000 *plus* a $10,000 bonus *plus* a five-year contract and
an offer to record in any part of the world the band chose.
Predictably, they did not choose Bangkok or Vladivostok, but
London, where in the early months of 1968 they cut a single
and an album. Then they set off for a European tour. All this
was slightly marred by all sorts of personal conflicts and the
band, now back in California, is in the process of splitting and
re-forming. Split or not, they have produced some of the few
really strong and worthwhile albums of late sixties' rock.

Albums/CHILDREN OF THE FUTURE (April 1968):
Children Of The Future; Pushed Me To It; You've Got The
Power; In My First Mind; Key To The Highway; Beauty Of
Time Is That It's Snowing; Baby's Callin' Me Home; Steppin'
Stone; Roll With It; Junior Saw It Happen; Fanny Mae.
SAILOR (October 1968): *Song For Our Ancestors; Dear*
Mary; My Friend; Living In The U.S.A.; Quicksilver Girl;
Lucky Man; Gangster Of Love; You're So Fine; Overdrive;
Dime-A-Dance Romance. BRAVE NEW WORLD (June
1969).

Singles/*Sittin' In Circles/Roll With It* (April 1968); *Living In The U.S.A./Quicksilver Girl* (September 1968); *My Dark Hour/Song For Our Ancestors* (June 1969).

MINDBENDERS/*Eric Stewart (piano, guitar, drums), Paul Hancox (guitar, drums), James O'Neill (guitar), Graham Gouldman (guitar).*
Previous Member: Wayne Fontana.
An English group, their *Groovy Kind Of Love* was a big international hit in 1966. They have yet to come up with anything like it.

Album/A GROOVY KIND OF LOVE (August 1966): *Groovy Kind Of Love; One Fine Day; Seventh Son, Just A Little Bit; Trickie Dickie; Little Nightingale; Way You Do The Things You Do; Can't Live With You; Can't Live Without You; All-Night Worker; Love Is Good; You Don't Know About Love; Don't Cry Anymore.*

Single/*It's Getting Harder All The Time/Off And Running.*

JONI MITCHELL/Tall, pale, slim, frail, the very model of a lady folk singer, Joni didn't emerge as a personality until 1968 with an album and some delicate personal appearances. But she was a name to be reckoned with from the moment some big names—Judy Collins, Buffy Sainte-Marie, Tom Rush and Dave Van Ronk—started doing her material a year before. Her *Both Sides Now* is one of the most beautiful songs of this decade, whether it's rasped out by Dave Van Ronk or honeyed out by Miss Collins, with tinkling bells in the background. *Urge For Going* is what Mitchell audiences scream for. She's probably the most talented lady songwriter about, though not quite as big a singer as a writer.

Albums/JONI MITCHELL (March 1968): *I Had A King; Michael From Mountains; Night In The City; Marcie; Nathan La Franeer; Sisotowbell Lane; Dawntreader; Pirate Of Penance; Song To A Seagull; Cactus Tree.* CLOUDS (April 1969): *Tin Angel; Chelsea Morning; I Don't Know Where I Stand; That Song About The Midway; Roses Blue; The Gallery; I Think I Understand; Songs To Aging Children Come; The Fiddle And The Drum; Both Sides Now.*

Single/*I Had A King/Night In The City* (January 1968).

MOBY GRAPE/*Jerry Miller (lead guitar), Peter Lewis (second lead guitar), Bob Mosley (bass), Don Stevenson (drums).*
Previous Member: Skip Spence (rhythm guitar).

Moby Grape's entrance into pop music was nothing if not spectacular—five singles and an album all released at once in one big overwhelming promotion in May, 1967. It made people very nervous, but it meant the Grape never had to go through all the agonies of making a name for itself like other groups. The sound was distilled from folk, blues, country, rock, rhythm and blues, bluegrass and soul. Three guitarists, four singers, clean country rock with harmonious and even psychedelic overtones. It couldn't possibly go wrong —and didn't. There were no stars or featured performers; everything very equal and level. Bass player Bob Mosley, drummer Don Stevenson and lead guitarist Jerry Miller came from a group called the Frantics. Peter Lewis, who had been a folk singer and had also been with a group called, not surprisingly, Peter and the Wolves, made the fourth in the initial jam sessions. Later, Skip Spence, once drummer for the Jefferson Airplane, now a rhythm guitarist, joined. They were in San Francisco, so they went the usual Avalon and Fillmore route. Then came that record contract (and reports of a launching party with so many imported Hawaiian orchids that one man slipped and broke his leg). The first Moby Grape album was pleasantly innocuous and undistinguished except for the fact that all the material was written by the Grape, each member having written at least one cut. It was an easy listening record with no surprises. And perhaps that explains why the second album is full of gimmicks and novelties. The two-record set had one whole section called *Grape Jam,* which was just that, the Grape jamming with organist Al Kooper (borrowed from Blood, Sweat and Tears) and guitarist Mike Bloomfield (borrowed from the Electric Flag). Though the idea came through as a little pretentious, the two outside musicians put the Grape on their toes and had them playing better than usual. In any case, it was the first of the recorded jams. Another first was a track that had to be played at 78 rpm. Otherwise, the Grape was its usual competent self, a little freer, a little deeper than before, but still a psychedelic version of the Dave Clark Five or any other

of those "safe" groups that abounded from 1964 on. In the summer of 1968 Skip Spence made a sudden and mysterious exit. The group continued as a quartet for a while and then disbanded. Spence is now recording solo and so are some of the others.
(see SKIP SPENCE)

Albums/MOBY GRAPE (May 1967): *Hey Grandma; Mr. Blues; Fall On You; 8:05; Come In The Morning; Omaha; Naked, If I Want To; Someday; Ain't No Use; Sitting By The Window; Changes; Lazy Me; Indifference.* WOW/GRAPE JAMS (April 1968): *Murder In My Heart For The Judge; Bitter Wind; Can't Be So Bad; Three-Four; Place And The Time; Motorcycle Irene; Rose-Colored Eyes; Funky-Tunk; Miller's Blues; He; Just Like Gene Autry, A Foxtrap; Naked, If I Want To;* Above Titles Plus "Grape Jam" Featuring Guest Artists With Moby Grape At Jam Session. MOBY GRAPE '69 (March 1969): *Ooh Mama Ooh; Ain't That A Shame; I Am Not Willing; It's A Beautiful Day Today; Hoochie; Trucking Man; If You Can't Learn From My Mistakes; Captain Nemo; What's To Choose; Going Nowhere; Seeing.* TRULY FINE CITIZEN.

Singles/*Omaha/Someday* (May 1967); *Fall On You/Changes* (May 1967); *Sitting By The Window/Indifference* (May 1967); *8:05/Mr. Blues* (May 1967); *Hey Grandma/Come In The Morning* (May 1967); *Bitter Wind/Can't Be So Bad* (June 1968); *If You Can't Learn From My Mistakes/Trucking Man* (March 1969).

THE MONKEES/*Mickey Dolenz (guitar, lead vocals, drums), Davy Jones (vocals, tambourine), Michael Nesmith (bass).*
Previous Member: Peter Tork (guitar).
The cynicism with which it was done was incredible and created a lot of resentment. Four boys would be cast in Beatle-like roles, and each installment in the fall 1966 tv series would be done as much like *A Hard Day's Night* as humanly possible. Nobody really minded that the Monkees, as this new group was called, were manufactured entirely in cold blood and for bluntly commercial reasons. But when, never having played together before, their records hit the top of the

charts on the strength of what seemed like nothing more than tv exposure and a good sound financial push, the bitterness from other struggling groups was overwhelming. The story went that they were being told what to play note by note, that it had all been worked out for them, and that half the time on the records *they* weren't playing but the Candy Store Prophets, experienced musicians (with Bobby Hart of the Hart and Boyce team which produced and wrote many of the Monkees' early hits), were. Today, merely to mention this possibility brings on the wrath of several million Monkee fans who regard even the suggestion as treason. But it really no longer matters whether the Monkees did play every note themselves on those early singles or not.

The four boys were brought together one way or another (the story that they all answered an ad in *Variety* is sometimes contradicted) and told they would star in a weekly tv series about a rock group. It was one of the Beatles who pointed out that just getting out that weekly episode was a full-time job and that it wasn't fair to expect the group to be monster musicians as well. And they said it too, that they were hired as *actors*, actors who would portray musicians, and that musical background would help but that that wasn't what it was about. So then why put out singles if they weren't musicians? The answer to that is why not? The public bought, didn't they? And in the beginning it was like that. The Monkees were treated as one big hype. It was very hard on the boys. Not so much on Davy, who was basically an actor (he'd been very big on Broadway as the Artful Dodger in *Oliver*). Not so much on Mickey, who also was a former child actor and had starred in the *Circus Boy* tv series. But on Mike Nesmith and Peter Tork, who had paid a few dues in the music scene, it was rough. The point was in the beginning, with the series and the publicity, there hadn't been *time* to get together musically. But there was pressure to get a single out, so everyone did the best he could, and if that involved a little help from professional musicians, it wasn't the first time or the last time it had happened and with much more established groups than the poor old Monkees. Still, there was no doubt, and they were the first to admit it at the start, that they weren't four musical geniuses.

Mickey Dolenz had been a lead singer with a group called

the Missing Links and he could play guitar and had started to play drums before he became a Monkee but, well, he was no Ginger Baker. Davy Jones played a little guitar and he'd sung in *Oliver* and Screen Gems had tried unsuccessfully to make him a solo singer before the Monkees. Peter Tork did that whole Greenwich Village coffeehouse circuit and had a lot of musical know-how. And Mike Nesmith was also performing professionally before the Monkees. After a while it got to be a matter of pride for the Monkees to master their own instruments, so when things were a little settled in the summer of 1967 they got together a live "act" with which they toured the country proving they could provide a pleasant evening's entertainment as well as anyone. The tour won them a lot of respect from people who had previously dismissed them as a non-group. It was not that they were so fantastic, though they certainly were entertaining and competent, but that they were willing to face an audience and be judged like any other group was to their credit. Somewhere in all this they got away from their plastic image into something a bit earthier. Individual personalities started to emerge. Nesmith's stint as a folk singer and comedian at Los Angeles' Troubadour stood him in good stead. (Later, when the Monkees were established, he wrote, produced and conducted an instrumental album of serious music, *THE WICHITA TRAIN WHISTLE*). Dolenz did his James Brown imitation. Jones has Broadway ambitions. Tork is all gentleness and peace. It was the music people who first discovered that the Monkees were good guys. Everyone else followed. By 1968 it was distinctly *not done* to put down the Monkees. And to top things, they did a rather nice album that suggested there was more than tv exposure selling their singles for them. The end of 1968 saw their film *Head*, which finally established them as, if not exactly underground heroes, then underground pets. Early in 1969 Peter Tork left the group, but the Monkees decided to continue as a trio. Their latest album, *INSTANT REPLAY*, was recorded without Tork, and the group is supposedly much tighter now. Only time will tell if a barrel of three Monkees is as much fun as a barrel of four.

Albums/THE MONKEES (October 1966): *Theme From The Monkees; Saturday's Children; I Wanna Be Free; Tomorrow's*

Gonna Be Another Day; Poppa Jean's Blues; Take A Giant Step; Last Train To Clarksville; This Just Doesn't Seem To Be My Day; Let's Dance On; I'll Be True To You; Sweet Young Thing; Gonna Buy Me A Dog. MORE OF THE *MONKEES* (January 1967): *I'm A Believer; Steppin' Stone; She; When Love Come Knockin' (At Your Door); Mary, Mary; Hold On Girl; Your Auntie Grizelda; Look Out (Here Comes Tomorrow); Kind Of Girl I Could Love; Day We Fall In Love; Laugh; Sometime In The Morning.* MONKEES' HEADQUARTERS (June 1967): *You Told Me; I'll Spend My Life With You; Forget That Girl; Band 6; You Just May Be The One; Shades Of Gray; I Can't Get Her Off My Mind; For Pete's Sake; Sunny Girlfriend; Zilch; No Time; Early Morning Blues And Greens; Randy Scouse Git; Mr. Webster.* PISCES, AQUARIUS, CAPRICORN AND JONES, LTD. (November 1967): *Words; Salesman; She Hangs Out; Door Into Summer; Love Is Only Sleeping; Cuddly Toy; Hard To Believe; What Am I Doing Hangin' 'Round; Daily Nightly, Don't Call On Me; Star Collector; Medley; Pleasant Valley Sunday; Peter Percival Patterson's Pet Pig Porgy.* THE BIRDS, THE BEES, AND THE MONKEES (April 1968): *Dream World; Valleri; Auntie's Municipal Court; We Were Made For Each Other; P.O. Box 9847; The Poster; I'll Be Back Up On My Feet; Writing Wrongs; Daydream Believer; Tapioca Tundra; Zir And Zam; Magnolia Simms.* HEAD (December 1968): *Opening Ceremony; Porpoise Song (Theme From Head); Ditty Diego-War Chant; Circle Sky; Supplicio; Can You Dig It; Neck Gravy; Superstitious; As We Go Along; Dandruff; Daddy's Song; Pull; Long Title: Do I Have Do All Over Again; Swami-Plus Strings.* INSTANT REPLAY (March 1969): *Through The Looking Glass; Don't Listen To Linda; I Won't Be The Same Without Her; Me Without You; Just A Game; Don't Wait For Me; You & I; While I Cry; Tear Drop City; Girl I Left Behind Me; Man Without A Dream; Shorty Blackwell.*

Singles/*Last Train To Clarksville/Take A Giant Step* (August 1966); *I'm A Believer/Steppin' Stone* (November 1966); *A Little Bit Me, A Little Bit You/Girl I Knew Somewhere* (March 1967); *Pleasant Valley Sunday/Words* (July 1967); *Daydream Believer/Goin' Down* (October 1967); *Valleri/*

Tapioca Tundra (February 1968); *D. W. Washburn/It's Nice To Be With You* (May 1968). *As We Go Along/Pornoise Song* (October 1968); *Listen To The Band/Someday Man* (April 1969).

MOODY BLUES/*Justin Hayward (replaced Denny Laine) (lead vocals, 12-string guitar, acoustic & electric guitar, sitar, tablas, piano, mellotron, harpsichord, percussion), Mike Pinder (mellotron, piano, harpsichord, cello, acoustic & bass guitar, autoharp), John Lodge (replaced Clint Warwick) (bass & acoustic guitar, cello, tambourine, snare drum, vocals), Ray Thomas (flute, soprano saxophone, vocals), Graeme Edge (drums, timpani, tambourine, tablas, piano).*
The Moody Blues are a group that illustrate perfectly the vagaries of the life of a rock band and the ups and downs in its popularity. Coming hot on the heels of the big English rock explosion of 1964, they clinched their popularity with the American public by touring with the Beatles and getting the all-time great exposure for a good but second-string English group. The strange, hurt voice of Denny Laine kept the group's songs on the charts. Then, inexplicably, a slump. Staleness, public inconstancy—it could have been anything. When in 1966 Denny Laine left to go solo, there was not much left. That was when the band, with Denny's replacement, Justin Hayward, did what many good bands have done to get themselves together: they split to Belgium for three months constructive retreat. When they returned to England they were a whole new group, and with absolutely nothing to lose set about making the highly experimental *DAYS OF FUTURE PASSED*. Until then, no rock group had even considered working together with classical musicians on the major scale the Moodies chose when they combined forces with the London Festival Orchestra, taking the best from both musical worlds. The experiment was a sensational success. Now, instead of being one of a hundred just-above-average pop groups, the Moody Blues had status, the status of all groups big enough to take risks. On their next album, *IN SEARCH OF THE LOST CHORD*, they didn't need a symphony orchestra, they became it, playing something like thirty-three instruments themselves.
Albums/MOODY BLUES NO. 1 (July 1965): *I Go Crazy;*

And My Baby's Gone; Go Now; It Ain't Necessarily So; It's Easy Child; Can't Nobody Love You; I Had A Dream; Let Me Go; I Don't Want To Go On Without You; From The Bottom Of My Heart; True Story; Bye Bye Burd. DAYS OF FUTURE PASSED (March 1968): *Nights In White Satin; Dawn Is A Feeling; Another Morning; Peak Hours; Forever Afternoon (Tuesday); Sun Set; Twilight Time.* IN SEARCH OF THE LOST CHORD (September 1968): *Departure; Ride My See-Saw; House Of Four Doors; Dr. Livingstone, I Presume; Legend Of A Mind; Voices In The Sky; Best Way To Travel; Visions Of Paradise; Actor; Word; Om.* ON THE THRESHOLD OF A DREAM (May 1969).

Singles/*Go Now/It's Easy Child; Fly Me High/I Really Haven't Got The Time; Cities/Nights In White Satin; Another Morning/Forever Afternoon (Tuesday); Never Comes The Day/So Deep Within You* (May 1969).

MOOG SYNTHESIZER/Invented by Robert Moog (rhymes with vogue), the instrument—a machine that in theory can do anything a musician can by reproducing any sound electronically—looks something like an organ and needs two pairs of hands and two pairs of feet to play it. The Moog has not yet done a full rock album (though it has been used on them) but it has done a Bach album (*SWITCHED-ON BACH* in August, 1968) with realistic sounding trumpet, oboe and organ sounds. With the coming of the Moog synthesizer, will symphony orchestras become obsolete?

VAN MORRISON/Former lead singer of Them, Van Morrison took off for a solo career in 1967. A strong singer and a writer, he is just starting to get recognition and exposure. (see THEM)

Albums/BLOWIN' YOUR MIND (1968): *Brown-Eyed Girl; He Ain't Give You None; Who Drove The Red Sports Car; Goodbye Baby; T. B. Sheets; Spanish Rose; Ro Ro Rosey; Midnight Special.* ASTRAL WEEKS (December 1968): *Astral Weeks; Beside You; Sweet Thing; Cyprus Avenue; Young Lovers Do; Madame George; Ballerina; Slim Slow Slider.*

Singles/*Brown-Eyed Girl/Goodbye Baby; Chick-A-Boom/Ro Ro Rosey.*

MOTHER EARTH/ *Lonnie Castille (drums), Powell St. John (harp), Tracy Nelson (vocals), Martin Fierro (saxophone).*
Mother Earth is a Texas blues and soul band that features "intellectual body rock," which means lots of body movement. Tracy Nelson, a tiny girl, has a huge voice in the Janis Joplin range.

Albums/ REVOLUTION (soundtrack): *Revolution; Stranger In My Own Home Town.* LIVING WITH THE ANIMALS (November 1968): *Marvel Group; Mother Earth; I Did My Part; Living With The Animals; Down So Low; Cry On; It Won't Be Long; My Love Will Never Die; Goodnight Nelda Grebe, The Telephone Company Has Cut Us Off; Kingdom Of Heaven (Is Within You).*

Singles/ *Down So Low/ Goodnight Nelda Grebe* (December 1968); *I Did My Part/ Mother Earth* (April 1969).

MOTHERS (OF INVENTION)/ *Ray Collins (vocals), Frank Zappa (lead guitar), Roy Estrada (bass), Jimmy Carl Black (rhythm guitar), Ian Underwood (piano, saxophone), Don Preston (piano), Motorhead Sherwood (saxophone, tambourine), Bunk Gardner (saxophone, drums).*
Previous Members: Billy Mundi, Alice Stuart, Henry Vestine, Steve Mann, Elliot Ingber, Jim Fielder, James Guercio.
The look that was bizarre and shocking on them in 1966 was a look that barely raised eyebrows by 1968. On the surface, the Mothers' performances were built around ugliness—ugly players, bearded and menacing like something out of an old pirate movie; ugly music; ugly lyrics; ugly gestures; ugly noises. The motive: satire. And all of it done with great sophistication. The Mothers were as fascinating as monster movies, and they had a social message too. Their first album, *FREAK OUT,* was unlike anything that was happening in American music in 1966. It grew on the public like an evil fungus. *FREAK OUT* was not just social and musical satire. It was the first rock album produced as if it were a single piece of music. (It was a full year before the Beatles made this concept commercially acceptable with *SERGEANT PEPPER.*)

Zappa started with a high school band in the fifties. In the sixties, when the English invasion was in full force and it wasn't fashionable to be freaky, he and some other musicians had a freaky group called Captain Glasspack and his Magic Mufflers. After much coming and going and switching of instruments and switching of roles, they became the Mothers of Invention. Ian Underwood, the pianist, has a master's degree in music. Euclid James "Motorhead" Sherwood started off as an equipment manager and now plays baritone sax. Musicians came and went in the Mothers with such frequency that for a while it looked as if every band in rock was to be made up of ex-Mothers (well, several: Henry Vestine of Canned Heat, James Guercio, who now produces the Buckinghams, James Fielder of Blood, Sweat and Tears, Billy Mundi of Rhinoceros). The Mothers' style and technique borrows very cleverly from everything from early rock to the modern classical composers. They use props and "visual aids" to bring to rock a whole new element of art, theatre and audience participation. When they worked for five consecutive months at a Greenwich Village theatre they called their show *Absolutely Free,* a name that invariably attracted more customers than most. Later it was the title of a more sophisticated second album, which contained two Mothers' classics: *Brown Shoes Don't Make It* and *America Drinks and Goes Home.* There was in this album a preoccupation with vegetables not generally found in popular music. The Mothers' third album, a SERGEANT PEPPER parody called WE'RE *ONLY IN IT FOR THE MONEY,* stated that the ugliest part of a person's body might very well be his mind. Lyricist Zappa has always had a great deal to tell the hippies, the middle class and every other target of his satire. Even his titles carry his message: *Chrome Plated Megaphone of Destiny* and *Nasal Retentive Calliope Music.*

The Mothers, being a little older than most current rock groups, did a lot of their high living in the fifties and their songs reflect their nostalgia for that era. *CRUISIN' WITH RUBEN AND THE JETS,* is straight fifties rock and roll with appropriate teen-love high-school-dance lyrics, the whole album underlining their biggest talent—musical satire. The idea is to destroy the top-forty concept of radio, and ease the listener into "serious" music. Significantly, the Mothers made the album best-seller lists without any sort of top-forty radio play. Significantly again, a still unreleased three-record set is called *NO COMMERCIAL POTENTIAL*. It includes the sounds of New York policemen breaking into a Mothers recording session—taped only because no one had switched off the machine during the surprise visit.

Albums/FREAK OUT (August 1966): *Hungry Freaks, Daddy; I Ain't Got No Heart; Who Are The Brain Police; Go Cry On Somebody Else's Shoulder; Motherly Love; How Could I Be Such A Fool; Wowie Zowie; You Didn't Try To Call Me; Any Way The Wind Blows; I'm Not Satisfied; You're Probably Wondering Why I'm Here; Trouble Comin' Every Day; Help, I'm A Rock; Return Of The Son Of Monster Magnet.* ABSOLUTELY FREE (May 1967): *Plastic People; Duke Of Prunes; Amnesia Vivace; Duke Regains His Chops; Call Any Vegetable; Soft-Sell Conclusion; Status Back Baby; Son Of Suzy Creamcheese; Brown Shoes Don't Make It; America Drinks And Goes Home; Uncle Bernie; Invocation And Ritual Dance Of The Young Pumpkin; America Drinks.* WE'RE ONLY IN IT FOR THE MONEY (January 1968): *Are You Hung Up; Who Needs The Peace Corps; Concentration Moon; Mom And Dad; Bow Tie Daddy; Harry, You're A Beast; What's The Ugliest Part Of Your Body; Absolutely Free; Flower Punk; Nasal Retentive Calliope Music; Let's Make The Water Turn Black; Idiot Bastard Son; Lonely Little Girl; Take Your Clothes Off When You Dance; Mother People; Hot Poop; Chrome Plated Megaphone Of Destiny.* LUMPY GRAVY (May 1968): (Frank Zappa conducts Abnuceals Emuukha Electric Symphony Orchestra and Chorus) *Lumpy Gravy* (2 Parts). CRUISING WITH RUBEN AND THE JETS (November 1968): *Cheap Thrills; Love Of My Life; How Could I Be Such A Fool; Deseri; I'm Not Satisfied; Jelly Roll Gum Drop; Anything; Later That Night; You Didn't Try To Call Me; Fountain Of Love; "No. No. No."; Anyway The Wind Blows; Stuff Up The Cracks* UNCLE MEAT (April 1969).

Singles/*Big Leg Emma/Why Don't You Do Me Right* (April 1967); *Lonely Little Girl/Mother People* (November 1967); *Anyway The Wind Blows/Jelly Roll Gum Drop* (December 1968).

MOTOWN (see DETROIT SOUND)

THE MOVE/ *Bev Bevan (drums), Trevor Burton (lead vocals, rhythm guitar), Chris "Ace" Kefford (bass guitar), Carl Wayne (guitar, vocals), Roy Wood (lead guitar, vocals, banjo, sitar, autoharp).*

The Move, which is still scarcely known in the U.S., is a very big group in England, where like the Who it goes in for what can only be called rock and wreck. Because it came in 1967, after the Who were established, it had to do them one better, so instead of wrecking instruments as do the Who, the Move smash television sets (old ones), pianos and cars. Once they destroyed an effigy of British Prime Minister Wilson, which contributed usefully to a publicity campaign designed to make them come across as a junior version of the Rolling Stones. Musically, they used to go in for high four-part harmonies though their sound has become more aggressive. Apart from the smashings their big asset was Ace Kefford, who had a face so thin it sometimes looked like a skull, blond frizzy Afro-Annie hair and steel-rimmed glasses. In 1968 Kefford left (for a rest in a nursing home said the English music papers). The group has had its eye on America.

Singles/ *Night Of Fear/ The Disturbance* (January 1967); *I Can Hear The Grass Grow/ Wave The Flag And Stop The Train* (March 1967); *Flowers In The Rain/ The Lemon Tree (Here We Go Round)* (February 1968); *Something/ Yellow Rainbow; Fire Brigade/ Walk Upon The Water.*

MUGWUMPS/ *Cass Elliot, Denny Doherty, Zal Yanovsky, James Hendricks.*

Mugwump, an Indian word, means "a person who is neutral on a controversial issue." The Mugwumps were around in 1964, Beatles year, singing very sophisticated folky stuff that was a sort of combination Mama-Papa/ Lovin' Spoonful, but obviously that wasn't the year for it. Music had to be allowed to do its loud rock thing before it could come back to this. Cass and Jim wrote. Cass later went on to join the Mamas and the Papas, and Jim (who was her husband and is, of course, not Jimi Hendrix) later headed the Lamp of Child-hood and now sings solo. Denny joined Cass in the Mamas and the Papas and Zal left, too, to join the Lovin' Spoonful (with John Sebastian, who can be heard playing harp on several cuts of the Mugwumps' album). The record, marked clearly "an historic recording," was released in 1967, only when the Spoonful and the Mamas and the Papas had become top record sellers.

(See LOVIN' SPOONFUL, MAMAS AND THE PAPAS)

Album/THE MUGWUMPS (June 1967): *Searchin'; I Don't Wanna Know; I'll Remember Tonight; Here It Is Another Day; Do You Know What I Mean; You Can't Judge A Book By The Cover; Everybody's Been Talkin'; Do What They Don't Say; So Fine.*

Single/*Season Of The Witch/My Gal* (May 1967).

THE MUSIC EXPLOSION/*Jamie Lyons (lead vocals), Don (Tudor) Atkins (lead guitar), Rick Nesta (rhythm guitar), Butch Stahl (bass guitar, organ), Bob Avery (drums, harmonica).*

They come from Ohio and had a big hit in *Little Bit O' Soul* in 1967. Lead singer Jamie Lyons, who is still very young, is the one who's considered to have star potential.

Album/LITTLE BIT O' SOUL (July 1967): *Let Yourself Go; Everybody; Light Of Love; What Did I Do To Deserve Such A Fate; Good Time Feeling; One Potato Two; Little Bit O' Soul; Can't Stop Now; Patch Of Dawn; Sha La La La; Love, Love, Love, Love, Love; 96 Tears.*

Singles/*Little Bit O' Soul/I See The Light* (April 1967); *Can't Stop Now/Sunshine Games* (August 1967); *Hearts And Flowers/We Gotta Go Home* (September 1967).

NASHVILLE SOUND/In Nashville they say there's no such thing as a "Nashville sound," which is odd, because the musicians and recording engineers down there are making a comfortable living providing it. They say there's no Nashville sound, just the happy, easy rapport of men who have worked together so long that communication is perfect and spontaneous. But that's not entirely right, for when those same men are flown to other places to play for recording sessions, it's just not the same. Oh, but that's because they're at their best when they're on their own comfortable home ground, they explain. So all right, it's not just something in the air, as some English musicians found when they went to record there, with their own musicians. Those who come from far away to get the Nashville sound say it is a combination of three factors: the studio musicians, the relaxed atmosphere of the southern capital, and the cheerful mixture of homespun rawness and sheer professionalism of Nashville's country musicians.

Nashville has three lives. First and foremost it's the capital of country music with hundreds of recording and publishing companies and Grand Ole Opry every Friday and Saturday night. Secondly, long before the current country boom in rock, Nashville became a center for ailing singers, a place where they could go to bring a new fresh sound to their albums. Finally there is the Nashville where Buffy Sainte-Marie, Leonard Cohen, Joan Baez, Nancy Sinatra, Ian and Sylvia, and the Union Gap among others have gone to make albums. This new wave was started by Bob Dylan, who was persuaded by his producer, an old Nashville man named Bob Johnston, to cut some albums there—with great success. It was Dylan and the Byrds who brought a Nashville feel into rock—Dylan with *JOHN WESLEY HARDING* and his latest *NASHVILLE SKYLINE,* and the Byrds with *SWEET-HEART OF THE RODEO.*

The Nashville sound uses light, feathery-textured drums, the sounds of banjos and fiddles and dobros (steel guitars) found in traditional country music, and the ching-ching-ching of guitars; and the musicians are always open to innovations within this framework. There are fine studio musicians at the Motown studios of Detroit and the Stax studios of Memphis, all with their own sound, but nowhere are there as many good session musicians in one place working better together than in Nashville.

NAZZ/*Robert "Stewkey" Antoni (organ, piano, lead vocals), Todd Rundgren (guitar), Carson van Osten (bass guitar), Thom Mooney (drums).*

The Nazz is a hard-rock group that appeared on the music scene early in 1968. It was one of the few new *young* groups with the emphasis on early Beatle freshness and wholesomeness rather than on the San Francisco flower-child bearded look that was then dominating. The sound was very clean—a few Beach Boys harmonies here, an appealing touch of the Bee Gees there. The four thin Philadelphia boys played a nice, competent, slightly eclectic rock, write all their own songs and have had the advantage of highly sophisticated management. But splits in 1969 suggested they wouldn't see out the year. Todd Rundgren, writer-guitarist, has already gone solo.

Albums/ THE NAZZ (October 1968): *Open My Eyes; Back Of Your Mind; See What You Can Be; Hello It's Me; Wildwood Blues; If That's The Way You Feel; When I Get My Plane; Lemming Song; Crowded; She's Goin' Down.* NAZZ NAZZ (May 1969): *Forget All About It; Not Wrong Long; Rain Rider; Gonna Cry Today; Meridian Leeward; Under The Ice; Hang On Paul; Kiddie Boy; Featherbedding Lover; Letters Don't Count; Beautiful Song.*

Singles/ *Hello It's Me/ Everybody's Talkin'* (August 1968). *Under The Ice/ Not Wrong Long* (April 1969).

FRED NEIL/ In the age of hype, autohype and superhype, Fred Neil, composer, guitarist, folk singer, blues singer, folk-rock singer, is the victim of *underhype*. He is great and everyone inside rock knows it. Outside, so few know it that his record company was driven to one desperate and inspired piece of promotion: Buy-one-Fred-Neil-record-and-if-you-like-it-we'll-send-you-another-one-for-nothing. They figured, quite rightly, that by the time you had two Neil records you would be hopelessly hooked. All right, if he's so good, how come he ain't rich? The answer is you don't get rich unless you play the game. You have to make records, often. And promote them, almost continually. Play clubs, do concerts, tours and as many magazine interviews as the traffic will stand. Fred Neil lives very happily in Miami. He's not about to give that up for the concert tour hassle if he can help it.

Neil came from the late fifties-early sixties Village scene when folk was slowly but surely being seduced by rock, though it didn't know it. Not all of it succumbed, and what's left is proud but sorry. Fred Neil is somewhere in between all that. He had his following of Village musicians, just kids hanging out in the Kettle of Fish, and now those kids are John Sebastian and Cream's producer, Felix Pappalardi. Neil wrote a lot of songs then, and still does. His blues-based songs— which he sings in a rich, warm, deep, suffering voice—

are all about life, love and the high price you pay for enjoying both. And they turn up in funny places like on the Youngbloods' first album (which, coincidentally, Pappalardi produced).

Peter, Paul and Mary have recorded his songs. So have Nilsson, Kenny Rankin, the Lovin' Spoonful and about seventy others. He is talked about admiringly where musicians gather and really looked up to for refusing to play the rock game. (The Jefferson Airplane has two songs about him: *Ballad of You and Me and Pooneil* and *House at Pooneil Corner.*) He's probably one of the most important singer-composers around.

Albums/BLEECKER & MAC DOUGAL: *Travelin' Shoes; The Water Is Wide; Yonder Comes The Blues; Candy Man; Handful Of Gimme; Gone Again; Bleecker & MacDougal; Blues On The Ceiling; Sweet Mama; Little Bit Of Rain; Country Boy; Other Side To This Life; Mississippi Train.* FRED NEIL (January 1967): *The Dolphins; I've Got A Secret; That's The Bag I'm In; Badi-Da; Faretheewell; Green Rocky Road; Sweet Cocaine; Everything Happens; Everybody's Talkin' Cynicrust-Petefredjohn Raga.* FRED NEIL SESSIONS (January 1968): *Felicity; Please Send Me Someone To Love; Merry Go Round; Look Over Yonder; Fools Are A Long Time Coming; Looks Like Rain; Roll On Rosie.* TEAR DOWN THE WALLS: *I Know You Rider; Red Flowers; Tear Down The Walls; Weary Blues; Toy Balloon; Baby; Morning Dew; I'm A Drifter; Linin' Track; I Got 'Em; Wild Child In A World Of Trouble; Dade County Jail Lonesome Valley.*

Singles/*Dolphins/I've Got A Secret* (May 1967); *Felicity/ Please Send Me Someone To Love* (September 1968); *Everybody's Talkin'/That's The Bag I'm In* (October 1968)

RICK NELSON is the perfect example of how every singer in the immediate post-Elvis period was cast in the Elvis mold (just as later groups in the post-Beatle period were cast in the Beatle mold). Rick's greatest popularity came in 1959, with fan clubs all over the world (like Paul Anka, he shrewdly nurtured an international following), and although he started his rock career as a lark (he was then in his parents' tv series) he was a big success in his time. He never stopped recording and made some country albums in 1966 and 1967. In 1968 he headlined at the Latin Quarter (following the Everly Brothers and Brenda Lee), bringing in no end of nostalgic customers and almost everyone who had been in their teens and early twenties in Rick's heyday. In 1969 he made a quiet comeback at Los Angeles' Ash Grove that may well be the beginning of a serious new career.

Albums/RICKY (1958). RICK NELSON (November 1958). RICKY SINGS AGAIN (October 1959). RICK IS 21. BEST SELLERS BY RICK. MILLION SELLERS BY RICK NELSON. LONG VACATION. RICK NELSON (July 1963). RICK NELSON SINGS FOR YOU (January 1964). VERY THOUGHT OF YOU (October 1964). BEST ALWAYS (June 1965). LOVE AND KISSES (January 1966). RICK NELSON (June 1966). BRIGHT LIGHTS AND COUNTRY MUSIC (July 1966). SPOTLIGHT ON RICK (January 1965). ON THE FLIP SIDE (January 1967). COUNTRY FEVER (June 1967). ANOTHER SIDE OF RICK (January 1968).

Singles/*Be-Bop Baby/Stood Up; Poor Little Fool/Lonesome Town; Travelin' Man/My Bucket's Got A Hole In It; Hello Mary Lou/Wonder Like You; It's Up To You/Teen Age Idol; Young Emotions/That's All; It's Late/Never Be Anyone Else But You; Believe What You Say/Young World; I Got A Woman/You Don't Love Me Anymore; Gypsy Woman/String Along; Fools Rush In/Down Home; For You/That's All She Wrote; I Wonder/Very Thought Of You; Lonely Corner/There's Nothing I Can Say; Don't Breathe A Word/Happy Guy; Mean Old World/When The Chips Are Down; Come Out Dancin'/Yesterday's Love; Love And Kisses/Say You Love Me; Fire Breathin' Dragon/Your Kind Of Lovin'; Louisiana Man/You Just Can't Quit; I'm Called Lonely/Take A City Bride; Moonshine/Suzanne On A Sunday Morning; Dream Weaver/Baby Close Its Eye; Don't Blame It On Your Wife/Promenade In Green.*

BOB NEUWIRTH/Probably best known as Bob Dylan's road manager during the English tour filmed in *Don't Look Back,* Bob Neuwirth started as a country folk singer and in 1968 made a still unreleased country album that was the talk of the West Coast.

THE NEW LOST CITY RAMBLERS/*Mike Seeger (fiddle),*
Tom Paley (banjo), John Cohen (guitar).
They are still playing the fast fiddle music that was revived in
the early sixties, just before the rock explosion hit the folk
people. A lot of today's rock people, people like the Spoonful's John Sebastian, were just growing up musically when this
music was being played at every college and folk club. You
can still hear the New Lost City Ramblers in the music
Sebastian is writing today, and there are echoes of them in
Dylan's Nashville records. In fact, if you hear the New Lost
City Ramblers playing, you realize that many of today's rock
stars who originally came out of folk lean toward their country and bluegrass sound.

Albums/NEW LOST CITY RAMBLERS: *Old Joe Clark;*
Old Molly Hair; Nick Nack Song; Country Blues; If I Love;
Sail Away Ladies; 12 Other Titles. NEW LOST CITY RAM-
BLERS, II: *Tom Cat Blues; Dallas Rag; Sailor On The Deep*
Blue Sea; Other Titles. NEW LOST CITY RAMBLERS, III:
17 Songs. NEW LOST CITY RAMBLERS, IV: *Black Moun-*
tain Rag; Roll In My Sweet Baby's Arms; Talking Hard
Luck; Railroad Blues; Weaveroom Blues; Baltimore Fire;
Willy; Poor Boy; Red Rocking Chair; Hold That Woodpile
Down; Three Men Went A-Hunting; Johnson Boys; Hot
Corn; Lady of Carlisle; Man Who Wrote Home Sweet Home
Never Was A Married Man; Sal Got A Meatskin; My Long
Journey Home; Fly Around My Pretty Little Miss; Hogeye.
NEW LOST CITY RAMBLERS, V (March 1964): *Run*
Mountain; Take Me Back To The Sweet Sunny South; Black
Jack David; Molly Put The Kettle On; Carter Blues; Coo Coo
Bird; Keno The Rent Man; Cindy; Have A Feast Here
Tonight; Crow Black Chicken; Billy Grimes The Rover;
Frankie Silver; Stackerlee; Dollar's All I Crave; Miller's Will;
Story That The Crow Told Me. NEW LOST CITY RAM-
BLERS, VI. "NEW" NEW LOST CITY RAMBLERS: *John*
Dee; Lisa Jane; Train No. 45; Rambler's Blues; Tennessee
Cat; Danville Girl; 12 Other Titles. DEPRESSION SONGS
(February 1960). AMERICAN MOONSHINE AND PRO-
HIBITION (March 1963): *Virginia Bootlegger; Moonshiner;*
Goodbye Old Booze; Old Home Brew; I've Still Got 99; 12
Other Titles. GONE TO THE COUNTRY (March 1964).

NEW LOST CITY RAMBLERS INSTRUMENTALS (November 1964). RURAL DELIVERY NO. 1 (August 1965): *Going Down The River; Cyclone Of Rye Cove; Sweet Willie; I've Always Been A Rambler; Old Joe Bone; Automobile Trip Through Alabama; Bachelor Blues; Train On The Island; Pretty Polly; Soldier & The Lady; Gold Watch & Chain; Days Of My Childhood Plays; Fishing Creek Blues; Hungry Hash-House; Rubber Neck Blues; Twenty-One Years; Rosa Le McFall.* REMEMBRANCES OF THINGS TO COME (February 1967): *Soldier's Joy; Titanic; Single Girl; Rock About My Saro Jane; I'm Lonesome; Dark & Stormy Night; He Is Coming To Us Dead; New Lost Hometown Blues; Black Bottom Strut; Cat's Got The Measles; Lord Bateman.* NEW LOST CITY RAMBLERS WITH COUSIN EMMY (April 1968): *Little Joe; Ruby; Bowling Green; Johnny Booker; Dance All Night;* Others.

NEW VAUDEVILLE BAND/The New Vaudeville Band was one of the first to inject humor and mad-campery into pop. They treat prewar favorites with an airy wit that makes the young giggle and the old wipe a nostalgic tear away. Their one big hit (number one in the U.S. and recorded by more than fifty people, including Petula Clark, Dizzy Gillespie, Lawrence Welk, Frank Sinatra, Rudy Vallee, Nancy Wilson, Sandy Nelson, David McCallum and the Bob Crewe Generation) was *Winchester Cathedral,* but they do very well with their saucy line of comic rock in live performances and albums.

Albums/WINCHESTER CATHEDRAL: *Winchester Cathedral; Lili Marlene; Oh, Donna Clara; I Can't Go Wrong; Tap Your Feet; Nightingale Sang In Berkeley Square; That's All For Now Sugar Baby; Whispering; There's A Kind Of Hush; Your Love Ain't What It Used To Be.* NEW VAUDEVILLE BAND ON TOUR: *Finchley Central; Shine On Harvest Moon; I Wonder Who's Kissing Her Now; So Tired; Reflections; Thoroughly Modern Millie; Peek-A-Boo; If I Had A Talking Picture Of You; Shirl; Sadie Moonshine; Amy.*

Singles/*Anniversary Song/The Bonnie & Clyde; Fourteen Lovely Women/Green Street Green; Winchester Cathedral/Peek-A-Boo.*

Also Appear On/ENGLAND'S GREATEST HITS: *Winchester Cathedral.*

NEW YORK ELECTRIC STRING ENSEMBLE/On its first album out, late in 1967, the New York Electric String Ensemble plays Bach and Purcell on two electric guitars and an electric bass. It's an interesting experiment, and strangely enough the instruments usually associated with rock do quite well for baroque music, too. It's too early yet to see if the electric revolution will spread further into the world of serious concert music, but it's not impossible.

Album/NEW YORK ELECTRIC STRING ENSEMBLE (December 1967).

NEW YORK ROCK AND ROLL ENSEMBLE/*Dorian Rudnytsky (piano, cello, trumpet, French horn, guitar), Michael Kamen (piano, English horn, harpsichord, clarinet, oboe, guitar, organ, lead vocals), Martin Fulterman (drums), Brian Corrigan (guitar, lead vocals), Clifford Nivison (lead guitar).* Three of them are Juilliard musicians. It gives them class, an excuse to wear tie and tails and startle people, and it means they can play a sonata for oboe and cello under a rock chorus. The New York Rock and Roll Ensemble formed in the spring of 1967, which makes it the first (but not the last: Ars Nova followed) group to marry rock to the baroque renaissance. *Billboard* put it most succinctly when it said, "It takes guts to open a Greenwich Village discotheque set with an oboe duet. It takes guts to follow the duet with a Bach trio for two oboes and a cello. It takes guts to then drift into a rock program. And it takes considerable talent and ingenuity to carry it off." And that's just what they did at Trude Heller's.

Predictably, they included *A Whiter Shade of Pale* in the program that night, but the Bach was done with oboe and cello. They also did *Dock of the Bay* and *Sunshine of Your Love,* which to say the least proved they were versatile. And though they do all that better than anyone else, they're never smug—something they've learned, all five of them, from years of playing in other rock groups. They are all either from Tom's River, New Jersey, or from New York. Michael Kamen, who plays oboes and things, sings like Wilson Pickett

and Otis Redding and looks like a decadent Roman emperor
(and he's only nineteen). Whenever they do a rock standard,
they try to do it *their* way. They claim, like Leonard Cohen,
and like so many others drawn to rock, that it's the idea of
the mass audience that appeals to them. They may be playing
with classical orchestras (which the Juilliard three still do),
but they obviously enjoy playing rock too.

Albums/NEW YORK ROCK AND ROLL ENSEMBLE
(August 1968): *Intro; Sounds Of Time; Began To Burn; Mr.
Tree; Monkey; Trio Sonata No. 1 In C; Poor Pauline; Alla
Breve Fugue (2nd Movement); She's Gone; You Know
What It's Like; Pick Up In The Morning; Studeao Atlantis;
The Seasons; Question Mark.* FAITHFUL FRIENDS
(August 1969).

Singles/*Suddenly/Kiss Her Once* (1968); Pick Up In The
Morning/Thing To Do (1968).

NEWBEATS/Their single *Bread and Butter* was probably one
of the dancing songs to come out of the 1965–66 discotheque
era. They seemed to fade out after that.

Albums/BIG BEAT SOUNDS (November 1966): *I Can't
Hear You No More; Birds Are For The Bees; Mother-In-
Law; Baby Let's Play House; Break Away (From That Boy);
Great Balls Of Fire; Poison Pen; Hey-O-Daddy-O; Find Ya
Somewhere Else; Better Watch Your Step; The Natural;
Human Kindness.* BREAD AND BUTTER (November
1966): *Bread And Butter; Bye Bye Love; It's In His Kiss;
Everything's Alright; I'm Blue; So Fine; Thou Shalt Not
Steal; There Oughta Be A Law; Pink Dally Rue; Patent On
Love; Tough Little Buggy; Ain't That Lovin' You Baby.*
RUN, BABY, RUN (November 1966): *Run, Baby, Run;
Oh, Pretty Woman; Hang On Sloopy; Help; Little Child; It's
Really Goodbye; Oh, Girls, Girls; Satisfaction (I Can't Get
No); This Old Heart; Come See About Me; Mean Woolly
Willie; Lookin' For Love.*

Singles/*Better Watch Your Step/Birds Are For The Bees;
Little Child/I Can't Hear You No More; Run, Baby, Run/
Mean Woolly Willie; Shake Hands/Too Sweet To Be Forgot-
ten; Crying My Heart Out/Short On Love; Bird Dog/Evil
Eva; My Yesterday Love/Patent On Love; So Fine/Top*

Secret; Hide The Moon/It's Really Goodbye; Don't Turn Me Loose/You And Me And Happiness; Bad Dreams/Swinger; Bread And Butter; I've Been A Long Time Loving You/Michelle De Ann (August 1968); *Girls And The Boys/Ain't That Lovin' You* (December 1968); *Great Balls Of Fire/Thou Shalt Not Steal* (June 1969).

RANDY NEWMAN/He sings like a mixer full of half-dried concrete, all rough and ragged. But although he is a songwriter and not a singer, his first album, in 1968, full of half-bitter little ironies sung in that gravelly voice, won him a fierce following. His best known song is the one sung by Judy Collins, *I Think It's Gonna Rain Today.* Ex-Animal Alan Price has an album out in England, half of which is Newman songs. There are people who believe the Beatles' *When I'm 64* wouldn't have been possible without Newman, and certainly it is in the tender and laconic Newman style. An interesting point about the men who write the songs for the new music is that they are no longer content to take a back seat but make a point of recording their own material, even if their voices are not what voices are supposed to be. Bob Dylan, no doubt, made this possible. Once you had gotten hooked on his voice you were ready for anything. Los Angeles-based Newman is an equally acquired taste.

Album/RANDY NEWMAN (June 1968): *Love Story; Bet No One Ever Hurt This Bad; Living Without You; So Long Dad; I Think He's Hiding; Linda; Laughing Boy; Cowboy; Davy The Fat Boy; Beehive State; I Think It's Going To Rain Today.*

Single/*I Think It's Going To Rain Today/Beehive State* (May 1968).

NICE/*Brian "Blinky" Davison (drums), Keith Emerson (organ), Lee Jackson (bass), David O'List (lead guitar, vocals).*
That they have gone in for quite a bit of shock rock is not surprising, for the Nice are managed by former Rolling Stones manager Andrew Oldham. In their New York debut at Steve Paul's The Scene in 1968, they stripped to the waist and whipped each other during performances—and played thereafter to packed houses. In England they stabbed an

American flag with knives, stomped on it and burned it on stage. The organ player has been known to tap-dance on the keys with remarkably musical results. The June, 1968, American flag-burning got them banned from London's Royal Albert Hall for life. By July they were being criticized for promoting their English single, *America,* with a poster that showed the group holding children upon whose faces had been superimposed photographs of the late President Kennedy, the late Senator Robert Kennedy and the late Dr. Martin Luther King Jr. The Nice started as a backup group and made their first appearance at the 1967 Windsor Blues Festival, freaking out the whole audience. It was then that they decided to go out on their own. Their sound ranges from Chinese music to Schönberg but is mainly a very forceful blend of rock, jazz and blues.

Albums/THE THOUGHTS OF EMERLIST DAVJACK (February 1968): *Flower King Of Flies; Thoughts Of Emerlist Davjack; Bonnie K; Rondo; War And Peace; Cry Of Eugene; Tantalising Maggie; Dawn.* ARS LONGA VITA BREVIS (March 1969): *America-2nd Amendment; Daddy Where Did I Come From; Little Arabella; Happy Freuds; Intermezzo From "Karalia Suite"; Don Edito El Gruva; Ars Longa Vita Brevis-Prelude; 1st Movement-Awakening; 2nd Movement-Realization; 3rd Movement-Acceptance "Brandenburger"; 4th Movement-Denial; Coda-Extension To The Big Note.*

Singles/*Thoughts Of Emerlist Davjack/Azial (Angel Of Death)* (January 1968); *America-2nd Amendment/Diamond Hard Blue Apples Of The Moon* (November 1968).

NICO/Originally an Andy Warhol superstar (that is, one of the repertory company of strolling players that people his films), Nico moved into the world of music when Warhol did. When he got himself a group, the Velvet Underground, she became its singer. Eventually she went solo, accompanying herself with a small portable organ. At Steve Paul's The Scene she was billed as the Moon Goddess, and she does have an air of tall, pale mystery partially justifying that name. Only recently, though, has she revealed a not so pale gift for songwriting, and her new album features all her own songs

sung in a deep, flat, moon goddess voice with suitable liturgic instrumentation by Velvet Underground's John Cale.
(see VELVET UNDERGROUND)

Albums/VELVET UNDERGROUND AND NICO (March 1967): *Sunday Morning; I'm Waiting For The Man; Femme Fatale; Venus In Furs; Run, Run, Run; All Tomorrow's Parties; Heroin; There She Goes Again; I'll Be Your Mirror; European Son To Delmore Schwartz; Black Angel's Death Song.* CHELSEA GIRL (July 1967): *Fairest Of The Seasons; These Days; Little Sister; Winter Song; It Was A Pleasure Then; Chelsea Girls; I'll Keep It With Mine; Wrap Your Troubles In Dreams; Somewhere There's A Feather; Eulogy To Lenny Bruce.* THE MARBLE INDEX (September 1968): *Prelude; Lawns Of Dawn; No One Is There; Aries' Song; Facing The Wing; Julius Caesar (Momento Hode); Frozen Warnings; Evening Of Light.*

NILSSON (Harry Nilsson)/He first attracted Beatle attention (and therefore world attention) with *You Can't Do That,* a clever collage of at least twelve Beatles songs. Derek Taylor, the Beatles' legendary press officer, heard about it and played it to John Lennon. Lennon, on his May, 1968, U.S. visit, talked of nothing else to anyone who would listen. But Nilsson, who lives in Los Angeles, is too delicate and too clever for instant stardom (or as Frank Kofsky of *Jazz and Pop* shrewdly pointed out, he's a jazz singer, really, and that's the kiss of death in rock). His first album, *PANDEMONIUM SHADOW SHOW,* which came out in December, 1967, used twenty voices—all his. His range is about three octaves and he does two-, three-, and four-part harmonies with these voices, even taking on the intricate harmonies of *She's Leaving Home.* He's been around for a long time—the Ronettes did two of his early songs and the Modern Folk Quartet another. The Monkees' *Cuddly Toy* is his, as is the Yardbirds' *Ten Little Indians,* and Blood, Sweat and Tears did his song *Without Her.* (Lana Cantrell, The Turtles, Jack Jones, Lulu, Herb Alpert and Rick Nelson also do Nilsson songs.) No one has quite worked him out except for one thing—he's not just a good singer, he's a good group.

Albums/PANDEMONIUM SHADOW SHOW (December 1967): *Ten Little Indians; 1941; Cuddly Toy; She Sang*

Hymns Out Of Tune; You Can't Do That; Sleep Late, My Lady Friend; She's Leaving Home; There Will Never Be; Without Her; Freckles; It's Been So Long; River Deep, Mountain High. AERIAL BALLET (August 1968): *Good Old Desk; Don't Leave Me; Together; Mr. Richland's Favorite Song; Little Cowboy; Everybody's Talkin'; I Said Goodbye To Me; Mr. Tinker; One; Wailing Of The Willow; Bath.*

Single/*Everybody's Talkin'*/*Rainmaker* (May 1969).

1910 FRUITGUM COMPANY/*Frank Jeckell (lead vocals, rhythm guitar), Pat Karwan (vocals, lead guitar), Mark Gutkowski (vocals, organ), Floyd Marcus (vocals, drums).*
Their name came from a crumpled chewing-gum wrapper found in the pocket of an old suit jacket. Their first song, in 1968, was a teenybopper number called *Simon Says* and they did that deliberately because, let's face it, it was one way to get on the charts. And it did make the charts—impressively. So did their next *1-2-3 Red Light*. They'd like to change directions, they say. They don't want to do teenybopper music forever. Well, we'll see.

Albums/SIMON SAYS: *Simon Says; May I Take A Giant Step (Into Your Heart); Keep Your Thoughts On The Bright Side; Bubble Gum World; Story Of Flipper; Pop Goes The Weasel; Year 2001; Magic Windmill; Poor Old Mr. Jensen; Happy Little Teardrops; Soul Struttin'.* 1, 2, 3 RED LIGHT (September 1968): *1, 2, 3 Red Light; Book; 9, 10 Let's Do It Again; Yummy, Yummy, Yummy; Mighty Quinn; Lookin' Back; Song Song; Shirley Applegate; Sister John; Take Away; Blue Eyes And Orange Skies.* INDIAN GIVER (March 1969).

Singles/*May I Take A Giant Step (Into Your Heart)*/*Mr. Jensen* (1968); *1, 2, 3, Red Light*/*Sticky, Sticky* (1968); *Simon Says*/*Reflections From The Looking Glass* (1968); *No Good Annie*/*Special Delivery* (May 1969).

THE NITTY GRITTY DIRT BAND/*Ralph Barr (guitar, clarinet, banjo), Chris Darrow (replaced Bruce Kunkel) (guitar, banjo, fiddle, mandolin), Jimmie Fadden (replaced Hanna's brother) (washtub bass, jug, harmonica, drums, trombone, euphonium), Jeffrey Hanna (washboard, harmoni-*

ca, guitar, lead vocals), John McEuen (replaced Jackson Browne) (banjo, guitar, washtub bass, harmonica, piano, comb, Jew's harp), Les Thompson (guitar, banjo, kazoo, mandolin).

The Nitty Gritty Dirt Band is a throwback to the mad music of Spike Jones, of the jug bands, of the English skiffle bands that the Beatles came out of—that is, zany, homemade music, with the sort of comedy that popped up occasionally in bands like the New Vaudeville Band, the Bonzo Dog Doo Dah Band and the Jim Kweskin Jug Band. Goodtime, old-time music, with a lot of country influences.

The group started early in 1966 and went through many personnel changes, at one stage adding drums, electric bass and piano for a modern sound, an addition they later regretted. Jackson Browne, the legendary writer-singer, was with the group for a while. In 1967 they had a hit with their first release, *Buy For Me The Rain*. In 1968 they had a starring role in *Paint Your Wagon*, the first pop group to get a major role in a high-budget Hollywood musical. Shortly afterward several members decided to go into a different sound and the group split up.

Albums/THE NITTY GRITTY DIRT BAND (February 1965): *Buy For Me The Rain; Euphoria; Melissa; You Took The Happiness; Hard-Hearted Hannah; Holding; Song To Jutta; Candy Man; Dismal Swamp; I Wish I Could Shimmy Like My Sister Kate; Crazy Words, Crazy Tune; You're Gonna Get It In The End.* RICOCHET (August 1967): *Shadow Dream Song; Ooh Po Pe Do Girl; Coney Island Washboard; Put A Bar In My Car; It's Raining Here In Long Beach; I'll Search The Sky; Truly Right; Tide Of Love; Happy Fat Annie; I'll Never Forget What's Her Name; Call Again; The Teddy Bear's Picnic.* RARE JUNK (April 1968): *Reason To Believe; End Of The Line; Sadie Green The Vamp Of New Orleans; Willie The Weeper; Hesitation Blues; Collegiana; Dr. Heckle And Mr. Jibe; Cornbread And 'Lasses; Number And A Name; Mournin' Blues; These Days.* ALIVE (March 1969): *Crazy Words, Crazy Tunes; Fat Boys; Candy Man; Foggy Mountain Breakdown; Alligator Man; Buy For Me The Rain; Rock Me Baby; Goodnight, My Love, Pleasant Dreams.*

Singles/*Buy For Me The Rain*/*Candy Man* (February 1967); *Truly Right*/*The Teddy Bear's Picnic* (June 1967); *These Days*/*Collegiana* (July 1968).

STEVE NOONAN/A folk singer (from California) who has moved into the folk-flavored art song. His nervous first album made in 1968 is *not* a good example of his singing, but it is a good example of what a good songwriter he is (he wrote *Buy For Me the Rain,* which was a hit for the Nitty Gritty Dirt Band). He's one of those people everyone in the know feels must be watched carefully.

Album/STEVE NOONAN (March 1968): *Leaning Back And Laughing; Tide Of Love; All Your Flowers; She's A Flying Thing; Back Alley Dream Street Song; Tumble Down; Street Singer; The Painter; Shadow Dream Song; Buy For Me The Rain; Trusting Is A Harder Thing.*

LAURA NYRO/She is a 20-year-old white New Yorker who sings like a 55-year-old black lady from Mississippi. The experts say she will do for soul pop what Dylan did for folk. Apart from her two sweet-sad albums whose lyrics have a lot of Donovan and Dylan in them, she wrote *Stoned Soul Picnic* for the Fifth Dimension, giving them back the soul sound they'd abandoned, not to mention a major hit. Although she herself has yet to come up with that same sort of smash single, many people sing her songs and her albums are highly successful.

Albums/MORE THAN A NEW DISCOVERY (February 1967): *Wedding Bell Blues; Goodbye Joe; Billy's Blues; And When I Die; Stoney End; Lazy Susan; Hands Off The Man; Buy And Sell; He's A Runner; Blowin' Away; I Never Meant To Hurt You; California Shoe-Shine Boys.* ELI AND THE THIRTEENTH CONFESSION (April 1968): *Luckie; Lu; Sweet Blindness; Poverty Train; Lonely Woman; Eli's Comin'; Timer; Stoned Soul Picnic; Emmie; Woman's Blues; Once It Was Alright Now (Farmer Joe); December's Boudoir; The Confession.*

Singles/*And When I Die*/*Flim Flam Man* (April 1967); *Eli's Coming*/*Sweet Blindness; Save The Country*/*Timer; Stoney End*/*Flim Flam Man* (November 1968); *And When I Die*/*I Never Meant To Hurt You* (March 1969).

PHIL OCHS/Bob Dylan was not the only one to be a poet, politician, singer, composer, news commentator and arch satirist in one big, beautiful, exploitable package. Somewhat contemporary with and subsequent to Dylan and the protest boom was then New York based, Texas-born Phil Ochs, whose first album, in 1964, *ALL THE NEWS THAT'S FIT TO SING*, established him as the first of the singing journalists He thought like a journalist, wrote like one, rhymed what he came up with, set it to music and sang it. When the topical song faded in 1966, so did Phil, but not for long.

When the topic was drugs, not politics, he still wrote his story, freaked it a little around the edges and sang it in that same flat, deadpan, throwaway little-boy-lost voice. Political revolutions, psychedelic revolutions—as long as someone was marching someone to the tumbrils it called for a song. There are those who'd like to believe Ochs is finished because he has never gone electric or Eastern or anything. There are others who think he hasn't even gotten started. There's too much there to write off. Ochs is currently doing what most wise men do from time to time: recharging his batteries.

Albums/ALL THE NEWS THAT'S FIT TO SING (April 1964): *One More Parade; Thresher; Talking Vietnam; Lou Marsh; Power And The Glory; Celia; Bells; Automation Song; Ballad Of William Worthy; Knock On The Door; Talking Cuban Crisis; Too Many Martyrs; Bound For Glory; What's That I Hear.* I AIN'T MARCHING ANYMORE (February 1965): *I Ain't Marching Anymore; In The Heat Of The Summer; Draft Dodger Rag; That's What I Want To Hear; That Was The President; Iron Lady; The Highwayman; Links On The Chain; Hills Of West Virginia; The Men Behind The Guns; Talking Birmingham Jam; Ballad Of The Carpenter; Days Of Decision; Here's To The State Of Mississippi.* PHIL OCHS IN CONCERT (April 1966): *I'm Going To Say It Now; Bracero; Ringing Of Revolution; Is There Anybody Here; Canon Of Christianity; There But For Fortune; Cops Of The World; Santo Domingo; Changes; Love Me, I'm A Liberal; When I'm Gone.* PLEASURES OF THE HARBOR (November 1967): *Cross My Heart; Flower Lady; Outside Of A Small Circle Of Friends; I've Had Her; Miranda; The Party; Pleasures Of The Harbor; The Crucifixion.*

TAPE FROM CALIFORNIA (September 1968): *Tape From California; White Boots Marching In A Yellow Land; Half A Century High; Joe Hill; War Is Over; Harder They Fall; When In Rome; Floods Of Florence.* REHEARSALS FOR RETIREMENT (March 1969).

Singles/*Harder They Fall/War Is Over* (October 1967); *Cross My Heart/Flower Lady* (October 1967); *Outside Of A Small Circle Of Friends/Miranda* (December 1967); *My Life/World Began In Eden & Ended In Los Angeles* (June 1969).

ODETTA (Odetta Felious)/A folk singer with a voice so strong that every filling in your mouth aches when she hits her top notes. When the first stirrings of the folk boom started in 1956, she was there, and she's been there ever since doing everything from Christmas spirituals to *Strawberry Fields Forever.* She's one of the few early folk people who are still around—doing extremely well, and still into everything that's happening.

Albums/MY EYES HAVE SEEN (July 1959): *Poor Little Jesus; Bald-Headed Woman; I Know Where I'm Going; I've Been Driving On Bald Mt.; Motherless Children; Water Boy; Ox Driver Song; Down On Me; No More Cane On The Brazos Saro Jane; Three Pigs; Jumpin' Judy; Battle Hymn Of The Republic.* ODETTA AT TOWN HALL (March 1962): *Let Me Ride; The Fox; Santy Anna, Devilish Mary; Another Man Done Gone; He Had A Long Chain On; He's Got The Whole World In His Hands; Take This Hammer; Ox Driver; Hound Dog; Carry It Back To Rosie;* Three Others & Medley. ODETTA (May 1963): *John Henry; Old Cotton Fields At Home; Run, Come See Jerusalem; Frozen Logger; Old Blue; Water Boy; Santy Anna; I Was Born About 10,000 Years Ago; Car-car Song; I've Been Buked & I've Been Scorned; No More Cane On The Brazos; Pay Day At Coal Creek; Rock Island Line.* ODETTA SINGS FOLK SONGS (August 1963): *900 Miles; Blowing In The Wind; Maybe She Go, I Never Will Marry; Yes I See; Why Oh Why; Shenandoah; Golden Vanity; Roberta; All My Trials; Anthem Of The Rainbow; This Little Light Of Mine.* ONE GRAIN OF SAND (November 1963): *Sail Away Ladies; Moses, Moses;*

Midnight Special; Rambler Gambler; Cotton Fields; Ain't No Grave; Roll On, Buddy; Rambling Round Your City; Special Delivery Blues; Come All Ye Fair & Tender Ladies; Cool Water; She Moved Through The Fair; One Grain Of Sand. ODETTA AT THE GATE OF HORN: *Deep River; Chilly Winds; Take This Hammer; Midnight Special; He's Got The Whole World In His Hands; Sail Away Ladies, Sail Away; Gallows Pole; Lowlands; The Fox; Maybe She Go; Lass From The Low Country; Timber; Greensleeves; Devilish Mary; All The Pretty Little Horses.* ODETTA SINGS DYLAN (March 1965): *Baby, I'm In The Mood For You; Long Ago & Far Away; Don't Think Twice, It's All Right; Tomorrow Is A Long Time; Masters Of War; Walkin' Down The Line; Times They Are A-Changin'; With God On Our Side; Long Time Gone; Mr. Tambourine Man.* BALLAD FOR AMERICANS (September 1965): *This Land; On Top Of Old Smokey; Dark As A Dungeon; Hush Little Baby; Payday At Coal Creek; Great Historical Bum; Going Home; Pastures Of Plenty.* ODETTA IN JAPAN (December 1965): *If I Had A Hammer; Kaeshite Okure Ima Suguni; The Fox; Chilly Winds; No More Cane On The Brazos; One Man's Hands; On Top Of Old Smokey; Sakura; Hush Little Baby; Why Oh Why; Joshua Fit The Battle Of Jericho; We Shall Overcome.* ODETTA (May 1967): *Give Me Your Hand; Strawberry Fields Forever; Love Songs Of The Nile; Oh My Babe; Oh Papa; Little Red Caboose; Child Of God; Turn Me 'Round; African Prayer; Little Girl Blue; Hogan's Alley.* BEST OF ODETTA (May 1967): *Mule Skinner Blues; If I Had A Ribbon Bow; Shame & Scandal; Buked & Scorned; Joshua; He's Got The Whole World In His Hands; The Fox; Lass From The Low Country; Devilish Mary; Take This Hammer.* ODETTA AT CARNEGIE HALL (August 1967): *If I Had A Hammer; John Riley; John Henry; Hold On; Prettiest Train;* Ten Other Titles. ODETTA SINGS THE BLUES (January 1968): *Hawd, Oh Lord; Believe I'll Go; Oh, Papa; How Long Blues; Hogan's Alley; Leavin' This Mornin'; Oh, My Babe; Yonder Come The Blues; Make Me A Pallet On Your Floor; Go Down Sunshine; Nobody Knows You When You're Down And Out.*

OHIO EXPRESS/*Douglas Grassel (rhythm guitar), Tim Cor-*

*win (drums), Dean Kastran (bass guitar), Jim Pfayler (or-
gan), Dale Powers lead guitar).*
They started when they were still in high school and still living
with their families in Ohio. *Beg, Borrow and Steal,* their first
hit, was very soulful rock. But they had a bigger hit with
Yummy, Yummy, Yummy, which immediately became the
living and breathing example of how in 1968, when rock was
never more progressive, shlock rock still could and did dominate the charts both in America and in England. It's still
possible to use a big shlock hit to publicize and finance a
group into bigger and better things, and Ohio Express is only
one of many groups that has chosen that particular way up.
(See BUBBLEGUM MUSIC)

Albums/BEG, BORROW AND STEAL (April 1968): *Beg,
Borrow & Steal; And It's True; Had To Be Me; Let Go; Soul
Struttin'; Try It; I Know We'll Be Together; I Find I Think
Of You; Stop, Take A Look Around; Hard Times; It's Too
Groovy.* YUMMY YUMMY YUMMY (September 1968):
*Yummy, Yummy, Yummy; Down At Lulu's; Winter Skies;
Into This Time; First Grade Reader; Mary Anne; Turn To
Straw; Vacation; She's Not Coming Home; It's A Sad Day;
The Time You Spent With Me.* MERCY (May 1969).

Singles/*Beg, Borrow & Steal/Maybe; Soul Struttin'/Try It;
Yummy, Yummy, Yummy/Zig Zag; Down At Lulu's/She's
Not Comin' Home; Chewy Chewy/Firebird* (October 1968);
Mercy/Roll It Up (March 1969).

ROY ORBISON/What is the secret of Roy Orbison's success?
He's not beautiful or even grotesquely arresting. His stage act
is nonexistent. When singers all went hairy, Texas-born Orbison stayed pompadoured. A lone cowboy dressed in black
with a pale face and perennial shades, he had an air that
managed to be both sinister and old-fashioned. Yet he's
constantly touring; he has the most fanatic fan clubs in
England and Australia; and even in America, where he
doesn't have major hits anymore, he still has an impressive
following.

Orbison started in 1956 in the Elvis days and never really
outgrew them. He's the last person anyone would think of
trying to make a star and yet his sweet-sad songs attract not

just record buyers, but other singers, especially, during the early rock boom, people like the late Buddy Holly, Jerry Lee Lewis, and the Everly Brothers. He toured with the Beatles when he was big and they weren't. He toured with Elvis when Elvis was still a country singer, not a rock star. Nashville claims Orbison as a country singer, but he has to this day a lot of the mood of early rock. There must have been a million country singers trying to make it in rock after Elvis. Orbison, in his puzzling way, was one of the few who actually did. (See CANDYMEN)

Albums/ROY ORBISON, GREATEST HITS (October 1962); IN DREAMS (March 1964): *In Dreams; Shahdaroba; No One Will Ever Know; Dream; All I Have To Do Is Dream; Lonely Wine; Sunset; Blue Bayou; Gigolette; My Prayer; Beautiful Dreamer.* THERE IS ONLY ONE ROY ORBISON (October 1965): *Ride Away; You Fool You; Two Of A Kind; If You Can't Say Something Nice; This Is Your Song; I'm In A Blue, Blue Mood; Claudette; Afraid To Sleep; Sugar And Honey; Summer Love; Big As I Can Dream; Wondering.* ORBISONGS (December 1965): *Pretty Woman; Dance; Say You're My Girl; Good Night; Night Life; Let The Good Times Roll; I Get So Sentimental; Wedding Day; Yo Te Amo Maria; Sleepy Hollow; 22 Days; I'll Be A Legend In My Time.* ORBISON WAY (February 1966): *Crawling Back; It Ain't No Big Thing; Time Changed Everything; This Is My Land; The Loner; Maybe; Breakin' Up Is Breakin' My Heart; Go Away; New Star; Never; It Wasn't Very Long Ago; Why Hurt The One Who Loves You.* CLASSIC ROY ORBISON (August 1966): *You'll Never Be Sixteen Again; Pantomime; Twinkle Toes; Losing You; City Life; Wait; Growing Up; Where Is Tomorrow; I'll Never Get Over You; Going Back To Gloria; Just Another Name For Rock And Roll; Never Love Again.* VERY BEST OF ROY ORBISON (August 1966): *Only The Lonely; Cryin'; Running Scared; It's Over; Candy Man; Oh Pretty Woman; Blue Angel; In Dreams; Dream Baby; Mean Woman Blues.* ROY ORBISON SINGS DON GIBSON (January 1967): *Legend In My Time; I'm Hurting; Oh, Such A Stranger; Same Street; Far Far Away; Big-Hearted Me; Sweet Dreams; Blue, Blue Day; What About Me; Give Myself A Party; Too Soon To Know;*

Lonesome Number One. FASTEST GUITAR ALIVE (June 1967): *Whirlwind; Medicine Man; River, Fastest Guitar Alive; Rollin' On; Pistolero; Good Time Party; Heading South; Best Friend; There Won't Be Many Coming Home.* CRY SOFTLY LONELY ONE (November 1967): *She; Communication Breakdown; Cry Softly Lonely One; Girl Like Mine; It Takes One (To Know One); Just Let Me Make Believe; Here Comes The Rain, Baby; That's A No No; Time To Cry; Memories; Only Alive.* ROY ORBISON AT THE ROCK HOUSE: *Rock House; You're My Baby; Mean Little Mama; This Kind Of Love; Devil Doll; It's Too Late; Tryin' To Get To You; Sweet And Easy To Love; I Never Knew; You're Gonna Cry; Ooby Dooby; Problem Child.* EARLY ORBISON: *She Wears My Ring; Blue Avenue; Cry; Bye Bye Love; Great Pretender; I Can't Stop Loving You; I'll Say It's My Fault; Love Hurts; Raindrops; Come Back To Me (My Love); Summer Song; Pretty One.* MORE OF ROY ORBISON'S GREATEST HITS: *It's Over; Blue Bayou; Indian Wedding; In Dreams; Lana; Falling; Workin' For The Man; Mean Woman Blues; Pretty Paper; Leah; Borne On The Wind; What'd I Say.* ROY ORBISON'S MANY MOODS (April 1969): *Truly, Truly True; Unchained Melody; More; I Recommend Her; Heartache; Amy; What Now My Love; Good Morning, Dear; Walk On; Try To Remember; Yesterday's Child.*

Singles/*Paper Boy/With The Bug; Pretty One/Up Town, Here Comes That Song Again/Only The Lonely; Blue Angel/Today's Teardrops; I Can't Stop Loving You/I'm Hurtin'; Running Scared/Love Hurts; Crying/Candy Man; The Actress/Dream Baby; The Crowd/Mama; Leah/Workin' For The Man; In Dreams/Shahdaroba; Blue Bayou/Mean Woman Blues; Beautiful Dreamer/Pretty Paper; Distant Drums/Falling; Indian Wedding/It's Over; Oh Pretty Woman/Yo Te Amo Maria; Pistolero/Cry Softly Lonely One* (June 1967): *Born To Be Loved By You/Shy Away* (January 1968); *Flowers/Walk On.*

ORIENT EXPRESS is one of the few rock groups entitled to play Near Eastern rock. It is made up of a French oud player, a Belgian guitarist and a Persian drummer. They have one album out. The group now works out of New York's East Village.

Album/THE ORIENT EXPRESS (January 1969): *Train To Bombay; For A Moment; Layla; Azaar; Caravan Of Silk; Birds Of India; Cobra Fever; Dance For Me; A Little Star; Impulse (42 Drums); Fruit Of The Desert.*

BUCK OWENS AND HIS BUCKAROOS/Buck Owens is a country singer from Texas who has made a pledge to stay country. His mood is country, his costume and style country, his following (enormous) country, but his beat has been delighting educated rock fans for some years. Most of the country people who "defected" to rock, like, say, Elvis Presley, stayed in rock, or anyway didn't go back to country till rock gave them the bounce. But Owens, who has won more awards than any artist in the history of country music and accounts for more than several million sales, has seduced rock fans to country instead of the other way around. In any case, with the 1968 merging of rock and country (the Byrds, Bob Dylan, the Band), Owens has come in for more than even his usual large share of attention.

Albums/FABULOUS COUNTRY MUSIC SOUND OF BUCK OWENS. BUCK OWENS (March 1961). BUCK OWENS SINGS HARLAN HOWARD (August 1961). YOU'RE FOR ME (October 1962). ON THE BANDSTAND (June 1963). BUCK OWENS SINGS TOMMY COLLINS (November 1963). BEST OF BUCK OWENS (June 1964). TOGETHER AGAIN (October 1964). I DON'T CARE (December 1964). I'VE GOT A TIGER BY THE TAIL (May 1965). INSTRUMENTAL HITS OF BUCK OWENS AND THE BUCKAROOS (August 1965). BEFORE YOU GO/NO ONE BUT YOU (August 1965). ROLL OUT THE RED CARPET (March 1966). DUST ON MOTHER'S BIBLE (June 1966). CARNEGIE HALL CONCERT (September 1966). OPEN UP YOUR HEART (February 1967). AMERICA'S MOST WANTED BAND (May 1967). BUCK OWENS IN JAPAN (June 1967). YOUR TENDER LOVING CARE (September 1967). IT TAKES PEOPLE LIKE YOU (January 1968). BEST OF BUCK OWENS, VOL. 2 (April 1968). NIGHT ON THE TOWN

(May 1968). SWEET ROSIE JONES (August 1968). GUI-
TAR PLAYER (October 1968). BUCK OWENS IN LON-
DON (June 1969).

Singles/ *Act Naturally/Over And Over Again; Love's Gonna
Live Here/Getting Used To Losing You; I Don't Care/Don't
Let Her Know; I've Got A Tiger By The Tail/Cryin' Time; I
Want No One But You/Before You Go; Gonna Have
Love/Only You; Buckaroo/If You Want A Love; Santa
Looked A Lot Like Daddy/All I Want For Xmas Dear Is
You; Waitin' In Your Welfare Line/In The Palm Of Your
Hand; Think Of Me/Heart Of Glass; Open Up Your Heart/
No More Me And You; Together Again/My Heart Skips A
Beat; You're For Me/Above And Beyond; Your Tender
Loving Care/What A Liar I Am; It Takes People Like
You/You Left Her Lonely Too Long; How Long Will My
Baby Be Gone/Everybody Loves Somebody; Sam's
Place/Don't Ever Tell Me Goodbye; Sweet Rosie Jones/Hap-
py Times Are Here Again; Under Your Spell Again/Tired Of
Livin'; Together Again/My Heart Skips A Beat; Down On
The Corner Of Love/Sweetheart In Heaven; Johnny B.
Goode/Maybe If I Close My Eyes* (May 1969).

VAN DYKE PARKS/Whether Van Dyke Parks is a genius,
or merely pretentious, is still being argued on the patios of
Los Angeles and the balconies of Manhattan. Late in 1967 he
did an album so incredible people are still reeling. Both music
and lyrics bristled with musical puns that allude to everything
from Debussy and Mahler to the Andrews sisters. And obviously this small bespectacled person had a breathtaking command of music as a medium. Certainly he's done well recording Harper's Bizarre and writing some songs for them. But
a lot of his fame rests on an eight-month collaboration with
another genius, Brian Wilson of the Beach Boys, a collaboration which was going to produce, between *PET SOUNDS* and
SMILEY SMILE, a superalbum, but for some reason (nobody knows what it is) it was scrapped. Since then everyone
has been afraid to put down Parks in case he turns out to be
the genius of the century. Financially his album was a disaster. It cost a lot to make and sold comparatively few copies.
But if nothing else, it's a landmark in pop experiment.

Album/SONG CYCLE (November 1967): *Vine Street; Palm Desert; Widow's Walk; Laurel Canyon Boulevard; The All Golden; Van Dyke Parks; Public Domain; Donovan's Colours; The Attic; By The People; Pot Pourri.*

PAUL AND PAULA/Now out of the business, Paul and Paula were best known for their 1963 number one single *Hey Paula,* which might have been forgotten by now had it not been revived by that much respected archivist Tiny Tim, who does the number, straight out of pop's teenage love period, singing as usual both voices. The duo might have gone on to become a Simon and Garfunkel or a Sonny and Cher or even a Peter and Gordon had they stuck out the early English invasion, but like so many other American groups who were just beginning to make their mark when the British took over, they gave up without a fight.

Singles/*Hey Paula/Something Old, Something New; First Quarrel/Young Lovers; All These Things/Wedding.*

THE PAUPERS/*Skip Prokop (vocals, drums), Adam Mitchell (rhythm guitar, drums, lead vocals), Chuck Beal (lead guitar, mandolin), Brad Campbell (replaced Denny Gerrard) (bass guitar, drums, vocals).*

In 1967 the word was around that the Paupers were the group to watch. (This was just after the same word got around about the Doors.) They came from Canada where they had been a top group since forming in the summer of 1966. They had original songs by Prokop and Mitchell, a hard-rock sound with folky overtones, a ten-minute bass solo at the end of every set, and three sets of drums. They came out of Canada and were signed up, on the spot, by Bob Dylan's manager. But all that promise wasn't kept. In 1969 the group disbanded.

Albums/MAGIC PEOPLE (September 1967): *Magic People; It's Your Mind; Black Thank You Package; Let Me Be; Think I Care; One Rainy Day; Tudor Impressions; Simple Deeds; My Love Hides Your View; You And Me.* ELLIS ISLAND (September 1968): *South Down Road; Cairo Hotel; Can't Go On; Another Man's Hair On My Razor; Numbers; Oh That She Might; Yes I Know; Ask Her Again; Julliana.*

Singles/ *Let Me Be*/ *Simple Deeds* (February 1967); *Tudor Impressions*/ *One Rainy Day* (May 1967); *Black Thank You Package*/ *Magic People* (July 1967); *Think I Care*/ *White Song* (November 1967); *Another Man's Hair On My Razor*/ *Cairo Hotel* (November 1968).

TOM PAXTON/The trouble with Tom Paxton is that he's been too good too long and people take him for granted in a way they never would if he had appeared on the scene for the first time ever in 1969. In 1964 he may have been singing along with other folk singers that his lady was a wild flying dove, but he was also doing a good deal of singing journalism with *What Did You Learn in School Today?* and *Daily News*. His *Lyndon Johnson Told the Nation* anticipated President Johnson's unpopular period by several years. He is easily music's wittiest singer (*Talking Vietnam Pot Luck Blues*). Inspired by the often topical songs of Pete Seeger and Woody Guthrie, he has been a huge influence on all protest singers, especially Bob Dylan, Joan Baez, Judy Collins and Phil Ochs.

Albums/RAMBLIN' BOY (October 1964): *Job Of Work; Rumblin' In The Land; What Did You Learn In School Today; When Morning Breaks; Daily News; Last Thing On My Mind; Harper; Fare Thee Well, Cisco; I Can't Help But Wonder Where I'm Bound; High Sheriff Of Hazard; My Lady's A Wild, Flying Dove; Standing On The Edge Of Town; I'm Bound For The Mountains And The Sea; Goin' To The Zoo; Ramblin' Boy.* AIN'T THAT NEWS (October 1965): *Ain't That News; The Willing Conscript; Lyndon Johnson Told The Nation; Hold On To Me Babe; Name Of The Game Is Stud; Bottle Of Wine; The Natural Girl For Me; We Didn't Know; Goodman, Schwerner And Chaney; Buy A Gun For Your Son; Every Time; Georgie On The Freeways; Sully's Pail; I'm The Man Who Built The Bridges.* OUTWARD BOUND (September 1966): *Leaving London; Don't You Let Nobody Turn You 'Round; My Son John; King Of My Backyard; One Time And One Time Only; When You Get Your Ticket; All The Way Home; Is This Any Way To Run An Airline; This World Goes 'Round And 'Round; I Followed Her Into The West; Talking Pop Art; I Believe, I Do; Outward Bound.* MORNING AGAIN (May 1968):

*Jennifer's Rabbit; Mr. Blue; Victoria Dines Alone; Hooker;
So Much For Winning; Pot Luck Blues; Talking Viet Nam;
Clarissa Jones; Morning Again; Thousand Years; Now That
I've Taken My Life.*

PEACHES AND HERB/*Herb Fame, Francine Barker (replaced Marlene Mack who replaced Francine "Day" Barker).*
Peaches and Herb are the sweethearts of soul. They must be,
with five hits in 1967 all built around the theme of love and
kisses. *Let's Fall In Love* was their first; then *Close Your
Eyes, Love Is Strange, For Your Love* and *Two Little Kids.*
It was a year when golden duets looked as if they would be
big on the charts (Otis Redding and Carla Thomas also
teamed up). If white duos have not done as well as black
ones, it may be because there seems to be a little bit more bite
in the banter of the latter.

Albums/LET'S FALL IN LOVE (January 1967): *Tenderly;
Let's Fall In Love; Don't Know Why; Melody Of Love; True
Love; Anniversary Song; Falling In Love With Love; As Time
Goes By; Can't Help Falling In Love; Always; I'm In The
Mood For Love; Let Me Call You Sweetheart.* FOR YOUR
LOVE (July 1967): *For Your Love; Things I Want To Hear;
I Love How You Love Me; Embraceable You; Everybody
Loves A Lover; It's True I Love You; Answer Me My Love;
Door Is Still Open To My Heart; I Need Your Love So
Desperately; My Life; Count On Me.* GOLDEN DUETS
(December 1967): *Two Little Kids; Rockin' Good Way; Let
It Be Me; What's The Matter With You Baby; Something
You Got; Somethin' Stupid; Love Is Strange; Baby (You Got
What It Takes); Mockingbird; We Belong Together; I Want
To Stay Here; I Do.* PEACHES AND HERB'S GREATEST
HITS (July 1968): *United; Let's Fall In Love; Two Little
Kids; We've Got To Love One Another; For Your Love;
Close Your Eyes; What A Lovely Way; Love Is Strange; I
Need Your Love So Desperately; Ten Commandments Of
Love; It's True I Love You.*

Singles/*We're In This Thing Together/Let's Fall In Love*
(August 1966); *Close Your Eyes/I Will Watch Over You*
(March 1967); *For Your Love/I Need Your Love So Des-
perately* (June 1967); *Love Is Strange/It's True I Love You*
(September 1967); *Two Little Kids/We've Got To Love One*

Another (November 1967); *The Ten Commandments Of Love/What A Lovely Way* (February 1967); *United/Thank You* (April 1968); *Let's Make A Promise/Me And You* (October 1968); *We've Got To Love One Another/So True* (December 1968); *Close Your Eyes/For Your Love* (March 1969).

PEANUT BUTTER CONSPIRACY/*Al Brackett (bass), Bill Wolff (replaced Lance Fent) (guitar, harmonica), John Merrill (rhythm guitar), Sandi Robinson (female vocals), Jim Voight (drums).*
The Peanut Butter Conspiracy emerged in California early in 1967 as one of the first of what were eventually to be hundreds of groups with trippy names. Their music was a blend of blues, rock and raga—the West Coast sound that was then still reasonably new and had yet to spread East. Their first album was named after their superpromotable slogan, *THE PEANUT BUTTER CONSPIRACY IS SPREADING*. Their notable singles were *It's a Happening Thing* and *Turn On a Friend (to the Good Life)*. Some of the novelty appeal they had at the beginning of their career faded somewhat when groups with trippier names, trippier songs and trippier music eventually overtook them.

Albums/THE PEANUT BUTTER CONSPIRACY IS SPREADING (March 1967): *It's A Happening Thing; Then Came Love; You Can't Be Found; Twice Is Life; Second-Hand Man; Why Did I Get So High; Dark On You Now; The Market Place; You Should Know; Most Up Till Now; You Took Too Much*. THE GREAT CONSPIRACY (December 1967): *Turn On A Friend; Lonely Leaf; Pleasure; Too Many Do; Living, Loving Life; Invasion Of The Poppy People; Captain Living Dream; Ecstasy; Time Is After You; Wonderment*.

Singles/*It's A Happening Thing/Twice Is Life* (January 1967); *Dark On You Now/Then Came Love* (March 1967); *Floating Dream/Time Is After You; I'm A Fool/It's So Hard* (November 1968).

Also Appear On/WEST COAST LOVE-IN: *Time Is After You; One-Nine-Six-Seven; Big Bummer; Floating Dream; Dark On You Now; Roses Gone*.

PEARLS BEFORE SWINE/*Tom Rapp (guitar, vocals), Jim Bohannon (replaced Roger Crissinger) (organ, piano, clavinette, marimba), Wayne Harley (banjo, autoharp, mandolin, vibraphone), Lane Lederer (bass, guitar).*

We already know about acid rock. What the underground group called Pearls Before Swine sings is acid *folk*, that is, folk music affected by the discoveries of an LSD-influenced generation. This four-man Florida-born group is best known for *Uncle John*, as bitter a cry against the injustices of American society as anything that came out of the protest-folk and protest-rock era. The alternative is offered in songs like *Drop Out* and *I Shall Not Care*, the only possible stand the young and innocent of the Pearls Before Swine world can take in a society they see as cold, heartless and totally wrong.

Albums/ONE NATION UNDERGROUND (October 1967):

Another Time; Playmate; Ballad To An Amber Lady; (Oh Dear) Miss Morse; Drop Out; Morning Song; Regions Of May; Uncle John; I Shall Not Care; The Surrealist Waltz. BALAKLAVA (November 1968): *Trumpeter Landfrey; Translucent Carriages; Images Of April; There Was A Man; I Saw The World; Guardian Angels; Suzanne; Lepers And Roses; Florence Nightingale . . .; Ring Thing.*

DAVID PEEL AND THE LOWER EAST SIDE/*David Peel (vocals), Harold C. Black (tambourine), Larry Adam (guitar), Billy Joe White (guitar), George Cori (washtub bass).*

A singer and songwriter, David Peel was discovered in 1968 singing at an impromptu Sunday afternoon hootenanny (yes, they still used the word in 1968 from time to time) in Washington Square. And not only that, he was recorded there. He had first surfaced with banana-smoking campaigns at the 1967 Central Park Be-ins, then became a street singer with a portable audience that acted as an answering chorus. Their first album, *HAVE A MARIJUANA*, for which Peel wrote the lyrics and music, starts with David just rapping in a general way and then using a song to make a more specific point. The talk and songs are of drugs and sex, winos and tourists. It is probably the first time a performance of street theatre has gone on record. His *Up Against the Wall* is true urban folk.

Album/HAVE A MARIJUANA (January 1969): *Mother, Where Is My Father; I Like Marijuana; Here Comes A Cop; I've Got Some Grass; Happy Mother's Day; Up Against The Wall; I Do My Bawling In The Bathroom; The Alphabet Song; Show Me The Way To Get Stoned; We Love You.*

PENNY WHISTLERS/A group of girls who play only the folk and never the rock circuit—unusual in the late sixties, when rock and folk chose to intermingle (and almost couldn't help it). The intricate harmonies of the Eastern European folk songs they do have intrigued rock musicians like Al Kooper, but so far no rock *singers* have attempted them.

Albums/PENNY WHISTLERS (April 1966): Collection of 15 Folk Songs From Bulgaria, Macedonia, Czechoslovakia And Others. COOL DAY AND CROOKED CORN (May 1967): Collection of Russian, Bulgarian, Polish, Yiddish and Other Folk Songs.

PENTANGLE/*Terry Cox (drums), Bert Jansch (guitar), Jacqui McShee (vocals), John Renbourn (vocals, guitar), Danny Thompson (bass).*
It has never seemed exactly fair that the rockers and the ravers went on to make all the money when the quiet folk singers, who had been there right from the start, struggled along with tiny ingroup audiences just because they were unwilling to sell out to the new big sound. As hard rock receded and the music scene became more and more receptive to other sounds and other styles, groups like the Pentangle emerged.
The group's sound is pre-Beatles folk, soft and gentle and musically literate. Only one amplified instrument is used, a guitar, and even that not too often. The drummer will climb out of his perch to perform on the glockenspiel. The two singers, both well-known English folk singers, perform together and separately in pure folk style. Bert Jansch, the legendary guitarist who inspired Donovan, and many others, is the fourth member of the group; and the fifth member, a rarity in the pop-rock world, is a bass player who plays acoustic stand-up bass. It's not rock but ultrasophisticated folk, and from its acceptance on a 1969 U.S. tour, it would seem that

this English group has opened up the way for other folk ensembles rather than the usual folk soloist.

Album/THE PENTANGLE (October 1968): *Let No Man Steal Your Thyme; Bells; Hear My Call; Pentangling; Mirage; Way Behind The Sun; Bruton Town; Waltz.*

Single/*Let No Man Steal Your Thyme/Way Behind The Sun* (October 1968).

CARL PERKINS/When a country singer called Elvis Presley moved into something very new called rock and roll many other singers followed him, but some also had thought of the same thing at the same time. When Elvis was just beginning, Carl Perkins was doing a rocking country thing (that was later the basis for rock and roll). He wrote a song called *Blue Suede Shoes* and released his own version of it at an unfortunate time—just when Elvis was making his first astonishing impact on the charts. *Blue Suede Shoes* might have been a number one record if Elvis hadn't just come up with *Heartbreak Hotel*, which hugged that number one spot for weeks. Later it was too late, and when the song did make it, it was with Presley singing it. Of the big three at Memphis' Sun Records (Perkins, Presley and Johnny Cash), Perkins was the only one who never made it on the million dollar international level, though like the others he had what it took. He now does what a lot of former rock stars who started as country singers do—he's back in the country circuit, traveling with Johnny Cash.

Albums/CARL PERKINS: *Blue Suede Shoes; Movie Magg; Sure To Fall; Gone, Gone, Gone; Honey Don't; Only; Tennessee; Your True Love; Wrong Yo Yo; Everybody's Trying To Be My Baby; Matchbox; Boppin' The Blues.* INTO CARL PERKINS.

Singles/*Blue Suede Shoes/Money Don't; All Mama's Children/Boppin' The Blues; For A Little While/Help Me Find My Baby; Let My Baby Be/Monkeyshine.*

Also Appears On/COUNTRY SALUTE TO HANK WILLIAMS. GOLDEN SOUNDS OF COUNTRY MUSIC: *Pointed Toe Shoes.* MILLION SELLERS: *Blue Suede Shoes; Boppin' The Blues.* OLDIES BUT GOODIES, VOL 4: *Blue Suede Shoes.*

PETER AND GORDON (Peter Asher and Gordon Waller)/
An early English duo, Peter and Gordon came over with the
first English invasion of 1964. Peter had the distinction of
being the brother of Jane Asher, then girl friend of Beatle
Paul McCartney. They got the first number one record with
McCartney's *World Without Love* after the Beatles' first
triumphant entry into the U.S. charts in 1964. Another of
their big hits was a song called *Woman* by Bernard Webb, an
unknown songwriter. After a suitably coy and modest silence,
Paul McCartney announced that he, in fact, was Bernard
Webb and he had just wondered if a Beatle song by another
writer would make it. Apparently it did. Subsequent hits were
more in the clever, novelty line. Peter worked as a producer
for the Beatles' Apple Corps and was head of the Artists
and Repertoire (A & R) department. He has since left. Gordon sings solo. Both still sing together for records.

Albums/WORLD WITHOUT LOVE (August 1964): *Lucille;
Five Hundred Miles; If I Were You; Pretty Mary; Trouble In
Mind; Tell Me How; World Without Love; You Don't Have
To Tell Me; Leave My Woman Alone; All My Trials; Last
Night I Woke.* I DON'T WANT TO SEE YOU AGAIN
(November 1964): *I Don't Want To See You Again; Nobody
I Know; My Babe; Willow Garden; Two Little Love Birds;
Land Of Oden; Freight Train; Love Me, Baby; Soft As The
Dawn; Leave Me Alone; Lonely Avenue.* PETER AND
GORDON—I GO TO PIECES (April 1965): *I Go To
Pieces; Sleepless Nights; Tears Don't Stop; If You Wish; All
Shook Up; Whatcha Gonna Do 'Bout It; Good Morning
Blues; Someone Ain't Right; A Mess Of Blues; I Still Love
You; I Don't Care What They Say.* TRUE LOVE WAYS
(July 1965): *Don't Pity Me; Cry To Me; To Know You Is
To Love You; I Told You So; Who's Lovin' You; Any Day
Now; Crying In The Rain; Hurtin' Is Lovin'; Broken Prom-
ises; When The Black Of Your Eyes Turn To Grey; True
Love Ways.* WOMAN (February 1966): *Woman; Wrong
From The Start; As Long As I Have You; Let It Be Me;
Green Leaves Of Summer; High Noon; I Know A Man;
Black, Brown And Gold; 3:10 To Yuma; Somewhere; There's
No Living Without Your Loving.* BEST OF PETER AND

GORDON (May 1966): *A World Without Love; True Love Ways; If I Were You; I Told You So; To Know You Is To Love You; Don't Pity Me; I Go To Pieces; I Don't Want To See You Again; Love Me, Baby; If You Wish; Woman.* PETER AND GORDON SING AND PLAY THE HITS OF NASHVILLE TENNESSEE (September 1966): *I've Got A Tiger By The Tail; Sweet Dreams; Before You Go; Please Help Me, I'm Falling; I'm So Lonesome I Could Cry; The Race Is On; My Heart Skips A Beat; Lonely Street; Send Me The Pillow You Dream On; I Forgot More Than You'll Ever Know; Memphis.* LADY GODIVA (January 1967): *Lady Godiva; The Exodus Song; Young And Beautiful; When I Fall In Love; A Taste Of Honey; Baby I'm Yours; Love Is A Many-Splendored Thing; Morning's Calling; Start Trying Someone Else; If I Fell; Till There Was You.* KNIGHT IN RUSTY ARMOUR (March 1967): *Knight In Rusty Armour; Stranger With A Black Dove; To Show I Love You; A Boy With Nothing; My First Day Alone; Colour Blue; The Flower Lady; I Would Buy You Presents; Baby What You Want Me To Do; Homeward Bound; Young Girl Of Sixteen.* PETER AND GORDON—IN LONDON FOR TEA (June 1967): *London At Night; The Jokers; I'm Your Puppet; Here Comes That Hurt Again; You've Got Your Troubles; Sally Go 'Round The Roses; Sunday For Tea; Red, Cream And Velvet; Stop, Look And Listen; Please Help Me, I'm Falling; Goodbye My Love.* HOT, COLD AND CUSTARD (August 1968): *I Feel Like Going Out; Freedom Is A Breakfast Food; Never Ever; The Magic Story Of The Park Keeper And His Fairy Godmother; Sipping Wine; Greener Days; You've Had Better Times; The Quest For The Holy Grail; She Needs Love; Uncle Hartington; Cos You're A Star.*

Singles/*Speak For Me*/*Little Nonie* (Gordon Waller) (1963); *Never Ever*/*Greener Days* (March 1964); *You've Had Better Times*/*Sipping My Wine* (March 1965); *A World Without Love*/*Nobody I Know* (August 1965); *Woman*/*Wrong From The Start* (January 1966); *Lady Godiva*/*Morning's Calling* (September 1966); *To Show I Love You*/*Someone Else* (November 1966); *Knight In Rusty Armour*/*Flower Lady* (January 1967); *Sunday For Tea*/*Hurtin' Is Love* (May 1967); *There's No Living Without Your Loving*/*Stranger*

With A Black Dove (June 1967); *I Go To Pieces/Love Me Baby* (June 1967).

PETER, PAUL AND MARY/*Peter Yarrow (tenor vocals), Paul Stookey (baritone vocals), Mary Travers (female vocals).*
In the summer of 1961 Fred Weintraub had opened a new place in the Village, the Bitter End, and he'd taken all these advertisements to say that the trio he had there, Peter, Paul and Mary, were the greatest thing that had happened in years. Who really believes that sort of talk from a guy who owns the place? Besides, the real folk action was all up at Gerdes' Folk City and Izzy Young's Folklore Centre, and the few folk people who did venture over to the Bitter End didn't think the two bearded guys and the blonde Villagey looking chick were very *authentic*. A small circle of friends hung around, of course, the still undiscovered Dylan among them. But this was 1962, and folk music wasn't where it was happening as far as money went. What was happening on the uptown music charts was the twist, Neil Sedaka and the Monster Mash.

The story of Peter, Paul and Mary begins with Albert Grossman, today the formidable manager of Dylan, Janis Joplin, the Band, Richie Havens, Butterfield, and Odetta, but previously known mainly for running the early Newport Folk Festivals. Folk performers had gotten into the charts from time to time, but only because of one good song, not as a consistent pattern. One big exception was the Kingston Trio, whose success made it clear that there was room at the top for a certain sort of processed pop folk. It was Grossman's inspiration to improve on the all-male Kingston Trio formula by teaming up two men and one girl, matching them carefully, visually as well as vocally. That was when Joan Baez was starting to move and Mary, blonde, long-haired gypsy that she was, was cast in the same mold. And there are people who say that if they didn't know better they'd suspect the Machiavellian Grossman arranged for facial surgery to heighten the resemblance between Peter and Paul. As for the names, could a man hope for better? Would they have had a chance as Marvin, Seymour and Shirley?

The rest is history. The PPM sound was a huge commercial

success, and every single a hit. There were mutterings among the folk purists that they had sold out musically, but what the purists didn't know then was that Peter, Paul and Mary's success would open the doors for a massive folk take-over and, later, for Dylan, folk rock and a whole new American music scene that wasn't dominated by Tin Pan Alley. Their first big hit was a song by Pete Seeger that folk people had known for years (*If I Had A Hammer*). And now here were busboys whistling it and jukeboxes blaring it. And when Bob Dylan happened in a small way, Peter, Paul and Mary, now thoroughly established, were able to make him happen in a *big* way by making *Blowin' In The Wind* one of the top ten songs in the nation. They did a lot of other things that opened up a lot of other doors, directly and indirectly, including making it possible for a lot of folk people to make comfortable livings by letting the American public at large know folk was good entertainment.

Musically, the trio stuck to a predictable but very smooth and professional formula. From time to time they did introduce a new writer as they had Dylan. (One of their newest finds is the gifted Gary Shearston, who wrote *Sometime Lovin'*, which in fact he sings best himself.) The other interesting role Peter, Paul and Mary played was a political one. Generally, singers at the top of the charts had previously stayed out of politics. Peter, Paul and Mary sang at rallies and marches, in the good old folk tradition, but with the additional advantage of a huge public following. They did have a hammer, they had a bell, they had a song to sing, and they sang it where it counted.

Albums/PETER, PAUL AND MARY (May 1962): *This Train; Bamboo; It's Raining; If I Had My Way; Cruel War; Lemon Tree; If I Had A Hammer; Autumn To May; Where Have All The Flowers Gone.* PETER, PAUL AND MARY— MOVING (March 1963): *Settle Down; Gone The Rainbow; Flora; This Land Is Your Land; Pretty Mary; Puff; Tiny Sparrow; Man Come Into Egypt; Old Coat; Big Boat; Morning Train; A'Soalin'.* PETER, PAUL AND MARY—IN THE WIND (December 1963): *Very Last Day; Hush-A-Bye; Long Chain On; Rocky Road; Tell It On The Mountain; Polly Von; Stewball; All My Trials; Don't Think Twice, It's All Right;*

Freight Train; Quit Your Lowdown Ways; Blowin' In The Wind. PETER, PAUL AND MARY IN CONCERT (March 1965): *Times They Are A-Changin'; A'Soalin'; Blue; 500 Miles; Three Ravens; One Kind Favor; Car-Car; Blowin' In The Wind; Puff (The Magic Dragon); Jesus Met The Woman; Le Deserteur; Oh, Rock My Ship; Paultalk; Single Girl; There Is A Ship; It's Raining; If I Had My Way; If I Had A Hammer.* SONG WILL RISE (May 1965): *When The Ship Comes In; Jimmy Whalen; Come And Go With Me; Gilgarry Mountain; Ballad Of Spring Hill; Motherless Child; Wasn't That A Time; Monday Morning; Cuckoo; Talkin' Candy Bar Blues; San Francisco Bay Blues; For Lovin' Me.* SEE WHAT TOMORROW BRINGS (December 1965): *If I Were Free; Betty And Dupree; Rising Of The Moon; Early Mornin' Rain; Jane, Jane; Because All Men Are Brothers; Hangman; Brother, Can You Spare A Dime; The First Time Ever I Saw Your Face; Tryin' To Win; On A Desert Island (With You In My Dreams); Last Thing On My Mind.* PETER, PAUL AND MARY ALBUM (October 1966): *And When I Die; Sometime Lovin'; Pack Up Your Sorrows; King Of Names; For Baby (For Bobbie); Hurry Sundown; Other Side Of This Life; Good Times We Had; Kisses Sweeter Than Wine; Norman Normal; Mon Vrai Destin; Well, Well, Well.* ALBUM 1700 (September 1967): *Rolling Home; Leaving, On A Jet Plane; No Other Name; Weep For Jamie; House Song; I Dig Rock And Roll Music; Great Mandella; If I Had Wings; I'm In Love With A Big Blue Frog; Whatshername; Bob Dylan's Dream; Song Is Love.* LATE AGAIN (1968): *Apologize; Yesterday's Tomorrow; Moments Of The Soft Persuasion; There's Anger In The Land; Too Much Of Nothing; Love City; Hymn; She Dreams; Tramp On The Street; I Shall Be Released; Reason To Believe; Rich Man Poor Man.* PETER, PAUL & MOMMY (May 1969).

Singles/*If I Had A Hammer/Lemon Tree* (1962); *Blowin' In The Wind/Puff* (1963); *I Dig Rock & Roll Music/Great Mandella* (1967); *Too Much Of Nothing/House Song* (1968); *Love City/Yesterday's Tomorrow* (September 1968); *500 Miles/I Dig Rock And Roll Music* (November 1968); *Day Is Done/Make Believe Town* (April 1969).

WILSON PICKETT/One of the big soul kings of music, he

started as a gospel man and singer of spirituals, first solo, then with the Falcons, one of Detroit's top groups. Then he discovered he had a talent for writing rhythm and blues songs—and for singing them. His first single after he went solo again in 1963, one of his own songs, *If You Need Me*, was a hit at once and still is a classic. It has been recorded by everyone from the Stones to Tom Jones. Since then, nearly all the singles he has done (many of them his own compositions) have become not just hits but all-time rock classics. Among the most notable are *In the Midnight Hour, Mustang Sally, Land of 1,000 Dances, Ninety-Nine and A Half* and *I'm a Midnight Mover*. There isn't a rock group with soul leanings that hasn't performed these songs and borrowed more than a little from Pickett. He's probably solely responsible for the 1967-69 "soulization" of literally thousands of young white rock groups that a few years ago wouldn't even have known what the word meant—and possibly still don't.

Albums/ IN THE MIDNIGHT HOUR: *In The Midnight Hour; Teardrops Will Fall; Take A Little Love; For Better Or Worse; I Found A Love; That's A Man's Way; I'm Gonna Cry; Don't Fight It; Take This Love I've Got; Come Home Baby; I'm Not Tired; Let's Kiss & Make Up.* EXCITING WILSON PICKETT: *634-5789; Ninety-Nine And A Half (Won't Do); In The Midnight Hour; Land Of 1,000 Dances; Something You Got; Barefootin'; Mercy, Mercy; You're So Fine; Danger Zone; I'm Drifting; It's All Over; She's So Good To Me.* WICKED PICKETT: *Mustang Sally; New Orleans; Sunny; Ooh Poo Pah Doo; Everybody Needs Somebody; She Ain't Gonna Do Right; Knock On Wood; Time Is On My Side; Up Tight Good Woman; You Left The Water Running; Three Time Loser; Nothing You Can Do.* SOUND OF WILSON PICKETT: *Soul Dance No. 3; Funky Broadway; I Need A Lot Of Loving Every Day; I Found A Love; You Can't Stand Alone; Mojo Mamma; Love Is A Beautiful Thing; I Found The One; Something Within Me; I'm Sorry About That.* BEST OF WILSON PICKETT: *In The Midnight Hour; Don't Fight It; Soul Dance Number Three; 634-5789; Ninety-Nine And A Half (Won't Do); Land Of 1,000 Dances; I Found A Love; Funky Broadway; Mustang Sally; Everybody Needs Somebody To Love; If You Need Me; It's*

Too Late. I'M IN LOVE: *I'm In Love; Stagger Lee; Jealous Love; That Kind Of Love; Hello Sunshine; Don't Cry No More; We've Got To Have Love; Bring It On Home; She Is Looking Good; I've Come A Long Way.* MIDNIGHT MOVER: *I'm A Midnight Mover; It's A Groove; I'm Gonna Cry; Remember, I Been Good To You; Deborah; I Found A True Love; Down By The Sea; Trust Me; Let's Get An Understanding; For Better Or Worse.* GREAT WILSON PICKETT HITS: *If You Need Me; I'm Gonna Love You; Baby Don't Weep; Peace Breaker; Down To My Last Heartbreak; Roberts Monkey Beat; I Can't Stop; I'll Never Be The Same; Baby Call On Me; Give Your Lovin' Right Now; It's Too Late.*

Singles/ *Come Home Baby/ Take A Little Love* (March 1965); *I'm Not Tired/ In The Midnight Hour* (April 1965); *634–5789/ That's A Man's Way* (January 1966); *Don't Fight It/ It's All Over* (April 1966); *Danger Zone/ Ninety-Nine And A Half* (April 1966); *Land Of 1,000 Dances/ You're So Fine* (July 1966); *Mustang Sally/ Three Time Loser* (November 1966); *Everybody Needs Somebody To Love/ Nothing You Can Do* (January 1967); *I Found A Love* (Part I)/ *I Found A Love* (Part 2) (March 1967); *Soul Dance Number Three/ You Can't Stand Alone* (May 1967); *Funky Broadway/ I'm Sorry About That* (July 1967); *I'm In Love/ Stagger Lee* (November 1967); *I've Come A Long Way/ Jealous Love* (February 1968); *She's Lookin' Good/ We've Got To Have Love* (April 1968); *Deborah/ I'm A Midnight Mover* (August 1968); *For Better Or Worse/ I Found A True Love* (August 1968); *I Wish I Knew (How It Would Feel To Be Free)/ It's Just A Matter Of Time* (September 1968); *For Better Or Worse/ I Found A True Love* (September 1968); *People Make The World (What It Is)/ Man And A Half* (November 1968); *Search Your Heart/ Hey Jude* (December 1968); *Born To Be Wild/ Toe Hold* (May 1969).

Also Appears On/ HISTORY OF RHYTHM & BLUES, VOL. 6: *I'm Gonna Cry.* ORIGINAL GOLDEN BLUES GREATS: *If You Need Me.* SATURDAY NIGHT AT THE UPTOWN: *If You Need Me; I'm Gonna Cry.* SOLID GOLD SOUL, VOL. 1: *Don't Fight It; In The Midnight Hour.* SOLID GOLD SOUL, VOL. 2: *634–5789; Danger Zone.*

SUPER HITS, VOL. 1: *Mustang Sally; In The Midnight Hour.* SUPER HITS, VOL. 2: *Funky Broadway.* SUPER SOUL: *If You Need Me; Baby Don't Weep.* THIS IS SOUL: *Land of 1,000 Dancers.*

PINK FLOYD/*Rick Wright (organ, piano, cello, fiddle), Nick Mason (drums), Roger Waters (bass guitar, piano, beat frequency oscillator), Dave Gilmore (replaced Syd Barret) (lead guitar), Mick Lowe (lights).*
Pink Floyd caused much excitement in England early in 1967 by being the first English rock group to come on stage with a light show. They were also one of the first English groups to play San Francisco style psychedelic rock. Since then, trying to understand the music of the Pink Floyd has become a sort of underground hobby in England. As with most experimental groups, it was difficult to decide what was sheer lack of control and what was courageous dabbling in the music of the future. They have been highly praised by some big names in music and dismissed as psychedelic muzak by others. In America, where psychedelic music and light shows started, the Pink Floyd never had quite the impact they had in England. Their experiments involve pure electronic sound, freaky electrical piano and an ethereal organ.
Albums/PINK FLOYD (April 1968): *Gnome; See Emily Play; Chapter 24; Pow R Toch; Interstellar Overdrive; Take Up Thy Stethoscope And Walk; Lucifer Sam; Matilda Mother; Scarecrow.* SAUCERFUL OF SECRETS (September 1968): *Let There Be More Light; Remember A Day; Set The Controls For The Heart Of The Sun; Corporal Clegg; Saucerful Of Secrets; See Saw; Jugband Blues.*

Singles/*Arnold Layne/Candy And A Currant Bun; Scarecrow/See Emily; Flaming/The Gnome.*

ELVIS PRESLEY/The Elvis Presley story has been told so often that it is sometimes difficult to remember that he is alive and well and thriving in Hollywood making film after film after film. Perhaps the reason most of what is written about him has that flat, dead quality of a past event is that Elvis in a sense "died" when he withdrew from the live concert circuit. And both his record releases and films, of which there are

many, have a posthumous quality, as have the nostalgic pieces
that are written about him from time to time. One of those
nostalgic biographers, Kurt Von Meier, pointed out that Elvis
was most alive in his immediate prestardom period. It started
with the release, in 1954, of *Mystery Train* coupled with *I
Forgot To Remember To Forget* on the Sun label in Memphis. The disc made the top of the local country charts and
Elvis went on tour on the country circuit as a promising
newcomer. Within a year he headed his own country and
western shows and might very well have gone on to be a
major country and western star had not the major companies
started to take an interest in him.

He went of course to the highest bidder, RCA Victor,
which had taken note that Elvis' abilities were not confined to
country and western but included rhythm and blues and
general pop potential (most of his singles were backed by
lively rhythm and blues numbers, a not too usual procedure in
the country field). Early in 1956 RCA released *Heartbreak
Hotel*—and pop, rhythm and blues, and country and western
customers rushed to buy it. It was, at this stage, just about
unheard-of to crack three such different markets—perhaps
one or the other and pop, but not all three. (Ironically, one
other singer achieved the same feat at the same time, Carl
Perkins, with a song he had written himself, *Blue Suede
Shoes,* and if anything less sensational than *Heartbreak Hotel*
had been around, the Perkins song might have made it.
Instead, it had its big success only when Presley recorded it
himself some months later.)

So he'd gotten the music down. Then there was the show.
According to Bo Diddley, who was a rock and roll star when
Elvis was still an electrician, Presley was out front at the
Apollo night after night watching him and the rest of the
show—and everyone knows that the gyrations at the Apollo
are something to behold. Elvis learned a lot from those
performers and quickly assimilated their movements. Perhaps
for the public there was some sort of surprise in seeing a
white man move the way black men had been moving for
years. Whatever it was, Elvis' bumps and grinds were new to
the teen audiences of the time, and wildly erotic. Mothers
were horrified to see those frankly copulatory demonstrations
right there on the home television screens. All the adult

uneasiness that had been accumulating, as earthy "race" music spilled out into the teen market, finally had a focus. Elvis and his obscene hips would have to go. Well, of course it never was that way. The hips stayed and so did he. And so did his music.

Albums/HEARTBREAK HOTEL: *Heartbreak Hotel; I Was The One; Money Honey; I Forgot To Remember To Forget.* ELVIS PRESLEY: *Blue Suede Shoes; I'm Counting On You; I Got A Woman; One-Sided Love Affair; I Love You Because; Just Because; Tutti Frutti; Tryin' To Get To You; I'm Gonna Sit Right Down And Cry (Over You); I'll Never Let You Go (Little Darlin'); Blue Moon; Money Honey.* ANY WAY YOU WANT ME: *Mystery Train; I Don't Care If The Sun Don't Shine; Any Way You Want Me; I'm Left, You're Right, She's Gone.* ELVIS: *Rip It Up; Love Me; When My Blue Moon Turns To Gold Again; Long Tall Sally; First In Line; Paralyzed; So Glad You're Mine; Old Shep; Ready Teddy; Anyplace Is Paradise; How's The World Treating You; How Do You Think I Feel.* STRICTLY ELVIS: *Long Tall Sally; First In Line; How Do You Think I Feel; How's The World Treating You.* LOVE ME TENDER: *Love Me Tender; Let Me; Poor Boy; We're Gonna Move.* JUST FOR YOU: *I Need You So; Have I Told You Lately That I Love You; Blueberry Hill; Is It So Strange.* JAILHOUSE ROCK: *Jailhouse Rock; Young And Beautiful; I Want To Be Free, Don't Leave Me Now; Baby I Don't Care.* LOVING YOU: *Loving You; Party; Teddy Bear; True Love; Lonesome; Cowboy; Hot Dog; Mean Woman Blues; Got A Lot O' Livin' To Do; Blueberry Hill; Don't Leave Now; Have I Told You Lately That I Love You; I Need You.* CHRISTMAS WITH ELVIS. FOLLOW THAT DREAM: *Follow That Dream; What A Wonderful Life; I'm Not The Marrying Kind; Angel.* KID GALAHAD: *King Of The Whole Wide World; This Is Living; Riding The Rainbow; Home Is Where The Heart Is; I Got Lucky; Whistling Tune.* EASY COME, EASY GO: *Easy Come, Easy Go; Love Machine; Yoga Is As Yoga Does; You Gotta Stop; Sing You Children; I'll Take Love.* REAL ELVIS: *Don't Be Cruel; I Want You, I Need You, I Love You, Hound Dog; My Baby Left Me.* PEACE IN THE VALLEY: *Peace In The Valley; It Is No Secret; I Believe; Take My*

Hand, Precious Lord. ELVIS' GOLDEN RECORDS (March 1958): *Hound Dog; Loving You; All Shook Up; Love Me; Heartbreak Hotel; Jailhouse Rock; Too Much; Don't Be Cruel; That's When Your Heartaches Begin; Teddy Bear, Anyway You Want Me; Love Me Tender; Treat Me Nice; I Want You, I Need You, I Love You.* KING CREOLE (September 1958): *Trouble; Crawfish; King Creole; As Long As I Have You; Hard-Headed Woman; Dixieland Rock; Don't Ask Me Why; Lover Doll; Young Dreams; Steadfast, Loyal And True; New Orleans.* ELVIS' CHRISTMAS ALBUM: *Santa Claus Is Back In Town; White Christmas; Here Comes Santa Claus (Right Down Santa Claus Lane); I'll Be Home For Christmas; Blue Christmas; Santa Bring My Baby Back To Me; Oh Little Town Of Bethlehem; Silent Night, Peace In The Valley; I Believe; Take My Hand, Precious Lord; It Is No Secret (What God Can Do).* ELVIS SAILS VIVA LAS VEGAS: *If You Think I Need You; C'mon Everybody; I Need Somebody To Lean On; Today, Tomorrow And Forever.* TICKLE ME: *I Feel That I've Known You Forever; Slowly But Surely; Night Rider; Put The Blame On Me; Dirty Feeling.* TOUCH OF GOLD, VOL. 1: *Hard-Headed Woman; Good Rockin' Tonight; Don't; I Beg Of You.* TOUCH OF GOLD, VOL. 2: *Wear My Ring Around Your Neck; Treat Me Nice; One Night; That's Alright.* TOUCH OF GOLD, VOL. 3: *All Shook Up; Don't Ask Me Why; Too Much; Blue Moon Of Kentucky.* ELVIS PRESLEY, FOR LP FANS ONLY (February 1959): *That's All Right; Lawdy Miss Clawdy; Mystery Train; Playing For Keeps; Poor Boy; My Baby Left Me; I Was The One; Shake, Rattle And Roll; I'm Left, You're Right, She's Gone; You're A Heartbreaker.* A DATE WITH ELVIS (July 1959): *Blue Moon Of Kentucky; Young And Beautiful; (You're So Square) Baby I Don't Care; Milkcow Blues Boogie; Baby Let's Play House; Good Rockin' Tonight; Is It So Strange; We're Gonna Move; I Want To Be Free; I Forgot To Remember To Forget.* 50,000,000 ELVIS FANS CAN'T BE WRONG—ELVIS' GOLDEN RECORDS, VOL. 2 (November 1959): *One Night; I Need Your Love Tonight; I Beg Of You; Now And Then There's A Fool Such As I; Don't; Wear My Ring Around Your Neck; My Wish Came True; I Got Stung; A Big Hunk O' Love; Doncha' Think It's Time.* ELVIS

IS BACK! (April 1960): *Make Me Know It; Fever; The Girl Of My Best Friend; I Will Be Home Again; Dirty, Dirty Feeling; Thrill Of Your Life; Soldier Boy; Such A Night; It Feels So Right; Girl Next Door Went Walking; Like A Baby; Reconsider Baby.* G. I. BLUES (September 1960): *Tonight Is So Right For Love; What's She Really Like; Frankfort Special; Wooden Heart; G. I. Blues; Pocketful Of Rainbows; Shoppin' Around; Big Boots; Didja' Ever; Blue Suede Shoes; Doin' The Best I Can.* HIS HAND IN MINE (November 1960): *His Hand In Mine; I'm Gonna Walk Dem Golden Stairs; In My Father's House (Are Many Mansions); Milky White Way; Known Only To Him; I Believe In The Man In The Sky; Joshua Fit The Battle; He Knows Just What I Need; Swing Down Sweet Chariot; Mansion Over The Hilltop; If We Never Meet Again; Working On The Building.* SOMETHING FOR EVERYBODY (May 1961): *Put The Blame On Me; Judy; There's Always Me; Give Me The Right; It's A Sin; Sentimental Me; Starting Today; Gently; I'm Comin' Home; In Your Arms; I Want You With Me; I Slipped, I Stumbled, I Fell.* BLUE HAWAII (September 1961): *Blue Hawaii; Almost Always True; Aloha-Oe; N) More; Can't Help Falling In Love; Rock-A-Hula Baby; Moonlight Swim; Ku-u-i-Po (Hawaiian Sweetheart); Ito Eats; Slicin' Sand; Hawaiian Sunset; Beach Boy Blues; Island Of Love; Hawaiian Wedding Song.* POT LUCK (May 1962): *Kiss Me Quick; Just For Old-Time's Sake; Gonna Get Back Home Somehow; Such An Easy Question; Steppin' Out Of Line; I'm Yours; Something Blue; Suspicion; I Feel That I've Known You Forever; Night Rider; Fountain Of Love; That's Someone You Never Forget.* GIRLS, GIRLS, GIRLS (November 1962): *Girls, Girls, Girls; I Don't Wanna Be Tied; Where Do You Come From; I Don't Want To; We'll Be Together; A Boy Like Me, A Girl Like You; Earth Boy; Return To Sender; Because Of Love; Thanks To The Rolling Sea; Song Of The Shrimp; The Walls Have Ears; We're Coming In Loaded.* IT HAPPENED AT THE WORLD'S FAIR (March 1963): *Beyond The Bend; Relax; Take Me To The Fair; They Remind Me Too Much Of You; One Broken Heart for Sale; I'm Falling In Love Tonight; Cotton Candy Land; A World Of Our Own; How Would You Like To Be; Happy Ending.* ELVIS' GOLDEN RECORDS, VOL. 3 (August

1963): *It's Now Or Never; Stuck On You; Fame And Fortune; I Gotta Know; Surrender; Are You Lonesome Tonight; Good Luck Charm; Anything That's Part Of You; She's Not You; I Feel So Bad; His Latest Flame; Little Sister.* FUN IN ACAPULCO (November 1963): *Fun In Acapulco; El Toro; Marguerita; The Bullfighter Was A Lady; I Think I'm Gonna Like It Here; Bossa Nova, Baby; Guadalajara; Vino, Dinero Y Amor; You Can't Say No In Acapulco; Love Me Tonight; Slowly But Surely; There's No Room To Rhumba In A Sports Car; Mexico.* KISSIN' COUSINS (April 1964): *Kissin' Cousins; Barefoot Ballad; Catchin' On Fast; Once Is Enough; One Boy Two Little Girls; Smokey Mountain Boy; Tender Feeling; There's Gold In The Mountains; Anyone Could Fall In Love With You; Kissin' Cousins (Number 2); Echoes Of Love; It's A Long Lonely Highway.* ROUSTA-BOUT (October 1964): *Roustabout; Little Egypt; Poison Ivy League; Hard Knocks; It's A Wonderful World; Big Love Big Heartache; One-Track Heart; It's Carnival Time; Carny Town; There's A Brand New Day On The Horizon; Wheels On My Heels.* GIRL HAPPY (March 1965): *Girl Happy; Spring Fever; Fort Lauderdale Chamber Of Commerce; Startin' Tonight; Cross My Heart And Hope To Die; The Meanest Girl In Town; Puppet On A String; I've Got To Find My Baby; You'll Be Gone; Wolf Call; Do Not Disturb; Do The Clam.* ELVIS FOR EVERYONE (July 1965): *Your Cheatin' Heart; Summer Kisses, Winter Tears; Finders Keepers, Losers Weepers; Memphis, Tennessee; For The Millionth And The Last Time; Santa Lucia; I Met Her Today; In My Way; Forget Me Never; Sound Advice; When It Rains, It Really Pours; Tomorrow Night.* HARUM SCARUM (November 1965): *Harem Holiday; Golden Coins; Hey Little Girl; My Desert Serenade; Kismet; Go East Young Man; So Close Yet So Far; Mirage; Shake That Tambourine; Animal Instinct; Wisdom Of The Ages.* FRANKIE AND JOHNNY (April 1966): *Frankie And Johnny; Come Along; Petunia, The Gardener's Daughter; Chesay; What Every Woman Lives For; Look Out, Broadway; Beginner's Luck; Down By The Riverside; And When The Saints Go Marching In; Shout It Out; Hard Luck; Please Don't Stop Loving Me; Everybody Come Aboard.* PARADISE, HAWAIIAN STYLE (June 1966): *Paradise, Hawaiian Style; This Is My Heaven;*

*Scratch My Back; House Of Sand; A Dog's Life; Datin';
Queenie Wahine's Papaya; Drums Of The Islands; Stop
Where You Are; Sand Castles.* SPINOUT (October 1966):
*Spinout; Stop, Look And Listen; Adam And Evil; All That I
Am; Never Say Yes; Am I Ready; Beach Shack; Smorgas-
bord; I'll Be Back; Tomorrow Is A Long Time; Down In The
Alley; I'll Remember You.* HOW GREAT THOU ART (Feb-
ruary 1967): *How Great Thou Art; In The Garden; Stand By
Me; Farther Along; Without Him; So High; Where Could I
Go But To The Lord; By And By; If The Lord Wasn't
Walking By My Side; Run On; Where No One Stands Alone;
Crying In The Chapel; Somebody Bigger Than You And I.*
DOUBLE TROUBLE (May 1967): *Double Trouble; Long-
Legged Girl; Baby, If You'll Give Me All Your Love; Could I
Fall In Love; City By Night; Old MacDonald; It Won't Be
Long; I Love Only One Girl; There Is So Much World To
See; Never Ending; Blue River; What Now, What Next,
Where To.* CLAMBAKE (October 1967): *Big Boss Man;
You Don't Know Me; House That Has Everything; Guitar
Man; Who Needs Money; Clambake; Confidence; Hey, Hey,
Hey; Girl I Never Loved; How Can You Lose What You
Never Had; Singing Tree; Just Call Me Lonesome.* ELVIS'
GOLDEN RECORD, VOL. 4 (January 1968): *Love Letters;
Witchcraft; It Hurts Me; Ask Me; What'd I Say; Please Don't
Drag That String Around; Indescribably Blue; You're The
Devil In Disguise; Lonely Man; Mess Of Blues; Ain't That
Loving You Baby; Just Tell Her Jim Said Hello.* SPEEDWAY
(August 1968): *Speedway; Your Time Hasn't Come Yet,
Baby; Who Are You; He's Your Uncle Not Your Dad; Let
Yourself Go; Five Sleepyheads; Western Union; Mine; Going
Home; Suppose.* ELVIS (December 1968): *Trouble; Guitar
Man; Lawdy Miss Clawdy; Baby What You Want Me To Do;
Heartbreak Hotel; Hound Dog; All Shook Up; Can't Help Fall-
ing In Love; Jailhouse Rock; Love Me Tender; Where Can I
Go But To The Lord; Over My Head; Saved; Blue Christmas;
One Night; Memories; Nothingville; Big Boss Man; Guitar
Man; Little Egypt; If I Can Dream.* ELVIS SINGS "FLAM-
ING STAR" (April 1969): *Flaming Star; Night Life Do The
Vega Tiger Man; 5* Other Titles.

Singles/*Mystery Train/I Forgot To Remember To Forget;*

Blue Moon Of Kentucky/That's All Right (August 7, 1954); *Good Rockin' Tonight/I Don't Care If The Sun Don't Shine; Milkcow Blues Boogie/You're A Heartbreaker; Baby Let's Play House/I'm Left, You're Right, She's Gone; Heartbreak Hotel/I Was The One* (1956); *I Want You, I Need You, I Love You/My Baby Left Me; Hound Dog/Don't Be Cruel; Blue Suede Shoes/Tutti Frutti; Blue Moon/Just Because; One-Sided Love Affair/Money Honey; Shake, Rattle And Roll/Lawdy, Miss Clawdy* (1959); *Love Me Tender/Anyway You Want Me; Too Much/Playing For Keeps; All Shook Up/That's When Your Heartaches Begin; Jailhouse Rock/ Treat Me Nice; Teddy Bear/Loving You; Don't/I Beg Of You; Wear My Ring Around Your Neck/Doncha' Think It's Time; Don't Ask Me Why/Hard-Headed Woman; One Night/I Got Stung; Fool Such As I/I Need Your Love Tonight; My Wish Came True/Big Hunk O' Love; Stuck On You/Fame And Fortune; It's Now Or Never/Mess Of Blues; Are You Lonesome Tonight/I Gotta Know; Surrender/Lonely Man; I Feel So Bad/Wild In The Country; His Latest Flame/Little Sister; Can't Help Falling In Love/Rock-A-Hula Baby* (1961); *Good Luck Charm/Anything That's Part Of You; Just Tell Her Jim Said Hello/She's Not You; Return To Sender/Where Do You Come From; Kiss Me Quick/Suspicion* (1962); *One Broken Heart For Sale/They Remind Me Too Much Of You* (1963); *Devil In Disguise/Please Don't Drag That String Around; Witchcraft/Bossa Nova Baby; I Believe In The Man In The Sky/Crying In The Chapel; Kissin' Cousins/It Hurts Me* (1964); *Such A Night/Never Ending; Viva Las Vegas/What'd I Say; Blue Christmas/Santa Claus Is Back In Town; Do The Clam/You'll Be Gone; Ain't That Loving You Baby/Ask Me; Wooden Heart/Puppet On A String; Joshua Fit The Battle Of Jericho/Known Only To Him; Milky White Way/Swing Down Sweet Chariot; Easy Question/It Feels So Right; I'm Yours/Long Lonely Highway; Blue River/Tell Me Why; Frankie And Johnny/Please Don't Stop Loving Me; Love Letters/Come What May, Spinout/All That I Am* (1966); *How Would You Like To Be/If Every Day Was Like Christmas; Fools Fall In Love/Indescribably Blue; Long-Legged Girl/That's Someone You Never Forget; Judy/There's Always Me; Big Boss Man/You Don't Know Me; Guitar Man/Hi Heel Sneakers; Stay*

Away/U.S. Male; Your Time Hasn't Come Yet, Baby/Let Yourself Go; We Call On Him/You'll Never Walk Alone; Almost In Love/Little Less Conversation; Edge Of Reality/If I Can Dream; His Hand In Mine/How Great Thou Art (April 1969); *In The Ghetto/Any Day Now* (April 1969).

ALAN PRICE SET/*Alan Price (lead vocals, organ, piano, vibes, guitar), Clive Burrows (alto, baritone & tenor sax, drums, flute, double bass), Steve Gregory (tenor sax, flute), John Walters (trumpet, flugelhorn), Rod "Boots" Slade (bass guitar), Little Roy (alto, baritone & tenor sax, drums, flute, double bass).*

Alan Price was the organist on the Animals' *House of the Rising Sun*, which was the number one record in America for three weeks in September, 1964, and the first record by an English group to make it in that spot after the Beatles. Alan, a vital part of the Animals sound, left the following year to form his own band (the Animals had been the Alan Price Combo when Eric Burdon joined them). His songs were hits in England, and he would have been bigger in the States but for work-permit difficulties that prevented his band from accompanying him when he was due to appear at Steve Paul's The Scene in 1968. His one American album was widely praised as an example of what a good rock vocalist can do without electronic tricks.

Albums/THIS PRICE IS RIGHT (January 1968): *House That Jack Built; She's Got Another Pair Of Shoes; I Put A Spell On You; On This Side Of Goodbye; So Long Dad; Bet No One Ever Hurt So Bad; Shame; Simon Smith And His Amazing Dancing Bear; Biggest Night Of Her Life; Hi-Lili, Hi-Lo; Don't Do That Again; To Ramona; Living Without You; Happy Land.*

Singles/*I Put A Spell On You/Lechyd-Da* (April 1966); *Hi-Lili, Hi-Lo/Take Me Home* (August 1966); *Simon Smith And His Amazing Dancing Bear/Tickle Me* (March 1967); *The House That Jack Built/Who Cares* (August 1967); *Shame/Don't Do That Again* (November 1967); *Not Born To Follow/To Ramona* (February 1968).

LLOYD PRICE wrote and sang some of the bounciest songs of the fifties. His *Lawdy Miss Clawdy* (which started as a radio commercial) was a classic. There was *Just Because, Where Were You On Our Wedding Day?* and his million seller, *Stagger Lee.* Price toured all over the world taking with him the sound that was later to form the basis for much of the rock that sprang up in other countries. Mike Smith of the Dave Clark Five has a particularly Lloyd Price sound and of course every rock singer worth his salt has recorded *Lawdy Miss Clawdy,* including Elvis Presley, the Hollies, Johnny Rivers and Sandy Nelson.

Albums/EXCITING LLOYD PRICE: *Stagger Lee; I Wish Your Picture Was You; Talking About Love; What Do You Do To My Heart; You Need Love; Mailman Blues; Where Were You (On Our Wedding Day); Why; Lawdy Miss Clawdy; Oh, Oh, Oh; Foggy Day; Just Because.* MR. PERSONALITY: *All Of Me; I Only Have Eyes For You; Time After Time; Personality; I'm Gonna Get Married; Mary Anne; Yakte-Yak-Bing-Bang; Dinner For One; Is It Really Love; Poppaschun; I Want You To Know; Have You Ever Had The Blues.* MR. PERSONALITY SINGS THE BLUES: *Ain't Nobody's Business; Please Send Me Someone To Love; Kidney Stew; I Cover The Waterfront; Talk To Me; I've Got The Blues; Just To Hold Your Hand; Sittin' Here And Rockin'; I Don't Need Nobody; Feeling Lowdown; I'm A Lonely Man; Down For The Count.* FANTASTIC LLOYD PRICE: *What Is This Thing Called Love; Blue Skies; Because Of You; Undecided; Let's Fall In Love; Don't Blame Me; In A Shanty In Old Shanty Town; Mean To Me; Don't Take Your Love From Me; Jeepers Creepers; Little Volcano; Five Foot Two.* MR. PERSONALITY'S BIG 15: *Personality; Three Little Pigs; Where Were You; Come Into My Heart; Never Let Me Go; Lady Luck; Have You Ever Had The Blues; Is It Really Love; I'm Gonna Get Married; You Need Love; Won't Cha Come Home; Lawdy Miss Clawdy; Just Because; Stagger Lee.* LLOYD PRICE SINGS THE MILLION SELLERS: *Ain't That Just Like A Woman; Will You Love Me Tomorrow; Save The Last Dance For Me; Shop Around; At Last; Corrina, Corrina; Hoochie Coochie Coo; He Will Break Your Heart; I Count The Tears; Once In A While; Spanish Harlem; C'est Si Bon.* LLOYD PRICE, COOKIN': *'Deed I Do; Since I Fell For You; Blues In The Night; Summertime; Is You Or*

Is You Ain't My Baby; Straighten Up And Fly Right; I Cried For You; That's Why Tears Come And Go; I'll Always Be In Love With You; It's Only A Paper Moon; Rainbow Joe; Frim Fram Sauce. LLOYD SWINGS FOR SAMMY: *Woman; Fly Me To The Moon; Come Home; Don't Cry; Nice & Easy; Oh Lady Luck; Baby Please Don't Go; Gone (You're Gone); Ebb Tide; Meet In The Bottom; I Love You; Amen.*

Singles/*Why*/*Just Because; Stagger Lee*/*You Need Love; Personality*/*Have You Ever Had The Blues; Just Because*/*Personality; Man Who Took The Valise Off The Floor Of Grand Central Station At Noon*/*I Won't Cry Anymore.*

Also Appears On/ALL STAR CAST. ALAN FREED'S TOP 15: *Lawdy Miss Clawdy.* ORIGINAL RHYTHM & BLUES HITS. MILLION OR MORE: *Just Because; Stagger Lee.*

P. J. (JIM) PROBY/In 1964 in London he was the bad boy of pop—skintight pants ripping on stage, raving maniac performances. He now claims the pants split once accidentally and people expected it after that. Besides, raving paid off then. Today, broke and dispirited, he's kissed the screaming scene good-bye, lopped off most of his Tiny Tim hairdo, and thinks he might try the cabaret circuit where other old rockers like Tom Jones are thriving. But he *was* one of the original freakout kids in rock and should be remembered for that.

Albums/SOMEWHERE (March 1965): *Somewhere; Just Call And I'll Be There; Que Sera, Sera; Stagger Lee; Linda Lu; Together; Rockin' Pneumonia And The Boogie Woogie Flu; Glory Of Love; Masquerade Is Over; Hold Me; Zing, Went The Strings Of My Heart; Question.* P. J. PROBY (August 1965): *That Means A Lot; I Will; Mission Bell; Nearness Of You; Lonely Weekends; If I Loved You; Let The Water Run Down; She Cried; Secret Love; I Will Come To You; Lonely Teardrops; With These Hands.* ENIGMA (February 1967): *Niki Hokey; Shake Shake Shake; Reach Out I'll Be There; That's The Tune; Out Of Time; Don't Forget About Me; People, That's Why; I Wanna Thank You Baby; I'm Twenty-Eight; Angelica; I Can't Make It Alone; You Make Me Feel Like Someone.* PHENOMENON (August 1967): *Just Holding On; Mama Told Me Not To Come; Work With Me*

Annie; Ling Ting Tong; Honey Hush; Straight Up; Butterfly High; She's Looking Good; You Can't Come Home Again; Pretty Girls Everywhere; Good Rockin' Tonight; Sanctification. WHAT'S WRONG WITH MY WORLD (August 1968): *What's Wrong With My World; Cry Baby; Turn Her Away; Give Me Time; Mary In The Morning; I'm Coming Home; And The Sun Will Shine; Why, Baby, Why; I've Got My Eyes On You; When Love Has Passed You By; I Apologize Baby; It's Your Day Today.*

Singles/*Somewhere/Just Like Him* (December 1964); *I Apologize/Rocking Pneumonia* (March 1965); *Mission Bell/Stagger Lee* (April 1965); *That Means A Lot/Let The Water Run Down* (June 1965); *Maria/Good Things Are Coming My Way* (December 1965); *My Prayer/Wicked Woman* (March 1966); *I Can't Make It Alone/If I Ruled The World* (September 1966); *Niki Hokey/Good Things Are Coming My Way* (December 1966); *You Can't Come Home Again/Work With Me Annie* (May 1967); *Just Holding On/Butterfly High* (August 1967); *It's Your Day/I Apologize Baby* (March 1968); *What's Wrong With My World/Turn Her Away* (June 1968).

PROCOL HARUM/*Mathew Charles Fisher (organ), Robbie Trower (replaced Ray Royer) (lead guitar), Dave Knights (bass), B. J. Wilson (replaced Bobby Harrison) (drums), Gary Brooker (piano, organ, trombone, piano, accordion).*
The name Procol Harum is Latin for "beyond these things," and the group's material gave a hint of having more serious content than is usually found in rock. Their biggest hit was built around a Bach cantata. This was not the first time Bach had appeared in a popular single (the Toys' *Lovers' Concerto* was an earlier rock version of a Bach tune), but this was something more. Keith Reid's lyrics were a surrealistic mixture of vestal virgins, flying ceilings and fandangos. The musicians who put it all to music decided to sing it above and around a Bach cantata, *Sleepers Awake.* There was no group, just a bunch of musicians, and an especially fine organist. The result was *A Whiter Shade of Pale,* a record that in the spring of 1967 sold two and a half million copies within a few weeks of its release. Never was a group less

ready for success. The personnel on the original record was changed almost immediately. There were traumas and counter-traumas, complaints from the press about lack of cooperation, every conceivable hassle that a group could possibly encounter.

Nothing was more eagerly awaited than the album, especially since *SERGEANT PEPPER* had just come out. The album *PROCOL HARUM* was said to have been hastily thrown together—written, arranged, recorded, mixed and released within a week and a half—but it never sounded that way. The few people who inevitably found it disappointing at first were to change their minds later. Keith Reid's beautiful lyrics were still there; the tempo of the record was slow, with all the dignity and mystery of a black mass. Robin Trower's guitar sounded like a voice in terror. This was one of the first groups to use two keyboard instruments together continually. The sound was very reminiscent of Dylan's *HIGHWAY 61 REVISITED* and *BLONDE ON BLONDE,* which also used the rich combination of piano and organ.

Meanwhile the group did not go the usual tour route in England but by October 1967 had visited America, where they were moderately but not sensationally successful. The trouble was no singles and no image. A second tour, early in 1968, was more successful, and the third tour in October 1968, coinciding with the release of the second album, established them once and for all as an important group. The second album, *SHINE ON BRIGHTLY,* was notable for an eighteen-minute first-person track describing both the destrucion and reconstruction of the narrator's ego. Like all Procol Harum lyrics, it was written by Keith Reid and took four months to put together and record. The other tracks are a supplement to rather than a development of the themes of the first album. On stage, singer, pianist and composer Gary Brooker dominates the rather static performances of the group.

Albums/PROCOL HARUM—A WHITER SHADE OF PALE (August 1967): *Whiter Shade Of Pale; She Wandered Through The Garden Fence; Something Following Me; Mabel; Cerdes (Outside The Gates Of); Salad Days; Conquistador; Kaleidoscope; Repent Walpurgis; A Christmas Camel.*

SHINE ON BRIGHTLY (November 1968): *Quite Rightly So; Shine On Brightly; Skip Softly; Wish Me Well; Rambling On; In Held Twas In I; Magdalene.* SALTY DOG (April 1969).

Singles/*Good Captain Clack/Hamburg* (March 1966); *In The Wee Small Hours Of Sixpence/Quite Rightly So* (October 1966); *A Whiter Shade Of Pale/Lime Street Blues* (May 1967); *Salty Dog/Long Gone Geek* (June 1969).

PRODUCERS/Record production, which once was a mere technician's job, somewhere in the late sixties became an art form. Records came out, like the Beach Boys' *Good Vibrations* late in 1966, with arrangements that were difficult if not impossible to do in live performance. And inevitably the question was raised: did a performer have the right to put on record a sound he could not reproduce in person? And if so, who was the star—the performer or the producer and engineer? Or both? The Beatles, typically, provided one answer when, after they came out with *SERGEANT PEPPER,* a masterpiece of electronic art, they announced they would no longer appear in person. It's still being argued how much of the Beatles' art is theirs and how much credit is due their producer, George Martin. He is jokingly but accurately referred to as the Fifth Beatle. *SERGEANT PEPPER,* which wouldn't have been possible without him, is a catalog of the hundreds of possibilities that have remained untapped in the recording studio.

So fascinating is the work of the producer that serious rock musicians have moved into the field. Harry Nilsson and Lee Michaels not only perform but also produce their own material. The Who's Peter Townshend has had a recording studio built into his home so he can, at his leisure, go into the further potentials of tape, amplification, double tracking, etc. The Beach Boys' Brian Wilson's real genius lies in production. And Jimi Hendrix is also a very talented producer. Producers like Bob Crewe (the Four Seasons), Felix Pappalardi (Cream, Youngbloods), Jimmy Miller (Rolling Stones, Traffic), Paul Rothchild (the Doors), Tom Wilson (Simon and Garfunkel), and Bob Johnson (Bob Dylan) are stars in their own right. Fans recognize them, magazines write about them, they actively influence the direction music is moving in. Country-oriented Bob Johnson persuaded Dylan to record in Nashville; Jerry Wexler brought out the "real" Aretha. The producer, as much as the star, decides when double tracking (or triple tracking or quadruple tracking) will work and when it won't; when trickery is too much trickery; what changes have to be made in the layer after layer of sound that goes into the making of even the simplest single these days; what sidemen to use; what arranger to use; whether the sound should be clean or muddy.

Experts say they can detect when certain producers have been at work—like Mickie Most, for example. Most has a distinctly *clean* commercial sound, and he has a lot to do with what material is recorded and how it's done (he works with Herman, Donovan and recently Lulu). The king of all producers however is Phil Spector, who did twenty-eight records between 1962 and 1966, eighteen of which sold more than a million copies. His records were so commercially successful that not everyone was able to see the amount of artistry Spector was putting into them. He was the first to put elaborate walls of sound behind vocals. More goes on in his records than in anybody else's, and although just about everyone who followed him tried to copy him no one really succeeded. The Beatles are as indebted to his ideas as anyone.

The roles of producer and arranger, producer and manager, performer and producer, often overlap though as music becomes more and more intricate in the studio. The producer will suggest to the arranger that there should be a little more noise in one spot, a little less in another, and what sort of noise it should be. He can make things louder, softer, faster, slower, closer, more distant. In a way he is the conductor of the symphony of studio sound. Meanwhile, there are groups who manage to reproduce in person what they do in the studio (United States of America brought elaborate recording equipment on stage for just this purpose). Others, like the Moody Blues, who play many instruments on their albums, find this impractical live, so they work at getting a similar sound, as close as they can come, with available instruments.

There are groups however with an uncanny knack for reproducing live what other groups can do only in a studio. One of these is the much underrated Candymen, who astonished audiences in The Scene in the summer of 1967 by reproducing the Beatles' *Day in the Life* and the Beach Boys' *Good Vibrations* with every effect as easily as if they were bellowing out *Louie Louie* or *Gloria*. But few groups can do this As rock becomes more complicated, producers' roles grow more important. A day could well come when the producer will be not just the *real* but the *only* star of the performance, twiddling knobs and mixing sounds.

PSYCHEDELIC MUSIC (see ACID ROCK)

THE PSYCHEDELIC STOOGES (now **THE STOOGES**)/A Detroit rock group that combines politics, comedy and music, the Psychedelic Stooges have been described as having the spirit of W. C. Fields, the Three Stooges, the Marx Brothers and Elvis Presley. They were discovered in 1968.

GARY PUCKETT AND THE UNION GAP (formerly UNION GAP/*Gary Puckett (vocals), Dwight Bement (tenor sax), Kerry Chater (bass guitar), Paul Wheatbread (drums), Gary "Mutha" Withem (piano)*.
The Union Gap, formed in California in 1967, has had three million dollar best sellers in a row in less than a year. If all three are the same song sung sideways, as the ungracious insist, it only goes to show how much the public liked it the first time. The strong voice of Gary Puckett is the basis for the group's sound and will outlast mere fads—even the gimmickry of the group's Civil War uniforms.

Albums/THE UNION GAP (January 1968): *Woman, Woman; M'Lady; By The Time I Get To Phoenix; Raindrops; I Want A New Day; Believe Me; You Better Sit Down, Kids; My Son; Kentucky Woman; To Love Somebody; Don't Make Promises*. GARY PUCKETT AND THE UNION GAP (May 1968): *Young Girl; Lady Madonna; Kiss Me Goodbye; Pleasure Of You; Dreams Of The Everyday Housewife; I'm Losing You; Honey (I Miss You); Mighty Quinn; Wait Till The Sun Shines On You; Since You've Been Gone; Say You Don't Need Me*. INCREDIBLE (October 1968): *Over You; Now And Then; I'm Just A Man; Can You Tell; Common Cold; If The Day Would Come; Lady Willpower;*

Reverend Posey; Give In; Take Your Pleasure; I've Done All I Can.

Singles/*Woman, Woman*/*Don't Make Promises* (September 1967); *Young Girl*/*I'm Losing You* (February 1968); *Lady Willpower*/*Daylight Stranger* (May 1968); *If The Day Would Come*/*Over You* (October 1968).

BERNARD PURDIE has played drums on three record sessions a day, six days a week, for the last three years. When the Rolling Stones wanted a session drummer, they got the man they call the hitmaker, "Pretty" Purdie. Listen to his drumming on Tim Rose's *Hey Joe*. It explains everything.

QUICKSILVER MESSENGER SERVICE/*John Cipollina (guitar), Gary Duncan (guitar), David Freiberg (bass), Gregory Elmore (drums).*
One of the first of the San Francisco rock bands, Quicksilver assembled when the rock scene was just beginning in San Francisco at the end of 1965. They played mostly for the citizens of Haight-Ahsbury at free concerts and for the patrons of the Fillmore and the Avalon at the height of San Francisco's flower period in 1966 and 1967. They did not record until quite late in their careers, turning down offers until they considered themselves entirely together and ready to record. When their album did come out, it wasn't quite what anyone who knew their work expected. There was a brilliant cut of folk-singer Hamilton Camp's *Pride of Man* but everything else was very Electric Flag, which is not surprising since two members of the Electric Flag helped produce the album. John Cipollina, the guitarist, came on like Bloomfield —not that there was anything wrong with that, but with that and overtones of Country Joe, Procol Harum, the Vanilla Fudge, the Dead, the Airplane and Eric Clapton, not much of the original hard-rock/deep-blues combination of the group came through. The group also did four cuts on the soundtrack album of the film *Revolution.*

Albums/QUICKSILVER MESSENGER SERVICE (May 1967): *Pride Of Man; Light Your Windows; Gold And Silver; Dino's Song; It's Been Too Long; Fool.* HAPPY TRAILS (March 1969): *Who Do You Love; When You*

Love; Where You Love; How You Love; Which Do You Love; Mona; Maiden Of The Cancer Moon; Calvary; Happy Trails.

Singles/*Dino's Song/Pride Of Man* (May 1968); *Stand By Me/Bears* (November 1968).

RAGA ROCK/The term raga rock was introduced early in 1966—not by the Byrds, who had started using a sitar in *Eight Miles High,* but by an imaginative publicist in charge of publicizing that single. The Byrds were shocked at this musical sacrilege, but the term stayed and from then on was used to describe any piece of rock music that featured a sitar or a sitar sound produced by another instrument, or any sort of Indian or even faintly Oriental sound—and from 1966 on, there was plenty of that.

Actually a raga is a piece of Indian music that follows a particular and strict form (in pretty much the same way a Shakespearean sonnet does). There have been many hundreds written and some are over a thousand years old.

LYNNE RANDELL/There is a whole tradition in rock of small bouncy blondes with large bouncy voices. Lynne Randell is one. She used to be Australia's number one girl singer and owes her U.S. fame to a tour with the Monkees in 1967 and to appearances on Rascals and Who tours in Hawaii.

Single/*The Right To Cry/An Open Letter* (August 1968).

KENNY RANKIN/He has a warm and loving voice, tender, gentle lyrics, a folk sound with string orchestration—the whole mood that was pioneered by Donovan and the Bee Gees.

Album/MIND DUSTERS (November 1967): *Cotton Candy Sandman; Dolphin; It Never Changes; Every Passing Moment; Song For A Winter's Night; My Carousel; Tambourine Man; Peaceful; Come Away Melinda; Girl I Left Behind; Minuet.*

Single/*Dolphin/Peaceful* (October 1967).

THE RASCALS (formerly THE YOUNG RASCALS)/ *Eddie Brigati (vocals), Felix Cavaliere (organ), Gene Cornish (guitar), Dino Danelli (drums).*

If you were a kid in New Jersey you might have heard about the Young Rascals very early in February, 1965, when they played the Choo Choo Club in Garfield, New Jersey. Even then, as a new group, they weren't amateurs. Dino had done a lot of work since the age of fifteen with jazz people and later with a band backing Sandy Scott in Las Vegas. Felix had also backed Miss Scott and had been one of Joey Dee's Starlighters (after the twist had died). And Gene and Eddie were also Starlighters (Eddie's brother was an original in that group). So even then they were something to listen to. But if you weren't around New Jersey but had social aspirations, you might have known of them that 1965 summer when they played the Barge, the first of the big discotheques at the Hamptons on Long Island. It was *the* place to go that summer and it was also considered very chic in those circles to have a Rascal or two in tow. ("So cute, my dear," said the jet-set ladies, not realizing they had just gotten their first taste of being a groupie.)

If you were around early in 1966 and you hadn't seen the Young Rascals in the smaller New York clubs, well, you had to have seen them in any one of a score of concerts (including James Brown's Madison Square Garden debut) where they would come on in (plus fours and silly Lord Fauntleroy outfits) to do a very soulful, frantic and raunchy *Good Lovin'*. The song was probably the most played single on discotheque jukeboxes, especially at the black discos like the Dom in New York's East Village, where they tended to play only black music (Stevie Wonder and all that) but invariably included the Rascals, who were white. They always did the number even better live than on record, and that whole discotheque exposure in 1966 made them.

They went to England for a while where their black sound predictably flipped out black-oriented prestige groups like the Stones and the Animals. Back in America they were soon playing to the sort of packed houses you thought only the Beatles got. With *Groovin'* they went into a quiet stage but they came out of it for *People Got To Be Free* (1968), one of those stirring let's-all-be-brothers songs that featured Felix in his most Ray Charles voice. The Rascals were so successful that by 1968 they were the most imitated of any American group. Although the four are much admired and liked, they've never come through as superheroes or even superstars. In New York you'd see them at The Scene chatting up girls with just that touch of anxiety you'd never expect to find in one of America's top groups. Later, when they suddenly went psychedelic in the wardrobe department, all guru jackets, beads and afghan coats, it looked like a desperate effort to make the "in" scene, but beads or not they remained exactly what they were, four lovable, unpretentious boys.

Albums/ YOUNG RASCALS (March 1966): *Good Lovin';
Slow Down; Baby Let's Wait; Just A Little; I Believe; Do
You Feel It; Like A Rolling Stone; Mustang Sally; I Ain't
Gonna Eat Out My Heart Anymore; In The Midnight Hour.*
COLLECTIONS (November 1966): *What Is The Reason;
Since I Fell For You; I've Been Lonely Too Long; No Love
To Give; Love Lights; Mickey's Monkey; Come On Up; Too
Many Fish In The Sea; More; Nineteen-Fifty-Six; Love Is A
Beautiful Thing; Land Of 1,000 Dances.* GROOVIN' (July
1967): *Girl Like You; Groovin'; I'm So Happy Now; Find
Somebody; How Can I Be Sure; If You Knew; I Don't Love
You Anymore; You Better Run; Place In The Sun; It's Love;
Sueño.* ONCE UPON A DREAM (January 1968): *Easy
Rollin'; Rainy Day; Please Love Me; It's Wonderful; I'm
Gonna Love You; My Hawaii; My World; Silly Girl; Singin'
The Blues Too Long; Sattva; Once Upon A Dream.* THE
RASCALS' GREATEST HITS (TIME PEACE) (June
1968): *Groovin'; How Can I Be Sure; Lonely Too Long; In
The Midnight Hour; I Ain't Gonna Eat Out My Heart
Anymore; Good Lovin'; You Better Run; Come On Up;
Mustang Sally; Love Is A Beautiful Thing; Girl Like You;
It's Wonderful; Easy Rollin'; Beautiful Morning.* FREEDOM
SUITE (March 1969): *America The Beautiful; Me & My
Friends; Any Dance'll Do; Look Around; Ray Of Hope;
Island Of Love; Of Course; Love Was So Easy To Give;
People Got To Be Free; Baby I'm Blue; Heaven; Adrian's
Birthday; Cute; Boom.*

Singles/ *I Ain't Gonna Eat Out My Heart Anymore/ Slow
Down* (November 1965); *Good Lovin'/ Mustang Sally* (February 1966); *Love Is A Beautiful Thing/ You Better Run*
(May 1966); *What Is The Reason/ Come On Up* (August
1966); *I've Been Lonely Too Long/ If You Knew* (January

1967); *Groovin'/Sueño* (April 1967); *A Girl Like You/It's Love* (June 1967); *Groovin' (Italian)/Groovin' (Spanish)* (July 1967); *How Can I Be Sure/I'm So Happy Now* (August 1967); *It's Wonderful/Of Course* (November 1967); *Beautiful Morning/Rainy Day* (March 1968); *People Got To Be Free/My World* (August 1968); *Ray Of Hope/Any Dance'll Do* (December 1968); *Away Away/See* (May 1969).

LOU RAWLS/Primarily a pop singer with a touch of the blues, Lou Rawls originally sang gospel and made a sensational debut with Dick Clark at the Hollywood Bowl in 1959. In 1961 he did an album of soulful blues, *STORMY MONDAY,* with a jazz pianist and by 1963 had made the Downbeat Jazz Polls. His style is rough and belting and never too far from the blues. And he keeps getting hits.

Albums/BLACK & BLUE (December 1962): *Roll 'Em Pete; I'd Rather Drink Muddy Water; How Long, How Long Blues; Trouble I'm Mind; Everyday I Have The Blues; St James Infirmary; Black And Blue; Kansas City; Goin' To Chicago; World Of Trouble; Six Cold Feet Of Ground; Strange Fruit.* STORMY MONDAY: *Stormy Monday; God Bless The Child; See See Rider; Willow Weep For Me; I'm Gonna Move To The Outskirts Of Town; T'ain't Nobody's Business If I Do; In The Evening; I'd Rather Drink Muddy Water; Lost And Lookin'; Sweet Love.* TOBACCO ROAD (December 1963): *Tobacco Road; Cotton Fields (Ledbetter); Rockin' Chair; Stormy Weather; Ol' Man River; Blues For A Four String Guitar; St. Louis Blues; Georgia On My Mind; Sentimental Journey; Summertime.* NOBODY BUT LOU (February 1965); *If I Had My Life To Live Over; Into Each Life Some Rain Must Fall; Whispering Grass; Two Tickets West; It's Monday Every Day; Power Of Love, Nobody But Me; For You My Love; If It's The Last Thing I Do; Gee Baby, Ain't I Good To You; Blues For The Weepers.* LOU RAWLS AND STRINGS (September 1965): *What'll I Do; My Buddy; Du Bist Die Liebe; Margie; Fool Such As I; Three O'clock In The Morning; Me And My Shadow; Cold, Cold Heart; I'll See You In My Dreams; Nothing Really Feels The Same; Charmaine.* LOU RAWLS "LIVE" (March 1966): *Stormy Monday; Tobacco Road; St.*

James Infirmary; Southside Blues; Love Theme From The Sandpiper; I'd Rather Drink Muddy Water; Goin' To Chicago Blues; In The Evening When The Sun Goes Down; Girl From Ipanema; I Got It Bad And That Ain't Good; Street Corner Hustlers' Blues; World Of Trouble. PILGRIM TRAVELERS: *Wade In The Water; Sweet Chariot; Jesus Be A Fence Around Me; If He Holds Your Hand; Didn't It Rain; That's Heaven To Me; Stand By Me Father; Motherless Child; Did You Stop To Pray This Morning; Walking In The Light Of The Lord; Poor Pilgrim Of Sorrow.* SOULIN' (August 1966): *Whole Lotta Woman; Love Is A Hurtin' Thing; So Hard To Laugh, So Easy To Cry; You're The One; Don't Explain; What Now My Love; Old Folks; Autumn Leaves; On A Clear Day; Breaking My Back (Instead Of Using My Mind); Medley.* CARRYIN' ON! (December 1966): *Mean Black Snake; Walking Proud; Devil In Your Eyes; Find Out What's Happening; You Can Bring Me All Your Heartaches; Woman Who's A Woman; Life That I Lead; Yesterday; Trouble Down Here Below; You're Gonna Hear From Me; Something Stirring In My Soul; On Broadway.* TOO MUCH (April 1967): *Dead End Street; Yes, It Hurts (Doesn't It); Uphill Climb To The Bottom; I Just Want To Make Love To You; You're Takin' My Bag; Then You Can Tell Me Goodbye; Twelfth Of Never; Righteous Woman Monologue; I Wanna Little Girl; Why (Do I Love You So); I'll Take Time; You're Always On My Mind; Dead End Street Monologue.* THAT'S LOU (July 1967): *When Love Goes Wrong; What Are They Doing About Today; Problems; Love That I Give; Street Of Dreams; I Don' Love You Anymore (How Do You Say); Hard To Get Thing Called Love; They Don't Give Medals (To Yesterday's Heroes); Monologues: Reminiscing; Ear Bender.* MERRY CHRISTMAS HO! HO! HO!: *Little Drummer Boy; Good Time Christmas; Have Yourself A Merry Little Christmas; Little Boy Dear; Christmas Is; Santa Claus Is Coming To Town; Merry Christmas, Baby; Christmas Song; Christmas Will Really Be Christmas; What Are You Doing New Year's Eve; Child With A Toy.* FEELIN' GOOD (February 1968): *The Letter; My Ancestors; For What It's Worth; Even When You Cry; Hang-Ups; Evil Woman; My Son; Feelin' Good; Encore; I'm Gonna Use What I Got (To Get What I Need); Gotta Find A Way.*

YOU'RE GOOD FOR ME (August 1968): *Down Here On The Ground; I Want To Hear It From You; Beautiful Friendship; Baby I Could Be So Good At Lovin' You; Soul Serenade; You're Good For Me; Life Time; Life Time Monologue; Ol' Man River; I'm Satisfied; One For My Baby (And One More For The Road).* BEST OF LOU RAWLS (August 1968): *Love Is A Hurtin' Thing; Southside Blues; Tobacco Road; It Was A Very Good Year; My Ancestors; Dead End Street; World Of Trouble; Three O'clock In The Morning; Street Corner Hustler's Blues; Trouble Down Here Below.* WAY IT WAS, THE WAY IT IS (May 1969).

Singles/*Love Is A Hurtin' Thing/Memory Lane; Trouble Down Here Below/The Life That I Lead; Dead End Street Monologue/Yes It Hurts Doesn't It; Show Business/When Love Goes Wrong; Three O'clock In The Morning/Stormy Monday; Tobacco Road/Blues For A Four String Guitar; Love Is A Hurtin' Thing/Memory Lane; Little Drummer Boy/A Child With A Toy; My Ancestors/Evil Woman; You're Good For Me/Soul Serenade; Down Here On The Ground/I'm Satisfied (Duffy Theme); The Split/Why Can't I Speak* (November 1968).

Also Appears On/CENTRAL PARK MUSIC FESTIVAL: *On Broadway; Love Is A Hurtin' Thing; They Don't Give Medals.* SUPER OLDIES (June 1968): *Dead End Street; Love Is A Hurtin' Thing.* SUPER SOUL-DEES (September 1967): *Tobacco Road.* SUPER SOUL-DEES, VOL. 2 (June 1968): *Love Is A Hurtin' Thing; Dead End Street.*

OTIS REDDING/When they buried him, he was only twenty-six. It was the end of 1967, and everyone knew, and had known for some time, that 1968 was going to be his year, the year he really got there—and stayed there. Because there was something else everyone knew by then, that there was no topping him. Otis Redding was born in Dawson, Georgia, in 1941, but while still young he moved to Macon, the home of Little Richard. And it was Little Richard's success that encouraged him. It all began in 1962, when Otis was driving someone else to a recording session and just happened to mention that he sang too. He cut some things right at the end of the session and although they liked him they thought he

was a bit too country for a rhythm and blues man. The song
he had just tossed off in twenty minutes was *These Arms of
Mine.*

Little Richard and Sam Cooke were Otis' boyhood idols.
On his first album, he came on a bit like Little Richard. And
he liked to do intense Sam Cooke numbers, especially the
unforgettable *Shake,* the performance of which is still with
anyone who saw him do it at the 1967 Monterey Pop
Festival.

They had to take over the Macon City Auditorium to find a
place for all the people at Otis Redding's funeral. James
Brown. Joe Tex. Sam and Dave. Wilson Pickett. Four thousand five hundred men and women weeping inside the auditorium and who knows how many waiting in the streets. Booker
T played the organ and Johnny Taylor sang. Musicians used
to love to work with Otis. He was the king at the Stax-Volt
studios in Memphis. One reason there are still so many tracks
of his in the can is that he loved to work and cut what he
could whenever he had time. Among his earliest fans and
promoters were the Rolling Stones, who turned people on to
him who might never have encountered him otherwise. The
Stones did a lot of his songs, and he did one of theirs,
Satisfaction, in a way that made people wonder whether it
mightn't have been his song all along. The story was told that
the Stones had "bought" *Satisfaction* from Otis. But Steve
Cropper of the MG's with whom Otis worked so harmoniously, told Jann Wenner of *Rolling Stone* magazine that the story
was "completely false." He said they all sat around and
listened to the Stones version for five minutes, then cut their
own. That was all there was. Never mind the compliment paid
to Otis; it was an even greater compliment to the Stones.

Soul moved out of the rhythm and blues charts into the pop
and rock charts in 1965. Otis was working hard then, but it
took Aretha Franklin to open things up properly in 1967 and
really take over. Otis had released his own brilliantly aggressive version of his song *Respect* in mid-1965, but the general
white public (apart from the soul freaks) didn't get to hear it
till 1967, when Aretha had a million seller with it. And
Arthur Conley, his protégé, made it to number one with
another Otis song, *Sweet Soul Music.* In 1967 England's
Melody Maker, which had voted Elvis Presley top male

vocalist for eight straight years, named Otis number one. It was obvious that rhythm and blues, soul, or any other bag was too small to hold him. He was just getting started. And even without his singles and other people's versions of them, there were the albums, the definitive one being a *DICTIONARY OF SOUL*. But the others had titles that, in the light of that plane crash in 1967, the crash of that new private plane that plunged Otis and five of the Bar-Kays into the icy waters of Lake Pomona that December, well, they were titles that would make a strong man weep looking back. *HISTORY OF OTIS REDDING. THE IMMORTAL OTIS REDDING.*

Owning that private plane of his—a symbol that showed he'd made it and didn't have to tour in a bus—was a big triumph and just a small sign of what was ahead for him, and this was his first tour in it. He was just leaving a concert at Madison, Wisconsin, and heading for Cleveland, Ohio, when it went down only four miles from the Madison Municipal Airport on Sunday, December 10. Four thousand five hundred people were at the funeral. Sugar Pie Desanto and Percy Sledge and Gene Chandler and Mabel John. Otis had a plan to bring back Fats Domino and Little Richard and Big Joe Turner and Clyde McPhatter, to get them out of their 1950s thinking into a 1960s groove and watch them take over the charts again. Most of his songs were about chicks and missing them. But his last song, *Dock of the Bay* (ironically the only one that sold a million) was personal, introspective and, perhaps because it was posthumous, the one for which he'll be remembered.

Albums/ DICTIONARY OF SOUL: *Day Tripper; Tennessee Waltz; My Lover's Prayer; Fa, Fa, Fa, Fa, Fa; I'm Sick Y' All; Sweet Lorraine; Try A Little Tenderness; She Put The Hurt On Me; Ton Of Joy; You're Still My Baby; Hawg For You; Love Have Mercy.* DOCK OF THE BAY: *Tramp; Dock Of The Bay; I Love You More Than Words Can Say; Let Me Come On Home; Open The Door; Don't Mess With Cupid; Glory Of Love; I'm Coming Home; Huckle-Buck; Nobody Knows You When You're Down & Out; Ole Man Trouble.* GREAT OTIS REDDING SINGS SOUL BALLADS: *That's How Strong My Love Is; Chained & Bound; Woman, Lover, A Friend; Your One & Only Man; Nothing*

Can Change This Love; For Your Precious Love; It's Too Late; I Want To Thank You; Come To Me; Home In Your Heart; Keep Your Arms Around Me; Mr. Pitiful. HISTORY OF OTIS REDDING: I've Been Loving You Too Long; Try A Little Tenderness; These Arms Of Mine; Pain In My Heart; My Lover's Prayer; Respect; Mr. Pitiful; Fa, Fa, Fa, Fa, Fa; Shake; I Can't Turn You Loose; Security; Satisfaction. IMMORTAL OTIS REDDING: I've Got Dreams To Remember; You Made A Man Out Of Me; Nobody's Fault But Mine; Hard To Handle; Thousand Miles Away; Fool For You; Happy Song; Think About It; Amen; Waste Of Time; Champagne & Wine. OTIS BLUE: Ole Man Trouble: Respect; Change Gonna Come; Down In The Valley; I've Been Loving You Too Long; Shake; My Girl; Satisfaction; You Don't Miss Your Water; Wonderful World; Rock Me Baby. PAIN IN MY HEART: Pain In My Heart; Dog; Stand By Me; Hey Hey Baby; You Send Me; I Need Your Lovin'; Louie, Louie; These Arms Of Mine; Something Is Worrying Me; Security; Tha's What My Heart Heeds; Lucille. LIVE IN EUROPE: Respect; Can't Turn You Loose; I've Been Loving You Too Long; My Girl; Shake; These Arms Of Mine; Satisfaction; Fa, Fa, Fa, Fa, Fa; Day Tripper; Try A Little Tenderness. SOUL ALBUM: Just One More Day; It's Growing; Cigarettes & Coffee; Chain Gang; Nobody Knows You When You're Down & Out; Good To Me; Scrach My Back; Treat Her Right; Everybody Makes A Mistake; Any Ole Way; 634–5789. KING AND QUEEN: Knock On Wood; Tramp; Let Me Be Good To You; Tell It Like It Is; When Something Is Wrong With My Baby; Lovey Dovey; New Year's Resolution; It Takes Two; Are You Lonely For Me Baby; Bring It On Home To Me; Ooh Carla, Ooh Otis. HERE COMES SOME SOUL FROM OTIS REDDING AND JOE CURTIS: Gettin' Hip; Your Mini Skirt; Gamma Lama; Let Me Make It Up To You; 6 Other Titles. IN PERSON AT THE WHISKEY-A-GO-GO (November 1968): I Can't Turn You Loose; Pain In My Heart; Just One More Day; Mr. Pitiful; These Arms Of Mine; I'm Depending On You; Any Ole Way; Satisfaction; Poppa's Got A Brand New Bag; Respect.

Singles/Pain In My Heart/Something Is Worrying Me (October 1963); *Come To Me/Don't Leave Me This Way* (February 1964); *I Want To Thank You/Security* (April 1964), *Chained And Bound/Your One And Only Man* (September 1964); *Ole Man Trouble/Respect* (April 1965); *I'm Depending On You/I've Been Loving You Too Long* (April 1965); *I Can't Turn You Loose/Just One More Day* (November 1965); *Any Ole Way/Satisfaction* (February 1966); *Don't Mess With Cupid/My Lover's Prayer* (May 1966); *Fa-Fa-Fa-Fa-Fa/Good To Me* (September 1966); *I'm Sick Y'All/ Try A Litle Tenderness* (November 1966); *I Love You More Than Words Can Say/Let Me Come On Home* (March 1967); *Shake/You Don't Miss Your Water* (April 1967); *Glory Of Love/I'm Coming Home* (June 1967); *Dock Of The Bay/Sweet Lorraine* (January 1968); *Happy Song (Dum-Dum)/Open The Door* (April 1968); *Amen/Hard To Handle* (June 1968); *Fat Girl/Shout Bamalama; Mr. Pitiful/That's How Strong My Love Is; I've Got Dreams To Remember/Nobody's Fault But Mine* (September 1968); *Direct Me/Papa's Got A Brand New Bag* (December 1968); *Can't Turn You Loose/Love Man* (May 1969).

Also Appears On/APOLLO SATURDAY NIGHT: *Pain In My Heart; These Arms Of Mine.*

HELEN REDDY/A top singer in Australia, Helen Reddy came to the U.S. in 1966 and in 1967 became one of the first nightclub singers to introduce works by Simon and Garfunkel (*Feelin' Groovy*) and Donovan (*Catch The Wind*) into an act intended for adult audiences. Before long many other singers were doing it, but when she started, places like Mr. Kelly's in Chicago had never heard anything quite like it.

Single/*One Way Ticket/Go.*

JIMMY REED is a Chicago city bluesman who, like Muddy Waters and Howlin' Wolf, originally came from Mississippi, home of the country blues.

Albums/NEW JIMMY REED ALBUM (March 1967): *Big Boss Man; I Wanna Know; Got No-where To Go; Two Ways To Skin; Heartaches And Troubles; Tell Me What You Want Me To Do; Honey I'll Make Two; You Don't Have To Go; Don't Play Me Cheap; Two Sides To Every Story; I'm Just*

Trying To; Two Heads Are Better Than One. SOULIN' (November 1967): *Buy Me A Hound Dog; Feel Like I Want To Ramble; I Wake Up At Daybreak; Peepin' And Hidin'; Don't Press Your Luck Woman; I'm Not Going To Let You Down; I'm Knockin' On Your Door; Crazy About Oklahoma; Cousin Peaches; Ain't No Time For Fussin'; Dedication To Sonny.* BIG BOSS MAN (March 1968): *Give Up And Let Me Go; I'm Leavin'; Shame, Shame, Shame; Run Here To Me Baby; Life Is Funny; Two In One Blue; My Baby Told Me; Five Years Of Good Lovin'; When Two People In Love; I've Got To Keep On Rollin'; When I Woke Up This Morning.* SOMETHIN' ELSE (September 1968): *Go On To School; My First Plea; String To Your Heart; Down In Virginia;* 6 Others.

Singles/ *Buy Me A Hound Dog/Crazy About Oklahoma; Got No Where To Go/Two Ways To Skin (A Cat).*

JIM REEVES/ A prolific country singer, Jim Reeves died in a plane crash in 1964 and left many tapes behind. He has had posthumous hits all over the world but the most surprising was *Distant Drums* which in 1967, in the middle of a rock boom, leaped to number one place on the English charts.

Albums/ JIM REEVES (December 1957). GIRLS I HAVE KNOWN (August 1958). GOD BE WITH YOU (April 1959). SONGS TO WARM THE HEART (September 1959). ACCORDING TO MY HEART (June 1960). INTIMATE (August 1960). TALL TALES AND SHORT TEMPERS (April 1961). TALKIN' TO YOUR HEART (November 1961). COUNTRY SIDE OF JIM REEVES (April 1962). TOUCH OF VELVET (June 1962). WE THANK THEE (August 1962). GENTLEMAN JIM (March 1963). INTERNATIONAL JIM REEVES (September 1963). GOOD 'N' COUNTRY (December 1963). HE'LL HAVE TO GO (April 1964). KIMBERLY JIM (April 1964). MOONLIGHT AND ROSES (July 1964). BEST OF JIM REEVES (August 1964). HAVE I TOLD YOU LATELY THAT I LOVE YOU (December 1964). JIM REEVES WAY (March 1965). JIM REEVES UP THROUGH THE YEARS (September 1965). BEST OF JIM REEVES, VOL. 2 (February 1966). DISTANT DRUMS (July 1966). YOURS SIN-

CERELY, JIM REEVES (December 1966). BLUE SIDE OF LONESOME (June 1967). MY CATHEDRAL (December 1967). TOUCH OF SADNESS (May 1968). JIM REEVES, ON STAGE (October 1968).

TERRY REID/*Terry Reid (guitar, vocals), Keith Webb (drums), Peter Shelley (organ).*
A nineteen-year-old with the face of a Cockney angel and the voice of a hard-rocking barrow boy, Terry Reid came from England with his trio late in 1968 with a repertoire of old favorites like *Season Of The Witch* and *Summertime Blues*, all sung with sunshiny freshness. Mickie Most, who produced their album and has already performed multimillion dollar miracles for the baby-faced Lulu and the saintly Donovan, seems to be moving Reid in the same direction—a clean, young, highly professional sound touched, but not spoiled, by good, practical commercialism.

Album/BANG, BANG YOU'RE TERRY REID (December 1968): *Bang, Bang (My Baby Shot Me Down); Tinker Tailor; Erica; Without Expression; Sweater; Something's Gotten Hold Of My Heart; Season Of The Witch; Writing On The Wall; Summertime Blues; When You Get Home; Loving Time.*

THE REMAINS/*Barry Tashian (lead guitar, vocalist), Chip Damiani (drums), Vern Miller Jr. (trumpet, tuba, guitar, French horn, acoustic and electric bass), William Henry Briggs III (electric organ, electric piano).*
As Barry and the Remains, this tight hard-rock group (of four Boston University dropouts) reigned supreme in New England for over two years (1965-67). Internal strife, as well as difficulty in expressing themselves in a recording studio, eventually led the group to disband. Barry Tashian, the lead guitarist of the Remains, is still regarded in some circles as one of the foremost rock musicians of this decade.

Album/THE REMAINS (May 1967): *Heart; Lonely Week-End; Don't Look Back; Why Do I Cry; Diddy Wah Diddy; You Got A Hard Time Coming; Once Before; Thank You; Time Of Day; Say You're Sorry.*

Single/*Diddy Wah Diddy/Once Before.*

REPARATA AND THE DELRONS/*Mary Aiese, Loraine Mazzola, Nanette Licari.*
Reparata and the Delrons are an example of how unpredictable the rock scene can be. Once a brief hit in the U.S. (with *Tommy* and *When A Teenager Cries*) the group was forgotten, or so it seemed, till their *Captain Of My Ship* was number one on the English charts in May 1967. Although they are American this all-girl trio is still big in England, and still comparatively neglected in the States.

Singles/*I Believe*/*It's Waiting There For You* (August 1967); *Captain Of Your Ship*/*Toom Toom (Is A Little Boy)* (January 1968); *Panic*/*Saturday Night Didn't Happen* (April 1968); *Weather Forecast*/*You Can't Change A Young Boy's Mind* (July 1968); *Heaven Only Knows*/*Summer Laughter* (September 1968).

PAUL REVERE AND THE RAIDERS/*Mark Lindsay (lead vocals, saxophone), Paul Revere (piano, organ), Freddie Weller (replaced Michael "Smitty" Smith) (lead guitar), Joe Junior Correro (replaced Jim "Harpo" Valley, who had replaced Drake Levin) (drums), Charlie Coe (replaced Philip "Fang" Volk) (bass guitar).*
For years Paul Revere and the Raiders were on television every single day, camping it up in their revolutionary uniforms of jackets and tights. Any other group would have died of overexposure. But the Raiders became an integral part of the young girlhood of every American teeny of that period. They were the first rock group with Columbia to have a million dollar gold album (*JUST LIKE US*, 1966), and inevitably there was much looking down of noses by supercilious rivals as Revere and his boys stuck to the well-rehearsed formulas (choreographed down to the last shuffle kick) that the audiences adored. Actually, their witty stage act, on television and live, was a nice piece of rock theatre and comedy rock, and many of their songs that made the charts deserved to be there.

They started as a hard-rock group, the Downbeats, in Portland, Oregon, in 1962, complete with piped collarless suits and swept-back pompadours. They became famous for the dances they ran in that area in 1963. (Revere was a shrewd businessman then, as he is now.) They had a version of a song called *Louie, Louie* which might have made some national impact had not another local group, the Kingsmen, got in first with their version. The song went on to be a hit and a rock classic, but at least the Raiders' version got them a record contract. After that there were a million hassles to get themselves established.

Dick Clark's tv show, *Where The Action Is*, did it for them in April 1965, and there they were, instant superstars. Since then there have been personnel changes, but Mark Lindsay, one of America's few really big rock idols, stayed, as did Revere. Neither the image nor the sound has changed much (except to become slightly more sophisticated); the appeal is always frankly to the very young, but the group has to have top marks for durability in the face of a chaotically changing scene. They are probably one of the great financial successes to come out of rock.
(see BROTHERHOOD)

Albums/HERE THEY COME (August 1965): *You Can't Sit Down; Money (That's What I Want); Louie, Louie; Do You Love Me; Big Boy Pete; Oo Poo Pah Doo; Sometimes; Gone; Time Is On My Side; A Kiss To Remember You.* JUST LIKE US (March 1966): *Steppin' Out; Doggone; Out Of Sight; Baby, Please Don't Go; I Know; Night Train; Just Like Me; Catch The Wind; Satisfaction (I Can't Get No); I'm Crying; New Orleans; Action.* IN THE BEGINNING (April 1966): *Shake, Rattle And Roll; Don't Be Cruel; Linda Lu; So Fine; Blues Stay Away; Work With Me Annie; Mojo Workout; Rinky Dink; Hey Baby; Hard Tonk; Irresistible You; Crisco.* MIDNIGHT RIDE (July 1966): *Kicks; There's Always Tomorrow; Little Girl In The 4th Row; Ballad Of A Useless Man; I'm Not Your Stepping Stone; There She Goes; All I Really Need Is You; Get It On; Louie, Go Home; Take A Look At Yourself; Melody For An Unknown Girl.* SPIRIT OF '67 (January 1967): *Good Thing; All About Her; Louise; In My Community; Why Why Why (Is It So Hard); Oh To Be A Man; Hungry; Undecided Man; 1001 Arabian Nights; Our Candidate; Great Airplane Strike.* PAUL REVERE AND THE RAIDERS GREATEST HITS (June 1967): *Ups & Downs; Steppin' Out; Just Like Me; Louie, Louie; Louie Go Home; Kicks; Hungry; Great Airplane Strike; Good Thing;*

Legend Of Paul Revere; Melody For An Unknown Girl.
REVOLUTION (October 1967): *Him Or Me—What's It
Gonna Be; I Had A Dream; Reno; Upon Your Leaving;
Mo'reen; I Hear A Voice; Wanting You; Gone—Movin' On;
Tighter; Make It With Me; Ain't Nobody Who Can Do It
Like Leslie Can.* GOIN' TO MEMPHIS (April 1968): *Boo-
galoo Down Broadway; Every Man Needs A Woman; My
Way; One Night Stand; Love You So; Soul Man; I Don't
Want Nobody; Cry On My Shoulder; I'm A Loser Too; Peace
Of Mind; No Sad Songs; Goin' To Memphis.* SOMETHING
HAPPENING (September 1968): *Happening Intro; Too
Much Talk; Don't Take It So Hard; Good Times; Happens
Every Day; Communications; Burn Like A Candle; Free; Get
Out Of My Mind; Happening '68; Love Makes The World Go
'Round; Observation From Flight 285.* CHRISTMAS
PRESENT...& PAST (November 1967): *Wear A Smile At
Christmas; Jingle Bells; Brotherly Love; Rain, Sleet, Snow;
Peace; Valley Forge; Dear Mr. Claus; Macy's Window;
Christmas Spirit; Heavy Christmas Message.*

Singles/*Louie, Louie*/*Louie Go Home; Great Airplane Strike*/
Hungry; Ups & Downs/*Good Thing; Steppin' Out*/*Him Or
Me—What's It Gonna Be; I Had A Dream*/*Upon Your
Leaving; Do Unto Others*/*Peace Of Mind; Brotherly Love
*/*Rain, Sleet, Snow; Happening '68*/*Too Much Talk; Don't
Take It So Hard*/*Observation From Flight 285; Cinderella
Sunshine*/*It's Happening* (October 1968); *I Don't Know*/*Let
Me* (May 1969).

RHINOCEROS/*John Finley (vocals), Michael Fonfara (organ), Alan Gerber (piano), Doug Hastings (guitar), Billy
Mundi (drums), Danny Weis (guitar), Jerry Penrod (bass).*
What would happen if you took the best musicians you could
find, locked them in a room together and threw away the key?
Rhinoceros is a group made up of the seven best musicians
that Doors' producer Paul Rothchild could find in 1968, and
when the story got around Los Angeles the group got itself a
nickname: Supergroup. Well, heavens, no one wants to start a
career with *that* name to live up to so it was changed to
Rhinoceros. But they still *thought* supergroup—seven stars in
search of a sound that worked. At their first New York
appearance, at a free concert in Central Park, they really

freaked the entire audience (reportedly 20,000 people)
Eventually, after some very sophisticated playing around, they
finished up with a strong rock-soul-gospel-blues combination.

Album/RHINOCEROS (November 1968): *When You Say
You're Sorry; Same Old Way; Apricot Brandy; That Time Oʃ
The Year; You're My Girl (I Don't Want To Discuss It); I
Need Love; I've Been There; Belbuekus; Along Comes To-
morrow; I Will Serenade You.*

RHYTHM AND BLUES was a nice way of saying "race
music," which was what black popular music was called for a
long time. It grew up out of jazz, gospel and the blues and
was a far, far cry from the pop songs that dominated the
pre-Elvis white charts. Rock and roll was born only when
whites became intrigued with black music and sought out
recordings of it. Soon white artists, noting the sharp rise in
sales of those records, took to studying black charts to see
what they could find. Elvis was among the first to combine
sounds from the black charts with his own country-music
background. That was rock and roll. Others followed and
before long hundreds of white artists were "covering" songs
from the black rhythm and blues charts. Once in a while the
original record would hit the white charts, but very rarely.
Eventually more and more black artists started crossing into
white charts, but there is still an active rhythm and blues
chart which features many names barely known to the white
public. Once in a while, but very rarely, a white performer
makes it on those rhythm and blues charts.

CLIFF RICHARD/Anyone who thinks tne English music
scene began with the Beatles should know that there was an
English, as well as an American, scene that they sprang from.
The big figure in the 1958 English scene, when the Beatles
were growing up, was a seventeen-year-old former $10-a-
week office boy, Harry Webb, who sang under the name of
Cliff Richard. Almost overnight, this mini-Presley (ducktail
and all) had a hit on the English charts, *Move It.* From
Favorite New Singer Under Twenty-One he went on to a gold
disk, films and performances for England's Royal Family.
After that it was Top British Male Singer, more films, more
awards, more records. He was a major rock star in England

with riots and all, but never in America, mainly because he was the best of what was essentially a very dull English music scene. As the Beatles' star rose, his huge popularity inevitably declined, but not as much as one would think, the English being a loyal and sentimental lot. So he's still big in England with the special status of a former idol. A few years ago he was converted to Christianity and now makes religious films wearing neat suits, horn-rimmed specs and a semi-Beatle haircut.

THE RIGHTEOUS BROTHERS/*Bobby Hatfield, Jimmy Walker (replaced Bill Medley).*
The Righteous Brothers were among the first to produce what was later to be dismissed contemptuously as "blue-eyed soul," but theirs was a blue-eyed soul that the brown-eyed soul boys dug and played on their own radio stations. Together since 1962 (and once produced by the great Phil Spector), the boys split in July, 1968, so that Medley could go solo. No one since has been able to come up with that same mixture of jazz, gospel, rhythm and blues, rock and roll, and spiritual.

Albums/RIGHT NOW (December 1963): *Let The Good Times Roll; My Babe; Bye Bye Love; B-Flat Blues; Little Latin Lupe Lu; My Prayer; In That Great Gettin' Up Mornin'; Georgia On My Mind; Koko Joe; I'm So Lonely; Love Or Magic; Fee-Fi-Fidily-I-Oh.* SOME BLUE-EYED SOUL: *Baby, What You Want Me To Do; I Just Want To Make Love To You; Bring Your Love To Me; My Tears Will Go Away; Fanny Mae; Something's Got A Hold On Me; This Little Girl Of Mine; Try To Find Another Man; Night Owl; For Your Love.* THIS IS NEW: *Justine; Burn On Love; I Still Love You; Gotta Tell You How I Feel; I Need A Girl; You Can Have Her; Cryin' Blues; At My Front Door; If You're Lying You'll Be Crying; There She Goes.* BEST OF THE RIGHTEOUS BROTHERS: *Georgia On My Mind; Little Latin Lupe Lu; For Your Love; Try To Find Another Man; You Can Have Her; Justine; I Just Want To Make Love To You; Fanny Mae; Something's Got A Hold On Me; My Prayer; Let The Good Times Roll; Bye Bye Love; At My Front Door; This Little Girl Of Mine.* YOU'VE LOST THAT LOVIN' FEELIN': *You've Lost That Lovin' Feelin'; Ol' Man River; Summertime; What'd I Say; Angels Listened*

In; Ko Ko Mo; Look At Me; Over And Over; Sick And Tired; Soul City; There's A Woman. JUST ONCE IN MY LIFE: *Just Once In My Life; Big Boy Pete; See That Girl; Unchained Melody; You Are My Sunshine; Sticks And Stones; Great Pretender; Oo-Oo-Pah-Doo; You'll Never Walk Alone; Guess Who; The Blues.* BACK TO BACK (August 1966): *Ebb Tide; God Bless The Child; Hung On You; Hot Tamales; Hallelujah, I Love Her So; She's Mine, All Mine; For Sentimental Reasons; White Cliffs Of Dover; Loving You; Without A Doubt; Late, Late Night.* SOUL AND INSPIRATION (June 1966): *You're My Soul And Inspiration; He Will Break Your Heart; Stand By; In The Midnight Hour; He; I'm Leaving It Up To You; Turn On Your Love Lights; Hey Girl; Mine All Mine; Change Is Gonna Come; Bring It On Home To Me; Rat Race.* GO AHEAD AND CRY (September 1966): *Go Ahead And Cry; Save The Last Dance For Me; Something You Got; I've Got The Beat; I Believe; Let It Be Me; What Now My Love; Big Time Ben; Island In The Sun; Stagger Lee; Things Didn't Go Your Way; Drown In My Own Tears.* SAYIN' SOMETHIN' (March 1967): *Along Came Jones; On This Side Of Goodbye; Don't Fight It; I; Yes Indeed; Harlem Shuffle; Soulville; Hold On, I'm Comin'; Man Without A Dream; Will You Love Me Tomorrow; Jimmy's Blues.* RIGHTEOUS BROTHERS GREATEST HITS (October 1967): *Great Pretender; Unchained Melody; You've Lost That Lovin' Feelin'; Ebb Tide; Hung On You; Georgia On My Mind; You'll Never Walk Alone; Just Once In My Life; See That Girl; Guess Who; White Cliffs Of Dover; For Sentimental Reasons.* SOULED OUT (November 1967): *Been So Nice; Stranded In The Middle Of No Place; If Loving You Is Wrong; Here I Am; It's Up To You; So Many Lonely Nights Ahead; I Don't Believe In Losing; You Bent My Mind; Someone Like You; Without You I'd Be Lost; Love Keeps Callin' My Name.* RIGHTEOUS BROTHERS STANDARDS (March 1968): *That Lucky Old Sun; That's All; My Darling Clementine; All The Way; Country Boy; If I Ruled The World; Without A Song; Since I Fell For You; Come Rain Or Come Shine; Secret Love; Somewhere.* ONE FOR THE ROAD (August 1968): *Let The Good Times Roll; You're My Soul And Inspiration; Little Latin Lupe Lu; My Babe· You'll Never*

*Walk Alone; That Lucky Old Sun; Oldies But Goodies Medley
And Gospel Medley.*

Singles/*My Tears Will Go Away*/*Georgia On My Mind;
Bring Your Love To Me*/*I Need A Girl; There's A Woman*/
You've Lost That Lovin' Feelin'; The Blues/*Just Once In My
Life; Unchained Melody*/*Hung On You, Ebb Tide*/*For Senti-
mental Reasons, She's Mine All Mine*/*White Cliffs Of Dover;
Georgia On My Mind*/*You've Lost That Lovin' Feelin';
He*/*Ebb Tide; Just Once In My Life*/*White Cliffs Of Dover;
Soul And Inspiration*/*Little Lupe Lu; Been So Nice*/*Stranded
In The Middle Of No Place* (August 1967); *That Lucky Old
Sun*/*My Darling Clementine* (November 1967); *Here I
Am*/*So Many Lonely Nights Ahead* (January 1968).

Also Appears On/SWINGIN' SUMMER: *Justine.*

THE ROBBS/*Dee Robb, Joe Robb, Bruce Robb, Craig Robb.*
Three clean-cut long-haired brothers and a clean-cut long-
haired lookalike cousin, the Robbs originated in Florida. In
1961 and 1962 they were backing Del Shannon, Bobby
Vinton, Brian Hyland and Gene Pitney, then the reigning
kings of the pop scene. In 1964-65 they toured with the Dave
Clark Five and in the summer of 1966 became practically
regulars on Dick Clark's television show, "Where the Action
Is," winning themselves a teeny following despite the lack of
national chart activity.

Album/THE ROBBS (October 1967). *Violets Of Dawn;
Race With The Wind; Next Time You See Me; Cynthia
Loves; Girls, Girls; Bittersweet; See Jane Run· In A Funny
Sort Of Way; Rapid Transit; Jolly Miller.*

Singles/*Girls, Girls*/*Violets Of Dawn* (September 1967);
Castles In The Air/*I Don't Want To Discuss It* (1968);
Changin' Winds/*Good Time Song* (December 1968).

SMOKEY ROBINSON AND THE MIRACLES/Smokey
is three geniuses in one: Smokey the songwriter, the performer
and the producer. He is Mr. Music, Dylan, Lennon and Pappalardi in one glistening package. Why have Smokey and the
Miracles never become as well known as others with fewer
and less spectacular hits to their credit? Put it down to indifferent publicity Those who love him—many but never enough
—say it shouldn't matter But that's debatable.

Albums/HI, WE'RE THE MIRACLES: *Who's Lovin' You; Depend On Me; Heart Like Mine; Shop Around; Won't You Take Me Back; 'Cause I Love You; Your Love; After All; Way Over There; Money; Don't Leave Me.* COOKIN' WITH THE MIRACLES: *Embraceable You; Everybody's Gotta Pay Some Dues; Mama; You Never Miss A Good Thing; That's The Way I Feel; Ain't It Baby; Determination; Broken Hearted; Only One I Love; I Can't Believe.* I'LL TRY SOMETHING NEW: *I'll Try Something New; Speak Low; What's So Good About Goodbye; I've Got You Under My Skin; On The Street Where You Live; Love That Can Never Be; If Your Mother Only Knew; I've Been Good To You; He Don't Care About Me; This I Swear, I Promise.* FABULOUS MIRACLES: *You've Really Got A Hold On Me; I've Been Good To You; Such Is Love, Such Is Life; I Can Take A Hint; Won't You Take Me Back; Love She Can Count On; Whatever Makes You Happy; Heartbreak; Happy Landing; Your Love.* MIRACLES ON STAGE: *Mighty Good Lovin'; You've Really Got A Hold On Me; Happy Landing; Love She Can Count On; I've Been Good To You; Way Over There; What's So Good About Goodbye.* MIRACLES DOIN' MICKEY'S MONKEY: *Land Of 1,000 Dances; Monkey Time; Dancing Holiday; Dance What You Wanna; Watusi; Twist; I Gotta Dance To Keep From Crying; Do You Love Me; Twist And Shout; Mickey's Monkey; Groovy Thing.* MIRACLES GREATEST HITS—FROM THE BEGINNING (March 1966): *Got A Job; Mama Done Told Me; Money (I Need Some); I Cry; Bad Girl; I Love You Baby; Way Over There; You Can Depend On Me; I Need A Change; All I Want Is You; Who's Lovin' You; Shop Around; What's So Good About Goodbye; I've Been Good To You; I'll Try Something New; You've Really Got A Hold On Me; Love She Can Count On; Mickey's Monkey; I Gotta Dance To Keep From Crying; I Like It Like That; That's What Love Is Made Of; Would I Love You.* GOING TO A GO-GO (March 1966): *Tracks Of My Tears; Going To A Go-Go; Ooo, Baby, Baby; My Girl Has Gone; In Case You Need Me; Choosey Beggar; Since You Won My Heart; From Head To Toe; All That's Good; My Baby Changes Like The Weather; Let Me Have Some; Fork In The Road.* AWAY WE A-GO-GO (April 1967): *Whole Lot Of Shakin' In My*

Heart; I'm The One You Need; You Don't Have To Say You Love Me; Save Me; Oh Be My Love; Can You Love A Poor Boy; Beauty Is Only Skin Deep; I Just Don't Know What To Do With Myself; Baby Baby; Walk On By; Swept For You, Baby; More, More, More Of Your Love. MAKE IT HAPPEN (December 1967): *More Love; Love I Saw In You Was Just A Mirage; You Must Be Love; After You Put Back The Pieces; Dancing's Alright; On The Outside; It's A Good Feeling; Don't Think It's Me; Tears Of A Clown; Soulful Shack; My Love Is Your Love; My Love For You.* MIRACLES' GREATEST HITS WITH SMOKEY ROBIN-SON (January 1968): *I Second That Emotion; Tracks Of My Tears; Going To A-Go-Go; Love I Saw In You Was Just A Mirage; Oooh Baby Baby; My Girl Has Gone; Come On Do The Jerk; Whole Lot Of Shakin' In My Heart; I'm The One You Need; More Love; Choosey Beggar; Save Me.*

Singles/*Shop Around/Who's Lovin' You; Mighty Good Lovin'/Broken Hearted; Everybody's Gotta Pay Some Dues/I Can't Believe; What's So Good About Goodbye/I've Been Good To You; You Never Miss A Good Thing/I'll Try Something New; If Your Mother Only Knew/Way Over There; You've Really Got A Hold On Me/Happy Landing; I Can Take A Hint/Love She Can Count On; Mickey's Monkey/What Ever Makes You Happy; Such Is Love, Such Is Life/I Gotta Dance To Keep From Crying; Heartbreak Road/Man In You; I Like It Like That/You're So Fine And Sweet; Would I Love You/That's What Love Is Made Of; Baby Don't You Go/Come On And Do The Jerk; All That's Good/Oooh Baby Baby; Fork In The Road/Tracks Of My Tears; Since You Won My Heart/My Girl Is Gone; Going To A-Go-Go/Choosey Beggar; Whole Lot Of Shakin' In My Heart/Oh, Be My Love; I'm The One You Need/Save Me; Love I Saw In You Was Just A Mirage/Come Spy With Me; Swept For You/More Love; I Second That Emotion/You Must Be Love; If You Can Want/When The Words From Your Heart Get Caught In Your Throat; Give Her Up/Special Occasion.*

ROCK MANAGERS/You could put Colonel Tom Parker up on a stage, let him talk, charge admission and you'd have a big star. Or you could put Albert Grossman in a film and he would upstage the leading man. Brian Epstein was a shy man, they say, but when he forgot that and was feeling self-assured and a little arrogant, he too could go in for some delicious bits of stage business.

Perhaps not all managers have a star inside them clamoring to get out, perhaps there are some good ones who are small drab uninteresting businessmen, but few spring to mind immediately. The great managers of great acts are almost invariably great acts themselves. It is a pity they have to stay behind the scenes, at least as far as audiences are concerned. Elvis Presley's manager, Colonel Tom Parker, is more than a shrewd financial adviser and tactician. He has never lost the air of carnival barker, which is how he started out. Albert Grossman made Bob Dylan a star (not to mention Peter, Paul and Mary and a bunch of others), but in "Don't Look Back" he almost steals the limelight from his client. His wheelings and dealings are as much a part of the Dylan story as the lyrics of *Positively Fourth Street*. As for Brian Epstein, the Beatles' biography makes clear what a major role his faith, persistence and levelheadedness played in their success.

And yet: Grossman, successful as he is, never did find another Dylan; Parker never found another Elvis (though he has been reported casting covetous eyes at England's hip-swivelling Tom Jones); Epstein searched and searched but none of his groups got anywhere near the Beatles; Andrew Oldham, who managed the Stones to fame and fortune, had smaller successes with smaller groups but never repeated the Stones coup. What does all this mean? That any good manager has only one good star in him? That the Presleys and Dylans would have made it regardless?

Was it the Beatles or Epstein? Dylan or Grossman? Presley or Parker? The answer is—it must be—that it takes two to create that rare chemistry that makes a great match. The star has to have it, but the manager has to *know* it. The manager has to have the same sort of instinctive sense of timing *off* stage that the star has *on* stage.

The relationship between manager and star is not an easy one. Some stars in the end have preferred to manage themselves. The Beatles did after Epstein died. The Stones now work without the man who got them together. Jefferson Airplane, once managed by Fillmore impresario Bill Graham, now look after themselves. Others thrive on a relationship where one man takes care of all sordid business details, money matters, tax payments, everything that takes away much needed energy from performing.

Tim Buckley could not hope to function without Herbie Cohn, who also manages the Mothers. Harold Leventhal has Judy Collins, Arlo Guthrie, and Pete Seeger in his stable, among others. Kit Lambert and Chris Stamp had the vision to pilot The Who to glory. Ex-Animals Chas Chandler and Mike Jeffrey saw the potential in Jimi Hendrix when he was an unknown guitarist. Steve Paul carried his discovery, Johnny Winter, financially until he got him his half a million dollar record contract. And if in all these men there is a personal flamboyance, well, so there should be. Presenting an act or a performer to the public is as flamboyant an act as getting up on a stage and singing. But in the manager, the artist has to be a businessman as well. Not many make it in that perfect combination but those who do are probably as much the real stars of rock as the people they represent.

ROCK MUSICALS/By the end of 1968, in spite of all the talk about rock and the new music, the big rock musical had still to be done. There had been a few brave tries. One of the first, maybe *the* first, was Megan Terry's *Viet Rock* in the fall of 1966, a serious play about Vietnam with satiric rock songs specially written for it. The first actual rock musical, in which a rock group appeared on stage, was Tom Sankey's *The Golden Screw,* which played off-off-Broadway, then off-Broadway, and told the story of a folk-rock singer whose career was not unlike Bob Dylan's. The off-Broadway season of 1967 yielded a rock musical of sorts, *Your Own Thing,* while 1968 brought *Hair,* which was described as a rock musical but was actually rather like most other musicals on Broadway as far as listening went.

ROCK POOL/The notion of a rock pool came up late in 1968 as more and more groups split apart from the pressures and demands of touring, making the charts, meeting album deadlines and other group duties. Frank Zappa was one of the first to talk (in *Rolling Stone* magazine) about the possibility of different musicians getting together for just one concert.

No rehearsals, just spontaneity and mutual challenging and, of course, a unique never-to-be-repeated sound and experience. (Also no boredom, no hassles, none of the strain of constant tedious touring.) Others took the idea up, thinking it could probably work well for recording anyway. A Moby Grape album, *GRAPE JAM*, brought the group together in a spontaneous jam session with two musicians from other bands, Mike Bloomfield from the Electric Flag and Al Kooper from Blood, Sweat and Tears. Another product of a rock pool was *SUPER SESSION* with Bloomfield, Kooper, and Steve Stills of the by then defunct Buffalo Springfield. The album was a best seller. It had exactly the loose and relaxed quality Zappa had been talking about. Whether jams with lesser names will sell as well, whether the idea of a concert jam will appeal to entrepreneurs is still unknown. But the idea of the rock pool is already spreading, perhaps mainly because of its appeal to good and energetic musicians.

ROCK REVIVAL/In the middle of 1968 in England there was a mild but interesting revival of early rock that was marked by the triumphant return of Bill Haley and the Comets, a brief fashion for leather and studs (but not greased-back hairdos), and a brisk reissue of many early rock records, including four albums (and forty-seven tracks) of the late Buddy Holly. At the Haley concert there was no question of rock *revival;* one look around at the motorcycles outside, and the pompadours and the blue suede shoes, and you knew that there were whole pockets of the world where rock had never died. There have been attempts to revive rock in the U.S., and a growing interest in music roots and sources suggests that this would be well received. What people don't realize is that Little Richard, Fats Domino, Chuck Berry, Jerry Lee Lewis and all the others never did stop working when the fiercest flames of their popularity died down. They're ready for a rock revival any time we are.

JIMMIE RODGERS was a country singer whose fusion of pop, folk, country, blues and jazz opened the way for singers like Elvis Presley and Johnny Cash. He died in 1933 at the age of thirty-five, but in the six years before his death he sold millions of records; today he is considered the founder of country music.

Albums/NEVER NO MO' BLUES. TRAIN WHISTLE BLUES. (January 1959). MY ROUGH AND ROWDY WAYS (June 1960). JIMMIE THE KID (June 1961). COUNTRY MUSIC HALL OF FAME (August 1962). SHORT BUT BRILLIANT LIFE OF JIMMIE RODGERS (June 1963). MY TIME AIN'T LONG (August 1964). BEST OF THE LEGENDARY JIMMIE RODGERS (March 1965).

ROLLING STONES/*Mick Jagger (lead vocals, harmonica), Keith Richard (lead guitar, vocals), Brian Jones (rhythm guitar, harmonica, sitar), Charlie Watts (drums), Bill Wyman (bass guitar).*

When the Beatles were still four sweet little moptop dolls in 1964, and we didn't know then that they were going to grow into more than faces on a Woolworth's charm bracelet, the Stones did not come on, as almost everyone else on the English scene did, as moptop imitations. Even at that early, early stage they did their own thing. And their thing was the full slummy English lout barrow-boy gutter-rat routine. Mean, moody and magnificent (as was once said about Jane Russell).

While the 1964 Beatles looked as if they had been personally scrubbed down by Brian Epstein himself, the 1964 Rolling Stones looked as if they had been sent to bed every night for a week with the same clothes on and no supper. By the time they hit Beatle-sated, Hermit-sated America, they looked different, not to say positively menacing. This immediately established them as personalities at a time when so many hairy groups had come through that they had all eventually become faceless. Their music had much the same impact. The Beatles' songs had been rinsed and hung out to dry. The Stones had never seen soap and water. And where the adorable little windup Beatle moptops wanted no more than to hold a hand, the hateful rasping Stones were bent on rape, pillage and plunder. Well, at least satisfaction. At that stage, both the Beatles and the Stones were doing English imitations of American music (there certainly wasn't any English music worth imitating then), but the Stones were basing their music on an earlier, earthier and less polished period than the period the Beatles were concentrating on.

English groups were into raunchy American blues before the Stones (there was a long tradition of that), but they had always done it in a very removed way—a little too earnest, a little too intent and reverent. Not Jagger. No one had ever seen a white man move on stage the way Jagger moved. Later, like Elvis, whom he completely overshadowed, he was to become the prototype for stage sexuality, the most imitated singer in rock. Right from the start he parodied himself completely, but that worked *for* him, not against him. His lips and no-hips drove every relevant point home; a not-so-distant relative of the Shangri-las' Leader of the Pack, he laid it all on the line.

Most of the girls who watched had never before had the word put on them quite so explicitly. It was heady stuff for fourteen-year-old virgins, and others besides. And the publicity played it up, although it is hard to say where manager Andrew Oldham's shrewdness left off and the Stones' own natural boorishness began. In any case, they were never photographed to look pretty; they seemed under orders not to smile and their music was full of disdain for women, morals, parents and under-assistant West Coast promotion men.

What started off as a series of straight pinches from a variety of black blues musicians of the past eventually came out as the Stones sound. Even in the first three albums, where they were simply searching for a musical identity in their vast repertoire of soul music, rhythm and blues, and Chicago blues, they were producing what was then the heaviest music to come out of England in that 1964-early 1965 period. They started to find themselves in mid-1965 in their fourth album, *OUT OF OUR HEADS* (stopping only to pay tribute to some heroes, Sam Cooke and Otis Redding), continuing the process with *DECEMBER'S CHILDREN*, where it was clear from the growing number of Mick Jagger-Keith Richard compositions that a Stones "personality" was emerging in unambiguous lyrics and music. *BIG HITS (HIGH TIDE AND GREEN GRASS)* in the spring of 1966 was the wrap-up of that time, their sort of farewell to the first golden era.

AFTERMATH, that summer, saw something quite new. The Stones had made every point they needed to make. Now they could relax. Some of the brute force was gone now, to be replaced by tenderness, impatience and more than a touch of the sardonic. Guitarist Brian Jones played dulcimer and, in *Paint It Black*, sitar, which had hardly been used then in rock except by the Beatles and Byrds. There was early fuzz-tone in *Think* and a most un-Stones-like Elizabethan mood prevailed, just mocking enough to make it believable. A live album followed and *BETWEEN THE BUTTONS*, where the Stones told it all (*Let's Spend The Night Together* and *Something Happened To Me Yesterday*), then *FLOWERS* in the summer of 1967, a farewell to the second golden era.

The second golden era was marked by the highly publicized 1967 bust, the first *big* drug bust in English rock. They didn't have the sort of public image that a bust would hurt and the uncharitable never stopped insisting that manager Oldham had engineered it all, but the bust *was* a jolt to them, and two further busts of Brian Jones, harrowing, to say the least. Out of all this private confusion emerged the Stones' answer to the Beatles' *SERGEANT PEPPER* album—*THEIR SATANIC MAJESTIES REQUEST*, an album that induced more visions than anything coming out of San Francisco in the height of the psychedelic revolution. The album was not entirely a critical success and the two hard-rock singles that followed suggested a possible return to their earlier styles.

Their new album, *BEGGAR'S BANQUET*, bears this out. It is a comeback, a great rock and roll album with no pretenses, Dylanesque lyrics, and a country and western mood. For the big people in rock, 1968 was the year for a return to simplicity, and that seems to be what happened with the Rolling Stones. For a while, all seemed well. Then in June 1969, a shock: Brian Jones left to do his own music. His replacement was Mick Taylor, formerly of John Mayall's Blues Breakers. A few weeks later Brian was found dead in his swimming pool.

The group is still strong and together. Jagger is becoming a film star (*Performance* and *Ned Kelly*). But nothing is the same. How could it be?

Albums/THE ROLLING STONES (May 1964): *Not Fade Away; Route 66; I Just Want To Make Love To You; Honest I Do, Now I've Got A Witness; Little By Little; I'm*

King Bee; Carol; Tell Me; Can I Get A Witness; You Can Make It If You Try; Walking The Dog. 12 X 5 (October 1964): *Around And Around; Confessin' The Blues; 2120 So. Michigan Avenue; Empty Heart; Time Is On My Side; Good Times, Bad Times; It's All Over Now; Under The Boardwalk; Grown Up Wrong; Congratulations; If You Need Me; Susie Q.* THE ROLLING STONES NOW (February 1965): *Heart Of Stone; Everybody Needs Somebody To Love; Little Red Rooster; Oh Baby We Got A Good Thing Goin'; Down Home Girl; You Can't Catch Me; What A Shame; Down The Road A Piece; Off The Hook; Pain In My Heart; Surprise, Surprise; Mona (I Need You Baby).* OUT OF OUR HEADS (July 1965): *Mercy Mercy; Hitch Hike; Last Time; That's How Strong My Love Is; Good Times; I'm All Right; Satisfaction (I Can't Get No); Cry To Me; Under Assistant West Coast Promotion Man; Play With Fire; Spider And The Fly; One More Try.* DECEMBER'S CHILDREN (November 1965): *Get Off My Cloud; Blue Turns To Grey; She Said Yeah; Talkin' About You; You Better Move On; Look What You've Done; The Singer Not The Song; Route 66; I'm Free; As Tears Go By; Gotta Get Away; I'm Moving On.* BIG HITS (HIGH TIDE AND GREEN GRASS) (March 1966): *19th Nervous Breakdown; Satisfaction (I Can't Get No); Last Time; As Tears Go By; Time Is On My Side; It's All Over Now; Tell Me; Heart Of Stone. Get Off My Cloud; Not Fade Away; Good Times, Bad Times; Play With Fire.* AFTER-MATH (June 1966): *Paint It Black; Stupid Girl; Lady Jane; Think; Under My Thumb; Doncha Bother Me; Flight; High And Dry; It's Not Easy; I Am Waiting; Going.* GOT "LIVE" IF YOU WANT IT (November 1966): *Have You Seen Your Mother, Baby, Standing In The Shadow; Under My Thumb; Get Off My Cloud; Lady Jane; I've been Loving You Too Long; Fortune Teller; Last Time; 19th Nervous Breakdown; Time Is On My Side; I'm Alright; Satisfaction (I Can't Get No); Not Fade Away.* BETWEEN THE BUTTONS (January 1967): *Ruby Tuesday; Let's Spend The Night Together; Yesterday's Papers; Connection; All Sold Out; She Smiled Sweetly; Cool And Collected; My Obsession; Who's Been Sleeping Here; Complicated; Miss Amanda Jones; Something Happened To Me Yesterday.* FLOWERS (June 1967): *Ruby Tuesday; Have You Seen Your Mother, Baby; Let's Spend*

The Night Together; Lady Jane; Out Of Time; My Girl; Back Street Girl; Please Go Home; Mother's Little Helper; Take It Or Leave It; Ride On Baby; Sittin' On A Fence. THEIR SATANIC MAJESTIES REQUEST (November 1967): *Sing This All Together; Citadel; In Another Land; 2000 Man; Sing This All Together (See What Happens); She's A Rainbow; The Lantern; Gomper; 2000 Light Years From Home; On With The Show.* BEGGARS BANQUET (November 1968): *Sympathy For The Devil; No Expectations; Dear Doctor; Parachute Woman; Jig-Saw Puzzle; Street Fighting Man; Prodigal Son; Stray Cat Blues; Factory Girl; Salt Of The Earth.*

Singles/*I Wanna Be Your Man/Stoned* (February 1964); *Not Fade Away/I Wanna Be Your Man* (March 1964); *Tell Me (You're Coming Back)/I Just Want To Make Love To You* (June 1964); *It's All Over Now/Good Times, Bad Times* (July 1964); *Time Is On My Side/Congratulations* (September 1964); *Heart Of Stone/What A Shame* (December 1964); *The Last Time/Play With Fire* (March 1965); *Satisfaction/The Under Assistant West Coast Promotion Man* (May 1965); *Get Off My Cloud/I'm Free* (September 1965); *As Tears Go By/Gotta Get Away* (December 1965); *19th Nervous Breakdown/Sad Day* (February 1966); *Paint It Black/Stupid Girl* (April 1966); *Mother's Little Helper/Lady Jane* (June 1966); *Have You Seen Your Mother, Baby, Standing In The Shadow/Who's Driving My Plane* (September 1966); *Let's Spend The Night Together/Ruby Tuesday* (December 1966); *We Love You/Dandelion* (August 1967); *She's A Rainbow/2000 Light Years From Home* (December 1967); *In Another Land/The Lantern* (November 1967); *Jumpin' Jack Flash/Child Of The Moon* (May 1968); *Street Fighting Man/No Expectations* (August 1968); *Honky Tonk Women/You Can't Always Get What You Want* (July 1969).

RONETTES/There are two kinds of lady singers—the angels and the devils. The angels sing ethereal songs in ethereal voices and wear long, loose gowns. The devils sing earthy songs in earthy voices and their gowns fit where gowns should fit. The Ronettes were every teenage boy's dream of a teenage devil in triplicate. Brazen, shapely and without any illusions about men and sex. They were like girlie magazines come alive and set to music. Their song *Do I Love You* made the boys feel like men. Nothing psychedelic there, just straight from the hip or wherever. The Ronettes were Phil Spector creations, and Phil Spector knew, better than anyone, what made a record sell, what popular music was all about. The Beatles adored them and had them on their 1966 tour—more, one suspects, because *they* wanted to hear them sing than because they thought their audiences wanted to.

Albums/RONETTES: *Be My Baby; Walking In The Rain; Do I Love You; Baby I Love You; Breakin' Up; Chapel Of Love; So Young; What'd I Say; You Baby; How Does It Feel; When I Saw You; I Wonder.* RONETTES: *He Did It; Silhouettes; Good Girls; The Memory; You Bet I Would; I'm Gonna Quit While I'm Ahead; I'm On The Wagon; Recipe For Love; My Guiding Angel; I Want A Boy; What's So Sweet About Sweet Sixteen.*

Singles/*Be My Baby/Tedesco And Pitman; Baby I Love You /Miss Joan And Mr. Sam; Big Red/Breakin' Up; Do I Love You/Bebe And Su Su; How Does It Feel/Walking In The Rain; Blues For My Baby/Born To Be Together; Is That What I Get For Loving You/Oh, I Love You; When I Saw You/I Can Hear Music.*

Also Appear On/TODAY'S HITS: *Be My Baby.*

ROONEY BROTHERS/*Mickey Rooney Jr. (guitar, bass, organ, piano, drums), Teddy Rooney (guitar, bass, organ, piano, drums), Timothy Rooney (guitar, piano).*
They started in show business as tv performers and actors on shows such as "The Mickey Mouse Club" and "Playhouse 90." But since they are part of the rock generation they decided to form a band. They have recorded two singles but for some reason known only to their record company they have not received any real promotion or airplay. Maybe being the sons of a famous star is not as helpful as it could be.

Singles/*Georgie/Just A Friend* (December 1967); *I'm Left To Wondering/I'm Wondering* (April 1968).

TIM ROSE/When he first hit New York, Tim Rose organized the Big Three with Mama Cass Elliott and James Hendricks (not Jimi Hendrix), a folk trio that cut two singles and made a name and reputation—but no money. The group folded after a year and Tim Rose was not heard from again until Jimi Hendrix had one of his first hits in England in 1967 with Rose's arrangement of a traditional song, *Hey Joe. Morning Dew,* which Rose co-authored, was also recorded by everyone from Jeff Beck to the Grateful Dead to Lulu. In 1968 Rose made an album that went over well with the folk-and-blues people, all rough intensity and all his own material. He is greatly admired in England and Europe.

Albums/TIM ROSE (December 1967): *I Got A Loneliness; I'm Gonna Be Strong; I Gotta Do Things My Way; Fare Thee Well; Eat, Drink And Be Merry; Hey Joe; Morning Dew; Where Was I; You're Slipping Away From Me; Long Time Man; Come Away, Melinda.* THROUGH ROSE COLORED GLASSES.

Singles/*Hey Joe/King Lonely The Blue* (May 1966); *I Got A Loneliness/I'm Gonna Be Strong* (December 1966); *Morning Dew/You're Slipping Away From Me* (February 1967); *Come Away, Melinda/Long Time Man* (November 1967); *Long-Haired Boy/Looking At A Baby* (August 1968). *Angela/Whatcha Gonna Do* (March 1969).

DIANA ROSS AND THE SUPREMES (formerly THE SUPREMES)/*Diana Ross, Mary Wilson, Cindy Birdsong (replaced Florence Ballard).*
You always get the feeling when you read newspaper interviews with the Supremes, the world's most famous and highest-paid female trio, that they are keeping a secret. The talk is always about clothes and wigs and families. Never about their music or their feelings. They are not, as someone described them, Aretha in triplicate. They're too slim and chic for that and it comes out in their voices. If they must be compared with anyone, they're like three black Marlene Dietrichs. Diana Ross is Supervamp, all soft purring, but with claws.

When Diana and the Supremes move it's in the beautiful but predictable steps they have choreographed inside their minds. And yet it's that very timing and planning that makes them exciting, like a woman who has planned every detail of what she'll wear, and she knows you know, but you are flattered that she has gone to that trouble for you. Audiences are flattered at the obvious hours, days of rehearsals that lie behind every Supremes appearance. Every single sells, every album sells. The Supremes epitomize the machinelike precision of the Motown sound. Everything is worked out for them and they don't buck the system.

Although they didn't give the Motown writing team of Holland/Dozier/Holland their first hit (Martha and the Vandellas did that), the two teams have worked together in perfect harmony. Holland/Dozier/Holland have a formula. Ross/Wilson/Birdsong sing to that formula.

In the part of Detroit Diana and Mary came from (Cindy is from New Jersey) a lot of girls were harmonizing, in church, for fun, for amateur contests. They were in their senior year at high school just when Berry Gordy was getting the whole Motown operation under way in 1960, and they auditioned for him then. When they finished school (he wouldn't take them until they had), he let them sing background. He had other fine female trios but this was the one with the magic. They fit perfectly into the Motown image of sophisticated soul—everything very cool, very clear, no last-minute deviations in the recording studios.

It was all very assembly line, like the job former Motown head Gordy had had in an auto plant (and there are always cracks made about that). But there are people who have to be told what to do and people who are best left to themselves. The Supremes need to be told, but give them their thing to do and they'll do it with flawless perfection, though not without a certain sharp bitchy passion.

Then Stax in Memphis came out with a rival sound that was earthier, fiercer and more erotic. The Supremes had provided the only black sound the mass public was ready for in 1964-66, the sophisticated, commercialized, polished-down sound. It took rock musicians' interest in funkier black music (an interest that was there in 1964 and 1965, but only started emerging publicly in interviews when these musicians were more securely established in 1966, 1967 and 1968) to ready the field for the less sophisticated, gustier sound of Memphis. By 1968 there was a feeling that Motown was too predictable and commercial and watered down, and slowly but surely the interest started to swing back to Memphis. It won't put Motown or the Supremes out of business, but it will be interesting to see if the Motown machine learns anything from Memphis soul.

Albums/ MEET THE SUPREMES (December 1963): *Your Heart Belongs To Me; Who's Lovin' You; Baby Don't Go; Buttered Popcorn; You Bring Back Memories; I Want A Guy; Let Me Go The Right Way; Time Changes Things; Play A Sad Song; Never Again; Seventeen.* WHERE DID OUR LOVE GO (August 1964): *Where Did Our Love Go; Baby Love; Run, Run, Run; Come See 'Bout Me; Long Gone Lover; When The Love Light Starts Shinin' Through His Eyes; I'm Giving You Your Freedom; Your Kiss Of Fire; Breathtaking Guy; He Means The World To Me; Standing At The Crossroads Of Love; Ask Any Girl.* A BIT OF LIVER-POOL (October 1964): *How Do You Do It; World Without Love; Hard Day's Night; Because; House Of The Rising Sun; Bits & Pieces; I Want To Hold Your Hand; Can't Buy Me Love; You've Really Got A Hold On Me; You Can't Do That; Do You Love Me.* COUNTRY, WESTERN & POP (February 1965): *Funny How Time Slips Away; Lazy Bones; You Didn't Care; Tumbling Tumbleweeds; Tears In Vain; My Heart Can't Take It No More; It Makes No Difference Now; You Need Me; Rock & Roll Banjo Band; Sunset; Baby Doll.* MORE HITS (July 1965): *Nothing But Heartaches; Stop In The Name Of Love; Back In My Arms Again; Ask Any Girl; Mother Dear; Honey Boy; Whisper You Love Me Boy; Only Time I'm Happy; He Holds His Own; Who Could Ever Doubt My Love; I'm In Love Again; Heartaches Don't Last Always.* WE REMEMBER SAM COOKE (April 1965): *You Send Me; Nothing Can Change This Love; Cupid; Chain Gang; Bring It On Home To Me; Only Sixteen; Havin' A Party; Shake; Wonderful World; A Change Is Gonna Come; Good News.* SUPREMES AT THE COPA (November 1965): *Baby Love; Stop, In The Name Of Love; Put On A Happy Face; Sam Cooke Medley; I Am A Woman; Girl From Ipanema; Make Someone Happy; Come See About Me; Rock A Bye Your Baby With A Dixie Melody; Queen Of The House; Somewhere; Back In My Arms Again; You're Nobody Till Somebody Loves You.* MERRY CHRISTMAS (November 1965): *Santa Claus Is*

Comin' To Town; Children's Christmas Song; Born Of Mary; Rudolph The Red-Nosed Reindeer; Little Drummer Boy; White Christmas; Silver Bells; My Favorite Things; Joy To The World; Twinkle Twinkle Little Me; My Christmas Tree; Little Star. I HEAR A SYMPHONY (February 1966): *My World Is Empty Without You; I Hear A Symphony; Yesterday; Without A Song; With A Song In My Heart; Stranger In Paradise; Lover's Concerto; Any Girl In Love; Wonderful, Wonderful; Unchained Melody; He's All I've Got; Everything Is Good About You.* SUPREMES A-GO-GO (August 1966): *You Can't Hurry Love; I Can't Help Myself; Love Is Like An Itchin' In My Heart; Hang On Sloopy; These Boots Are Made For Walkin'; Put Yourself In My Place; Get Ready; This Old Heart Of Mine; Money; Come & Get These Memories; Baby I Need Your Lovin'; This Old Heart Of Mine; Shake Me, Wake Me (When It's Over).* SING HOLLAND, DOZIER, HOLLAND (January 1967): *Love Is Here & Now You're Gone; Your Keep Me Hangin' On; You're Gone (But Always In My Heart); Mother You, Smother You; Heat Wave; I Guess I'll Always Love You; Going Down For The Third Time; I'll Turn To Stone; It's The Same Old Song; Remove This Doubt; Love Is In Our Hearts; There's No Stopping Us Now.* SUPREMES SING ROGERS AND HART (May 1967): *Mountain Greenery; Blue Moon; Lady Is A Tramp; My Funny Valentine; Where Or When; This Can't Be Love; Lover; My Romance; My Heart Stood Still; Falling In Love With Love; Thou Swell; Dancing On The Ceiling.* SUPREME'S GREATEST HITS (August 1967): *Happening; You Keep Me Hangin' On; Nothing But Heartaches; You Can't Hurry Love; Run, Run, Run; Come See About Me; Baby Love; I Hear A Symphony; Where Did Our Love Go; My World Is Empty Without You; Ask Any Girl; Stop, In The Name Of Love; Back In My Arms Again; When The Love Light Starts Shinin' Through His Eyes; Whisper You Love Me; Love Is Here & Now You're Gone; Love Is Like An Itchin' In My Heart; There's No Stopping Us Now; Standing At The Crossroads Of Love; Everything's Good About You.* REFLECTIONS (March 1968): *Forever Came Today; In & Out Of Love; What The World Needs Now Is Love; Reflections; I'm Gonna Make It; Ode To Billie Joe; I Can't Make It Alone; Bah-Bah-Bah; Up-Up & Away; Love (Makes Me Do*

Foolish Things); Then; Misery Makes Its Home In My Heart.
FUNNY GIRL (August 1968): *If A Girl Isn't Pretty, Music Makes Me Dance; Don't Rain On My Parade; His Love Makes Me Beautiful; Cornet Man; Sadie, Sadie; I'm The Greatest Star; Funny Girl; People; I Am A Woman.* LIVE AT TALK OF THE TOWN (August 1968): *Medley; With A Song In My Heart; Stranger In Paradise; Wonderful, Wonderful; Without A Song; Stop In The Name Of Love; Come See About Me; My World Is Empty Without You; Baby Love; Love Is Here And Now You're Gone; More; You Keep Me Hanging On; Michelle; Yesterday; In And Out Of Love; Lady Is A Tramp; Let's Get Away From It All; The Happening; Thoroughly Modern Millie; Second-Hand Rose; Mame; You're Nobody Till Somebody Loves You.* LOVE CHILD (December 1968); *How Long Has That Evening Train Been Gone; Some Things You Never Get Used To; He's My Sonny Boy; Love Child;* Others.

Singles/ *He's All I've Got/Love Is Like An Itching In My Heart; Your Heart Belongs To Me/Seventeen* (May 1962); *Let Me Go The Right Way/Time Changes Things* (November 1962); *My Heart Can't Take It No More/You Bring Back Memories* (February 1963); *A Breath-Taking Guy/Rock & Roll Banjo Man* (June 1963); *When The Lovelight Starts Shining/Standing At The Crossroads Of Love* (November 1963); *Run, Run, Run/I'm Giving You Your Freedom* (February 1964); *Baby Love/Ask Any Girl* (September 1964); *Where Did Our Love Go/He Means The World To Me* (June 1964); *Come See About Me/Always In My Heart* (October 1964); *Stop! In The Name Of Love/I'm In Love Again* (February 1965); *Back In My Arms Again/Whisper You Love Me Boy* (April 1965); *Nothing But Heartaches/He Holds His Own* (July 1965); *I Hear A Symphony/Who Could Ever Doubt My Love* (October 1965); *Children's Christmas Song/Twinkle, Twinkle Little Me* (November 1965); *My World Is Empty Without You/Everything's Good About You* (December 1965); *Love Is Like An Itching In My Heart/He's All I Got* (April 1966); *You Can't Hurry Love/Put Yourself In My Place* (July 1966); *You Keep Me Hangin' On/Remove This Doubt* (October 1966); *Love Is Here & Now You're Gone/There's No Stopping Us*

Now (January 1967); *The Happening/All I Know About You* (March 1967); *Reflections/Going Down For The Third Time* (July 1967); *In And Out Of Love/I Guess I'll Always Love You* (October 1967); *Forever Came Today/Time Changes Things* (February 1968); *Some Things You Never Get Used To/You've Been So Wonderful To Me* (May 1968); *Love Child/Will This Be The Day* (October 1968); *I'm Gonna Make You Love Me/Place In The Sun* (December 1968); *Beginning Of The End/Composer* (April 1969); *No Matter What Sign You Are/Young Folks* (June 1969).

Also Appears On/MOTORTOWN REVUE IN PARIS: *Stop In The Name Of Love; Somewhere; Baby Love.* 16 ORIGINAL BIG HITS, VOL I: *Your Heart Belongs To Me.* VOL 2: *Lovelight In His Eyes; Buttered Popcorn.* VOL 3: *Breathtaking Guy.* VOL 4: *Baby Love; Let Me Go The Right Way* VOL 5: *Where Did Our Love Go; Come See About Me* VOL 6: *Stop In The Name Of Love.* VOL 7: *I Hear A Symphony; Back In My Arms Again.* VOL 8: *My World Is Empty Without You; You Can't Hurry Love.*

ROTARY CONNECTION/A four-man-two-woman group that specializes, like the Vanilla Fudge, in slow-motion, intense, strung-out interpretations of the material of others, especially the Rolling Stones and Bob Dylan. Rotary Connection sings *Lady Jane* even slower than the Stones. Sometimes considered imitations of Vanilla Fudge imitations, they still remain interesting and may be instrumental in bringing back into fashion interpretation rather than the scramble for sometimes inferior original material just for originality's sake.

Albums/ROTARY CONNECTION (February 1968): *Amen·Rapid Transit; Turn Me On; Pink Noise; Lady Jane; Like A Rollin' Stone; Soul Man; Sursum Mentes; Didn't Want To Have To Do It; Black Noise; Memory Band; Ruby Tuesday; Rotary Connection.* ROTARY CONNECTION (October 1968): *Life Could; Teach Me How To Fly; V. I. P.; I Took A Ride; Let Them Talk; Aladdin; I Feel Sorry; Magical World; I Must Be There; Paper Castle.* PEACE AT LEAST (December 1968): *Opening Round; Silent Night; Christmas Love; Last Call For Peace; Shopping Bay Menagerie; Christ-*

mas Child; Peace At Least; Santa's Little Helpers; Sidewalk Santa; Three Other Titles.

Singles/ *Like A Rollin' Stone/Turn Me On* (February 1968); *Paper Castle/Teach Me How To Fly; Magical World/Aladdin* (November 1968).

THE ROYAL GUARDSMEN/ *Chris Nunley (lead vocals), Barry "Snoopy" Winslow (vocals, rhythm guitar), Tom Richards (lead guitar), Bill Balogh (guitar), Billy Taylor (organ), John Burdett (drums).*
Their song depicting Snoopy (the *Peanuts* dog) fighting the Red Baron became a million seller in three weeks. One month later they did a sequel to it. And one year later, *Snoopy's Christmas.* Some people question the Royal Guardsmen's imagination.

Albums/ SNOOPY VERSUS THE RED BARON: *Snoopy Versus The Red Baron; Li'l Red Riding Hood; Battle Of New Orleans; Alley Oop; Bo Diddley; Peanut Butter; Jolly Green Giant; Liberty Valence; Road Runner; Sweetmeats Slide.* RETURN OF THE RED BARON: *Return Of The Red Baron; Gimme Some Lovin'; I'm A Man; So You Want To Be A Rock & Roll Star; Airplane Song; Any Wednesday; Shot Down; I'm Not Gonna Stay; Om; Searchin' For The Good Times; I Need You Girl; Leaving Me.* SNOOPY AND HIS FRIENDS: *Snoopy's Christmas; Snoopy Versus The Red Baron; Return Of The Red Baron; I Say Love; Airplane Song; Down Behind The Lines; It's Sopwith Camel Time;* Other titles.

Singles/ *Snoopy Versus The Red Baron/I Needed You; Return Of The Red Baron/Sweetmeats Slide; Airplane Song/ Om; So Right/Wednesday; It Kinda Looks Like Christmas/Snoopy's Christmas; Baby Let's Wait/Biplane Evermore; Down Behind The Lines/Snoopy For President; I Say Love/I'm Not Gonna Stay; Magic Window/Mother Where's Your Daughter* (April 1969).

OTIS RUSH/ A Chicago blues guitarist now in his thirties, Otis Rush influenced many of the young blues guitarists today, particularly Elvin Bishop of the Paul Butterfield Blues Band. Although he's been known and admired on the blues circuit since he started touring in 1956 and is popular in England where he played in 1966, he is only just beginning to get a name in rock circles.

Singles/*Homework*/*I Have To Laugh; I'm Satisfied*/*So Many Roads, So Many Trains.*

Also Appears On/BLUES, VOL. 2 (June 1963): *So Many Roads, So Many Trains.* CHICAGO/THE BLUES/TODAY, VOL. 2 (April 1966): *Everything's Gonna Turn Out Alright; It's A Mean Old World; I Can't Quit You Baby; Rock; It's My Own Fault.*

TOM RUSH/He came out of the flourishing folk-music scene in Cambridge, Massachusetts, which had produced Jim Kweskin and the influential Eric Von Schmidt as well as the first of the commercially big-time lady folk singers, Joan Baez. Early Tom Rush, like early Joan Baez, was pure folk, and if there *was* a Boston sound it was Tom Rush in the middle sixties. When folk started to go electric in 1965, so did Rush, whose austere white New England sound suddenly took on the black colorations of Bo Diddley. *TAKE A LITTLE WALK WITH ME*, made early in 1966, was electric Tom Rush. Long before everyone else discovered Joni Mitchell, Rush did a beautifully produced version of what is probably her best song, *Urge For Going.* It was high on the Boston charts though sadly not on the national ones. *THE CIRCLE GAME*, is folk, 1968 style—thoughtful, romantic and mostly contemporary material.

Albums/TOM RUSH (December 1963). TOM RUSH (March 1965): *Long John; If Your Man Gets Busted; Do Re Mi; Milk Cow Blues; Cuckoo; Black Mountain Blues; Poor Man; Solid Gone; When She Wants Good Lovin'; I'd Like To Know; Jelly Roll Baker; Windy Hill; Panama Limited.* BLUES/SONGS/BALLADS (May 1965): *Alabama Bound; More Pretty Girls; Sister Kate; Original Talking Blues; Pallet On The Floor; Drop Down Mama; Rag Mama; Barb'ry Allen; Cocaine; Come Back Baby; Stackerlee; Baby Please Don't Go.* TAKE A LITTLE WALK WITH ME (June 1966): *You Can't Judge A Book By The Cover; Who Do You Love; Love's Made A Fool Of You; Too Much Monkey Business; Money Honey; On The Road Again; Joshua Gone*

Barbados; Statesboro Blues; Turn Your Money Green; Sugar Babe; Galveston Flood. CIRCLE GAME (March 1968): *Tin Angel; Something In The Way She Moves; Urge For Going; Sunshine Sunshine; Glory Of Love; Shadow Dream Song; Circle Game; So Long; Rockport Sunday; No Regrets.*

Single/*Urge For Going/Sugar Babe* (1967).

MITCH RYDER (and the DETROIT WHEELS)/They used to be Billy Lee and the Rivieras in Detroit till producer Bob Crewe wisely renamed them. Ryder is one of those white singers who is still doing every trick in the fifties' rhythm and blues book. Even though the Detroit Wheels came and went, Mitch was still socking it to his female fans with enormous success in 1967, proving that even then there was a market for sweaty, barechested, hard-rock, bump-and-grind sexuality.

Albums/TAKE A RIDE (April 1967): *Jenny Take A Ride; Come See About Me; I'll Go Crazy; Please, Please, Please; Shake A Tail Feather; Let Your Lovelight Shine; I Hope; Just A Little Bit; Sticks And Stones; Bring It On Home To Me; Baby Jane (Mo-Mo Jane).* BREAKOUT (April 1967): *Little Latin Lupe Lu; Breakout; In The Midnight Hour; Walking The Dog; I Had It Made; Oo Papa Do; I Like It Like That; You Got Your Kicks; Shakin' With Linda; Stubborn Kind Of Fellow; Any Day Now; I Need Help.* SOCK IT TO ME (July 1967): *Sock It To Me, Baby; I Can't Hide It; Takin' All I Can Get; Slow Fizz; Walk On By; I Never Had It Better; Shakedown; Face In The Crowd; I'd Rather Go To Jail; Wild Child.* WHAT NOW MY LOVE (November 1967): *What Now My Love; Let It Be Me; I Make A Fool Of Myself; Born To Lose; If You Go Away; Whole Lotta Shakin' Goin' On; Sally Go Round The Roses; Browneyed Handsome Man; I Need Lovin' You; That's It, I Quit (I'm Movin' On).* ALL MITCH RYDER HITS: *Joy; Takin' All I Can Get; Sock It To Me, Baby; Devil With The Blue Dress On And Golly Miss Molly; Breakout; Jenny Take A Ride; Little Latin Lupe Lu; Too Many Fish In The Sea & Three Little Fishes; In The Midnight Hour.*

Singles/*Baby Jane/Jenny Take A Ride; I Hope/Little Latin Lupe Lu; Breakout/I Need Help; Takin' All I Can/You Got Your Kicks; Devil With A Blue Dress On And Good Golly*

*Miss Molly/I Had It Made; I Never Had It Better/Sock It To
Me, Baby; One Grain Of Sand/Too Many Fish In The Sea
And Three Little Fishes; I'd Rather Go To Jail/Joy; You Are
My Sunshine/Wild Child; Come See About Me/Face In The
Crowd; Ruby Baby/You Get Your Kicks; Blessing In Dis-
guise/What Now My Love; I Make A Fool Of Myself/Per-
sonality—Chantilly Lace; I Need Lovin' You/Lights Of
Night; Baby I Need Your Loving/Ring Your Bell* (December
1968).

BUFFY SAINTE-MARIE/Although she insists only five
percent of the songs she sings are protesting anything, Buffy
Sainte-Marie, a Cree Indian, sings one of the most bitter protest songs ever: *My Country 'Tis Of Thy People You're Dying*, which tells of the atrocities American Indians suffered at
the hands of the white man. Her anti-war song *Universal
Soldier* is a classic and much recorded. She can sing an old
folk standard like *Sir Patrick Spens* and then move into a
contemporary song like Joni Mitchell's *Circle Game. I'M
GONNA BE A COUNTRY GIRL AGAIN*, was made in
April 1968 in Nashville. Buffy, who grew up in Maine, moved
into the folk places of New York in 1963. She is now one of
the giants of the contemporary folk circuit.

Albums/IT'S MY WAY (March 1964): *Now That The Buf-
falo's Gone; Old Man's Lament; Ananias; Mayoo Sto Hoon;
Cod'ne; Cripple Creek; Universal Soldier; You're Gonna
Need Somebody On Your Bond; Babe In Arms; He Lived
Alone In Town; Incest Song; Eyes Of Amber; It's My Way.*
MANY A MILE (February 1965): *Must I Go Bound;
Fishermen; Groundhog; On The Banks Of Red Roses; Fixin'
To Die; Come All Ye Fair And Tender Girls; Until It's Time
For You To Go; Piney Wood Hills; Welcome Welcome
Emigrante; Broke Down Girl; Johnny Be Fair; Maple Sugar
Boy; Lazarus; Many A Mile.* LITTLE WHEEL, SPIN AND
SPIN (April 1966): *Little Wheel, Spin And Spin; House
Carpenter; Waly, Waly; Rolling Log Blues; My Country 'Tis
Of Thy People You're Dying; Men Of The Fields; Timeless
Love; Sir Patrick Spens; Poor Man's Daughter; Lady Mar-
garet; Sometimes When I Get To Thinkin'; Winter Boy.* FIRE
AND FLEET AND CANDLELIGHT (June 1967): *Circle
Game; Seeds Of Brotherhood; Summer Boy; Lyke Wake Dirge;*

Song To A Seagull; Doggett's Gap; Wedding Song; 97 Men In This Here Town Would Give A Half A Grand In Silver Just To Follow Me Down; Lord Randall; The Carousel; T'es Pas Un Autre; Hey, Little Bird; Little Boy Dark Eyes; Reynardine. I'M GONNA BE A COUNTRY GIRL AGAIN (April 1968): *I'm Gonna Be A Country Girl Again; He's A Pretty Good Man If You Ask Me; Uncle Joe, A Soulful Shade Of Blue; From The Bottom Of My Heart; Sometimes When I Get To Thinkin'; The Piney Wood Hills; Now That The Buffalo's Gone; They Gotta Quit Kickin' My Dawg Around; Tall Trees In Georgia; The Love Of A Good Man; Take My Hand For Awhile; Gonna Feel Much Better When You're Gone.*

Single/*Circle Game*/*Until It's Time For You To Go* (July 1967).

SAM AND DAVE (Sam Moore and Dave Prater)/Now that Otis Redding is dead, Sam and Dave are probably the best soul performers around—particularly live, when everything is high voltage and energy. On record, too, they have come up with some of the great soul classics, like *Soul Man* and *Hold On, I'm Coming*, all typical of the drive and excitement that artists at Stax-Volt generate, especially when working with the "house band" Booker T and the MG's. Sam has the memorable high lead voice but the two together bring their numbers to dramatic fierce conclusions (even though, according to *Rolling Stone*, they don't speak to or about each other except when they're working on stage).

Albums/HOLD ON, I'M COMING: *Hold On, I'm Coming; If You Got The Lovin'; I Take What I Want; Ease Me; I Got Everything I Need; Don't Make It So Hard On Me; It's A Wonder; Don't Help Me Out; Just Me; You Got It Made; Blame Me.* DOUBLE DYNAMITE: *You Got Me Hummin'; Said I Wasn't Gonna Tell Nobody; That's The Way It's Gotta Be; When Something Is Wrong With My Baby; I'm Your Puppet; Soothe Me; Just Can't Get Enough; Sweet Pains; Sleep Good Tonight; I Don't Need Nobody; Home At Last; Use Me.* SOUL MEN: *Soul Man; May I, Baby; Broke Down Piece Of Man; Let It Be Me; Hold It, Baby; I'm With You; Don't Knock It; Just Keep Holding On; Good Runs The Bad Away; Rich Kind Of Poverty; I've Seen What Loneliness Can*

Do. I THANK YOU: *I Thank You; Everybody Got To Believe In Somebody; These Arms Of Mine; Wrap It Up; If I Didn't Have A Girl Like You; You Don't Know What You Mean To Me; Don't Turn Your Heater On; Talk To The Man; Love Is After Me; Ain't That A Lot Of Love; Don't Waste That Love; Lucky Old Sun.*

Singles/*Hold On, I'm Coming/I Got Everything I Need; If You Got The Loving/Said I Wasn't Gonna Tell Nobody; You Got Me Hummin'/Sleep Good Tonight; Small Portion Of Your Love/When Something Is Wrong With My Baby; I Can't Stand Up For Falling Down/Soothe Me; Soul Man/May I Baby; Wrap It Up/I Thank You; This Is Your World/You Don't Know What You Mean To Me; Still Is The Night/Can't You Find Another Way (Of Doing It); Everybody Got To Believe In Somebody/If I Didn't Have A Girl Like You.*

TOMMY SANDS/Elvis Presley couldn't be everywhere, so from 1956 on, little Presleys sprang up like mushrooms after a spring rain. Tommy Sands, an Elvis friend, got his break when he played a little Elvis in NBC's play *The Singing Idol* in January 1958, a role that had already been turned down by Elvis. His contributions to the early rock period were songs like *Teenage Crush* and *Cutie Wootie*. He was briefly married to Nancy Sinatra.

SAVOY BROWN BLUES BAND/*Chris Youlden (vocals), Bob Hall (piano), Kim Simmonds (lead guitar), Dave Peverett (rhythm guitar), Rivers Jobe (bass guitar), Roger Earle (drums).*
The Savoy Brown Blues Band is one of half a dozen English bands that conscientiously play American blues, careful to be faithful to the original. Not valid, say some who prefer to hear the original. Historically interesting, say others. The band's appearance in the United States contributed to the revived interest in blues roots, just as Fleetwood Mac, Ten Years After, John Mayall's Blues Breakers and other English and American blues bands did. For those sated by uncompromising hard rock, blues were a welcome change. And the English should be given credit for it, even if it was a borrowed sound.

Albums/GETTING TO THE POINT (September 1968): *Flood In Houston; Stay With Me Baby; Honey Bee; The Incredible Gnome Meets Jaxman; Give Me A Penny; Mr. Downchild; Getting To The Point; Big City Lights; You Need Love.* BLUE MATTER (July 1969): *Train To Nowhere; Tolling Bells; She's Got A Ring In His Nose And A Ring On Her Hand; Vicksburg Blues; Don't Turn Me From Your Door; May Be Wrong; Louisiana Blues; It Hurts Me Too.*

Also Appear On/ANTHOLOGY OF BRITISH BLUES (September 1968).

SCAFFOLD/*Roger McGough, John Gorman, Mike McGear.* A group with Paul McCartney's brother as lead singer would, one would think, be predestined for, at the very least, a modest success. But the Scaffold, which features Paul's brother Mike, is not that sort of group, nor is Mike, who calls himself Mike McGear, that sort of brother. Scaffold specializes in satire and sophisticated comedy. One of its three members is Roger McGough, a much respected Liverpool poet. Another, John Gorman, is bald and lugubrious and an unlikely type for teen idolatry. Scaffold was busy playing dates (including the Edinburgh Festival) long before their act-closing number, *Thank U Very Much,* became a hit. Old man McCartney, who was a pianist with the Jimmy Mack Jazz Band and who bought Paul his first guitar, couldn't have been happier than when his second son (a hairdresser's apprentice) made it.

Album/THANK U VERY MUCH (October 1968): *Long Strong Black Pudding; Two Days One Day, Three Blind Jellyfish; Thank U Very Much; Ide B The First; Do You Remember; Knees Up Mother Brown (Knees Down Mother Brown); One, Two, Three; Today; Please Sorry; Jelly Covered Cloud.*

Single/*Thank U Very Much/Ide B The First* (August 1968).

SEA TRAIN/*Andy Kulberg (bass, flute), Roy Blumenfeld (drums), Richard Greene (violin, viola), John Gregory (vocals, lead guitar), Don Kretmar (replaced Andy Musar) (saxophone, bass), Jim Roberts (vocals).*
Sea Train is half the answer to the question "Whatever hap-

pened to the Blues Project?" Andy Kulberg and Roy Blumenfeld were what was left of the Blues Project in 1967 when Al
Kooper and Steve Katz took off to form Blood, Sweat and
Tears, and Danny Kalb just took off. The sound is sometimes
Blues Project, but there is another dimension to it when you
consider one of the five members, Richard Greene, is the
ex-fiddler from the Jim Kweskin Jug Band. The general
feeling after their 1968 debut at the old Blues Project home
base, the Cafe Au Go Go, was that they weren't cooking yet
but they might be soon. The band now works out of Mill
Valley, California, not out of New York. That's supposed to
be just the place to get bands together.
(see BLUES PROJECT)

Album/SEA TRAIN (December 1968): *Sea Train; Let The
Duchess No; Pudding St.; Portrait Of The Lady As A Young
Artist; As I Lay Losing; Rondo; Sweet Creek's Suite; Outwear
The Hills.*

Single/*As I Lay Losing/Let The Duchess No* (November
1968).

JOHN SEBASTIAN/Founder, writer, harp player and lead
singer for the Lovin' Spoonful, John Sebastian left the group
in 1968 to go solo. Before the Spoonful he had played
harmonica on endless folk albums, Eric Andersen's, Judy
Collins's, and with a group called the Mugwumps. He recorded
his first solo album in 1968, played a large part in Cass
Elliott's first solo album at the same time, and also in that
year wrote several songs for *Jimmy Shine*, a Broadway musical starring Dustin Hoffman. Sebastian, author of most of the
Spoonful hits, is currently less interested in performing than in
writing and plans to devote himself to Broadway musicals.
(see LOVIN' SPOONFUL)

Album/JOHN B. SEBASTIAN (August 1969).

Single/*Room Nobody Lives In/She's A Lady* (December
1968).

THE SEEDS (SKY SAXON'S BLUES BAND/*Sky Saxon
(lead vocals), Daryl Hooper (piano, organ), Jan Savage
(guitar), Rick Andridge (drums).*
The Seeds were a Los Angeles group that in the wake of the

1967 flower power movement followed up with flower music. It sounded much like other music but the floral lyrics went over big with the flower children. When flower power faded, so did the Seeds.

Albums/THE SEEDS (June 1966): *Can't Seem To Make You Mine; No Escape; Lose Your Mind; Evil Voodoo; Girl I Want You; Pushin' Too Hard; Try To Understand; Nobody Spoil My Fun; It's A Hard Life; You Can't Be Trusted; Excuse, Excuse; Fallin' In Love.* WEB OF SOUND (October 1966): *The Farmers; Tripmaker; Pictures And Designs; I Tell Myself; Faded Picture; Rollin' Machine; Just Let Go; Up In Her Room.* FUTURE (August 1967): *Thousand Shadows; March Of The Flower Children; Travel With Your Mind; Painted Doll; Flower Lady And Her Assistant; Six Dreams; Out Of The Question; Where Is The Entrance; Way To Play; Now A Man; Two Fingers Pointing On You; Fallin'.* FULL SPOON OF SEEDY BLUES (1967) (By Sky Saxon's Blues Band): *Pretty Girl; Moth And The Flame; I'll Help You; Cry Wolf; Plain Spoken; Gardner; One More Time Blues; Creepin' About; Buzzin' Around.* MERLIN'S MUSIC BOX (December 1967): *Mr. Farmer; No Escape; Satisfy You; Up In Her Room; Night Time Girl; Gypsy Plays His Drums; Can't Seem To Make You Mine; Mumble Bumble; Nine Million Daily Making Love; Forest Outside Your Door; Pushin' Too Hard.*

Singles/*Can't Seem To Make You Mine/Daisey Mae; Pushin' Too Hard/Try To Understand; No Escape/Mr. Farmer; March Of The Flower Children/Thousand Shadows; Six Dreams/Wind Blows Your Hair.*

PETE SEEGER/Someone said he was born too early. If Pete Seeger had been twenty instead of fifty during the sixties' folk boom he might be a multimillionaire now. But without Seeger there would probably not have *been* a folk boom. We'd still be singing about teenage love. Seeger was not too early, he was just in time. Already it's difficult for a new generation to realize that there was a time when folk music was an "inside" small-circle thing, with people swapping songs and turning each other on to whatever new finds they had just collected. Pete Seeger was one of the people who kept that feeling going all those years. (There were others who did the same thing in their own way—John Jacob Niles, Woody Guthrie, Leadbelly, Alan Lomax—but Seeger, the most active, combined the lot.)

Seeger set the stage for the early folk boom of 1956 when companies like the now powerful Elektra were just getting started and the Clancy Brothers and Odetta, to their amazement, found that folk music paid. Pete Seeger was the big daddy of the hootenanny, of the popularity of folk in colleges, of everything that was happening around the fountain in Washington Square Park. When the folk boom grew, most folk singers, many of them Seeger disciples, grew with it, but Seeger was left behind. The reason: his left-wing political views got him blacklisted from tv. Meanwhile the tide was changing—Kingston Trio, Joan Baez, Peter, Paul and Mary, Dylan, Judy Collins—Seeger's children were coming into their own (Joanie turning the masses on to folk by using many Seeger techniques).

For a multitude of reasons Seeger was never destined to make one of his own songs a hit, and he himself never made the charts, though he must have sold millions of albums. It was Peter, Paul and Mary who made his song *If I Had A Hammer* famous around the world, and so many of his songs are sung so often it's difficult to remember they originally came from him. He is part of anyone who ever picked up a guitar and even some who didn't (Marlene Dietrich sang his *Where Have All The Flowers Gone)*. He sowed the seed for protest songs.

Nothing demonstrated more dramatically than the 1968 Woody Guthrie Memorial Concert how very much did spring from Seeger (who was himself influenced by Leadbelly and Guthrie). And there are enough people carrying on the tradition. When Baez at the Fillmore or Guthrie at Forest Hills urges you to sing along, it's Seeger's ghost overseeing the concert—and the nice part of it is Seeger still lives to enjoy it.

Albums/AMERICAN FAVORITE BALLADS. AMERICAN FOLK SONGS FOR CHILDREN. AMERICAN GAME AND ACTIVITY SONGS FOR CHILDREN. BROADSIDES. CHAMPLAIN VALLEY SONGBAG. DARLING COREY. FRONTIER BALLADS. GAZETTE. GERMAN

FOLK SONGS. GOOFING-OFF SUITE. GUITAR: FOLK-SINGERS GUIDE. HOOTENANNY AT CARNEGIE HALL. HOW TO PLAY THE FIVE STRING BANJO. LONESOME VALLEY. PETE SEEGER AT VILLAGE GATE. PETE SEEGER SAMPLER. SING OUT. HOOTE-NANNY. SLEEP TIME. SONGS OF STRUGGLE AND PROTEST. SONGS TO GROW ON. SONGS OF THE SPANISH CIVIL WAR—SONGS OF THE LINCOLN BATTALION. 12 STRING GUITAR. PETE SEEGER CONCERT. SONGS OF THE LINCOLN AND INTER-NATIONAL BRIGADES. WE SHALL OVERCOME (November 1963). BADMEN. I CAN SEE A NEW DAY (November 1964). STRANGERS AND COUSINS (April 1965). BIG BILL BROONZY AND PETE SEEGER (June 1965). PETE SEEGER ON CAMPUS (June 1965). PETE SEEGER, FOLK MUSIC (October 1965). CHILDREN'S CONCERT AT TOWN HALL. PETE SEEGER (November 1965). GOD BLESS THE GRASS (January 1966). DAN-GEROUS SONGS (June 1966). WAIST DEEP IN THE BIG MUDDY (June 1967). PETE SEEGER'S GREATEST HITS (October 1967). AMERICAN INDUSTRIAL BAL-LADS. IN PERSON AT THE BITTER END. FREIGHT TRAIN (October 1964). LOVE SONGS FOR FRIENDS AND FOES. RAINBOW DESIGN (May 1960). PETE SEEGER SINGS LEADBELLY. TALKING UNION. WIMOWEH AND OTHER SONGS. WITH VOICES TO-GETHER WE SING. 3 SAINTS, 4 SINNERS AND 6 OTHER PEOPLE (July 1968).

Singles/*Little Boxes/ Where Have All The Flowers Gone; Waist Deep In The Big Muddy/ Down By The Riverside.*

THE SEEKERS/*Judith Durham, Athol Guy, Keith Potger, Bruce Woodley.*
If there hadn't been the Seekers some shrewd manager would have invented them. One cuddly girl-next-door type (complete with nose-crinkling smile) and three sober cats who looked like bank tellers. They came from Australia, singing nice harmonies for their supper on a boat bound for England. The English squares liked them immediately because they represented something they could understand and feel secure

with. As for the rest, well, it was a good clean sound and the tunes were catchy.

Their sound was, for lack of a better name, pop-folk with the strong and vibrant voice of Judith Durham giving it definition and added distinction. They didn't really click in America until *Georgy Girl* (done for the film in 1966), which went on to become a White Rock radio commercial. After that there was success wherever you looked: back in Australia, where they visited in triumph, in England, with tv show after tv show, and in America. But by the summer of 1968, inexplicably, they were tired of it all. They had never meant to stay together, they said. Durham of the exceptional voice says she'll sing solo. Bruce Woodley, who wrote *Red Rubber Ball* with Paul Simon, will probably come to America to write songs. Their last hit in England was called *The Carnival Is Over*, and it was.

Albums/THE NEW SEEKERS (April 1965): *This Little Light Of Mine; Morning Town Ride; The Water Is Wide; Well, Well, Well; Lady Mary; We're Moving On; The Ox Driving Song; Kumbaya; Blowin' In The Wind; Chilly Winds; What Have They Done To The Rain.* A WORLD OF OUR OWN (July 1965): *A World Of Our Own; Don't Think Twice, It's All Right; The Leaving Of Liverpool; This Land; Two Summers; The Times They Are A-Changin'; Just A Closer Walk With Thee; Don't Tell Me My Mind; Allentown Jail; Four Strong Winds; You Can't Tell The World.* GEORGY GIRL (February 1967): *Georgy Girl; Yesterday; The Last Thing On My Mind; All Over The World; Red Rubber Ball; Well, Well, Well; Come The Day; Island Of Dreams; Turn, Turn, Turn; Louisiana Man; California Dreamin'.* BEST OF THE SEEKERS (May 1967): *Morningtown Ride; World Of Our Own; Walk With Me; Carnival Is Over; Sinner Man; Times They Are A-Changin'; I'll Never Find Another You; When The Stars Begin To Fall; Some Day, One Day; Turn, Turn, Turn; We're Moving On.* SEEKERS SEEN IN GREEN (November 1967): *Love Is Kind, Love Is Wine; The Sad Cloud; 59th Street Bridge Song (Feelin' Groovy); If You Go Away; All I Can Remember; Chase A Rainbow (Follow Your Dream); Angeline Is Always Friday; When*

The Good Apples Fall; Cloudy; Can't Make Up My Mind; Rattler; Colours Of My Life.

Singles/*I'll Never Find Another You/Open Up Them Pearly Gates* (March 1965); *Someday, One Day/Nobody Knows The Trouble I've Seen* (March 1966); *Georgy Girl/When The Stars Begin To Fall* (October 1966); *Walk With Me/Morningtown Ride* (January 1967); *I Wish You Could Be Here/On The Other Side* (August 1967); *When The Good Apples Fall/Myra* (September 1967); *Love Is Kind, Love Is Wine* (November 1967).

SHADOWS/One of the great (and few) English instrumental groups that date back to the English pre-Beatle period, the Shadows were once the backing group for Cliff Richard (an early English mini-Presley). They recently celebrated their tenth anniversary in the business by announcing they would disband. Their hits included *Apache, Man of Mystery, F.B.I.* and *Wonderful Land.*

Albums/SURFING WITH THE SHADOWS: *Dance On; Stranger; Man Of Mystery; Kinda Cool; Bo Diddley; Rumble; Kon Tiki; F. B. I.; Frightened City; 1861; Are They All Like You; Atlantis.* THE SHADOWS KNOW: *Rise And Fall Of Flingle Blunt; That's The Way It Goes; Dakota; Tonight; Temptation; French Dressing; In The Mood; Theme For Young Lovers; Chattanooga Choo Choo; Don't It Make You Feel Good; Lonely Bull; Zambesi.*

Singles/*F.B.J./Frightened City; Kon Tiki/Man Of Mystery; Stars Fell On Stockton/Wonderful Land; Guitar Tango/What A Lovely Tune; Rumble/Dance On; Rise And Fall Of Flingle Blunt/Theme For Young Lovers; Rhythm And Greens/Miracle.*

THE SHANGRI-LAS/From time immemorial the bitch goddess has haunted and fascinated man. And so, of course, has the girl next door. The Shangri-las were both, a real bargain for the boy who wanted everything in a girl and the girl who wanted to be that everything. They played it soft and tough at the same time. Their toughest song was *Leader of the Pack.* (He was the head of the motorcycle gang and she was his tough mama. Then he dies. Tough mama goes soft, but not for long. You know whoever gets to be the next leader gets her too. Teased hair, doe eyes, ankle bracelet and all.) It was the necrophilia of it all that shocked the adults, not the funkiness of three bitchy white girls who told it straight out that in motor-bike gangs you don't just hold hands. The Shangri-las were akin to Clyde Barrow's Bonnie, in a reversal of the proverbial image, the velvet hands in the iron gloves.

Albums/GOLDEN HITS OF THE SHANGRI-LAS (December 1966): *Leader Of The Pack; Past Present & Future; Train From Kansas City; Heaven Only Knows; Remember; Out In The Streets; I Can Never Go Home Anymore; Give Him A Great Big Kiss; Long Live Our Love; Give Us Your Blessing; Sophisticated Boom Boom; What Is Love.* LEADER OF THE PACK: *Leader Of The Pack; Remember Walking In The Sand; Shout; Twist & Shout; Maybe;* Other titles. SHANGRI-LAS '65: *Give Us Your Blessings; You Cheated, You Lied; Out In The Streets; Right Now And Not Later; Never Again; Sophisticated Boom Boom; I'm Blue; Heaven Only Knows; Train From Kansas City; What's A Girl Supposed To Do; The Boy; Dum Dum Ditty.*

Singles/*Footsteps On The Roof/Take The Time; Give Him A Great Big Kiss/Long Live Our Love; Give Us Your Blessing/Remember Walkin' In The Sand; Hate To Say I Told You So/Wishing Well; I'll Never Learn/Sweet Sounds Of Summer; I Can Never Go Home Anymore/Leader Of The Pack; Paradise/Past Present & Future; It's Easier To Cry/Remember; He Cried/Dressed In Black; Right Now And Not Later/Train From Kansas City; Shout/Maybe; The Boy/Out In The Streets; Twist And Shout/Give Him A Great Big Kiss; Sophisticated Boom Boom/Long Live Our Love.*

Also Appear On/RED BIRD GOLDIES: *Remember Walkin' In The Sand; Give Him A Great Big Kiss; Leader Of The Pack.* SUPER OLDIES VOL. I: *I Can Never Go Home Anymore.*

RAVI SHANKAR/When he made his solo debut in America as a classical sitarist in October 1956, he could not have known that some ten years later he would be as popular with rock fans as with the followers of Indian music. It all started in 1965 when Beatle George Harrison played a little sitar in

Norwegian Wood after having taken lessons from Ravi Shankar. That's all that was needed for a full-blown sitar craze to hit rock; and as Harrison became more and more hooked on India, a passion for everything Indian from curry to gurus followed. By 1967 Shankar concerts were packed with the young, every small-time musician had his own imported sitar to tinker with (though it had taken Shankar about thirty years of constant practice just to get started) and the Indian sound (raga rock) permeated major and minor hits as well as every single struggling to make the charts. Much to Shankar's dismay Indian music came to be closely associated with drugs, and all he could do was protest that the music alone could get the listener high, a fact Indians have known for centuries. Now an electric sitar is on the market and the fad has died down, but it will be a long time before Mr. Shankar's influence is no longer felt in the rock sound.

SANDIE SHAW/She is very popular on the English rock scene more because she has been around so long than because she is any sort of innovator, though her style is pleasant enough. She has never caught on in the U.S. in the way her closest competitors, Dusty Springfield and Petula Clark, have.

Albums/SANDIE SHAW (April 1965): *I'll Stop At Nothin'; It's In His Kiss; Lemon Tree; Downtown; Talk About Love; Always Something There To Remind Me; Girl Don't Don't Come; Baby I Need Your Loving; Gotta See My Baby Every Day; Don't Be That Way; Stop Feeling Sorry For Yourself; Everybody Loves A Lover.* ME (February 1966): *You Don't Love Me No More; I Don't Need That Kind Of Lovin'; Do You Mind; How Glad I Am; Till The Night Begins To Die; Too Bad You Don't Want Me; One Day; When I Fall In Love.*

Singles/*Hide All Emotion/Think Sometimes About Me* (December 1966); *I Had A Dream Last Night/Puppet On A String* (April 1967).

SHOCK ROCK/It's a growing medium. It's what you don't bring your parents to. The Fugs are shock rock—their hilarious parodies of obscenity (visual and verbal) are obscene and shocking to the unhip. The Mothers are shock rock. Just looking at Frank Zappa's face in *Life* magazine's 1968 rock issue put more than half the U.S. population in shock. Wait till they hear what he *sounds* like. It used to be that just looking freaky was enough to qualify for the shock-rock label, or at least that was the way it was for the Fugs and the Mothers, the world's ugliest rock groups (not counting England's Bonzo Dog Doo Dah Band). But that was when rock bands were pretty. With the San Francisco explosion everyone started looking freaky and the shock groups were pushed to further and further extremes. Jimi Hendrix is shock rock when he caresses his guitar strings with his tongue and teeth—and double shock rock the days he mounts the guitar and sets it on fire. The Who were shock rock at first. Buddy Miles is shock rock just standing there. Arthur Brown and anyone else who sets his headgear on fire is shock rock. It can be lyric content or visual impact, but if it shocks, it's shock rock. And there's going to be a lot more of it.

SILVER APPLES/*Dan Taylor (drums), Simeon (simeon)*. They made their debut in mid-1968 in Mickey Ruskin's superhip restaurant, Max's Kansas City, Dan Taylor pounding away on two sets of tuned drums while Simeon played an odd electronic instrument that sounds like four or more instruments at once, which he made himself and which he calls a simeon (and indeed, why shouldn't he?). The sounds are ear-shattering, some tunes, some not. Is this the music of the future?

Album/SILVER APPLES: *Oscillations; Dancing Gods; Dust; Program; Velvet Cave; Whirly-Bird; Misty Mountain; Lovefingers; Seagreen Serenades.*

Single/*Confusion/You & I* (December 1968).

SIMON AND GARFUNKEL (Paul Simon and Art Garfunkel)/Everybody loves a Cinderella story and Simon and Garfunkel are it. In 1957, when everything in rock is Elvis, these two precocious sixteen-year-old schoolboys in Queens, New York, come up with a hit, *Hey Schoolgirl*. They have flattop haircuts and call themselves Tom and Jerry. They get to play on the Dick Clark show. But they turn out to be more or less a one-hit wonder, and within a year they're has-beens.

Weep for their disappointment. Years later, now it's the sixties folk boom and Bob Dylan has just made *Blowin' in the Wind* and *The Times They Are A-changin'*, the two boys, now calling themselves Simon and Garfunkel, make a folk album with Dylan songs and some Simon songs. They call it *WEDNESDAY MORNING, 3 A.M.* Well, no one's heard of Simon and Garfunkel and late in 1964 everyone and his brother is recording Dylan, so nothing happens with the album. Simon splits for England where American folk singers at least have novelty value. But meanwhile, the Cinderella story. (Do things *really* happen like this?)

A disc jockey has fallen in love with one cut on *WEDNES-DAY MORNING* and keeps playing it. Tom Wilson, a producer at Columbia who's nobody's fool, has watched the folk-rock explosion of 1965 and sees his chance. He gets the gentle folky single *Sounds of Silence* and adds the standard rock backing of drums, bass and electric guitar. And before you can say Simon and Garfunkel, it's a hit record, a number one hit. What happens is that the folkies buy because it's one of theirs and the rockers think they're buying a new kind of rock, which it is. Now that the market has been opened up for that fetching little combination, there's no stopping Simon and Garfunkel. (In a way, it's the success of the Kingston Trio all over again, folk pop, folk made acceptable by nice tuneful harmonizing.)

Paul Simon writes some of the loveliest melodies around, and his *Feelin' Groovy (59th Street Bridge Song)* is one of the best songs ever. And not *all* the lyrics sound as if they came out of a college yearbook, though their cleverness is often exasperating. The big point is the records sell. The two boys with a bomb on their hands in 1964 are selling records by the millions and picking up as much as $50,000 a concert. They are asked to do the sound track for a Mike Nichols film, *The Graduate*. They are growing moustaches. They're very American college student and American college students can identify with them. The criticisms have been that they're too bland, too sophomoric, too commercial, too safe, that they don't have and never will have the magic of a Bob Dylan. Unfair. They made a whole new gentle thing in rock possible, opened up the doors for a whole lot of melodic sound, and are heading for interesting places.

Albums/WEDNESDAY MORNING, 3 A.M. (October 1964): *You Can Tell The World; Last Night I Had The Strangest Dreams; Bleecker Street; Sparrow; Benedictus; Sounds Of Silence; He Was My Brother; Peggy-O; Go Tell It On The Mountain; Sun Is Burning; Times They Are A-Changin'; Wednesday Morning, 3 A.M.* SOUNDS OF SILENCE (February 1966): *Sounds Of Silence; Leaves They Are Green; Blessed; Kathy's Song; Somewhere They Can't Find Me; Angie; Richard Cory; Most Peculiar Man; April Come She Will; I Am A Rock; We've Got A Groovy Thing Goin'.* PARSLEY, SAGE, ROSEMARY AND THYME (September 1966): *Scarborough Fair/Canticle; Homeward Bound; Patterns; Emily, Whenever I May Find Her; Big Bright Green Pleasure Machine; Poem On The Underground Wall; Cloudy; Dangling Conversation; Simple Desultory Philippie (Or How I Was Robert McNamar'd Into Submission); 59th Street Bridge Song; Flowers Never Bend With The Rainfall; 7 O'Clock News/Silent Night.* THE GRADUATE/Soundtrack (March 1968): *Sounds Of Silence; Singleman Party Foxtrot; Mrs. Robinson; Sunporch Cha-Cha-Cha; On The Strip; Scarborough Fair; April Come She Will; The Folks; Great Effect; Big Bright Green Pleasure Machine; Whew.* BOOKENDS (April 1968): *Bookends Theme; Save The Life Of The Child; America; Overs; Voices Of Old People; Old Friends; Fakin' It; Punky's Dilemma; Hazy Shade Of Winter; At The Zoo; Mrs. Robinson.*

Singles/*We've Got A Groovy Thing Goin'/Sounds Of Silence* (September 1965); *Homeward Bound/Leaves That Are Green* (January 1966); *That's My Story/Tijuana Blues* (March 1966); *Dangling Conversation/Big Bright Green Pleasure Machine* (July 1966); *Sounds Of Silence/Homeward Bound* (September 1966); *A Hazy Shade of Winter/Emily Whenever I May Find Her* (October 1966); *At The Zoo/ The 59th Street Bridge Song (Feelin' Groovy)* (February 1967); *Fakin' It/You Don't Know Where Your Interest Lies* (July 1967); *Scarborough Fair/April Come She Will* (February 1968); *Mrs Robinson/Old Friends/Bookends* (April 1968); *Baby Driver/The Boxer* (April 1969).

EDDIE SIMON AND THE GUILD LIGHT CAGE/Eddie Simon (younger brother of Simon and Garfunkel's Paul

Simon) heads a two-boy, two-girl group that emerged in 1968.

Single/ *14th Annual Fun And Pleasure Fair*/*Cloudy* (1968).

NANCY SINATRA/Until her boots took to walking sadistically all over gentlemen, no one wanted to know anything about Frank Sinatra's little girl. She was Nancy with the smiling face and she would have stayed that way forever but for the inspiration of one Lee Hazlewood who in 1966 thought it was about time Nancy let some of her bitterness (one divorce and five years of trying to make the charts and a lot of hassles) come through in her voice. His instructions were to let it all hang out. The result was a new growly-voiced Nancy, full of rage and fury and a growly Duane Eddy guitar in the background confirming she meant it when she sang that her boots were made for walking and they'd walk right over you. (The song was in the best country tradition of women who had had it up to here with their men.) Every woman identified, every man dug her spirit. Nothing the new Nancy did after that quite lived up to *Boots*, but she was mean and wasted and deliciously disillusioned in *Sugar Town* and a few others. Hazlewood stuck with her as producer, writer, arranger and singing partner, and kept her in the same gutsy groove.
(see LEE HAZLEWOOD)

Albums/BOOTS (February 1966): *These Boots Are Made For Walkin'; It Ain't Me Babe; As Tears Go By; Day Tripper; So Long Babe; I Move Around; In My Room; Run For Your Life; Lies; Flowers On The Wall; If He'd Love Me.* HOW DOES THAT GRAB YOU? (April 1966): *Love Theme From "The Sandpiper"; Not The Lovin' Kind; Sorry 'Bout That; Time; Sand; Crying Time; My Baby Cried All Night Long; Let It Be Me; Call Me; Bang, Bang; How Does That Grab You, Darlin'.* NANCY IN LONDON (July 1966): *On Broadway; The End; Step Aside; I Can't Grow Peaches On A Cherry Tree; Summer Wine; Wishin' And Hopin'; This Little Bird; Shades; More I See You; Hutchinson Jail; Friday's Child.* SUGAR (December 1966): *Sugar Town; Sweet Georgia Brown; Hard-Hearted Hannah; Vaga-*

*bond Shoes; Oh, You Beautiful Doll; All By Myself; Coastin';
Mama Goes Where Papa Goes; Let's Fall In Love; What'll I
Do; Limehouse Blues; My Buddy; Button Up Your Overcoat.*
COUNTRY MY WAY (July 1967): *Jackson; Oh Lonesome
Me* (with Lee Hazlewood); *It's Such A Pretty World Today;
Get While The Gettin's Good; Walk Through This World
With Me; When It's Over; Lay Some Happiness On Me;
Lonely Again; By The Way (I Still Love You), End Of The
World, Help Stamp Out Loneliness.* MOVIN' WITH NAN-
CY: *Things* (with Dean Martin); *Jackson; Some Velvet
Morning* (with Lee Hazlewood); *I Gotta Get Out Of This
Town; Who Will Buy; Wait Till You See Him; See The Little
Children; Up Up And Away; Friday's Child; This Town;
What'd I Say.* NANCY AND LEE (February 1968): *You've
Lost That Lovin' Feeling; Greenwich Village Folksong Sales-
man; My Elusive Dreams; Summer Wine; Storybook Chil-
dren; I've Been Down So Long; Sundown, Sundown; Jackson;
Some Velvet Morning; Sand; Lady Bird.* NANCY (April
1969).

Singles/*In Our Time/Leave My Dog Alone; You Only Live
Twice/Jackson; Lightning's Girl/Until It's Time for You To
Go; Lady Bird/Sand; This Town/Tony Rome; Oh Lonesome
Me/Velvet Morning; Boots/Love Eyes; See The Little Chil-
dren/100 Years; Sugar Town/Summer Wine; Jackson/Sum-
mer Wine; Happy/Nice 'N' Easy; Old Devil Moon/Good
Time Girl* (November 1968). *Here We Go Again/Memories*
(April 1969).

SITAR/A 700-year-old instrument from India, the sitar is
over four feet long with a lengthy teakwood neck that sprouts
with tuning pegs and two resonators, one on each end, both
made of dried gourds. It has six or seven strings for playing
and eleven to thirteen auxiliary (drone) strings that vibrate
sympathetically. Although it is the most popular stringed
instrument of India it is extremely difficult to play, as young
American rock musicians who bought one during the sitar fad
of 1966–67 soon discovered. Sitar music is based on im-
provisation and is extremely complex. Some Westerners describe the sound as resembling the yowling of cats. But to the
initiated, the high thin whine is hypnotic and highly expres-
sive and a five-hour concert is considered almost too short.

The sitar craze in rock began when George Harrison used the instrument in 1965 on *Norwegian Wood*. The Yardbirds had already used a sitar *sound,* but not the sitar itself (they got their "Eastern" sound by plugging their guitar into a fuzz box and elongating the notes). The Byrds, who had introduced George Harrison to the sitar, also experimented with it and used it in *Eight Miles High* in 1966. And the Rolling Stones used it in *Paint It Black* in 1966. After that everyone who could used it, or something like it, to produce an Indian sound which, to many people, suggested the reveries and raptures of a psychedelic experience.
(see RAVI SHANKAR)

ELECTRIC SITAR was designed by guitarist Vincent Bell in the middle of the raga-rock era of 1966–67 to make every man an instant sitarist. Although the Indian sound is there, complete with characteristic drone effects, it looks like and is played like a guitar. The sitar itself is very complicated, but anyone who can play a guitar can play an *electric* sitar (it's even tuned like a standard guitar). You don't have to spend a lifetime mastering its six play strings and the thirteen sympathetic strings used for special effects. The electric sitar also solved the problem of how to produce sitar sounds while on the road, the authentic sitar usually being too large and cumbersome to travel with. It can be heard in Richie Havens' *Run Shaker Life Run* and the Animals' *Monterey,* among many others.

SKIFFLE/A loose combination of rhythm and blues and country music, Skiffle was a fad in England during the late fifties. It was very easy to play with homemade instruments like combs and chest basses, and with its goodtimey quality and genial amateurishness, it bore a close resemblance to the jug bands that sprang up in America about that time. It was made to be played in small coffee shops and coincided with the rise of the espresso coffee shops in London. Much of the cheery quality of the Beatles music can be directly traced to the fact that they had a skiffle group in high school.

PERCY SLEDGE/He had a big hit in 1966 with his first super-soulful, *When A Man Loves A Woman* (recorded by, among others, a super-soulful Mae West). He never created quite that sensation again.

Albums/WHEN A MAN LOVES A WOMAN (May 1966): *When A Man Loves A Woman; You're Pouring Water On A Drowning Man; Love Makes The World Go Round; Love Me Like You Meant It; My Adorable One; Put A Little Lovin' On Me; Love Me All The Way; When She Touches Me (Nothing Else Matters); Thief In The Night; You Fooled Me; Success.* WARM AND TENDER SOUL (August 1966): *It Tears Me Up; Warm And Tender Love; You Really Got A Hold On Me; I'm Hanging Up My Heart For You; That's How Strong My Love Is; Sweet Woman Like You; Love Me Tender; So Much Love; I Stand Accused; Oh How Happy; Heart Of A Child.* PERCY SLEDGE WAY (July 1967): *Dark End Of The Street; You Send Me; I Had A Talk With My Woman; What Am I Living For; I've Been Loving You Too Long; Drown In My Own Tears; My Special Prayer; Just Out Of Reach; Pledging My Love; You Don't Miss Your Water.* TAKE TIME TO KNOW HER (January 1968): *Take Time To Know Her; Feed The Flame; Out Of Left Field; Cover Me; Come Softly To Me; Sudden Stop; Spooky; Baby Help Me; It's All Wrong But It's Alright; High Cost Of Leaving; Between These Arms; I Love Everything About You.*

Singles/*When A Man Loves A Woman/ Love Me Like You Meant It* (March 1966); *Warm And Tender Love/Sugar Pudding* (June 1966); *Heart Of A Child/It Tears Me Up* (August 1966); *Baby Help Me/We've Got That Something Wonderful* (January 1967); *It Can't Be Stopped/Out Of Left Field* (March 1967); *Love Me Tender/What Am I Living For* (May 1967); *Hard To Believe/Just Out Of Reach* (July 1967); *Cover Me/Behind Every Great Man There's A Woman* (November 1967); *Take Time To Know Her/It's All Wrong But It's Alright* (March 1968); *Between These Arms/Sudden Stop* (August 1968).

SLY AND THE FAMILY STONE/*Sly Stone (organ, vocals), Rose Stone (electric piano, vocals), Freddie Stone (guitar, vocals), Larry Graham, Jr. (bass, vocals), Greg Errico (drums), Jerry Martini (saxophone, flute, accordion, piano,*

clarinet, tambourine), *Cynthia Robinson (trumpet, vocals).*
Sly and the Family Stone are probably the first example of
what might eventually become a whole new movement—
psychedelic soul, the almost inevitable fate, come to think of
it, for anyone young, lively and impressionable singing soul in
psychedelic San Francisco. *Rolling Stone* magazine pointed
out that it was also the first McLuhan soul group. The group
specializes in surprises. Four people sing lead and the switch
from tenor to bass can happen just about mid-sentence, and
again to soprano a second later. Musical puns abound—
snatches of old hits, theirs and others, weave in and out of the
arrangements. Three bars of *Eleanor Rigby* pop up in a song
about plastics ("All the plastic people, where *do* they all come
from?"). In a song called *Chicken,* which is not about poultry
at all, voices cluck like ruffled hens in an overcrowded
barnyard. Every song crackles with puns, jokes and mad
flashes. The whole raving soul apparatus is there, but once
that framework is defined, everything else is ingenious new-
rock madness, especially Sly's snide lyrics which deal with
such non-soul subjects as groupies. Sly and the Family
Stone demonstrate perfectly what will happen to music as old
established groupings break down—its members are male *and*
female, black *and* white, soulful *and* freaky.

Albums/WHOLE NEW THING (October 1967): *Underdog;
If This Room Could Talk; Run, Run, Run; Turn Me Loose;
Let Me Hear It From You; Advice; I Cannot Make It; Trip
To Your Heart; I Hate To Love Her; Bad Risk; That Kind Of
Person; Dog.* DANCE TO THE MUSIC (March
1968):*Dance To The Music; Higher; I Ain't Got Nobody
(For Real); Ride The Rhythm; Color Me True; Are You
Ready; Don't Burn Baby; I'll Never Fall In Love Again;
Medley.* LIFE (July 1968): *Dynamite; Chicken; Plastic Jim;
Fun; Into My Own Thing; Harmony; Life; Love City; I'm An
Animal; M'Lady; Jane Is A Groupee.* STAND (April 1969):
*Stand!; Don't Call Me Nigger, Whitey; I Want To Take You
Higher; Somebody's Watching You; Sing A Simple Song;
Everyday People; Sex Machine; You Can Make It If You
Try.*

Singles/*Dance To The Music/Let Me Hear It From You* (November 1967); *Life/M'Lady* (June 1968); *Everyday Peo-*

ple/Sing A Simple Song (November 1968); *Stand/I Want To Take You Higher* (April 1969).

SMALL FACES/*Steve Marriot (lead vocals, guitar), Ronnie "Plonk" Lane (bass guitar), Kenny Jones (drums), Ian McLagan (organ).*
Although they didn't make their major impact in the U.S. until 1968, they were very much in the English pop scene of 1966. In England their physical smallness, natty mod look, perkiness and sheer accessability made them number one group with all the new young fans who were already finding the Beatles and Stones too old and too remote to identify with. As rock started getting increasingly complicated (and, some complained, pretentious) and older groups retired from the frenzied public life and the frequent live appearances, the Small Faces emerged looking for all the world like the very kids they were playing to—innocent, childlike and vulnerable. For a while, it was just their look and the rave rock they went in for. But in 1967 both music and lyrics started getting extremely sophisticated without losing their quality of innocence. In *Itchycoo Park* people got high and touched the sky. *Lazy Sunday,* ultrasophisticated rave rock, has Steve Marriot solicitously asking a neighbor, "How's your bird's lumbago?" (Their second American album made history in record packaging. It came in a *round* instead of the usual square sleeve.) Early in 1969 they looked like they would split up.

Albums/THERE ARE BUT FOUR SMALL FACES (February 1968): *Itchycoo Park; Talk To You; Up The Wooden Hills; My Way Of Giving; I'm Only Dreaming; I Feel Much Better; Tin Soldier; Get Yourself Together; Show Me The Way; Here Comes The Nice; Green Circles; Have You Ever Seen Me (Tell Me).* OGDENS' NUT GONE (September 1968): *Ogdens' Nut Gone Flake; Afterglow; Long Agos And Worlds Apart, Rene; Song Of A Baker; Lazy Sunday; Happiness Stan; Rollin' Over; The Hungry Intruder; The Journey; Mad John; Happydaystoytown.*

Singles/*Itchycoo Park/I'm Only Dreaming* (September 1967); *Tin Soldier/I Feel Much Better* (February 1968); *Lazy Sunday/Rollin' Over* (April 1968).

BESSIE SMITH/Her heyday ran from about 1919 to her death after a car accident in 1937. An incomparable blues singer of great passion and power, she was the first of the big, beautiful red-hot ravers. When you hear Aretha Franklin, Janis Joplin or Tina Turner, you know some, at least, of Bessie Smith still lives.

HANK SNOW/One of the legendary greats in country and western music. *I'm Movin' On* was his first and most famous song.

SOFT MACHINE/*Michael Ratledge (organ, piano), Robert Wyatt (lead vocals, drums, bass guitar, piano, trumpet, cello), Kevin Ayers (vocals, lead guitar, bass guitar).*
The Soft Machine is a three-man English group that defies musical classification. The jazz people won't touch them because they have long hair and look like pop people. The pop people think they're not commercial enough. The avant-garde music people are intrigued but undecided. The group says they play avant-garde jazz but they call it pop because that's the only way people will come to hear it. They are one of the very few (and were one of the first) English groups to work closely with a light show, Mark Boyle's Sensual Laboratory. They created a minor sensation in St. Tropez when they appeared as part of a giant happening in August, 1966. But they didn't hit the United States until 1968, when they played in the Museum of Modern Art's jazz series (their long sets and improvisations didn't go over with some of the critics who found them just too avant-garde). They have been called the Futuristic Beatles, and years from now, when we fully understand their combinations of John Cage, Stockhausen, Cecil Taylor and Ornette Coleman, we might agree.
Albums/THE SOFT MACHINE (December 1968): *Hope For Happiness; Joy Of The Toy; Hope For Happiness (Reprise); Why Am I So Short; So Boot If At All; A Certain Kind; Save Yourself; Priscilla; Lullabye Letter; We Did It Again; Plus Belle Qu'une Poubelle; Why Are We Sleeping; Box 25/4 Lid.*
SOFT MACHINE, VOL. 2 (June 1969).

SOFT ROCK/Somewhere in the beginning of 1966 with the Mamas and the Papas and the Lovin' Spoonful, rock became gentler, softer. By 1967 and 1968 soft rock became part of the best-seller charts—Simon and Garfunkel, Tim Hardin, Donovan, The Zombies, the new Moody Blues, Procol Harum. All express gentle sentiments, nothing frantic. Some people see soft rock as the sellout: hard rock made easy listening, hard rock with its teeth drawn and its vitality removed to make it more commercial. Others see it as the non-violence of the new music. Both interpretations are valid. The point is rock doesn't have to be noisy anymore.

SOFT WHITE UNDERBELLY/ *Albert Buchard (drums), Andrew Winters (bass guitar), Donald Roeser (lead guitar), Allen Lanier (organ, keyboard, rhythm guitar), Les Braunstein lead vocals).*

After a year of retreat on Long Island for some cautious musical simmering, Soft White Underbelly, a rock group with mysterious Near Eastern overtones, emerged in 1969 with a record contract and a mildly mystical underground reputation.

SONNY (see SONNY & CHER)

Album/INNER VIEWS (August 1968): *I Just Sit There; I Told My Girl To Go Away; I Would Marry You Today; My Best Friend's Girl Is Out Of Sight; Pammie's On A Bummer.*

Singles/*Laugh At Me/Tony; Revolution Kind/Georgia And John Quetzal; I Told My Girl To Go Away/Misty Roses; My Best Friend's Girl Is Out Of Sight/Pammie's On A Bummer.*

SONNY & CHER/A husband and wife duo as teenage idols? Unthinkable. Sonny and Cher Bono pulled off this unlikely coup in 1965 by suddenly making marriage seem like the grooviest thing possible. To adults, all that conjugal bliss on display on stage veered close to the distasteful. To the young it was frankly beautiful—and contagious. To watch Sonny and Cher love each other was to feel loved by them and indeed they always encouraged flesh contact with their fans The other thing about Sonny and Cher was that they were not just an ordinary husband and wife, but a *rebel* pair, constantly being asked to leave restaurants and hotels because of their appearance—he in long hair, bell bottom pants and furry vests; she also in bell bottoms which went on to set a whole teen and then pre-teen style (in fact, when the first of the genus teenybooper stepped out in 1965, she was wearing "Cher pants" and they have been a teeny uniform ever since).

Socially, then, Sonny and Cher, working out of Los Angeles, were a massive influence. kids identified with them, tried to look like them, and relished the financial success that enabled them to thumb their noses at hotel managers and headwaiters. Musically, what got them moving was that new combination of folk and rock that the Byrds and the Turtles were pioneering in Los Angeles. But while these two groups were doing it by rocking folk material like Dylan, Sonny and Cher did it with their own material. To some *I Got You, Babe* seemed like an obvious imitation of Dylan folk rock. Never mind, it was a huge hit and well timed.

Gradually it became apparent that the voice of the team was not Sonny but Cher. Cher worked increasingly as a solo singer, with no apparent dismay on the part of Sonny, who continued to write songs for her, to conduct the business of being a star duo, and to play straight man on stage, lending his voice when the occasion called for it. When the union of folk and rock became something to be taken so much for granted that the term folk rock dropped out of popular use, Sonny and Cher still sold records.

By the time the other rich freaks happened in Los Angeles (the Mamas and the Papas, the Doors and others), they simply settled back to being an essential part of a very lively music scene where the people in the long hair and the bell bottoms had completely taken over. When celebrities like the BeeGees or Twiggy and Justin visited, it was Sonny and Cher who would host the star-studded parties. Gradually the eccentric costuming of the pair began to seem less eccentric, partly because everyone was wearing it by then and partly because with success, everything they owned became so much more lush and luxurious that even *Vogue* took to featuring them on its pages.

Sonny and Cher (who had once recorded as Caesar and Cleo) no longer are quite what they were in the early days; too many other people are being rebels both socially and musically. But they're still immensely popular, and exactly who they were was revealed at the huge soul-together in the summer of

1968 when Cher, in evening dress (she'd always worn pants in the old days), and Sonny, in exquisite silk Nehru jacket, announced they were going to become parents—to 40,000 fans. It seemed only right that that announcement should have been made from the stage of Madison Square Garden to an audience of 40,000. (Sadly, Cher lost the expected heir— she had lost a child in 1967 too—but you can bet that when the next one's along, the announcement will be made at the very least from the Hollywood Bowl).

Albums/LOOK AT US (August 1965): *I Got You Babe; Unchained Melody; Then He Kissed Me; Sing C'est La Vie; It's Gonna Rain; 500 Miles; Just You; Letter; Let It Be Me; You Don't Love Me; You Really Got A Hold On Me; Why Don't They Let Us Fall In Love,* WONDROUS WORLD OF SONNY AND CHER (January 1966): *Summertime; Tell Him; I'm Leaving It All Up To You; But You're Mine; Bring It On Home To Me; Set Me Free; What Now My Love; Leave Me Be; I Look For You; Laugh At Me; Turn Around; So Fine.* IN CASE YOU'RE IN LOVE (February 1967): *Beat Goes On; Groovy Kind Of Love; Podunk; You Baby; Monday; Love Don't Come; Little Man; We'll Sing In The Sunshine; Living For You; Misty Roses; Stand By Me; Cheryl's Going Home.* GOOD TIMES (April 1967): *I Got You Babe; It's The Little Things; I'm Gonna Love You; Good Times; Trust Me; Just A Name; Don't Talk To Strangers.* BEST OF SONNY AND CHER (July 1967): *Beat Goes On; What Now My Love; I Got You Babe; Little Man; Just You; Let It Be Me; Beautiful Story; It's The Little Things; But You're Mine; Sing C'est La Vie; Laugh At Me; Living For You.* THIS GOOD EARTH (May 1968).

Singles/*Letter/Spring Fever; Sing C'est La Vie/Just You* (March 1965); *I Got You Babe/It's Gonna Rain* (May 1965); *But You're Mine/Hello* (November 1965); *What Now My Love/I Look For You* (January 1966); *Leave Me Be/ Have I Stayed Too Long* (May 1966); *Little Man/Monday* (September 1966); *Beat Goes On/Love Don't Come* (December 1966); *Podunk/Beautiful Story* (April 1967); *It's The Little Things/Plastic Man* (May 1967); *Don't Talk To Strangers/It's The Little Things* (July 1967); *You And Me/Good Combination* (January 1968).

Also Appear On/BABY DON'T GO (November 1965): *Baby Don't Go; Walkin' The Quetzal.* SMASH SOUNDS: *Beat Goes On.*

SOPWITH CAMEL/An early San Francisco group, Sopwith Camel came on like a mini Lovin' Spoonful ("so relaxed they could make the Spoonful sound uptight" was one comment). That wasn't a bad way to come on in the 1966–67 dawn of American happy music, but they were sharply criticized for being camp, cute, commercial and too quaintly old-timey. (In 1968 Tiny Tim, who's as quaint and old-timey as they come, did their first hit, *Hello, Hello,* which proves the point.) They were very good live, active in the San Francisco music scene, but their record company encouraged them to do the faintly satirical campy stuff because that was what sold. Their producer, Erik Jacobsen, had produced nine straight top ten singles for the Lovin' Spoonful and might be forgiven for encouraging them in that direction. Besides, their prolific writer, Peter Kramer, sang in a very lilting John Sebastian style.

Hello, Hello was a huge hit and big things were expected of Sopwith Camel, artistically and commercially, but somehow success was too much for them. It brought pressures they hadn't even imagined existed. And they fell apart never to come back together again. All that is left is the prolific Kramer, now writing for Jacobsen's publishing company, Great Honesty, so that gentle Kink-like whimsy and country string sound is not lost forever.

Album/SOPWITH CAMEL (August 1967): *Hello, Hello; Frantic Desolation; Saga Of The Low Down Let Down; Little Orphan Annie; You Always Tell Me Baby; Maybe In A Dream; Cellophane Woman; Things That I Could Do With You; Walk In The Park; The Great Morpheum; Postcard From Jamaica.*

Singles/*Little Orphan Annie/Postcard From Jamaica; Great Morpheum/Saga Of The Low Down Let Down.*

SOUL/You have it—or you don't. Either way you can't define it. If you've lived through enough, if pain has been your constant companion and despair has seeped into your heart, lungs and guts so that no matter what good times come later they're always colored by that extra dimension of sorrow, if it's so much a part of you that you can't sing or play without it coming through, then you may start to understand what goes into a performance by Aretha Franklin, or B. B. King, or Otis Redding. A lot of black singers have soul. Some white singers give superb imitations of soul, but that's all. There are moments in the performances of Eric Burdon, Tim Buckley, Stevie Winwood, Tim Hardin and others when the skin and the flesh are ripped off and you can see their bared hearts beating. But they're still just moments. Aretha and Otis and the others sing like that *all* the time.

THE SOUL SURVIVORS/*Kenneth Jeremiah (vocals), Richard Ingui (vocals), Charles Ingui (vocals), Paul Venturini (organ), Edward Leonetti (guitar), Joey Forgione (drums).*
The Soul Survivors, who come from New York, were originally a vocal act called the Dedications; three of them were, anyway. In 1966 they decided to get drums, guitar and organ to back them and they became the Soul Survivors. Their first record, *Expressway To Your Heart,* was a number one record. Black rhythm and blues stations played it frequently—until they discovered the group was white. They're one of the few white soul groups that made it. (And they say their soul and inspiration came from the Righteous Brothers and, of course, the Rascals).

Album/*WHEN THE WHISTLE BLOWS ANYTHING GOES* (July 1967): *Expressway To Your Heart; Respect; Change Is Gonna Come; Please, Please, Please; Hey Gyp And The Rydle; Do You Feel It; Too Many Fish In The Sea; Shake; Dathon's Theme; Taboo.*

Singles/*Dathon's Theme/ Explosion (In My Soul)* (November 1967); *Expressway To Your Heart/Hey Gyp* (June 1967); *Impossible Mission/Poor Man's Dream* (February 1968); *Turn Out The Fire/Walkin'* (October 1968).

SOUND TRACKS AND FILM SCORES/The great rock sound track has yet to happen. Although the most interesting to date is the track for the Peter Fonda-Dennis Hopper film, *Easy Rider,* which included a song written by Bob Dylan and the Byrds' Roger McGuinn, and several already familiar but highly appropriate rock singles.

Many people felt that the Beatles' *Help* and *Hard Day's Night* were it, the great rock sound tracks, and perhaps they were. But many things have been tried since. Manfred Mann's score for *Up the Junction,* for example, has been much praised. Mostly though, rock and films have skirted around each other very dubiously.

No one fainted over Paul McCartney's score for *The Family Way* (starring Hayley Mills) or the Byrds' music for *Don't Make Waves* (starring Claudia Cardinale and Tony Curtis). Cream played on *The Savage Seven.* Tom Jones sang the title song of *What's New, Pussycat?* over the credits. The Seekers sang the title song of *Georgy Girl* over the credits. The Lovin' Spoonful appeared in *What's Up, Tiger Lily?* The Yardbirds appeared in Antonioni's *Blow-up,* Clear Light in *The President's Analyst* (starring James Coburn). Rock songwriting team Mann and Weil did the music for *Wild in the Streets.* Beatle George Harrison did a sound track for a film called *Wonderwall.* Simon and Garfunkel did some songs (but not the entire track) for Mike Nichols' *The Graduate.* Tim Buckley worked on the score of *Changes* (which Leonard Cohen turned down feeling it was more Buckley than Cohen). Spencer Davis and Stevie Winwood's Traffic collaborated on *Here We Go Round the Mulberry Bush.*

All that sounds like a lot of musical activity but it isn't. Although several rock stars have made films (the Beatles, the Monkees, Dave Clark, Herman's Hermits, Sonny and Cher) fewer than one would imagine have worked out. On the whole, groups don't make good films. And so far nor does the popular music theme.

You Are What You Eat is more a music and hippie happening collage than a film about rock. The mid-fifties rock and roll films (*Rock Around The Clock*) were out-and-out exploitation, not that there was anything wrong with that per se. A film called *Revolution* featured Country Joe and the Fish, the Quicksilver Messenger Service, Steve Miller Blues Band and Mother Earth; the sound track was released as an album. Booker T Jones of Stax records' famous Booker T and the MG's composed and arranged the score for a soul drama directed by Jules Dassin called *Uptight,* with his group performing in their characteristic Memphis style. *Festival* about the Newport Folk Festival, *Don't Look Back* about Bob Dylan and *Monterey Pop* about the 1967 Monterey Pop Festival are the only three films which have tried to capture musical performance and personality.

What is ahead is promising, though. Not the Stones' brief appearance in Godard's film *Sympathy for the Devil* but Mick Jagger's star role in *Performance* and his followup (with Marianne Faithfull) in *Ned Kelly* is expected to establish him as a film *actor*. Ringo Starr seems set for a film career with *Candy* and *The Magic Christian*. Arlo Guthrie has two films coming up. Paul Jones was less successful with *Privilege*, a film about a pop star.

Cher will act, not sing, under husband Sonny's direction. Papa John Phillips will produce a film about poet Percy Shelley, king of the nineteenth century hippies. Whether there'll be a John Phillips soundtrack set to Percy Shelley lyrics is something we'll just have to wait and see. *Anything* is possible in the magical world of the top forty.

SPACE/This is the first group specializing in Afro-Caribbean rock, which isn't surprising since they originated in Puerto Rico where, under the name of The Living End, they were the island's number one rock group. They have one single out, *Keep Free*, and now live in New York.

Single/*Keep Free*/*Keep Free* (January 1969).

SPANKY AND OUR GANG/*Elaine "Spanky" McFarlane (electric jug, washboard, lead vocals, tambourine), Nigel Pickering (guitar, bass), Malcolm Hale (guitar, trombone, vocals), John Seiter (drums), Kenny Hodges (replaced Geoffrey Myers) (bass guitar, vocals), Lefty Baker (lead guitar, tenor vocals).*

They laughed when Spanky stood up to sing. Too fat to be another Grace Slick, they said, and not fat enough to be another Cass Elliott. The whole business of having a girl in a group is a very delicate one. Theoretically she should be a freak or a belle and either way with the voice of an angel. But *Sundays Will Never Be The Same* took off and so did Spanky and Our Gang, offering the same pop-folk sound that made the Seekers so popular (and before them Peter, Paul and

Mary, the Kingston Trio and even the Weavers, all of whom offered essentially listenable harmonies). Interestingly enough, since Spanky and Our Gang more and more new groups have added girl singers to their lineup.

Albums/SPANKY AND OUR GANG (August 1967): *Making Every Minute Count; Sunday Will Never Be The Same; Commercial; Lazy Day; Brother Can You Spare A Dime; Byrd Avenue; Definitions Of Love; Distance; If You Could Only Be Me; Come Open Your Eyes; Trouble; Jet Plane.* LIKE TO GET TO KNOW YOU (April 1968): *Swingin' Gate· Prescription For The Blues; Three Ways From Tomorrow; My Bill; Sunday Mornin'; Echoes (Everybody's Talkin'); Suzanne; Stuperflabbergasted; Like To Get To Know You, Chick-A-Ding-Ding; Stardust.* SPANKY AND OUR GANG (January 1969): *Anything You Choose; And She's Mine; Hong Kong Blues; Nowhere To Go; Give A Damn; But Back Then; Leopardskin Phones; Mecca Flat Blues; Without Rhyme Or Reason; Jane; 1–3–5–8; Since You've Gone.*

Singles/*Sunday Will Never Be The Same/Distance* (March 1967); *Making Every Minute Count/If You Could Only Be Me* (August 1967); *Lazy Day/Byrd Avenue (It Ain't Necessarily)* (November 1967); *Sunday Morning/Echoes (Everybody's Talkin'* (January 1968); *Like To Get To Know You/Three Ways From Tomorrow* (April 1968); *Give A Damn/Swinging Gate* (July 1968); *Yesterday's Rain/Without Rhyme Or Reason* (November 1968).

SKIP (Alexander) SPENCE/He was the Moby Grape drummer but his musical ambitions were wider so he left the group and produced a solo album in 1969.

Album/OAR (July 1969): *Little Hands-Cripple Creek-Diana; Margaret-Tiger Rug; Wade Down; War In Peace; Broken Heart; All Come To Meet Her; Books Of Moses; Dixie Peach Promenade; Lawrence Of Euphoria; Grey-Afro.*

SPIRIT/*Mark Andes (bass, vocals), Randy California (lead guitar), Ed Cassidy (drums), Jay Ferguson (vocals), John Locke (piano).*
Spirit, which started in California in the summer of 1967, has

the advantage of having a drummer with fifteen years' experience in jazz, country, and even (this must be a first in rock) opera. With his shaved head he is probably the shortest-haired drummer in rock. But he plays well, going through amazing facial contortions, in rhythm, while playing. Spirit is one of the handful of bands trying to close the gap between jazz and rock. The whole sound is mellow and flowing, with a gentle bluesy piano and guitar riffs that glide from one note to another. A cut from their first album, *MECHANICAL WORLD,* moved to number one in Miami in August, 1968. Lou Adler, bearded Mamas and Papas mentor, created the group. Mark Andes, formerly with Canned Heat, does a lot of the writing.

Albums/SPIRIT (February 1968): *Fresh Garbage; Uncle Jack; Mechanical World; Taurus; Girl In Your Eye; Straight Arrow; Topanga Windows; Gramophone Man; Water Woman, Great Canyon Fire; In General Elijah.* FAMILY THAT PLAYS TOGETHER (January 1969): *I Got A Line On You; It Shall Be; Drunkard; Poor Richard; Silky Sam; Darlin' If; It's All The Same; Jewish; Dream Within A Dream; She Smiles; Aren't You Glad.*

Singles/*Mechanical World/Uncle Jack* (February 1968); *I Got A Line On You/She Smiles* (November 1968).

SPOOKY TOOTH/*Mike Harrison (piano, vocals), Luther James Grosvenor (lead guitar), Greg Ridley (bass), Michael Kellie (drums), Gary Wright (organ, lead vocals).*
Spooky Tooth, a group that arrived on the English scene in 1968, has something of Traffic and something of Procol Harum. What they have from Traffic is probably the result of sharing a producer with them (and with the Stones), young American Jimmy Miller. What they have from Procol Harum is a harpsichord-organ combination (which is not to say that they copped it from Procol Harum) that *sounds* like them at times, and to sound like Procol Harum can never be anything but good. Besides the harpsichord-organ combination, Spooky Tooth has Gary Wright's very individual and distinctive falsettos and the deep grinding voice of Mike Harrison. The group is one of the few Anglo-American mixtures in England (Jimi Hendrix Experience is another). Singer-organist Wright is from New Jersey.

Albums/SPOOKY TOOTH (September 1968): *It's All About A Roundabout; Tobacco Road; It Hurts You So; Forget It, I Got It; Bubbles; Society's Child; Love Really Changed Me; Here I Lived So Well; Too Much Of Nothing; Sunshine Help Me.* SPOOKY TWO (July 1969): *Waitin' For The Wind; Feelin' Bad; I've Got Enough Heartaches; Evil Woman; Lost In My Dream; That Was Only Yesterday; Better By You, Better Than Me; Hangman, Hang My Shell On A Tree.*

DUSTY SPRINGFIELD (Mary O'Brien)/Dusty Springfield is one of the very few English girl singers to have made the international big time. She used to be a country and western girl, in gingham and frilled petticoats, singing with a family group, but she went solo and fell under the spell of Motown at a time when all of England (and really the world) was dazzled by Motown. In fact, she was one of the people who turned the English public and many of its musicians on to what was coming out of Detroit. Her first big international hit, *You Don't Have to Say You Love Me,* reflected her growing soulfulness. In 1967–68 she went all out on the glamour bandwagon with a new image (fantastic blonde wigs and eye makeup that reportedly took three hours to put on). She then broke ties with her English manager and announced that America was where it was at. Once England's top girl singer, she's now working at being the same in America, busily recording in Memphis with Aretha's producer—and doing well.

Albums/DUSTY SPRINGFIELD'S GOLDEN HITS (November 1966): *All I See Is You; You Don't Have To Say You Love Me; Wishin' And Hopin'; In The Middle Of Nowhere; My Coloring Book; Goin' Back; All Cried Out; I Only Want To Be With You; I Just Don't Know What To Do With Myself; Little By Little; Losing You; Stay Awhile.* LOOK OF LOVE (November 1967): *What's It Gonna Be; Look Of Love; Give Me Time; They Long To Be Close To You; If You Go Away; Sunny; Come Back To Me; Welcome Home; Small Town Girl; Take Me For A Little While; Chained To A Memory.* STAY AWHILE/I ONLY WANT TO BE WITH YOU (December 1967): *Stay Awhile; Mockingbird; Mama Said; I Only Want To Be With You; You Don't Own Me; 5 Others.* DUSTY IN MEMPHIS (February

1969): *Just A Little Lovin'; So Much Love; Son-Of-A-Preacher Man; I Don't Want To Hear It Anymore; Don't Forget About Me; Breakfast In Bed; Just One Smile; Windmills Of Your Mind; In The Land Of Make Believe; No Easy Way Down; I Can't Make It Alone.*

Singles/Small Town Girl/What's It Gonna Be; Sweet Ride/ No Stranger Am I; Wishin' And Hopin'/Stay Awhile; I Only Want To Be With You/All Cried Out; You Don't Have To Say You Love Me/All I See Is You; Look Of Love/I'll Try Anything; Just A Little Lovin'/Son-Of-A-Preacher Man (November 1968); I Don't Want To Hear It Anymore/ Windmills Of Your Mind (April 1969).

THE STAPLE SINGERS/*Pop Roebuck Staples (vocals, guitar), Cleo Staples (vocals), Pervis Staples (vocals), Mavis Staples (contralto vocals).*
The Staple Singers are gospel singers that used to appear fairly regularly on the folk-festival circuit, but only in 1968, when the rock concert scene had become highly flexible, did they start singing to the mass rock audiences. At a Fillmore East concert featuring the English rock group Traffic, audiences were startled to find themselves clapping along with the irresistible gospel rhythms of the Staples family, and even more startled to hear the group singing Dylan anti-war songs. But Dylan is an old friend from their old folk-festival days and his *John Brown* (written for them in 1962) and *Hard Rain's Gonna Fall* are staples in their repertoire.

Albums/AMEN: *More Than A Hammer & Nail; He's Got The Whole World In His Hands; My Jesus Is All; This Train; Praying Time; Be Careful Of Stones That You Throw; Samson & Delilah; Nobody's Fault But Mine; Mary Don't You Weep; As An Eagle Stirreth Her Nest; Amen; Do Something For Yourself.* FOR WHAT IT'S WORTH: *Father Let Me Ride; Deliver Me; He; If I Had A Hammer; For What It's Worth; Are You Sure; Wade In The Water; I'm The Light Of The World; Jacob's Ladder; Good News.* FREEDOM HIGHWAY: *Freedom Highway; What You Gonna Do; Take My Hand Precious Lord; When I'm Gone; Help Me Jesus; We Shall Overcome; When The Saints Go Marching In; The Funeral; Build On That Shore; Tell Heaven; He's All Right.*

PRAY ON: *It's Been A Change; Waiting For My Child; How Great Thou Art; Wish I Had Answered; Tramp On The Street; When Was Jesus Born; Pray On; Glory, Glory, Hallelujah; Lord's Prayer; Had No Room; John Brown.* WHY: *Why; King Of Kings; Step Aside; If I Could Hear My Mother Pray Again; What Are They Doing (In Heaven Today); Will The Circle Be Unbroken; I've Been Scorned; I'm Gonna Tell God; My Sweet Home; Move Along Train.* WHAT THE WORLD NEEDS NOW IS LOVE: *What The World Needs Now Is Love; Don't You Let Nobody Turn You Around; Place In The Sun; I Wonder Why; Let That Liar Alone; Let's Get Together; Crying In The Chapel; Downward Road; A Hard Rain's A-Gonna Fall; Nothing Lasts Forever; People Get Ready.* STAPLE SINGERS (October 1968): *Sit Down Servant; Good News; It May Be The Last Time; Too Close; Don't Drive Me Away; Don't Knock; Somebody Save Me; Pray On; God's Wonderful Love; Downward Road.*

Singles/*Are You Sure/For What It's Worth; Deliver Me/He, Freedom Highway/Funeral; Hammer & Nails/Samson & Delilah; It's Been A Change/Why; Let's Get Together/Power Of Love; Nothing Lasts Forever/Crying In The Chapel; Ghetto/Got To Be Some Changes Made* (December 1968).

Also Appear On/GOLDEN GOSPEL HITS, VOL 1: *Sit Down.* NEWPORT FOLK FESTIVAL—1964, VOL. 2: *I Wish I Had Answered; Don't Drive Me Away; Pray On, My Child.*

STATUS QUO/*Mike Rossi (lead guitar, vocals), Roy Lynes (organ, piano, vocals), Alan Lancaster (bass), John Coghlan (drums), Rick Parfitt (rhythm guitar, vocals).*
Pictures of Matchstick Men and *Ice in the Sun* caused a stir on the U.S. charts in mid-1968. They were sung by this English group that has been around since 1965 without a hit—in fact, with five flop singles. One song that might have made it was called *Almost But Not Quite There*, but it was banned in England, for the title alone.

Album/MESSAGES FROM THE STATUS QUO (October 1968): *Technicolor Dreams; Spicks And Specks; Pictures Of Matchstick Men; Elizabeth Dreams; When My Mind Is Not Live; Paradise Flat; Sunny Cellophane Sky; Gentleman Joe's Sidewalk Cafe; Ice In The Sun; Black Veils.*

Singles/*Pictures Of Matchstick Men/Gentleman Joe's Sidewalk Cafe; Ice In The Sun/When My Mind Is Not Live, Technicolor Dreams* (December 1968).

TOMMY STEELE (Tommy Hicks)/In September, 1956, not long after Elvis had become an international sensation, a sailor named Tommy Hicks was causing a sensation in London coffee shops singing his version of *Heartbreak Hotel.* It was the time of the Teddy Boys in England. He was the first of the English rock idols and the first to fulfill the dream of all fading teen idols—namely, to finish up on Broadway and in Hollywood. Today he is an Anglo-American movie star; he has done both stage and film versions of *Half A Sixpence* and co-starred with Petula Clarke in *Finian's Rainbow.*

Album/EVERYTHING'S COMING UP BROADWAY! (June 1967): *Something's Coming; Hey There; If I Were A Bell; Hey Look Me Over; The Girl That I Marry; Too Close For Comfort; Everything's Coming Up Roses; I Talk To The Trees; I Wish I Were In Love Again; Happy Talk; They Say It's Wonderful; There Once Was A Man.*

Single/*Half A Sixpence/If The Rain's Got to Fall* (March 1968).

JEREMY STEIG AND THE SATYRS/They were part of what in 1967 and 1968 was optimistically being called the jazz-rock frontier. But flautist Steig and his excellent group were jazz, not rock. One can only suppose they took up the gimmicky (for a jazz group, anyway) name in order to play the popular circuit more easily and give the young a chance to listen to something different. This leads to some speculation: would rock fans listen to jazz or classical music if the performers were costumed appropriately—long hair, moustaches, tinted spectacles and beads? Steig has to be commended for extending a hand to the new musicians. He plays long and dreamily on one of Richie Havens' records to the happy advantage of both.

Album/JEREMY AND THE SATYRS (March 1968): *In The World Of Glass Teardrops; Foreign Release; She Didn't Even Say Goodbye; Do It; Superbaby; First Time I Saw You,*

Baby; Lovely Child Of Tears; Movie Show; Mean Black Snake; Canzonetta; Satyrized.

Single/*Lovely Child Of Tears*/*Movie Show* (March 1968).

STEPPENWOLF/*Goldy McJohn (organ), Jerry Edmonton (drums), Michael Monarch (lead guitar), John Moreve (replaced John Russel Morgan) (bass), John Kay (lead vocals).*
It wasn't their fault, but they originally came on hot and heavy as the Sparrow, a group that started in mid-1965 in Toronto. They were then victims of an expensive publicity campaign for which they weren't quite ready. They dissolved in June 1967 and came back in 1968 with a hipper style and a hipper name—Steppenwolf. There was a smash single, *Born To Be Wild,* followed by three smash albums. The sound combined electronic hard rock and white soul, and on the first albums there were tributes to the king of hard rock, Chuck Berry, and to blues. The tribute to blues is a musical documentary of the evolution of the blues, a cross section through the layers of its development from early country blues to the present day. The Sparrow was a blues group but Steppenwolf has used the blues merely as a foundation for its own hard-rock sound, with the guitar constantly on fuzz and a driving Hammond organ that never overwhelms John Kay's grating voice.

Albums/STEPPENWOLF (January 1968): *Sookie, Sookie; Everybody's Next One; Berry Rides Again; Hootchie Kootchie Man; Born To Be Wild; Your Wall's Too High; Desperation; The Pusher; A Girl I Knew; Take What You Need; The Ostrich.* STEPPENWOLF THE SECOND (October 1968): *Faster Than The Speed Of Life; Tighten Up Your Wig; None Of Your Doing; Spiritual Fantasy; Don't Step On The Grass; 28; Magic Carpet Ride; Disappointment Number; Lost And Found By Trial And Error; Hodge Podge Strained Through A Leslie; Resurrection; Reflections.* STEPPEN-WOLF "AT YOUR BIRTHDAY PARTY" (March 1969): *Don't Cry; Chicken Wolf; Lovely Meter; Round And Down; It's Never Too Late; Sleeping Dreaming; Jupiter Child; She'll Be Better; Cat Killer; Rock Me; God Fearing Man; Mango Juice; Happy Birthday.*

Singles/*Sookie, Sookie*/*Take What You Need* (February

1968); *Born To Be Wild/Everybody's Next One; Girl I Knew/The Ostrich; Magic Carpet Ride/Sookie Sookie; Happy Birthday/It's Never Too Late* (May 1969).

KARLHEINZ STOCKHAUSEN/A German composer now in his forties, Stockhausen was one of the pioneers in electronic music. Experimentally inclined rock musicians are very much into his sounds and his attitudes—revolutionary thoughts about creating "octaves" in volume as well as pitch.

STONE COUNTRY/*Dan Barry (bass), Don Beck (5-string banjo, 12-string guitar, mandolin, bass), Doug Brooks (rhythm guitar), Dennis Conway (spoons, drums), Steve Young (lead guitar), Richard Lockmiller (rhythm).*
This California group emerged in 1968, after all of the members had played in other groups for varying lengths of time. They play a combination of rock and roll, country and western, folk, folk rock, pop and country rock, which covers just about everything, and even has its own name, mod country.

Album/STONE COUNTRY: *Love Psalm; 'Lizabeth Peach; Mantra; Life Stands Daring Me; Magnolias; Everywhere I Turn; Woman Don't You Weep; Time Isn't There Anymore; Ballad Of Bonnie And Clyde; Love You Save (May Be Your Own); Why Baby Why; Angelica.*

Single/*Million Dollar Bash/Wheels On Fire.*

STONE PONEYS (see LINDA and the STONE PONEYS)

STRAWBERRY ALARM CLOCK/*Mark Weitz (organ), Lee Freeman (vocals, drums, harp, flute, sax, bagpipes), Ed King (lead guitar), Gary Lovetro (bass), George Bunnell (bass), Randy Seol (drums).*
Critic Robert Christgau was the first to point out that "popular" rock (rock appealing to the widest possible rock audience) varies geographically. In the South, it might be John Fred and the Playboys. In the East, it might be the Vagrants. But in the West, it's something sweetly pseudo-psychedelic like the Strawberry Alarm Clock. In other words, even the masses get a mini-contact-high out on the West Coast and that's

what the Strawberry Alarm Clock, which emerged in 1967 *after the psychedelic revolution,* is about. If you want to be pompous you can say they're a combination of jazz, hard rock, raga and classical rock. But really they're faintly psychedelic pop rock, heightened by publicity pictures posed in among a lot of Indian paisley and a contrived but hypnotic hit, *Incense and Peppermints.*

Albums/PSYCH-OUT: *Storybook; Boenzee Cryque; Seeds.* INCENSE & PEPPERMINTS: *World's On Fire; Birds In My Tree; Lose To Live; Strawberries Mean Love; Rainy Day Mushroom Pillow; Paxton's Back Street Carnival; Hummin' Happy; Pass Time With Sac; Incense And Peppermints; Unwind With The Clock.* WAKE UP, IT'S TOMORROW (September 1968): *Tomorrow; Sit With The Guru; Nightmares Of Percussion; Soft Skies, No Lies; They Saw The Fat One Coming; Curse Of The Witches; Go Back (You're Going The Wrong Way); Pretty Song From Psych-Out; Black Butter, Past; Black Butter, Present; Black Butter, Future.* WORLD IN A SEA SHELL (December 1968): *Sea Shell; Blues For A Young Girl Gone; An Angry Young Man; A Million Miles Away; Home Sweet Home; Lady Of The Lake; Barefoot In Baltimore; Wooden Woman; Heated Love; Love Me Again; Eulogy; Shallow Impressions.*

Singles/*Incense And Peppermints/Birdman Of Alkatrash; Birds In My Tree/Tomorrow; Pretty Song From "Psych-Out"/Sit With The Guru; Angry Young Man/Barefoot In Baltimore; Paxton's Back Street Carnival/Sea Shell* (November 1968); *Good Morning Starshine/Me & The Township* (April 1969).

SUMMER ROCK/Does the weather affect music? Apparently so. Every summer something happens to music to celebrate the season. From the days of Chubby Checker's *Let's Twist Again Like We Did Last Summer* to Every Mother's Son's invitation to the fisherman's daughter, there is a non-stop surge of summer rock from the first day of June. Most of summer rock is frankly schlock rock, music deliberately designed to cash in on the season's mood, but the summer sound has seeped through to such songs as *What a Day for a Daydream* by the Lovin' Spoonful and the Mamas and Papas'

California Dreaming (predictably, southern California is very open to it; surf music is just one part of the summer-rock phenomenon). The Rascals' *Grooving* is quality summer rock. Even as far away as rainy gloomy England, something of America's summer sound has managed to travel the Atlantic. You sometimes hear it in the Kinks—but not too often anywhere else. Other examples of summer rock are: *Sumertime Blues, Lazy Hazy Days of Summer, Summer in New York* (Imaginations), *Summer Love Song* (Dr. West's Medicine Show & Jug Band).

THE SUNSHINE COMPANY/*Mary Nance (tambourine, lead vocals), Maury Manseau (lead vocals, guitar, piano, autoharp), Larry Sims (guitar, vocals), Merel Bregante (drums, vocals), Douglas "Red" Mark (lead guitar, violin, tenor vocals).*
In the wake of the happy music revolution of the Mamas and the Papas, the Lovin' Spoonful, Harper's Bizarre and the Turtles (all of them influenced by the Kinks and the happy Good-Day-Sunshine period of the Beatles) came the Sunshine Company, all happy harmonies. The California-based group started as a duo with Mary Nance and Maury Manseau doing a sort of Ian and Sylvia thing. Larry Sims and his guitar made it a trio. Eventually they were joined by two young musicians from a surf band. By June, 1967, the five were the Sunshine Company. The first single they cut, but never released, was *Up, Up and Away*, which another group was to make a number one record. The next single, *Happy,* made the charts. There was something very California and sunshiny about their sound, which is basically vocal (Clairol used it for their haunting *Summer Blonde* commercials). Jackson Browne and Steve Gillette both write for them. And it was Gillette's *Back on the Street Again* that got them on the charts once again. Unlike most girl singers, Mary does harmony mostly and lead vocals only sometimes and likes it that way. The group became a sextet in December, 1968, when they added Dave Hodgkins on acoustical guitar.

Albums/HAPPY IS THE SUNSHINE COMPANY (September 1967): *Children Could Help Us Find The Way; Up Up*

And Away; I Need You; Just Beyond Your Smile; I Just Want To Be Your Friend; Four In The Mornin'; Warm In My Heart; A Year Of Jaine Time; Rain; Love Is A Happy Thing; Back On The Street Again; Happy. THE SUNSHINE COMPANY (February 1968): *Look, Here Comes The Sun; Reflections On An Angel; Love, That's Where It Is; Sunday Brought The Rain; I Can't Help But Wonder; I, To We, And Back Again; It's Sunday; You Don't Know Her Like I Do; Your Heart Is Free Just Like The Wind; If You Only Knew; Darcy Farrow; Without Really Thinking.* SUNSHINE AND SHADOWS (December 1968): *To Put Up With You; Let's Get Together; I'm Gonna Love You; Ways & Means; Stitch In Time Saves None; Love Poem; Wingate Square Springtime Meadows; Willie Jean; Out On The Town; I Hate Pigeons; Sunshine Theme; Bolero.*

Singles/*Happy/Blue May* (May 1967); *Back On The Street Again/A Year Of Jaine Time* (October 1967); *It's Sunday/Look, Here Comes The Sun* (January 1968); *On A Beautiful Day/Darcy Farrow* (June 1968); *Willie Jean/Love Poem* (October 1968).

THE SUPREMES (see DIANA ROSS and the SUPREMES)

THE SURFARIS/*Pat Connolly (lead vocals, bass), Jim Fuller (lead guitar), Bob Berryhill (rhythm guitar), Ron Wilson (drums), Jim Pash (saxophone, clarinet, guitar).*
Like the Beach Boys, the Surfaris were California schoolboys with a love of the surf and a talent for making music. They were part of the post-Beach Boys surf-music boom. *Wipe Out* in 1963 was a million seller. When it all ended, these boys moved into another California sound—folk rock—but it wasn't the same as the good old happy surfing days.

Albums/WIPE OUT (July 1963): *Wipe Out; Wiggle Wobble; Torquay; Tequila; You Can't Sit Down; Green Onions; Wild Weekend; Teen Beat; Yep; Memphis; Surfer Joe; Walk, Don't Run.* SURFARIS PLAY WIPE OUT (November 1963): *Wipe Out; Point Panic; Surfer Joe; Waikiki Run; That Man; Surfing Drums; Similau; Jack The Ripper; I'm A Hog For You; Surf Scene; Misirlou; Surfaris Stomp.* IT AIN'T ME BABE (September 1965): *It Ain't Me Babe; California*

Girls; Like A Rolling Stone; Satisfaction; All I Really Want To Do; Concrete And Clay; You Were On My Mind; Down In The Boondocks; I Want Candy; You Tell Me Why; You Turn Me On; Shakin' All Over.

Singles/*Wipe Out/Surfer Joe; Chicago Green/Show Biz; Search/Shake; Point Panic/Waikiki Run; Boss Barracuda/Dune Buggy; I'm A Hog For You/Wipe Out.*

Also Appear On/GOLDEN INSTRUMENTALS (August 1967): *Wipe Out.*

SURFING MUSIC/Someone once defined surf music as wet rock and roll. Surf music was born in California with the Beach Boys in 1962. Everyone knows the story. The Wilson brothers and assorted friends and relatives, not a group then, got together, wrote a song about surfing, sang it, recorded it, had a small local hit with it and went on to make three huge consecutive national hits on the same theme. The ball the Beach Boys got rolling with *Surfin' Safari* (a Brian Wilson-Mike Love 1962 composition) and *Surfin' USA* (written by Chuck Berry in 1963) was quickly picked up by Jan and Dean, whose *Surf City* in 1963 was the first of a long line of Jan and Dean surf hits. When people talked about California sound in those days they didn't mean acid rock, they meant the Beach Boys' *Fun, Fun, Fun,* the Surfaris' *Wipe Out* and Jan and Dean covering the world of surf and drag racing. The songs were about beach dollies and ho-daddies and marked the first time in music history that a sport actually had its own music. Surf music had a nice summer sound and was a good beat to drive to. It had the kind of high, summery harmonies that the Beach Boys used, and the thing to do, of course, was to sound as if the sound had just happened on a sandy beach. It grew and grew so that at one stage even Chubby Checker had a surf record out. A comedy album, *MY SON THE SURF NUT,* had numbers like *The Teenage Surfing Vampire* and *Some Gremmie Stole My Hair Bleach.* By 1964, when the novelty wore off, hot-rod music took over, but California lost its supremacy with the arrival of the Beatles and the new sound of folk rock in 1965. Jan and Dean turned to something called folk 'n' roll; the Beach Boys went sophisticated and even the Surfaris recorded an album called *IT AIN'T ME*

BABE. But surfing music comes back every year with each new batch of summer rock; its tingling harmonies live on in the Mamas and the Papas, the Fifth Dimension, the Cowsills.

Albums/SURF CITY (Jan and Dean); SURFARIS PLAY WIPE OUT (Surfaris); SURFER GIRL (Beach Boys); SURFER'S CHOICE (Dick Dale); SURFER'S STOMP (Marketts); SURFING (Ventures); SURFIN' BONGOS (Bongo Tenns and the Preston Epps); SURFIN' SAFARI (Beach Boys); SURFIN' U. S. A. (Beach Boys); SURFIN' WITH BO DIDDLEY (Bo Diddley); SURFIN' WITH THE ASTRONAUTS (Astronauts); SURFIN' WITH THE CHALLENGERS (Challengers); SURFING WITH THE SHADOWS (Shadows); SURF'S UP (Challengers).

THE SWEET INSPIRATIONS/*Cissy Drinkard Houston, Myrna Smith, Sylvia Shemwell, Estelle Brown.*
The Sweet Inspirations started off as a background group working anonymously for six years in literally hundreds of sessions (as many as three different ones a day), before they were given their name and, in 1967, their chance to work as featured performers. They have two albums out: *SWEET INSPIRATIONS,* which came out in the spring of 1968, and *CISSY DRINKARD AND THE SWEET INSPIRATIONS SING SONGS OF FAITH AND INSPIRATION.* The four girls, who come from a gospel background, can be heard particularly on many Atlantic records, and especially those of Aretha Franklin.

Albums/SWEET INSPIRATIONS (1968): *Oh, What A Fool I've Been; Blues Stay Away From Me; Don't Let Me Lose This Dream; Do Right Woman, Do Right Man; Knock On Wood; Don't Fight It; Sweet Inspiration; Let It Be Me; I'm Blue; Reach Out For Me; Here I Am (Take Me); Why (Am I Treated So Bad).* CISSY DRINKARD AND THE SWEET INSPIRATIONS SING SONGS OF FAITH AND IN-SPIRATION: *What A Friend; I Shall Know Him; Swing Low; Guide Me; Looking On The Bright Side; Pilgrims Of Sorrow; He'll Fight; Without A Doubt; 23rd Psalm; Down By The River Side.* WHAT THE WORLD NEEDS NOW IS LOVE (November 1968): *Alfie; What The World Needs*

Now Is Love; To Love Somebody; Watch The One Who Brings You The News; Am I Ever Gonna See My Baby Again; Unchained Melody; You Really Didn't Mean It, Walkin' My Shoes; Where Did It Go; I Could Leave You Alone; That's How Strong My Love Is; I Don't Want To Go On Without You.

Singles/*I Don't Want To Go On Without You/Why; Let It Be Me/When Something Is Wrong With My Baby; I've Been Loving You Too Long/That's How Strong My Love Is; Don't Fight It/Oh, What A Fool I've Been; Do Right Woman, Do Right Man/Reach Out For Me; I'm Blue/Sweet Inspirations; Crying In The Rain/Everyday Will Be Like A Holiday* (April 1969).

TEENY ROCK/In 1966 teeny rock had a small boom with Gary and the Hornets (then made up of three Ohio brothers: Greg Calvert, twelve, Gary, eleven, on guitar and Steve, six, on drums). The Bantams were Mike Kirchner, twelve, brother Jeff, ten, and Fritz, nine, who sang out of Venice, California. Since then the novelty of teeny rock has died down a little, though groups in that age bracket continue to thrive, not on lucrative record contracts, but on regular dance gigs in smaller towns. The younger members of the Cowsills were the closest to teeny rock in the 1967–68 era.

TEMPTATIONS/*Mel Franklin, Otis Williams, Eddie Kendricks, Paul Williams, Dennis Edwards (replaced David Ruffin) (lead vocals).*
The Temptations signed with Berry Gordy in 1960, and by the time they had their first big hit in 1964, *The Way You Do The Things You Do,* they were one of those polished groups that Gordy's Motown puts out in the image of its superstar group, the Four Tops. The Temptations break records wherever they play. They are always asked to return. They never *need* hits (though they have them: *Beauty Is Only Skin Deep, Since I Lost My Baby* and so on). They are all tall, slim and sharper than a serpent's tooth on stage. When they got to play the Copa in 1968, always the crowning glory for a Motown group, they knew they had arrived. Lead singer David Ruffin has left to go solo.

Albums/MEET THE TEMPTATIONS (March 1964): *Way You Do The Things You Do; Paradise; May I Have This Dance; Dream Come True; I Want A Love I Can See; Farewell My Love; Your Wonderful Love; Just Let Me Know; Slow Down Heart; Further You Look, The Less You See; Check Yourself; Isn't She Pretty.* TEMPTATIONS SING SMOKEY (February 1965): *My Girl; Way You Do The Things You Do; You Beat Me To The Punch; You've Really Got A Hold On Me; Baby, Baby I Need You; What Love Has Joined Together; You'll Lose A Precious Love; It's Growing; Who's Loving You; What's So Good About Goodbye; Way Over There; Depend On Me (You Can).* TEMP-TIN' TEMPTATIONS (November 1965): *Since I Lost My Baby; Girl's Alright With Me; Just Another Lonely Night; My Baby; You've Got To Earn It; Everybody Needs Love; Girl (Why You Wanna Make Me Blue); Don't Look Back; I Gotta Know Now; Born To Love You; I'll Be In Trouble; You're The One I Need.* GETTIN' READY (June 1966): *Say You; Little Miss Sweetness; Ain't Too Proud To Beg; Get Ready; Lonely, Lonely Man Am I; Too Busy Thinking About My Baby; I've Been Good To You; It's A Lonely World Without Your Love; Fading Away; Who You Gonna Run To; You're Not An Ordinary Girl; Not Now I'll Tell You Later.* TEMPTATION'S GREATEST HITS (November 1966): *Beauty Is Only Skin Deep; My Girl; Get Ready; Girl's Alright With Me; Girl (Why You Wanna Make Me Blue); Way You Do The Things You Do; Ain't Too Proud To Beg; My Baby; It's Growing; Since I Lost My Baby; Don't Look Back; I'll Be In Trouble.* TEMPTATIONS—LIVE (March 1967): *My Girl; Beauty Is Only Skin Deep; I Wish You Love; Ol' Man River; Get Ready; Fading Away; My Baby; Baby, Baby I Need You; Don't Look Back; Medley.* WITH A LOT O' SOUL (July 1967): *You're My Everything; All I Need; I'm Losing You; Ain't No Sun Since You've Been Gone; No More Water In The Well; It's You That I Need; Save My Love For A Rainy Day; Just One Last Look; Sorry Is A Sorry Word; Now That You've Won Me; Two Sides To Love; Don't Send Me Away.* IN A MELLOW MOOD (August 1967): *Taste Of Honey; Hello Young Lovers; For Once In My Life; Somewhere; Old Man River; I'm Ready For Love; Try To Remember; Who Can I Turn To; What Now My Love; That's*

Life; With These Hands; Impossible Dream. I WISH IT
WOULD RAIN (April 1968); *I Wish It Would Rain; I Truly
Truly Believe; I Could Never Love Another; Gonna Give Her
All The Love I Got; Cindy; Please Return Lour Love To Me;
Fan the Flame; He Who Picks A Rose; Why Did You Leave
Me Darling; This Is My Beloved; I've Passed This Way Be-
fore; No Man Can Love Her Like I Do.*

Singles/*Dream Come True/Isn't She Pretty* (March 1962);
Paradise/Slow Down Heart (October 1962); *I Want A Love I
Can See/The Further You Look The Less You See* (March
1963); *Farewell My Love/May I Have This Dance* (June
1963); *The Way You Do The Things You Do/Just Let
Me Know* (January 1964); *I'll Be In Trouble/The Girl's
Alright With Me* (April 1964); *Girl (Why You Wanna
Make Me Blue)/Baby, Baby I Need You* (August 1964);
My Girl/Nobody But My Baby (December 1964); *It's
Growing/What Love Has Joined Together* (March 1965);
Since I Lost My Baby/You Got To Earn It (June 1965);
My Baby/Don't Look Back (September 1965); *Get
Ready/Fading Away* (February 1966); *Ain't Too Proud
To Beg/You'll Lose A Precious Love* (May 1966); *Beauty Is
Only Skin Deep/You're Not An Ordinary Girl* (August
1966); *I Know I'm Losing You/I Couldn't Cry If I Wanted
To* (November 1966); *All I Need/Sorry Is A Sorry Word*
(April 1967); *You're My Everything/I've Been Good To
You* (June 1967); *Loneliness Made Me Realize (It's You
That I Need)/Don't Send Me Away* (September 1967); *I
Wish It Would Rain/I Truly Truly Believe* (December 1967);
*I Could Never Love Another After Loving You/Gonna Give
Her All The Love I've Got* (April 1968); *Please Return Your
Love To Me/How Can I Forget* (July 1968); *Cloud
Nine/Why Did She Have To Leave Me* (November 1968);
Don't Let The Joneses Get You Down/Since I've Lost You
(May 1969).

TEN YEARS AFTER/*Leo Lyons (bass), Alvin Lee (guitar,
vocals), Chick Churchill (organ), Ric Lee (drums).*
They're from England and they made their U.S. debut in
1968 (the year all the English blues bands finally arrived).
They describe their sound as progressive blues but it contains
a lot of boogie and Count Basie. Actually it crosses the fine

dividing line between blues and jazz, but instead of coming on hot and hard like the blues-influenced bands (Cream, Canned Heat, etc.) that were big in 1968, the group projects a sound that is light and fast and easy, which is not to say lightweight. The American audiences liked them and their unpompous musical attitudes.

Albums/TEN YEARS AFTER (August 1967): *I Want To Know; I Can Keep From Crying Sometimes; Adventures Of A Young Organ; Spoonful; Losing The Dogs; Feel It For Me; Love Until I Die; Don't Want You, Woman; Help Me.* UNDEAD (August 1968): *I May Be Wrong, But I Won't Be Wrong Always; Woodchoppers Ball; Spider In My Web; Summertime; Shantung Cabbage; I'm Going Home.* STONED-HENGE (March 1969): *Going To Try; I Can't Live Without Lydia; No Title; Woman Trouble; Skoobly-Oobly-Doobob; Hear Me Calling; Sad Song; Three Blind Mice; Faro; Speed Kills.*

SONNY TERRY (Saunders Teddell)/A singer and harmonica player now in his fifties, Sonny Terry has been singing and playing country blues with Brownie McGee since the thirties. It was impossible to be around the folk scene of the fifties and sixties without hearing Sonny Terry and his harmonica. He has influenced countless members of the folk and rock generation.

Albums/BACK COUNTRY BLUES (with Brownie McGhee): *Gone Baby Gone; Tell Me Baby; Sittin' Pretty; Bottom Blues; Dissatisfied Blues; Diamond Ring; Way I Feel; So Much Trouble; When It's Love Time; I'd Love To Love You; Love's A Disease; My Fault.* BLUES AND SHOUTS (With Brownie McGhee): *John Henry; I'm A Stranger; Cornbread And Peas; Louise; I Done Done; Meet You In The Morning; Poor Boy From Home; Something's Wrong At Home; Hudy Ledbelly; Take This Hammer; Baby's Gone; Lose Your Money.* FIRST MEETIN' (With Lightnin' Hopkins, Brownie McGhee, Big Joe Williams): *Ain't Nothin' Like Whiskey; Penitentiary Blues; If You Steal My Chickens You Can't Make Them Lay; First Meetin'; How Long Has It Been Since You've Been Home; Wimmin From Coast To Coast.* HOME TOWN BLUES (With Brownie McGhee): *Mean Old*

Frisco; Man Ain't Nothin' But A Fool; Woman Is Killing Me; Crying The Blues; Forgive Me; Sittin' On Top Of The World; Goin' Down Slow. JUST A CLOSER WALK WITH THEE (With Brownie McGhee): *Just A Closer Walk With Thee, Children, Go Where I Send Thee; What A Beautiful City; Glory Glory; If I Could Hear My Mother Pray; I'm Going To Shout; I Shall Not Be Moved; If You See My Savior; You Can't Hide; Packing Up; Get Right, Church; Some Of These Days.* SONNY AND BROWNIE AT SUGAR HILL (With Brownie McGhee): *Hooray, Hooray, This Woman Is Killing Me; Born To Live The Blues; Just About Crazy; I Got A Little Girl; Up, Sometimes Down; Keep On Walking; Baby I Knocked On Your Door; Baby, I Got My Eye On You; I Feel All Right Now; Worry, Worry, Worry; Sweet Woman Blues.* SONNY TERRY: *Cornbread, Meat And Molasses; It Takes A Chain Gang Man; Ham And Eggs; Lost John; Chain Gang Blues; Betty And Dupree; Stackhole Rock Me Momma; Chain Gang Special; Long John; Pick A Bale Of Cotton; Red River.* SONNY TERRY AND HIS MOUTH HARP: *Greyhound Bus; You Don't Want Me Blues; Others.* SONNY TERRY AND BROWNIE McGHEE: *I Got Fooled; No Need Of Running; I Feel So Good; Thinkin' And Worryin'; I Love You Baby; California Blues; Walkin' And Lyin' Down; I Have Had My Fun; First And Last Love; Christine; Whoopin' And Squallin'; Water Boy Cry; Motherless Child; Sportin' Lee.* SONNY TERRY, HARMONICA AND VOCAL SOLOS: *Alcoholic Blues; Beautiful City; Lost John; Fine False; Women's Blues; Shortnin' Bread; Stomp; Hollers.* SONNY TERRY'S NEW SOUND: *Shortnin' Bread; My Baby's Gone; Skip To My Lou; Plus 10 Other Titles.* SONNY TERRY'S WASHBOARD BAND: *Woman Is Killing Me; Custard Pie Blues; Diggin' My Potatoes; Crazy Man Blues; Wine-Headed Woman; Sonny's Jump; Baby Changed The Lock On The Door; Louise.*

JOE TEX/His first love was country and western, and although he's a soul man, Joe Tex works out of Nashville and is probably responsible for some of the occasional soulfulness that gets into that town's music. He's been around since the early sixties, but he's currently part of the new wave, the soul wave, that has taken over from the English boom of

1964–66 and the San Francisco boom of 1967–68. Like many other soul men, he's glad enough for the Beatles, who saved a dying and very white rock scene by giving America back some of its own black music via Liverpool. Without the Beatles' and other English groups' reverence for black American music, the 1968 soul and blues boom might not have happened. Chuck Berry might have been forgotten. The English borrowed but they gave credit, and by 1968 everyone wanted to hear the originals. Of course Tex is only one of a score of soul men, but as he pointed out drily in a recent interview, there's room for everybody. James Brown can't be everywhere.

Albums/TURN BACK THE HANDS. BEST OF JOE TEX (January 1965). HOLD ON (July 1965). HOLD WHAT YOU'VE GOT. NEW BOSS. LOVE YOU SAVE. I'VE GOT TO DO A LITTLE BIT BETTER. BEST OF JOE TEX. LIVE AND LOVELY. BUYING A BOOK.

Singles/*Don't Play/You Keep Her; All I Could Do Was Cry/ Baby, You're Right; Fresh Out Of Tears/Hold What You've Got; You Got What It Takes/You Better Get With It; Don't Let Your Left Hand Know/Woman Can Change A Man; Build Your Love/One Monkey Don't Stop No Show; Funny Bone/I Want To; Close The Door/Sweet Woman Like You; If Sugar Was As Sweet As You/Love You Save; I'm A Man/S.Y.S.L.J.F.M. (Letter Song); I Believe I'm Gonna Make It/You Better Believe It, Baby; I've Got To Do A Little Bit Better/What In The World; Papa Was Too/Truest Woman In The World; Show Me/Woman Sees A Hard Time; I'm Going And Get It/Woman Like That, Yeah; Woman's Hands/See See Rider; Skinny Legs And All/Watch The One; Don't Give Up/I'll Make Every Day Christmas; Men Are Gettin' Scarce/You're Gonna Thank Me, Woman; I'll Never Do You Wrong/Wooden Spoon; Betwixt And Between/ Chocolate Cherry; Buying A Book/Chicken Crazy* (March 1969).

THEM/*Jim Armstrong (guitar, sitar, drums), David Harvey (drums), Alan Henderson (bass), Ray Elliot (organ), Ken McDowell (replaced Van Morrison) (lead vocals).*
The original Them with Van Morrison started in Ireland in

1963, one of the few Irish groups to make an international
name for itself. It was also one of the first rock groups to use
an organ and preceded the sound of later organ-based groups
like Traffic, the Band and Steppenwolf. Until he went solo,
Morrison, with his harsh voice and off phrasing, was the focus
of the group His version of Dylan's *It's All Over Now Baby
Blue* (on the group's second American album) best demon-
strates his style. Morrison wrote *Gloria*, which the Shadows of
Night made a hit and which was to go on to become another
generations' *Louie Louie*, a standard for dance bands. It was
blues rock in the best tradition of the Stones' *Route 66* and
the Doors' *Back Door Man*. Like many English groups they
received little attention during their first U.S. tour. This and
internal difficulties caused the group to disband.

Albums/THEM (August 1965): *Here Comes The Night; Mys-
tic Eyes; Don't Look Back; Little Girl; One Two Brown Eyes;
Gloria; One More Time; If You And I Could Be As Two; I
Like It Like That; I'm Gonna Dress In Black; Route 66; Go
On Home Baby*. THEM AGAIN (March 1967): *Call My
Name; Turn On Your Lovelight; Bad Or Good; How Long
Baby; Don't You Know; My Lonely Sad Eyes; Bring 'Em On
In; Something You Got; Out Of Sight; I Can Only Give You
Everything; It's All Over Now Baby Blue; Could You, Would
You*. NOW AND THEM (April 1968): *I'm Your Witch
Doctor; What's The Matter Baby; Truth Machine; Square
Room; You're Just What I Was Looking For Today; Dirty
Old Man; Nobody Loves You When You're Down And Out;
Walking In The Queen's Garden; I Happen To Love You;
Come To Me*. TIME OUT, TIME IN, FOR THEM (October
1968): *Time Out For Time In; She Put A Hex On You; Bent
Over You; Waltz Of The Flies; Back Where I Started; We've
All Agreed To Help; Market Place; Just One Conception; I
Got A Woman; Lost*.

Singles/*Secret Police/Gloria's Dream; Richard Correy/Don't
You Know; Don't Start Crying Now/I Can Only Give You
Everything; Gloria/Baby Please Don't Go; All For Myself/
Here Comes The Night; If You And I Could Be As
Two/Mystic Eyes; Bring 'Em On In/Call My Name; I Hap-
pen To Love You/Walking In The Queen's Garden; Square
Room/But It's Alright*.

CARLA THOMAS/She started in the WDIA Teen Town Singers but slid into the big time with the Memphis Sound, sometimes with Otis Redding, who sang sweet snarly duets with her that were more like catfights, but elegant ones. She's had hit after hit after hit after hit but seems to be leaving the field to Aretha these days.

Albums/GEE WHIZ (June 1961): *Gee Whiz; Dance With Me; Lovely Way To Spend An Evening; You Love; Fools Fall In Love; To The Aisle; Look Of My Own; It Ain't Me; Masquerade Is Over; Promises; Love We Shared; For You.* COMFORT ME (January 1966): *Comfort Me; No Time To Lose; Yes, I'm Ready; Lover's Concerto; I'm For You; What The World Needs Now; Let It Be; A Woman's Love; Will You Love Me Tomorrow; Forever; Move On Drifter; Another Night Without My Man.* CARLA (September 1966): *B-A-B-Y; I Fall To Pieces; What Have You Got To Offer Me; I'm So Lonesome I Could Cry; You Don't Have To Say You Love Me; Fate; Looking Back; Red Rooster; Let Me Be Good To You; I Got You, Boy; Baby What You Want Me To Do; For Your Love.* KING AND QUEEN (March 1967): *Knock On Wood; Tramp; Let Me Be Good To You; Tell It Like It Is; When Something Is Wrong With My Baby; Lovey Dovey; New Year's Resolution; It Takes Two; Are You Lonely For Me, Baby; Bring It On Home To Me; Ooh Carla, Ooh Otis.* QUEEN ALONE (May 1967): *Any Day Now; Stop Thief; I Take It To My Baby; I Want To Be Your Baby; Something Good (Is Going To Happen To You); When Tomorrow Comes; I'll Always Have Faith In You; All I See Is You; Unchanging Love; Lie To Keep Me From Crying; Give Me Enough (To Keep Me Going).*

Singles/*For You/Gee Whiz* (November 1960); *Love Of My Own/Promises* (April 1961); *In Your Spare Time/Wish Me Good Luck* (August 1961); *I Kinda Think He Does/Masquerade Is Over* (December 1961); *I Can't Take It/Bring It On Home To Me* (September 1962); *Life To Live/What A Fool I've Been* (March 1963); *That's Really Some Good/Night Is The Right Time* (April 1964); *Don't Let The Love Light Leave/A Woman's Love* (October 1964); *Every Ounce Of Strength/Stop, Look What You're Doing* (November 1964); *Boy Named Tom/I've Got No*

Time To Lose (November 1964); *How Do You Quit/Puppet* (January 1965); *When You Move You Lose/We're Tight* (August 1965); *Comfort Me/I'm For You* (December 1965); *Birds And Bees/Never Let You Go* (January 1966); *Let Me Be Good To You/Another Night Without A Man* (March 1966); *B-A-B-Y/What Have You Got To Offer Me* (July 1966); *All I Wanted For Christmas Is You/Winter Snow* (November 1966); *It Started To Grow/Something Good (Is Going To Happen)* (December 1966); *Unchanging Love/When Tomorrow Comes* (March 1967); *Tell It Like It Is/Tramp* (April 1967); *I'll Always Have Faith In You/Stop Thief* (May 1967); *Knock On Wood/Let Me Be Good To You* (July 1967); *Picking Up The Pieces/Separation* (December 1967); *Lovey Dovey/New Year's Resolution* (January 1968); *A Dime A Dozen/I Want You Back* (March 1968); *Where Do I Go/I've Fallen In Love* (September 1968).

T.I.M.E./*Larry Byrom (guitar), Bill Richardson (guitar), Pat Couchois (replaced Steve Rumph) (drums), Richard Tepp (replaced Nick St. Nicholas) (bass).*
A rock quartet that was first heard at the Electric Circus in 1968

Albums/T.I.M.E. (June 1968); *Take Me Along; Make It Alright; Let The Colors Keep On; Tripping Into Sunshine; Love You, Cherish You; You Changed It All; Make Love To You; I Really Love You; Finders Keepers; What Can It Be; I Can't Find It; Label It Love*. SMOOTH BALL (February 1969): *Preparation G; Leavin' My Home; See Me As I Am; I Think You'd Cry; I'll Write A Song; Lazy Day Blues; Do You Feel It; Flowers; Morning Came; Trust In Men Everywhere*.

Singles/*Make It Alright/Take Me Along* (March 1968); *Tripping Into Sunshine/What Would Life Be Without It*.

TINY TIM (Herbert Khaury)/Financially, 1968 was the year of Tiny Tim, with $50,000-a-week engagements at Las Vegas, a best-selling album, English concerts, adulation, world fame, the whole long, glittering, predictable star trip. But Tiny Tim had been performing for years before that in

Greenwich Village clubs like the Fat Black Pussycat and the Page Three, and his act then was much as it is now. First Tiny himself: tall, thin, hawk-nosed, with hair well down below his shoulders (this as far back as 1962, when the only people who wore long hair were girls). His face powdered into a pearly pallor, a delicate pastel circle of coral rouge on each cheek. His grin huge and disarming, as the falsetto notes of a long-forgotten soprano and a long-forgotten song trilled from his throat. Even in the early days, it was impossible to think he was not a put-on. But as the years wore on it became obvious that Tiny was not a comedian, or a joke. He was a living archive of songs of a period that had fallen into oblivion, a human jukebox of the songs of the twenties to the fifties, and even earlier—and not only the songs, but the style in which they were sung.

Since he had a rich and flexible baritone as well as a pure (if occasionally comic) soprano, he was able to sing not just male and female voices separately but also duets. The Jeanette MacDonald-Nelson Eddy duet was a standard in his repertoire. He loved duets that showed off his versatility, so Sonny and Cher and Paul and Paula imitations were among his favorites, with the two voices often seeming to blend. Such virtuosity could not fail to bring applause, and when it did, which was often, Tiny would respond with a Shirley Temple gesturette, fingers delicately touching lips as though to blow the babiest of kisses. Offstage too everyone was called Mister or Miss, no coarseness of any sort was indulged in, and the word "dear" recurred constantly, gentling and sweetening his every pronouncement.

For years Tiny Tim had his following, but it was a small, loyal in-group, not the world. One day he stumbled into Steve Paul's club, The Scene, where he so enchanted the clientele that he was booked on the spot for 365 days a year. The fee was modest, though more than he'd received in the past, but the exposure was fantastic. Every rock musician in the world makes the scene at The Scene. And Tiny's fan club grew. Peter Townshend of the Who decided to record him in London. Others had similar plans. Then it happened. Tiny Tim, who had made records under other names, got a serious, big-company record contract.

To promote his album he was put on several national television shows. Now a nation was seeing him. Old ladies fainted at hearing those songs again. Little children shrieked with delight at the sight of him. Trendy young executives pronounced him camp. Flower people said he was a beautiful person. Here and there were people who thought he couldn't be for real, that the whole thing was a brilliant invention—as though any mere writer or idea man could have dreamed up Tiny Tim's dialogue, or his pumpkin-seed habit, or his deliciously dated gallantry and romantic worship of the fair sex, or his perpetual showering, or anything.

Musically, Tiny's range is wide, enabling him to sing to *Mister* Dylan one of his own songs sung in the style of *Mister* Rudy Vallee, and then one of *Mister* Vallee's songs sung in the style of *Mister* Dylan. He has a perfect sense of showmanship, of comedy, of timing. And somewhere in Queens is a mother who for years had to explain her son to the neighbors ("How come, if he's so good, he ain't rich?"). Tiny's success vindicated all that. You make fifty thousand a week, it's okay if you wear your hair long.

Albums/GOD BLESS TINY TIM (May 1968): *Welcome To My Dream; Tip-Toe Thru The Tulips With Me; Livin' In The Sunlight, Lovin' In The Moonlight; On The Old Front Porch; Viper; Stay Down Here Where You Belong; Then I'd Be Satisfied With Life; Strawberry Tea; Other Side; Ever Since You Told Me That You Love Me; Daddy, Daddy, What Is Heaven Like; Coming Home Party; Fill Your Heart; I Got You, Babe; This Is All I Ask.* TINY TIM'S 2ND ALBUM (November 1968): *Come To The Ball; My Dreams Are Getting Better All The Time; We Love It; When I Walk With You; Community; She's Just Laughing At Me; Have You Seen My Little Sue; Christopher Brady's Old Lady; Great Balls of Fire; Neighborhood Children; Can't Help But Wonder Where I'm Bound; It's Alright Now; Medley; I'm Glad I'm A Boy; My Hero; As Time Goes By.*

Singles/*Tip-Toe Thru The Tulips With Me/Fill Your Heart* (May 1968). *Be My Love/Hello Hello* (September 1968).

LIBBY TITUS/One of the few solo singers to come out in 1968 (though groups were putting a lady up front like so many imitation Jefferson Airplanes that year), she did a beautiful sensitive album that included the Beatles' *Fool On The Hill*, Joni Mitchell's *Michael From The Mountains* (that Michael, whoever he is, certainly gets on the acetates; there isn't a chick singer around who can resist singing that song), a Tim Hardin song, a John Sebastian song and one of the few really effective versions of the BeeGees' *Holiday*—all this and her company decided not to release the album because it would need too much promotion. Libby is one third ingenue, one third socialite, one third hippie, with a head full of Medusa hair, like a thousand snakes. Not exactly difficult to promote.

TOM AND JERRY/(see SIMON AND GARFUNKEL)

TRAFFIC/*Stevie Winwood (piano, organ, auto-organ), Chris Wood (flute, tenor, alto and soprano sax) Jim Capaldi (drums, piano) Dave Mason (bass guitar, sitar).*
Someone once asked Jerry Wexler, who produces Aretha and is therefore in a position to know *something* about soul, what he had to say about white soul and he said two words: Stevie Winwood. The voice, guitar, organ and piano of Traffic, Stevie is white, frail, English and one of the Renaissance men of rock—writer, arranger, performer.

The Traffic story starts with the Spencer Davis story. Davis started a group in 1963 with three others, two of whom were brothers already playing together. One of those brothers was Stevie, aged fifteen. Like the Beatles, he came out of the skiffle craze of 1959 (though he was only eleven when he was in a skiffle band). He had lived and breathed American blues from the start, learned from the record collections of friends. It was Stevie's voice, his songs, his organ and piano work that made Spencer Davis's band. *I'm A Man* and *Gimme Some Loving*, two of Stevie's songs done under the Davis umbrella, were so black and strong it took a lot of adjusting to get used to the fact that they were coming from a seventeen-year-old English kid from Birmingham. In 1967 Stevie decided to leave Davis (life on the road was bringing him down) and start his own group.

With maturity and wisdom you don't find even in older musicians, Stevie took himself and his new musicians off to a quiet country cottage in Berkshire to work and get themselves together as people, as a band, as musicians. Photographers were barred. Reporters were barred. Under assistant promotion men were barred. It was all peace and quiet there, with green grass, and roaring logs on the fire at night. An idyllic setting that was immediately reflected in the first Traffic singles, *Paper Sun* and *Hole in My Shoe* and in everything else that followed. You could see it in the way Stevie smiled, a smile with no tensions, or with the way his group moved physically on stage. They worked together so perfectly with so much telepathy and trust that sometimes the audience felt a little left out.

For a long time Traffic looked like it would be a great band, a nicely balanced blend of three or four good musicians (depending on whether Dave Mason was in or out that week). Winwood's voice was strong; Capaldi's drums were strong; Chris Wood on flute, Mason on sitar and Winwood on organ were gentle and peaceful. Traffic was in the process of changing the whole mood of popular music when Mason left, leaving a trio that worked well only when it was the then unusual organ-drums-flute combination. In the traditional guitar, bass, drums grouping it was invariably too thin. When Mason returned, all seemed to be saved and the group never seemed happier. They started to get away from the blues that had put them on the map with Spencer Davis. But Traffic wasn't to last and at the height of their popularity, to everyone's surprise, the group split, Winwood to join Clapton and Baker in Blind Faith, the other three to try and work out a combination of their own.

Albums/MR. FANTASY (March 1968): *Dear Mr. Fantasy; Paper Sun; Hole In My Shoe; Dealer; Coloured Rain; No Face, No Name And No Number; Heaven Is In Your Mind; House For Everyone; Berkshire Poppies; Giving To You; Smiling Phases; We're A Fade, You Missed This.* TRAFFIC (October 1968): *You Can All Join In; Pearly Queen; Don't Be Sad; Who Knows What Tomorrow Will Bring; Feeling Alright; Vagabond Virgin, 40,000 Headmen; Cryin' To Be Heard; No Time To Live; Means To An End.*
Singles/*Here We Go 'Round The Mulberry Bush/Mr. Fantasy,* (April 1968): *Paper Sun/Coloured Rain; Smiling Phases/Hole In My Shoe; Feelin' Alright/Withering Tree* (October 1968).

TREMELOES/ *Ricky West (lead guitar), Len "Chip" Hawkes (bass), Alan Blakeley (rhythm guitar), Dave Munden (drums).*
"We're only in it for the money" isn't just the Mothers' motto. It's also the motto of the Tremeloes and they *mean* it. They've been around for ten years and used to back an English singer called Brian Poole. When he split, the group's fortunes dropped, but picked up again with *Here Comes My Baby,* which was a major hit not just in England and America but in Australia, South America and Europe as well.

The three original Tremeloes, a rather rugged lot, not exactly pretty-boy types, say the new look given to the group by the addition of good-looking young "front man" Chip Hawkes did the trick. So now they work fifty-two weeks a year almost seven days a week, with one aim only: to please as many people as possible with no nonsense about "moving in new musical directions." They say they'll move where the money is, that's all. Their stage act is all clever harmonies, falsettos and bright upbeat songs (with an occasional tongue-in-cheek revival of an old rock number), and no one's asked for his money back yet.

Albums/HERE COMES MY BABY (July 1967): *Here Comes My Baby; Run Baby Run; My Town; What A State I'm In; Loving You (Is Sweeter Than Ever); Good Day Sunshine; You Shake Hands (And Come Out Crying); When I'm With Her; Even The Good Times Are Bad.* TREMELOES ARE HERE AND BRIAN POOLE (August 1967): *I Want Candy; Michael Row The Boat Ashore; I Could Make You Love Me; Heard It All Before; You Can't Sit Down; Hands Off; Rag Doll; Times Have Changed; Well, Who's That; Love Me Baby; Uncle Willie; Chills.* EVEN THE BAD TIMES ARE GOOD/SILENCE IS GOLDEN (December 1967): *Even The Bad Times Are Good; Silence Is Golden; Cool Jerk; Too Many Fish In The Sea; Jenny's All Right; Round And Round; Running Out; Sing Sorta Swingle; Sunshine Games; Let Your Hair Hang Down; Come On Home.* SUDDENLY YOU LOVE ME (March 1968): *Suddenly You Love Me; Such A Happy Song; You Don't Know Like I Know; Negotiations In Soho Square; Suddenly Winter; Show Me; Norman Stanley James St. Claire; Be Mine; I'm With*

You All The Way; I Take What I Want; Reach Out, I'll Be There. TREMELOES '58/'68 WORLD EXPLOSION: *Peggy Sue; Every Day; The Lion Sleeps Tonight; Rag Doll; I'll See You There; Willy And The Hand Jive; Helulie Helulie; Girl From Nowhere; Alley Oop; Traveling Circus; Ain't Nothing But A House Party.*

Singles/*Good Day Sunshine/What A State I'm In* (September 1966); *Here Comes My Baby/Gentleman Of Pleasure* (February 1967); *Silence Is Golden/Let Your Hair Hang Down* (May 1967); *Even The Bad Times Are Good/Jenny's All Right* (September 1967); *Suddenly You Love Me/Suddenly Winter* (January 1968); *Girl From Nowhere/Helulie Helulie; My Little Lady/All The World To Me* (October 1968); *Up, Down, All Around/Hello World* (April 1969).

TROGGS/An English group, the Troggs turned out one of the rock classics of 1966, *Wild Thing,* the perfect song for anyone who wanted to come on supersexy. (One version of the song was a clever imitation of the late Robert Kennedy done by the Hardly Worth It Players, which delighted the young Senator as much as anyone.) They seemed to specialize in songs that got banned, like *I Can't Control Myself.* Their *Love Is All Around* is gentle and on safer ground. But everyone's missing the wild things.

Albums/WILD THING (August 1966): *Wild Thing; From Home; Just Sing; Hi Hi Hazel; Lost Girl; Evil; With A Girl Like You; Jungle Jangle; When I Am With You; I Want You; Your Love; Our Love Will Be There.* LOVE IS ALL AROUND (April 1968): *Love Is All Around; Night Of The Long Grass; Gonna Make You; Any Way That You Want Me; 66-5-4-3-2-1; When Will The Rain Come; Little Girl; I Can't Control Myself; Girl In Black; Give It To Me; Cousin Jane.*

Singles/*Wild Thing/With A Girl Like You* (April 1966); *Gonna Make You/Can't Control Myself* (September 1966); *I Want You/With A Girl Like You; Give It To Me/You're Lying; Any Way You Want Me/66-5-4-3-2-1; Girl In Black/Night Of The Long Grass; Love Is All Around/When Will The Rain Come; You Can Cry If You Want To/There's*

Something About You; Surprise, Surprise/Cousin Jane (September 1968).

TULLY/*Michael Carlos (organ), Robert Taylor (drums), Richard Lockwood (sax, flute), John Blake (bass), Jerry Wilson (vocals).*
The group that played for the Australian production of *Hair* (June 1969), Tully has the organ sound that made Traffic, Procol Harum and The Band distinctive. They are yet another example of the world-class music that is being played outside the American Top Forty.

IKE AND TINA TURNER/Although they are American, Ike and Tina Turner are much bigger names in England than at home, partly because their sensational 1966 single, *River Deep, Mountain High*, took off there as it never did in the United States. Some say it is the most passionate performance ever to be put on record until Aretha came along. While much of the credit has to go to producer Phil Spector, whose great triumph it was, one has only to see Tina Turner in live performance to see what raw material Spector was lucky enough to have to start with. The easiest way to describe Tina Turner is to say that she doubles in intensity whatever any other singer is capable of—her screams and wails are faster and more uninhibited, her boogaloos are double the speed.

Ike is an integral part of the act, not just because he plays guitar (and how) and sings (less, lately), but because the whole performance is *for* him. Tina, all skintight glitter and sequins and long hair whipping about in primitive frenzy, is making the definitive statement about what it means to be a woman. Behind her are the Ikettes, purring and sophisticated. While recordings released in America have simply not done Ike and Tina justice, in England and Europe they are superstars.

Albums/IKE AND TINA TURNER—REVUE "LIVE" (1964): *Please, Please, Please; Feel Good; Love Of My Man; Think; Drown In My Own Tears; I Love The Way You Love; Your Precious Love; All In My Mind; I Can't Believe What You Say.* IKE AND TINA TURNER "LIVE" (January 1965): *Finger Poppin'; Good Times; Twist And Shout;*

Something's Got A Hold On Me; Hi-Heel Sneakers; I Can't Stop Loving You; Tell The Truth; You Are My Sunshine. IKE AND TINA TURNER SHOW—VOLUME 2 (December 1966): *Shake A Tail Feather; You Must Believe In Me; Ooh Poo Pah Doo; Early In The Morning; All I Can Do Is Cry; Somebody Somewhere Needs You; Keep On Pushing; It's All Over; You're No Good; Fool For You.* RIVER DEEP-MOUNTAIN HIGH (March 1969).

Singles/*Tin Top House/Two Is A Couple; Can't Change A Break Up/Stagger Lee And Billy; Dear John/I Made A Promise Up Above; It's Gonna Work Out Fine/Prancing; Please Don't Hurt Me/Worried And Hurtin' Inside; River Deep—Mountain High/I'll Keep You Happy; Man Is A Man Is A Man/Two To Tango; Cash Box Blues/I'll Never Need More Than This; It Sho' Ain't Me/We Need An Understanding* (August 1968); *Too Hot To Hold/You Got What You Wanted* (October 1968); *I'm Gonna Laugh You Right Out Of My Life/You've Got Too Many Ties That Bind* (March 1969); *Grumbling/I've Been Loving You Too Long* (April 1969).

JOE TURNER/He started his career as a blues singer in the twenties when he was still a teenager in Kansas City. In the late thirties and forties he was part of the boogie-woogie craze. In the fifties he moved into rock with such classics as *Honey Hush, Sweet Sixteen, Corrine Corrina.* His biggest song, *Shake, Rattle and Roll,* was taken up by Bill Haley, Elvis Presley, Sam Cooke and others who made their reputations with it.

Albums/JOE TURNER: *Honey Hush; Sweet Sixteen; Chains Of Love; Shake, Rattle And Roll; Flip, Flop And Fly; Corrine Corrina; Chicken And The Hawk; Hide And Seek; Feeling Happy; Well All Right; Oke-She-Moke-She-Pop; Boogie Woogie Country Girl; Midnight Special Train; Crawdad Hole.* ROCKIN' THE BLUES (December 1958): *We're Gonna Jump For Joy; Teen Age Letter; Still In Love; Blues In The Night; After Awhile; TV Mama;* 7 Other Titles. BIG JOE IS HERE (November 1959): *Wee Baby Blues; Rock Awhile; Baby I Still Want You; Chill Is On; Poor Lover's Blues; Don't*

You Cry; Ti-Ri-Lee; Married Woman; Midnight Cannonball; After My Laughter Came Tears; I'll Never Stop Loving You; Bump Miss Susie. BIG JOE RIDES AGAIN (August 1960): *Switchin' In The Kitchen; Nobody In Mind; I Get The Blues When It Rains; When I Was Young; Until The Real Thing Comes Along; Rebecca; Don't You Make Me High; Time After Time; Pennies From Heaven; Here Comes Your Iceman.* JUMPIN' THE BLUES (September 1962). BEST OF JOE TURNER (August 1963): *Shake, Rattle And Roll; Chains Of Love; Flip, Flop And Fly; Honey Hush; Chicken And The Hawk; Midnight Special Train; Oke-She-Moke-She-Pop; Corrine Corrina; Cherry Red; St. Louis Blues; Boogie Woogie Country Girl; Crawdad Hole; Ti-Ri-Lee; TV Mama.* JOE TURNER (THE BLUES WILL MAKE YOU HAPPY TOO): *Hollywood Bed; Whistle Stop Blues; Last Goodbye Blues; Howlin' Winds; I'm Still In The Dark; Miss Brown Blues; Sally Zu Zaz; Rock Of Gibraltar Blues; Milk And Butter Blues; That's When It Really Hurts; I'm In Sharp When I Hit The Coast; Ooowee Baby.* BOSS OF THE BLUES: *Cherry Red; Roll 'Em Pete; I Want A Little Girl; Low Down Dog; Wee Baby Blues; How Long Blues; You're Driving Me Crazy; St. Louis Blues; Morning Glories; Piney Brown Blues.* CARELESS LOVE: *S. K. Blues; Johnson And Turner Blues; Watch That Jive; Nobody In Mind; Lucille; Rocks In My Bed; Careless Love; Playboy Blues; I Got Love For Sale; Sunday Morning Blues; Mad Blues.* SINGING THE BLUES (October 1967): *Well Oh Well; Joe's Blues; Bluer Than Blue; Big Wheel; Poor House; Piney Brown Blues; Mrs. Geraldine; Since I Was Your Man; Roll 'Em Pete; Cherry Red.*

Singles/*Honey Hush/Crawdad Hole; Shake, Rattle And Roll/ You Know I Love You; Flip, Flop And Fly/Ti-Ri-Lee; Hide And Seek/Midnight Cannonball; Chicken And The Hawk/Morning Noon And Night; Boogie Woogie Country Girl/Corrine Corrina; Lipstick, Powder And Paint/Rock-A-While; Feeling Happy/Midnight Special; Teen Age Letter/ Wee Baby Blues; Blues In The Night/Jump For Joy; Tomorrow Night/Honey Hush; Chains Of Love/My Little Honey Dripper; Big Wheel/Bluer Than Blue; I've Been Up On The Mountain/I Love You Baby* (December 1968).

TURTLES/*Howard Kaylan (lead vocals), Johnny Barbata (drums), Jim Pons (bass, vocals), Al Nichol (lead guitar, vocals), Mark Volman (vocals).*
Previous Member: Jim Tucker (rhythm guitar).
The group started in Los Angeles in 1965, just when the whole concept of marrying folk and rock was developing in that city. The Byrds had just had a huge hit with *Mr. Tambourine Man,* the first rock version of a Dylan song. And when the Turtles put out their version of Dylan's *It Ain't Me Babe,* it couldn't have been more timely. They had a best seller on their hands immediately, and a national reputation. It was enough to get them into every major rock club in America and England, and it really surprised everyone that they weren't able to come up with another hit, since they were that happy combination of good music and good commercial sound.

In 1967 they finally did have a hit with one of the biggest records of the year, *Happy Together,* a happy, sunshiny single that both the upper and lower echelons of rock approved of. Follow-ups like *She'd Rather Be With Me, You Know What I Mean* and *She's My Girl* used the same sunny vocal harmonies with hints of the old California surf sound. They had more hits, played clubs, played the White House, but never did become the giants of the American scene they could have been.

Albums/IT AIN'T ME BABE (September 1965): *It Ain't Me Babe; Like A Rolling Stone; It Was A Very Good Year; Wanderin' Kind; Eve Of Destruction; Your Maw Said You Cried; Glitter And Gold; Let Me Be; Let The Cold Winds Blow; Walk In The Sun; Last Laugh; Love Minus Zero.* YOU BABY (March 1966): *You Baby; Let Me Be; Down In Suburbia; Give Love A Trial; Flyin' High; I Know That You'll Be There; House Of Pain; Just A Room; I Need Some One; Pallbearing, Ballbearing World; All My Problems; Almost There.* HAPPY TOGETHER (March 1967): *Happy Together; Makin' My Mind Up; Guide For The Married Man; Think I'll Run Away; Walking Song; Me About You; She'd Rather Be With Me, Too Young To Be One; Person Withou. A Care; Like The Seasons; Rugs Of Woods And Flowers.* TURTLES' GOLDEN HITS (October 1967): *Hap-*

py Together; You Know What I Mean; You Baby; It Ain't Me Babe; She'd Rather Be With Me; So Goes Love; Let Me Be; Grim Reaper Of Love; Can I Get To Know You Better; Outside Chance; Is It Any Wonder. THE TURTLES PRESENT THE BATTLE OF THE BANDS (December 1968): *Battle Of The Bands; The Last Thing I Remember; Elenore; Too Much Heartsick Feeling; Oh Daddy; Buzz Saw; Surfer Dan; I'm Chief Kamanawanalea (We're The Royal Macadamia Nuts); You Showed Me; Food; Chicken Little Was Right; Earth Anthem (All).*

Singles/*It Ain't Me Babe/Almost There* (May 1965); *Let Me Be/Your Maw Said You Cried* (September 1965); *You Baby/Wanderin' Kind* (October 1965); *Grim Reaper Of Love/Come Back* (March 1966); *We'll Meet Again/An Outside Chance* (April 1966); *Making My Mind Up/Outside Chance* (June 1966); *Can I Get To Know You Better/Like The Seasons* (July 1966); *Happy Together/Like The Seasons* (November 1966); *She'd Rather Be With Me/Walking Song* (February 1967); *Guide For The Married Man/Think I'll Run Away* (February 1967); *You Know What I Mean/Rugs Of Woods And Flowers* (May 1967); *She's My Girl/Chicken Little Was Right* (September 1967); *Sound Asleep/Umbassa And The Dragon* (February 1968); *Story Of Rock And Roll/Can't You Hear The Cows* (May 1968); *Elenore/Surfer Dan* (September 1968).

THE TWIST/You put one foot out and pretend you're stubbing out a cigarette butt on the floor with the big toe. At the same time, you move your hands and body as though you're drying every inch of your back with an invisible towel. That's the Twist. It took first New York, then America, then the world by storm. The year was 1961. White teenagers had been dancing it at least a year. Black teenagers must have been dancing it longer, since the original record by Hank Ballard, *The Twist,* the one Chubby Checker was to make famous, was out in 1955. In New York there was the Peppermint Lounge where kids, fairly tough kids, used to come and dance it. Café society looking for a new kick "discovered" it and the next thing the leather boys and the girls in the blonde beehives knew, the ringside seats were being taken over by such notables as Greta Garbo, Noel Coward, Elsa Maxwell and Tennessee Williams, not to mention Natalie Wood, the Duke and Duchess of Windsor and a thousand other hangers-on.

By bringing dancing back in for adults it completely altered the mood of the charts, selling records that were good to dance to to people who had never bought a record in their lives. They twisted to everything from the *Blue Danube Waltz* to *Hava Nagila,* and in some parts of the world, Russia for instance, they have never stopped twisting and probably never will.

(see CHUBBY CHECKER)

Albums/THE TWIST (Ray Anthony And The Bookends). TWIST & SHOUT (Isley Brothers). TWIST POLKA (Ray Henry). TWIST WITH BOBBY DARIN (Bobby Darin). TWIST WITH THE VENTURES (Ventures). TWISTING THE NIGHT AWAY (Sam Cooke). TWISTIN' WITH DUANE EDDY (Duane Eddy). TWISTING WITH THE CADILLACS (Cadillacs).

CONWAY TWITTY/The name was ridiculous, but even so, for stage purposes, more effective than his real name, Harold Jenkins. Back in 1956 when facsimiles of Elvis Presley were springing up everywhere, Conway was one. He didn't like the name much, but after his *It's Only Make Believe* sold a million copies in late 1958, he said that the name didn't really sound so bad. (And in the Broadway musical *Bye Bye Birdie,* the Presley-like teen idol bears the name of Conway Birdie.)

Albums/CONWAY TWITTY'S GREATEST HITS (May 1960): *It's Only Make Believe; Danny Boy; Hurt In My Heart; Heavenly; I'll Try; Lonely Blue Boy; Half Way To Heaven; Is A Blue Bird Blue; Mona Lisa; What Am I Living For; She's Mine.* CONWAY TWITTY SINGS (February 1966): *Ribbon Of Darkness; Green, Green Grass Of Home; Wine; Other Woman; Truck Drivin' Man; Together Forever; That Kind Of Girl; I'll Have Another Cup Of Coffee; Tips Of My Fingers; Guess My Eyes Were Bigger Than My Heart; That's What It's Like To Be Lonesome; Honky Tonk Man.* CONWAY TWITTY COUNTRY (January 1968): *Working Girl; But I Dropped It; Things Have Gone To Pieces; Walk*

Me To The Door; Two Of The Usual; Life Turned Her That Way; Go Woman Go; Don't Put Your Hurt In My Heart; Walk Through This World With Me; I Threw Away The Rose; Wound Time Can't Erase; Funny. HERE'S CONWAY TWITTY (April 1968): *Dim Lights, Thick Smoke; Skip A Rope; Sing Me Back Home; Image Of Me; I Don't Mind; Tender Years; Jambalaya; By The Time I Get To Phoenix; You Sure Know How To Hurt A Friend; Sensitive Heart; Take Me As I Am.* LOOK INTO MY TEARDROPS (June 1968): *Don't You Believe Her; Almost Persuaded; I Don't Want To Be With Me; I Made Her That Way; Wild Side Of Life; There Stands The Glass; Look Into My Teardrops; If You Were Mine To Lose; Fraulein; Take Me; Before I'll Set Her Free; Another Man's Woman.* NEXT IN LINE: *Mama Tried; Next In Line; D-I-V-O-R-C-E; With Pen In Hand; Us; I Told My World To Go Away; Ain't It Sad To Stand And Watch Love Die; I Started Loving You Again; Folsom Prison Blues; Things I Lost In You; I'm Checking Out:* DARLING, YOU KNOW I WOULDN'T LIE (April 1969).

Singles/*Danny Boy/Mona Lisa; It's Only Make Believe/Lonely Blue Boy; Before I'll Set Her Free/I Don't Want To Be With Me; Darling You Know I Wouldn't Lie/Table In The Corner; Dim Lights, Thick Smoke/Image Of Me; Don't Put Your Hurt In My Heart/Walk Me To The Door; Funny (But I'm Not Laughing)/Working Girl; Guess My Eyes Were Bigger Than My Heart/Honky Tonk Man; If You Were Mine To Lose/Look Into My Teardrops; I'm Checking Out/Next In Line; That Kind Of Girl/Together Forever; Bad Girl/I Love You More Today* (April 1969).

TYRANNOSAURUS REX/*Marc Bolan (lead vocals, guitar), Steve Took (vocals).*
Tyrannosaurus Rex is the underground group of 1968 England. Bolan, who writes the songs, sings a high-pitched vibrato that rattles and wails like a witch doctor in a jungle horror movie. He looks innocent, sings evil. He and Steve Took sing around each other in a way that makes you either hate them or love them.

Single/*Child Star/Deborah* (June 1968).

THE U.F.O.'s/Ann Sternberg (bass guitar), Lisa Kindred *(lead vocals, rhythm guitar), Diane Tribuno (lead guitar), Laurie Stanton (drums).*
The U.F.O.'s were one of the very few all-girl groups in rock, working mainly in the May-June 1966 period out of the West Coast.

ULTIMATE SPINACH/*Ian Bruce-Douglas (lead vocals, bells, chimes), Barbara Hudson (vocals, electric guitar, kazoo, guitar), Keith Lahteinen (vocals, drums, tabla, bass drums), Richard Nese (bass), Geoffrey Winthrop (vocals, lead guitar, electric sitar).*
Ultimate Spinach was one of the three Boston groups that found themselves being promoted as the Boston sound when in fact there *was* no Boston sound. It was not an unsurmountable disadvantage, but it took a second album to establish them as experimental and quite talented, if a little too serious about it all. The material is all their own, and they have to be given credit for trying (though not always with success) to break out of the narrowness of the usual pop-rock formula with some interesting lyrics, in the Mothers-Country Joe style, and a wide range of instruments.
Albums/ULTIMATE SPINACH (March 1968): *Ego Trip; Sacrifice Of The Moon; Plastic Raincoats/Hung-Up Minds; Hip Death Goddess (Ballad Of The); Your Head Is Reeling; Dove In Hawk's Clothing; Baroque Number 1; Funny Freak Parade; Pamela.* BEHOLD AND SEE (June 1968): *Gilded Lamp Of Cosmos; Visions Of Your Reality; Jazz Thing; Mind Flowers; Where You're At; Suite; Genesis Of Beauty; Fifth Horseman Of The Apocalypse; Fragmentary March Of The Green.*

UNION GAP (see GARY PUCKETT and the UNION GAP)

UNITED STATES OF AMERICA/*Joseph Byrd (synthesizer), Dorothy Moskowitz (vocals), Craig Woodson (tabla, electronic & African drums), Gordon Marron (electric violin, vocals), Rand Forbes (unfretted bass).*
United States of America was apparently too good to last, or before its time, or the victim of one or another dreaded

rock-group disease. It played avant-garde electronic rock, which at that time (1968) had not appeared on the scene as much as one might have expected. The group came from California out of a score of influences, not the least of which was the work of contemporary experimental composers like John Cage.

Joseph Byrd, the group leader, is a legendary figure in serious modern music, a producer of happenings, an experimental composer, a conductor, arranger, producer and a man who has studied such things as acoustics and psychology of music. Dorothy Moskowitz, the group's singer-lyricist, among other things has studied composition and production and has conducted avant-garde happenings and experimental concerts. The group's drummer, Craig Woodson, is no ordinary drummer either, having studied everything from African drums to Indian tabla, with intensive experiments with electronic drums (he wanted to find a way to miniaturize them so they could be carried easily and operated by push button).

The rest of the group was equally sophisticated. Gordon Marron not only played an electronically adapted violin but also composed, arranged and sang in the group. A device on his violin could raise it or drop it an octave. There were also gadgets called distortion amplifiers, ring modulators, tape echo units—all designed to alter the texture of the sound. These were available not just for recorded performances but for live ones, giving Marron the choice of something like ten different pedals to push for a variety of distorted sound effects. Even the bass player, Rand Forbes, was an experimental composer, and his instrument, an unfretted instead of fretted bass, was more difficult to play while having greater range and potential.

Perhaps what went wrong with the United States of America, with an abundance of riches, was that their music was too contrived, too mechanical, too cerebral. Even the lyrics were exceptionally literate and meaningful. One song, *The American Way of Love,* dealt most explicitly with the activities of homosexual prostitutes on New York's notorious 42nd Street. Their album met with a mixed reception. Unbelieving enthusiasm on one hand, and boredom on the other. That alone would not have meant the end of the group. No doubt other factors were involved. And whatever they were, the United

States of America, born in the fall of 1967, did not go anywhere near lasting out the year.

Album/UNITED STATES OF AMERICA (March 1968): *American Metaphysical Circus; Hard Coming Love; Cloud Song; Garden Of Earthly Delights; I Won't Leave My Wooden Wife For You, Sugar; Where Is Yesterday; Coming Do Down; Love Song For The Dead Che; Stranded In Time; American Way Of Love* (3 parts).

THE VAGRANTS/*Jay Storch (organ), Peter Sabatino (vocals), Leslie West (guitar), Roger Mansour (drums), Larry West (bass).*
All over America, all over the world in fact, are groups like the Vagrants. Their role is somehow to close the huge gap between rock audiences and superstar groups. For every Beatles and Rolling Stones there are a thousand Vagrants doing a Beatles thing, a Rolling Stones thing, a thing of whoever is fashionable and popular. For those who can't get to see the real thing, here is a close approximation thereof. For every fan who can't get to meet the superstars, here is a local group they *can* meet.

From this kind of start, which is the way most rock groups start anyway, the Vagrants built a following of their own. On Long Island they are *it*, the New York sound, hard rock with the currently fashionable psychedelic trimmings. They would not go over the same way in California because California has its own Vagrants, like the Strawberry Alarm Clock (a national hit did big things for them, just as a national hit could do big things for the Vagrants). Groups like the Vagrants, who work constantly and tend to move with the popular demands of the times, are generally criticized for not being "serious" about music.

Singles/*I Love You, Love You*/*Respect* (March 1967); *Beside The Sea*/*Sunny Summer Rain* (August 1967); *And When It's Over*/*I Don't Need Your Lovin'* (January 1968).

DINO VALENTI (Chester Powers)/Dino Valenti is one of those living legends. He worked in a carnival for seventeen years, was a trapeze artist for three of them, sang around the clubs of Los Angeles for years, but never made a record because he wanted it to be perfect when he did. (The story was that he kept making them, refusing to have them released, dropping them and making more.) He spent nearly a year in jail for possession of amphetamine and sold his rights to his most successful song, *Let's Get Together,* to get money to get out of jail. It's one of the most recorded songs ever (the song's composer is listed as Chester Powers)—the Youngbloods, Jefferson Airplane, Quicksilver Messenger Service have all done it. He also co-wrote *Hey Joe.* But his album, finally out in 1968, has none of this—just strange, mysterious, intimate songs that sneak up behind you. "An underground Bob Dylan," said critic Ralph Gleason. Well, he has that curly Dylan look anyway. "A five-year-dead Orphan Annie," said Emmet Lake of the *East Village Other.* Yes, he's a songwriting legend, and a one-year-in-gaol-for-amphetamine legend, and a macrobiotics-solar-energy legend, but mainly he's a ladies' man legend. It was San Francisco radio personality Tom Donahue who said simply: "If every chick Dino's ever known buys the record, it will be number one."

Album/DINO (October 1968): *Time; Something New; My Friend; Listen To Me; Me And My Uncle; Tomorrow; Children Of The Sun; New Wind; Everything Is Gonna Be OK; Test.*

RITCHIE VALENS (Richard Valenzuela)/When Ritchie Valens died in the 1959 plane crash that killed Buddy Holly and Big Bopper, he was only nineteen—but he was already one of the legends of the golden age of rock. His father had been a Latin guitar player. While he was still a schoolboy, his widowed mother put up her mortgage money to rent a hall for a dance at which Ritchie would provide the music. When the dance made a profit he started having them three times a month and was so good he was signed up by Bob Keene, a veteran bandleader with his own record company. Keene still remembers how his song *Come On, Let's Go* typified his impatience and energy. *La Bamba,* which Valens also wrote and which made Trini Lopez a star, is still a rock standard and is one of the few examples of Latin rock. Even when rock got sophisticated, you could still hear echoes of Ritchie Valens.

Albums/RITCHIE VALENS: *Bluebirds Over The Mountain;
Come On, Let's Go; Hi Tone; Donna; Bamba; We Belong
Together; Boney Maronie; Dooby-Dooby Wah; In A Turkish
Town; Ooh, My Head; That's My Little Suzie; Framed.*
RITCHIE: *Stay Beside Me; Cry, Cry, Cry; Big Baby Blues;
Paddi-Wack Song; My Darling Is Gone; Hurry Up; Little
Girl; Now You're Gone; Fast Freight; Ritchie's Blues; Rock-
in' All Night.* RITCHIE VALENS IN CONCERT AT PAC-
OIMA JR. HIGH: *Come On, Let's Go; Donna; Summertime
Blues; From Beyond; La Bamba; Rhythm Song; Malaguena;
Rock Little Darlin'; Let's Rock And Roll; Guitar Instrumen-
tal.* RITCHIE VALENS MEMORIAL ALBUM: *Donna; We
Belong Together; From Beyond; In A Turkish Town; Stay
Beside Me; Malaguena; Bluebirds Over The Mountain; La
Bamba; Come On, Let's Go; Rockin' All Night; Cry, Cry,
Cry; Hurry Up.*

Singles/*Come On, Let's Go/Framed; La Bamba/Donna; In
A Turkish Town/That's My Little Suzie; Little Girl/We
Belong Together; Big Baby Blues/Stay Beside Me; Cry, Cry,
Cry/Paddi-Wack Song.*

FRANKIE VALLI/He dared to do what other lead singers
talk of doing but never do. A member of the Four Seasons,
Frankie Valli stepped out in 1967 to make some solo singles
and a solo album while still continuing to work with the
group. He may not realize it, but with all the current talk of
musicians' pools and cross-fertilization in rock and superses-
sions, it may have been he who opened the way for singers
and instrumentalists with occasional solo yearnings and an
equal need for group security.
(see FOUR SEASONS)

Albums/FRANKIE VALLI SOLO (July 1967): *Can't Take
My Eyes Off You; Sun Ain't Gonna Shine (Anymore); Hurt
Yourself (You're Gonna); My Funny Valentine; Secret Love;
Ivy; My Mother's Eyes; Trouble With Me; You're Ready;
Proud One.* TIMELESS (1968): *By The Time I Get To
Phoenix; Expression Of Love; For All We Know; Sunny;
Watch Where You Walk; To Give; Eleanor Rigby; Fox In A
Bush; September Rain; Make The Music Play; Stop And Say
Hello; Donnybrook.*

Singles/*Can't Take My Eyes Off You*/*I Make A Fool Of Myself* (June 1967); *To Give (The Reason I Live)*/*Watch Where You Walk* (1968).

DAVE VAN RONK/In the sixties, an age of lyric tenors, falsettos and angelic boy singers, Dave Van Ronk, who sings like a combination truck driver-lumberjack, seems strangely out of time and out of place. But if you've ever heard him after an evening of Judy Collins-Joan Baez sweetness, and if you've heard what he does with Joni Mitchell's *Both Sides Now*, giving it the gritty third dimension of a man who's been there, then you know *his* time is coming.

Albums/DAVE VAN RONK, FOLKSINGER: *Samson And Delilah; Cocaine Blues; You've Been A Good Old Wagon; Fixin' To Die; Hang Me, Oh Hang Me; Long John; Chicken Is Nice; He Was A Friend Of Mine; Sometimes I Feel Like A Motherless Child; Stagger Lee; Mr. Noah; Come Back Baby; Lazarus.* IN THE TRADITION (February 1964): *Sister Kate; Kansas City Blues; Hesitation Blues; Green Rocky Road; See See Rider; St. Louis Tickle; Rocks And Gravel; Cake Walking Babies From Home; Ace In The Hole; Death Letter Blues; If I Had To Do It All Over Again, I'd Do It All Over You; Whoa Back Buck.* DAVE VAN RONK AND THE RAGTIME JUG STOMPERS (March 1964): *Everybody Loves My Baby; Stealin'; Take It Slow And Easy; St. Louis Tickle; Sister Kate; Moritat; Diggin' My Potatoes; Temptation Rag; Shake That Thing; K. C. Moan; Georgia Camp Meeting; You're A Viper.* INSIDE DAVE VAN RONK. JUST DAVE (August 1964): *Candy Man; Frankie's Blues; Bad Dream Blues; Pastures Of Plenty; Didn't It Rain; Wanderin'; God Bless The Child; Blue Monday; Baby, Let Me Lay It On You; House Of The Rising Sun.* NO DIRTY NAMES (December 1966): *One Meatball; One Of These Days; Song Of The Wandering Aengus; Keep It Clean; Zen Koans Gonna Rise Again; Freddie; 'Bout A Spoonful; Midnight Hours Blues; Statesboro Blues; Mean World Blues; Blues Chante; Old Man; Alabama Song.* DAVE VAN RONK SINGS BALLADS, BLUES AND A SPIRITUAL: *Duncan And Brady; Black Mountain Blues; In The Pines; My Baby's So Sweet; Winnin' Boy; Twelve Gates To The City; If You*

Leave Me Pretty Momma; Backwater Blues; Careless Love; Betty And Dupree; K. C. Moan; How Long. DAVE VAN RONK SINGS THE BLUES (July 1965): *River Come Down; Bed Bug Blues; Yas-Yas-Yas; Tell Old Bill; See That My Grave Is Kept Clean; George And The IRT; Hesitation Blues; Hootchy Koochy Man; Sweet Substitute; Dink's Song; Just A Closer Walk With Thee; Come Back Baby; Spike Driver's Blues; Willie The Weeper; Standing By The Window.* DAVE VAN RONK AND THE HUDSON DUSTERS (April 1968): *Alley Oop; Head Inspector; Swinging On A Star; Mr. Middle; Chelsea Morning; Clouds (From Both Sides Now); Keep Off The Grass; Dink's Song; New Dreams; Cocaine; Romping Through The Swamp.* GAMBLER'S BLUES: *Duncan And Brady; Black Mountain Blues; In The Pines; My Baby's So Sweet; Twelve Gates To The City; Winnin' Boy; If You Leave Me Pretty Momma; Backwater Blues; K. C. Moan; Betty And Dupree; Careless Love; John Henry; How Long; Gambler's Blues.*

Singles/*Dink's Song*/*Head Inspector* (October 1967); *Clouds*/*Romping Through The Swamp* (February 1968).

Also Appears On/TAKE A TRIP WITH ME: BLUES PROJECT: *Bad Dream Blues; Don't You Leave Me Here.* BLUES AT NEWPORT (1963): *That Will Never Happen No More; Gambler's Blues.*

VANILLA FUDGE/*Carmine Appice (drums), Tim Bogert (bass), Vincent Martell (bass guitar), Mark Stein (organ).*
If you had been around at George Harrison's house in the summer of 1967, you would have heard an astonishing version of the Beatles' *Eleanor Rigby.* It sounded as if the tempo had been slowed down by as much as four times—or if not the tempo, then you. (And if not you *before* you heard it, then certainly you *after* you heard it.) That was Vanilla Fudge. They were just another white Long Island hard-rock group but they were interpreting contemporary rock songs so uniquely even the Beatles were sitting up and taking notice. That summer George Harrison played their album to anyone who would listen.

Their first single, an incredibly slow-motion version of the Supremes' fast-paced hit *You Keep Me Hanging On,* was a

huge hit in England (and not a hit in the United States till a
full year later for reasons no one has ever understood). It was
Vanilla Fudge at their most musically effective, the song
seemingly destined to go on forever. *Eleanor Rigby,* too,
seemed to have been put on a rack and stretched out and
tortured to a point where the tension was no longer bearable.
The same applied to another Beatles song, *Ticket To Ride,*
and Sonny and Cher's *Bang Bang.*

Vanilla Fudge made the whole notion of interpretation interesting again. (The Rotary Connection copied what the Fudge
would sound like copying the Stones with a version of *Lady
Jane* stretched out so thin it was breaking.) But in live
performance it was harder to take. That mixture of overpow-
ering Rascals organ and psychedelic Hendrix guitar, all those
slow build-ups and crescendos, those lulls and storms, every
bit of it copied by a hundred other white Long Island
hard-rock groups—it finally got to be too much for everyone
except the fans of what the Fudge termed "psychedelic
symphonic rock."

Albums/VANILLA FUDGE (July 1967): *You Keep Me
Hanging On; Ticket To Ride; People Get Ready; She's Not
There; Bang Bang; Illusions Of Childhood* (3 parts); *Take
Me For A Little While; Eleanor Rigby.* BEAT GOES ON
(January 1968): *Sketch; Beat Goes On; Fur Elise; Moonlight
Sonata; 18th Century Variations On A Theme By Mozart;
Voices In Time; The Merchant; Game Is Over.* RENAIS-
SANCE (July 1968): *She Cried . . . When I Was A Boy;
Thoughts; Paradise; That's What Makes A Man; Faceless
People; Spell Comes After; Season Of The Witch.* ROCK &
ROLL (July 1969): *Need Love; Lord In The Country; I
Can't Make It Alone; Street Walking Woman; Churchbells
of St. Martins; The Windmills Of Your Mind; If You Gotta
Make A Fool Of Somebody.*

Singles/*Look Of Love/Where Is My Mind* (January 1968);
Come By Day, Come By Night/You Keep Me Hangin' On
(June 1968); *Thoughts/Take Me For A Little While* (September 1968); *Season Of The Witch* (2 Parts) (December
1968); *People/Some Velvet Morning* (May 1969).

EDGAR VARESE/A composer now in his eighties, Varese
went in for extremes of dissonance, unusual instrumentation

and electronic instruments. Frank Zappa likes to drop his name into conversations, especially when he's with someone who obviously thinks he's nothing but an ignorant hippie. Zappa says Varese has influenced the Mothers' sound.

VELVET UNDERGROUND/ *Lou Reed (lead guitar, vocals), Sterling Morrison (bass & rhythm guitar), Maureen Tucker (percussion), Doug Yule (guitar, organ, vocals).*
Previous Members. Nico (vocal), John Cale (piano, bass, electric viola).

It takes some of the magic away when you realize that when Andy Warhol found them in 1965 they were called the Falling Spikes, and before that the Warlocks. And certainly it seemed at that time as though Warhol, anxious to get into everything while his name was red-hot and flashing, had picked up just any group, given them a fancy name with a double meaning (*Velvet Underground* was the title of a bizarre, sado-masochistic book) and told them to get out there and freak out the paying customers. That's how it seemed but it really wasn't that way at all.

After you heard them you knew it was they who enhanced Warhol's image and not necessarily the other way around (though his famous name did help). They were ever so much more than their master's voice. First of all, most of their good songs were written *before* they met Warhol, not at all under his influence. Secondly, they had a whole long history of good musicianship, longer than most other American groups. Lou Reed had been studying piano seriously since the age of five. John Cale was a child prodigy in England, doing his own compositions for BBC at the age of eight and classically trained from an even earlier age. Sterling Morrison played classical trumpet from the age of ten. Maureen Tucker, one of the very few girl drummers in rock and the only one in a top group, got her training in an all-girl rock band. So if they were overshadowed at first by Warhol, and then by the tall blonde dream-like Nico, that was misleading.

Their role in the beginning was to tour in Warhol's porta-ble total environment show, *The Exploding Plastic Inevitable.* This was the first show to incorporate music, dancers, films, lights, projection, environment and *people* (there was no audience, the people were part of the show). When everyone else got their discotheques tuned in to all that action and the multi-media experience stopped being new, Warhol lost interest. But the band continued. Their first album came out with a Warhol banana on the cover; the second cover looked all black (but held in certain light a skull becomes visible). Everything else was pure Velvet.

The important thing about the Velvet Underground was that in 1966 and 1967 they were as far away as a group could possibly be from the world of incense and peppermints and lollipops and even earnest teenage protest. Theirs was the dim underworld of drugs and sexual perversion, of heroin addiction and the desperate loss of hope that goes with it. Their concern was with death and violence. They were singing about a world that exists and that they knew. *Venus in Furs* was about sado-masochism. *Heroin* didn't have to code words to get its meaning across. Musically they were very advanced, using sounds and voices in a way most groups didn't start using till 1968. They were using whips on stage before the Nice and Dave Dee, and with far more sinister intent. Oozing evil and lubricity, they made every other group look like kid stuff, and they made a lot of people nervous. Their records were never played on commercial stations. There is no word for their sound but sometimes it seems as if a *presence* has taken it over, perhaps even His Satanic Majesty himself. You can easily imagine someone performing black masses with the Velvet Underground's albums. Not for the kiddies.

Albums/VELVET UNDERGROUND AND NICO (March 1967): *Sunday Morning; I'm Waiting For The Man; Femme Fatale; Venus In Furs; Run, Run, Run; All Tomorrow's Parties; Heroin; There She Goes Again; I'll Be Your Mirror; European Son To Delmore Schwartz; Black Angel's Death Song.* WHITE LIGHT/WHITE HEAT (January 1968): *White Light/White Heat; The Gift; Lady Godiva's Operation; Here She Comes Now; I Heard Her Call My Name; Sister Ray.* THE VELVET UNDERGROUND (April 1969): *Candy Says; What Goes On; Some Kinda Love; Pale Blue Eyes; Jesus; Beginning To See The Light; I'm Set Free; That's The Story Of My Life; The Murder Mystery; Afterhours.*

Singles/*Here She Comes Now/White Light/White Heat* (November 1967); *Jesus/What Goes On* (May 1969).

GENE VINCENT/Originally a country performer, Gene Vincent was one of the early rock originals. He began his career only months after Presley and was the embodiment of the whole leather and motor-bike movement immortalized on film by Marlon Brando in *The Wild One* and Jimmy Dean in *Rebel Without A Cause*. This was in the fifties, when it was still very new and when the idea of a man singing in a leather jacket rather than a tuxedo was wildly exciting, more than slightly erotic, and a major victory in the early struggles of teenagers for identity and a world of their own. Ten years later teenagers were to laugh off this period as the greasy teenage rock era, but their own flower-bell-incense rock wouldn't have been possible without it. In any case, literally millions of youths never did move out of this heady time but remained fixated, duck-tail haircut and all, on the fifties forever. Among them is a musician called Richard Starkey, who as a drummer with Rory Storm and the Hurrycanes had toured England with Vincent. Today, as Ringo Starr, Starkey is a living symbol of the music of the sixties, but when he talks about Vincent and that tour his eyes light up and you know inside he's still one of the fifties rockers.

Single/*Be-Bop-A-Lula*/*Lotta Lovin'*.

ERIC VON SCHMIDT is one of those legendary names that crop up from a past when blues singers and folk singers were not as well-known as they are today. He was around in the early sixties singing folk blues and greatly impressing many young singers, particularly Bob Dylan. Now in his thirties, he comes out of hiding from time to time, although he works mainly as a painter and illustrator these days. Whatever singing he does is for his own pleasure and not for the usual commercial outlets. There is a move, however, to coax him out of semi-retirement, and the heightened interest in blues may finally tempt him.

Albums/FOLK BLUES (January 1964): *Crow Jane; Gulf Coast Blues; Brave Wolfe; Junco Partner; De Kalb Blues; Lolita; Jack O'Diamonds; Champagne Don't Hurt Me Baby; Buffalo Skinners; He Was A Friend Of Mine; Cocoa Beach Blues; Down On Me; Titanic*. ERIC VON SCHMIDT SINGS (March 1965).

WAH WAH PEDAL/You push the wah-wah pedal with your foot and it goes from full treble to full bass and back again, giving your guitar a wah-wah sound. Jimi Hendrix and Eric Clapton have made it an important, if overworked, part of the 1968–69 sound.

WALKER BROTHERS/*Gary Leeds (drums), Scott Engel (electric bass, vocals), John Maus (guitar, vocals).*
The Walker Brothers were a phenomenon in the 1966–67 English pop scene—three young Americans (not brothers) who were more English than the English, long, lean, beautiful, long-haired, ruffled and frilled, and, for that period anyway, probably more popular than the Beatles even. And what is more remarkable is that in America they were (and are) practically unheard of. Musically, they did an Everly Brothers type harmony. Visually, they went in for all that dramatic fingerpointing that you would think was overdone by now, but they did it well and the English fans loved the total involvement of their performances. Scott, who was always being named number one bachelor on the popularity polls, had one of the great faces and voices of rock—and a long string of wildly emotional hassles that served only to enhance his magic. At the height of their success, the Walker Brothers announced they couldn't take it any longer. All three went solo (joining up only for, of all things, the occasional tour in Japan where they were very popular). Drummer Leeds (now known as Gary Walker) and Scott have solo careers and hope eventually to make it back in America.

Album/INTRODUCING THE WALKER BROTHERS (January 1966): *Make It Easy On Yourself; Dancing In The Street; Pretty Girls Everywhere; My Ship Is Comin' In; Doin' The Jerk; Love Her; I Don't Want To Hear Anymore; Love Minus Zero; Land Of 1,000 Dances; There Goes My Baby; Here Comes The Night; You're All Around Me.*

Also Appear On/ENGLAND'S GREATEST HITS (May 1968): *The Sun Ain't Gonna Shine Anymore.*

JERRY JEFF WALKER/In 1968, a year that might very well mark the beginning of the end of the group syndrome and the renaissance of the solo singer, Jerry Jeff Walker enjoyed popularity. After years of solo work on the road, he had helped form a group, Circus Maximus, in 1966, but when the group moved to a jazz-soul sound, Walker left to get back to what he felt was his own natural musical mood, Dylanesque country folk rock. His long song, called *Mr. Bojangles,* achieved something like the underground success of Arlo Guthrie's *Alice's Restaurant,* and he was on his way.

Albums/ MR. BOJANGLES (September 1968): *Gypsy Song Man; Mr. Bojangles; Little Bird; I Makes Money (Money Don't Make Me); Round And Round; I Keep Changin'; Maybe Mexico; Broken Toys; The Ballad Of The Hulk; My Old Man.* DRIFTIN' WAY OF LIFE (May 1969): *Driftin' Way Of Life; Morning Song To Sally; Shell Game; Ramblin', Scramblin'; No Roots In Ramblin'; Old Road; North Cumberland Blues; Let It Ride; Fading Lady; Gertrude; Dust On My Boots.*

Single/*Mr. Bojangles/Round And Round* (June 1968).

JOHN WALKER (John Maus)
Single/*Annabella/You Don't Understand Me.*
(see WALKER BROTHERS)

SCOTT WALKER (Scott Engel) (see WALKER BROTHERS)
Albums/ALONER (March 1968): *Big Hurt; Such A Small Love; You're Gonna Hear From Me; Through A Long And Sleepless Night; Always Coming Back To You; When Joanna Loved Me; Amsterdam; Mathilde; My Death; Montague Terrace; Angelica; Lady Came From Baltimore.* SCOTT VOL. 2 (July 1968): *Jackie; Best Of Both Worlds; Black Sheep Boy; Amorous Humphrey; Plugg; Next; Girls From The Streets; Plastic Palace People; Wait Until Dark; Girls And The Dogs; Windows Of The World; Bridge; Come Next Spring.*

T-BONE WALKER/Born in Texas in 1913, T-Bone (Aaron) Walker has been singing the blues for a long time and making records since the age of sixteen. When the big swing bands were picking up on blues singers, Walker and Leadbelly were way up there. He sang with Les Hites' California dance band, dressing up in flashy gold suits and doing splits on stage. He was supposedly the first dance band singer of his time to accompany himself on an electric, jewel-studded guitar. B.B. King ("father" of many of today's guitarists) says he got a lot of his style from T-Bone Walker. Apart from having written countless all-time great blues songs like *Stormy Monday*, he still plays clubs, but has yet to be discovered by the generation that has only just discovered B.B. King.

Albums/ SINGING THE BLUES: *Glamour Girl; Hustle; Alimony Blues; News For My Baby; Love Is Just A Gamble; I'm Still In Love With You; I'm About To Lose My Mind; I Got The Blues; Everytime; Bye, Bye, Baby; I'll Understand; Teenage Baby.* THE TRUTH: *Treat Your Daddy Well; You Ought To Know Better; Let Your Hair Down Baby; Old Time Used To Be; You Don't Love Me And I Don't Care; It Ain't No Right In You; I Ain't Your Fool No More; Don't Let Your Heartache Catch You Crying; I Don't Be Jiving; Hate To See You Go; Takes A Lot Of Know-How.* T-BONE BLUES: *Two Bones And A Pick; Mean Old World; T-Bone Shuffle; Stormy Monday Blues; Blues For Marili; T-Bone Blues; Shufflin' The Blues; Evenin'; Play On, Little Girls; Blues Rock; Papa Ain't Salty.* STORMY MONDAY BLUES: *I'm Gonna Stop This Night Life; Little Girl, Don't You Know; Every Night I Have To Cry; I'm Still In Love With You; Cold Hearted Woman; Treat Me So Low Down; Stormy Monday; Confusion Blues; I Gotta Break, Baby; Flower Blues.* FUNKY TOWN: *Goin' To Funky Town; Party Girl; Why My Baby; Jealous Woman; Going To Build Me A Playhouse; Long Skirt Baby Blues; I Wish My Baby; Struggling Blues; I'm In An Awful Mood.*

Single/ *Confusion Blues/ Every Night I Have To Cry.*

Also Appears On/ ROCK AND ROLL FOREVER: *T-Bone Shuffle.*

DIONNE WARWICK (Dionne Warrick)/ In 1962 she was singing on demonstration records and in background groups. Today she's hardly ever off the charts. A lot of it has to do with Burt Bacharach and Hal David, both of whom write good songs for her and produce her records. She came out of gospel and used to travel around with her own group, the Gospelaires. At the end of 1968 (just to show how things come round full circle) she planned to release a gospel album featuring the famous Drinkard Singers (who happen to be her relatives). She has done *Alfie, Message To Michael* and a lot of other pop hits, but the only one that sold a million was *Valley of the Dolls.*

Albums/ANYONE WHO HAD A HEART: *Anyone Who Had A Heart; Don't Make Me Over; Shall I Tell Her; I Cry Alone; Any Old Time Of Day; Getting Ready For The Heartbreak; Oh Lord, What Are You Doing To Me; Mr. Heartbreak; Put Yourself In My Place; I Could Make You Mine; This Empty Place; Please Make Him Love Me.* HERE I AM: *Here I Am; Looking With My Eyes; Are You There (With Another Girl); Don't Go Breaking My Heart; If I Ever Make You Cry; How Can I Hurt You; Once In A Lifetime, This Little Light; Window Wishing; In Between The Heartaches; I Loves You Porgy; Long Come A Short Night* HERE WHERE THERE IS LOVE: *Alfie; Trains & Boats & Planes; Here Where There Is Love; I Just Don't Know What To Do With Myself; Go With Love; What The World Needs Now Is Love; As Long As He Needs Me; Blowing In The Wind; I Never Knew What You Were Up To; I Wish You Love.* MAKE WAY FOR DIONNE WARWICK: *House Is Not A Home; You'll Never Get To Heaven; People; They Long To Be Close To You; Last One To Be Loved; Land Of Make Believe; Reach Out For Me; Walk On By; Get Rid Of Him; Wishin' & Hopin'; I Smiled Yesterday; Make The Night A Little Longer.* PRESENTING DIONNE WARWICK: *This Empty Place; Don't Make Me Over; It's Love That Really Counts; I Cry Alone; Zip-A-Dee-Doo-Dah; Wishin' & Hopin'; Make The Music Play; If You See Bill; Unlucky, Love Of A Boy; I Smiled Yesterday; Make It Easy On Yourself.* SENSITIVE SOUND OF DIONNE WARWICK (June 1965): *Don't Say I Didn't Tell You So; Wives & Lovers; Unchained Melody; Who Can I Turn To; How Many Days; Is There Another Way; Where Can I Go; You Can Have Him; That's Not The Answer; Only The Strong; Forever My Love.* VALLEY OF THE DOLLS & OTHERS (May 1968): *Valley Of The Dolls; As Long As There's An Apple; Silent Voices; For The Rest Of My Life; Do You Know The Way To San Jose; Where Would I Go; Let Me Be*

Lonely; You're My World; Up-Up And Away; Walking Backwards Down The Road. DIONNE WARWICK: *You'll Never Walk Alone; I Believe In You; One Hand, One Heart; Way You Look Tonight; Something Wonderful; Anything You Can Do; Summertime; Baubles, Bangles & Beads; My Favorite Things; She Loves Me; My Ship.* DIONNE WARWICK IN PARIS: *Message To Michael; I Love Paris; C'est Si Bon; You'll Never Get To Heaven; Walk On By; O, Yeah, Yeah, Yeah; Good Life; Vie En Rose; What'd I Say; House Is Not A Home.* DIONNE WARWICK'S GOLDEN HITS: *Walk On By; Anyone Who Had A Heart; Don't Make Me Over; This Empty Place; Wishin' & Hopin'; I Smiled Yesterday; It's Love That Really Counts; Any Old Time Of Day; Make It Easy On Yourself; Reach Out For Me; You'll Never Get To Heaven.* WINDOWS OF THE WORLD: *Windows Of The World; Walk Little Dolly; Another Night; Beginning Of Loneliness; I Say A Little Prayer; There's Always Something There To Remind Me; You're Gonna Hear From Me; Somewhere; Taking A Chance On Love; What's So Good About Goodbye.* MAGIC OF BELIEVING: *Magic Of Believing; Battle Hymn Of The Republic; Somebody Bigger Than You & I; Jesus Will; Old Landmark; Blessed Be The Name Of The Lord; Grace; Steal Away; In The Garden; Who Do You Think It Was.* PROMISES, PROMISES (December 1968): *Promises, Promises; This Girl Is In Love With You; Little Green Apples; Where Is Love; Who Is Gonna Love Me; Whoever You Are, I Love You; Where Am I Going; Wanting Things; Lonely In My Heart; Yesterday I Heard The Rain.* SOULFUL (March 1969): *I've Been Loving You Too Long; People Got To Be Free; You've Lost That Lovin' Feelin'; People Get Ready; Do Right Woman; Hey Jude; I'm Your Puppet; You're All I Need To Get By; We Can Work It Out; Hard Days Night.*

Singles/*Alfie/Window Wishing; Always Something There To Remind Me/Who Is Gonna Love Me; Another Night/Go With Love; Any Old Time Of Day/Unchained Melody; Anyone Who Had A Heart/Love Of A Boy; Are You There With Another Girl/You'll Never Get To Heaven; Beginning Of Loneliness/Somewhere; Do You Know The Way To San Jose/Let Me Be Lonely; Don't Ever Say I Didn't Tell*

You/Who Can I Turn To; Don't Make Me Over/I Smiled Yesterday; Good Life/Wives & Lovers; Here I Am/Summertime; Here, Where There Is Love/Message To Michael; A House Is Not A Home/One Hand, One Heart; How Many Days Of Sadness/Reach Out For Me; I Just Don't Know What To Do With Myself/Trains & Boats & Planes; I Say A Little Prayer/Valley Of The Dolls; Last One To Be Loved/People; Love/Make It Easy On Yourself; Only The Strong, Only The Brave/You'll Never Walk Alone; Please Make Him Love Me/Walk On By; Put Yourself In My Place/What The World Needs Now Is Love; This Little Light/What'd I Say; Walk Little Dolly/Windows Of The World; What's Good About Goodbye/Wishin' & Hopin'; Promises, Promises/Whoever You Are* (1968); *April Fools/Slaves* (May 1969).

Also Appears On/GREATEST ON STAGE: *What'd I Say.* GREATEST SING THEIR SOUL FAVORITES: *Don't Make Me Over; Wishin' & Hopin'.* MURRAY THE K—5TH BEATLE. WHAT'S NEW PUSSYCAT: *Here I Am.*

MUDDY WATERS (McKinley Morganfield)/One of the Rolling Stones' earliest singles was an old Muddy Waters' song, *I Just Want To Make Love To You* (written by Willie Dixon). Someone should issue a single with Mick Jagger's version on one side and Muddy's on the other and let them fight it out, because in those two cuts is the whole story of how the young English musicians of 1962, 1963 and 1964 took the American sound of the Mississippi Delta over to England and then sent it back across the Atlantic with love and admiration. And a whole generation grew up believing that that was the *English* sound. By 1968, after Jagger, Eric Clapton, Mike Bloomfield and others had talked freely and, yes, worshipfully, of their roots and influences, Muddy Waters' name, already revered in blues circles, started to become known to the general public.

A singer, guitarist and songwriter now in his fifties, Muddy appeared in 1968 at Steve Paul's The Scene, at the Cafe Au Go Go, at the Schaefer Festival in Central Park, establishing where that sound had come from in the first place—from the flat Mississippi cotton country where he grew up, and later from Chicago, where he sang to the homesick Mississippians who had migrated there. In the Delta he'd learned to play guitar with the distinctive whining sound that the Stones used in *Little Rooster* and that so many others have copied since (many of them imagining it was the Stones they were copying). And Cream did his *Rollin and Tumblin'* on *FRESH CREAM*. The debt blues-rock owes Muddy Waters is massive.

Albums/BEST OF MUDDY WATERS (August 1958): *Louisiana Blues; Honey Bee; I Just Want To Make Love To You; I Can't Be Satisfied; She Moves Me; Long Distance Call; I'm Ready; Rollin' Stone; Hoochie Coochie; Standing Around Crying; I Want You To Love Me; Still A Fool.* MUDDY WATERS SINGS "BIG BILL" BROONZY: *Tell Me Baby; Southbound Train; When I Get To Thinking; Just A Dream; Double Trouble; I Feel So Good; I Done Got Wise; Mopper's Blues; Lonesome Road Blues; Hey, Hey.* MUDDY WATERS AT NEWPORT (December 1960): *I Got My Brand On You; I'm Your Hoochie Coochie Man; Baby, Please Don't Go; Soon Forgotten; Tiger In Your Tank; I Feel So Good; Got My Mojo Working* (2 Parts); *Goodbye Newport Blues.* FOLK SINGER (March 1964): *My Home Is In The Delta; Long Distance; My Captain; Good Morning School Girl; You Gonna Need My Help; Cold Weather Blues; Big Leg Woman; Country Boy; Feel Like Going Home.* REAL FOLK BLUES (February 1966): *Mannish Boy; Screamin' And Cryin'; Just To Be With You; Walking In The Park; Same Thing; Walking Blues; Canary Bird; Gypsy Woman; Rollin' And Tumblin'; Forty Days And Forty Nights; You Can't Lose What You Never Had; Little Geneva.* MUDDY, BRASS AND THE BLUES (November 1966): *Corrine, Corrina; Piney Brown Blues; Black Night; Trouble In Mind; Going Back To Memphis; Betty And Dupree; Sweet Little Angel; Take My Advice; Trouble; Hard Loser.* MORE REAL FOLK BLUES (February 1967): *Sad Letter; Gonna Need My Help; Whiskey Blues; Down South Blues; Train Fare Blues; Kind-Hearted Woman; Appealing Blues; Early Morning Blues; Too Young To Know; She's All Right; My Life Is Ruined; Honey Bee.* SUPER BLUES (June 1967) (With Bo Diddley and Little Walter): *Long Distance Call; Who Do You Love; I'm A Man Bo Diddley; You Can't Judge A Book*

*By It's Cover; I Just Want to Make Love To You; My Babe;
You Don't Love Me.* SUPER SUPER BLUES BAND (February 1968) (With Howlin' Wolf and Bo Diddley): *Long
Distance Call; Sweet Little Angel; Ooh, Baby; Wrecking My
Love; Goin' Down Slow; Spoonful; Diddley Daddy; Red
Rooster.* ELECTRIC MUD (October 1968): *I Just Want To
Make Love To You; Hoochie Coochie Man; Let's Spend The
Night Together; She's All Right; I'm A Man; Herbert Harper's Free Press; Tom Cat; Same Thing.*

Singles/*Just Make Love To Me/Oh Yes; Mannish Boy/
Young Fashion Ways; Diamonds At Your Feet/Don't Go No
Farther; Clouds In My Heart/Oh Wee; She's Into Something/Take The Bitter With The Sweet; Recipe For
Love/Tell Me Baby; I Feel So Good/When I Get To Thinkin'; I'm Your Doctor/Read My Way; Love Affair/Look What
You've Done; Meanest Woman/Tiger In Your Tank;
Lonesome Room Blues/Messin' With The Man; Going Home
/Tough Times; You Shook Me/Muddy Waters Twist; Little
Brown Bird/You Need Love; Five Long Years/Twenty-Four
Hours; The Same Thing/You Can't Lose What You Ain't
Never Had; Short Dress Woman/My John The Conquer
Root; Put Me In Your Lay Away/Still A Fool; My Dog
Can't Bark/I Got A Rich Man's Woman; Corrine Corrina/Hoochie Coochie Man; When The Eagle Flies/Bird Nest
On The Ground.*

THE WEAVERS/Looking back now, it is obvious that from
a mass-market point of view the Weavers happened too early.
Their version of Leadbelly's 1931 song *Goodnight Irene* was
number one for thirteen weeks in 1950, a particularly amazing achievement when you consider the 1950 charts were
dominated by Patti Page, Mario Lanza, Doris Day, Bing
Crosby, Perry Como, the Andrews Sisters and Eddie Fisher.
(It was the year of *Rudolph the Red-Nosed Reindeer* and
Mona Lisa.) They also managed to make the charts with
Woody Guthrie's *So Long It's Been Good To Know You* and
On Top of Old Smokey and they were the first *big* folk group
to sell well outside folk circles. Nevertheless it was too soon,
for one reason or another, for the overwhelming success that
was to meet the Kingston Trio a decade or so later. But the

Weavers did set the stage for scores of other folk groups that made it commercially as the folk revival gathered momentum from 1956 onward; and just about everything that happened in the first half of the sixties (when folk took over completely)—everything from Joan Baez, Dylan, protest folk rock and the Byrds—came from the Seeger-influenced Weavers of the fifties.
(see PETE SEEGER)

Albums/WEAVERS AT HOME (August 1958). BEST OF THE WEAVERS (July 1959). FOLK SONGS AROUND THE WORLD (December 1959). WEAVERS ALMANAC (April 1962). WEAVERS REUNION (December 1963). WEAVERS REUNION, VOL. 2 (August 1965). WEAVERS SONGBOOK (October 1967). TRAVELING ON WITH THE WEAVERS. WEAVERS ON TOUR.

Singles/*Jig Along Home/Join Into The Game; Across The Wide Missouri/On Top Of Old Smokey; Goodnight Irene/ Midnight Special.*

JUNIOR WELLS is one of the best of the young Chicago bluesmen around today (and it was in his band that guitarist Buddy Guy rose to fame). He was always well known in Chicago (he used to play harp for Muddy Waters) but got his national reputation only after he went on the road in 1966. His *HOO DOO MAN BLUES* LP was named Blues Album of the Year by *Jazz* magazine. He made his name internationally when he traveled with the American Blues Festival in Europe. Lately he has been fusing blues and soul in what may turn out to be an up-to-date version of the Chicago blues, and which, even if it sounds a little blasphemous to purists, may bring black "soul" audiences back to the blues they long ago wrote off as being too raw and unsophisticated.

Albums/JUNIOR WELLS' CHICAGO BLUES BAND (HOO DOO MAN BLUES) (March 1966): *Snatch It Back And Hold It; Ships On The Ocean; Good Morning Schoolgirl; Hound Dog; In The Wee Wee Hours; Hey Lawdy Mama; Hoo Doo Man Blues; Early In The Morning; We're Ready; You Don't Love Me Baby; Chittlins Con Carne; Yonder Wall.* IT'S MY LIFE, BABY! (December 1966): *It's My*

Life, Baby; It's So Sad To Be Lonely; Country Girl; You Lied To Me; Look How Baby; Stormy Monday; Shake It Baby; Checking On My Baby; Early In The Morning; Stomach Ache; Slow, Slow; Everything's Going To Be Alright. COM-IN' AT YOU (June 1968): *Stop Breakin' Down; Somebody's Tippin' In; Five Long Years; Mystery Train; So Sad This Mornin'; When My Baby Left Me; Little By Little; Tobacco Road; Worried Life Blues; I'm Your Hoochie Coochie Man; You Don't Love Me.* YOU'RE TUFF ENOUGH (July 1968): *You're Tuff Enough; It's All Soul; Gonna Cramp Your Style; Where Did I Go Wrong; That'll Hold Me; Sweet Darling Think It Over; Up In Heah; You Are The One; You Ought To Quit That; Messin' With The Kid; The Hippies Are Trying; Junior's Groove.*

Single/*It's A Man Down There*/*Girl You Lit My Fire* (October 1968).

Also Appears On/CHICAGO/THE BLUES/TODAY (Vol. 1) (April 1966): *Tribute To Sonny Boy Williamson; It Hurts Me Too; Messin' With The Kid; Vietcong Blues; All Night Long.*

MARY WELLS/A Motown Miss with class, Mary Wells faded out of the scene when she became a Missus—and a Mom. In 1963 she was the first female rhythm and blues singer to make it big in the regular pop charts. Songs like *My Guy, The One Who Really Loves You* and *You Beat Me To The Punch* made her a big favorite with, among many others, the Beatles, who named her as their favorite girl singer and had her touring with them in England. She returned the compliment with an album called *LOVE SONGS TO THE BEATLES.* After a long time out of the picture she signed with a new record company in 1968, released a new single, *The Doctor,* and is beginning what hopefully will be an impressive comeback.

Albums/BYE BYE BABY: *Bye Bye Baby; I Don't Want To Take A Chance; Shop Around; I'm Gonna Stay; Let Your Conscience Be Your Guide; Come To Me; I Love The Way You Love; Bad Boy; I'm So Sorry; Please Forgive Me.* ONE WHO REALLY LOVES YOU: *One Who Really Loves You; Two Wrongs Don't Make A Right; You Beat Me To The*

Punch; I've Got A Notion; Day Will Come; Strange Love; You're My Desire; I'll Still Be Around; She Don't Love You; Drifting Love. TWO LOVERS: *Two Lovers; Laughing Boy; Was It Worth It; No Love; Guess Who; My Two Arms Plus You Equals Tears; Goody, Goody; Stop Right Here; Looking Back; Operator.* MARY WELLS ON STAGE: *To Lovers; Laughing Boy; I Don't Want To Take A Chance; Bye Bye Baby; One Who Really Loves You; Old Love; Operator; You Beat Me To The Punch.* MARY WELLS GREATEST HITS: *Two Lovers; What's Easy For Two Is Hard For One; One Who Really Loves You; My Guy; Bye Bye Baby; You Beat Me To The Punch; Old Love; You Lost The Sweetest Boy; What Love Has Joined Together; Laughing Boy; Your Old Stand By; Oh Little Boy.* MARY WELLS SINGS MY GUY: *My Guy; He's The One I Love; Whisper You Love Me Boy; Does He Love Me; How, When My Heart Belongs To You; He Holds His Own; My Baby Just Cares For Me; I Only Have Eyes For You; You Do Something To Me; It Had To Be You; If You Love Me, Really Love Me; At Last.* VIN-TAGE STOCK: *My Guy; You Beat Me To The Punch; Two Lovers; When I'm Gone; One Who Really Loves You; He's The One I Love; Guarantee (For A Lifetime); Honey Boy; Everybody Needs A Love; I'll Be Available; One Block From Heaven; Goodbye And Good Luck.* TWO SIDES OF MARY WELLS: *Satisfaction (I Can't Get No); Love Makes The World Go Round; In The Midnight Hour; My World Is Empty Without You; Good Lovin'; Dear Lover; Where Am I Going; Shangri-La; On A Clear Day; Love Theme From 'The Sandpiper'; Boy From Ipanema; Sunrise, Sunset.* LOVE SONGS TO THE BEATLES: *He Loves You; Do You Want To Know A Secret; Yesterday; Ticket To Ride; Help; And I Love Him; Please Please Me; All My Lovin'; Can't Buy Me Love; I Should Have Known Better; Eight Days A Week; I Saw Him Standing There.* MARVIN AND MARY TO-GETHER: *Once Upon A Time; What's The Matter With You Baby; Deed I Do; Until I Met You; After The Lights Go Down Low; Together; Squeeze Me; For Sentimental Reasons; You Came A Long Way From St. Louis; Late Late Show.* SERVIN' UP SOME SOUL (September 1968): *Can't Get Away From Your Love; Apples, Peaches, Pumpkin Pie; Two Lovers' History; Don't Look Back; Woman In Love; Make*

Me Yours; Bye Bye Baby; Stagger Lee; Soul Train; Doctor; 500 Miles; Sunny.

Singles/*Bye Bye Baby/Please Forgive Me; I Don't Want To Take A Chance/I'm So Sorry; Come To Me/Strange Love; I'm Gonna Stay/One Who Really Loves You; Old Love/You Beat Me To The Punch; Two Lovers/Operator; Laughing Boy/Two Wrongs Don't Make A Right; What Love Has Joined Together/Your Old Stand By; You Lost The Sweetest Boy/What's Easy For Two Is Hard For One; My Guy/Oh Little Boy; Once Upon A Time/What's The Matter With You Baby; Dear Love/Can't You See (You're Losing Me); Keep Me In Suspense/Such A Sweet Thing; Fancy Free/Me And My Baby; Set My Soul On Fire/Coming Home; Doctor/Two Lovers' History.*

Also Appears On/MOTOR-TOWN REVUE, Vols. 1 & 2. MOTOWN HITS. NOTHING BUT A MAN: *You Beat Me To The Punch; Bye Bye Baby.* 16 ORIGINAL BIG HITS: Vol. 1—*One Who Really Loves You; You Beat Me To The Punch.* Vol. 2—*You Lost The Sweetest Boy; Bye Bye Baby.* Vol. 3—*What's Easy For Two Is Hard For One.* Vol. 4— *Two Lovers; My Guy; What's The Matter With You Baby* (with Marvin Gaye); *Once Upon A Time* (with Marvin Gaye). TAMLA SPECIAL: *Bye Bye Baby.*

MAE WEST/She is better known as an actress, comedienne and sort of souped-up sexpot from way back, when saying "Come up and see me some time, tall, dark and handsome" was terribly naughty. That Mae West would do a rock and roll record at the age of seventy-five came as a surprise to some, and that it wasn't an aging freak thing came as an even greater surprise to most. But there it is. At seventy-five she sings Dylan and Lennon-McCartney as well as anyone. The lady has always been one of the better blues singers about (only her undulating figure and flashing innuendos distracted from her voice). Now she's discovered that all you have to do to sing rock and roll is double the blues beat. The Beatles' *Day Tripper,* which she sings, is about exactly the sort of shady lady Mae knows better than anyone. And Dylan's *If You Gotta Go,* another of the star tracks on her album, tells of a situation that existed long before the composer was born.

When you compare Miss West's wiser, sadder versions to the originals, you know what people mean about older women. She could read a telephone book and make it sound like a list of her lovers.

Albums/FABULOUS MAE WEST: *Love Is The Greatest Thing; I'm In The Mood For Love; My Daddy Rocks Me; Pecado; All Of Me; Frankie & Johnny; I Want You, I Need You; They Call Me Sister Honky Tonk; Guy What Takes His Time; Criswell Predicts; Havana For A Night; If I Could Be With You.* WAY OUT WEST: *Treat Him Right; When A Man Loves A Woman; You Turn Me On; Shakin' All Over; If You Gotta Go; Lover, Please Don't Fight; Day Tripper; Nervous; Twist & Shout; Boom Boom; Mae Day.*

Also Appears On/THOSE WONDERFUL GIRLS (Of Stage, Screen & Radio): *Easy Rider's Gone.* MERMAN-WEST-ROBERTI: *Guy What Takes His Time; Easy Rider's Gone; I'm No Angel; I Found A New Way To Go To Town; I Want You, I Need You; They Call Me Sister Honky Tonk.*

WHITE BLUES BANDS/Can white men play the blues? More words (and bitter quarrels) have come out on this subject than just about any other since the late sixties blues revival got under way. Regardless of whether they can play them or have the right to play them, the fact remains they *do* play them. The Paul Butterfield Blues Band was the first of the white blues bands and it did much to popularize blues with a whole segment of the white population that had never heard them before. Butterfield and his original guitarist, Mike Bloomfield, never hesitated to talk about where these blues came from in the first place. In fact, Bloomfield just about singlehandedly (well, with a little help from Eric Clapton) made names of blues originals like B.B. King and Muddy Waters known to a generation that had grown up hearing black sounds only from white singers. Meanwhile there were many white blues singers working within the framework of the early sixties folk scene—Eric Von Schmidt, Fred Neil, early Tim Hardin. From this sort of background came the Blues Project, which did a nice job of popularizing the material of Muddy Waters and Howlin' Wolf, among others.

Slowly but surely more white blues bands sprang up in

America, always with a solid following, but not really hitmakers. Then came the small blues boom of 1968 when Canned Heat got on the charts, the Steve Miller Band made an impact, and blues bands like Linn County, Siegel-Schwall, Colwell-Winfield started appearing on the regular rock circuits. In England there had always been a white blues scene— John Mayall's Blues Breakers, which was the most uncompromising fanatically faithful to the original; the early Animals, early Yardbirds and early Stones. But only after Cream (whose guitarist, Eric Clapton, had started with Mayall and the Yardbirds) became popular in America in 1968 did the white English blues bands start touring the U.S.

All this time the argument raged. Whites shouldn't sing blues because they hadn't paid their dues. (Yes, they had. No, they hadn't.) Why listen to imitations when you can hear the original? (Why not? Why not both?) Besides, a whole segment of the black population found blues old-fashioned and were glad enough to leave them to the whites. And while the words flew, the black blues artists found themselves increasingly in demand on the pop-rock-blues circuits and a new generation found out about Albert King, B.B. King, Buddy Guy, Muddy Waters and Howlin' Wolf. Maybe white men can't play blues, maybe they can. But they should at least be credited for bringing the blues back up front and getting black blues artists back into the popular spotlight where people can decide for themselves who can play and who can't.

BUKKA WHITE/One of the early legendary country blues singers from whom the city blues singers learned their craft. White is one of the grandfathers of today's blues.
Albums/BUKKA WHITE (September 1964). BUKKA WHITE, VOL. 1 (August 1966).

THE WHO/*Peter Townshend (guitar), John Entwistle (bass), Keith Moon (drums), Roger Daltrey (lead vocals).*
The Who are so English it's difficult to imagine them the essentially American stars they have now become. You can't even start to understand the Who unless you lived in the England they came from. They're summer dances in Brighton, and whole weekends of mod-rocker riots, and all those old rock and roll Eddie Cochran songs like *Summertime*

Blues that were always more popular there than here. There was Roger Daltrey, always more mannequin than singer, throwing the mike around his head so the mods could see every line of that new jacket. Who could understand that without understanding England's mod revolution and the glorious faddish tyranny of clothes that overtook the British working boy? And Keith Moon, the mad drummer? Listen, it's one thing to kick over the drums in America, just to be different, just to have a gimmick, because there's plenty of bread here to buy more. But in England where forty dollars a week is not a bad wage at all, the violence and madness have to be for real. And Entwistle the bass man, isn't he perhaps a little *too* sane?

At the helm, controlling the whole Who sound and playing the Fourth Stooge, Peter Townshend and the meanest-looking guitar in all of rock. The great hand is poised high, as high as it will go, only so it can swoop down on the strings like an angry hawk, ready to snatch its prey. The great face, that can be gentle and whimsical or haughtily aristocratic, grimaces horribly. The guitar is put through such terrors that when in the end it's smashed to bits by its enraged tormentor, you heave a sigh of relief for the suffering that is finally over. Ho, ho, says Peter Townshend about all that, it's simply brilliant showmanship. In the days when he felt he couldn't measure up, he covered his deficiencies with an extravagance of gesture that, he says modestly, has fooled everyone ever since. You really don't ever realize how well he's playing because his performances are so visually seductive. So are Roger Daltrey's, a singer in the best mincing, primping, foppish Mick Jagger tradition. And though the Who sound pretty good on record, you still feel you are missing something because they are rock theatre first, and that's how it should be.

They were originally called the Highnumbers, and they came out in 1963, a little after the Yardbirds and the Stones. Chris Stamp (who is actor Terence's brother) and Kit Lambert were two boys in search of a group, their heads full of Brian Epstein fantasies, when they first clapped eyes on the scruffy Highnumbers. First they changed the name. The Who, how could you ever go wrong with that? (Who? The Who.) The group's distinctive mark then was Townshend's jacket, made from the English flag, the Union Jack. Now those were the days when a new band had to fight for recognition, and while clothes were already pretty interesting and Roger Daltrey's florals and ruffles were giving the fans more than their money's worth, there had to be more than that. (No one else, it must be remembered, at that time had anything made from the Union Jack—no ashtrays, no wastepaper baskets, no shopping bags, no whole shops of Union Jack merchandise in London as there are now. No, that was what Peter Townshend's jacket started.) But with the emergence of pop art at that time, Peter's Union Jack jacket was a sensation. And one of the saddest moments ever came at Murray the K's Easter Show, during the Who's brief first U.S. season, when a Who fan sat in the front row in a Union Jack red-white-and-blue shirt, and Peter Townshend, in velvet or something, just *looked* at him. By then Townshend was sick to death of the flag, but to the fan it was as shocking as if Townshend had come on stage without his famous nose.

In any case, with the ready-made audience of mods waiting for them in England, the Who clicked. *My Generation* became the national anthem of the under-twenty-fives in England and a number one record there. But in 1966, when Lambert and Stamp came over to sell their boys to America, all anyone was getting excited about over here was Herman's Hermits. When the Who did play Murray the K's Easter Show a year later, it was on a sort of guest basis—they got to do two numbers. No one knew them in the U.S., so their records, including *My Generation,* got no airplay, which in turn meant that no one got a chance to know them. They started to make their name after the Monterey Pop Festival later in 1967, when their guitar-smashing and smoke-amplifier act went over better than the ritual burning of Jimi Hendrix's guitar. *Happy Jack,* a nicely characteristic single, all wry humor and perky tune, quickly established them as a group to be taken seriously musically as well as theatrically.

Since then, Who singles have continued to be wry and perky, Townshend's lyrics almost always telling a little story with a beginning, a middle and an end. They were the first of the now popular three-instrument groups (drums, bass and lead guitar) and the first to popularize the creative use of feedback (though whether they were the first to use it is still being argued out with the Yardbirds). The big thing was the orgy of destruction at the end—drums kicked, guitars smashed, amplifiers and microphones wrenched from their places and ominously smoking and sputtering electric leads. Once in a while Townshend wouldn't break his guitar totally (he claims the whole thing started accidentally, because he felt like smashing a guitar, and that to this day he doesn't smash unless he wants to) and now and then a smoke bomb was planted to add to the fun, but the rock and wreck part of the act was always a refreshing change from the blandness of the Dave Clark Five and Herman's Hermits.

By 1968 the Who were stars. The gimmickry never blinded anyone to the true talent of the Who. The singles were making it, the albums were selling. *A Quick One While He's Away* was a very complicated twelve-minute rock opera. A whole album was done as a BBC radio show with commercials. *TOMMY*, a rock opera, is about a deaf and blind boy who's seduced by his uncle, but because Townshend wrote it and the boy is deaf and blind, the seduction becomes just another interesting experience. Townshend is one of the great musicians of the new music, not of the blues or some other era's music like most of the greats, but of rock and pop itself and all of its future possibilities.

Albums/THE WHO SINGS MY GENERATION (June 1966): *Out In The Street; I Don't Mind; The Good's Gone; La La La Lies; Much Too Much; My Generation; Kids Are Alright; The Ox; Please, Please, Please; It's Not True; A Legal Matter; Instant Party.* HAPPY JACK (June 1967): *Run Run Run; Boris The Spider; I Need You; Whiskey Man; Cobwebs And Strange; So Sad About Us; Happy Jack; Don't Look Away; See My Way; Quick One While He's Away.* THE WHO SELL OUT (February 1968): *I Can See For Miles; Armenia City In The Sky (Heinz Baked Beans); Mary-Anne With The Shaky Hands; Odorono; Tattoo; Our Love Was, Is; I Can't Reach You (Spotted Henry); Relax; Silas Stingy; Sunrise; Real.* MAGIC BUS (October 1968): *Disguises; Run Run Run; Dr. Jekyll And Mr. Hyde; I Can't Reach You; Our Love Was, Is; Call Me Lightning; Magic Bus; Someone's Coming; Doctor, Doctor; Bucket T.; Pictures Of Lily.* TOMMY (June 1969).

Singles/*Substitute/Waitin' For A Pig; Bald Headed Woman/ I Can't Explain; Anytime You Want Me/Anyway Anyhow Anywhere; My Generation/Out In The Street; Kids Are Alright/Legal Matter; I'm A Boy/In The City; Happy Jack/ Whiskey Man; Pictures Of Lily/Doctor, Doctor; I Can See For Miles/Mary-Anne With The Shaky Hands; Dr. Jekyll And Mr. Hyde/Call Me Lightning; Magic Bus/Someone's Coming; Pinball Wizard/Dogs* (Part 2) (March 1969).

HANK WILLIAMS/In 1968 there was suddenly a lot of talk in rock circles about country music, and the term country rock was used about some of the best albums to come out that year. Suddenly a lot of people who had never thought one way or another about country music started digging into its albums to see what it was about. One of the best examples of what country music is about is Hank Williams, who died in 1953 at the age of twenty-nine. Country-music fans have not recovered to this day, and when you hear his songs or read his story it's easy to see why. He was an Alabama farm boy who sang in the church choir and got turned on to music at the age of eight, when someone gave him a guitar. By the time he was fourteen he had gotten together a group, was playing at dances and was a regular on radio. From there he went on to Nashville's famous Grand Ole Opry, which was broadcast nationally every Saturday night. Hank was a star.

He was tall, dark and good-looking, a beautiful, gentle singer. And he wrote literally hundreds of hits. At first for others who were more well known in the world of popular music, hits like *Hey Good Lookin'* and *Your Cheatin' Heart,* but eventually for himself, getting himself as high on the pop charts as he had been on the country and western. Then his marriage fell apart and so did he. There was talk of alcohol and drugs, and to this day no one is sure if they were what killed him, but it really doesn't matter.

Today you hear echoes of Hank Williams in so many singers, often in Tim Hardin, who has the same gentle voice overlaid with unexpressed pain. Sometimes you hear him for a moment in the work of the Spoonful or the Buffalo Springfield, and in fact in all the groups where the early influences were country. His songs were enormously popular with everyone from Louis Armstrong, Fats Domino and Teresa Brewer to

Jerry Lee Lewis and Elvis Presley. *Your Cheatin' Heart* has
been recorded by at least fifty people. *Cold, Cold Heart,
Jambalaya* and *Ramblin' Man* were among the biggest of his
hits. He was very hard working and productive and it's almost
impossible to comprehend, looking at the long list of his
albums (some released after his death) and hearing the
legends about his life, that he was so young when he died.

Albums/LONESOME SOUND (March 1960). WAIT FOR
THE LIGHT (October 1960). HANK WILLIAMS'
GREATEST HITS (February 1961). SPIRIT OF HANK
WILLIAMS (August 1961). ON STAGE (March 1962).
GREATEST HITS, VOL. 2 (July 1962). VERY BEST OF
HANK WILLIAMS (November 1963). GREATEST HITS,
VOL. 3 (March 1964). VERY BEST OF HANK
WILLIAMS, VOL. 2 (July 1964). HANK WILLIAMS
STORY (December 1964). COUNTRY WESTERN FLA-
VOR, VOL. 1 (May 1965). HANK WILLIAMS (May
1965). LOST HIGHWAY (October 1964). HANK
WILLIAMS SINGS KAW-LIGA (July 1965). MR. AND
MRS. HANK WILLIAMS (January 1966). COUNTRY
WESTERN FLAVOR, VOL. 2 (July 1966). LUKE THE
DRIFTER (August 1966). HANK WILLIAMS WITH
STRINGS, VOL. 1 (September 1966). HANK WILLIAMS
AND HANK WILLIAMS JR. (November 1966). MORE
HANK WILLIAMS WITH STRINGS (February 1967). IM-
MORTAL HANK WILLIAMS (April 1967). I WON'T BE
HOME NO MORE (September 1967). HANK WILLIAMS
WITH STRINGS, VOL. 3 (March 1968). IN THE BEGIN-
NING (August 1968). HANK WILLIAMS, VOL. 2. I SAW
THE LIGHT. UNFORGETTABLE HANK WILLIAMS.
HANK WILLIAMS LIVES AGAIN. LET ME SING A
BLUE SONG. WANDERIN' AROUND; I'M BLUE IN-
SIDE. FIRST, LAST AND ALWAYS.

Singles/*Cold, Cold Heart*/*I'm So Lonesome I Could Cry;
Dear John*/*Long Gone Lonesome Blues; Half As Much*/
Honky Tonk Blues; Hey Good Lookin'/*Why Don't You Love
Me; House Of Gold*/*I Can't Help It; I'll Never Get Out Of
This World Alive*/*Jambalaya; Just Waitin'*/*Roly Poly; Kaw-
Liga*/*Ramblin' Man; Your Cheatin' Heart*/*Lovesick Blues;*

Moanin' The Blues/You Win Again; My Bucket's Got A Hole In It/My Son Calls Another Man Daddy.

HANK WILLIAMS JUNIOR/Son of the late Hank Williams, Hank Junior has a song he sings called *Standing In The Shadows (Of A Very Famous Man)* and that really is it. At the age of fourteen he recorded an album of his father's songs (his father started at fourteen too), and in the same year did a second. In the next two years, apart from other albums (one with Connie Francis), he recorded two albums *with* his father—eerie electronic wizardry made it possible for Hank Junior to sing along with his dad's tapes. Since then he has moved away from those shadows a little and is singing other country songs. It is in live appearance that he has the most impact, mainly because to this day no one wants to forget Hank Senior, and Junior brings back the memories.
(see HANK WILLIAMS)

Albums/HANK WILLIAMS JR. (SINGS THE SONGS OF HANK WILLIAMS) (March 1964): *Long Gone Lonesome Blues; Your Cheatin' Heart; I'm So Lonesome I Could Cry; I'm A Long Gone Daddy; Cold Cold Heart; You Win Again; Hey, Good Lookin'; Moanin' The Blues; I Can't Help It; There'll Be No Teardrops Tonight; Jambalaya; Mansion On The Hill.* YOUR CHEATIN' HEART (October 1964): *Your Cheatin' Heart; Hey, Good Lookin'; I'm So Lonesome I Could Cry; I Saw The Light; Jambalaya; Ramblin' Man; Cold, Cold Heart; Kaw-Liga; I Can't Help It; Long Gone Lonesome Blues; You Win Again.* GREAT COUNTRY FA-VORITES (WITH CONNIE FRANCIS) (November 1964): *Send Me The Pillow That You Dream On; Bye Bye, Love; Wolverton Mountain; Please Help Me, I'm Falling; Singing The Blues; Walk On By; If You've Got The Money, I've Got The Time; Mule Skinner Blues; Making Believe; Blue Blue Day; No Letter Today; Wabash Cannonball.* HANK WILLIAMS JR. AND HANK WILLIAMS SR. (SINGING TOGETHER IN A RECORDING MIRACLE)—VOL. 1 (April 1965): *I Won't Be Home No More; Lovesick Blues; May You Never Be Alone; Move It On Over; Lost Highway; Crazy Heart; Wedding Bells; Honky Tonk Blues; (I Heard*

That) Lonesome Whistle; Why Don't You Love Me; Mind Your Own Business; I Just Don't Like This Kind Of Livin'. BALLADS OF THE HILLS AND PLAINS (September 1965): *The River; Doc Holiday; Cowpoke; Stampede; Blood's Thicker Than Water; The Blizzard Rainmaker; Streets Of Laredo; Black Lightning; Big Twenty; Eyes Of Death; I'm Afraid.* BLUES MY NAME (March 1966): *Salt Lake City; Good Leavin' Alone; Cry Cry Darling; Weary Blues From Waitin'; Wrong Doin' Man; These Boots Are Made For Walkin'; It's Written All Over Your Face; When You're Tired Of Breaking Others' Hearts; Blue's My Name; Low As A Man Can Go; Old Frank; So Easy To Forgive Her (But So Hard To Forget).* HANK WILLIAMS JR. AND HANK WILLIAMS SR.—VOL. 2 (May 1966): *My Sweet Love Ain't Around; I'll Be A Bachelor 'Til I Die; Window Shopping; My Bucket's Got A Hole In It; I Can't Help It; Howlin' At The Moon; My Son Calls Another Man Daddy; Moanin' The Blues; Kaw-Liga; Baby We're Really In Love; Why Should We Try Anymore; I'll Never Get Out Of This World Alive.* COUNTRY SHADOWS (July 1966): *Standing In The Shadows; Almost Nearly But Not Quite Plumb; Guess What, That's Right, She's Gone; Is It That Much Fun To Hurt Someone; I Can Take Anything; Truck Drivin' Man; Endless Sleep; You're Runnin' My Life; Pecos Jail; In The First Place; I Went To All That Trouble For Nothin'; Going Steady With The Blues.* MY OWN WAY (April 1967): *I'm In No Condition; Just Another Town; I'm Gonna Break Your Heart; Moods Of Mary; That's How I Wanted It To Be; What A Heck Of A Mess; I Can't Take It No Longer; Next Best Thing To Nothing; Nobody's Child; Waitin' For Money From Home; Kiowa Jones.* BEST OF HANK WILLIAMS JR. (October 1967): *Standing In The Shadows; I'm In No Condition; Next Best Thing To Nothing; Long Gone Lonesome Blues; Endless Sleep; I Can't Take It No Longer; Nobody's Child; I'm Gonna Break Your Heart; It's Written All Over Your Face; Hanging My Teardrops Out To Dry; That's How I Wanted It To Be.* MY SONGS (January 1968): *No Meaning And No End; Three Miles To Right; I Can't Decide; I Wouldn't Change A Thing About You; I Ain't Sharin' Sharon; Prison Of Memories; Your Love's Like A Stranger; Funny Feelings; Wandering Astray; Young Man's*

Fancy; Hanging My Teardrops Out To Dry. LUKE THE DRIFTER, JR. (November 1968): *I Was With Red Foley; I Dreamed About Mama Last Night; Glass; Fly Trouble; On Trial; At The First Fall Of Snow; Uncle John; Please Make Up Your Mind; Help Me Understand; Everythin's Okay; My Home Town Circle 'R'.* LUKE THE DRIFTER, JR. (April 1969).

Singles/*I'm Gonna Break Your Heart/I'm In No Condition* (April 1967); *Next Best Thing To Nothing/Nobody's Child* (July 1967); *I Wouldn't Change A Thing About You/No Meaning And No End* (November 1967).

JACKIE WILSON/He is one of the few singers who has made the journey out of soul into pop, or rather popularity. Whatever he records sells. He began his career in 1953, one year after graduating from high school in Detroit, as lead singer of Billy Ward's Dominoes. In 1957 he went solo and since then has done nothing but break records everywhere from the Apollo to the Copa, with the Sahara and the Fontainbleau in between. In 1961, when he was twenty-six, he was shot and critically wounded by a woman he said was a fan. Happily, he survived.

Albums/LONELY TEARDROPS (1958). DOGGIN' AROUND (1959). NIGHT (1960). JACKIE SINGS THE BLUES (May 1960). SO MUCH (July 1960). TRY A LITTLE TENDERNESS (1961). YOU AIN'T HEARD NOTHIN' YET (February 1961). BY SPECIAL REQUEST (October 1961). SHAKE A HAND (1962). JACKIE WILSON AT THE COPA (August 1962). BODY AND SOUL (April 1962). JACKIE WILSON SINGS THE WORLD'S GREATEST MELODIES (January 1963). BABY WORK OUT (April 1963). DANNY BOY (1964). SOMETHIN' ELSE (August 1964). NO PITY (1965). SOUL TIME (April 1965). SPOTLIGHT ON JACKIE WILSON (September 1965). WHISPERS (1966). SOUL GALORE (February 1966). HIGHER AND HIGHER (1967). HE'S SO FINE. HITSVILLE. JUMPIN' JACK. MERRY XMAS FROM JACKIE WILSON. MILLION-AIRS. JACKIE WILSON. WOMAN, A LOVER, A FRIEND. MANUFACTURERS OF SOUL (April 1968). I GET THE SWEETEST FEELING (October 1968).

Singles/*Ask/I'll Be Satisfied; Night/Doggin' Around; Woman, A Lover, A Friend/All My Love; Baby Work Out/I'm Going Crazy; Say I Do/Shake A Hand; Baby Get It/New Breed; Be My Girl/Big Boss Line; Be My Love/I Believe; Brand New Thing/Soul Galore; Call Her Up/Kickapoo; Danny Boy/Soul Time; Fairest Of Them All/Whispers; Give Me Back My Heart/Squeeze Her-Tease Her; Haunted House/I'm Travelin' On; He's A Fool/Shake, Shake, Shake; I Believe I'll Love On/Lonely Teardrops; I Don't Want To Lose You/Just Be Sincere; I Get The Sweetest Feeling/Nothing But Heartaches; I'm So Lonely/No Pity; I'm The One To Do It/Higher And Higher; I've Got To Get Back/3 Days, 1 Hour, 30 Minutes; I've Lost You/Those Heartaches; Oh Holy Night/Silent Night; Please Don't Hurt Me/Think Twice; Say I Do/Shake A Hand; She's Alright/Watch Out; Since You Showed Me How To Be Happy/Who Who Song; Yes Indeed/When The Saints Go Marching In; Respect/Uptight; Chain Gang/For Your Precious Love; Somebody Up There Likes You/You Can Count On Me; For Once In My Life/You Brought About A Change In Me* (October 1968).

MURRY WILSON/Rock father of the century. He was a California machinery salesman who gave it all up to open a music publishing firm and sign his three teenage sons to a record contract with Capitol. The firm, Sea of Tunes, is now one of the most prosperous in the world, and his three sons a sizable part of the Beach Boys. He managed them for the first two and a half years. After he left them late in 1964, they managed themselves and have done so ever since. Recently Mr. Wilson put out an album, *THE MANY MOODS OF MURRY WILSON*, designed to show the world that composer son Brian is not the only genius in that talented family.

Albums/MANY MOODS OF MURRY WILSON (November 1967): *Love Won't Wait; Happy Song; Broken Heart; Warmth Of The Sun; Leaves; Plumber's Tune; Painting With Teardrops; Italia; Islands In The Sky; Just 'Round The River Bend; Betty's Waltz; Heartbreak Lane.*

Singles/*Leaves/Plumber's Tune* (1967).

WIND IN THE WILLOWS/*Gil Fields (drums), Harris Wiener (organ, vocals), Peter Brittain (lead guitar, vocals),*

Steve De Phillips (bass, vocals), Paul Klein (lead vocals),
Deborah Harry (vocals), Ida Andrews (bassoon, fife, electric
flute, vocals).
Wind in the Willows first appeared in 1968, a year when good
groups, and well-promoted ones, glutted the market. They
featured a strong beat and a harmony of anything up to six
voices with instruments played to resemble the voices.

Album/WIND IN THE WILLOWS (July 1968): *Moments*
Spent; Uptown Girl; So Sad (To Watch Good Love Go Bad);
My Uncle Used To Love Me But She Died; There Is But One
Truth, Daddy; Friendly Lion; Park Avenue Blues; Djini Judy;
Little People; She's Fantastic And She's Yours; Wheel Of
Changes.

JOHNNY WINTER/Somewhere in the deep heart of
America at this very moment is a man or woman, black,
white or brindle, who, if properly promoted, properly pack-
aged, properly booked and handled, could be bigger than
Elvis and the Beatles put together. The question is where? Or,
if you like, who? When the December 1968 issue of *Rolling
Stone* mentioned almost in passing, in an article on the Texas
scene, a totally unknown cross-eyed albino who played Delta
blues, New York club owner Steve Paul snapped like a
divining rod that had at last found water. He left on the first
plane to Texas and didn't return until he'd tracked down the
pale thin cowboy with the pale white hair and the black, black
voice.

Johnny Winter may not be exactly the legendary unknown
destined to reign as the greatest song hero since Bob Dylan,
but he was an exciting discovery to make early in 1969 when
everyone had seen everything except a cross-eyed albino who
could sing. Columbia Records believed in him to the extent of
a six figure contract and his lean white presence and silky hair
brought an unexpected new twist to a musical scene already
heavily dominated by a Black is Beautiful philosophy.

Once the first flurry of excitement was over, however, the
big question that needed to be raised was, could Johnny
Winter have made it if he'd been, say, Jewish and from
Chicago, like Mike Bloomfield? Yes, said the ecstatic *New
York Times.* Well . . .? said the doubters. All in all, it became

one of the more pleasant subjects to argue about in that drab winter.

America's first albino bluesman learned his sound from the black radio stations he listened to as a child. When he first became a professional entertainer in Texas (Johnny Winter and the Black Plague, he called himself and his group—later renamed It and Them with his brother Edgar) he played little blues, just hits of the time, rhythm and blues and soul material. Nobody played blues for fun or profit in the rock and roll decade (1956–66). Then the blues revival of 1967–68 got underway and when Steve Paul, entrepreneur extraordinaire of the New York music scene, met the albino boy wonder of the Lone Star State, his big selling point was that Johnny had a right to sing the blues, just like anyone else.

By mid-1969 Winter's vintage blues had clicked with most of the insiders and tastemakers, barring the one or two who always dissent fashionably. Then the mass media moved in and billed him, to everyone's astonishment, as the most talented and irresistible freak since Tiny Tim. If the pitch didn't show where he was at musically, it at least sold a lot of records and nobody, but nobody (not Dylan, not the Beatles, not anyone) is ever likely to knock *that*.

Albums/THE PROGRESSIVE BLUES EXPERIMENT: *Rollin' And Tumblin'; Tribute To Muddy; I Got Love If You Want It; Bad Luck And Trouble; Help Me; Mean Town Blues; Broke Down Engine; Black Cat Bone; It's My Own Fault; Forty-Four.* JOHNNY WINTER: *I'm Yours And I'm Hers; Be Careful With A Fool; Dallas; Mean Mistreater; Leland Mississippi; Good Morning Little School Girl; When You Got A Good Friend; I'll Drown In My Tears; Back Door Friend.*

Single/*I'm Yours And I'm Hers/I'll Drown In My Tears* (June 1969).

HOWLIN' WOLF (Chester Arthur Burnett)/When people talk about the English groups of 1963–64 giving Americans back their own sound, they probably mean the sound of Chicago blues man Howlin' Wolf. The Yardbirds did one of his songs, *Smokestack Lightnin'*, on their first English album (though it was released on their second album in the U.S.).

He had a great deal of influence on the early Stones (*Little Red Rooster* was his), on most English blues bands, on Cream, Spoonful and of course on American white blues bands like the Paul Butterfield Blues Band, Canned Heat and the now defunct Blues Project. At the 1966 Folk Festival in Newport, Howlin' Wolf brought the house down with *You Go, I Go With You*, a song of his that most people there had never heard anyone but the Blues Project do. That confrontation with an original is something few of them were likely to forget.

Albums/MOANIN' IN THE MOONLIGHT: *Moanin' At Midnight; How Many More Years; Smokestack Lightnin'; Baby How Long; No Place To Go; All Night Boogie; Evil; I'm Leavin' You; Moanin' For My Baby; I Asked For Water (She Gave Me Gasoline); Forty-four; Somebody In My Home.* TUNE BOX: *Shake For Me; Red Rooster; You'll Be Mine; Who's Been Talkin'; Wang-Dang-Doodle; Little Baby; Spoonful; Going Down Slow; Down In The Bottom; Back Door Man; Howlin' For My Baby; Tell Me.* REAL FOLK BLUES—HOWLIN' WOLF (April 1966): *Killing Floor; Louise; Poor Boy; Sittin' For Top Of The World; Nature; My Country Sugar Mama; Tail Dragger; Three Hundred Pounds Of Joy; Natchez Burnin'; Built For Comfort; Ooh, Baby Hold Me; Tell Me What I've Done.* MORE REAL FOLK BLUES —HOWLIN' WOLF (April 1967): *Just My Kind; I've Got A Woman; Work For Your Money; I'll Be Around; You Can't Be Beat; You Gonna Wreck My Life; I Love My Baby; Neighbors; I'm The Wolf; Who Will Be Next; Rocking Daddy; I Have A Little Girl.*

Singles/*Moanin' For My Baby/I Didn't Know; Change My Ways/I'm Leaving You; Howlin' Blues/I Better Go Now; You Gonna Wreck My Life/Natchez Burnin'; Tell Me/Who's Been Talking; Howlin' For My Darling/Spoonful; Back Door Man/Wang-Dang-Doodle; Red Rooster/Shake For Me; Going Down Slow/You'll Be Mine; Just Like I Treat You/I Ain't Superstitious; Tail Dragger/Hidden Charms; Killing Floor/Louise; Tell Me What I've Done/Ooh Baby; Don't Laugh At Me/I Walked From Dallas; I Had A Dream/Pop It To Me.*

STEVIE WONDER (formerly LITTLE STEVIE WONDER)/
He was "Little" Stevie Wonder when he made his sensational
microbopper's debut in 1963, at the age of twelve, with *I Call
It Pretty Music, Fingertips* and an album predictably called
TWELVE YEAR OLD GENIUS. But he engraved himself
once and for all on the public consciousness as an adult with
the metric pyrotechnic *Uptight* that dominated the post-twist
1965–66 discotheque era, a song it was impossible *not* to
dance to. He plays piano, drums, harmonica, clarinet and
organ and has managed to retain a vibrant mood and speed in
spite of a lifetime of blindness and a childhood in a Detroit
slum where there are still a million Stevie Wonders, an army
of black child troubadours warbling away at soul ballads,
waiting to be discovered, at every street corner.

Albums/ 12 YEAR OLD GENIUS: *Fingertips* (Two Parts);
*Soul Bongo; Drown In My Own Tears; La La La La La;
Masquerade Is Over (I'm Afraid); Hallelujah! I Love Her
So; Don't You Know.* TRIBUTE TO UNCLE RAY: *Hallelu-
jah I Love Her So; Ain't That Love; Mary Ann; Don't You
Know; Masquerade; My Baby's Gone; Frankie And Johnny;
Drown In My Own Tears; Come Back Baby; Sunset.* JAZZ
SOUL: *Fingertips; Square; So Bongo; Manhattan At Six;
Some Other Time; Wandering; Session 112; Bam; Paulsby.*
WITH A SONG IN MY HEART: *Dream; With A Song In
My Heart; Get Happy; Put On A Happy Face; When You
Wish Upon A Star; Smile; Make Someone Happy; Without A
Song; On The Sunny Side Of The Street; Give Your Heart A
Chance.* AT THE BEACH: *Red Sails In The Sunset; Party
At The Beach; Happy Street; Beachcomber; Castles In The
Sand; Beyond The Sea; Sad Boy; Beachstomp; Hey, Harmoni-
ca Man.* UPTIGHT (May 1966): *Uptight (Everything's
Alright); Nothing's Too Good For My Baby; Love A Go-Go;
Ain't That Asking For Trouble; Blowin' In The Wind; Hold
Me; Teach Me Tonight; I Want My Baby Back; Pretty Little
Angel; Contract On Love; With A Child's Heart.* DOWN TO
EARTH (December 1966): *Place In The Sun; Bang Bang;
Thank You Love; Mr. Tambourine Man; Hey Love; Sixteen
Tons; Down To Earth; Sylvia; Lonesome Road; My World Is
Empty Without You; Angel Baby; Be Cool, Be Calm & Keep
Yourself Together.* I WAS MADE TO LOVE HER (May

1967): *I Was Made To Love Her; My Girl; I Got A Witness; Baby Don't You Do It; Respect; I Pity The Fool; Send Me Some Lovin'; I'd Cry; Everybody Needs Somebody; Fool For You; Please, Please, Please; Every Time I See You I Go Wild.* SOMEDAY AT CHRISTMAS (November 1967): *Someday At Christmas; What Christmas Means To Me; Silver Bells; Christmas Song; Little Drummer Boy; Ave Maria;* Others. STEVIE WONDER, GREATEST HITS (March 1968): *Uptight; I Was Made To Love Her; I'm Wondering; Hey Love; Place In The Sun; Blowin' In The Wind; Contract On Love; Workout Stevie, Workout; Fingertips; Hey Harmonica Man; Nothing's Too Good For My Baby; Castles In The Sand.*

Singles/*I Call It Pretty Music* (Part I)/*I Call It Pretty Music* (Part II) (August 1963); *Little Water Boy/La La La La La* (October 1962); *Contract On Love/Sunset* (December 1962); *Fingertips* (Part I)/*Fingertips* (Part II) (May 1963); *Workout Stevie, Workout/Monkey Talk* (September 1963); *Castles In The Sand/He's A Good Guy* (January 1964); *Hey Harmonica Man/This Little Girl* (May 1964); *Sad Boy/Happy Street* (September 1964); *Kiss Me Baby/Tears In Vain* (March 1965); *High Heel Sneakers/Funny* (August 1965); *Uptight/Purple Raindrops* (November 1965); *Nothing's Too Good For My Baby/With A Child's Heart* (March 1966); *Blowin' In The Wind/Ain't That Asking For Trouble* (May 1966); *A Place In The Sun/Sylvia* (October 1966); *Someday At Christmas/The Miracles Of Christmas* (November 1966); *Travelin' Man/Hey Love* (February 1967); *I Was Made To Love Her/Hold Me* (May 1967); *I'm Wondering/Everytime I See You I Go Wild* (September 1966); *Shoo-Be-Doo-Be-Doo-Da-Day/Why Don't You Lead Me To Love* (March 1968); *You Met Your Match/My Girl* (June 1968);

Also Appears On/MOTORTOWN REVUE IN PARIS (May 1966): *High Heel Sneakers; Funny How Time Slips Away; Fingertips.* 16 ORIGINAL BIG HITS: VOL 1: *Contract On Love; Sunset.* VOL 2: *Fingertips.* VOL 3: *Hey, Harmonica Man.* VOL. 6: *Uptight.* VOL. 7: *Place In The Sun.* VOL. 8: *Travelin' Man.*

THE WONDER WHO/*Frankie Valli (vocals), Bob Gaudio (vocals), Tommy De Vito (vocals), Joe Long (vocals).*

Not to be confused with the Who, the Wonder Who was a name the Four Seasons recorded under for two singles, just for fun. It is surprising that more bands don't do this, particularly those that are fixed in a commercial groove and secretly long to break out in other directions.
(see FOUR SEASONS)

Singles/ *Around And Around/ Lonesome Road; Don't Think Twice/ Till Somebody Loves You.*

BRENTON WOOD/ One of those singers who has the rich voice, the good timing and the potential to step into the shoes of the late Sam Cooke.

Album/ OOGUM BOOGUM: *Oogum Boogum Song; Little Bit Of Love; I'm The One Who Knows; Come Here Girl; I Like The Way You Love Me; Birdman; Psychotic Reaction; Runnin' Wild; I Think You've Got Your Fools Mixed Up; Best Thing I Ever Had; Gimme Little Sign; Take A Chance.*

Singles/ *Cross The Bridge/ Molly Malone; I Want Love/ Good Lovin'; Oogum Boogum Song/ I Like The Way; Gimme Little Sign/ I Think You've Got Your Fools Mixed Up; Baby You Go It/ Catch You On The Rebound; Lovey Dovey Kinda Lovin'/ Two Time Loser; Me And You/ Some Got It, Some Don't.*

Also Appears On/ SUPER SOUL: *Hideaway.*

ZAL YANOVSKY is alive and well in Toronto, and that isn't quite good enough for all the American fans he acquired when he was guitarist (and stand-up funnyman) for the Lovin' Spoonful, from its inception in 1965. His leaving in 1967 was the beginning of the end for the group. He made a solo single, *As Long As You're Here,* on which he was backed by four guitarists, six saxophones, four trombones, three trumpets, piano, organ, drums and jew's harp and three female singers. The flip side was that whole instrumental track played backwards. It wasn't a very good record but he deserved top marks for effort. He also made an album that insisted he was alive and well in Argentina. In the Spoonful he was replaced by Jerry Yester, who was both handsome and talented, but there was no replacing Zal, a great maniac figure in cowboy hat and shaggy ankle-length furs. It was something like replacing Groucho Marx, possible but not probable. (see LOVIN' SPOONFUL)

Single/*As Long As You're Here/Ereh Er' Ouy Sa Gnol.*

YARDBIRDS/*Jimmy Page (replaced Jeff Beck who replaced Eric Clapton) (lead guitar), John Paul Jones (replaced Paul "Sam" Samwell-Smith) (bass, organ), Robert Plante (replaced Keith Relf) (vocals), John Bonnham (replaced Jim McCarty) (drums).*
Previous Member: Chris Dreja (rhythm guitar).
In late 1963-early 1964 when the English "scene" was having its birth pangs, the Yardbirds followed the Rolling Stones into the Crawdaddy Club (by day the somewhat staid Richmond Cricket Club) as house band. Like the early Stones, they used standard material—Bo Diddley, Isley Brothers, Muddy Waters, Sonny Boy Williamson—always remaining more faithful to the original than the improvisation/variation-prone Stones. This was important at a time when the concept of original material was not as overworked as it was to become in 1967–69. Also, man for man, the Yardbirds were better instrumentalists than the Stones were then.

The original Yardbirds came out of a parent group called the Metropolis Blues Quartet, which featured Chris Dreja on rhythm guitar, Paul "Sam" Samwell-Smith on bass, Jim McCarty on drums, and Keith Relf doing vocals. They were joined by a very straight-looking crew-cut Eric Clapton who played lead guitar, and they became the Yardbirds. Now of course what the Stones had over them, even then, was the charisma of their lead singer, Mick Jagger. And although the Yardbirds were better musicians in 1963–64, the Stones were better performers, and their rival factions used to fight it out rather bitterly at times.

By 1964 the Beatles had hit America, the Rolling Stones had hit America, everyone English and his brother had hit America (including some of the worst groups in England) and the Yardbirds, like some other good, even great groups, found themselves lost in the shuffle. A lot of things went wrong. Their first British album was recorded live at the famous Marquee Club where they used to play every Sunday night.

The ten tracks were fine, but to fit them all on the album they had to be speeded up, only a little, but enough to make the music almost unrecognizable to hard-core Yardbird fans. And the tragedy was that that album *was* the Yardbirds—*Five Long Years, Louise, Smokestack Lightning, I'm A Man.*

During that time the Yardbirds happened on to what they called a rave-up, a long wild instrumental break, sometimes as long as thirty minutes, during which all the attention was focused on guitarist Clapton (for a change, since singer Relf was the natural star of the group). The rave-ups were Eric's big chance. He took off and the audience flew with him. His whole personality changed during these breaks, and because they weren't ever as long and as frequent as he wanted them (or needed them) to be, he eventually left—for John Mayall's group, which was even more tradition-oriented than the Yardbirds. Later, when he formed Cream, it was obvious that Eric was a breaker of new ground, and the Yardbirds merely excellent tillers of already-cultivated soil.

The tradition of the rave-up stayed with the Yardbirds. Much, much later the long instrumental breaks started to be associated with the dance scene of San Francisco and as a result were given the name of psychedelic. By 1968 people were saying with admiration that the Yardbirds had been the first to get into a psychedelic "bag." Clapton was replaced by Jeff Beck, another guitarist extraordinaire, who was eventually to leave, too, and start his own group. He was succeeded by Jimmy Page, one of the best session men in England (who is said to be on anywhere from fifty to ninety percent of the records released in England in the 1963–65 days).

In America the Yardbirds were never as lucky as other, often lesser, groups. Their first album here, *FOR YOUR LOVE,* was full of material they thought (or were made to think) was most suitable for American audiences. The material was more modern than material they had done in England. The second American album seemed to be designed to correct this, with new material on one side (the *Evil Hearted You* side), but with older material—Muddy Waters and Bo Diddley tracks from their first English album—on the other (this time they were presented at their normal speed). Because they were recorded when Clapton was still with the group he is, naturally, featured on them, even though he had left by the time the album was released. The problem was, though, that this material was wildly exciting in England where no one had access to the originals. Americans seemed to prefer the "modern" Yardbirds. (With the 1968 blues revival this was to change, but too late for the old Yardbirds.)

In 1968 the Yardbirds announced they were splitting. One of the best groups to come out of England, one of the most concerned with music, they influenced the development of every group that came out of the English scene from the Beatles to the Who.

(see LED ZEPPELIN)

Albums/FOR YOUR LOVE (June 1965): *For Your Love; I'm Not Talking; I Ain't Got You; Got To Hurry; I Ain't Done Wrong; I Wish You Would; Certain Girl; Sweet Music; Good Morning Little Schoolgirls; My Girl Sloopy.* HAVING A RAVE UP WITH THE YARDBIRDS (November 1965): *I'm A Man; You're A Better Man Than I; Evil-Hearted You; Still I'm Sad; Heart Full Of Soul; Train Kept A-Rollin'; Smokestack Lightning; Respectable; Here 'Tis.* YARDBIRDS WITH SONNY BOY WILLIAMSON (March 1966): *Bye, Bye Bird; Pontiac Blues; Take It Easy Baby; I Don't Care No More; Do The Weston; Mister Downchild; 23 Hours Too Long; Out Of Water Coast; Baby Don't Worry.* OVER UNDER SIDEWAYS DOWN (July 1966): *Lost Woman; Over Under Sideways Down; I Can't Make Your Way; Farewell; Hot House Of Omagarashid; Jeff's Boogie; He's Always There; Turn Into Earth; What Do You Want; Ever Since The World Began.* YARDBIRDS' GREATEST HITS (March 1967): *Shapes Of Things; Still I'm Sad; New York City Blues; For Your Love; Over Under Sideways Down, I'm A Man; Happenings Ten Years Ago; Heart Full Of Soul; Smokestack Lightning; I'm Not Talking.* LITTLE GAMES (July 1967): *Little Games; Smile On Me; White Summer; Tinker, Tailor, Soldier, Sailor; Glimpses; No Excess Baggage; Drinking Muddy Water; Only The Black Rose; Stealing, Stealing; Little Soldier Boy.*

Singles/*I Wish You Would/A Certain Girl* (August 1964); *Shapes Of Things/I'm A Man* (February 1966); *For Your Love/Heart Full Of Soul* (March 1966); *Nazz Are Blue/ Happenings Ten Years Ago* (November 1966); *Little Games/*

Puzzles (March 1967); *Over Under Sideways Down/ Happenings Ten Years Ago* (May 1967); *Ha, Ha, Said The Clown/Tinker, Tailor, Soldier, Sailor* (July 1967); *Drinking Muddy Water/Ten Little Indians* (October 1967); *Goodnight Sweet Josephine/Think About It* (March 1968).

YELLOW PAYGES/*Dan Hortter (lead vocals, harmonica), Dan Gorman (drums), Bill Ham (lead guitar), Bob Barnes (bass guitar).*
A California rock group whose arrival in 1968 was greeted ecstatically by AT&T. A highly lucrative tieup with the telephone book was inevitable.

Album/THE YELLOW PAYGES — Volume 1 (March 1969): *The Two Of Us; Little Woman; Friends; Boogie Woogie Baby; Crowd Pleaser; Moonfire; Devil Woman; Never Put Away My Love For You; I'm A Man; Here 'Tis.*

Singles/*Our Time Is Running Out/Sweet Sunrise; Crowd Pleaser/You're Just What I Was Looking For Today* (November 1968); *Judge Carter/Childhood Friends* (December 1968).

JERRY YESTER/He replaced Zal Yanovsky in the Lovin' Spoonful in 1967. An able musician and the producer of Tim Buckley's *GOODBYE AND HELLO,* Jerry Yester was barely settled in when the Spoonful folded. He has, however, done some solo singles, but their success was more critical than financial.
(see LOVIN' SPOONFUL)

Singles/*Ashes Have Turned/Sound Of Summer Showers, Garden Of Imagining/I Can Live Without You.*

THE YOUNGBLOODS/*Jesse Colin Young (bass, vocals), Joe Bauer (drums), Banana (electric piano, guitar, vocals).*
Previous Member: Jerry Corbitt (lead guitar, bass).
In 1967 everyone hailed the Youngbloods (country-blues-jazz-rock) as the biggest thing since the Spoonful—the same tightness and free-swinging humor. Banana, the electric piano player (and perhaps the "electrical banana" of Donovan's *Mellow Yellow*) had the same touch of madness as the Spoonful's Yanovsky. Lead singer Jesse Colin Young had had

a whole separate career as a blues folksinger before turning to rock. Drummer Joe Bauer was a jazz drummer converted to rock by hearing the Beatles. (In rock he had to learn to play less intricately.) Jerry Corbitt, the original lead guitarist, sang ragtime, and their first hit, *Grizzly Bear,* was twenties rock or what a cunning publicist dubbed "rag and roll." When Corbitt left, Banana took on the guitar chores. Now the former Boston group does a three-voice harmony thing. They made Dino Valenti's *Get Together* a hit. Although they are produced by ace producer Felix Pappalardi and have moved away from the tensions of New York to peaceful San Francisco, the Youngbloods are still not up there with the supergroups. Those things take time.

Albums/THE YOUNGBLOODS (January 1967): *Grizzly Bear; All Over The World (La-La); Statesboro Blues; Get Together; One Note Man; Other Side Of This Life; Tears Are Falling; Four In The Morning; Foolin' Around (The Waltz); Ain't That Lovin' You, Baby; See See Rider.* EARTH MUSIC (October 1967): *Euphoria; All My Dreams Blue; Monkey Business; Dreamer's Dream; Sugar Babe; Long And Tall; I Can Tell; Don't Play Games; Wine Song; Fool Me; Reason To Believe.* ELEPHANT MOUNTAIN (April 1969): *Darkness, Darkness; Smug; On Sir Francis Drake; Sunlight; Beautiful; Turn It Over; Rain Song; Trillium; Quicksand; Black Mountain Breakdown; Sham; Ride The Wind.*

Singles/*Grizzly Bear/Tears Are Falling* (January 1967); *Merry-Go-Round/Foolin' Around* (March 1967); *Euphoria/The Wine Song* (May 1967); *Get Together/All My Dreams Blue* (July 1967); *Fool Me/I Can Tell* (October 1967); *Quicksand/Dreamer's Dream* (January 1968).

ZOMBIES/*Rod Argent (piano, organ, harmonica, violin, clarinet, vocals), Hugh Grundy (drums), Paul Atkinson (guitar, violin, harmonica), Chris White (bass guitar, double bass, vocals), Colin Blunstone (guitar, tambourine, lead vocals).*
When the Beatles gave America the English sound in 1964, they opened up a transatlantic door in music. One of those early English groups to pass through that door was the Zombies. Led by pianist-composer Rod Argent, they came up with a subtle style of minor-mood tunes that were unlike

anything that had yet come in from England and certainly unlike anything that was happening in America. *Tell Her No* and *She's Not There* were two of their major hits which earned them a small but loyal American following. It was small because immigration problems prevented the group from ever appearing in America.

After a while the group dropped out of sight, although they left their mark on literally hundreds of groups—not just other subtle minor-mood groups like the Kinks, but also such unlikely and distinct groups as the Left Banke and Procol Harum. Eventually a whole new music generation grew up without ever having heard them. The release of a new LP in 1968 showed that the Zombies were alive and well, and the sound as good as ever. Their new sound is tender and wistful but despite its critical success the group is reportedly folding. The Zombies will go down in history as one of the most underrated groups in rock.

Albums/ THE ZOMBIES (January 1965): *She's Not There; Summertime; It's Alright With Me; You've Really Got A Hold On Me; I Don't Want To Know; Sometimes; I've Got My Mojo Working; Woman; Tell Her No; Work 'n' Play; Can't Nobody Love You; What More Can I Do.* ODYSSEY AND ORACLE (July 1968): *Care Of Cell 44; A Rose For Emily; Maybe After He's Gone; Beechwood Park; Brief Candles; Hung Up On A Dream; Changes; I Want Her She Wants Me; This Will Be Our Year; Butcher's Tale (Western Front 1914); Friends Of Mine; Time Of The Season.*

Singles/ *She's Not There/You Make Me Feel So Good* (August 1964); *Tell Her No/Leave Me Be* (December 1964); *She's Coming Home/I Must Move* (March 1965); *Whenever You're Ready/I Love You* (August 1965); *Remember You/Just Out Of Reach* (September 1965); *Is This The Dream/Don't Go Away* (February 1966); *Indication/How Were We Before* (June 1966); *Care Of Cell 44/Maybe After He's Gone* (November 1967); *Butcher's Tale: Western Front 1914/This Will Be Our Date* (June 1968); *Time Of The Season/Friends Of Mine* (November 1968). *Conversation On Floral Street/Imagine The Swan* (May 1969).

APPENDIX

CASH BOX TOP ALBUMS (1960–1968)

1960

*1. THE SOUND OF MUSIC—ORIGINAL B'WAY CAST—COLUMBIA

*2. The Button Down Mind of Bob Newhart—Warner Bros. Warner Bros.

*3. Sold Out—The Kingston Trio—Capitol

*4. Heavenly—Johnny Mathis—Columbia

*5. 60 Years of Music America Loves Best—RCA Victor

6. Encore of Golden Hits—The Platters—Mercury

*7. Here We Go Again—The Kingston Trio—Capitol

8. Elvis Is Back—Elvis Presley—RCA Victor

*9. Theme From A Summer Place—Percy Faith—Columbia

10. Nice 'N' Easy—Frank Sinatra—Capitol

*11. Belafonte At Carnegie Hall—Harry Belafonte—RCA Victor

*12. Faithfully—Johnny Mathis—Columbia

13. String Along—The Kingston Trio—Capitol

14. Connie Francis Sings Italian Favorites—MGM

15. Brenda Lee—Decca

1961

1. CAMELOT—ORIGINAL B'WAY CAST—COLUMBIA

*2. EXODUS—FILM TRACK—RCA VICTOR

3. GREAT MOTION PICTURE THEMES—VARIOUS ARTISTS—UNITED ARTISTS

*4. G.I. Blues—Elvis Presley—RCA Victor

5. Sound Of Music—Original B'way Cast Columbia

6. Never On Sunday—Film Track—United Artists

*7. Calcutta—Lawrence Welk—Dot

8. Knockers Up—Rusty Warren—Jubilee

*9. Button Down Mind Strikes Back—Bob Newhart—Warner Bros.

*10. Encore Of Golden Hits—Platters—Mercury

11. Button Down Mind—Bob Newhart—Warner Bros.

These titles won Gold Record awards (based on cumulative sales).

*12. Nice & Easy—Frank Sinatra—Capitol
 13. Make Way—Kingston Trio—Capitol
 14. T.V. Sing Along With Mitch—Mitch Miller—Columbia
 15. All The Way—Frank Sinatra—Capitol
 16. Something For Everybody—Elvis Presley—RCA Victor
*17. Exodus—Mantovani—London
*18. String Along—Kingston Trio—Capitol
 19. Sinatra's Swingin' Session—Frank Sinatra—Capitol
 20. Goin' Places—Kingston Trio—Capitol
 21. Genius + Soul = Jazz—Ray Charles—Impulse
 22. Johnny's Moods—Johnny Mathis—Columbia
 23. Wonderland By Night—Bert Kaempfert—Decca
 24. Brenda Lee—Brenda Lee—Decca
*25. Happy Times Sing-Along—Mitch Miller—Columbia
 26. Ring-A-Ding-Ding—Frank Sinatra—Reprise
 27. Last Date—Lawrence Welk—Dot
 28. Judy At Carnegie Hall—Judy Garland—Capitol
 29. Tonight In Person—Limelighters—RCA Victor
 30. Carnival—Original B'way Cast—MGM
 31. Yellow Bird—Lawrence Welk—Dot
 32. Stars For A Summer Night—Various Artists—Columbia
 33. Portrait Of Johnny—Johnny Mathis—Columbia
*34. Memories Are Made Of This—Ray Connif—Columbia
 35. Rick Is 21—Rick Nelson—Imperial
 36. Sinatra Swings—Frank Sinatra—Reprise
 37. Solid & Raunchy—Bill Black—Hi
*38. Belafonte Returns To Carnegie Hall—Harry Belafonte—RCA Victor
 39. This Is Brenda—Brenda Lee—Decca
 40. Genius Hits The Road—Ray Charles—ABC Paramount
 41. Exodus To Jazz—Eddie Harris—Vee Jay
 42. Bobby Darin Story—Bobby Darin—Atco
 43. Quarter To Three—U.S. Bonds—Legrand
 44. 60 Years Of Music—Vol. II—Various Artists—RCA Victor
 45. Come Swing With Me—Frank Sinatra—Capitol
 46. Darin At The Copa—Bobby Darin—Atco
 47. The Astronaut—Bill Dana (Jose Jiminez)—Kapp
 48. Unsinkable Molly Brown—Orig. B'way Cast—Capitol

49. Paul Anka's Big 15—Paul Anka—ABC Paramount
50. I'll Buy You A Star—Johnny Mathis—Columbia

1962

*1. WEST SIDE STORY—SOUNDTRACK—COLUMBIA
*2. CAMELOT—ORIGINAL CAST—COLUMBIA
*3. BLUE HAWAII—ELVIS PRESLEY—VICTOR
*4. Joan Baez, Vol. 2—Vanguard
*5. Modern Sounds In C&W Music—Ray Charles—ABC-Paramount
*6. Peter, Paul & Mary—WB
 7. Your Twist Party—Chubby Checker—Parkway
*8. Judy At Carnegie Hall—Judy Garland—
*9. Time Out—Dave Brubeck—Columbia
10. Doin' The Twist At The Peppermint Lounge—Joey Dee—Roulette
11. Twist—Chubby Checker—Parkway
12. Moon River—Andy Williams—Columbia Victor
*13. Breakfast At Tiffany's—Soundtrack—Victor
*14. Stranger On The Shore—Acker Bilk—Atco
15. The Stripper—David Rose—MGM
16. College Concert—Kingston Trio—Capitol
17. A Song For Young Love—Lettermen—Capitol
18. Music Man—Soundtrack—WB
*19. Flower Drum Song—Soundtrack—Decca
20. Pot Luck—Elvis Presley—Victor
21. I Left My Heart In San Francisco—Tony Bennett—Columbia
22. Runaround Sue—Dion—Laurie
23. Moon River—Lawrence Welk—Dot
*24. Best Of The Kingston Trio—Capitol
25. Hatari—Soundtrack—Victor Cast—Columbia
27. No Strings—Original Cast—Columbia
28. I Remember Tommy—Frank Sinatra—Reprise
29. Let There Be Drums—Sandy Nelson—Imperial
30. Rome Adventure—Soundtrack—WB
31. Close Up—Kingston Trio—Capitol
32. Portrait Of Johnny—Johnny Mathis—Columbia

33. Sinatra & Strings—Capitol
34. Live It Up—Johnny Mathis—Columbia
35. Bashin' Jimmy Smith—Verve
*36. Ray Charles' Greatest Hits—ABC-Par.
37. Something Special—Kingston Trio—Capitol
38. Roses Are Red—Bobby Vinton—Epic
39. State Fair—Soundtrack—Dot
40. Behind The Button-Down Mind—Bob Newhart—WB
41. George Maharis Sings—Epic
42. Your Request Sing-Along—Mitch Miller—Columbia
43. It Keeps Right On A-Hurtin'—Johnny Tillotson—Cadence
44. Never On Sunday—Connie Francis—MGM
45. Midnight In Moscow—Kenny Ball—Kapp
46. Great Motion Picture Themes—UA
47. 'S Continental—Ray Conniff—Columbia
48. Lovers Who Wander—Dion—Laurie
49. Tonight—Ferrante & Teicher—UA
50. Do The Twist With Ray Charles—Atlantic
51. Jazz Samba—Stan Getz & Charlie Byrd—Verve

1963

*1. West Side Story—Soundtrack—Columbia
2. Peter, Paul & Mary—Warner Bros.
*3. Movin'—Peter, Paul & Mary—Warner Bros.
4. Joan Baez In Concert—Vanguard
*5. I Left My Heart In San Francisco—Tony Bennett—Columbia
*6. Moon River—Andy Williams—Columbia
7. Lawrence Of Arabia—Soundtrack—Colpix
8. Pot Luck—Elvis Presley—RCA Victor
*9. Days Of Wine And Roses—Andy Williams—Columbia
10. Barbra Streisand Album—Columbia
11. Bye Bye Birdie—Soundtrack—RCA Victor
12. Jazz Samba—Stan Getz—Verve
13. How The West Was Won—Soundtrack—MGM
14. I Wanna Be Around—Tony Bennett—Columbia
15. Roy Orbison's Greatest Hits—Monument
*16. Surfin' U.S.A.—Beach Boys—Capitol
*17. Oliver!—Original Cast—RCA Victor

18. Kingston Trio—#16—Capitol
19. Songs I Love To Sing—Frank Fontaine—ABC-Paramount
*20. Think Ethnic—Smothers Bros.—Mercury
21. Our Man In Hollywood—Henry Mancini—RCA Victor
22. Richard Chamberlain Sings—MGM
23. Fly Me To The Moon—Joe Harnell—Kapp
24. Johnny's Newest Hits—Johnny Mathis—Columbia
25. James Brown At The Apollo—King
26. Broadway My Way—Nancy Wilson—Capitol
27. Surfing—Ventures—Dolton
28. Cleopatra—Soundtrack—20th Century Fox
29. Alley Cat—Bent Fabric—Atco
30. Trini Lopez At PJ's—Reprise
31. Sincerely Yours—Robert Goulet—Columbia
*32. Themes For Young Lovers—Percy Faith—Columbia
33. Hail The Conquering Nero—Peter Nero—RCA Victor
34. Shut Down—Beach Boys—Capitol
35. Sinatra-Basie—Reprise
36. 1962's Greatest Hits—Billy Vaughn—Dot
37. It Happened At The World's Fair—Elvis Presley—RCA Victor
38. I Love You Because—Al Martino—Capitol
39. New Frontier—Kingston Trio—Capitol
40. My Son The Celebrity—Allan Sherman—Warner Bros.
41. 1962's Early Hits—Lawrence Welk—Dot
42. Tell Tall Tales—New Christy Minstrels—Columbia
*43. Music Man—Soundtrack—Warner Bros.
44. Blue Velvet—Bobby Vinton—Epic
45. Hobo Flats—Jimmy Smith—Verve
46. Latin Rendevous—Mantovani—London
47. Happy Beat—Ray Conniff—Columbia
48. Paul & Paula Sing For Young Lovers—Philips
*49. Ring Of Fire—Johnny Cash—Columbia
50. Sunny Side—Kingston Trio—Capitol

1964

*1. Meet The Beatles—Capitol
*2. Honey In The Horn—Al Hirt—RCA Victor

  3. West Side Story—Soundtrack—Columbia
 *4. The Second Barbra Streisand Album—Columbia
 *5. Blowin' In The Wind—Peter, Paul & Mary—Warner Bros.
 *6. Hello Dolly—Original Cast—RCA Victor
 *7. The Barbra Streisand Album—Columbia
  8. Peter, Paul & Mary—Warner Bros.
  9. Louie, Louie—Kingsmen—Wand
 10. Catch A Rising Star—John Gary—RCA Victor
 11. Movin'—Peter, Paul & Mary—Warner Bros.
 *12. Pink Panther—Henry Mancini—RCA Victor
 13. Charade—Henry Mancini—RCA Victor
 *14. Funny Girl Original Cast—Capitol
 *15. Hello Dolly—Louis Armstrong—Kapp
 16. Introducing The Beatles—Vee Jay
 17. Days Of Wine And Roses—Andy Williams—Columbia Columbia
 *18. Ramblin'—New Christy Minstrels—Columbia
 19. Shut Down Vol.II—Beach Boys—Capitol
 *20. Cotton Candy—Al Hirt—RCA Victor
 21. Today—New Christy Minstrels—Columbia
 *22. Joan Baez In Concert—Vanguard
 *23. The Beatles Second Album—Capitol
 *24. Getz/Gilberto—Stan Getz & Joao Gilberto—Verve
 *25. The Singing Nun—Soeur Souire—Philips
 *26. Call Me Irresponsible And Other Academy Award Winners—Andy Williams—Columbia
 *27. Glad All Over—Dave Clark Five—Epic
 *28. Trini Lopez At P.J.'s—Reprise
 29. Wives And Lovers—Jack Jones—Kapp
 30. Little Deuce Coupe—Beach Boys—Capitol
 *31. Roy Orbison's Greatest Hits—Monument
 32. Hard Day's Night—Soundtrack—United Artists
 33. Bye Bye Birdie—Soundtrack—RCA Victor
 34. Bach's Greatest Hits—Swingle Singers—Philips
 35. Something Special For Young Lovers—Ray Charles Singers—Command
 36. Lawrence Of Arabia—Soundtrack—Colpix
 37. How The West Was Won—Soundtrack—MGM
 38. I Left My Heart In San Francisco—Tony Bennett—Columbia

39. Blue Velvet—Bobby Vinton—Epic
40. All Summer Long—Beach Boys—Capitol
41. Washington Square—Village Stompers—Epic
42. Curb Your Tongue, Knave—Smothers Bros.
43. Fun In Acapulco—Elvis Presley—RCA Victor
44. Painted Tainted Rose—Al Martino—Capitol
45. Think Ethnic—Smothers Bros.—Mercury
*46. Sinatra's Sinatra—Reprise
47. Beatle Song Book—The Hollyridge Strings—Capitol
48. Ingredients In A Recipe For Soul—Ray Charles—ABC Paramount
49. Tender Is The Night—Johnny Mathis—Mercury
*50. Something New—The Beatles—Capitol

1965

*1. Mary Poppins—Soundtrack—Buena Vista
*2. My Fair Lady—Soundtrack—Columbia
*3. Fiddler On The Roof—Original Cast—RCA Victor
4. Where Did Our Love Go—Supremes—Motown
5. Goldfinger—Soundtrack—United Artists
*6. People—Barbra Streisand—Columbia
*7. Sound of Music—Soundtrack—RCA Victor
*8. Beatles '65—Capitol
*9. Beach Boys in Concert—Capitol
*10. Dear Heart—Andy Williams—Columbia
*11. Beach Boys Today—Capitol
*12. Bringing It All Back Home—Bob Dylan—Columbia
*13. Introducing Herman's Hermits—MGM
*14. Best of Al Hirt—RCA Victor
15. Rolling Stones Now—London
*16. The Return of Roger Miller—Smash
17. A Song Will Rise—Peter, Paul & Mary—Warner Bros.
*18. My Name Is Barbra—Barbra Streisand—Columbia
*19. Blue Midnight—Bert Kaempfert—Decca
20. Hello Dolly—Original Cast—RCA Victor
*21. Whipped Cream & Other Delights—Tijuana Brass—A&M
*22. Herman's Hermits On Tour—MGM
23. Louie Louie—Kingsmen—Wand
*24. Beatles VI—Capitol

25. Roustabout—Elvis Presley—RCA Victor
26. Joan Baez #5—Vanguard
27. Girl Happy—Elvis Presley—RCA Victor
*28. Everybody Loves Somebody—Dean Martin—Reprise
29. Bobby Vinton's Greatest Hits—Epic
30. Dear Heart & Other Songs About Love—Henry Mancini —RCA Victor
31. Yesterday's Gone—Chad & Jeremy—World Artists
32. You've Lost That Lovin' Feelin'—Righteous Bros.— Philles
33. Just Once In My Life—Righteous Bros.—Philles
34. The Roar Of The Greasepaint—Original Cast—RCA Victor
35. The Genius Of Jankowski—Horst Jankowski—Mercury
36. 12 x 5—Rolling Stones—London
*37. Ramblin' Rose—Nat King Cole—Capitol
38. L-O-V-E—Nat King Cole—Capitol
39. Hard Day's Night—Soundtrack—United Artists
40. Marianne Faithfull—London
*41. Peter, Paul & Mary In Concert—Warner Bros.
*42. Summer Days & Summer Nights—Beach Boys—Capitol
*43. Sugar Lips—Al Hirt—RCA Victor
*44. All Summer Long—Beach Boys—Capitol
45. Your Cheating Heart—Soundtrack—MGM
*46. My Love Forgive Me—Robert Goulet—Columbia
*47. Out Of Our Heads—Rolling Stones—London
*48. My Fair Lady—Andy Williams—Columbia
49. Downtown—Petula Clark—Warner Bros.
50. That Honey In The Horn Sound—Al Hirt—RCA Victor

1966

1. Sound of Music—Soundtrack—RCA
2. Whipped Cream and Other Delights—Herb Alpert & Tijuana Brass—A&M
*3. Going Places—Herb Alpert & Tijuana Brass—A&M
*4. Dr. Zhivago—Soundtrack—MGM
*5. South of the Border—Herb Alpert & Tijuana Brass— A&M
*6. The Best of Herman's Hermits—MGM
*7. The Best of the Animals—MGM

*8. What Now My Love—Herb Alpert & Tijuana Brass—A&M

*9. Lonely Bull—Herb Alpert & Tijuana Brass—A&M

*10. Why Is There Air?—Bill Cosby—Warner Bros.

11. Fiddler on the Roof—Original Cast—RCA Victor

*12. If You Can Believe Your Eyes and Ears—Mamas & Papas—Dunhill

*13. Big Hits (High Tide and Green Grass)—Rolling Stones—London

*14. My Name is Barbra, Two—Barbra Streisand—Columbia

*15. September of My Years—Frank Sinatra—Reprise

*16. Rubber Soul—Beatles—Capitol

*17. Wonderfulness—Bill Cosby—Warner Bros.

*18. The Dave Clark Five's Greatest Hits—Epic

*19. Strangers in the Night—Frank Sinatra—Reprise

20. Spanish Eyes—Al Martino—Capitol

*21. Lou Rawls Live—Capitol

*22. Aftermath—Rolling Stones—London

*23. Golden Hits of Roger Miller—Smash

*24. Somewhere My Love—Ray Conniff Singers—Columbia

*25. Just Like Us—Paul Revere & the Raiders—Columbia

*26. Ballad of the Green Berets—S/Sgt. Barry Sadler—RCA Victor

27. Mary Poppins—Soundtrack—Buena Vista

28. Out Of Our Heads—Rolling Stones—London

*29. December's Children (and Everybody's)—Rolling Stones—London

30. Boots—Nancy Sinatra—Reprise

*31. Houston—Dean Martin—Reprise

32. That Was the Year That Was—Tom Lehrer—Reprise

33. Pet Sounds—Beach Boys—Capitol

*34. Help—Beatles—Capitol

*35. Soul and Inspiration—Righteous Brothers—Verve

36. Shadow of Your Smile—Johnny Mathis—Mercury

*37. Mame—Original Cast—Columbia

38. Crying Time—Ray Charles—ABC Paramount

39. My Fair Lady—Soundtrack—Columbia

40. Man of La Mancha—Original Cast—Kapp

*41. Revolver—Beatles—Capitol

*42. Midnight Ride—Paul Revere & the Raiders—Columbia

43. Beach Boys Party—Capitol

*44. Sounds of Silence—Simon & Garfunkel—Columbia
*45. The Young Rascals—Atlantic
*46. Yesterday & Today—Beatles—Capitol
 47. Thunderball—Original Motion Picture Soundtrack—United Artists
 48. Turn, Turn, Turn—Byrds—Columbia
 49. Daydream—Lovin' Spoonful—Kama Sutra
 50. Hold On—Herman's Hermits—MGM

1967

 1. Dr. Zhivago—Soundtrack—MGM
 2. Sound of Music—Soundtrack—RCA
*3. A Man & A Woman—Soundtrack—United Artists
*4. More of the Monkees—Colgems
*5. Sgt. Pepper's Lonely Hearts Club Band—Beatles—Capitol
*6. Surrealistic Pillow—Jefferson Airplane—RCA
*7. S.R.O.—Herb Alpert & Tijuana Brass—A&M
*8. The Monkees—Colgems
*9. Monkees Headquarters—Colgems
*10. Doors—Elektra
*11. Sounds Like—Herb Alpert & Tijuana Brass—A&M
*12. Revenge—Bill Cosby—Warner Bros.
*13. I Never Loved A Man—Aretha Franklin—Atlantic
*14. Mamas & Papas Deliver—Dunhill
*15. The Best of Lovin' Spoonful—Kama Sutra
*16. Born Free—Andy Williams—Columbia
 17. Collections—Young Rascals—Atlantic
 18. Whipped Cream & Other Delights—Herb Alpert & Tijuana Brass—A&M
 19. Wonderfulness—Bill Cosby—Warner Bros.
*20. Release Me—Engelbert Humperdinck—Parrot
*21. That's Life—Frank Sinatra—Reprise
*22. Flowers—Rolling Stones—London
*23. Insight Out—Association—Warner Bros.
*24. Born Free—Roger Williams—Kapp
*25. Paul Revere & The Raiders Greatest Hits—Columbia
*26. Between the Buttons—Rolling Stones—London
*27. Spirit of '67—Paul Revere & The Raiders—Columbia
*28. My Cup Runneth Over—Ed Ames—RCA

*29. Bob Dylan's Greatest Hits—Columbia
 30. Supremes Sing Holland, Dozier, Holland—Motown
 31. Cabaret—Original Cast—Columbia
 32. Groovin'—Young Rascals—Atlantic Experience—Reprise
 33. 4-Tops-Live—Motown
 34. Diana Ross & Supremes Greatest Hits—Motown
 35. Aretha Arrives—Aretha Franklin—Atlantic
*36. The Byrds' Greatest Hits
 37. Here Where There Is Love—Dionne Warwick—Scepter
*38. Ode To Billie Joe—Bobby Gentry—Capitol
 39. Album 1700—Peter Paul & Mary—Warner Bros.
 40. Claudine—Claudine Longet—A&M
 41. Are You Experienced—Jimi Hendrix Experience—Warner Bros.
 42. Temptations-Live—Gordy
*43. Mamas & Papas—Dunhill
 44. Georgy Girl—Seekers—Capitol
 45. Reach Out—4 Tops—Motown
 46. In The Arms of Love—Andy Williams—Columbia
 47. Bee Gees 1st—Atco
 48. There's a Kind of a Hush All Over the World—Herman's Hermits—MGM
 49. 4 Tops Greatest Hits—Motown
 50. Vanilla Fudge—Atco

1968

*1. Disraeli Gears—Cream—Atco
*2. The Graduate—Original Soundtrack—Columbia
*3. Are You Experienced—Jimi Hendrix Experience—Reprise
*4. Bookends—Simon & Garfunkel—Columbia
*5. Look Around—Sergio Mendes & Brasil 66—A&M
*6. Parsley, Sage, Rosemary & Thyme—Simon & Garfunkel—Columbia
 7. Lady Soul—Aretha Franklin—Atlantic
*8. The Beat Of The Brass—Herb Alpert & Tijuana Brass—A&M
*9. Magical Mystery Tour—Beatles—Capitol
*10. Blooming Hits—Paul Mauriat—Philips

*11. Honey—Bobby Goldsboro—United Artists
*12. Wheels Of Fire—Cream—Atco
 13. Dr. Zhivago—Original Soundtrack—MGM
*14. The Rascal's Greatest Hits/Time Peace—Atlantic
*15. The Good, The Bad, And The Ugly—Original Sound-
     track—United Artists
*16. Axis: Bold As Love—Jimi Hendrix Experience—Reprise
 17. Aretha Now—Aretha Franklin—Atlantic
*18. To Russell, My Brother, Whom I Slept With—Bill
     Cosby—Warner Bros.
*19. Herb Alpert's Ninth—Herb Alpert & Tijuana Brass—
     A&M
 20. Realization—Johnny Rivers—Imperial
 21. A Tramp Shining—Richard Harris—Dunhill
 22. Steppenwolf—Dunhill
*23. John Wesley Harding—Bob Dylan—Columbia
*24. Waiting For The Sun—Doors—Elektra
*25. Feliciano—Jose Feliciano—RCA
 26. Sounds Of Silence—Simon & Garfunkel—Columbia
*27. The Birds The Bees & The Monkees—Colgems
 28. Lettermen . . . . And Live!—Capitol
 29. Diana Ross & The Supremes Greatest Hits—Motown
 30. I Wish It Would Rain—Temptations—Gordy
*31. Pisces, Aquarius, Capricorn & Jones Ltd.—Monkees—
     Colgems
*32. Camelot—Original Soundtrack—Warner Bros.
 33. Sound Of Music—Original Soundtrack—RCA
 34. In-A-Gadda-Da-Vida—Iron Butterfly—Atco
 35. Sgt. Pepper's Lonely Heart's Club Band—Beatles—
     Capitol
 36. Papas & Mamas—Mamas & Papas—Dunhill
*37. Their Satanic Majesties Request—Rolling Stones—Lon-
     don
 38. The Turtle's Golden Hits—White Whale
*39. Johnny Cash At Folsom Prison—Columbia
 40. Birthday—Association—Warner Bros./7 Arts
*41. Vanilla Fudge—Atco
 42. History Of Otis Redding—Volt
 43. God Bless Tiny Tim—Reprise
*44. Cheap Thrills—Big Brother & Holding Co.—Columbia

45. By The Time I Get To Phoenix—Glen Campbell—Capitol
46. Who Will Answer—Ed Ames—RCA
47. The Dock Of The Bay—Otis Redding—Volt
48. The Unicorn—Irish Rovers—Decca
49. Music From A Fistfull of Dollars, For A Few Dollars More & The Good, The Bad, & The Ugly—Hugo Montenegro—RCA
50. Dionne Warwick's Golden Hits—Part One—Scepter

CASH BOX TOP SINGLES (1949–1968)

1949

1. Forever And Ever—Russ Morgan Orch.
2. Riders In The Sky—Vaughn Monroe
3. Again—Gordon Jenkins Orch.
4. Forever And Ever—Perry Como
5. Cruising Down The River—Blue Barron Orch.
6. Cruising Down The River—Russ Morgan Orch.
7. Again—Vic Damone
8. So Tired—Russ Morgan Orch.
9. Lavender Blue—Dinah Shore
10. Buttons And Bows—Dinah Shore

1950

1. Goodnight Irene—Gordon Jenkins & The Weavers
2. It Isn't Fair—Sammy Kaye
3. Third Man Theme—Anton Karas
4. Mule Train—Frankie Laine
5. Mona Lisa—King Cole
6. Music, Music, Music—Teresa Brewer
7. I Wanna Be Loved—Andrew Sisters
8. I'd've Baked A Cake—Eileen Barton
9. I Can Dream Can't I—Andrews Sisters
10. That Lucky Old Sun—Frankie Laine

1951

1. Tennessee Waltz—Patti Page
2. How High The Moon—Les Paul & Mary Ford
3. Too Young—Nat "King" Cole
4. Be My Love—Mario Lanza
5. Because Of You—Tony Bennett
6. On Top Of Old Smokey—Weavers & Terry Gilkyson
7. If—Perry Como
8. Sin—Four Aces
9. Come On-A My House—Rosemary Clooney
10. Mockin' Bird Hill—Les Paul & Mary Ford

1952

1. Cry—Johnny Ray
2. Blue Tango—Leroy Anderson

3. Anytime—Eddie Fisher
4. Delicado—Percy Faith
5. Kiss Of Fire—Georgia Gibbs
6. Wheel Of Fortune—Kay Starr
7. Tell Me Why—Four Aces
8. I'm Yours—Don Cornell
9. Here In My Heart—Al Martino
10. Auf Wiedersehn Sweetheart—Vera Lynn

1953

1. Song From Moulin Rouge—Percy Faith ⎰ Tie
2. Till I Waltz With You—Teresa Brewer ⎱
3. April In Portugal—Les Baxter
4. Vaya Con Dios—Les Paul & Mary Ford
5. I'm Walking Behind You—Eddie Fisher
6. I Believe—Frankie Laine
7. You, You, You—Ames Bros.
8. Doggie In The Window—Patti Page
9. Why Don't You Believe Me—Joni James
10. Pretend—Nat "King" Cole

1954

1. Little Things Mean A Lot—Kitty Kallen
2. Hey There—Rosemary Clooney
3. Wanted—Perry Como
4. Young At Heart—Frank Sinatra
5. Sh-Boom—Crewcuts
6. Three Coins In The Fountain—Four Aces
7. Little Shoemaker—Gaylords
8. Oh, My Papa—Eddie Fisher
9. Secret Love—Doris Day
10. Happy Wanderer—Frank Weir

1955

1. Rock Around The Clock—Bill Haley & Comets
2. Davy Crocket—Bill Hayes
3. Cherry Pink And Apple Blossom White—Perez Prado
4 Melody Of Love—Billy Vaughn

5. Yellow Rose Of Texas—Mitch Miller
6. Ain't That A Shame—Pat Boone
7. Sincerely—McGuire Sisters
8. Unchained Melody—Al Hibbler
9. Crazy Otto—Johnny Maddox
10. Mr. Sandman—Chordettes

1956

1. Don't Be Cruel—Elvis Presley
2. The Great Pretender—Platters
3. My Prayer—Platters
4. The Wayward Wind—Gogi Grant
5. Whatever Will Be, Will Be—Doris Day
6. Heartbreak Hotel—Elvis Presley
7. Lisbon Antigua—Nelson Riddle
8. Canadian Sunset—Hugo Winterhalter
9. Moonglow & Picnic—Morris Stoloff
10. Honky Tonk—Bill Doggett
11. Memories Are Made Of This—Dean Martin
12. Poor People Of Paris—Les Baxter
13. Rock And Roll Waltz—Kay Starr
14. Hot Diggitty—Perry Como
15. Hound Dog—Elvis Presley
16. I Want You, I Need You, I Love You—Elvis Presley
17. Blue Suede Shoes—Carl Perkins
18. Why Do Fools Fall In Love—Teenagers
19. No Not Much—Four Lads
20. I Almost Lost My Mind—Pat Boone
21. Tonight You Belong To Me—Patience & Prudence
22. I'm In Love Again—Fats Domino
23. Allegheny Moon—Patti Page
24. Just Walking In The Rain—Johnnie Ray
25. Ivory Tower—Cathy Carr
26. Green Door—Jim Lowe
27. Love Me Tender—Elvis Presley
28. Band Of Gold—Don Cherry
29. Standing On The Corner—Four Lads
30. See You Later, Alligator—Bill Haley & Comets

31. Magic Touch—Platters
32. I'll Be Home—Pat Boone
33. True Love—Crosby & Kelly
34. A Tear Fell—Teresa Brewer
35. Flying Saucer—Buchanan & Goodman
36. On The Street Where You Live—Vic Damone
37. The Fool—Sanford Clark
38. Friendly Persuasion—Pat Boone
39. Blueberry Hill—Fats Domino
40. Song For A Summer Night—Mitch Miller
41. More—Perry Como
42. Singing The Blues—Guy Mitchell

1957

1. Tammy—Debbie Reynolds
2. Love Letters In The Sand—Pat Boone
3. It's Not For Me to Say—Johnny Mathis
4. Young Love—Sonny James—Tab Hunter
5. Chances Are—Johnny Mathis
6. Little Darlin'—Diamonds
7. Bye Bye Love—Everly Brothers
8. All Shook Up—Elvis Presley
9. So Rare—Jimmy Dorsey
10. Round and Round—Perry Como
11. Jailhouse Rock—Elvis Presley
12. Wake Up Little Susie—Everly Brothers
13. Diana—Paul Anka
14. Honeycomb—Jimmie Rodgers
15. Teddy Bear—Elvis Presley
16. Don't Forbid Me—Pat Boone
17. I'm Gonna Sit Right Down—Billy Williams
18. Come Go With Me—Del-Vikings
19. Silhouettes—Rays
20. Party Doll—Buddy Knox
21. Butterfly—Charlie Gracie—Andy Williams
22. You Send Me—Sam Cooke
23. Day-O—Harry Belafonte
24. Fascination—Jane Morgan
25. That'll Be The Day—Crickets

26. Banana Boat Song—Tarriers
27. A White Sport Coat—Marty Robbins
28. Too Much—Elvis Presley
29. Marianne—Easy Riders
30. I'm Walkin'—Fats Domino
31. Dark Moon—Gale Storm
32. Gone—Ferlin Husky
33. School Day (Ring Ring Goes The Bell)—Chuck Berry
34. Searchin'—Coasters
35. Whole Lot Of Shakin' Going On—Jerry Lee Lewis
36. April Love—Pat Boone
37. Be Bop Baby—Ricky Nelson
38. Rainbow—Russ Hamilton
39. My Special Angel—Bobby Helms
40. Teen Age Crush—Tommy Sands
41. Around The World—Victor Young—Mantovani
42. Send For Me—Nat "King" Cole
43. White Silver Sands—Don Rondo
44. Melodie D'Amour—Ames Bros.
45. Raunchy—Bill Justis—Ernie Freeman
46. Mr. Lee—Bobbettes
47. Old Cape Cod—Patti Page
48. Happy Happy Birthday Baby—Tune Weavers
49. Love Is Strange—Mickey & Sylvia
50. Little Bitty Pretty One—Thurston Harris

1958

1. Nel Blu Di Pinto Di Blu—Domenico Mudugno
2. It's All In The Game—Tommy Edwards
*3. Patricia—Perez Prado
4. All I Have To Do Is Dream—Everly Brothers
5. Bird Dog/Devoted to You—Everly Brothers
6. Little Star—Elegants
7. Witch Doctor—David Seville
8. Twilight Time—Platters
9. Tequila—Champs
10. At The Hop—Danny & The Juniors

*These titles won Gold Record awards (based on cumulative sales).

11. Return To Me—Dean Martin
*12. Catch A Falling Star—Perry Como
13. Purple People Eater—Sheb Wooley
14. Tea For Two Cha Cha—Warren Covington & T. Dorsey Orch.
*15. He's Got The Whole World In His Hands—Laurie London
16. Sail Along Silv'ry Moon—Billy Vaughn
17. Get A Job—Silhouettes
18. Poor Little Fool—Ricky Nelson
19. Yakety Yak—Coasters
*20. Tom Dooley—Kingston Trio
21. Rockin' Robin—Bobby Day
22. Topsy 11—Cozy Cole
23. Secretly—Jimmy Rodgers
24. Who's Sorry Now—Connie Francis
25. Wear My Ring Around Your Neck—Elvis Presley
26. It's Only Make Believe—Conway Twitty
27. Splish Splash—Bobby Darin
28. Don't—Elvis Presley
29. Chantilly Lace—Big Bopper
30. The Stroll—Diamonds
31. When—Kalin Twins
32. Just A Dream—Jimmy Clanton
33. Susie Darlin'—Robin Luke
34. Tears On My Pillow—Little Anthony & Imperials
35. Lollipop—Chordettes
36. Everybody Loves A Lover—Doris Day
*37. Hard Headed Woman—Elvis Presley
38. Big Man—Four Preps
39. Chanson D'Amour—Art & Dotty Todd
40. Oh Julie—Crescendos
41. Sweet Little Sixteen—Chuck Berry
42. To Know Him Is To Love Him—Teddy Bears
43. Fever—Peggy Lee
44. My True Love—Jack Scott
45. Twenty Six Miles—Four Preps
46. Sugartime—McGuire Sisters
47. Do You Wanna Dance—Bobby Freeman
48. The End—Earl Grant
49. Rebel-'Rouser—Duane Eddy

50. It's Too Soon To Know—Pat Boone
51. Looking Back—Nat "King" Cole

1959

1. Mack The Knife—Bobby Darin
2. Battle Of New Orleans—Johhny Horton
3. Venus—Frankie Avalon
4. Lonely Boy—Paul Anka
5. There Goes My Baby—Drifters
6. Personality—Lloyd Price
7. Three Bells—Browns
8. Put Your Head On My Shoulder—Paul Anka
9. Sleepwalk—Santo & Johnny
10. Come Softly To Me—Fleetwoods
11. Stagger Lee—Lloyd Price
12. Dream Lover—Bobby Darin
13. Kansas City—Wilbert Harrison
14. Smoke Gets In Your Eyes—Platters
15. Charlie Brown—Coasters
16. Mr. Blue—Fleetwoods
17. A Fool Such As I—Elvis Presley
18. Don't You Know—Della Reese
19. A Big Hunk O' Love—Elvis Presley
20. What A Difference A Day Makes—Dinah Washington
21. Quiet Village—Martin Denny
22. Pink Shoelaces—Dodie Stevens
23. Just A Matter Of Time—Brook Benton
24. Sea Of Love—Phil Phillips
25. A Teenager In Love—Dion & Belmonts
26. I'm Gonna Get Married—Lloyd Price
27. Sorry (I Ran All The Way Home)—Impalas
28. ('Til) I Kissed You—Everly Brothers
29. Primrose Lane—Jerry Wallace
30. Deck Of Cards—Wink Martindale
31. Kookie Kookie (Lend Me Your Comb)—Edd Byrnes & Connie Stevens
32. Seven Little Girls (Sittin' In The Back Seat)—Paul Evans & Curls
33. Lipstick On Your Collar—Connie Francis
34. Lavender Blue—Sammy Turner
35. The Happy Organ—Dave "Baby" Cortez

36. Hawaiian Wedding Song—Andy Williams
37. Waterloo—Stonewall Jackson
38. Red River Rock—Johnny & The Hurricanes
39. Teen Beat—Sandy Nelson
40. My Heart Is An Open Book—Carl Dobkins. Jr.
41. Since I Don't Have You—Skyliners
42. Gotta Travel On—Billy Grammer
43. Frankie—Connie Francis
44. Chilren's Marching Song—Cyril Stapleton/Mitch Miller
45. Lonely Street—Andy Williams
46. Donna—Ritchie Valens
47. Tiger—Fabian
48. Heartaches By The Numbers—Guy Mitchell
49. Sixteen Candles—Crests
50. Broken Hearted Melody—Sarah Vaughan

1960

*1. Theme From A Summer Place—Percy Faith
 2. It's Now Or Never—Elvis Presley
 3. Save The Last Dance For Me—Drifters
 4. The Twist—Chubby Checker
 5. Itsy Bitsy Teenie Bikini—Brian Hyland
 6. I'm Sorry—Brenda Lee
 7. Stuck On You—Elvis Presley
 8. He'll Have To Go—Jim Reeves
 9. Cathy's Clown—Everly Brothers
10. Running Bear—Johnny Preston
11. Walk, Don't Run—Ventures
12. Everybody's Somebody's Fool—Connie Francis
13. Handy Man—Jimmy Jones
14. My Heart Has A Mind Of Its Own—Connie Francis
15. Only The Lonely—Roy Orbison
16. Teen Angel—Mark Dinning
17. El Paso—Marty Robbins
18. Chain Gang—Sam Cooke
19. Kiddio—Brook Benton
20. Please Help Me, I'm Falling—Hank Locklin
21. Greenfields—Brothers Four
22. Night—Jackie Wilson
23. Good Timin'—Jimmy Jones

24. Baby (You Got What It Takes)—Brook Benton—Dinah Washington
25. Wild One—Bobby Rydell
26. Mr. Custer—Larry Verne
27. Sink The Bismarck—Johnny Horton
28. Sweet Nothin's—Brenda Lee
29. Puppy Love—Paul Anka
30. I Want To Be Wanted—Brenda Lee
31. Paper Roses—Anita Bryant
32. Because They're Young—Duane Eddy
33. Alley-Oop—Hollywood Argyles/Dante & Evergreens
34. Way Down Yonder In N.O.—Freddie Cannon
35. Why—Frankie Avalon
36. Burning Bridges—Jack Scott
37. Where Or When—Dion & Belmonts
38. Finger Poppin' Time—Hank Ballard & Midnighters
39. Volare—Bobby Rydell
40. Theme From The Apartment—Ferrante & Teicher
41. Devil Or Angel—Bobby Vee
42. You Talk Too Much—Jon Jones
43. Heartaches By The Number—Guy Mitchell
44. A Rockin' Good Way—Brook Benton & Dinah Washington
45. White Silver Sands—Bill Black's Combo
46. It's Time To Cry—Paul Anka
47. You Got What It Takes—Marv Johnson
48. What In The World's—Jack Scott
49. The Big Hurt—Toni Fisher
50. Harbor Lights—Platters

1961

  1. Exodus—Ferrante & Teicher (UA)
*2. Calcutta—Lawrence Welk—(Dot)
  3. Will You Love Me Tomorrow—Shirelles (Scepter)
  4. Tossin' & Turnin'—Bobby Lewis (Beltone)
  5. Wonderland By Night—Bert Kaempfert—(Decca)
  6. Are You Lonesome Tonight—Elvis Presley (RCA)
  7. Travelin' Man—Rickey Nelson (Imperial)
  8. Michael—Highwaymen (UA)
  9. Runaway—Del Shannon (Bigtop)
10. Last Date—Floyd Cramer—(RCA)

11. Blue Moon—Marcels (Colpix)
12. Boll-Weevil Song—Brook Benton (Mercury)
13. North To Alaska—Johnny Horton—(Columbia)
14. Pony Time—Chubby Checker—(Parkway)
15. 100 Lbs. Of Clay—Gene McDaniels (Liberty)
16. Mother-in-law—Ernie K-Doe (Minit)
17. Raindrops—Dee Clark (Veejay)
18. He Will Break Your Heart—Jerry Butler—(Vee Jay)
19. Quarter To Three—U.S. Bonds—(Legrand)
20. A Thousand Stars—Dathy Young (Indigo)
21. Running Scared—Roy Orbison (Monument)
22. Wooden Heat—Joe Dowell—(Smash)
23. Take Good Care Of My Baby—Bobby Vee (Liberty)
24. Wheels—Billy Vaughn (Dot)
25. Shop Around—Miracles (Tamla)
26. Last Night—Mar-Keys (Satellite)
27. Daddy's Home—Shep & Limelites (Hull)
28. Cryin'—Roy Orbison (Monument)
29. Where The Boys Are—C. Francis (MGM)
30. Apache—Jorgen Ingmann (Atco)
31. Don't Worry—Marty Robins (Columbia)
32. Surrender—Elvis Presley—(RCA)
33. I've Told Every Little Star—Linda Scott (Canadian American)
34. Mountain's High—Dick & Deedee (Liberty)
35. Hats Off To Larry—Del Shannon—(Big Top)
36. Moody River—Pat Boone—(Dot)
37. Stay—Maurice Williams—(Herald)
38. Calendar Girl—Neil Sedaka—(RCA)
39. But I Do—Clarence Henry—(Argo)
40. Dedicated To The One I Love—Shirelles (Scepter)
41. Poetry In Motion—Johnny Tillotson—(Cadence)
42. Yellow Bird—Lawrence Welk—(Dot)
43. Stand By Me—Ben E. King (Atco)
44. New Orleans—U.S. Bonds (Legrand)
45. You're Sixteen—Johnny Burnette—(Liberty)
46. Angel Baby—Rosie & The Originals (Decca)
47. Sailor—Lolita (Kapp)
48. Dum-Dum—Brenda Lee—(Decca)
49. I Like It Like That—Chris Kenner—(Instant)
50. Rubber Ball—Bobby Vee—(Liberty)

1962

1. Twist—Chubby Checker (Parkway)
2. Stranger On The Shore—Acker Bilk (Atco)
3. Peppermint Twist—Joey Dee & Starlighters (Roulette)
4. Mashed Potato Time—Deedee Sharp (Cameo)
5. Moon River—Henry Mancini (RCA)
*6. I Can't Stop Loving You—Ray Charles (ABC)
7. You'll Lose a Good Thing—Barbara Lynn (Jamie)
8. The Stripper—David Rose (MGM)
9. The Wanderer—Dion (Laurie)
*10. The Lion Sleeps Tonight—Tokens (RCA)
11. Johnny Angel—Shelly Fabares (Coplix)
12. The One Who Really Loves You—Mary Wells (Motown)
13. Ramblin' Rose—Nat "King" Cole (Capitol)
14. Hey Baby—Bruce Channel (Smash)
15. Locomotion—Little Eva (Dimension)
16. Duke of Earl—Gene Chandler (Vee Jay)
*17. Roses Are Red—Bobby Vinton (Epic)
18. Do You Love Me—Contours (Gordy)
19. Soldier Boy—Shirelles (Scepter)
20. Sherry—Four Seasons (Vee Jay)
21. Walk On By—Lerory Van Dyke (Mercury)
22. I Know—Barbara George (AFO)
23. It Keeps Right On A-Hurtin'—Johnny Tillotson (Cadence)
24. Midnight In Moscow—Kenny Ball (Kapp)
25. Let Me In—Sensations (Argo)
26. Monster Mash—Bobby Pickett (Garpax)
27. Palisades Park—Freddy Cannon (Swan)
*28. Can't Help Falling In Love—Elvis Presley (RCA)
29. Twist And Shout—Isley Bros. (Wand)
30. Twistin' The Night Away—Sam Cooke (RCA)
31. Surfin' Safari—Beach Boys (Capitol)
32. Breaking Up Is Hard To Do—Neil Sedaka (RCA)
33. Run To Him—Bobby Vee (Liberty)
34. Green Onions—Booker T. & MG's (Stax)
35. Wolverton Mountain—Claude King (Columbia)
36. Love Letters—Ketty Lester (Era)
37. Town Without Pity—Gene Pitney (Musico)

39. Please Mr. Postman—Marvelettes (Tamla)
40. Alley Cat—Bent Fabric (Atco)
41. Patches—Dickey Lee (Smash)
42. Good Luck Charm—Elvis Presley (RCA)
*43. Big Bad John—Jimmy Dean (Columbia)
44. Tuff—Ace Cannon (Hi)
45. Goodbye Cruel World—James Darren (Colpix)
46. Dear Lady Twist—Gary U.S. Bonds (Laurie)
47. Party Lights—Claudine Clark (Chancellor)
48. Sealed With A Kiss—Brian Hyland (ABC—Paramount)
49. She Cried—Jay & The Americans (UA)
50. Norman—Sue Thompson (Hickory)

1963

1. Limbo Rock—Chubby Checker (Parkway)
2. Go Away Little Girl—Steve Lawrence (Columbia)
3. End Of The World—Skeeter Davis (RCA)
4. Blue Velvet—Bobby Vinton (Epic)
5. Telstar—Tornadoes (London)
6. I Will Follow Him—Little Peggy March (RCA)
7. Rhythm Of The Rain—Cascades (Valiant)
8. Can't Get Used To Losing You—Andy Williams (Columbia)
9. Fingertips—Little Stevie Wonder (Tamla)
10. Return To Sender—Elvis Presley (RCA)
11. Up On The Roof—Drifters (Atlantic)
12. So Much In Love—Tymes (Parkway)
13. He's So Fine—Chiffons (Laurie)
*14. Hey Paula—Paul & Paula (Philips)
15. Big Girls Don't Cry—Four Seasons (Vee Jay)
16. Surfin' U.S.A.—Beach Boys (Capitol)
17. Walk Right In—Rooftop Singers (Vanguard)
18. Walk Like A Man—Four Seasons (Vee Jay)
19. If You Wanna Be Happy—Jimmp Soul (S.P.Q.R.)
20. Easier Said Than Done—Essex (Roulette)
21. My Boyfriend's Back—Angels (Smash)
22. Mockingbird—Inez Foxx (Symbol)
23. Our Day Will Come—Ruby & Romantics (Kapp)
24. Puff The Magic Dragon—Peter, Paul & Mary (WB)

25. Ruby Baby—Dion DiMuci (Columbia)
26. Surf City—Jan & Dean (Liberty)
27. I Love You Because—Al Martino (Capitol)
28. You're The Reason I'm Living—Bobby Darin (Capitol)
29. Sukiyaki—Kyu Sakamoto (Capitol)
30. It's My Party—Lesley Gore (Mercury)
31. The Night Has A Thousand Eyes—Bobby Vee (Liberty)
32. Blame It On the Bossa Nova—Edyie Gorme (Columbia)
33. Pipeline—Chantays (Dot)
34. Two Faces Have I—Lou Christie (Roulette)
35. You Can't Sit Down—Dovells (Parkway)
36. Surfer Girl—Beach Boys (Capitol)
37. Lonely Bull—Tijuana Brass (A&M)
38. Hello Stranger—Barbara Lewis (Atlantic)
*39. Blowing In The Wind—Peter, Paul & Mary (WB)
40. Wild Weekend—Rockin' Rebels (Swan)
41. If I Had A Hammer—Trini Lopez (Reprise)
42. Heat Wave—Martha & The Vandellas (Gordy)
43. Tell Him—Exciters (UA)
44. Be My Baby—Ronettes (Philles)
45. Wipe Out—Surfaris (Dot)
46. You Really Got A Hold On Me—Miracles (Tamla)
47. From A Jack To A King—Ned Miller (Fabor)
48. My Dad—Paul Petersen (Colpix)
49. Bobby's Girl—Marcie Blaine (Seville)
50. Candy Girl—Four Seasons (Vee Jay)

1964

*1. I Want To Hold Your Hand—Beatles (Capitol)
2. She Loves You—Beatles (Swan)
3. Hello Dolly—Louis Armstrong (Kapp)
*4. Oh, Pretty Woman—Roy Orbison (Monument)
5. I Get Around—Beach Boys (Capitol)
6. Louie, Louie—Kingsmen (Wand)
7. My Guy—Mary Wells (Motown)
8. Blue Velvet—Bobby Vinton (Epic)
9. Glad All Over—Dave Clark Five (Epic)
*10. Everybody Loves Somebody—Dean Martin (Reprise)
11. Dominique—Singing Nun (Philips)

12. There I've Said It Again—Bobby Vinton (Epic)
13. Love Me Do—Beatles (Capitol)
14. She's A Fool—Lesley Gore (Mercury)
15. Where Did Our Love Go—Supremes (Motown)
16. Java—Al Hirt (RCA)
17. People—Barbra Streisand (Columbia)
*18. A Hard Day's Night—Beatles (Capitol)
19. Since I Fell For You—Lenny Welch (Cadence)
20. Forget Him—Bobby Rydell (Cameo)
21. Under The Boardwalk—Drifters (Atlantic)
22. It's All Right—Impressions (ABC)
23. Love Me With All Of Your Heart—Ray Charles Singers (Command)
24. Chapel Of Love—Dixiecups (Red Bird)
25. Little Children—Billy J. Kramer & Dakotas (Imperial)
26. Bread And Butter—Newbeats (Hickory)
27. I'm Leaving It Up To You—Dale & Grace (Montel)
28. Dawn (Go Away)—Four Seasons (Philips)
*29. Rag Doll—Four Seasons (Philips)
30. Suspicion—Terry Stafford (Crusader)
31. Popsicles & Icicles—Murmaids (Chattahoochee)
32. Washington Square—Village Stompers (Epic)
33. A World Without Love—Peter & Gordon (Capitol)
34. Can I Get A Witness—Marvin Gaye (Tamla)
35. I Can't Stay Mad At You—Skeeter Davis—(RCA)
36. Wishin' And Hopin'—Dusty Springfield (Philips)
37. Please, Please Me—Beatles (Capitol)
38. You Don't Have To Be A Baby To Cry—Caravelles (Smash)
*39. Sugar Shack—Jimmy Gilmer (Dot)
40. Busted—Ray Charles (ABC)
41. Walkin' The Dog—Rufus Thomas (Stax)
42. You Don't Own Me—Lesley Gore (Mercury)
43. Hey Little Cobra—Rip Chords (Columbia)
44. Deep Purple—Nino Tempo & April Stevens (Atco)
45. Fools Rush In—Rick Nelson (Decca)
46. Don't Let The Rain Come Down—Serendipity Singers (Philips)
47. Out Of Limits—Marketts (WB)
48. Walk On By—Dionne Warwick (Scepter)
49. Nitty Gritty—Shirley Ellis (Congress)

50. Cry Baby—Garnett Mimms & Enchanters (UA)

1965

1. Back In My Arms Again—Supremes (Motown)
*2. Wooly Bully—Sam The Sham & The Pharos (MGM)
3. Mr. Lonely—Bobby Vinton (Epic)
4. I Can't Help Myself—Four Tops (Motown)
*5. Satisfaction—Rolling Stones (London)
*6. Downtown—Petula Clark (WB)
7. You've Lost That Lovin' Feeling—Righteous Bros. (Philles)
8. Come See About Me—Supremes (Motown)
9. The In Crowd—Ramsey Lewis (Cadet)
10. You Were On My Mind—We Five (A & M)
*11. Help—Beatles (Capitol)
12. Crying In The Chapel—Elvis Presley (RCA)
13. Love Potion #9—Searchers (Kapp)
*14. I Got You Babe—Sonny & Cher (Atco)
15. This Diamond Ring—Gary Lewis & Playboys (Liberty)
16. My Girl—Temptations (Gordy)
"17. King Of The Road—Roger Miller (Smash)
18. Hang On Sloopy—McCoys (Bang)
*19. I Feel Fine—Beatles (Capitol)
20. The Birds & The Bees—Jewel Akins (Era)
21. The Jerks—Larks (Money)
22. Can't You Hear My Heartbeat—Herman's Hermits (MGM)
23. Mrs. Brown You Have A Lovely Daughter—Herman's Hermits (MGM)
24. Stop In The Name Of Love—Supremes (Motown)
25. Eve of Destruction—Barry McGuire (Dunhill)
26. Mr. Tambourine Man—Byrds (Columbia)
27. What The World Needs Now Is Love—Jackie DeShannon (Liberty)
28. Shotgun—Jr. Walker & All Stars (Soul)
29. She's Not There—Zombies (Parrot)
30. Help Me Rhonda—Beach Boys (Capitol)
31. How Sweet It Is—Marvin Gaye (Tamla)
32. Unchained Melody—Righteous Bros. (Philles)
33. Ringo—Lorne Green (RCA)
34. Down In The Boonedocks—Billy Joe Royal (Columbia)

35. The Name Game—Shirley Ellis (Congress)
36. Ticket To Ride—Beatles (Capitol)
37. Going Out Of My Mind—Little Anthony & Imperials (DCP)
38. Like A Rolling Stone—Bob Dylan (Columbia)
39. I Know A Place—Petula Clark (WB)
40. Silhouettes—Herman's Hermits (MGM)
41. Red Roses For A Blue Lady—Bert Kaempfert (Decca)
42. I'll Never Find Another You—Seekers (Capitol)
43. Cara Mia—Jay & The Americans (UA)
44. Keep Searchin'—Del Shannon (Amy)
45. Count Me In—Gary Lewis & The Playboys (Liberty)
46. A Walk In The Black Forest—Horst Jankowski (Mercury)
47. Goldfinger—Shirley Bassey (UA)
48. I'm Telling You Now—Freddie & The Dreamers (Tower)
49. It Ain't Me Babe—Turtles (White Whale)
50. Jolly Green Giant—Kingsmen (Ward)

1966

*1. The Ballad Of The Green Berets—S/Sgt. Barry Sadler (RCA)
*1. California Dreamin'—Mamas & Papas (Dunhill)
*2. Sounds of Silence—Simon & Garfunkel (Columbia)
*3. Sunny—Bobby Hebb (Philips)
 4. Strangers In The Night—Frank Sinatra (Reprise)
 5. You Can't Hurry Love—Supremes (Motown)
 6. A Groovy Kind Of Love—Mindbenders—(Fontana)
 7. I Got You—James Brown—King
*8. Little Red Riding Hood—Sam The Sham & Pharaohs —MGM
 9. See You In September—Happenings—B. T. Puppy
10. Good Lovin'—Young Rascals—Atlantic
*11. We Can Work It Out—Beatles—(Capitol)
12. Up Tight—Stevie Wonder (Tamla)
13. You Don't Have To Say You Love Me—Dusty Springfield (Philips)
14. Kicks—Paul Revere & Raiders (Columbia)
*15. Lightnin' Strikes—Lou Christie (MGM)
*16. Cherish—Association (Valiant)

*17. Soul & Inspiration—Righteous Bros. (Verve)
*18. Hanky Panky—Tommy James & Shondells (Roulette)
*19. 96 Tears—? Question Mark & Mysterians (Cameo)
 20. Red Rubber Ball—Cyrkle (Columbia)
*21. Last Train To Clarksville—Monkees (Colgems)
 22. No Matter What Shape—T-Bones (Liberty)
 23. Cool Jerk—Capitols (Karen)
 24. Ain't Too Proud To Beg—Temptations (Gordy)
 25. Sunshine Superman—Donovan (Epic)
*26. These Boots Are Made For Walking—Nancy Sinatra (Reprise)
 27. Daydream—Lovin' Spoonful—Kama Sutra
*28. When A Man Loves A Woman—Percy Sledge (Atlantic)
 29. Over & Over—Dave Clark Five (Epic)
 30. A Taste Of Honey—Herb Alpert & Tijuana Brass (A&M)
*31. Monday Monday—Mamas & Papas (Dunhill)
 32. Paint It Black—Rolling Stones (London)
 33. Turn, Turn, Turn—Byrds (Columbia)
 34. Bus Stop—Hollies (Imperial)
 35. My Love—Petula Clark (Warner Bros.)
 36. Keep On Dancing—Gentrys (MGM)
 37. What Becomes Of The Broken Hearted—Jimmy Ruffin (Soul)
 38. 19th Nervous Breakdown—Rolling Stones—(London)
 39. Reach Out, I'll Be There—Four Tops (Motown)
*40. Summer In The City—Lovin' Spoonful (Kama Sutra)
 41. I Am A Rock—Simon & Garfunkel (Columbia)
 42. Let's Hang On—Four Seasons (Philips)
 43. Time Won't Let Me—Outsiders (Capitol)
*44. Paperback Writer—Beatles (Capitol)
 45. Barbara Ann—Beach Boys (Capitol)
 46. She's Just My Style—Gary Lewis & Playboys (Liberty)
 47. Bang Bang—Cher (Imperial)
 48. Crying Time—Ray Charles (ABC)
 49. Five O'Clock World—Vogues (Co & Ce)
 50. Somewhere My Love—Ray Conniff Singers (Columbia)

1967

*1. The Letter—Boxtops—Dell
*2. Light My Fire—Doors—Elektra

*3. Can't Take My Eyes Off You—Frankie Valli—Philips
*4. Ode to Billie Joe—Bobbie Gentry—Capitol
*5. To Sir With Love—Lulu—Epic
 6. Happy Together—Turtles—White Whale
*7. Windy—Association—Warner Bros.
*8. I'm A Believer—Monkees—Colgems
*9. Groovin—Young Rascals—Atlantic
*10. Respect—Aretha Franklin—Atlantic
*11. Georgy Girl—Seekers—Capitol
 12. I Think We're Alone Now—Tommy James & Shondells—Roulette
*13. Something Stupid—Frank & Nancy Sinatra—Reprise
*14. Soul Man—Sam & Dave—Stax
*15. Come Back When You Grow Up—Bobby Vee—Liberty
*16. Sweet Soul Music—Arthur Conley—Atco
*17. Ruby Tuesday—Rolling Stones—London
 18. King Of A Drag—Buckingham—USA
*19. A Little Bit Of Soul—Music Explosion—Laurie
 20. I Got Rhythm—Happenings—B. T. Puppy
 21. Reflections—Supremes—Motown
 22. Somebody To Love—Jefferson Airplane—RCA
 23. The Happening—Supremes—Motown
 24. She Rather Be With Me—Turtles—White Whale
 25. Come On Down To My Boat—Every Mother's Son—MGM
 26. I Was Made To Love Her—Stevie Wonder—Tamla
*27. Incense & Peppermints—Strawberry Alarm Clock—UNI
 28. Then You Can Tell My Goodbye—Casinos—Fraternity
 29. Apples, Peaches & Pumpkin Pie—Jay & Techniques—Smash
*30. A Little Bit Me, A Little Bit You—Monkees—Colgems
*31. The Rain, The Park & Other Things—Cowsills—MGM
 32. Mercy, Mercy, Mercy—Buckinghams—Columbia
*33. Never My Love—Association—Warner Bros.
 33. It Must Be Him—Vikki Carr—Liberty
*35. There's A Kind Of A Hush—Herman's Hermits—MGM
 36. We Ain't Got Nothing Yet—Blues Magoos—Mercury
 37. Dedicated To The One I Love—Mamas & Papas—Dunhill
 38. Don't You Care—Buckinghams—Columbia

39. This Is My Song—Petula Clark—Warner Bros.
40. Love Is Here & Now You're Gone—Supremes—Motown
41. Sock It To Me Baby—Mitch Ryder & Detroit Wheels—New Voice
42. Release Me—Englebert Humperdinck—Parrot
*43. All You Need Is Love—Beatles—Capital
44. Expressway To Your Heart—Soul Survivors—Crimson
*45. Penny Lane—Beatles—Capitol
46. Please Love Me Forever—Bobby Vinton—Epic
47. A Whiter Shade Of Pale—Procol Harum—Deram
48. Jimmy Mack—Martha Reeves & Vandellas—Gordy
*49. Baby I Love You—Aretha Franklin—Atlantic
*50. Snoopy Vs The Red Baron—Royal Guardsmen—Laurie

1968

*1. Hey Jude—Beatles (Apple)
*2. Love Is Blue—Paul Mauriat (Philips)
*3. Young Girl—Union Gap (Columbia)
*4. The Dock Of The Bay—Otis Redding (Volt)
*5. Mrs. Robinson—Simon & Garfunkel (Columbia)
*6. Honey—Bobby Goldsboro (United Artists)
*7. People Got To Be Free—Rascals (Atlantic)
*8. Green Tambourine—Lemon Pipers (Buddah)
*9. This Guy's In Love With You—Herb Alpert (A&M)
*10. Tighten Up—Archie Bell & Drells (Atlantic)
*11. Yummy, Yummy, Yummy—Ohio Express (Buddah)
*12. Harper Valley PTA—Jeannie C. Riley (Plantation)
*13. Judy In Disguise—John Fred & Playboys (Paula)
*14. Little Green Apples—O. C. Smith (Columbia)
*15. Hello I Love You—Doors (Elektra)
16. I've Gotta Get A Message To You—Bee Gees (Atco)
*17. A Beautiful Morning—Rascals (Atlantic)
*18. Cry Like A Baby—Box Tops (Mala)
19. The Ballad Of Bonnie & Clyde—Georgie Fame (Epic)
20. I Wish It Would Rain—Temptations (Gordy)
21. Lady Willpower—Gary Puckett & Union Gap (Columbia)
*22. Those Were The Days—Mary Hopkin (Apple)
23. Mony Mony—Tommy James & Shondells (Roulette)

*24. Simon Says—1910 Fruitgum Co. (Buddah)
*25. Bend Me Shape Me—American Breed (Acta)
  26. Jumpin Jack Flash—Rolling Stones (London)
*27. Lady Madonna—Beatles (Capitol)
*28. Sunshine Of Your Love—Cream (Atco)
  29. Stone Soul Picnic—5th Dimension (South City)
  30. Midnight Confessions—Grass Roots (Dunhill) ⎫
*30. Valleri—Monkees (Colgems) ⎬tie
                                            ⎭
  31. The Good The Bad And The Ugly—Hugo Montenegro (RCA)
  32. Fire—Arthur Brown (Track)
  33. MacArthur Park—Richard Harris (Dunhill)
  34. Turn Around, Look At Me—Vogues (Reprise)
  35. The Mighty Quinn—Manfred Mann (Mercury)
  36. Born To Be Wild—SteppenWolf (Dunhill)
  37. Light My Fire—Jose Feliciano (RCA)
  38. Grazin' In The Grass—Hugh Masekela (UNI)
  39. 1,2,3, Red Light—1910 Fruitgum Co. (Buddah)
  40. Slip Away—Clarence Carter (Atlantic)
  41. Over You—Gary Puckett & Union Gap (Columbia)
  42. Valley Of The Dolls—Dionne Warwick (Scepter)
  43. The Horse—Cliff Nobles & Co. (Phil L. A. of Soul)
  44. Girl Watchers—O'Kaysions (ABC)
  45. Angel Of The Morning—Merilee Rush (Bell)
  46. Reach Out Of The Darkness—Friend & Lover (Verve)
  47. Baby Now That I've Found You—Foundations (UNI)
  48. White Room—Cream (Atco)
  48. Goin' Out Of My Head/Can't Take My Eyes Off You —Lettermen (Capitol)
  49. Hurdy Gurdy Man—Donovan (Epic)
  50. The Unicorn—Irish Rovers (Decca)

BILLBOARD'S # 1 WEEKLY HITS

1950

1/7	RUDOLPH THE RED NOSED REINDEER, Gene Autry, Columbia
1/14	I CAN DREAM, CAN'T I? Andrew Sisters/A. Jenkins Ork., Decca
1/21	I CAN DREAM, CAN'T I? Andrew Sisters/A. Jenkins Ork.
1/28	I CAN DREAM, CAN'T I? Andrew Sisters/A. Jenkins Ork.
2/4	I CAN DREAM, CAN'T I? Andrew Sisters/A. Jenkins Ork.
2/11	RAG HOP, Ames Brothers, Coral
2/18	CHATTANOOGIE SHOE SHINE BOY, R. Foley, Decca
2/25	CHATTANOOGIE SHOE SHINE BOY, R. Foley
3/4	CHATTANOOGIE SHOE SHINE BOY, R. Foley
3/11	CHATTANOOGIE SHOE SHINE BOY, R. Foley
3/18	MUSIC! MUSIC! MUSIC!, T. Brewer, London
3/25	MUSIC! MUSIC! MUSIC!, T. Brewer
4/1	MUSIC! MUSIC! MUSIC!, T. Brewer
4/8	MUSIC! MUSIC! MUSIC!, T. Brewer
4/15	IF I KNEW YOU WERE COMING I'D'VE BAKED A CAKE, E. Barton, National
4/22	IF I KNEW YOU WERE COMING I'D'VE BAKED A CAKE, E. Barton
4/29	THIRD MAN THEME, A. Karas, London
5/6	THIRD MAN THEME, A. Karas
5/13	THIRD MAN THEME, A. Karas
5/20	THIRD MAN THEME, A. Karas
5/27	THIRD MAN THEME, A. Karas
6/3	THIRD MAN THEME, A. Karas
6/10	THIRD MAN THEME, A. Karas
6/17	THIRD MAN THEME, A. Karas
6/24	THIRD MAN THEME, A. Karas
7/1	THIRD MAN THEME, A. Karas
7/8	THIRD MAN THEME, A. Karas
7/15	MONA LISA, Nat King Cole & Trio, Capitol

7/22	MONA LISA, Nat King Cole & Trio
7/29	MONA LISA, Nat King Cole & Trio
8/5	MONA LISA, Nat King Cole & Trio
8/12	MONA LISA, Nat King Cole & Trio
8/19	GOODNIGHT IRENE, G. Jenkins/Weaver
8/26	GOODNIGHT IRENE, G. Jenkins/Weaver
9/2	GOODNIGHT IRENE, G. Jenkins/Weavers
9/9	GOODNIGHT IRENE, G. Jenkins/Weavers
9/16	GOODNIGHT IRENE, G. Jenkins/Weavers
9/23	GOODNIGHT IRENE, G. Jenkins/Weavers
9/30	GOODNIGHT IRENE, G. Jenkins/Weavers
10/7	GOODNIGHT IRENE, G. Jenkins/Weaver
10/14	GOODNIGHT IRENE, G. Jenkins/Weavers
10/21	GOODNIGHT IRENE, G. Jenkins/Weavers
10/28	GOODNIGHT IRENE, G. Jenkins/Weavers
11/4	GOODNIGHT IRENE, G. Jenkins/Weavers
11/11	GOODNIGHT IRENE, G. Jenkins/Weavers
11/18	HARBOR LIGHTS, S. Kaye, Columbia
11/25	HARBOR LIGHTS, S. Kaye, Columbia
12/2	THE THING, Phil Harris, Victor (RCA)
12/9	THE THING, Phil Harris
12/16	THE THING, Phil Harris
12/23	THE THING, Phil Harris
12/30	TENNESSEE WALTZ, Patti Page, Mercury

1951

1/6	TENNESSEE WALTZ, Patti Page, Mercury
1/13	TENNESSEE WALTZ, Patti Page
1/20	TENNESSEE WALTZ, Patti Page
1/27	TENNESSEE WALTZ, Patti Page
2/3	TENNESSEE WALTZ, Patti Page
2/10	TENNESSEE WALTZ, Patti Page
2/17	TENNESSEE WALTZ, Patti Page
2/24	TENNESSEE WALTZ, Patti Page
3/3	IF, Perry Como, Victor (RCA)
3/10	BE MY LOVE, Mario Lanza, Victor (RCA)
3/17	IF, Perry Como, Victor (RCA)
3/24	IF, Perry Como
3/31	IF, Perry Como

4/7   IF, Perry Como
4/14   IF, Perry Como
4/21   HOW HIGH THE MOON, L. Paul/M. Ford, Capitol
4/28   HOW HIGH THE MOON, L. Paul/M. Ford
5/12   HOW HIGH THE MOON, L. Paul/M. Ford
5/19   HOW HIGH THE MOON, L. Paul/M. Ford
5/26   HOW HIGH THE MOON, L. Paul/M. Ford
6/2   HOW HIGH THE MOON, L. Paul/M. Ford
6/9   HOW HIGH THE MOON, L. Paul/M. Ford
6/16   HOW HIGH THE MOON, L. Paul/M. Ford
6/23   TOO YOUNG, Nat (King) Cole, Capitol
6/30   TOO YOUNG, Nat (King) Cole
7/7   TOO YOUNG, Nat (King) Cole, Capitol
7/14   TOO YOUNG, Nat (King) Cole
7/21   TOO YOUNG, Nat (King) Cole
7/28   COME ON-A MY HOUSE, R. Clooney, Columbia
8/4   COME ON-A MY HOUSE, R. Clooney
8/11   COME ON-A MY HOUSE, R. Clooney
8/18   COME ON-A MY HOUSE, R. Clooney
8/25   COME ON-A MY HOUSE, R. Clooney
9/1   COME ON-A MY HOUSE, R. Clooney
9/8   BECAUSE OF YOU, Tony Bennett, Columbia
9/15   BECAUSE OF YOU, Tony Bennett
9/22   BECAUSE OF YOU, Tony Bennett
9/29   BECAUSE OF YOU, Tony Bennett
10/6   BECAUSE OF YOU, Tony Bennett
10/13 BECAUSE OF YOU, Tony Bennett
10/20 BECAUSE OF YOU, Tony Bennett
10/27 BECAUSE OF YOU, Tony Bennett
11/3   COLD, COLD HEART, Tony Bennett/P. Faith Orch., Columbia
11/10 COLD, COLD HEART, Tony Bennett/P. Faith Orch.
11/70 COLD, COLD HEART, Tony Bennett/P. Faith Orch.
11/24 COLD, COLD HEART, Tony Bennett/P. Faith Orch.
11/1   COLD, COLD HEART, Tony Bennett/P. Faith Orch.
11/8   COLD, COLD HEART, Tony Bennett/P. Faith Orch.
12/15 SIN, E. Howard, Mercury
12/22 SIN, E. Howard
12/29 CRY, Johnny Ray, OKeh

1952

1/5	CRY, Johnny Ray, OKeh
1/12	CRY, Johnny Ray
1/19	CRY, Johnny Ray
1/26	CRY, Johnny Ray
2/2	CRY, Johnny Ray
2/9	CRY, Johnny Ray
2/16	CRY, Johnny Ray
2/23	CRY, Johnny Ray
3/1	CRY, Johnny Ray
3/8	CRY, Johnny Ray
3/15	WHEEL OF FORTUNE, Kay Starr, Capitol
3/22	WHEEL OF FORTUNE, Kay Starr
3/29	WHEEL OF FORTUNE, Kay Starr
4/5	WHEEL OF FORTUNE, Kay Starr
4/12	WHEEL OF FORTUNE, Kay Starr
4/19	WHEEL OF FORTUNE, Kay Starr
4/26	WHEEL OF FORTUNE, Kay Starr
5/3	WHEEL OF FORTUNE, Kay Starr
5/10	WHEEL OF FORTUNE, Kay Starr
5/17	BLUE TANGO, L. Anderson, Decca
5/24	BLUE TANGO, L. Anderson
5/31	BLUE TANGO, L. Anderson
6/7	BLUE TANGO, L. Anderson
6/14	BLUE TANGO, L. Anderson
6/21	HERE IN MY HEART, Al Martino, BBS
6/28	HERE IN MY HEART, Al Martino
7/5	DELICADO, P. Faith/S. Freemen, Columbia
7/12	AUF WIEDERSHEH'N SWEETHEART, V. Lynn, London
7/19	AUF WIEDERSEH'N SWEETHEART, V. Lynn
7/26	AUF WIEDERSEH'N SWEETHEART, V. Lynn
8/2	AUF WIEDERSEH'N SWEETHEART, V. Lynn
8/9	AUF WIEDERSEH'N SWEETHEART, V. Lynn
8/16	AUF WIEDERSEH'N SWEETHEART, V. Lynn
8/23	AUF WIEDERSEH'N SWEETHEART, V. Lynn
8/30	AUF WIEDERSEH'N SWEETHEART, V. Lynn
9/6	AUF WIEDERSEH'N SWEETHEART, V. Lynn
9/13	YOU BELONG TO ME, Jo Stafford, Columbia
9/20	YOU BELONG TO ME, Jo Stafford
9/27	YOU BELONG TO ME, Jo Stafford

10/4   YOU BELONG TO ME, Jo Stafford
10/11   YOU BELONG TO ME, Jo Stafford
10/18   I WENT TO YOUR WEDDING, Patti Page, Mercury
10/25   I WENT TO YOUR WEDDING, Patti Page
11/1   I WENT TO YOUR WEDDING, Patti Page
11/8   I WENT TO YOUR WEDDING, Patti Page
11/15   I WENT TO YOUR WEDDING, Patti Page
11/22   IT'S IN THE BOOK, PARTS 1 & 2, J. Standley, Capitol
11/29   WHY DON'T YOU BELIEVE ME, Joni James, MGM
12/6   WHY DON'T YOU BELIEVE ME, Joni James
12/13   WHY DON'T YOU BELIEVE ME, Joni James
12/20   WHO DON'T YOU BELIEVE ME, Joni James
12/27   I SAW MOMMY KISSING SANTA CLAUS, J. Boyd, Columbia

1953

1/3   I SAW MOMMY KISSING SANTA CLAUS, J. Boyd, Columbia
1/10   DON'T LET THE STARS GET IN YOUR EYES, Perry Como, Victor
1/17   DON'T LET THE STARS GET IN YOUR EYES, Perry Como
1/24   DON'T LET THE STARS GET IN YOUR EYES, Perry Como
1/31   DON'T LET THE STARS GET IN YOUR EYES, Perry Como
2/7   DON'T LET THE STARS GET IN YOUR EYES, Perry Como
2/14   TILL I WALTZ AGAIN WITH YOU, T. Brewer, Coral
2/21   TILL I WALTZ AGAIN WITH YOU, T. Brewer
2/28   TILL I WALTZ AGAIN WITH YOU, T. Brewer
3/7   TILL I WALTZ AGAIN WITH YOU, T. Brewer
3/14   TILL I WALTZ AGAIN WITH YOU, T. Brewer
3/21   DOGGIE IN THE WINDOW, Patti Page, Mercury
3/28   DOGGIE IN THE WINDOW, Patti Page

4/4   DOGGIE IN THE WINDOW, Patti Page
4/11   DOGGIE IN THE WINDOW, Patti Page
4/18   DOGGIE IN THE WINDOW, Patti Page
4/25   DOGGIE IN THE WINDOW, Patti Page
5/2   DOGGIE IN THE WINDOW, Patti Page
5/9   DOGGIE IN THE WINDOW, Patti Page
5/16   SONG FROM MOULIN ROUGE, P. Faith/F. Sanders, Columbia
5/23   SONG FROM MOULIN ROUGE, P. Faith/F. Sanders
5/30   SONG FROM MOULIN ROUGE, P. Faith/F. Sanders
6/6   SONG FROM MOULIN ROUGE, P. Faith/F. Sanders
6/13   SONG FROM MOULIN ROUGE, P. Faith/F. Sanders
6/20   SONG FROM MOULIN ROUGE, P. Faith/F. Sanders
6/27   SONG FROM MOULIN ROUGE, P. Faith/F Sanders
7/4   SONG FROM MOULIN ROUGE, P. Faith, Columbia
7/11   SONG FROM MOULIN ROUGE, P. Faith
7/18   SONG FROM MOULIN ROUGE, P. Faith
7/25   I'M WALKING BEHIND YOU, Eddie Fisher, Victor
8/1   I'M WALKING BEHIND YOU, Eddie Fisher
8/8   VAYA CON DIOS, L. Paul/M. Ford, Capitol
8/15   VAYA CON DIOS, L. Paul/M. Ford
8/22   VAYA CON DIOS, L. Paul/M. Ford
8/29   VAYA CON DIOS, L. Paul/M. Ford
9/5   VAYA CON DIOS, L. Paul/M. Ford
9/12   VAYA CON DIOS, L. Paul/M. Ford
9/19   VAYA CON DIOS, L. Paul/M. Ford
9/26   VAYA CON DIOS, L. Paul/M. Ford
10/3   VAYA CON DIOS, L. Paul/M. Ford
10/10   ST. GEORGE AND THE DRAGONET, S. Freberg, Capitol
10/17   ST. GEORGE AND THE DRAGONET, S. Freberg
10/24   ST. GEORGE AND THE DRAGONET, S. Freberg
10 31   ST. GEORGE AND THE DRAGONET, S. Freberg

11/7	VAYA CON DIOS, L. Paul/M. Ford, Capitol
11/14	VAYA CON DIOS, L. Paul/M. Ford
11/21	RAGS TO RICHES, Tony Bennett, Columbia
11/28	RAGS TO RICHES, Tony Bennett
12/5	RAGS TO RICHES, Tony Bennett
12/12	RAGS TO RICHES, Tony Bennett
12/19	RAGS TO RICHES, Tony Bennett
12/26	RAGS TO RICHES, Tony Bennett

1954

1/2	OH MY PAPA, Eddie Fisher, Victor
1/9	OH MY PAPA, Eddie Fisher
1/16	OH MY PAPA, Eddie Fisher
1/23	OH MY PAPA, Eddie Fisher
1/30	OH MY PAPA, Eddie Fisher
2/6	OH MY PAPA, Eddie Fisher
2/13	OH MY PAPA, Eddie Fisher
2/20	OH MY PAPA, Eddie Fisher
2/27	SECRET LOVE, Doris Day, Columbia
3/6	SECRET LOVE, Doris Day
3/13	MAKE LOVE TO ME, J. Stafford, Columbia
3/20	SECRET LOVE, Doris Day, Columbia
3/27	MAKE LOVE TO ME, J. Stafford, Columbia
4/3	MAKE LOVE TO ME, J. Stafford
4/10	WANTED, Perry Como, Victor
4/17	WANTED, Perry Como
4/24	WANTED, Perry Como
5/1	WANTED, Perry Como
5/8	WANTED, Perry Como
5/15	WANTED, Perry Como
5/22	WANTED, Perry Como
5/29	WANTED, Perry Como
6/5	LITTLE THINGS MEAN A LOT, K. Kallen, Decca
6/12	LITTLE THINGS MEAN A LOT, K. Kallen
6/19	LITTLE THINGS MEAN A LOT, K. Kallen
6/26	LITTLE THINGS MEAN A LOT, K. Kallen
7/3	LITTLE THINGS MEAN A LOT, K. Kallen
7/10	LITTLE THINGS MEAN A LOT, K. Kallen
7/17	LITTLE THINGS MEAN A LOT, K. Kallen

7/24   LITTLE THINGS MEAN A LOT, K. Kallen
7/31   LITTLE THINGS MEAN A LOT, K. Kallen

8/7   SH-BOOM, Crew Cuts, Mercury
8/14   SH-BOOM, Crew Cuts
8/21   SH-BOOM, Crew Cuts
8/28   SH-BOOM, Crew Cuts
9/4   SH-BOOM, Crew Cuts
9/11   SH-BOOM, Crew Cuts
9/18   SH-BOOM, Crew Cuts
9/25   HEY THERE, R. Clooney, Columbia
10/2   HEY THERE, R. Clooney
10/9   HEY THERE, R. Clooney
10/16   HEY THERE, R. Clooney
10/23   HEY THERE, R. Clooney
10/30   HEY THERE, R. Clooney
11/6   THIS OLE HOUSE, R. Clooney, Columbia
11/13   I NEED YOU NOW, Eddie Fisher, Victor
11/20   I NEED YOU NOW, Eddie Fisher
11/27   I NEED YOU NOW, Eddie Fisher
12/4   MR. SANDMAN, Chordettes, Cadence
12/11   MR. SANDMAN, Chordettes
12/18   MR. SANDMAN, Chordettes
12/25   MR. SANDMAN, Chordettes

1955

1/1   MR. SANDMAN, Chordettes, Cadence
1/8   MR. SANDMAN, Chordettes
1/15   MR. SANDMAN, Chordettes
1/22   LET ME GO LOVER, J. Weber, Columbia
1/29   LET ME GO LOVER, J. Weber
2/5   HEARTS OF STONE, Fontane Sisters, Dot
2/12   SINCERELY, McGuire Sisters, Coral
2/19   SINCERELY, McGuire Sisters
2/26   SINCERELY, McGuire Sisters
3/5   SINCERELY, McGuire Sisters
3/12   SINCERELY, McGuire Sisters
3/19   SINCERELY, McGuire Sisters
3/26   BALLAD OF DAVEY CROCKETT, B. Hayes,
        Cadence

4/2   BALLAD OF DAVY CROCKETT, B. Hayes
4/9   BALLAD OF DAVY CROCKETT, B. Hayes
4/16   BALLAD OF DAVY CROCKETT, B. Hayes
4/23   BALLAD OF DAVY CROCKETT, B. Hayes
4/30   CHERRY PINK & APPLE BLOSSOM WHITE, P. Prado, Victor
5/7   CHERRY PINK & APPLE BLOSSOM WHITE, P. Prado
5/14   CHERRY PINK & APPLE BLOSSOM WHITE, P. Prado
5/21   CHERRY PINK & APPLE BLOSSOM WHITE, P. Prado
5/28   CHERRY PINK & APPLE BLOSSOM WHITE, P. Prado
6/4   CHERRY PINK & APPLE BLOSSOM WHITE, P. Prado
6/11   CHERRY PINK & APPLE BLOSSOM WHITE, P. Prado
6/18   CHERRY PINK & APPLE BLOSSOM WHITE, P. Prado
6/25   CHERRY PINK & APPLE BLOSSOM WHITE, P. Prado
7/2   CHERRY PINK & APPLE BLOSSOM WHITE, P. Prado, Victor
7/9   ROCK AROUND THE CLOCK, B. Haley, Decca
7/16   ROCK AROUND THE CLOCK, B. Haley
7/23   ROCK AROUND THE CLOCK, B. Haley
7/30   ROCK AROUND THE CLOCK, B. Haley
8/6   ROCK AROUND THE CLOCK, B. Haley
8/13   ROCK AROUND THE CLOCK, B. Haley
8/20   ROCK AROUND THE CLOCK, B. Haley
8/27   ROCK AROUND THE CLOCK, B. Haley
9/3   YELLOW ROSE OF TEXAS, M. Miller, Columbia
9/10   YELLOW ROSE OF TEXAS, M. Miller
9/17   YELLOW ROSE OF TEXAS, M. Miller
9/24   YELLOW ROSE OF TEXAS, M. Miller
10/1   YELLOW ROSE OF TEXAS, M. Miller
10/8   LOVE IS A MANY-SPLENDORED THING, Four Aces, Decca

10/15   YELLOW ROSE OF TEXAS, M. Miller, Columbia

10/22 LOVE IS A MANY-SPLENDORED THING, Four Aces, Decca
10/29 AUTUMN LEAVES, R. Williams, Kapp
11/5   AUTUMN LEAVES, R. Williams
11/12 AUTUMN LEAVES, R. Williams
11/19 AUTUMN LEAVES, R. Williams
11/26 SIXTEEN TONS, Tennessee Ernie, Capitol
12/3   SIXTEEN TONS, Tennessee Ernie
12/10 SIXTEEN TONS, Tennessee Ernie
12/17 SIXTEEN TONS, Tennessee Ernie
12/24 SIXTEEN TONS, Tennessee Ernie
12/31 SIXTEEN TONS, Tennessee Ernie

1956

1/7   SIXTEEN TONS, Tennessee Ernie Ford, Capitol
1/14   MEMORIES ARE MADE OF THIS, Dean Martin, Capitol
1/21   MEMORIES ARE MADE OF THIS, Dean Martin
1/28   MEMORIES ARE MADE OF THIS, Dean Martin
2/4   MEMORIES ARE MADE OF THIS, Dean Martin
2/11   MEMORIES ARE MADE OF THIS, Dean Martin
2/18   ROCK AND ROLL WALTZ, Kay Starr, RCA Victor
2/25   LISBON ANTIGUA, Nelson Riddle, Capitol
3/3   LISBON ANTIGUA, Nelson Riddle
3/10   LISBON ANTIGUA, Nelson Riddle
3/17   LISBON ANTIGUA, Nelson Riddle
3/24   POOR PEOPLE OF PARIS, Les Baxter, Capitol
3/31   POOR PEOPLE OF PARIS, Les Baxter
4/7   POOR PEOPLE OF PARIS, Les Baxter
4/14   POOR PEOPLE OF PARIS, Les Baxter
4/21   HEARTBREAK HOTEL, Elvis Presley, RCA Victor /I WAS THE ONE
4/28   HEARTBREAK HOTEL, Elvis Presley, RCA Victor /I WAS THE ONE
5/5   HEARTBREAK HOTEL, Elvis Presley, RCA Victor
5/12   HEARTBREAK HOTEL, Elvis Presley
5/19   HEARTBREAK HOTEL, Elvis Presley
5/26   HEARTBREAK HOTEL, Elvis Presley
6/2   HEARTBREAK HOTEL, Elvis Presley

6/9 HEARTBREAK HOTEL, Elvis Presley
6/16 WAYWARD WIND, Gogi Grant, Era
6/23 WAYWARD WIND, Gogi Grant
6/30 WAYWARD WIND, Gogi Grant
7/7 WAYWARD WIND, Gogi Grant
7/14 WAYWARD WIND, Gogi Grant
7/21 WAYWARD WIND, Gogi Grant
7/28 I WANT YOU, I NEED YOU, I LOVE YOU, Elvis
      Presley, RCA Victor
      /MY BABY LEFT ME
8/4 MY PRAYER, Platters, Mercury
      /HEAVEN ON EARTH
8/11 MY PRAYER, Platters, Mercury
      /HEAVEN ON EARTH
8/18 HOUND DOG, Elvis Presley, RCA Victor
      /DON'T BE CRUEL
8/25 HOUND DOG, Elvis Presley,
      /DON'T BE CRUEL
9/1 HOUND DOG, Elvis Presley
      /DON'T BE CRUEL
9/8 HOUND DOG, Elvis Presley
      /DON'T BE CRUEL
9/15 HOUND DOG, Elvis Presley
      /DON'T BE CRUEL
9/22 HOUND DOG, Elvis Presley
9/29 DON'T BE CRUEL, Elvis Presley
      /HOUND DOG
10/6 DON'T BE CRUEL, Elvis Presley
      /HOUND DOG
10/13 DON'T BE CRUEL, Elvis Presley
      /HOUND DOG
10/20 DON'T BE CRUEL, Elvis Presley
      /HOUND DOG
10/27 DON'T BE CRUEL, Elvis Presley
      /HOUND DOG
11/3 LOVE ME TENDER, Elvis Presley, RCA Victor
11/10 LOVE ME TENDER, Elvis Presley
      /ANY WAY YOU WANT ME
11/17 LOVE ME TENDER, Elvis Presley,
      /ANY WAY YOU WANT ME
12/1 LOVE ME TENDER, Elvis Presley

12/4   LOVE ME TENDER, Elvis Presley
12/8   SINGING THE BLUES, Guy Mitchell, Columbia
12/15   SINGING THE BLUES, Guy Mitchell
12/22   SINGING THE BLUES, Guy Mitchell
12/29   SINGING THE BLUES, Guy Mitchell

1957

1/5   SINGING THE BLUES, Guy Mitchell, Columbia
1/12   SINGING THE BLUES, Guy Mitchell
1/19   SINGING THE BLUES, Guy Mitchell
1/26   SINGING THE BLUES, Guy Mitchell
2/2   SINGING THE BLUES, Guy Mitchell
2/9   TOO MUCH, Elvis Presley, RCA Victor
        /PLAYING FOR KEEPS
2/16   TOO MUCH, Elvis Presley
2/23   TOO MUCH, Elvis Presley
3/2   YOUNG LOVE, Tab Hunter, Dot
3/9   YOUNG LOVE, Tab Hunter
3/16   YOUNG LOVE, Tab Hunter
3/23   YOUNG LOVE, Tab Hunter
3/30   PARTY DOLL, Buddy Knox, Roulette
4/6   ROUND AND ROUND, Perry Como, RCA Victor
4/13   ALL SHOOK UP, Elvis Presley, RCA Victor
4/20   ALL SHOOK UP, Elvis Presley
4/27   ALL SHOOK UP, Elvis Presley
4/29   ALL SHOOK UP, Elvis Presley
5/6   ALL SHOOK UP, Elvis Presley
5/13   ALL SHOOK UP, Elvis Presley
5/20   ALL SHOOK UP, Elvis Presley
5/27   ALL SHOOK UP, Elvis Presley
6/3   LOVE LETTERS IN THE SAND, Pat Boone, Dot
        /BERNARDINE
6/10   LOVE LETTERS IN THE SAND, Pat Boone
        /BERNARDINE
6/17   LOVE LETTERS IN THE SAND, Pat Boone
6/24   LOVE LETTERS IN THE SAND, Pat Boone
        /BERNARDINE
7/1   LOVE LETTERS IN THE SAND, Pat Boone
        /BERNARDINE

7/8 TEDDY BEAR, Elvis Presley, RCA Victor
     /LOVING YOU
7/15 TEDDY BEAR, Elvis Presley
     /LOVING YOU
7/22 TEDDY BEAR, Elvis Presley
     /LOVING YOU
7/29 TEDDY BEAR, Elvis Presley
     /LOVING YOU
8/5 TEDDY BEAR, Elvis Presley
     /LOVING YOU
8/12 TEDDY BEAR, Elvis Presley
     /LOVING YOU
8/19 TEDDY BEAR, Elvis Presley
     /LOVING YOU
9/2 TAMMY, Debbie Reynolds
9/2 TAMMY, Debbie Reynolds, Coral
9/9 DIANA, Paul Anka, ABC-Paramount
9/16 TAMMY, Debbie Reynolds, Coral
9/23 THAT'LL BE THE DAY, Crickets, Brunswick
9/30 HONEYCOMB, Jimmy Rodgers, Roulette
10/7 HONEYCOMB, Jimmy Rodgers
10/14 WAKE UP LITTLE SUSIE, Everly Bros., Cadence
10/21 JAILHOUSE ROCK, Elvis Presley, RCA Victor
     /TREAT ME NICE
10/28 JAILHOUSE ROCK, Elvis Presley
     /TREAT ME NICE
11/4 JAILHOUSE ROCK, Elvis Presley
     /TREAT ME NICE
11/11 JAILHOUSE ROCK, Elvis Presley
     /TREAT ME NICE
11/18 JAILHOUSE ROCK, Elvis Presley
     /TREAT ME NICE
11/25 JAILHOUSE ROCK, Elvis Presley
     /TREAT ME NICE
12/2 YOU SEND ME, Sam Cooke, Keen
     /SUMMERTIME
12/9 YOU SEND ME, Sam Cooke
     /SUMMERTIME
12/16 JAILHOUSE ROCK, Elvis Presley, RCA Victor
     /TREAT ME NICE
12/23 APRIL LOVE, Pat Boone, Dot

/WHEN THE SWALLOWS COME BACK TO CAPISTRANO

12/30   APRIL LOVE, Pat Boone, Dot

1958

1/6   AT THE HOP, Danny & The Juniors, ABC-Paramount

1/13   AT THE HOP, Danny & The Juniors

1/20   AT THE HOP, Danny & The Juniors

1/27   AT THE HOP, Danny & The Juniors

2/3   AT THE HOP, Danny & The Juniors

2/10   DON'T, Elvis Presley, RCA Victor
/I BEG OF YOU

2/17   DON'T, Elvis Presley
/I BEG OF YOU

2/24   DON'T, Elvis Presley
/I BEG OF YOU

3/3   DON'T, Elvis Presley
/I BEG OF YOU

3/10   DON'T, Elvis Presley
/I BEG OF YOU

3/17   TEQUILA, The Champs, Challenge

3/24   TEQUILA, The Champs

3/31   TEQUILA, The Champs

4/7   TEQUILA, The Champs

4/14   TEQUILA, The Champs

4/21   TWILIGHT TIME, Platters, Mercury

4/28   WITCH DOCTOR, David Seville, Liberty

5/5   WITCH DOCTOR, David Seville

5/12   ALL I HAVE TO DO IS DREAM, Everly Bros. Cadence
/CLAUDETTE

5/19   ALL I HAVE TO DO IS DREAM, Everly Bros.
/CLAUDETTE

5/26   ALL I HAVE TO DO IS DREAM, Everly Bros.
/CLAUDETTE

6/2   ALL I HAVE TO DO IS DREAM, Everly Bros.
/CLAUDETTE

6/9   PURPLE PEOPLE EATER, Sheb Wooley, MGM

6/16 PURPLE PEOPLE EATER, Sheb Wooley
6/23 PURPLE PEOPLE EATER, Sheb Wooley
6/30 PURPLE PEOPLE EATER, Sheb Wooley
7/7   PURPLE PEOPLE EATER, Sheb Wooley
7/14 PURPLE PEOPLE EATER, Sheb Wooley
7/21 HARD HEADED WOMAN, Elvis Presley, RCA
      Victor
      /DON'T ASK ME WHY
7/28 HARD HEADED WOMAN, Elvis Presley
      /DON'T ASK ME WHY
8/4   POOR LITTLE FOOL, Ricky Nelson, Imperial
8/11 POOR LTTLE FOOL, Ricky Nelson
8/18 VOLARE (NEL BLU DIPINTO DI BLU), Domen-
      ico Modugno, Decca
8/25 LITTLE STAR, Elegants, Apt
9/1   VOLARE (NEL BLU DIPINTO DI BLU), Domen-
      ico Modugno
9/8   VOLARE (NEL BLU DIPINTO DI BLU), Domen-
      ico Modugno
9/15 VOLARE (NEL BLU DIPINTO DI BLUE), Do-
      menico Modugno
9/22 VOLARE (NEL BLU DIPINTO DI BLU), Domen-
      ico Modugno
9/29 IT'S ALL IN THE GAME, Tommy Edwards, MGM
10/6 IT'S ALL IN THE GAME, Tommy Edwards
10/13 IT'S ALL IN THE GAME, Tommy Edwards
10/20 IT'S ALL IN THE GAME, Tommy Edwards
10/27 IT'S ALL IN THE GAME, Tommy Edwards
11/3 IT'S ALL IN THE GAME, Tommy Edwards
11/10 IT'S ONLY MAKE BELIEVE, Conway Twitty,
      MGM
11/17 TOM DOOLEY, Kingston Trio, Capitol
11/24 TOM DOOLEY, Kingston Trio, Capitol
12/1 TO KNOW HIM IS TO LOVE HIM, Teddy Bears,
      Dore
12/8 TO KNOW HIM IS TO LOVE HIM, Teddy Bears
12/15 TO KNOW HIM IS TO LOVE HIM, Teddy Bears
12/22 THE CHIPMUNK SONG, David Seville & The
      Chipmunks, Liberty
12/29 THE CHIPMUNK SONG, David Seville & The
      Chipmunks

1959

1/5	THE CHIPMUNK SONG, David Seville & Chipmunks, Liberty
1/12	THE CHIPMUNK SONG, David Seville & Chipmunks
1/19	SMOKE GETS IN YOUR EYES, Platters, Mercury
1/26	SMOKE GETS IN YOUR EYES, Platters
2/2	SMOKE GETS IN YOUR EYES, Platters
2/9	STAGGER LEE, Lloyd Price, ABC-Paramount
2/16	STAGGER LEE, Lloyd Price
2/23	STAGGER LEE, Lloyd Price
3/2	STAGGER LEE, Lloyd Price
3/9	VENUS, Frankie Avalon, Chancellor
3/16	VENUS, Frankie Avalon
3/23	VENUS, Frankie Avalon
3/30	VENUS, Frankie Avalon
4/6	VENUS, Frankie Avalon
4/13	COME SOFTLY TO ME, Fleetwoods, Dolphin
4/20	COME SOFTLY TO ME, Fleetwoods
4/27	COME SOFTLY TO ME, Fleetwoods
5/4	COME SOFTLY TO ME, Fleetwoods
5/11	THE HAPPY ORGAN, Dave (Baby) Cortez, Clock
5/18	KANSAS CITY, Wilbert Harrison, Fury
5/25	KANSAS CITY, Wilbert Harrison
6/1	THE BATTLE OF NEW ORLEANS, Johnny Horton, Columbia
6/8	THE BATTLE OF NEW ORLEANS, Johnny Horton
6/15	THE BATTLE OF NEW ORLEANS, Johnny Horton
6/22	THE BATTLE OF NEW ORLEANS, Johnny Horton
6/29	THE BATTLE OF NEW ORLEANS, Johnny Horton
7/6	THE BATTLE OF NEW ORLEANS, Johnny Horton, Columbia
7/13	LONELY BOY, Paul Anka, ABC-Paramount
7/20	LONELY BOY, Paul Anka
7/27	LONELY BOY, Paul Anka
8/3	LONELY BOY, Paul Anka

8/10   A BIG HUNK O' LOVE, Elvis Presley, RCA Victor
8/17   A BIG HUNK O' LOVE, Elvis Presley
8/24   THE THREE BELLS, Browns, RCA Victor
8/31   THE THREE BELLS, Browns
9/7   THE THREE BELLS, Browns
9/14   THE THREE BELLS, Browns
9/21   SLEEP WALK, Santo & Johnny, Canadian-American
9/28   SLEEP WALK, Santo & Johnny
10/5   MACK THE KNIFE, Bobby Darin, Atco
10/12   MACK THE KNIFE, Bobby Darin
10/19   MACK THE KNIFE, Bobby Darin
10/26   MACK THE KNIFE, Bobby Darin
11/2   MACK THE KNIFE, Bobby Darin
11/9   MACK THE KNIFE, Bobby Darin
11/16   MR. BLUE, Fleetwoods, Dolton
11/23   MACK THE KNIFE, Bobby Darin, Atco
11/30   MACK THE KNIFE, Bobby Darin
12/7   MACK THE KNIFE, Bobby Darin
12/14   HEARTACHES BY THE NUMBER, Guy Mitchell,
        Columbia
12/21   HEARTACHES BY THE NUMBER, Guy Mitchell,
        Columbia
12/28   WHY, Frankie Avalon, Chancellor

1960

1/4   EL PASO, Marty Robbins, Columbia
1/11   EL PASO, Marty Robbins
1/18   RUNNING BEAR, Johnny Preston, Mercury
1/25   RUNNING BEAR, Johnny Preston
2/1   RUNNING BEAR, Johnny Preston
2/8   TEEN ANGEL, Mark Dinning, MGM
2/15   TEEN ANGEL, Mark Dinning
2/22   THEME FROM A SUMMER PLACE, Percy Faith,
        Columbia
2/29   THEME FROM A SUMMER PLACE, Percy Faith
3/7   THEME FROM A SUMMER PLACE, Percy Faith
3/14   THEME FROM A SUMMER PLACE, Percy Faith
3/21   THEME FROM A SUMMER PLACE, Percy Faith
3/28   THEME FROM A SUMMER PLACE, Percy Faith
4/4   THEME FROM A SUMMER PLACE, Percy Faith

4/11	THEME FROM A SUMMER PLACE, Percy Faith
4/18	THEME FROM A SUMMER PLACE, Percy Faith
4/25	STUCK ON YOU, Elvis Presley, RCA Victor
5/2	STUCK ON YOU, Elvis Presley
5/9	STUCK ON YOU, Elvis Presley
5/16	STUCK ON YOU, Elvis Presley
5/23	CATHY'S CLOWN, Everly Brothers, Warner Bros.
5/30	CATHY'S CLOWN, Everly Brothers
6/6	CATHY'S CLOWN, Everly Brothers
6/13	CATHY'S CLOWN, Everly Brothers
6/20	CATHY'S CLOWN, Everly Brothers
6/27	EVERYBODY'S SOMEBODY'S FOOL, Connie Francis, MGM
7/4	EVERYBODY'S SOMEBODY'S FOOL, Connie Francis, MGM
7/11	ALLEY -OOP, Hollywood Argyles, Lute
7/18	I'M SORRY, Brenda Lee, Decca
7/25	I'M SORRY, Brenda Lee
8/1	I'M SORRY, Brenda Lee
8/8	ITSY BITSY TEENIE WEENIE YELLOW POLKA DOT BIKINI, Brian Hyland, Leader
8/15	IT'S NOW OR NEVER, Elvis Presley, RCA Victor
8/22	IT'S NOW OR NEVER, Elvis Presley
8/29	IT'S NOW OR NEVER, Elvis Presley
9/5	IT'S NOW OR NEVER, Elvis Presley
9/12	IT'S NOW OR NEVER, Elvis Presley
9/19	TWIST, Chubby Checker, Parkway
9/26	MY HEART HAS A MIND OF IT'S OWN, Connie Francis, MGM
10/3	MY HEART HAS A MIND OF IT'S OWN, Connie Francis
10/10	MR. CUSTER, Larry Verne, Era
10/17	SAVE THE LAST DANCE FOR ME, Drifters, Atlantic
10/24	I WANT TO BE WANTED, Brenda Lee, Decca
10/31	SAVE THE LAST DANCE FOR ME, Drifters, Atlantic
11/7	SAVE THE LAST DANCE FOR ME, Drifters
11/14	GEORGIA ON MY MIND, Ray Charles, ABC-Paramount
11/21	STAY, Maurice Williams & The Zodiacs, Herald

11/28	ARE YOU LONESOME TONIGHT, Elvis Presley,
12/5	ARE YOU LONESOME TONIGHT, Elvis Presley
12/12	ARE YOU LONESOME TONIGHT, Elvis Presley
12/19	ARE YOU LONESOME TONIGHT, Elvis Presley
12/26	ARE YOU LONESOME TONIGHT, Elvis Presley
12/31	ARE YOU LONESOME TONIGHT, Elvis Presley

1961

1/9	WONDERLAND BY NIGHT, Bert Kaempfert, Decca
1/16	WONDERLAND BY NIGHT, Bert Kaempfert
1/23	WONDERLAND BY NIGHT, Bert Kaempfert
1/30	(WILL YOU LOVE ME) TOMORROW, Shirelles, Scepter
2/6	(WILL YOU LOVE ME) TOMORROW, Shirelles
2/13	CALCUTTA, Lawrence Welk, Dot
2/20	CALCUTTA, Lawrence Welk
2/27	PONY TIME, Chubby Checker, Parkway
3/6	PONY TIME, Chubby Checker
3/13	PONY TIME, Chubby Checker
3/20	SURRENDER, Elvis Presley, RCA Victor
3/27	SURRENDER, Elvis Presley
4/3	BLUE MOON, Marcels, Colpix
4/10	BLUE MOON, Marcels
4/17	BLUE MOON, Marcels
4/24	RUNAWAY, Del Shannon, Big Top
5/1	RUNAWAY, Del Shannon
5/8	RUNAWAY, Del Shannon
5/15	RUNAWAY, Del Shannon
5/22	MOTHER-IN-LAW, Ernie K-Doe, Minit
5/29	TRAVELIN' MAN, Ricky Nelson, Imperial
6/5	RUNNING SCARED, Roy Orbison, Monument
6/12	TRAVELIN'MAN, Ricky Nelson, Imperial
6/19	MOODY RIVER, Pat Boone, Dot
6/26	QUARTER TO THREE, U.S. Bonds, Le Grand
7/3	QUARTER TO THREE, U.S. Bonds
7/10	TOSSIN' AND TURNIN', Bobby Lewis, Belton
7/17	TOSSIN' AND TURNIN', Bobby Lewis
7/24	TOSSIN' AND TURNIN', Bobby Lewis

7/31	TOSSIN' AND TURNIN', Bobby Lewis
8/7	TOSSIN'AND TURNIN', Bobby Lewis
8/14	TOSSIN' AND TURNIN', Bobby Lewis
8/21	TOSSIN' AND TURNIN', Bobby Lewis
8/28	WOODEN HEART (MUSSI DENN), Joe Dowell, Smash
9/4	MICHAEL, Highwaymen, United Artists
9/11	MICHAEL, Highwaymen
9/18	TAKE GOOD CARE OF MY BABY, Bobby Vee, Liberty
9/25	TAKE GOOD CARE OF MY BABY, Bobby Vee
10/2	TAKE GOOD CARE OF MY BABY, Bobby Vee
10/9	HIT THE ROAD JACK, Ray Charles, ABC-Paramount
10/16	HIT THE ROAD JACK, Ray Charles
10/23	RUNAROUND SUE, Dion, Laurie
10/30	RUNAROUND SUE, Dion
11/6	BIG BAD JOHN, Jimmy Dean, Columbia
11/13	BIG BAD JOHN, Jimmy Dean
11/20	BIG BAD JOHN, Jimmy Dean
11/27	BIG BAD JOHN, Jimmy Dean
12/4	BIG BAD JOHN, Jimmy Dean
12/11	PLEASE MR. POSTMAN, Marvelettes, Tamla
12/18	THE LION SLEEPS TONIGHT, Tokens, RCA Victor
12/25	THE LION SLEEPS TONIGHT, Tokens

1962

1/6	THE LION SLEEPS TONIGHT, Tokens, RCA Victor
1/13	THE TWIST, Chubby Checker, Parkway
1/20	THE TWIST, Chubby Checker
1/27	PEPPERMINT TWIST, Joey Dee & Starlighters, Roulette
2/3	PEPPERMINT TWIST, Joey Dee & Starlighters
2/10	PEPPERMINT TWIST, Joey Dee & Starlighters
2/17	DUKE OF EARL, Gene (Duke of Earl) Chandler, Vee Jay
2/24	DUKE OF EARL, Gene (Duke of Earl) Chandler

3/3	DUKE OF EARL, Gene (Duke of Earl) Chandler
3/10	HEY! BABY, Bruce Channel, Smash
3/17	HEY! BABY, Bruce Channel
3/24	HEY! BABY, Bruce Channel
3/31	DON'T BREAK THE HEART THAT LOVES YOU, Connie Francis, MGM
4/7	JOHNNY ANGEL, Shelley Fabares, Colpix
4/14	JOHNNY ANGEL, Shelley Fabares
4/21	GOOD LUCK CHARM, Elvis Presley, RCA Victor
4/28	GOOD LUCK CHARM, Elvis Presley, RCA
5/5	SOLDIER BOY, Shirelles, Scepter
5/12	SOLDIER BOY, Shirelles
5/19	SOLDIER BOY, Shirelles
5/26	STRANGER ON THE SHORE, Mr. Acker Bilk, Atco
6/2	I CAN'T STOP LOVING YOU, Ray Charles, ABC-Paramount
6/9	I CAN'T STOP LOVING YOU, Ray Charles
6/16	I CAN'T STOP LOVING YOU, Ray Charles
6/23	I CAN'T STOP LOVING YOU, Ray Charles
6/30	I CAN'T STOP LOVING YOU, Ray Charles
7/7	THE STRIPPER, David Rose & His Orch., MGM
7/14	ROSES ARE RED, Bobby Vinton, Epic
7/21	ROSES ARE RED, Bobby Vinton
7/28	ROSES ARE RED, Bobby Vinton
8/4	ROSES ARE RED, Bobby Vinton
8/11	BREAKING UP IS HARD TO DO, Neil Sedaka, RCA Victor
8/18	BREAKING UP IS HARD TO DO, Neil Sedaka
8/25	LOCO-MOTION, Little Eva, Dimension
9/1	SHEILA, Tommy Roe, ABC-Paramount
9/8	SHEILA, Tommy Roe
9/15	SHERRY, Four Seasons, Vee Jay
9/22	SHERRY, Four Seasons
9/29	SHERRY, Four Seasons
10/6	SHERRY, Four Seasons
10/13	SHERRY, Four Seasons
10/20	MONSTER MASH, Bobby (Boris) Pickett & The Crypt Kickers, Garpax
10/27	MONSTER MASH, Bobby (Boris) Pickett & The Crypt Kickers

11/3   HE'S A REBEL, Crystals, Philles
11/10   HE'S A REBEL, Crystals
11/17   BIG GIRLS DON'T CRY, Four Seasons, Vee Jay
11/24   BIG GIRLS DON'T CRY, Four Seasons
12/1   BIG GIRLS DON'T CRY, Four Seasons
12/8   BIG GIRLS DON'T CRY, Four Seasons
12/15   BIG GIRLS DON'T CRY, Four Seasons
12/22   TELSTAR, Tornadoes, London
12/29   TELSTAR, Tornadoes

1963

1/5   TELSTAR, Tornadoes, London
1/12   GO AWAY LITTLE GIRL, Steve Lawrence, Columbia
1/19   GO AWAY LITTLE GIRL, Steve Lawrence
1/26   WALK RIGHT IN, Rooftop Singers, Vanguard
2/2   WALK RIGHT IN, Rooftop Singers
2/9   HEY PAULA, Paul & Paula, Philips
2/16   HEY PAULA, Paul & Paula
2/23   HEY PAULA, Paul & Paula
3/2   WALK LIKE A MAN, Four Seasons, Vee Jay
3/9   WALK LIKE A MAN, Four Seasons
3/16   WALK LIKE A MAN, Four Seasons
3/23   OUR DAY WILL COME, Ruby & The Romantics, Kapp
3/30   HE'S SO FINE, Chiffons, Laurie
4/6   HE'S SO FINE, Chiffons
4/13   HE'S SO FINE, Chiffons
4/20   HE'S SO FINE, Chiffons
4/27   I WILL FOLLOW HIM, Little Peggy March, RCA Victor
5/4   I WILL FOLLOW HIM, Little Peggy March, RCA Victor
5/11   I WILL FOLLOW HIM, Little Peggy March, RCA
5/18   IF YOU WANNA BE HAPPY, Jimmy Soul, S.P.Q.R.
5/25   IF YOU WANNA BE HAPPY, Jimmy Soul
6/1   IT'S MY PARTY, Lesley Gore, Mercury
6/8   IT'S MY PARTY, Lesley Gore, Mercury

6/15	SUKIYAKI, Kyu Sakamoto, Capitol
6/22	SUKIYAKI, Kyu Sakamota
6/29	SUKIYAKI, Kyu Sakamota
7/6	EASIER SAID THAN DONE, Essex, Roulette
7/13	EASIER SAID THAN DONE, Essex
7/20	SURF CITY, Jan & Dean, Liberty
7/27	SURF CITY, Jan & Dean
8/3	SO MUCH IN LOVE, Tymes, Parkway
8/10	FINGERTIPS (Part II) Little Stevie Wonder, Tamla
8/17	FINGERTIPS (Part II) Little Stevie Wonder
8/24	FINGERTIPS (Part II) Little Stevie Wonder
8/31	MY BOYFRIEND'S BACK, Angels, Smash
9/7	MY BOYFRIEND'S BACK
9/14	MY BOYFRIEND'S BACK
9/21	BLUE VELVET, Bobby Vinton, Epic
9/28	BLUE VELVET, Bobby Vinton
10/5	BLUE VELVET, Bobby Vinton
10/12	SUGAR SHACK, Jimmy Gilmer & The Fireballs, Dot
10/19	SUGAR SHACK, Jimmy Gilmer & The Fireballs
10/26	SUGAR SHACK, Jimmy Gilmer & The Fireballs
11/2	SUGAR SHACK, Jimmy Gilmer & The Fireballs
11/9	SUGAR SHACK, Jimmy Gilmer & The Fireballs
11/16	DEEP-PURPLE, Nino Tempo & April Stevens, Atco
11/23	I'M LEAVING IT UP TO YOU, Dale & Grace, Montol-Michele
11/30	I'M LEAVING IT UP TO YOU, Dale & Grace
12/7	DOMINIQUE, Singing Nun, Philips
12/14	DOMINIQUE, Singing Nun
12/21	DOMINIQUE, Singing Nun
12/28	DOMINIQUE, Singing Nun
1/4	THERE I'VE SAID IT AGAIN, Bobby Vinton, Epic
1/11	THERE! I'VE SAID IT AGAIN, Bobby Vinton
1/18	THERE! I'VE SAID IT AGAIN, Bobby Vinton
1/25	THERE! I'VE SAID IT AGAIN, Bobby Vinton
2/1	I WANT TO HOLD YOUR HAND, Beatles, Capitol
2/8	I WANT TO HOLD YOUR HAND, Beatles
2/15	I WANT TO HOLD YOUR HAND, Beatles
2/22	I WANT TO HOLD YOUR HAND, Beatles
2/29	I WANT TO HOLD YOUR HAND, Beatles

1964

3/7	I WANT TO HOLD YOUR HAND, Beatles
3/14	I WANT TO HOLD YOUR HAND, Beatles
3/21	SHE LOVES YOU, Beatles, Swan
3/28	SHE LOVES YOU, Beatles
4/4	CAN'T BUY ME LOVE, Beatles, Capitol
4/11	CAN'T BUY ME LOVE, Beatles
4/18	CAN'T BUY ME LOVE, Beatles
4/25	CAN'T BUY ME LOVE, Beatles
5/2	CAN'T BUY ME LOVE, Beatles
5/9	HELLO DOLLY, Louis Armstrong, Kapp
5/16	MY GUY, Mary Wells, Motown
5/23	MY GUY, Mary Wells, Motown
5/30	LOVE ME DO, Beatles, Tollie
6/6	CHAPEL OF LOVE, Dixie Cups, Red Bird
6/13	CHAPEL OF LOVE, Dixie Cups
6/20	CHAPEL OF LOVE, Dixie Cups
6/27	A WORLD WITHOUT LOVE, Peter & Gordon, Capitol
7/4	I GET AROUND, Beach Boys, Capitol
7/11	I GET AROUND, Beach Boys
7/18	RAG DOLL, Four Seasons, Philips
7/25	RAG DOLL, Four Seasons, Philips
8/1	A HARD DAYS NIGHT, Beatles, Capitol
8/8	A HARD DAYS NIGHT, Beatles, Capitol
8/15	EVERYBODY LOVES SOMEBODY, Dean Martin, Reprise
8/22	WHERE DID OUR LOVE GO, Supremes, Motown
8/29	WHERE DID OUR LOVE GO, Supremes
9/5	THE HOUSE OF THE RISING SUN, Animals, MGM
9/12	THE HOUSE OF THE RISING SUN, Animals, MGM
9/19	THE HOUSE OF THE RISING SUN, Animals
9/26	OH, PRETTY WOMAN, Roy Orbison, Monument
10/3	OH, PRETTY WOMAN, Roy Orbison
10/10	OH, PRETTY WOMAN, Roy Orbison
10/17	DO WAH DIDDY DIDDY, Manfred Mann, Ascot
10/24	DO WAH DIDDY DIDDY, Manfred Mann
10/31	BABY LOVE, Supremes, Motown

17/7   BABY LOVE, Supremes
11/14 BABY LOVE, Supremes
11/21 BABY LOVE, Supremes
11/28 LEADER OF THE PACK, Shangri-Las, Red Bird
12/5   RINGO, Lorne Greene, RCA Victor
12/12 MR. LONELY, Bobby Vinton, Epic
12/19 COME SEE ABOUT ME, Supremes, Motown
12/26 I FEEL FINE, Beatles, Capitol

1965

1/2   I FEEL FINE, Beatles, Capitol
1/9   I FEEL FINE, Beatles
1/16   COME SEE ABOUT ME, Supremes, Motown
1/23   DOWNTOWN, Petula Clark, Warner Bros.
1/30   DOWNTOWN, Petula Clark
2/6   YOU'VE LOST THAT LOVING FEELING, Righteous Bros., Philles
2/13   YOU'VE LOST THAT LOVING FEELING, Righteous Bros.
2/20   THIS DIAMOND RING, Gary Lewis & Playboys, Liberty
2/27   THIS DIAMOND RING, Gary Lewis & Playboys
3/6   MY GIRL, Temptations, Gordy
3/13   EIGHT DAYS A WEEK, Beatles, Capitol
3/20   EIGHT DAYS A WEEK, Beatles
3/27   STOP! IN THE NAME OF LOVE, Supremes, Motown
4/3   STOP ! IN THE NAME OF LOVE, Supremes, Motown
4/10   I'M TELLING YOU NOW, Freddie & The Dreamers, Tower
41/7   I'M TELLING YOU NOW, Freddie & The Dreamers
4/24   GAME OF LOVE, Wayne Fontana & Mindbenders, Fontana
5/1   MRS. BROWN YOU'VE GOT A LOVELY DAUGHTER, Herman's Hermits, MGM
5/8   MRS. BROWN YOU'VE GOT A LOVELY DAUGHTER, Herman's Hermits

5/15   MRS. BROWN YOU'VE GOT A LOVELY DAUGHTER, Herman's Hermits
5/22   TICKET TO RIDE, Beatles, Capitol
5/29   HELP ME RHONDA, Beach Boys, Capitol
6/5   HELP ME RHONDA, Beach Boys
6/12   BACK IN MY ARMS AGAIN, Supremes, Motown
6/19   I CAN'T HELP MYSELF, Four Tops, Motown
6/26   MR. TAMBOURINE MAN, Byrds, Columbia
7/3   I CAN'T HELP MYSELF, Four Tops, Motown
7/10   (I Can't Get No) SATISFACTION, Rolling Stones, London
7/17   (I Can't Get No) SATISFACTION, Rolling Stones
7/24   (I Can't Get No) SATISFACTION, Rolling Stones
7/31   (I Can't Get No) SATISFACTION, Rolling Stones
8/7   I'M HENRY VIII, I AM Herman's Hermits, MGM
8/21   I GOT YOU BABE, Sonny & Cher, Atco
8/28   I GOT YOU BABE, Sonny & Cher
8/28   I GOT YOU BABE, Sonny & Cher
9/4   HELP, Beatles, Capitol
9/11   HELP, Beatles
9/18   HELP, Beatles
9/25   EVE OF DESTRUCTION, Barry McGuire, Dunhill
10/2   HANG ON SLOOPY, McCoys, Bang
10/9   YESTERDAY, Beatles, Capitol
10/16 YESTERDAY, Beatles
10/23 YESTERDAY, Beatles
10/30 YESTERDAY, Beatles
11/6   GET OFF OF MY CLOUD, Rolling Stones, London
11/13 GET OFF OF MY CLOUD, Rolling Stones
11/20 I HEAR A SYMPHONY, Supremes, Motown
11/27 I HEAR A SYMPHONY, Supremes,
12/4   TURN TURN TURN, Byrds, Columbia
12/11 TURN TURN TURN, Byrds
12/18 TURN TURN TURN, Byrds
12/25 OVER AND OVER, Dave Clark Five, Epic

1966

1/1   SOUNDS OF SILENCE, Simon & Garfunkel, Columbia
1/8   WE CAN WORK IT OUT, Beatles, Capitol

1/15   WE CAN WORK IT OUT, Beatles
1/22   SOUNDS OF SILENCE, Simon & Garfunkel, Columbia
1/29   WE CAN WORK IT OUT, Beatles, Capitol
2/5   MY LOVE, Petula Clark, Warner Bros.
2/12   MY LOVE, Petula Clark
2/19   LIGHTNIN' STRIKES, Lou Christie, MGM
2/26   THESE BOOTS ARE MADE FOR WALKIN', Nancy Sinatra, Reprise
3/5   BALLAD OF THE GREEN BERETS, THE, S/Sgt. Barry Sadler, RCA Victor
3/12   BALLAD OF THE GREEN BERETS, THE, S/Sgt. Barry Sadler
3/19   BALLAD OF THE GREEN BERETS, THE, S/Sgt. Barry Sadler
3/26   BALLAD OF THE GREEN BERETS, THE, S/Sgt. Barry Sadler
4/2   BALLAD OF THE GREEN BERETS, THE, S/Sgt. Barry Sadler
4/9   (You're My) SOUL AND INSPIRATION, Righteous Brothers
4/16   (You're My) SOUL AND INSPIRATION, Righteous Brothers
4/23   (You're My) SOUL AND INSPIRATION, Righteous Brothers
4/30   GOOD LOVIN', Young Rascals, Atlantic
5/7   MONDAY, MONDAY, Mamas & The Papas, Dunhill
5/14   MONDAY, MONDAY, Mamas & The Papas
5/21   MONDAY, MONDAY, Mamas & The Papas
5/28   WHEN A MAN LOVES A WOMAN, Percy Sledge, Atlantic
6/4   WHEN A MAN LOVES A WOMAN, Percy Sledge
6/11   PAINT IT, BLACK, Rolling Stones, London
6/18   PAINT IT, BLACK, Rolling Stones
6/25   PAPERBACK WRITER, Beatles, Capitol
7/2   STRANGERS IN THE NIGHT, Frank Sinatra, Reprise
7/9   PAPERBACK WRITER, Beatles, Capitol
7/16   HANKY PANKY, Tommy James & the Shondells, Riykette

7/23   HANKY PANKY, Tommy James & the Shondells
7/30   WILD THING, Troggs, Atco/Fontana
8/6   WILD THING, Troggs
8/13   SUMMER IN THE CITY, Lovin' Spoonful, Kama Sutra
8/20   SUMMER IN THE CITY, Lovin' Spoonful
8/27   SUMMER IN THE CITY, Lovin' Spoonful
9/3   SUNSHINE SUPERMAN, Donovan, Epic
9/10   YOU CAN'T HURRY LOVE, Supremes, Motown
9/17   YOU CAN'T HURRY LOVE, Supremes
9/24   CHERISH, Association, Valiant
10/1   CHERISH, Association
10/8   CHERISH, Association
10/15   REACH OUT I'LL BE THERE, Four Tops, Motown
10/22   REACH OUT I'LL BE THERE, Four Tops
10/29   96 TEARS, ? (Question Mark) & the Mysterions, Cameo
11/5   LAST TRAIN TO CLARKSVILLE, Monkees, Colgems
11/12   POOR SIDE OF TOWN, Johnny Rivers, Imperial
11/19   YOU KEEP ME HANGIN' ON, Supremes, Motown
11/26   YOU KEEP ME HANGIN' ON, Supremes
12/3   WINCHESTER CATHEDRAL, New Vauderville Band, Fontana
12/10   GOOD VIBRATIONS, Beach Boys, Capitol
12/17   WINCHESTER CATHEDRAL, New Vaudeville Band, Fontana
12/24   WINCHESTER CATHEDRAL, New Vauderville Band
12/31   I'M A BELIEVER, Monkees, Colgems

1967

1/7   I'M A BELIEVER, Monkees, Colgems
1/14   I'M A BELIEVER, Monkees
1/21   I'M A BELIEVER, Monkees
1/28   I'M A BELIEVER, Monkees
5/4   I'M A BELIEVER, Monkees
2/11   I'M A BELIEVER, Monkees

2/18   KIND OF A DRAG, Buckinghams, U.S.A.
2/25   KIND OF A DRAG, Buckinghams, U.S.A.
3/4   RUBY TUESDAY, Rolling Stones, London
3/11   LOVE IS HERE AND NOW YOU'RE GONE, Supremes, Motown
3/18   PENNY LANE, Beatles, Capitol
3/25   HAPPY TOGETHER, Turtles, White Whale
4/1   HAPPY TOGETHER, Turtles
4/8   HAPPY TOGETHER, Turtles
4/15   SOMETHIN' STUPID, Nancy Sinatra & Frank Sinatra, Reprise
4/22   SOMETHIN' STUPID, Nancy Sinatra & Frank Sinatra
4/29   SOMETHIN' STUPID, Nancy Sinatra & Frank Sinatra
5/6   SOMETHIN' STUPID, Nancy Sinatra & Frank Sinatra
5/13   THE HAPPENING, Supremes, Motown
5/20   GROOVIN', Young Rascals, Atlantic
5/27   GROOVIN', Young Rascals
6/3   RESPECT, Aretha Franklin, Atlantic
6/10   RESPECT, Aretha Franklin
6/17   GROOVIN', Young Rascals, Atlantic
6/24   GROOVIN', Young Rascals
7/1   WINDY, Association, Warner Bros.
7/8   WINDY, Association
7/15   WINDY, Association
7/22   WINDY, Association
7/29   LIGHT MY FIRE, Doors, Elektra
8/5   LIGHT MY FIRE, Doors
8/12   LIGHT MY FIRE, Doors
8/19   ALL YOU NEED IS LOVE, Beatles, Capitol
8/26   ODE TO BILLIE JOE, Bobbie Gentry, Capitol
9/2   ODE TO BILLIE JOE, Bobbie Gentry
9/9   ODE TO BILLIE JOE, Bobbie Gentry
9/16   ODE TO BILLIE, JOE, Bobbie Gentry
9/23   THE LETTER, Box Tops, Mala
9/30   THE LETTER, Box Tops
10/7   THE LETTER, Box Tops
10/14 THE LETTER, Box Tops
10/21 TO SIR, WITH LOVE, Lulu, Epic

10/28	TO SIR, WITH LOVE, Lulu
11/4	TO SIR, WITH LOVE, Lulu
11/11	TO SIR, WITH LOVE, Lulu
11/18	TO SIR, WITH LOVE, Lulu
11/25	INCENSE AND PEPPERMINTS, Strawberry Alarm Clock, Uni
12/2	DAYDREAM BELIEVER, Monkees, Colgems
12/9	DAYDREAM BELIEVER, Monkees
12/16	DAYDREAM BELIEVER, Monkees
12/23	DAYDREAM BELIEVER, Monkees
12/30	HELLO GOODBYE, Beatles, Capitol

Appendix listings reprinted with permission from *CASH BOX* Magazine's Best Selling Albums and Singles of Each Year and from the Hot 100 Charts of *BILLBOARD,* the International Music-Record Weekly. Our thanks.